REAL ESTATE
PRINCIPLES AND PRACTICES

ALFRED A. RING
Professor Emeritus
University of Florida

JEROME DASSO
H. T. Miner Chairholder in Real Estate
University of Oregon

9th edition

REAL ESTATE
PRINCIPLES AND PRACTICES

PRENTICE-HALL, INC, *Englewood Cliffs, New Jersey 07632*

Library of Congress Cataloging in Publication Data

RING, ALFRED A
    Real estate principles and practices.

    Includes bibliographies and index.
    1. Real estate business.   I. Dasso, Jerome J., joint author.   II. Title.
HD1375.R5   1981   346.7304'37   80-24512
ISBN   0-13-765958-X

Editorial/production supervision by Maureen Wilson
Cover and interior design by Jayne Conte
Cover photograph by Four by Five
Acquisitions editor: John Connolly
Manufacturing buyer: Gordon Osbourne

10 9 8 7 6 5 4 3 2 1

Prentice-Hall International, Inc., *London*
Prentice-Hall of Australia Pty. Limited, *Sydney*
Prentice-Hall of Canada, Ltd., *Toronto*
Prentice-Hall of India Private Limited, *New Delhi*
Prentice-Hall of Japan, Inc., *Tokyo*
Prentice-Hall of Southeast Asia Pte. Ltd., *Singapore*
Whitehall Books Limited, *Wellington, New Zealand*

Dedicated to the reader's understanding of real estate,
a much more complex subject than most realize,
and to the wise use of our land resources.

CONTENTS

ONE

DEFINING OWNERSHIP RIGHTS

TWO

CONVEYING OWNERSHIP RIGHTS

THREE

FINANCING REAL ESTATE

FOUR

REAL ESTATE MARKETS AND THE INVESTMENT CLIMATE

FIVE

REAL ESTATE INVESTMENT

SIX

REAL ESTATE OWNERSHIP AND ADMINISTRATION

SEVEN

APPENDICES

PREFACE

This book is designed for anyone preparing for a career in the business of real estate and/or seeking a clear understanding of the many considerations involved in acquiring and owning real estate. This book is also intended to provide a sound foundation for further study or research in real estate. The knowledge contained herein should enable anyone in the real estate business to realize greater professional capability and recognition. And the practice of real estate increasingly requires greater specialization and greater professional competence. Appraisal, brokerage, finance, management, and planning, in particular, are steadily obtaining greater professional recognition from the public.

Integrated Framework Introduced

Real Estate Principles and Practices, written by Philip A. Benson and Nelson L. North, was first published in 1922. Since then it has been periodically revised and updated to take account of important developments in real estate. The tradition of keeping current and of being the leading real estate text is maintained in this edition with a continued shift in emphasis to analysis for decision making and effective action in acquiring and owning realty.

The real estate ownership or investment cycle is introduced in this edition, to provide an integrated and continuing frame of reference for this analysis and action. Some people call this continuing analysis and action the real estate process. Using and administering realty to maximize self-interest of the investor, usually taken to mean maximizing wealth, is the assumed motivation or driving force of the cycle. Physical, institutional, and economic considerations are discussed as they pertain to this cycle. Concerns and functions of investors, appraisers, brokers, builders, developers, financiers, and managers are all related to this investment cycle. The result is a comprehensive and integrated approach to the study of real estate. With this approach, an investor or practitioner develops a continuous awareness of the needs of any particular transaction. And with full understanding of both the investor's viewpoint and the cycle, practitioners should be able to perform their functions in an effective and professional manner.

Organization and Content

This book is divided into six major parts, which represent important components of the ownership cycle: (1) defining rights, (2) conveying rights, (3) financing, (4) understanding markets and the investment climate, (5) analysis for investment value, and (6) ownership administration. The approach is, of necessity, very applied.

Important content from past editions has been retained, sometimes recast, and integrated into the ownership or decision-making cycle. For example, the chapter, "Federal Legislation Affecting Real Estate," has been incorporated into a chapter renamed "Long-Term Trends Affecting the Climate for Real Estate Investment." Some chapters have been sharply updated, for example, "Appraising for Market Value." And three chapters are almost completely new. Two of these are chapter 15, "Time Value of Money in Real Estate," and chapter 17, "Urban-Area Structure and Neighborhood Dynamics." The rationale of the organization and content is fully explained in chapter 1, "Introduction and Overview," which is also new.

Comment Concerning Use

Instructors familiar with past editions should have little difficulty adapting this edition to their courses. Chapters 1–14, 22, and 24–26 are most appropriate for a license preparation course. On the other hand, if an academic or professional emphasis is desired, chapters 1–4, 7, and 12–26 seem most suitable. It is not expected that all the contents would be covered in one term, whether a quarter or semester. An instructor's manual and a workbook, *Questions and Problems: Real Estate Principles and Practices,* are available to the users of this edition.

Some changes in format should be noted. Key terms are summarized, the bibliography is annotated, and discussion questions are provided at the end of each chapter. More illustrations are used than in the past.

Overall, every effort has been made to reflect the effect of changes in interpretations of constitutional, statutory, and common law on the ownership, financing transfer, and management of realty. These changes in real estate principles and practices are ongoing and are largely affected by the civil rights (affirmative action/equal opportunity) and consumer protection movements. This material is designed to provide accurate and authoritative information concerning real estate. However, please recognize that this material is not meant to be a rendering of accounting, legal, real estate, or other professional advice. If expert assistance is needed, the services of a competent professional person should be obtained.

This ninth edition is an outgrowth of the evolution of real estate thought that has been channeled to the authors from teachers of real estate courses at more than two hundred institutions of higher education. To these teachers who have so generously offered their constructive criticism go our grateful thanks. Please keep up the good work and let us know of other ways future editions can be better suited to your needs and purposes. Comments may continue to be sent to us in care of the publisher. Also, thanks go to the thousands of students who, through study and reading of this text, have offered valuable suggestions for further clarification and refinement of the subject matter.

Alfred A. Ring
Gainesville, Florida

Jerome Dasso
Eugene, Oregon

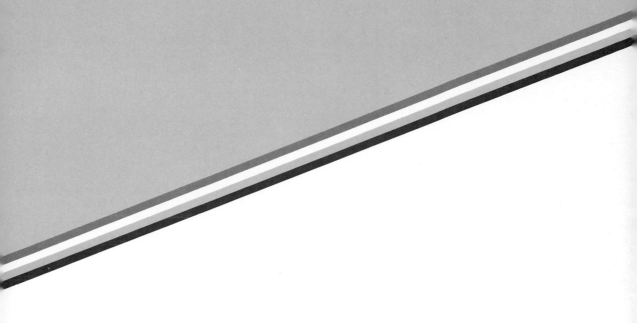

ACKNOWLEDGMENTS

Acknowledgment and grateful appreciation are extended to the following people who contributed directly or indirectly to the preparation of this work.

William Appleton
Richard F. Babcock
Joseph R. Bagby
Raleigh Barlowe
Byrl Boyce
Jim Brown
Lawrence E. Brown
William B. Brueggeman
Gary P. Cain
Neil G. Carn
Frederick E. Case
Walter H. Chudleigh, III
Richard Chumbley
John M. Clapp
Janet Clayton
Karel J. Clettenberg
John Connelly
Robert N. Corley

Susan Drake
Eugene F. Dunham, Jr.
James C. Downs, Jr.
James R. Fallain
M. Chapman Findley, II
William B. French
Jack Friedman
Richard T. Garrigan
George Gau
Caroll L. Gentry
James Graaskamp
Charles D. Gray
Francis J. Grey
Jerome Y. Halperin
Henry S. Harrison
John Heath, Jr.
Norbert Heath
Benjamin Henszey

Dudley S. Hinds
Herbert A. Huen
Jane Jacobs
Austin J. Jaffe
Kate Jones
Sanders A. Kahn
Stephen D. Kapplin
William N. Kinnard, Jr.
Daniel B. Kohlhepp
Charles O. Kroneke
Gerald Kuhn
William F. Landsea
William H. Langdon
Jack Lee
Howard Levine
Donald R. Levy
Bruce Lindeman
Robert L. Lyon
Victor Lyon
Paul G. Martin
W. M. McClellan
Katty McIntosh
John McMahon
Herbert A. Meistrich
Ivan J. Miestchovich, Jr.
Stephen D. Messner
Mike Miles
Norman G. Miller
Stanley F. Miller, Jr.
Carl M. Moser
Edward A. Moses
John Myers
Paul Nelson
Donald Nielsen
Nicholas Ordway
Max F. Pachl, Jr.

Stephen A. Pyhrr
Joseph Rabianski
Ronald L. Racster
Wade R. Ragas
Richard U. Ratcliff
Arnold L. Redman
John T. Reed
Michael Rice
William J. Robert
Stephen E. Roulac
Irving Schreiber
Arthur L. Schwartz, Jr.
Robert W. Semenow
Thomas W. Shafer
Harold Siegelaub
C. F. Sirmans
Dave Sirota
Wallace F. Smith
Jack Standeford
Joseph L. Steinberg
George Sternlieb
Raymond J. Struyk
Harold G. Trimble
Donald V. Valachi
James C. VanHorne
James Vernor
Robert L. Ward
Arthur E. Warner
James R. Webb
Paul F. Wendt
Robert J. Wiley
Wayne Winter
Larry E. Wofford
Lynn N. Woodward
Arthur L. Wright

Introduction and Overview

1

The first man, who, having enclosed a piece of ground, bethought of himself saying, *This is mine,* and found people willing to believe him, was the real founder of civil society.

Rousseau

Real estate has a myth and a reality much like the myth and the reality of the sirens of Greek mythology. The sirens, with their seductive singing, lured unwary sailors and adventurers to their deaths on rocky coasts. Real estate with its promise of exciting careers and quick riches entices many aspiring practitioners and unwary investors to their ruin on the reefs of ignorance and inexperience. Ulysses, with proper preparation, was able to hear the songs of the sirens while escaping the reality of their rocky coasts. In like manner, a newcomer to real estate, with proper preparation, may realize career goals and/or financial rewards while avoiding its hidden reefs.

Providing a sound foundation, or proper preparation, for maneuvering in the world of real estate is the overall purpose of this book. With this foundation, the reader will be able to make an informed decision as to whether to enter, and the best way to enter, this intriguing world. This chapter is intended as a guide or road map for the journey to this goal or purpose. Content, organization, basic assumptions, and key concepts of the book are all introduced here. This overview should make it easier for the reader to learn and retain the information and principles set forth. This chapter contains three major sections:

1. Overview of content
2. The real estate investment cycle
3. Decision making and administration in real estate

1

OVERVIEW OF CONTENT

As indicated, the overall purpose of this book is to provide a sound foundation for anyone interested in further study and/or business participation in real estate. The coverage of topics is broad and the depth is uniform. In addition, topics are organized by general subject area to make it easier to read, discuss, and fully understand the material. This section begins with a brief explanation of several key concepts and assumptions of this material and concludes with an explanation of the organization of the content and its underlying rationale.

The Meanings of Real Estate

The term *real estate* means different things to different people. It will therefore help to distinguish first among the three most common meanings. These three meanings, which are closely related in many ways and therefore have many interrelationships, are as follows:

1. A field of study
2. An occupation, profession, or form of business activity
3. A financial asset, commodity, or property

A FIELD OF STUDY. Real estate as a field of study concerns the description and analysis of the occupational, physical, legal, and financial aspects of land and permanent improvements on or to land. The purpose is greater knowledge and understanding of decisions and actions. Books, magazines, courses, and other educational activities focusing on real estate as a business or commodity fit into this definition. Thus, this entire book concerns real estate as a field of study.

A FORM OF BUSINESS ACTIVITY. When people devote their lives to real estate as their occupation, profession, or line of business activity, they are in "real estate." Appraisers, brokers, builders, lenders, planners, housing analysts, and investors are in real estate in this sense. In other words, real estate as a business activity focuses on human activities concerned with land and its use or improvement. Chapter 2 develops this meaning further.

A FINANCIAL ASSET. Real estate as a form of property or financial asset begins with the land and includes all "permanent" improvements on or to the land. Real estate accounts for roughly two-thirds of the tangible wealth of the United States. This asset or property concept is the most common meaning of real estate and is also the object or focus of all other meanings. Except for chapter 2, the remainder of this book is devoted to real estate as a financial asset. Unless otherwise indicated, the terms *real estate, realty,* and *real property* are used interchangeably in this book in referring to real estate as an asset or commodity.

Perspective

This book is for the reader who is interested both in the principles of real estate and in the practices of successful real estate investing. This book is also intended as a guide to those who may not have studied real estate before. The presentation is orderly and comprehensive. The perspective or viewpoint is that of an investor. For two major reasons, discussion centers on investment property. The first reason is that the laws concerning ownership, conveyance of ownership, and financing are essentially the same whether for a one-family residence or for an investment property. Therefore the reader mastering this material has basic preparation for either residential or commercial-investment real estate.

Second, readers of this book are expected to be interested in investing on their own account or in rendering competent, professional services to investors. The material is appropriate for either. Brief attention is also given to the social responsibility expected of anyone involved in real estate.

INVESTMENT ORIENTATION. The essentials of analyzing an income property and negotiating its acquisition or disposition are included. In effect, the reader takes the role of the investor. The tradeoff between avoiding risk and increasing rate-of-return is discussed relative to the typical investor's goal of wealth maximization. Ownership rights and their conveyancing are taken up early because these topics may be as serious a source of risk or loss as faulty analysis in making an investment. In addition, the investor is better off if he or she is able to communicate with, and negotiate through, brokers and other specialists on an equal-knowledge footing. The investor, in knowing the levels of performance to be expected from practitioners, also gains a considerable advantage in pursuing his or her goals.

PROFESSIONAL-SERVICES BENEFITS. The material provided herein is also appropriate for the reader interested in a career as a salesperson, broker, appraiser, builder, contractor, counselor, lender, planner, manager, housing analyst, escrow agent, or title analyst. An architect must know a client's needs and life style to design a suitable house. In the same sense, a professional must know a client's needs and goals to render the best possible service. Mastery of the content of this book should provide a better understanding of investment property, enabling the reader to convey a better image to clients, render a higher quality of services, and in turn earn higher fees. The material provided herein may also help the reader to select a specialty for a career in real estate.

SOCIAL RESPONSIBILITY. A sense of social responsibility is increasingly expected of real estate investors and specialists. Social responsibility means knowing and abiding by fair housing laws, zoning ordinances, and environmental regulations. It means reasonable effort to conserve energy and to use land wisely. It means being accountable for one's own decisions or actions relative to others. Issues involving social responsibility in real estate are therefore pointed up at appropriate places throughout the book.

Assumptions

Taking the perspective of the investor requires a number of basic assumptions. The most important assumption is that our investor is a **rational being** who behaves in a logical and reasonable manner toward the goal of maximizing **self-interest,** in this case, maximizing wealth. The concept of a rational being was developed shortly after World War II.[1] The "rational being" assumption makes the thought process or **decision-making process** of our investor logical and predictable. That is, acting in self-interest, the investor always selects the choice or alternative giving greatest personal advantage. This selection process is sometimes called "making a tradeoff."

Self-interest is neither good nor bad, desirable nor undesirable, per se. In a sense, self-interest is to people as gravity is to our world. We can curse gravity for keeping us from flying at will and requiring us to exert energy to conquer distance or elevation. But gravity also works to our advantage. It causes rain to fall and rivers to flow downhill. It keeps us on earth under predictable conditions and maintains our atmosphere. We even turn gravity to our advantage in our work and play when we irrigate land, ski, skydive, or play ball. Self-interest is a force or motivation that affects each of us in that it causes us to try to maximize our satisfactions in life. Toward this end we seek leisure, self-expression, travel, company of loved ones, thrills from skydiving, or social change. Most of us seek money (rents, profits, interest, wages) only as an intermediate goal. In our complex society, an entrepreneur seeking profits may be making a contribution to society as great as, or even greater than, a doctor seeking fees, a planner seeking wages, or a politician seeking power.

Self-interest tends to push real estate to its highest and best use. **Highest and best use** is that legal and possible employment which gives the greatest present value to realty while preserving its utility. A **land use** is that activity by which a parcel of realty is made productive (generates services of value), as in residential, commercial, or industrial uses.

A framework for financially administering real estate results from using the viewpoint of an investor as a rational being seeking to maximize self-interest. The effect is to provide the reader a model, or financial-management framework, for making decisions and for administering real estate.

Organization

As already indicated, this chapter gives an overview of the book, and chapter 2 explains real estate as a business. The balance of the book is devoted to the ownership of real estate as an asset or property and to the professional services that assist investors to achieve their goals. The book is divided into six parts with several chapters in each, as shown in figure 1–1. Each part has its own theme or rationale. Initially the emphasis is on considerations of ownership and conveyancing, with a gradual progression through financing, marketing, investing, and managing considerations. Each division represents an area of advance real estate study as law, finance, market analysis, investment analysis, and property management. Taken together, the divisions make up the real estate investment process. The process summarizes the essential and integrated information an investor needs for rational decision making and successful ven-

---

[1] The theory of "rational man" or "administrative man" was first conceived by Herbert A. Simon in *Administrative Behavior* (New York: Macmillan, 1947). Simon won the Nobel Prize in 1978 for his work in economics and decision theory.

tures into ownership of real estate. In turn, the many specialists providing real estate services can benefit greatly from an approach that emphasizes the importance of knowing and understanding the investor's goals. The approach, very simply, makes it possible for the specialist to tailor services to the investor's needs and purposes.

FIGURE 1–1
Organization of *Real Estate Principles and Practices,* 9th Ed.

<table>
<tr><td>1. Introduction and Overview</td><td></td><td>2. The Real Estate Business</td></tr>
<tr><td>**PART I**
Defining Ownership
Rights</td><td>**PART II**
Conveying Ownership
Rights</td><td>**PART III**
Financing
Real Estate</td></tr>
<tr><td>3. Property Descriptions and Characteristics
4. Real Property Ownership and Interests
5. Liens, Easements, and Other Encumbrances to Ownership
6. Governmental Limitations to Ownership</td><td>7. Contracts for the Sale of Real Estate
8. Title Closing
9. Title Assurance and Title Transfer
10. The Investor-Broker Relationship
11. Brokerage Operations and Practices</td><td>12. Mortgage Financing
13. Trust Deed, Land Contract, and Lease Financing
14. Real Estate Credit and Our Financial System
15. Time Value of Money in Real Estate</td></tr>
<tr><td>**PART IV**
Real Estate Markets and the Investment Climate</td><td>**PART V**
Real Estate Investment</td><td>**PART VI**
Real Estate Ownership and Administration</td></tr>
<tr><td>16. Long-Run Trends Affecting the Climate for Real Estate Investment
17. Urban-Area Structure and Neighborhood Dynamics
18. Real Estate Markets
19. Real Estate Market and Feasibility Analysis</td><td>20. Property Productivity Analysis
21. Federal Taxes Affecting Real Estate
22. Appraising for Market Value
23. Real Estate Investment Analysis
24. Property Development and Redevelopment</td><td>25. Property Management
26. Leases and Leasing
27. Home Ownership
28. Real Estate Trends and Outlook</td></tr>
</table>

DEFINING OWNERSHIP RIGHTS. Real property rights constitute the commodity of the real estate market. And anyone aspiring to ownership or to providing services for owners of real estate must certainly understand property rights. In fact, everyone in our society should know and understand real property rights because we are all touched by, and dependent on, real estate in some way. Hence, part I is devoted to defining the rights a land owner does and does not have.

Chapter 3 covers methods of describing individual parcels (units of ownership) of land or realty. A discussion of the physical and economic characteristics that make realty ownership units different from other commodities is included in this chapter. Chapter 4 explains the legal foundations of real property ownership. Chapters 5 and 6 explain private and public limits to ownership because what ownership does *not* include may be critical to successful ownership. If an investor understands the full nature of ownership, he or she is better qualified to engage in transactions involving ownership rights.

CONVEYING OWNERSHIP RIGHTS. Part II focuses on the legal and accounting considerations in transferring ownership rights. Agreements for the sale of real property must be in writing; the legal and essential elements of contracts are therefore explained in chapter 7. It helps to know how a transaction ends in explaining some of the intermediate steps; hence chapter 8 discusses title closing. **Title closing** is the point at which the money concerns of all parties must be accounted for, appropriate payments made, and transfer of ownership concluded. A potential owner wants to be sure of getting the best possible title, which is why chapter 9, on title and title assurance, is important. The type of deed by which a buyer gets title defines the legal guarantee toward protection of ownership that the seller offers; therefore deeds are fully explained in chapter 9. Brokers are frequently used in buying and selling or renting realty. Use of a broker involves a principal-agent relationship, an arrangement in which both parties are advised to be fully aware of their rights and obligations. Chapter 10, "The Investor-Broker Relationship," covers these rights and obligations. Chapter 11 summarizes the essential considerations of real estate brokerage operations.

FINANCING REAL ESTATE. Interest rates and capital flows, or credit, form a direct link between the national economy and local real estate market activity. Further, available credit is absolutely necessary for real estate sales or investment activity. Without credit, few investors would have the money to buy properties. And without credit, real estate might not offer a high enough rate of return to attract investment funds from alternative investments such as stocks and bonds. The terminology, instruments, methods of calculation, and institutions of real estate finance are covered in part III.

REAL ESTATE MARKETS AND THE INVESTMENT CLIMATE. Real estate is subject to social, economic, legal, and political forces. These forces cause many changes in both the short and the long run and provide the setting or climate of real estate and real estate markets.

In chapter 16 we look at long-run trends affecting real estate such as population and economic growth and steadily developing technology. In chapter 17, "Urban-Area Structure and Neighborhood Dynamics," we look at the way these forces cause formation of urban areas and change in our neighborhoods. Rent theory is discussed in these chapters as it affects urban growth and change. Our rational investor must understand real estate markets and market analysis in order to interpret and translate change into specific investment opportunities. Chapter 18 takes up the operation and functions of real estate markets. Chapter 19, "Real Estate Market and Feasibility Analysis," explains the process of collecting and evaluating information to identify possible investment opportunities. With real estate financial and market information in hand, our investor is ready to analyze these opportunities in more detail.

REAL ESTATE INVESTMENT. An understanding of the material in chapters 3 to 19 is a prerequisite to making a sound investment analysis of a specific property. In investment analysis, a property must first be evaluated for its ability to generate services of economic value, which topic is taken up in chapter 20, "Property Productivity Analysis." Tax considerations also enter into the analysis, hence "Federal Taxes Affecting Real Estate" is the title for chapter 21. The market value of the property is also important to an investor. It's not rational to pay more to buy or build a property than its value in the market. Appraising for market value is therefore the focus of chapter 22. Finally, all these considerations are brought together in chapter 23, "Real Estate Investment Analysis." The possibility of developing rather than buying an investment property is considered in more depth in chapter 24.

REAL ESTATE OWNERSHIP AND ADMINISTRATION. After acquisition or development, the property is "out of the market." It must then be merchandised, maintained, and sometimes modernized, which activities make up property management, as discussed in chapter 25. Leasing is a particularly important aspect of real estate management. An entire chapter, 26, "Leases and Leasing," is therefore devoted to the topic. Of course, some people invest for personal use only. The considerations of home ownership are taken up in chapter 27. Real estate is often owned for extended periods. We therefore devote our final chapter, 28, to the outlook for real estate as a body of knowledge, a field of business activity, and a commodity.

THE REAL ESTATE INVESTMENT CYCLE

Major subject areas, as shown in figure 1–1 are (1) defining ownerships, (2) conveyancing, (3) finance, (4) markets, (5) investment analysis, and (6) ownership administration. Each of these areas requires data-collection analysis and decisions of an investor. These topics may readily be reorganized into the real estate ownership or investment cycle.

The real estate investment cycle has three phases: (1) purchase or acquisition, (2) administration of ownership, and (3) sale or disposition. Every owner-investor goes through these phases. In fact, better investment decisions and results are realized if the cycle is looked at in its entirety in the acquisition phase. A major organization or investor may have properties in each phase. Thus, attention would have to be given to each phase at one time.

The ownership or investment cycle requires some reordering of the topics or decision areas from figure 1–1, as shown in figure 1–2. In looking at figure 1–2, note that much of the analysis and effort takes place in the acquisition phase. Once a property is acquired with a contract signed, financing arranged, and title closed, an investor is locked in. Acquisition may take only two or three months. On the other hand, the ownership administration phase requires only occasional major decisions, even though it may last for five or ten years or longer. Disposition may take several months or longer, measuring from the initial offering of the property to closing of the sale. Note that the main difference between the acquisition and disposition phases is that a specific investor is on the opposite side of the buy-sell contract.

In keeping with the investment cycle, much of our emphasis is on prepa-

FIGURE 1–2
The real estate investment cycle

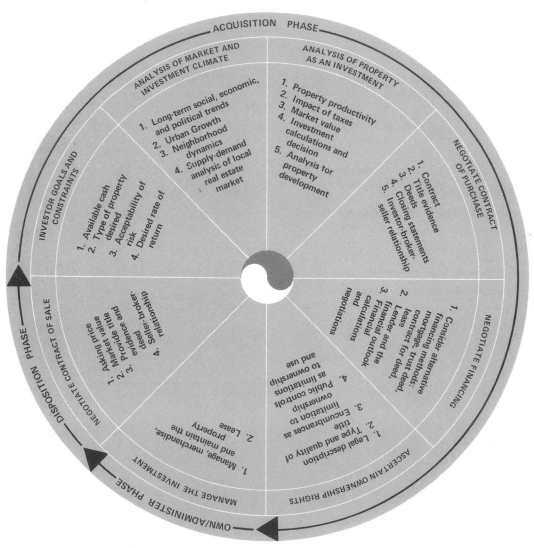

ration for a real estate investment. However, in practice the many topics considered are not so neatly organized. Rather, the topics must be considered on an interrelated basis. Thus, market analysis runs immediately into investment analysis and into negotiation for acquisition. And assuming a purchase contract, clear title has to be established at the same time that financing is being obtained. Failure of an investor to give proper attention to any one of these decision areas may mean less than the best possible return from the investment. The real estate investment cycle provides an organized framework for successful investing in much the same way that the decision-making process provides an orderly framework for rational thinking.

DECISION-MAKING AND ADMINISTRATIVE PROCESSES

Real estate is complex and relatively unique as a commodity. It has physical, legal, locational, and financial facets, which must all be analyzed prior to making decisions or taking actions about its use, purchase, sale, financing, or management. Therefore, a brief discussion of decision-making and administrative processes seems appropriate at this point. These processes are theoretically consistent with the financial-management framework and the real estate investment cycle. First, however, a few comments are appropriate to explain why real estate decisions are relatively unique or different from decisions about most other commodities.

The main characteristics that tend to make real estate decisions unique are as follows:

1. Real estate has high value, based on ability to generate services and income over an extended time period. The high value tends to be a market-limiting factor; that is, the ability of most people to own real estate is limited because of relatively low wealth or earning capacity.

2. Real estate has a long life. Land goes on forever. Buildings last for decades. And during the life of real estate, the services must be used as produced. Real estate services cannot be stored, to be used later, like toys, wheat, or cars. Each time period must stand on its own. If an apartment remains vacant during one month, the loss of rent cannot be recovered in the next.

3. Debt financing is usually necessary as well as desirable. It is necessary because most people cannot afford to purchase real estate outright; desirable because the use of credit means leverage and the possibility of a higher rate of return on any money invested. **Leverage,** or "trading-on-the-equity," results from borrowing money on a property at an interest rate lower than the property's rate of earning. This yields a higher rate of return to the owner's equity than would otherwise be earned. Leverage is illustrated, by example, in the chapters on real estate finance and investment.

4. Transaction costs, in terms of both time and money, are high. At a minimum several days are usually required to complete a real estate transac-

tion involving transfer of ownership. Several weeks is normal, and several months is not uncommon. A transaction cost of 6 or 7 percent of the value of a property is not unusual.

The Decision-Making Process

We make simple, everyday decisions about what to eat, wear or do, about whom to see, or where to go, by feel, habit, hunch, or intuition. And action flows out of the decision in a very natural manner. As situations become more complex, it becomes worthwhile to devote more time to identifying alternatives and their implications prior to making a decision and taking action. The benefits of a good decision or the costs of a bad decision, at some point, become great enough to justify spending extra time, money, and effort to reach the best choice. Choosing a career, a spouse, or a home are examples of such decisions. Higher costs of decision making are also justified in choosing a real estate investment.

A series of steps for orderly decision making have been identified. The series is called the decision-making process, the logical thought process, or the problem-solving process.[2] The steps are as follows:

1. *Recognize decision or problem situation.*   Based on objectives or experience, the need for a choice or some action becomes evident. For example, an investor recognizes that real estate probably offers greater returns than stocks and bonds. The investor's unstated objective is to maximize rate of return.

2. *Data collection.*   Collect all pertinent data or facts within reasonable limits, based on the importance of the problem and the time available to reach a decision. Our investor obtains data from securities dealers, real estate brokers, *The Wall Street Journal,* and other sources about various investment opportunities that are open.

3. *Problem identification.*   The collected information is studied, key issues or problems are identified, and possibly, subproblems are recognized. Our investor determines, for example, that real estate really does offer better rates of return and is therefore an alternative worth pursuing. Important subproblems become (1) getting more background in real estate ownership and investment, (2) learning about ownership and acquisition of titles, (3) finding out value trends in the community, (4) learning real estate finance because not enough money for 100 percent equity ownership is available, (5) learning tax implications of real estate ownership, (6) deter-

---

[2] For a current discussion of decision-making and administrative processes, see Herbert A. Simon, *The New Science of Management Decisions* (Englewood Cliffs, N.J.: Prentice-Hall, 1977) or E. Frank Harison, *The Managerial Decision-Making Process* (Boston: Houghton Mifflin, 1975). For early discussions of the decision-making and the executive or administrative processes, see the following: Peter F. Drucker, *The Practice of Management* (New York: Harper & Row, 1954); Chester I. Bernard, *The Functions of the Executive* (Cambridge, Mass.: Harvard University Press, 1953), and Simon, *Administrative Behavior.*

mining investment value of available properties, and (7) figuring out how to manage the properties, assuming acquisition.

4. *Posing alternatives.*   Possible solutions or modes of action are listed, and the probable implications of each are considered. For example, our investor now has the alternatives of not going into real estate at all, going in part way, or going in with all available assets. In short, it is a portfolio-management and estate-building situation.

5. *Make decision.*   The entire situation is reviewed, and a choice is made of that action likely to give the best result. In our example, the investor may decide to "try the water" by selling some stocks and bonds and acquiring an apartment building. At this point, action is called for.

The reader should be aware that the decision-making process is not as clean or clear-cut in practice as presented here. Much going back and forth, or interweaving, between the steps is likely. And, except for the last step, the sequence may not be exactly as indicated here. The important consideration is that data be collected and studied and alternatives identified, prior to reaching a decision. The steps ultimately boil down to answering three questions: (1) What problem is to be solved? (2) What are the alternative solutions? and (3) Which of the alternative solutions is the best?

The Administrative Process

The **administrative process** is an extension of the decision-making process; it is action oriented rather than analysis oriented. It usually involves achieving objectives through people. It involves a series of five steps.

1. *Deciding to achieve an objective.*   Effort and study are necessary in deciding to achieve an objective or desired result, in a complex situation. This combination of effort and study makes up the decision-making process. For our example, the investor's objective is to acquire an apartment building.

2. *Organize resources.*   Money and people must be mobilized to accomplish an objective. In our example, our investor must now plan for learning about real estate ownership, investment analysis, and business methods. Plans for the sale of stocks and bonds must also be made to release money for equity investment in the apartment building. The use of brokers, lenders, counselors, and appraisers may also be planned for.

3. *Exerting leadership.*   Action must be initiated or sparked to put a plan into action. The stockbroker must be told to sell; a real estate broker must be informed of the need for an apartment house; a counselor or appraiser may be engaged; and loan arrangements with a bank or savings and loan association may be made.

4. *Controlling operations.*   Efforts to achieve a desired objective must be coordinated and monitored on a continuing basis to assure conformance with the plan and achievement of the objective. Eventually, the stocks and bonds are sold, and an appropriate property is located, financed, and pur-

chased. Also, suitable arrangements must be made for the management of the property by either the owner or a hired manager.

5. *Periodic reevaluation.* On a more long-term basis, the process must be reviewed periodically to determine if the past choices are working out. In our example, this means comparing the rate of return from stocks and bonds with the rate of return from real estate. This is a portfolio-management strategy concern. More or larger real estate investments may eventually be desirable. And investment in different types of properties may become advantageous.

That is a very brief summary of the decision-making and administrative processes. For greater depth, the reader is referred to the sources cited. This summary is only intended to provide an approach or setting for much of the remainder of this book. Successful investment, on a continuing basis, does depend on selecting properties offering the greatest returns and on following through with a sound management system.

SUMMARY

Real estate has three common meanings: (1) a field of study, (2) a form of business activity, and (3) a financial asset, which is the object of the first two. The perspective of a rational investor who is seeking self-interest in real estate is to be used throughout this book. It is this self-interest that causes owners to use real estate in a way that gives it the greatest value, termed its highest and best use.

The next chapter covers real estate as a business. The balance of this book is divided into six divisions, or topics, each representing a major area of study of real estate. These divisions are: (1) defining ownership rights, (2) conveying ownership rights, (3) financing real estate, (4) determining the investment climate and the demand for real estate, (5) real estate investing, and (6) managing real estate. Taken together, these areas provide an integrated and comprehensive framework for the financial management of administration of real estate. This framework has many advantages for investors and specialists in real estate.

The administrative process has five steps: (1) deciding to achieve an objective (make decision), (2) organize resources, (3) exert leadership, (4) control operations, and (5) periodically reevaluate. The decision-making process is the first step in the administrative process. The decision-making process also has five steps: (1) recognize problem situation, (2) collect data, (3) identify the "real" problem, (4) pose alternatives, and (5) make decisions.

KEY TERMS

Administrative process

Decision-making process

Highest and best use

Land use

Leverage

Rational being

Self-interest

Title closing

Tradeoff

QUESTIONS FOR REVIEW AND DISCUSSION

1. List and distinguish among the three most common meanings of real estate.

2. What are the stated goals and assumptions of the rational investor of this chapter? How can the approach of the rational investor be helpful to anyone interested in making real-world investments in real estate?

3. What are the main concerns and goals of a real estate specialist? Is the rational-investor approach likely to be useful to someone interested in offering specialized real estate services? How?

4. Explain briefly the rationale for the order in which the six major divisions of this book are presented.

5. State and explain briefly at least three ways in which real estate decisions tend to be unique.

6. List the steps in the decision-making process.

7. List in order the steps in the executive or administrative process.

8. Do real estate investors and other specialists really have a social responsibility? Discuss.

9. In 150 words or less, write down your main objectives in studying real estate. Discuss your composition with others and revise as desired. Then save it until your immediate study or term is completed, as an administrative check on yourself.

REFERENCES

Harrison, E. Frank. *The Managerial Decision-Making Process.* Boston: Houghton Mifflin, 1975. Gives an overview of the decision-making process in an easily understood writing style. Many references cited. Includes glossary of terms.

Simon, Herbert A. *The New Science of Management Decisions.* Englewood Cliffs, N.J.: Prentice-Hall, 1977. An in-depth discussion of the administrative process; in some ways, an updated summary of Simon's earlier works. Of moderate reading difficulty.

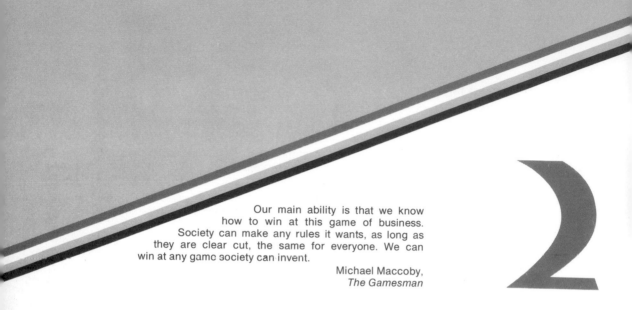

The Real Estate Business

Our main ability is that we know how to win at this game of business. Society can make any rules it wants, as long as they are clear cut, the same for everyone. We can win at any game society can invent.

Michael Maccoby,
The Gamesman

2

The activities and interaction of people involved in the buying, selling, exchanging, using, and improving of realty make up the real estate business and, in fact, actually make up the real estate market. The commodity involved is real estate rights. Many of the people in the real estate business have the same attitude as Michael Maccoby's gamesman. Thus, the real estate business is a game. Everyone must play, although at varying levels of intensity, because we all need space in which to live. Each community constitutes a field of play or a distinct market. Each person keeps his or her own score. To win is to maximize self-interest in real estate, and the prize may be satisfactions from home ownership, profits or returns on investment, or fees for services rendered. The rules of play come from several sources, including real estate law, licensing regulations, and professional and personal ethics.

The purpose of this chapter is to give an overview of the real estate game. The following major topics are discussed in this overview:

1. The players—market participants
2. The setting or field of play—market operation and characteristics
3. Player eligibility—requirements for entry
4. History of the game

THE PLAYERS

Four distinct groups or classes of players in the real estate game may be identified, as follows:

1. Finance and investment (lenders and investors, who are the primary decision makers and risk takers)
   (a) Equity investment
      (1) Owner-user
      (2) Owner-investor
   (b) Lender investment (primarily mortgage lending)
   (c) Leasehold investment
2. Brokerage services (brokerage personnel, who are the catalysts or facilitators)
   (a) Residential
   (b) Commercial investment
   (c) Industrial
   (d) Farm and land
3. Property development (developers, builders, contractors, who are specialized decision makers/risk takers)
   (a) Land subdivision
   (b) Contract construction
   (c) Speculative building
4. Specialized services (practitioners, who are the supporters or helpers) *soft goods*
   (a) Appraisal
   (b) Architecture
   (c) Counseling *lawyers –*
   (d) Education
   (e) Escrow
   (f) Insurance
   (g) Management
   (h) Planning
   (i) Title analysis

Finance and Investment

Members of the finance and investment groups are the primary decision makers in the real estate business. They put up the money and take the risks. They account for all major financial interests in the use and operation of real estate. Generally speaking, the values of the interests of the equity, lender, and leasehold (if any) interests amount to equal market value.

Most owner-users and owner-investors hold property for long-term benefits. Some even develop or improve property to realize these benefits. On the other hand, some owner-investors specialize in holding property for short periods in seeking speculative gains. The investment of most lenders is in the loan to the owner, which is secured by the property. The lender's main concerns then are that the property be kept operational and well-maintained and that the loan be repaid on schedule. Renters who live in or use property for an extended time, under a lease, hold an interest in the property, termed a **leasehold.** Rental payments must, of course, be paid to the owner for this occupancy.

Brokerage Services

Brokers act as catalysts or stimulants to the real estate market. That is, they make the market work by bringing buyers and sellers together, for a fee or commission. Together with investors and lenders, brokers are instrumental in carrying out the exchange function of the real estate market.

Property Development

Subdividers, contractors, and investor-**developers** add to the supply, or modify the existing supply, of real estate. They are decision makers specializing in making adjustments in the quality and quantity of space, which is the second major function of the real estate market. Contractors render improvement services for profit but have no ownership risks.

Specialized Services

People in the various real estate services groups are specialists who provide support services, technical expertise or know-how, usually for the finance and investment groups, on a fee or salary basis. **Appraisers** and **counselors** collect and analyze market information for the decision makers. Appraisers specialize in making value estimates; counselors, who have wider background and experience, give advice for a variety of decisions or actions. **Architects** design and oversee construction of real estate improvements. Real estate education is provided by people with many backgrounds at the licensure, professional, and college levels. Title analysts and insurance agents offer protection from loss to owners and lenders. **Escrow agents** hold money, legal instruments, and other valuables for contracting parties until all conditions pertinent to the contract have been satisfied. Title closing is the most usual situation where an escrow agent is used. **Managers** look after properties for owners. **Planners** coordinate development and change to protect the environment and to relate physical real estate to the social and economic needs of a community. Planners generally work for public agencies or very large private organizations.

An individual or an organization may belong in two or more of these groups at one time. That is, two or more hats may be worn at the same time. For example, a broker may also be a developer and an investor. Or an appraiser may also be a counselor and a teacher.

Professional Status

In the last half-century player specialization has developed rapidly because real estate is too broad for any one person or organization to master all its aspects. Professionalization has developed hand-in-hand with specialization because the experts want and need public recognition to set them apart. Professional recognition suggests (1) prestige and distinction, (2) greater sales acceptance in marketing services, and (3) social responsibility. In turn, new people entering the industry must develop expertise and obtain professional recognition to compete. Knowing the areas of specialization and the professional organizations is therefore a great advantage to a newcomer.

The major specializations and the main trade or professional organizations in real estate are shown in figure 2–1.

THE SETTING

Real estate business activity involves many types of properties, many buyers and sellers, and many specialists. Are there any generalizations that may be made to make it easier to understand what is going on; that is, to understand the operation of the real estate market? Fortunately, yes, there are several. Market functions may be identified and ex-

FIGURE 2–1
Major Areas of Specialization in Real Estate and Professional Organizations

Specialization	Organization
1. Appraising	American Institute of Real Estate Appraisers*
	American Society of Appraisers
	International Association of Assessing Officers
	Society of Real Estate Appraisers
2. Architecture	American Institute of Architects
3. Brokerage	Farm and Land Institute*
	International Real Estate Federation*
	National Association of Real Estate Brokers
	National Association of Realtors*
	Real Estate Securities and Syndication Institute*
	Realtors National Marketing Institute*
	Society of Industrial Realtors*
4. Building/Contracting	Associated General Contractors of America
	National Association of Home Builders
5. Counseling	American Society of Real Estate Counselors*
6. Developing	Urban Land Institute
7. Educating	American Real Estate and Urban Economics Association
8. Financing	American Bankers Association
	Mortgage Bankers of America
	National Association of Mutual Savings Banks
	U.S. League of Savings Associations
9. Insurance	American Institute for Property and Liability Underwriters
10. Managing	Institute of Real Estate Management*
11. Owning	National Apartment Owners Association
	National Association of Building Owners and Managers
12. Planning	American Planning Association

* Affiliates of the National Association of Realtors, 430 N. Michigan, Chicago, Ill. 60611.

plained. Broker specialization by property type is evident. Services are rendered on a specialized basis. And certain, unique aspects of the market, which make it appear disorganized and inefficient, may, in fact, be identified and explained. Taken together, these considerations provide the setting and largely determine the manner of play in the real estate game.

Functions Performed

The activity in the real estate market results in three very vital economic and social functions.

1. *Exchange,* resulting in the redistribution of space ownership and possibly the redetermination of space usage
2. *Space adjustment,* affecting both the amount and type of space available to the market
3. *Price and value information,* enabling market participants to be more knowledgeable for subsequent transactions

EXCHANGE. Exchange, and the possible reallocation of land and existing space to alternate uses based on rent-paying ability, is the most basic function of the real estate market. A sale occurs when it is mutually advantageous to both buyer and seller. The buyer prefers the property instead of the money. The seller prefers the money. The real estate market therefore reallocates property ownership and redistributes space usage according to the preferences of investors and users who have the financial capability. A lease also reallocates space. But in a leasing situation, only the rights of occupancy and use are exchanged for money.

In offering a property for sale, the owner, acting in self-interest, seeks to obtain the highest possible price. The asking price is therefore likely to be the maximum amount the seller thinks the property is worth. Each potential buyer shops the many properties available, seeking the one best suited to his or her needs. In addition to considering the price, the buyer needs to take physical, locational, social, legal, governmental, financial, and zoning considerations into account in making the determination of greatest suitability. The bidder able to use the property most effectively (earn the greatest profit) is also most able to pay the owner's price and thus is most likely to come to terms with the owner by offering the highest price, thereby getting the property. Thus, market competition keeps sale prices in line with actual or probable uses of properties and, in turn, tends to force properties to their highest and best uses. The *highest and best use* of a property is that legal and possible use giving the property its greatest value.

SPACE ADJUSTMENT. The market also operates to adjust the quality and quantity of space in response to changing social and economic needs of the community or area. Owners, managers, developers, and builders constantly seek to maximize the value of real estate under their control. For example, assume that the value of a property in a possible use, such as for offices, exceeds the value of the property in its current use plus the cost of conversion. A rational owner is likely to convert the property to office space in this circumstance. Also, if the value of new space exceeds the cost of providing it (site cost plus construction cost), additional land will be subdivided and new buildings will be erected. If, however, demand for space decreases and property values decline, little or no remodeling or new construction is likely to take place.

PROVIDING INFORMATION. The price paid for property in one transaction can help other market participants develop ideas about value for subsequent transactions. Value is partially determined in the market, for a given type of property, by comparing actual prices paid for similar type properties. Value is also partially determined by a buyer's needs and potential use of a property. An appraiser is often engaged to give an estimate of the market value (the most probable selling price) of a property. An estimate of market value in and of itself is relatively meaningless. The real purpose of determining market value, or making a judgment about market value, is making more reliable information available to an owner, to a bidder, or to someone else about to make a decision. Other information affecting value, also needed by a bidder, may have to be obtained from architects, planners, managers, or title analysts.

An appraiser or consultant collects and analyzes information in order to make a rather formal judgment of the market value or possible use of a specific property. The estimate may be used for a purchase decision, a mortgage-lending decision, or a condemnation action. Numerous other market participants, however, make judgments about market value and use them in many informal ways. Builders and developers make value judgments on structures to be built or projects to be undertaken. Many home buyers also make value judgments when they sign sales contracts without obtaining formal appraisals. Property managers make such judgments continually about properties under their control. The information and judgments may not always be accurate, but they do provide a basis for decisions or actions. The use of market information and the subsequent value judgments are important for the continuing stability and operation of the real estate market.

Market Characteristics and Their Implications

The real estate market appears disorganized and inefficient in comparison to the market for stocks and bonds. Much of this appearance stems from the unique nature of real estate as a commodity. The characteristics that are relatively unique and that are responsible for this somewhat disorganized and inefficient appearance are as follows:

1. Localized competition
2. Stratified demand
3. Decentralized transactions
4. Confidential transactions
5. Relatively uninformed participants
6. Supply fixed in short run

LOCALIZED COMPETITION. One physical characteristic of real estate as a commodity is its fixity, or immobility. Another is its heterogeneity, or lack of similarity. Immobility means that real estate cannot be moved from area to area in response to changes in supply-and-demand conditions. The lack of similarity and standardization (heterogeneity) means that a potential buyer must inspect each property of interest to fully understand its merits. That is, a buyer cannot generalize from one property to another. Both of these characteristics, fixity and heterogeneity, limit competition between properties. Property values therefore tend to be directly dependent on local demand. Localized competition is more true of residential properties than of commercial-investment and industrial properties because investors and industrialists are usually more knowledgeable and have greater reason to look around carefully before buying a property.

STRATIFIED DEMAND. People generally acquire or use real estate for a specific purpose. For example, a family looking for a detached home limits its search to one-family houses. A merchant seeking a property from which to sell furniture looks only at store buildings. An investor for dollar income looks only at rental properties. The market recognizes and responds to these specific needs of purchaser-investors in several ways. One response may be that the market for apartments is very active and the market for one-family residences very slow. The property classification system used in the market, as explained in the next section, reflects a second response. Specialization among brokerage and other market services reflects a third market response to stratified demand.

DECENTRALIZED TRANSACTIONS. Potential buyers need to visit each property of interest because of the lack of standardization of real estate. And because of the unique geographic location of each parcel, they must often travel great distances to visit all properties of interest. In turn, buyers and sellers make agreements whenever conditions seem right. These agreements may be drawn up and signed in a broker's office, in the buyer's home or place of work, or in a car at the time of a visit to the property itself. When a real estate sale is made, no central clearing house reports the price, as is usually done by the price quotations of the stock and bonds markets, which are printed in many daily newspapers.

CONFIDENTIAL TRANSACTIONS. Real estate buyers and sellers usually meet in private, and their offering and agreed prices are not freely disseminated as a rule. Nevertheless, people increasingly desire prices of completed transactions in subsequent sales talks. Public records do not necessarily indicate actual sale prices; many deeds only specify "ten dollars and other good and valuable consideration." In most states, deeds need not even be recorded if debt financing is not used, and the buyer moves into the property promptly after purchase. Recording is usually for the advantage of the buyer or lender. Only people closely associated with the market have relatively easy access to price and value information because of the confidential nature of the transactions. Decentralized and confidential transactions tend to make market information difficult to collect and therefore costly.

RELATIVELY UNINFORMED PARTICIPANTS. Most buyers and sellers engage in a sales transaction only once every several years. They do not fully understand real estate. They do not have access to price and value information because they are not associated with the market. There is no central source of information from which information may be purchased. And having information collected and analyzed is costly. Consequently, most owners and potential purchasers are not well prepared to engage in buying and selling property. A careful buyer cannot be sure of making an optimum choice in buying a property. And the price agreed upon may reflect differences in negotiating ability of the buyers and sellers as well as the relative merits of the property involved. Business firms, however, are increasingly using real estate specialists—negotiators—in buying and selling properties, to offset their own limitations. Lack of informed participants lowers the effectiveness of real estate markets.

SUPPLY FIXED IN SHORT RUN. A final characteristic of the real estate market is that supply is relatively fixed over a period of a few years. It takes from several weeks to several months or longer to build new structures. Conversion of existing properties or construction of new improvements is time consuming. In any given year, new construction generally accounts for only 2 or 3 percent of the total supply of space. Physical, legal, and financial obstacles all retard rapid expansion of supply in response to sharply increased demand. If demand decreases, the excess supply cannot be moved to another area or readily removed from the market. The consequence is sharp price increases for space in a community if demand runs too far ahead of supply. Alternatively, prices decrease if demand falls short of supply.

CONCLUDING COMMENT. Localized competition, stratified demand, decentralized and confidential transactions, and relatively fixed supply all cause the real estate market to be less than ideal. On the other hand, potential buyers and sellers usually do not have a tight time pressure regarding the completion of a transaction. A family just moving into a community does not, of course, have two or three years in which to find a place to live, but a family desiring a different home in the same community can generally take its time. Business firms are giving themselves more lead time and hiring more qualified personnel to realize better real estate decisions and locations. The point is that most participants do have time to consider alternatives and otherwise prepare for an advantageous transaction. Further, highly competent real estate service people are increasingly available to aid the buyers and sellers, for a fee of course.

Classes of Property Traded

The classes or kinds of real properties bought and sold in the real estate market are several. Each class represents a submarket that is often the basis of a brokerage specialization.

RESIDENTIAL. Residential real estate is generally considered to include one-family residences, multifamily residences up to six units, and vacant land or lots that might be improved for anything up to six dwelling units. These properties are included in this category whether located in a city, a suburb, or a rural area. Technically, larger multifamily properties are also residential, but because of their generally higher value and greater complexity, these larger properties are more frequently classified as commercial-investment properties.

COMMERCIAL INVESTMENT. Large apartment buildings, stores, shopping centers, office buildings, theaters, hotels and motels, vacant commercial sites, and other business properties, are termed commercial-investment real estate. Most commercial-investment properties are rental or income-producing properties. Commercial-investment properties are usually located in urban areas.

INDUSTRIAL. Industrial real estate includes factories, warehouses, utilities, and mines. Vacant industrial sites may also be included in this category. Large industrial properties are usually located in or near urban areas because of their dependence on an adequate labor supply. Industrial plants may sometimes be located and developed in rural areas if the availability of raw materials and power so dictates. Labor will be drawn to the plant and eventually an urban area will grow up around or near the plant.

RURAL (FARM AND LAND). Farms and ranches make up the bulk of rural properties that are bought and sold. Recreational properties are increasingly important and are tending to become a distinct class. Raw, vacant land near urban areas is typically included in the rural property category, although it might be ripe for conversion to residential, commercial, or industrial use.

SPECIAL PURPOSE. Churches, colleges and other education institutions, hospitals, cemeteries, nursing homes, and golf courses make up a category termed **special-purpose properties.** These properties are bought and sold only infrequently, and no specialization has developed around them. They tend, for the most part, to be located in or near urban areas.

PUBLIC. Public agencies need real estate for highways, post offices, parks, administration buildings, schools, and other public uses. Public properties are usually held for long periods of time and are sold only if excess. Public properties are frequently acquired under the power of eminent domain. **Eminent domain** is the right of a governmental agency to acquire property for public uses or purposes without the consent of the owner, upon payment of just compensation. For the most part, public properties are therefore not considered as being bought and sold in a free market. Many properties however, are often acquired for public use, and less often disposed of, by public agencies through the free market.

PLAYER ELIGIBILITY

People enter the real estate game from a wide variety of backgrounds. No license is required to become an equity investor, although money and a willingness to take risks are necessary. A source of money for loans is obviously necessary to become a lender. A leasehold position may be gained simply by entering into a rental contract. A license, know-how, and sometimes money are necessary to enter most other lines of real estate business activity. All states and/or provinces require all brokerage personnel to be licensed. Some states and/or provinces require builders, appraisers, counselors, and others rendering real estate services to be licensed.

Any one interested in becoming licensed may obtain necessary information by calling the local realtors' board or homebuilders' association. Alternately, a letter requesting licensing information might be sent to the real estate commissioner at the state or provincial capital.

Briefly, obtaining a license requires that an application be made and an examination be passed. An examination fee must usually be sent in with the application, along with other information or documentation. In general, a person must be a high school graduate or its equivalent, be at least eighteen years of age (in some states, twenty-one), and a citizen, to qualify to take the examination in the U.S. If you apply, the stage is set for the following events. Sometime after the application is submitted, a notice will be sent to you stating when and where the exam may be taken, plus any additional response expected of you. The results of the examination will be sent to you within several weeks of taking the exam. If you pass, the license fee may be mailed in and within a short time your license will be sent to you. If you did not pass, you may take the examination at a later time by paying a second fee. Several weeks are usually required for a license application to be processed. Hence, if you propose to take the exam upon finishing this book, you would be wise to request the application materials immediately.

ETHICS OF PLAY

People tend to do funny things when large amounts of money are involved. And real estate, being a high-value asset, involves large amounts of money. In order to protect the public as well as their own personal reputations, established practitioners and government regulators demand ethical behavior in real estate transactions. Ethical behavior results in a reputation for honesty and integrity and in avoidance of legal problems.

Licensed practitioners, particularly brokerage personnel, are subject to close and continuous scrutiny in their business practices. A breach of ethics may result in the loss of the license. A code of ethics covers three relationships:

1. Relations with the public, primarily people with whom business is conducted on other than a principal-agent basis (**customers**)
2. Relations with **principals,** primarily property owners (**clients**)
3. Relations with other practitioners (fellow workers)

An investor may reasonably expect certain minimum standards of behavior from licensed practitioners in each of these areas.

Relations with Customers

The public looks to brokers, appraisers, and contractors, as specialists and experts in real estate, for reliable information upon which to make decisions on buying, selling, building, and leasing property. The following are minimum standards for these specialists in other than principal-agent relationships:

1. Discrimination based on race, creed, sex, or place of national origin is to be avoided.

2. General knowledge of the field, such as planning, zoning, or economic trends, is to be current and reliable.

3. Pertinent facts about a parcel of real estate shall be clearly and accurately stated and shall not be concealed, exaggerated, misrepresented, or otherwise caused to be misleading.

4. No estimate of property value is to be made by an appraiser when employment or fee is contingent on the amount of the estimate.

5. Any oral or written estimate of the value of a property shall include the following items:
   (a) Estimate of value
   (b) Date of estimate
   (c) Interest appraised
   (d) Limiting conditions
   (e) Description of entire property
   (f) Basis of value estimate

Relations with Clients

In seeking and using the services of an agent-specialist, a great deal of trust is placed in the **agent.** Hence, the principal-agent relationship is extremely sensitive in an ethical sense. If the trust is violated, tighter regulation is likely. Some ethical guidelines to be expected by clients (principals) from practitioners-specialists (as agents) are as follows:

1. Market value should not be misrepresented to an owner, as in trying to list a property.

2. Upon accepting an agency agreement, a practitioner owes complete fidelity to the principal. Any and all conflicts of interest must be avoided in rendering services. Full disclosure must be made of any personal interest in the client's property by the agent.

 3. Compensation must not be accepted from more than one party in a transaction without full and prior disclosure to all parties in the transaction.

4. Owners-principals must be shown all offers as soon as they are received, whether from a prospective purchaser or another broker.

5. Any monies of principals-clients must be placed in special trust accounts until the transaction of concern is completed or terminated.

Relations with Fellow Practitioners

Principals have a right to expect their agents to build and maintain high levels of cooperation and communications with fellow personnel to further the principals' purposes. Ethics covering sensitive areas of cooperation and communication among brokerage personnel are as follows:

1. Brokerage personnel must willingly and fully disclose the nature of any listing to fellow sales personnel: open listing, exclusive right to sell, etc.

2. All pertinent facts, negotiations, and communications should be transmitted through the listing broker promptly to an owner.

Realtors'® Code of Ethics

The Code of Ethics of the National Association of REALTORS®, first adopted in 1913, contains detailed standards of professional conduct for brokerage and therefore embodies many of the above ethical principles. Personnel who belong to the National Association of REALTORS® agree to live up to the Code. Licensing examinations for both broker and **salesperson** sometimes include questions on the REALTORS'® Code. Aspiring licensees should therefore carefully read and study the Code, which can be found in the Appendix of this book.

HISTORY OF THE REAL ESTATE GAME

Real estate transactions date back to the Old Testament. Jeremiah tells of buying a field from his cousin, Hanamel, for seventeen shekels of silver. Leviticus, chapter 25, summarizes the ancient laws of real estate transactions.

Land subdivision and promotion is a part of our heritage in the United States. For example, George Washington and Robert Morris actively engaged in land speculation in the newly laid-out Washington, D.C. Morris, a signer of the Declaration of Independence, died in poverty after serving over three years in prison as a result of his "speculation." Until this century, most buy-sell transactions took place directly between an owner and a purchaser. After an agreement was made, lawyers were often called in to draw up the contract and to look after the details of the transaction.

At the beginning of this century, the real estate business was largely unorganized and fiercely competitive. The *caveat emptor* (let the buyer beware) spirit generally prevailed. But the use of brokers and agents had become an established practice. And the need for standardized brokerage practices and for trade ethics soon led to trade organizations known as *real estate boards*. The boards proved so successful that the National Association of Real Estate Boards was organized in 1908. In 1974, the association changed its name to the National Association of REALTORS® (NAR). Total membership in the NAR, as of 1980, is 755,650, as shown in figure 2–2.

FIGURE 2–2
Number of Real Estate Boards and Active Members of the National Association of REALTORS®

Year	Number of Boards	Realtor Members
1911	43	3,000
1920	225	10,077
1930	608	18,916
1940	458	14,162
1950	1,100	43,990
1960	1,370	68,818
1970	1,590	93,400
1980*	1,806	284,654

* Total 1980 membership, including Realtor Associates, was 755,650.

In 1917 both California and Oregon passed legislation requiring brokers and salespersons to be licensed to protect the public. All states and provinces now require brokers and salespersons to be licensed. Many states and provinces now also require other real estate specialists, such as contractors, appraisers, and managers, to be licensed.

In 1940, real estate and construction employed slightly over 2.5 million workers, making up 5.61 percent of total U.S. employment. Today (1980), real estate and construction employ 6.9 million workers, or 7.04 percent of the total U.S. employment of 98 million, and the value of new construction currently averages nearly 10 percent of the gross national product. This output includes from 1.5 to 3.0 million new dwelling units each year. (See figure 2–3.)

FIGURE 2–3
Construction and Real Estate Employment Relative to Total Employment in the United States, 1940–80

Year	Total Employment United States	Employment in Construction and Real Estate	Percent in Construction and Real Estate
1940	44,888,083	2,517,155	5.61
1950	56,239,449	4,014,790	7.14
1960	64,639,256	4,415,057	6.83
1970	77,308,792	5,003,049	6.47
1980 (est.)	98,000,000	6,900,000	7.04
Percent increase 1940–80	118.3	174.1	—

Source: U.S. Census of Population, 1940–1970, Detailed Characteristics. Calculations and some interpolations made by authors. Based on data from *Survey of Current Business,* December 1979.

SUMMARY

Real estate, in a sense, is a game in which everyone must play and in which the objective is to maximize personal benefits from realty. The players may be divided into four distinct groups: (1) finance and investment (the primary decision makers and risk takers), (2) brokerage services (catalysts and facilitators), (3) property development (specialized decision makers and risk takers), and (4) specialized services (supporters or helpers). Each community has its own real estate market or field of play. The commodity in this market is real-property rights.

The purpose of play, from an overall point of view, is to push real estate to its highest and best or most valuable use. The functions of the market are (1) exchange, (2) adjustment in amount and type of space, and (3) providing price and value information. Characteristics of the real estate market are local competition, stratified demand, decentralized and confidential transactions, relatively uninformed participants, and supply fixed, in the short run. The main classes of property and broker specializations are residential, commercial investment, industrial, and farm and land. Any competent adult may play the real estate game, though a license must be obtained to be eligible to render many of the services.

KEY TERMS

Agent	Escrow
Appraiser	Leasehold
Architect	Manager
Broker	Planner
Client	Principal
Contractor	REALTOR®
Customer	Salesperson
Developer	Special-purpose property
Eminent domain	Subdivider

QUESTIONS FOR REVIEW AND DISCUSSION

1. Name the four main classes or groups of participants in the real estate business and briefly explain the function of each.

2. List and explain briefly the three main market functions performed by the real estate business.

3. Identify and explain briefly the implications of at least five characteristics of the real estate market.

4. What are the purposes of real estate licensing laws? Of real estate ethics? Are the purposes achieved? Discuss.

5. Give three reasons for belonging to a profession. Are these reasons valid in real estate? Discuss.

6. Are higher or special educational requirements desirable for entry into the real estate business? What are the requirements in your state or province if any?

7. Most owners and potential owners are not well prepared to buy and sell property. Do you agree?

8. Do the various classes of real estate (residential, commercial-investment, etc.) have different-sized areas of market influence? If so, why? Discuss.

REFERENCES

Crowe, Kenneth C. *America for Sale.* Garden City, N.Y.: Doubleday, 1978. A general discussion of the purchase of property in America by the Arabs, the Japanese, and other foreign groups, which may affect our control of power. Interesting and easy to read.

Dasso, Jerome; Alfred A. Ring; and Douglas McFall. *Fundamentals of Real Estate.* Englewood Cliffs, N.J.: Prentice-Hall, 1977. Chapters 1–3 provide a more in-depth discussion of real estate as a business, a career, and a profession.

Halper, Emanuel B. *Wonderful World of Real Estate.* Boston; Warren, Gorham, and Lamont, 1975. A series of case studies about various facets of real estate (development, leasing, buying) written in a humorous style.

McMahan, John. *Property Development.* New York: McGraw-Hill, 1976. Chapters 1–3 discuss major trends affecting the property-development business: types of land-use activities and structures, governmental regulations, and industry organization. Vital information for anyone interested in property development.

Real Estate Review, vol. 8, nos. 3 and 4. Contain a series of three articles on the ethics and structure of real estate brokerage. "The Changing Structure of Residential Brokerage" by Norma G. Miller and "Broker's Liability: Cause for Concern" by Benjamin N. Henszey appear in the fall 1978 issue. "Rhetoric vs. Reality in Residential Real Estate Brokerage" by Ronald Bordessa appears in the winter 1979 issue. All three offer food for thought and discussion.

Thomas, Dana L. *Lords of the Land.* New York: Putnam's, 1977. Land development and promotion in American history. The style is anecdotal, breezy, and easy to read. The characters and content are fascinating.

ONE

DEFINING OWNERSHIP RIGHTS

Property Descriptions and Characteristics

> But that land—it is one thing that will still be there
> when I come back—land is always there.
> Pearl S. Buck
> *A House Divided*

3

Our system of accurate, clear, and complete property descriptions is important and necessary to an owner or investor for several reasons. It specifically identifies property, in a physical sense, for the establishment of boundaries, for the calculation of area, for noting location relative to other properties, and for transfer of title from one owner to another. In a legal sense, it allows for the identification of rights owned, for example, air rights, water rights, or mineral rights. It provides a basis for law and order, and, in turn, for rational decision making. In short, our system of property description is the basis for packaging real estate as a commodity in our real estate markets.

The purpose of this chapter is to explain our system of property rights, and its implications for real estate as a commodity. Toward this end, the material is divided into five sections:

1. From Mother Earth to real estate
2. Needed distinctions in describing real estate
3. Legal descriptions of real estate
4. Physical and economic characteristics of real estate
5. Land use and land-use competition

FROM MOTHER EARTH
TO REAL ESTATE

Real estate as a commodity consists of land and "permanent" improvements to the land. These improvements may be above or below the surface of the earth or may be something that affects the utility of a given parcel, such as adding fertilizer.

But, in the beginning, the earth was only land and water. There were few people relative to the amount of land. As the people increased in number and crowded more closely on the land, a system of property descriptions gradually became necessary. Initially, only surface rights were of concern. However, with time, a more complicated system of rights became necessary. Currently, rights of people in real estate go from air rights to surface rights to subsurface rights. The system of rights also provides for water rights and mineral rights. And a "right to light" (sunshine) appears to be evolving with our increasing dependence on solar power. The various rights and boundaries of use are shown in figure 3–1.

FIGURE 3–1
Real estate extends from the center of earth to the tops of the highest manmade improvements, above which common fly-over rights exist

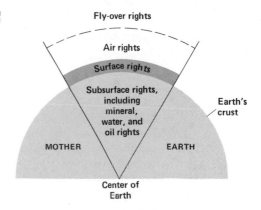

Legal ownership of a parcel of real estate includes possession and control of the minerals and substances below the earth's surface as well as the air and space above the surface. Thus, the boundaries of a parcel extend in the shape of an inverted pyramid from the center of Mother Earth to the limits of the sky, as suggested by figure 3–1.

In some cases, special rules must apply in determining water rights. The next two sections of this chapter give more detail about identifying and describing real property rights.

NEEDED DISTINCTIONS
IN DESCRIBING REAL ESTATE

Thus far, land, realty, real estate, and real property have been considered identical in meaning. And, for most purposes a distinction between them is not necessary. But, in fact, they are not identical. There are distinctions between them, which are sometimes subtle, sometimes obvious. **Land,** of course, really means the solid part of the earth not covered by water. **Realty** is a physical concept that includes land and land improvements and the natural assets of land like oil, water, and minerals. **Real estate** is somewhat more inclusive, meaning realty and the ownership and use of realty by people. **Real property** is realty that is owned, and ownership means the right to use or otherwise capture the benefits of controlling the physical real estate. Except in this immediate discussion, we shall continue to consider the four terms as identical in meaning.

Personalty is to personal property as realty is to real property. **Personalty,** therefore, means physical objects that are movable and not attached to the land, whereas personal property refers to ownership rights and privileges in movable things, such as cars, typewriters, or furniture.

So, how do we define real estate in specific situations? And what happens when the rights of ownership of realty are violated? A brief discussion of the following topics contains the answers for our purpose: (1) land and "permanent" improvements, (2) fixtures, and (3) trespass and encroachment.

Land and "Permanent" Improvements

Real estate includes "permanent" improvements on a site as well as the land itself. Thus, houses, stores, factories, office buildings, schools, outbuildings, fences, and landscaping, as improvements, are included. And, by law and tradition, conveying ownership of a parcel of land to another also conveys the improvements. In a similar sense, trees, natural vegetation, and assorted perennial plants, which do not require annual cultivation, are considered real estate. The term for them is *fructus naturales*. On the other hand, annual cultivated crops— e.g. corn, potatoes, and cotton—are considered personal property even though they are attached to the earth. They are called *fructus industriales* or **emblements.**

Fixtures

We know that realty includes not only the land and buildings thereon but also anything definitely or permanently affixed to the land and/or buildings. The latter group is known as **fixtures** and, like the land, is included in a sale or covered by a mortgage unless specifically excepted. There are also items known as *chattel fixtures,* which are personalty items annexed to or used with land but which retain their original character of personalty.

Whether or not an article is a fixture depends mainly on the intention of the person who placed it. In other words, a *fixture* is an item of personalty which meets certain tests of intention and is therefore legally classified as realty. The following criteria apply to each case and will aid in reaching a determination as to whether an item is a fixture.

1. *The reasonably presumable intent of the person placing the article.* The owner's statements to neighbors may show whether or not he intended the article to become a fixture. Also a conditional sales agreement may expressly state that the article is to remain personalty until fully paid for. So, too,

the courts will rule that if an article is usually intended to become a fixture, a person cannot claim a contrary intention and so violate the ordinary reasonable presumption.

2. *The method of annexation.* Generally if the article is specially adapted for use
   where placed, and if to remove it would leave the building or land incomplete, it is a fixture. The annexation may be actual, as with lighting,
   plumbing, and heating equipment; or constructive, as with awnings,
   screens, and blinds, which may or may not be in place.

3. *The relation of the parties.* Often the relation between the parties is such that
   the ordinary presumable intention is negated. For example, a permanent
   owner may be presumed to be permanently annexing the article. Although a tenant is ordinarily bound to leave articles fastened to the building, nevertheless, if the property is leased for business, it is a general rule
   that trade fixtures, such as shelves, counters, and showcases, do not become real fixtures. But such equipment must be removed before the lease
   expires, and a renewal that fails to state that the equipment is to be the
   tenant's property may deprive the tenant of ownership.

The determination is particularly important at the time of sale, of mortgaging,
of lease termination, and of assessment for property tax purposes. Fixtures are
considered a part of the realty at these times, but chattel fixtures are not.

Trespass and Encroachment

What happens when someone invades the real estate of another? Entering
on the land of another without permission is termed **trespass** and is illegal. The
offender may be sued for damages. **Encroachment** is having a building or some
other object intrude upon or into the space of an adjacent owner. For example,
wells are sometimes drilled at an angle to obtain oil from under a neighbor's
land. Trespass and encroachment both violate an owner's right to exclude others from real property.

LEGAL DESCRIPTIONS OF REAL ESTATE

A clear, adequate description of real es-
tate is essential for transactions and documents—from sales contracts to tax and
mortgage lien records to valid deeds. In almost all states the real estate must be
identifiable with reference only to the documents. Courts consider a description
legal if a competent surveyor can exactly locate the parcel of concern from the
description. In other words, a **legal description** is a specific and unique identification of a parcel of real estate that is recognized and acceptable in a court of law.

A street address is the simplest form of property description, but a street
address is not specific enough for most legal documents or for court purposes.
Other methods of legally describing real estate are therefore needed.

The three accepted methods of legally describing real estate are (1) metes
and bounds, (2) rectangular or government survey, and (3) recorded plat. A

fourth method, the state plane coordinate system, has been prepared and is gradually being accepted as a supplement to the above three methods. Each of these methods provides for a description suitable for use in a sales contract, mortgage, deed, or court of law. Description by recorded plat is used mostly in urban areas. Metes and bounds descriptions are also frequently used in urban areas for describing residential, commercial, and industrial parcels that have been split off and developed as distinct parcels. That is, the parcels are not part of a larger recorded plat. The governmental survey system is used mainly in rural areas for large parcels; it is too crude for smaller, urban parcels. Except for condominium descriptions, these methods describe land only and do not describe the improvements on a parcel.

Before taking up the methods, a brief discussion of the elements of surveying is appropriate.

Elements of Surveying

Several considerations are common to all systems of describing real estate. To begin with, any land description should contain (1) a definite point of beginning (P.O.B.), (2) definite corners or turning points, (3) specific directions and distances for sides or boundaries, (4) closure, or return to point of beginning, and (5) the area enclosed in accepted units of measurement. A *point of beginning* is the point of take off in describing real estate. Ideally, a P.O.B. ties into a larger system of property descriptions so that the resulting legal description relates the subject parcel to other parcels and to the rest of the world. In addition, a basic knowledge of units of measurement for angles or bearings, distances, and areas is needed in order to fully understand legal descriptions.

ANGLE MEASUREMENT. The full circle about a turning point contains 360 degrees. A *bearing* is a direction of measurement from an imaginary north-south line passing through a corner or turning point on a property. A bearing or angle of measurement is measured east or west of the imaginary line and cannot exceed 90 degrees. For example, assume that the circular diagram is properly oriented and set exactly over the corner point of a property. A line running just slightly north of due east might have a bearing of "north, 89 degrees east." A 3-degree more southerly line would have a bearing "south 88 degrees east." A minute, in angle measurement, equals 1/60 of a degree. See figure 3–2.

DISTANCE MEASUREMENT. Distance measurements in surveying have traditionally been in miles, rods, feet, and inches. A mile equals 5,280 feet or 320 rods. A *rod,* or stick 16½ feet in length, was a convenient unit of measurement in centuries past; it is not used much now because steel tapes are longer, faster, and more accurate.

AREA MEASUREMENT. Areas are most commonly measured in square feet, acres, and square miles or sections. An **acre** is a measure of land that contains 43,560 square feet. A square mile covers 640 acres. More detail on area measurements is given in the Appendix. The detail includes conversions to the metric system.

FIGURE 3–2

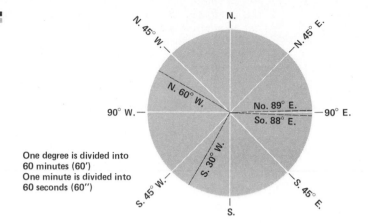

One degree is divided into
60 minutes (60′)
One minute is divided into
60 seconds (60″)

ELEVATION MEASUREMENT. A final element of surveying is elevation. Elevations are usually measured from mean sea level in New York Harbor, which is the basic elevation datum or point of reference for the United States. Elevations are important in establishing limits on heights of buildings and other structures and in setting grades for streets and highways. Condominium developments also depend on accurate elevation data.

Permanent reference points, called **bench marks,** are located throughout the country to aid surveyors in work involving elevations. That is, a surveyor may take an elevation from a local bench mark and need not measure from a basic bench mark in the city or area that is miles from the place of measurement. Bench mark locations may be obtained from the United States Geodetic Survey, if needed.

Metes and Bounds Descriptions

Metes and bounds descriptions are widely used in the eastern United States. They are also used throughout the country to describe irregular or non-platted tracts in conjunction with the rectangular survey system. **Metes and bounds** means measures and boundaries; the edges of a property are, of course, its limits or boundaries. A metes and bounds description can be highly accurate when it is developed and written by a competent surveyor who uses precision equipment. A metes and bounds description for a parcel, Z, shown in figure 3–3, might be as follows:

All that tract or parcel of land situated in the Town of East Hampton, County of Suffolk and State of New York, bounded and described as follows: BEGINNING at the junction of the westerly line of land of James McKinney and the southerly side of Further Lane, and running thence along the land of said James McKinney, south 18 degrees 17 minutes 30 seconds east 430 and 5/100 feet; thence along the land of said James McKinney north 71 degrees 42 minutes 30 seconds east, 383 and 52/100 feet to land of Rachel Van Houten; thence along the land of said Rachel Van Houten south 21 degrees 36 minutes 30 seconds east 895 and 82/100 feet to a point; thence still along the land of Rachel Van Houten south 21 degrees 16 minutes 20 seconds east 699 and 31/100 feet to the proposed Atlantic Avenue Highway, thence along said Atlantic Avenue south 72 degrees 42 minutes 40 seconds west 1387 and 50/100 feet; thence continuing along said Atlantic Avenue south 76 degrees 52 minutes 40 seconds west 264 and 85/100 feet to land of Edward J. McGuire; thence along the lands of said Edward J. McGuire north 17 degrees 33 minutes 40 seconds west 1297 and 28/100 feet, thence north 71 degrees 15 minutes 10 seconds east 4 feet; thence continuing along the land of said Edward J. McGuire north 17 degrees 48 minutes 50 seconds west 699 feet to Further Lane Highway; thence along said Further Lane Highway north 70 degrees 3 minutes 40 seconds east 624 and 92/100 feet; thence continuing along said Further Lane Highway south 85 degrees 33 minutes 20 seconds east 87 and 85/100 feet; thence continuing along said Further Lane Highway north 72 degrees 25 minutes 20 seconds east 447 and 38/100 feet to the point or place of beginning.

Containing by actual measurement as per survey dated April 10, 1971, of Nathan F. Tiffany 69.7349 acres. Atlantic Beach, New Jersey.

A variation of the metes and bounds system of identifying real estate is based on monuments. A **monument** is an identifiable landmark that serves as a corner of a property. A monuments description, which does not require exact measurements or directions, is acceptable whenever land is not too valuable and the expense of a detailed, accurate survey would be out of proportion to the

FIGURE 3–3

value of the land. Monuments descriptions are not widely used today, although at one time they were prevalent.

Monuments may be tangible or intangible. If tangible, they are either natural or artificial. Rivers, lakes, streams, trees, rocks, springs, and the like are natural monuments. Fences, walls, houses, canals, streets, stakes, and posts are artificial monuments. The center line of a street is an example of an intangible monument. Since all monuments are susceptible to destruction, removal, or shifting, they should be used only when necessary, and then every available identifying fact should be stated; for instance, not merely "a tree" but "an old oak tree." Thus, even after the tree has become a stump it may still be identified as oak and distinct from other trees.

A farm may be described without mention of metes or bounds per se. The farm of John Robinson at Pleasantville, Westchester County, New York, is bounded and described as follows:

Beginning at the dock on Indian Creek at the foot of Dock Road; thence along Dock Road to the point where said road is met by the fence dividing the farms of (the seller) and Jones, thence along said fence to the side of Indian Creek, and thence along said Indian Creek to the Dock, the point of beginning.

FIGURE 3–4

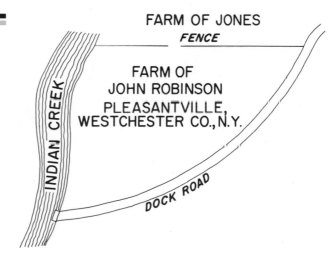

Rectangular or Government Survey Descriptions

The **rectangular or government survey system** was approved by the United States Congress in 1785 to establish a standardized system of property descriptions. It is relatively simple in operation, at least for rural lands, is easily the most general survey system, and is used in thirty states. The New England states, the Atlantic Coast states, and Texas are the main states not covered.

THE GENERAL FRAMEWORK. This system is based on surveying lines that run north and south, called **principal meridians,** and east and west, called **base lines.** Almost all sections of the country have a paired principal meridian and base line. These were established and given a name and number by the land office in Washington, D.C. A map showing the location of the several principal meridians and their base lines in the United States is given in figure 3–5.

FIGURE 3–5
Principal meridians and their base lines within the United States

To minimize errors in measurement caused by the curvature of the earth and the consequent converging of meridian lines as they extend north and south of the equator, surveyors divided the area into checks, or quadrangles, 24 miles on each side. These quadrangles reestablish an east-west distance of 24 miles at succeeding standard lines drawn parallel to the base line—north and south, called *standard parallels.* These checks are further subdivided into sixteen areas each measuring 6 miles by 6 miles, called **townships.** The townships containing an area of 36 square miles are again subdivided into **sections,** each a square mile containing 640 acres. And the sections were then divided into halves, quarters, or smaller subdivisions as the need called for to describe individual land holdings.

To identify the exact location of a given 36-square-mile area, the east-west rows, parallel to the base line, are numbered as **tiers** 1, 2, and so forth, north or south, of a given base line. The north and south columns, parallel to the meridians, are called **ranges** and are numbered 1, 2, and so forth, east or west of a principal meridian. The general system is illustrated in figure 3–6.

FIGURE 3–6
Designation of townships by tiers and ranges

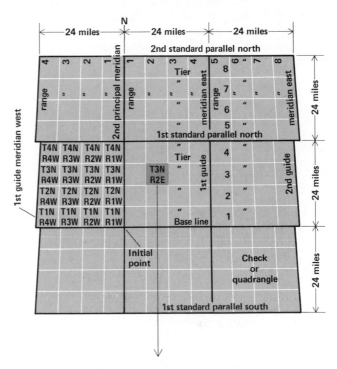

Sections in a township are identified by number and are related to adjoining sections, as indicated in figure 3–7.

FIGURE 3–7
Designation of Section 12 by Tier 3 North, Range 2 East, and location relative to other sections

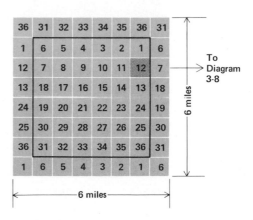

Because of the spherical shape of the earth, the meridians converge as one goes north—the north edge of a township is approximately 50 feet shorter than the south edge. To correct this error, as previously noted, the government established certain principal meridians and others, called **guide meridians,** which are adjusted at each standard parallel to make allowances for the earth's curvature. This problem really concerns only the surveyor and is mentioned simply so that the reader may not be confused in studying the diagram.

In describing a section, it is customary to state first the number of the section, then the township and range: "Section 12, Township 3 North, Range 2 East of the principal (named) meridian." It may be abbreviated: "Sect. 12, T. 3 N., R. 2 E., . . . County, State of. . . ."

SPECIFIC DESCRIPTION. The description of a part of a section is relatively simple. For example, the parcel designated by X in figure 3–8 is: Northeast one-

FIGURE 3–8
Measurements and subdivisions of a section

N.W. $\frac{1}{4}$, N.W. $\frac{1}{4}$, N.W. $\frac{1}{4}$
SEC. 12, T. 3N.
R. 2E., 2nd P.M.

10 acres

N.E. $\frac{1}{4}$, N.W. $\frac{1}{4}$
SEC. 12, T. 3N.
R. 2E., 2nd P.M.
40 acres
Parcel X

N.E. $\frac{1}{4}$, SEC. 12
T. 3N., R. 2E., 2nd P.M.
160 acres

S. $\frac{1}{2}$, N.W. $\frac{1}{4}$
SEC. 12, T. 3N.
R. 2E., 2nd P.M.

Center of section

12

Parcel Y

W. $\frac{1}{2}$, S.W. $\frac{1}{4}$
SEC. 12, T. 3N.
R. 2E., 2nd P.M.
80 acres

S.E. $\frac{1}{4}$, SEC. 12
T. 3N., R. 2E., 2nd P.M.
160 acres

1,320 feet   160 rods or 2,640 feet

1 mile

One rod = 16-½ feet
One mile = 320 rods or 5,280 feet
A square mile or section contains
640 acres
One acre contains 43,560 square feet

1 mile

fourth of the Northwest one-fourth of Section 12, etc. The parcel designated by Y is: West one-half of the Southwest one-fourth of Section 12, etc.

The acreage of each parcel can be determined quickly by working *backward* in the legal description from the section area of 640 acres. For example, areas of parcels X and Y are calculated as follows:

Parcel *X:* NE¼ of NW¼ of Section 12
(40)   (160)   (640)
Parcel *Y:* W½ of SW¼ of Section 12
(80)   (160)   (640)

Occasionally, a section is incomplete because it extends into the ocean, a lake, or a river. Since some parcels in the section are irregular in shape, a standard legal description based on the government survey system is not suitable for them. These incomplete lots are called *government lots* or *irregular lots.* A metes and bounds description is made up for the irregular parcel and is tied back to a point of beginning based on the rectangular survey system.

Recorded Plat Descriptions

The government survey system is extremely cumbersome for describing the small parcels commonly found in urban areas. The descriptions become much too involved. A more efficient and more widely accepted way of describing property is by recorded plat, as a subdivision or a condominium. A **plat** is a map or written plan showing actual or proposed property lines, buildings' setback lines, etc., entered into the public record, as, for example, a subdivision plat.

SUBDIVISION PLAT. Subdividing requires a very accurate initial survey map of a tract of land. The land is then divided into streets and lots and blocks. Easements and deed restrictions are also often either included on the subdivision map or filed with it. The map, easements, and deed restrictions are all entered into the public record as a plat. The map assigns numbers to the various blocks and lots for convenience of identification, and the map usually bears a subdivision title, the owner's and surveyor's names, the date of survey, and the date of approval by community or county officials. Figure 3–9 is a simple illustration of a small tract that the owner divided into lots.

The subdivision plat map describes exactly the size and location of each lot by the metes and bounds property description system. Once the subdivision plat map has been recorded, only the plat name need be referred to insofar as lots and blocks in the subdivision are concerned. Lot 8, Block 3 in Green Acres Subdivision, Rustic County, Wisconsin, would therefore constitute a complete and adequate legal description. Reference to the plat map would show the exact location, shape, size, and dimensions of the lot and give considerable additional information about it.

CONDOMINIUM PLAT. Condominium ownership is created by a special condominium law that permits individual interests or estates to be established within a total and larger property estate. The individual estates are technically established by use of vertical and horizontal planes (surfaces) that are usually identified vertically, such as the walls (not room partitions) of the unit and horizontally, such as the floors and ceilings of the unit. It is here that elevations

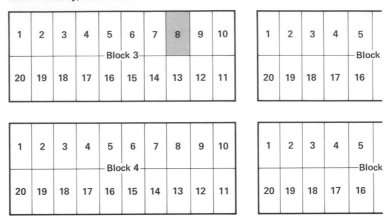

FIGURE 3–9
Green Acres subdivision,
Rustic County, Wisconsin

above sea level become critical. The exact location of the building or buildings on the site and the exact location of the unit within the buildings are described in the plat (location map) and in the architectural plans. Each is also described in legal language in a master deed. After all the individual unit estates have been described in the total property estate, all of what remains, such as the land and the structural parts of the buildings, become a common estate to be owned jointly by the owners of the individual unit estates. Thus, each condominium owner owns his or her individual unit estate and an undivided interest in the common estate.

Recording of the master deed extends the condominium laws of the state in which the condominium is located to the property. The master deed also establishes an association to look after the use and maintenance of the common estate. The association is governed by a board of directors or managers, elected from among the owners of the individual unit estates. Membership, with its attendant rights and responsibilities, applies to each unit in much the same sense that easements and deed restrictions apply to lots in a subdivision plat.

After recording, condominium units may be legally identified by reference to the plat or master deed. The complex three-dimensional descriptions need not be repeated in deeds, mortgages, or contracts.

The State Plane Coordinate System

The state plane coordinate system is intended to supplement other methods of describing real estate. The system provides a definite and very accurate means of identifying parcels, even if marks, monuments, and other points of origin are destroyed, moved, or otherwise obliterated.

The coordinate system is based on a system of coordinate grids for each state, with the state flattened mathematically into a level plane. Points in each grid are identified by longitude and latitude; thus the need for physical land-marks is avoided. Legal descriptions under the system are difficult for a lay person to interpret and understand. Therefore, property owners and lawyers are likely to continue to rely on traditional methods of describing realty. The system simply provides a certain means of locating critical points of beginning from which other methods of describing parcels may take off.

Description by Rights

Ownership may sometimes involve only air rights or riparian rights. Air rights are described in a similar manner to condominium rights. For example, rights of development over railroad tracks and cemeteries have been sold off in many larger cities. A legal description of air rights in a deed might convey all development rights 280 feet above mean sea level and up. To be useful, the description must also provide for the location and placement of footings and pillars among the railroad tracks, grave sites, and other surface uses, to support any structure built in the air space.

Riparian rights often are not subject to physical survey per se. If they are, the survey is only incidental to more complex legal considerations involving interaction with other property owners, relocation of streams, and the rights to shut off or restrict the flow of water. These rights should be expressed as clearly as possible in any legal document.

Encroachments, easements, and deed restrictions affect the rights of an owner, although they may not define the physical limits of the property. These should sometimes be considered equally important as physical descriptions in real estate transactions.

A seller must use care to convey only what is owned. Generally, this can best be accomplished by using the identical description under which the property was acquired.

If the acquiring description is believed to be erroneous, the words "more or less" may be used to compensate for a slight difference. "More or less" is a question of reasonableness. Sometimes a variance of a few inches is unreasonable, for example, in the width of a city lot, whereas a foot might not be unreasonable in the depth of the same lot. If the variance is reasonable, the seller can give good title under a description using the words "more or less." If "more or less" is used, the purchaser will often have the contract provide minimum dimensions or area, less than which will not be acceptable. If a house is standing on the lot, a small variance makes little difference, because the building will remain and produce rent, even if the description indicates slightly wider or narrower dimensions than the lot actually possesses.

CHARACTERISTICS OF REAL ESTATE

Once described, each parcel of real estate takes on several distinct attributes or characteristics. For ease of discussion, these characteristics are classified as physical, economic, and institutional. In practice, the distinction between the classes is sometimes uncertain. The physical attributes affect the economic and institutional, directly and indirectly, and, in turn, the behavior of people in using the realty. Institutions are laws, customs, and rules that affect the workings of the free economic market. These attributes are as follows:

Physical	Economic	Institutional
Immobility	Scarcity	Real property law
Indestructibility	Situs	Public regulation
Heterogeneity	Interdependence or modification	Local and regional custom
	Durability or fixity of investment	Associations and organizations

Physical Attributes

IMMOBILITY. Land is physically *immobile*—not movable in a geographic sense. Some of the *substance* of land—soil, minerals, oil—may be removed and transported, but the geographic location of a site remains fixed. An atomic bomb might destroy an entire city, but the geographic location of each parcel would be determinable by latitude and longitude, as we pointed out in discussing the state plane coordinate system. It is **immobility** that causes land to be classed as real estate. Because of immobility, too, the market for land tends to be local in character; demand must come to the site. Immobility results in the value of each parcel changing in direct response to changes in its environment, for better or for worse. Immobility also means that taxes may be levied against a parcel—and collected, in one way or another; the parcel cannot escape.

Buildings and other realty improvements are not necessarily immobile. But considerable expense must be incurred to move a house or other structure. This means, of course, that if the value of a site becomes great enough in a use inconsistent with the site's improvements, the improvements may be moved. In turn, the value of the improvements in a different location must exceed the cost of moving them.

INDESTRUCTIBILITY. Land, as space, cannot be destroyed; it goes on forever; it is *indestructible*. The **indestructibility** of land tends to popularize it as an investment. A sophisticated investor, of course, distinguishes between physical indestructibility and economic (value) durability. Physically, land may go on forever, but its value may be destroyed by changing conditions. For example, the value of certain locations may disappear almost completely, as happened in "ghost towns." On the other hand, the permanence of land and space means it may be used to support improvements, buildings, with extremely long lives. The buildings themselves, however, tend not to be indestructible—in a physical or a value sense.

HETEROGENEITY. No two parcels of land are exactly alike. Differences in location, size and shape, topography, and so forth cause realty to have the attribute of **heterogeneity** or unlikeness. Parcels may be highly similar in location, soil type, and appearance. The parcels may be economically alike and substitutable for one another. But geographically all parcels differ.

Heterogeneity has caused land to be legally declared a "nonfungible" (not substitutable) commodity requiring specific performance in contracts involving use or sale. **Specific performance** means that the terms of a contract must be specifically complied with, for example, a particular property must be conveyed and not a similar or substitute property. Heterogeneity is the basis of problems in pricing or valuing realty because comparison of site or property with similar but different properties is often a very complex undertaking.

Heterogeneity extends to buildings and other realty improvements. Structures usually differ in size, appearance, and complexity. Even if built to the same plan, workmanship and materials might differ slightly. At the very least, location and orientation are slightly different. In addition, differing owners and occupants lead to differing levels of use and maintenance.

Economic Attributes

SCARCITY. Inadequacy in supply means **scarcity.** The physical supply of land is fixed for all practical purposes. But there is no scarcity of land or space as such. However, certain types of land of a given quality and in a desired location may be in comparatively short supply. The supply of land for urban uses is generally in short supply; but with money, time, and effort, the supply can be increased in response to demand. Even so, the fear of an ever-increasing population outrunning a limited physical supply of land has caused periodic land booms and busts.

Land in the United States today is relatively less scarce than it was a decade ago, despite continued growth in total population and ever more extensive utilization of land and its mineral resources. The reason is the greater and more intensive use of land as a factor of production. The increase in the economic supply of land has had the practical effect of land and space production. This situation may be demonstrated by the following example:

At one time, cattle raising in many states required two or more acres of ground for each head of cattle. Improved pastures and the planting of better and more nutritious grasses have made it possible to graze two animals where only one could profitably feed before. Assuming that formerly two hundred acres of pasture land were needed to maintain a herd of one hundred cattle, the development of improved grasses thus doubles the economic land supply for cattle-growing purposes. In cities, too, use of steel and elevators make possible the skyscraper office buildings and multistory apartment structures that literally constitute a city in the sky. The prospects for further and still more intensive use of land and space make their scarcity of only relative importance. Whether land or buildings, increased demand means higher values. Higher food values mean better seeds or fertilizers can be developed and less productive lands can be cultivated. Higher space values mean new buildings or the modification of existing structures to accommodate the demand.

SITUS. The location of a parcel relative to other external land-use activities is called **situs.** Both physical and economic location are involved, with the economic relationships being the more important by far. Situs is the result of choices and preferences of individuals and groups in selecting sites. Differences in situs or relative locations cause otherwise similar parcels to have different uses and different values.

Factors influencing locational decisions of individuals and groups include direction of population growth, availability of services and utilities, shifts in centers of trade and manufacture, direction of prevailing minds, presence or lack of sunshine or shade, and changing standards in life styles. Another factor that affects locational choice is **accessibility**—the relative costs (in time, money, and effort) of getting to and from a property. When accessibility is good (the relative costs of movement are low) a property is said to have good situs or location. In turn, the property's value is likely to be high. Alternatively, poor or difficult accessibility generally leads to low values. The use of a parcel and the type of improvements or buildings added to a parcel are therefore a result of its situs or relative accessibility.

INTERDEPENDENCE OR MODIFICATION. The mutual interaction of uses, improvements, and values of parcels is called **interdependence.** In turn, interdependence means that the use and value of a given property is subject to **modification** by decisions and changes made about other properties. Thus, the development of a shopping center across the street strongly influences how I use my site. Or I may have a restaurant along a major highway that depends heavily on nearby motels for customers. Development of a by-pass route may severely cut the business of both the motels and my restaurant, with a consequent sharp drop in value of all properties. Under these conditions, the nature of the sites and their improvements would be secondary influences in determining their value.

DURABILITY OR FIXITY OF INVESTMENT. The long time required to recover costs to acquire a site and add improvements is termed **durability.** Once a site is purchased and labor and capital committed to build a structure, the investment is "set" or "fixed" for many years from the viewpoint of the community or of society. Durability is directly related to the concept of duration as used in other areas of finance and investments.[1] Drainage, sewage, electric, water and gas facilities, or buildings cannot as a rule be dismantled and shifted economically to locations in which they would be in greater demand. The investment "sunk" in the realty is slow in returning during the economic life of

---

[1]M. H. Hopewell and G. G. Kaufman, "Bond Price Volatility and Term to Maturity: A Generalized Respecification," *American Economic Review,* September 1973, pp. 749–53. Jack Clark Frances, *Investments: Analysis and Management,* 2nd ed. (New York: McGraw-Hill, 1976), pp. 206–8.

the improvements. Furthermore, the immobility and fixity of land and land investment make real estate vulnerable to rigid controls for taxation or various other social or political programs.

Durability of investment and immobility in location means that demand must come to the improvement and site. The property cannot move to satisfy demand in another city or area. Durability of investment does not preclude disposition of the property by one investor and acquisition by another. That is, the investment is not "set" for a specific owner.

Institutional Attributes

REAL PROPERTY LAW. Real estate has its own laws for the most part. Real estate is owned as real property rather than as personal property. We already touched briefly on the differences. Several subsequent chapters are devoted entirely to real-property law.

Ownership rights are the commodity that is bought, sold, or traded in the real estate market. And it is the rights of owners in real estate that make up the essence of real property law. Limitations to ownership include leases, liens, easements, and deed restrictions. Contracts to buy or sell real estate must be in writing to be enforceable. A deed must be used to transfer ownership. Real property law is as much a part of the commodity of real estate as is a site or a building. And flaws in ownership may offset value as readily or more readily than faults in a site or in construction.

PUBLIC REGULATION. In a fashion similar to real-property law, public regulation affects real estate. Community plans and zoning ordinances, rent controls, subdivision regulations, laws pertaining to mortgage finance, and building codes all go to shape the development and use of our realty. Building codes say what construction materials may or may not be used. Planning and zoning determine where land uses may locate. Rent controls limit how much may be charged in leasing space. Land-use controls indeed shape our buildings and our cities.

LOCAL AND REGIONAL CUSTOM. Cape Cod houses are prevalent in one community, almost nonexistent in another. New York City is relatively compact, while Los Angeles has been described as "seventeen cities in search of a city." Bicycles are an accepted mode of transportation in some areas, and firmly rejected in others. Though subtle, local attitudes and customs do influence the nature and appearance of real estate.

ASSOCIATIONS AND ORGANIZATIONS. The National Association of Realtors, the National Association of Homebuilders, and the Urban Land Institute all greatly influence the nature of the real estate business and the development of our communities. Homebuilders change their methods of construction in response to manuals published by the NAHB. The Urban Land Institute did much of the pioneer work to get planned unit developments, shopping centers, and curvilinear subdivisions accepted across the country. The National Associ-ation of Realtors emphasized higher ethics and promoted multiple-listing sys-tems to improve the real estate business. The Federal National Mortgage associ-ations, and other organizations cooperated to create and maintain secondary mortgage markets. Associations and organizations do greatly affect the nature of real estate as a commodity.

LAND USE AND LAND-USE COMPETITION

A **land use** is an activity that takes place on the surface of the earth, such as farming, manufacturing, trade, and recreation. As stated earlier, the activity that gives a site its greatest value is its highest and best land use. Highest and best use is the result of the quantity and quality of services or net income flows a property can generate under alterna-tive uses. Value is the present worth of these services or net-income flows. That legal, possible use that will preserve the utility of the property and yield the highest possible present value is the highest and best use for a site or a property at a given time.

The owner of each parcel, in self-interest, wants that use which gives greatest value to the parcel. And at any time, each parcel may be used for many uses. Land-use competition is the analysis and comparison of alternative uses to select that one which gives each property its greatest value. And over time, highest and best use may change as a result of technological, economic, or legal developments. Thus, the energy shortage or a revision in planning and zoning may result in a new highest and best use for a specific property.

Factors Influencing Use Selection

Some of the important considerations that enter into the determination of highest and best use are (1) land contour and elevation, (2) direction of pre-vailing winds, (3) nature of immediate environment, and (4) accessibility or the convenience of getting to the site. The importance of contour and elevation is self-evident; people like to visit or live in homes that are safe, high and dry, and have vistas of natural beauty. Prevailing winds influence development and de-sirability of location; therefore high-income residences tend to locate upwind, and industrial uses generating pollution often locate downwind to avoid public relations problems. The immediate environment influences highest and best use because, other things equal, people would sooner live or work in a desirable area than a run-down, blighted, or polluted area.

Good access roads, parking facilities, and bus and railroad transportation greatly affect the desirability of commercial and industrial sites. The reason is that access, or easier movement to related sites lowers costs of getting to related sites. Each user, or potential user, of a property takes the above factors into con-sideration in determining how much it's worth to use the site. This worth con-verts into how much rent will be paid for the use of the site.

Highest-and-Best-Use Calculations

A simplified case example will illustrate the determination of highest and best use. Suppose a vacant site in a given community can be developed under existing and reasonably anticipated zoning restrictions for residential purposes only. Suppose further that preliminary study and analysis of neighborhood characteristics and of housing demand narrow the choice of possible and profitable site improvements to one of the following type structures:

1. A single-story duplex building, each rental unit containing two bedrooms, living-dining room, kitchen, and tiled bath. Total improvements cost $75,000.

2. A three-family apartment building, each apartment containing two bedrooms, living-dining room, kitchen, and tiled bath. Total improvements cost $100,000.

Because the use of the site was prescribed by the zoning law for residential purposes, the determination still to be made is which of the alternate types of improvements described above constitutes the highest and best use. Under the definition of highest and best use, it is necessary to ascertain the income-producing capacity of the land under the alternate types of improvement and to find by the process of capitalization which income yields to land its highest present value. Based on prevailing rentals of similar residences in comparable neighborhoods of $600 a month per four-room-and-bath duplex units and $500 per month per four-room-and-bath apartment units, the procedure to derive land income and land value is calculated as shown in figure 3–10.

FIGURE 3–10
Analysis of Land Income and Land Value under Alternative Types of Improvements

Gross Annual Income	Single-Story Duplex	Triplex Apartment Building
Duplex units $600 x 2 x 12 (months) =	$14,400	
Three-family apartment $500 x 3 x 12 (months) =		$18,000
Less vacancy and credit losses and operating expenses (35%)	$5,040	6,300
Annual net operating income	$9,360	11,700
Less an 11% allowance for return on the investment in the buildings (9%) and recapture of the investment in the buildings (2%)		
Duplex—11% x $75,000	$8,250	
Triplex—11% x $100,000		11,000
Net income residual to land	$1,110	$700
Indicated market value of land capitalized at 9%		
Duplex—$1,110 ÷ .09	$12,333	
Triplex—$700 ÷ .09		$7,778

The valuation procedure outlined is one generally practiced by informed analysts to determine the present worth of land under the income or earnings residual approach to land value. Based on the analysis, as illustrated, the conclusion can be drawn that the highest and best use of the building site under value study is a single-story duplex to be constructed at a cost of $75,000 and renting at $600 per month per dwelling unit. Under this highest and best use the land warrants a present value of $12,333. Under the next best type of improvement or utilization both land income and land value decrease.

The above data could be processed in a different manner, using the time values of money techniques to ascertain the investment value of the alternative properties. Part V emphasizes analysis for an investment decision, including use of the time value of money or compound-interest techniques.

Because the market value of a given parcel of land, as demonstrated above, is based on the income attributable to land under its highest and best use, it is important that care be taken to differentiate between (1) income derived under a specific use or agreed-upon rental and (2) income that is warranted and residual to land when put to its optimum use and that remains after due economic shares have been allocated to labor (wages), coordination (entrepreneur costs or sacrifices), and capital (interest and capital returns).

The income that is attributable to land under its highest and best use is **market rent.** It is that rent that the land does or will produce if employed to its optimum capacity. Any other income agreed upon or arbitrarily assigned to land is **contract rent.** To the extent to which a contract rent fails to equal the market rent, a proportional share of land value is transferred from the owner to the user or tenant.

SUMMARY

In the beginning of history, land was freely available to anyone. The need for legal descriptions of real estate resulted from increasing numbers of people using the land. From the development of the concept of property, real estate, as property, may be divided into several types of rights: air, surface, subsurface, oil, mineral, and water. The terms, land, realty, real estate, and real property are generally used interchangeably although each has its own specific meaning. Realty refers to land and improvements as physical things. Realty is to real property as personalty is to personal property. A fixture is an item of personalty that meets the tests of intent, manner of annexation, and relation of the parties, and is therefore realty.

A legal description of real estate is a specific and unique identification of a parcel of realty that is acceptable in a court of law. The three accepted methods of describing real estate are (1) metes and bounds, (2) rectangular or government survey, and (3) recorded plat.

Physical attributes of a parcel of realty are immobility, indestructibility, and heterogeneity. Economic attributes are scarcity, durability of investment, interdependence, and situs. Institutional attributes include real property law, public regulations, local and regional customs, and pertinent associations and organizations. Each has its own implications for the parcel, all of which interact to affect the highest and best use of the parcel.

KEY TERMS

Accessibility

Acre

Base line

Bench mark

Contract rent

Durability of investment

Emblements

Encroachment

Fixity of investment

Fixture

Guide meridian

Heterogeneity

Immobility

Indestructibility

Interdependence

Land

Land use

Legal description

Market rent

Metes and bounds

Modification

Monument

Personalty

Plat

Principal meridian

Range

Realty

Real estate

Real property

Rectangular survey system

Scarcity

Section

Situs

Specific performance

Tier

Township

Trespass

QUESTIONS FOR REVIEW AND DISCUSSION

1. What is a fixture? When is the identification of a fixture important? When are the following fixtures: house key, storm windows, hot-water heater?

2. Explain the metes and bounds method of describing realty in detail. The government survey system. The recorded plat.

3. Are there any occasions where the above three methods or systems are not adequate to describe realty? Explain.

4. List three physical attributes of realty and explain the implications of each.

5. List at least three economic attributes of realty and explain the implications of each.

6. What is land-use competition? Explain, using an example, if necessary.

7. Discuss the implications of immobility of real estate relative to economic, social, and political forces or decisions.

8. How may the world's supply of "space" be increased? Explain.

9. Is all realty employed in its highest and best use? If not, why not? Discuss.

10. What effect of heterogeneity relative to real estate market adjustment or equilibrium exists?

11. What effects will adoption of the metric system have on legal descriptions of real estate, if any? Discuss.

12. The rectangular survey system is obsolete for describing real estate and should be replaced. Discuss.

REFERENCES

Breed, Charles B.; Alexander J. Bone; and Brother B. Austin Barry. *Surveying.* 3rd ed. New York: Wiley, 1979. A basic book in surveying and property descriptions. Technical in nature.

Corley, Robert N., and William J. Robert. *Principles of Business Law.* 11th ed. Englewood Cliffs, N.J.: Prentice-Hall, 1979. A comprehensive and clearly written text on basic business law, easily understood by the nonlawyer. Chapters 41 and 43 pertain to personal and real property.

Kratovil, Robert, and Raymond J. Werner. *Real Estate Law.* 7th ed. Englewood Cliffs, N.J.: Prentice-Hall, 1979. Real estate law for business people, presented in an interesting, easy-to-read, and ready-to-use format. Many cases cited. Chapters 1–5 particularly pertain to the development of the concept of real property.

Lusk, Harold F., and William B. French. *Law of the Real Estate Business.* 3rd ed. Homewood, Ill.: Richard D. Irwin, 1975. Principles of real estate law including history of real property ownership. Chapters 1 and 2 give in-depth treatment to rights in real estate and to the distinctions between real and personal property.

Real Property Ownership and Interests

Property has its duties as well as its rights.
Thomas Drummond,
Letter to the
Tipperary Magistrates, 1838

4

Real property rights and interests are the true commodity in the real estate market, even though attention is usually focused on the physical realty. The main rights of ownerships are control, possession and use, or enjoyment, exclusion and disposition. Rights in real estate may be divided in other ways, as discussed in the last chapter, to give air rights, surface rights, mineral rights, and the like. Ownership of real estate is sometimes considered as a bundle of rights. The bundle is wrapped in a government sheathing of law and order that serves to preserve, protect, and enforce the rights.

Knowledge of property rights is extremely important to an investor because decisions an owner may make or actions an owner may take are implied in the rights owned. Also, the relative completeness and clarity of ownership translates directly into risk of loss of ownership because of poor title. **Title** means ownership of property. Having high-quality title of the right type reduces investor risks and increases investor flexibility in administering the property. The following topics are covered in this chapter to provide the reader with adequate knowledge of rights and interests in real estate for investment decisions and actions:

1. Classes of ownership interests
2. Business or group ownership

3. Liens, easements, deed restrictions, and other encumbrances to ownership

4. Governmental or public limitations to ownership.

CLASSES OF OWNERSHIP INTERESTS

A possessory interest or right in real property is termed an **estate.** Estates are divided into two major classes: (1) freehold and (2) **leasehold.** A leasehold is also called a nonfreehold or less-than-freehold estate. A **freehold estate** is considered real property, because, for one thing, it continues for an indeterminate period of time. That is, title to a freehold estate may be held for the lifetime of its owner or of some other designated person. Title to most freehold estates is held for the lifetime of the owner (unless sold or otherwise disposed of) and then passed on to an heir of the owner. The most common freehold estates are fee simple, qualified fees, and life estates and remainders.

Less-than-freehold (leasehold) estates are not ownership interests and are regarded as personal property. Leasehold estates only endure for a determinate period of time, that is, for a period measured in years, months, weeks, or days.

Fee ownership and leasehold estates are often stated in terms of tenancy. That is, tenancy and estate are often used interchangeably in real estate, though they really do not mean the same thing. A **tenancy** is the manner of holding an interest in property. Again, an *estate* is a possessory right or interest held. Therefore, stating ownership by tenancy gives more specific information about the interest held. For example, identifying fee ownership as a **tenancy in common** or a leasehold estate as a periodic tenancy gives more complete information about the interest. A leasehold estate, by itself, may mean anything from a tenancy for years to a tenancy at sufferance.

It should be noted that every state has a law applying to transactions involving interests of any consequence in real property, called a **Statute of Frauds.** A Statute of Frauds requires, among other things, that any contract creating or transferring an interest in land or realty must be in writing to be enforceable at law. Oral testimony to alter or vary the terms of such written agreements is not admissible as evidence in court.

Estates in real estate have three important dimensions, as follows: (1) quantity or *completeness* of the interest, (2) *time* when interest is active and benefits are realized, and (3) *number* and *relationship* of the concerned parties. These dimensions are summarized in figure 4–1.

Completeness of Ownership

FEE SIMPLE. **Fee, fee simple,** and **fee simple absolute** all mean the same thing, namely, complete or absolute ownership of realty with unrestricted right of disposition, within certain limitations imposed by the government. Therefore fee simple is considered to be the most complete bundle of rights anyone can acquire. The governmental limitations are police power, eminent domain, taxation, and escheat. The owner of a fee simple may use it or dispose of it in any

FIGURE 4–1
Estates and tenancies in real property

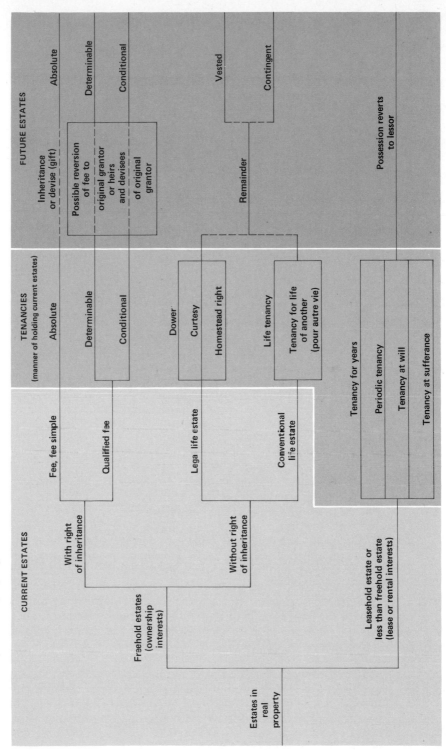

legal way, including passing it on to heirs or devisees by will. An owner may also encumber or lessen the estate by allowing mortgages and other liens, easements, deed restrictions, and leases to develop against it. In short, a fee simple owner may do anything with the property that does not interfere with the rights of others. For example, a nuisance may not be maintained, for instance, keeping pigs, goats, or chickens in an urban, residential neighborhood.

Most realty is held in fee simple, and the term *ownership* ordinarily means such a position. All other estates are less than fee simple, and in fact, are some portion of it. All the lesser parts, when gathered together, make up a complete fee. Splitting up the fee, "fee splitting," is usually in terms of completeness, time, or number of owners.

QUALIFIED FEE. A **qualified fee** is ownership in fee simple, with a limitation that may take title away from one person and place it with another. Two types of qualified fees exist: fee determinable and fee upon condition. Both give the holder all the benefits of full fee ownership subject to the happening of a future contingency that ends the rights if it occurs. The distinction between the two is that if the contingency occurs in a determinable fee the ownership automatically reverts to the grantor. In the fee upon a condition, the ownership may only be brought to an end by reentry. An illustration of these restricted fees or estate titles follows. If Brown deeds to Green for as long as the latter refrains from smoking, upon the occurrence of the limitation or condition, the fee is determinable if only by Green's lifespan, which constitutes the maximum length of years over which this restriction is operative. If property is deeded for as long as the use is for religious or educational purposes by a church or university, the fee is upon condition and might go on without end. These forms of holding are now seldom used.

CONVENTIONAL LIFE ESTATES. An ownership interest in real estate limited to the life of a certain person is a **life estate.** A **remainder** is the ownership interest that becomes effective at end of a life estate; that is, it is an interest of future ownership and possession. The person designated to receive the remainder interest is a remainderman. The creation of life estates is a common example of "fee splitting" by time. For example, a man gives land to A for his life, and at A's death it is to go to B. A, who is known as the life tenant, owns a life estate; that is, the full right in the property for life. And B takes a remainder, which is the right to receive and use the property at A's death. When A dies, the fee is reunited in B, who is then the owner of a fee simple interest. The life interest may be measured by the life tenant's own life or by that of any other person, termed *pour autre vie.* If the remainderman can be determined, the remainder is *vested;* if not, it is *contingent.* Let us take, for example, a gift to A for life, with the remainder to B. Because B's right to succeed is fixed, the possession merely being suspended until A's death, B has a vested remainder. But suppose the gift were to A and A's children after death, and that if A left no children, then B should take it. Here B's remainder is contingent because it cannot be determined whether B will ever receive the property until A's death, and B then might receive nothing if A leaves children.

A life tenant has certain rights and duties. The owner of a fee simple estate may let the property fall into disrepair or disuse. The life tenant, however, must think of the remainderman. Hence, the tenant is entitled to the income and use of the land, but is also obliged to keep the property in fair repair and pay the usual, normal carrying charges, including taxes. The life tenant must also pay the interest on any mortgage. Any buildings erected on the land usually become the property of the remainderman. Naturally, because the life tenant's rights cease at death, no rights extending beyond that event may be granted. Any deed would convey a right of possession ending then, and if the life tenant were to make a mortgage, the lien would expire at the end of the life estate.

LEGAL LIFE ESTATES. Under certain circumstances, life estates are created by operation of the law. Such estates are termed *legal life estates.* Dower, curtesy, and homestead rights are the basis for the creation of legal life estates.

The estate for life given by law to a wife in all real property owned by her husband at any time during marriage is termed **dower.** The requirements for dower are (1) a valid marriage, (2) ownership of real property by husband, and (3) his death. The interest attaches as soon as the property is acquired or the marriage takes place and cannot be cut off without the wife's consent. For this reason she usually joins with him in the deed when property is transferred by mutual consent. Upon his death her dower interest usually entitles her to a one-third life estate in all the real property owned by the husband, as a means of support after his death.

Curtesy is the interest given by law to a husband in real property owned by his wife. It is established by (1) a valid marriage and birth of a child, (2) sole ownership by the wife at her death, (3) her death, and (4) no disposition of the property by her will. This interest does not attach until the wife's death, and she may defeat it by deed in her lifetime or by her will, in either case without her husband's consent. If the curtesy right exists, it usually entitles the husband to all the net income as long as he lives.

During the husband's lifetime, the wife's dower rights are legally "inactive" or "inchoate." Until his death, the wife cannot sell, assign, transfer, or cancel this right except by release to a purchaser, which she generally does by joining in her husband's deed. On the other hand, the husband cannot circumvent the dower right, and any purchaser who acquires title to real property from the husband, in states where dower is effective, without search as to the existence and release of dower rights, may acquire a "clouded" title. Dower rights become "consummate" or active upon the husband's death, and the widow may thereafter dispose of her dower interests in any way she chooses, provided she elects dower rather than accept the will or a child's portion if her husband died intestate.

Dower and curtesy are survivors of ancient common law. With increasing use and recognition of tenancy by the entirety and community property, dower and curtesy are being phased out. And, in states where they are recognized, the division of the property between the parties by the court in a divorce terminates them.

A protection of residence that precludes its attachment or forced sale for nonpayment of debt, except for mortgage and tax liens, is a **homestead right,** also referred to as a *homestead exemption.* This exemption is not of common-law origin, and its details vary in the several states. It usually has two purposes: (1) to exempt the home from debt and (2) to provide a widow (sometimes a widower) with a home for life. In most states the value and area of the exempt homestead are limited. Usually it must be occupied as the family home, and a written declaration of homestead must be filed. It is then free from general claims for debts except those that are a lien on the property, such as taxes and mortgages.

As a rule, a homestead right exists in favor of a head of a family residing thereon, and may cover a maximum of 160 acres of land if outside or ½ acre if located within an incorporated city or town. A homestead right generally is not lost by a divorce if there are minor children whom the husband is bound to support, provided the spouse with custody does not abandon the homestead. Homesteads in a few states are exempt from taxes up to a stated amount of assessed value. It is not necessary that the owner be the head of a family in order to be entitled to a homestead exemption.

Freehold Tenancies

Realty may be owned by one or more persons. One person holding ownership gives *sole title,* and the owner holds the fee under a tenancy in severalty. Two or more people hold title together under tenancy by the entirety, community property, tenancy in common, or joint tenancy. Each of these forms of tenancy has distinct characteristics.

TENANCY BY THE ENTIRETY. Ownership of a property by a husband and wife, holding as one person, is a **tenancy by the entirety.** In many states validity is given to the rights under the common law, wherein a husband and wife are joined together as one person. Consequently, when they take title together, each becomes the owner of the entire property. They may take title to a piece of property as joint tenants or as tenants in common, but the presumption is that unless the instrument indicates to the contrary, a conveyance to them as husband and wife is intended to create a tenancy by the entirety. As tenants by the entirety, neither can convey the property or force a partition during the lifetime of the other. If either one dies, the entire property is owned by the survivor. This form of ownership is very useful in connection with the purchase of a home by a husband and wife, since it makes certain that the survivor will continue to own the home regardless of whether a will is drawn, or even if the will is contested successfully. A divorce is generally considered to convert a tenancy by the entireties into a tenancy in common. Tenancy by the entireties is not recognized in community-property states.

COMMUNITY PROPERTY. **Community property** is recognized as a form of ownership in eight states—Washington, Idaho, Nevada, California, Arizona, New Mexico, Texas, and Louisiana. The concept of community property is of Spanish origin and applies only to property held by spouses in a marriage. Thus, community property is not designated as a tenancy, though it is in effect.

The community-property system recognizes two kinds of property—community and separate—rather than personal and real. **Community property** means that title to any property acquired by a husband and wife during their marriage, individually or jointly, is held equally by each of them. The death of either gives full title to the survivor. **Separate property** is property owned by either the husband or wife before their marriage, or received by either after their marriage through gift or inheritance, which is specifically excluded from classification as community property. Separate property is free of any claim or interest by the other spouse. The owning spouse therefore has full ownership and control of separate property and may sell, will, or give the property away, or place a mortgage against it. Income or profit from separate property is also separate property. All property not classed as separate property is community property. Dower and curtesy are not recognized in community-property states.

The rules regarding community property are not uniform throughout the states that recognize this form of ownership. Under the community-property laws of most states, the wife is automatically entitled to one-half of the real and personal property, or income, of the husband, and the husband is entitled to the same share in the property of his wife. A divorce or mutual agreement dissolves the community ownership and divides the property between the two parties.

The development of a new law may be taking place as this is written. The issue is, Do unmarried cohabitants, or *par vivants,* also develop community-property rights? Lee Marvin, the actor, lived with a woman, Michelle Triola, for several years during which time she legally changed her last name to Marvin. Subsequently, they split up. She sued for one-half of his income during the period they lived together. The court ruled that Lee Marvin must only pay $104,000 "for rehabilitation purposes" in that no contract existed calling for the actor to share his assets. However, other cases indicate that where couples live together, share assets, and jointly invest, a property settlement is appropriate.

TENANCY IN COMMON. Ownership of realty by two or more persons, each of whom has an undivided interest, is called **tenancy in common.** Upon the death of one, ownership passes to the heirs or the devisees under the will of the deceased. The law expresses this principle by stating that there is no survivorship in a tenancy in common. That is, the surviving owner or owners do not become owners of the interest of the one who has died. This of course seems to be fair and reasonable and is the relationship presumed to be intended unless the instrument creating the ownership specifies to the contrary. It is this interest that is taken by two or more heirs inheriting the property of a deceased person or by two or more devisees under a will.

The owners in common may have equal shares, or the interests may differ in amount. They are entitled to share in the income and are obligated to contribute to expenses according to their shares. They may all join to sell the property, or one may sell his or her interest if he or she desires, in which case the purchaser becomes a tenant in common with the others. If one wishes the property sold and the others do not, an action may be brought for *partition,* in which event the property is sold at auction and each owner is paid a share of the proceeds.

JOINT TENANCY. Ownership of an undivided interest by two or more owners, with right of survivorship, is **joint tenancy.** That is, if one dies, his or her share or interest passes to the remaining owners. This form of ownership used to be favored by the law, but now the courts recognize a joint tenancy only when the instrument makes it clear that survivorship is intended—by the use of such appropriate words as "to the grantees, their survivor, survivor's heirs and assigns." For practical purposes it is nearly the same as a tenancy in common, with but two exceptions. (1) If the interest of one joint tenant is sold, the purchaser becomes a tenant in common with the remaining owner or owners. (2) Even in those states having dower, a joint tenant may convey a husband's interest free of his wife's dower. In practice, however, attorneys recommend that a wife join in the signing of a deed where real estate interests, no matter how ordered, are sold or transferred by a husband. For a joint tenancy to stand up under court contest, it must be proved that the joint owners have *equal* interests and have acquired title by a *single* deed, at the *same moment* of time, and that *possession* is identical and undivided. These are termed the *four unities* of joint tenancy. A breach of any of these unities is generally interpreted as creating a tenancy in common rather than a joint tenancy. Many states have passed laws to abolish joint tenancy, except that the right of survivorship may still be created if specified in the deed.

Leasehold Tenancies

A **lease** is an agreement giving possession and use of realty in exchange for a specified rental. The owner who rents the property is termed a *lessor* or *landlord*. The person to whom the property is rented is termed a *lessee* or *tenant*. The rental property, if owned as a fee simple estate, is termed a *leased fee*. A *leasehold* or *leasehold estate* is the right of possession and use of a tenant in a leased property. A leasehold estate is not an estate of inheritance; possession is returned to the lessor at the end of a lease.

The lease or rental agreement need not be in writing to create a leasehold interest. And a leasehold is considered personal property. Even so, the Statute of Frauds requires that a lease for more than one year be in writing and signed by both the lessor and the lessee to be enforceable. Leasehold estates are classified according to the tenancy involved. Again, tenancy means the manner or condition under which an estate or interest in real estate is held. Four distinct tenancies are possible in a leasehold estate, based on the strength and duration of the leasehold interest:

1. Tenancy for years
2. Tenancy from period to period, or periodic tenancy
3. Tenancy at will
4. Tenancy at sufferance

The rights of the lessee become weaker in going from a tenancy for years to a tenancy at sufferance.

TENANCY FOR YEARS. A leasing agreement for a specific or definite period of time is a *tenancy for years*. Such an agreement is usually for more than one year and is usually written. The time may actually be for one month, six months, one year, or more than one year. A written lease for nine months creates an estate or tenancy for years just as a lease for ninety-nine years does. In both cases, the time of occupancy and use is definite. The tenant is required to vacate the property and return possession to the landlord at the end of the lease, without notice being required of the landlord.

PERIODIC TENANCY. A tenancy of uncertain duration, for example, month to month or year to year, is termed a *periodic tenancy* or *tenancy from year to year*. The tenancy is usually from month to month in urban areas. The tenancy continues until the landlord or tenant gives notice of termination. Usually the rental period determines the length of notice required. That is, a week's notice is required to end a week-to-week tenancy. Only a month's notice is likely to be required to terminate a year-to-year tenancy however.

The acceptance of rental payments from a holdover tenant for years without a new lease agreement creates a tenancy from year to year. Courts generally hold that a holdover tenancy can never be longer than a year, probably because no new written contract is made. However, a tenant holding over from a tenancy for years, where rental payments are accepted monthly, is likely to create a month-to-month tenancy.

TENANCY AT WILL. When a tenant is allowed to holdover, subject to vacation or eviction at almost any time, with the consent of the landlord, a *tenancy at will* is created. The agreement traditionally could be terminated "at the will" of either party at any time, but almost all states now require that proper notice be given. This notice is important because a farm tenant might hold over and have crops planted. To evict the tenant before the crops could be harvested would be an injustice.

TENANCY AT SUFFERANCE. A lessee holding over without any justification other than the implied consent of the lessor creates a *tenancy at sufferance*. A tenancy at sufferance is the weakest possible estate in realty. In the past no notice to vacate was required of the landlord; however, many state statutes now require some notice to the tenant ordering that the premises be vacated.

BUSINESS OR GROUP OWNERSHIP

More intense use of land and space during recent years for recreational, business, and residential purposes has caused rapid development of condominium and cooperative forms of ownership in the United States. In addition, business use of real estate has long made it necessary for partnerships, corporations, syndicates, and trusts to own real estate.

Condominium

Condominium ownership is holding a fractional interest in a larger property, part of which is separate and unique to each owner (the condominium unit) and part of which is held in general by all the owners (the common elements). Condominium ownership is similar to holding by tenancy in common, except that a portion of the fractional share is held as a separate or divided interest. The larger property is, of course, the entire condominium development. The owner of a fractional share holds it in fee simple and may dispose of it without obligation to the other owner or owners.

Condominium ownership dates back to ancient Rome as a form of land tenure. Legislation introducing condominium ownership into the United States was passed in most states in the early 1960s. This form of ownership is most often used for residential properties. As a rule, the legislation requires the separate assessment and taxation of each space unit and its common interests. The legislation therefore stops the assessor from treating any part of the common elements of the property as a separate parcel for taxation purposes. As a rule, too, statutes bar the placement of mechanic's or other liens on the common elements of a structure held jointly by two or more condominium owners.

Under condominium coownership, each purchaser of an apartment receives an exclusive right to use, occupy, mortgage, and dispose of his or her particular apartment, plus an undivided interest in the areas and fixtures that serve all tenant owners in common. Each deed is subject to identical covenants and restrictions governing the repair and maintenance of the building. Condominium ownership gives great flexibility to the fee owner in matters concerning financing and sale of an individual residential unit and offers tax advantages identical to those enjoyed by owners of single-family structures. This method of ownership, however, as under a stock-cooperative venture, requires formation of a central administrative body to act on behalf of the condominium owners in matters that concern the common operations of the multiunit structure as an integral whole. Thus all condominium coowners are obligated to share the expenses of operation and maintenance, which are levied either as rent or as monthly assessments to each according to his or her share or value of ownership. Owners, too, are bound to observe recorded rules and regulations governing use and occupancy of both individually owned premises and those held in common. Although the condominium owner cannot be ousted or dispossessed (as can a defaulting tenant) for infraction of bylaws or regulations, he or she is nevertheless subject to court actions resulting from filing of liens against his or her fee interest or those actions necessary to compel compliance with terms of the declaration of ownership.

Condominium ownership may also be used to share in the operation of recreational, industrial, trade, or office facilities. The same rules of fee ownership of specific units of space and group ownership of common areas apply. Expenses of operation and maintenance must also be shared.

Cooperative

Ownership of shares in a cooperative venture, entitling the owner to occupy and use a specific space or unit, usually an apartment, under a proprietary lease is **cooperative ownership.** The cooperative form of mutual ownership differs from a condominium entity in that the ownership of the entire property (land and improvements) is acquired by a corporation. The corporation as a rule finances the purchase by placing a mortgage on the property for up to 70 or 80 percent of its value and obtaining the balance by the sale of equity shares in the corporation to the cooperative tenant owners. Each owner-occupant in effect holds a proprietary lease subject to liens, debts, and obligations incurred by the corporation.

A *proprietary lease* is an agreement, with the attributes of ownership, under which a tenant-shareholder in a cooperative occupies space designated according to the shares owned. The lease terms stipulate the payment of rent to the corporation to cover pro rata shares of the amounts necessary to meet mortgage debt, maintenance expenditures, property taxes, and building-related expenditures, such as hazard insurance and sinking-fund (replacement) reserves. Under condominium ownership each family unit is separately mortgaged and insured; a default in payment by one owner does not affect the ownership control of other owner-occupants. Under cooperative title ownership, the mortgage and the insurance are placed by the corporation on the entire property. And a default in payment by the corporation due to default in payment by some cooperative tenants affects occupancy and title of all cooperative participants.

Partnership

A **partnership** is an organizational arrangement whereby two or more people join together as coowners to conduct business for profit. A partnership operates as a business entity, with its own name, even though it is only an association of individuals. In other words, the partnership name is merely a convenient designation rather than the title of a distinct legal organization. According to the Uniform Partnership Act, unless stipulated otherwise, profits and losses are shared by the partners according to contributions of capital and expertise. In addition, all partners have unlimited liability in the event of extreme losses. The arrangement may be oral or written, but articles of partnership are usually drawn up for partnerships of consequence.

Two kinds of partnership interests are legally recognized: the general and the limited. The **general partner** operates and manages the business and may be held liable for all losses and obligations of the entity not met by the other partners. A **limited partner** is exempt by law from liability in excess of his or her contribution. A limited partner, also termed a *silent partner,* may not participate in operations and management under penalty of losing the exempt or limited liability status. A partnership arrangement with silent partners is generally referred to as a *limited partnership.* A limited partnership must have at least one general partner who conducts business for the entity.

A real estate partnership is usually kept relatively small (under twenty-five) in terms of number of partners. The general partner or partners act for the partnership in acquiring, managing, or developing and disposing of property. The limited partners then remain silent and often unknown outside the partnership. Unlimited liability of general partners means that, even though the partnership holds title to real estate, the effect is that the general partners hold title as tenants in common. When just a few real estate developers and investors buy and hold realty as a group, they do it as partners; this arrangement is sometimes called a **syndicate.**

Corporation

A **corporation** is a legal entity with rights of doing business that are essentially the same as those of an individual. The entity is owned by stockholders, who can be many in number, and has continuous existence regardless of any changes in ownership. A corporation limits the liability of owners to the amount invested in the organization. Substantial amounts of money may be raised from many investors by a corporation. A corporation ceases to exist only if dissolved according to proper legal process.

The major disadvantages of the corporate form for real estate ownership and investment purposes are that (1) costs of organizing and maintaining the corporation are relatively high; (2) profits are subject to double taxation—taxation of the corporation and taxation of the shareholder upon distribution; and (3) corporations are subject to more governmental regulation, at all levels, than most other forms of business organization.

Corporations have little difficulty in receiving and transferring real estate in most states because for business purposes corporations are recognized as individuals. A corporation enables many people to share ownership of realty, which may be held by the corporation under a tenancy in severalty.

A *subchapter S corporation,* which is a hybrid of the partnership and corporate forms of organization, is frequently used in holding real estate. A subchapter S is limited to ten shareholders, who enjoy the limited liability of the corporate form. At the same time, corporate profits are exempt from corporate income taxes if distributed to shareholders immediately at the end of each accounting period. Operating losses may also be passed through to shareholders for deduction on their tax returns. A subchapter S corporation is also called a *tax-option corporation;* the shareholders may elect to have profits retained by the corporation to be taxed at corporate rates.

Trust

A **trust** is a fiduciary arrangement whereby property is turned over to an individual or an institution, termed a *trustee,* to be held and administered for the profit and/or advantage of some person or organization, termed the *beneficiary*. The person setting up a trust is termed a *trustor* or *creator*. "Fiduciary" means based on faith and confidence, primarily in the trustee. The trustee acts for the trust, which may hold property in its own name, just as an individual or a corporation does. The trustee is obligated to act solely for the benefit of the beneficiary. Two kinds of trusts are mainly used in owning realty: a real estate investment trust and an express private trust.

A Real Estate Investment Trust (REIT) is like a corporation. People buy shares (of beneficial interest) and thereby join together for the ownership of real estate with limited liability. At the same time, double taxation of profits may be avoided by meeting the requirements of the trust laws. To qualify as a REIT, a trust must meet many requirements, the most important of which are as follows:

1. There must be at least 100 beneficiaries (trust shareholders), and 50 percent or more of the trust cannot be owned by 5 or fewer individuals.

2. At least 75 percent of the trust's assets must be in real property.

3. Not more than 25 percent of the value of a trust's total assets may be represented by securities.

4. Real property may not be held primarily for sale in the ordinary course of business. (For all practical purposes, this restriction excludes land development companies from trust-law exemption benefits.)

5. Income from assets that are held for less than 4 years cannot exceed 30 percent of total earnings.

6. At least 75 percent of the trust's gross income must be derived from real-property earning.

7. An additional 15 percent of gross income must come from either real estate or investment sources.

8. Ninety percent or more of earnings must be distributed to shareholders.

The wide distribution of ownership (more than 100 shareholders) makes initial organization of a REIT somewhat difficult. The 90 percent or greater distribution of profits to avoid double taxation means that the REIT must, for all practical purposes, attract new capital to grow.

An express private trust usually involves only a small number of beneficiaries, often a spouse and children. An express private trust may be created during one's lifetime (a living or *inter vivos* trust) or upon one's death (testamentary trust). The main advantages of a private trust are savings in estate taxes and extended protection for the beneficiary, who may not be familiar with business affairs.

Syndicate

A **syndicate,** or joint venture, is the coming together of individuals, and sometimes of individuals and organizations, to conduct business, and to make investments. A syndicate agreement usually takes partnership or corporate form. Personal and financial abilities are pooled because the syndicate members believe that as a group they will be able to accomplish ends that each could not undertake and complete by acting separately. A syndicate may also be formed when members want to limit individual investment in a project. A syndicate is not an organizational form per se in the sense of a corporation or trust. A syndicate, in fact, may have the legal form of a partnership, corporation, or trust. The term syndicate continues to be used because it connotes an organization that has limited goals, usually of an investment nature.

LIENS, EASEMENTS, DEED RESTRICTIONS, AND OTHER ENCUMBRANCES TO OWNERSHIP

Ownership rights of possession, control, and disposition may be encumbered (and imperiled) by contract or agreement. An **encumbrance** is a claim against clear title to, or a limitation on use of, a property. Encumbrances take several forms, as follows:

1. Liens
2. Easements
3. Deed restrictions
4. Licenses
5. Encroachments
6. Leases

The essence of all of these limitations is described here, including a comment on whether or not the limitation constitutes a serious encumbrance to clear title. Detailed explanations of all the limitations are given in subsequent chapters. Leases have already been briefly discussed and will not be covered here again.

Liens

A **lien** is a claim, enforceable at law, to have a debt or obligation satisfied out of property belonging to a debtor-owner. A lien therefore signifies a debtor-creditor relationship between the property owner and the lien holder. In most cases, a lien results from a contract entered into by an owner. A lien remains in effect against a property until removed by payment or by operation of law.

The most common voluntary lien is the **mortgage,** which is created when property is pledged as security for a loan. Other common liens are the mechanic's or material supplier's lien, the judgment lien, and the tax lien. Anyone performing work or furnishing materials toward the improvement of realty expects to be paid, of course. In the event of nonpayment, the worker or material supplier has a statutory claim for payment against the property, termed a *mechanic's lien.* A *judgment* is a court declaration of one individual's indebtedness to another, including the amount. A *judgment lien* means that a claim in the amount of the court declaration is placed against property owned by the debtor. A tax lien is a claim against property due to nonpayment of income, inheritance, or property taxes by an owner. A tax lien results from an implied contract in which the property owner owes tax payments to the government in return for protection, services, and other benefits received. The property-tax lien is the most common lien. A lien is an encumbrance to clear title unless otherwise provided for in a sales transaction.

Easements

An **easement** is a right or privilege to use the land of another for certain purposes, such as party driveways, ingress and egress, or drainage. Easements are nonpossessory, meaning that the holder of the easement does not have the right to occupy the property subject to the easement. Easements are usually created by deed or by contract. For example, a rancher may sell off a section of land near a river but include in the sales contract and deed an easement to obtain and move water across the alienated land. Easements may be terminated by abandonment, by mutual agreement between the property owner and the easement holder, or by consolidation of title to the property and the easement into one ownership. Easements, except those for utilities and services, are regarded as encumbrances to clear title in a sales transaction.

Deed Restrictions

A **deed restriction** is a covenant (promise) or condition entered into the public record to limit the nature or intensity of use of land or realty. For example, a property may be limited by a deed restriction to one-family residential use or to having no building smaller than 1,500 square feet. A deed restriction, in the form of a condition, creates a qualified fee estate. Deed restrictions are usually placed against property by a subdivider or developer at the time the development plans are entered into the public record. Deed restrictions are also created by including a provision regarding future use of the property in a deed conveying title to another. Deed restrictions that do not contain their own time limit (effective for thirty years from this date, for example) are terminated by the law of the state in which the property is located. A deed restriction may be, but need not be, an encumbrance to marketable title.

Licenses

A **license** is the privilege to use or enter on the premises, granted by someone in legal possession of realty. An example is the right to attend a ball game after purchase of a ticket. Permission to hunt or fish on a farmer's land is another example. License is not an interest in land and generally cannot be assigned to another. Since it is not an interest in land, license may be created orally. Also, as a general rule, a license may be terminated or canceled at the will of the property owner. A license is not usually considered an encumbrance to clear title of real estate.

Encroachments

An *encroachment* occurs when a building (or part of a building) or other object, such as a fence or driveway, illegally intrudes on or into public property or trespasses on or into private property. Extension of a garage overhang into an alley is an example. An abstract of title or title insurance policy is not likely to evidence an encroachment unless it existed and was picked up in a previous transaction. That is, a physical inspection of a property, and sometimes a survey as well, is needed to ascertain that an encroachment exists. An encroachment is a title encumbrance and must be cleared up for marketable title to be conveyed to a buyer.

GOVERNMENTAL OR PUBLIC LIMITATIONS TO OWNERSHIP

The system of property ownership in the United States is a mix of the feudal and allodial systems of ownership brought over from England. Under the *feudal system,* a king or sovereign owned all the land, with the subjects obtaining the use of the land in return for services and allegiance. The *allodial system* recognizes individual ownership only; that is, no proprietary or ownership rights are reserved by a sovereign authority. The mix of systems gives private ownership to the individual, with the state reserving the rights of police power, eminent domain, taxation, and escheat. The reservation of the four rights remains the same regardless of how the fee simple estate is split up.

The essential characteristics of the four public limitations to ownership are described here. Police power, eminent domain, and taxation are taken up in detail in a subsequent chapter. Escheat is not discussed further because of its relative lack of importance.

Police Power

Police power is a catchall term or concept meaning all those regulations of property that the courts consider consistent with due process of law. No compensation need be paid an owner for losses or damages suffered as a result of the exercise of police power. A government's right to exercise police power is based on considerations of public health, safety, morals, and welfare. Planning, zoning, building and housing codes; rent controls; and subdivision regulations are all imposed under the right of police power.

Eminent Domain

Eminent domain is the right of a governmental or quasi-governmental agency to take private property for public uses or purposes. The taking is without the consent of the owner and requires payment of reasonable or just compensation. The exercise of the right of eminent domain is termed **condemnation.** Eminent domain is based on the premise that an owner should sometimes be required to give up property, for fair or just compensation, so that the common good or welfare may be advanced.

Land is frequently acquired by public agencies through direct negotiations with the owner. The power of condemnation is always available, however, to enable public agencies to acquire title and possession by legal proceedings, if necessary. Land for streets, parks, schools and other public buildings, and for other public or social purposes is acquired through negotiation or eminent domain.

Taxation

Local and state governments exercise rights of property taxation to raise monies for operations and services that protect or otherwise benefit their citizenry. This taxation is on an *ad valorem* basis, meaning that the tax is levied according to the property's value, usually the market value. Services or benefits most usually provided for from the tax revenues are schools, police and fire protection, parks, libraries, street maintenance, and welfare payments to the elderly and the needy.

Escheat

Escheat is the reversion or automatic conveyance of realty to the state, upon the owner's death, when there is an absence of a will, heirs, or other legal claimants to title. Escheat is seldom exercised in fact because usually someone can be found who has a title claim. For all practical purposes, escheat is not a restriction on real estate. Escheat serves simply to keep property owned and productive, or "in the system." Land is considered too valuable to society to go unused.

SUMMARY

Real estate ownership includes control, possession and use, exclusion, and disposition. Holding title in fee simple is the most complete form of ownership; in fact, all the lesser rights or interests, when taken together, make up the fee simple title. A fee simple title may be split up by time to create life estates and remainders or leasehold estates and reversions. It may also be split up by number of owners as tenancy by the entirety, community property, tenancy in common, or joint tenancy. Business or group ownership may be held in several forms: condominium, cooperative, corporation, or trust. A syndicate actually has the legal form of a partnership, a corporation, or a trust.

Governmental limitations to ownership are police power, eminent domain, taxation, and escheat. Private limitations or encumbrances to clear title include liens, easements, deed restrictions, licenses, encroachments, and leases.

KEY TERMS

Community property	Leasehold estate
Condominium	License
Curtesy	Lien
Cooperative	Life estate
Condemnation	Limited partner
Corporation	Mortgage
Deed restriction	Partnership
Dower	Police power
Easement	Qualified fee
Eminent domain	Remainder
Encumbrance	Separate property
Estate	Statute of Frauds

Escheat

Fee, fee simple, fee simple absolute

Freehold estate

General partner

Homestead rights

Joint tenancy

Lease

Syndicate

Tenancy

Tenancy by the entirety

Tenancy in common

Tenancy in severalty

Title

Trust

QUESTIONS FOR REVIEW AND DISCUSSION

1. Define and distinguish among the following:
   (a) A freehold estate and a leasehold estate
   (b) A conventional life estate and a legal life estate
   (c) Estate and tenancy

2. Define and distinguish among the following:
   (a) Tenancy in severalty
   (b) Tenancy by the entirety
   (c) Tenancy in common
   (d) Joint tenancy
   (e) Community property

3. List and explain the four tenancies of leasehold estates.

4. List and distinguish among the four governmental limitations to private ownership of real estate.

5. List and explain at least four "voluntary" encumbrances of ownership to real estate.

6. Is government necessary for the existence of private property? Discuss.

7. Are there interests in real estate that do not involve ownership or possession? Discuss.

8. Compare condominium ownership with its Roman law origins, community property with its Spanish law origins, and tenancies with their English law origins. What are the similarities? What are the differences?

9. Are there any ways, other than those discussed in this chapter, that a fee might be split? Discuss.

10. Does condominium ownership make sense in a rural setting? If so, are there other forms of ownership that make more sense to accomplish the same purpose? Discuss.

11. Is the law concerning ownership of real estate changing? In what ways? Give examples.

REFERENCES

Corley, Robert N., and William J. Robert. *Principles of Business Law.* 11th ed. Englewood Cliffs, N.J.: Prentice-Hall, 1979. Provides comprehensive coverage of business law in precise but easily read style for nonattorney reader; shows relation of real property law to other areas of business law; also explains legal procedure. Chapter 43 pertains to real property.

Kratovil, Robert, and Raymond J. Werner. *Real Estate Law.* 7th ed. Englewood Cliffs, N.J.: Prentice-Hall, 1979. Covers most aspects of real estate law, written in a style easily understood by the nonlawyer. Many cases cited and examples given. See in particular, chapters 2, 4 and 6.

Lusk, Harold F., and William B. French. *Law of the Real Estate Business.* 3rd ed. Homewood, Ill.: Irwin, 1975. Covers most aspects of real estate law; written in a combination principles and case style. See chapters 2–4 regarding content of this chapter.

Liens, Easements, and Other Encumbrances to Ownership

5

Aspiration sees only one side of every question: possession many.
James Russell Lowell,
Among My Books

An **encumbrance** is a limitation on title due to either a defect in line of ownership or to some action, or nonaction, of the owner. An encumbrance is therefore a hindrance or obstacle to full title, which may be created voluntarily or involuntarily. Most encumbrances are created voluntarily. But some are created involuntarily by action of law as when an owner ignores someone's rights.

For example, in 1973, a law student in Sacramento, California, went to small claims court to recover a $50 cleaning deposit, plus $200 in damages. The owner refused to pay. In 1976 the property, a ninety-five-unit apartment complex valued at $1.5 million, was sold at auction to satisfy the claim. Only the student showed up at the auction, and in satisfaction of the default judgment, now put at $449, the student received a certificate of sale for the property. A one-year-and-one-day statutory period allowed for redemption of publicly auctioned property passed, without the certificate's being redeemed, so the student became the legal owner of the property, subject of course to the mortgage and other encumbrances against the property. Needless to say, investors need to know the causes and the implications of encumbrances.

The purpose of this chapter is to explain the rights and claims against title that may grow out of contractual relationships of an owner. Liens, easements, deed restrictions, and judgments are all discussed. Mortgages and leases are discussed only briefly because separate chapters are devoted to them.

LIENS

A **lien** is a claim, enforceable at law, to have a debt or obligation satisfied out of property belonging to another. Two parties are involved in a lien: the lien creditor and the lien debtor. The creditor holds the claim or lien. The debtor owns the property subject to the lien. The creditor, if not otherwise satisfied, may initiate an action at law to have the debtor's property sold to satisfy the claim.

Classification of Liens

Liens are classified as specific or general. A **general lien** affects all property of a debtor. A **specific lien** applies to only one or more designated properties. Specific liens, in their general order of importance, are as follows:

1. Mortgage
2. Tax and/or special assessment
3. Mechanic's and/or material supplier's
4. Vendee's
5. Vendor's
6. Attachment

General liens apply to both the personal and real property of a debtor. General liens include (1) state and federal taxes and (2) judgments (state and federal).

Priority of Liens

Liens generally rank in priority according to the order of their filing in the proper public office. For example, a mortgage lien recorded yesterday takes precedence over a vendee's lien entered into the public record today. Three exceptions exist to the general rule. The first exception is that tax or special assessment liens imposed by governmental authority take priority over all liens. The second exception concerns mechanic's and/or material supplier's liens that take precedence according to state statute.

The third exception to the general rule that liens take priority according to time of filing applies to judgment liens. A judgment lien is not good against the rights claimed under a deed or mortgage delivered prior to the court docket date of the judgment. This exception holds true even though the deed or mortgage is not recorded. The reason is that recording laws protect innocent purchasers and lenders for value. That is, buyers and lenders part with value (cash) when deeds or mortgages are delivered to them; and the buyers and lenders have relied upon the public record system in the transaction. Creditors, however, secure judgments without knowing fully what property a debtor owns. They assert an existing general claim in an action at law, which only becomes a lien when the court makes a decree. If the law were otherwise, buyers and lenders would have to be much more cautious or restrained in making transactions. Conditions resulting in restraint of trade are generally considered against public policy in our society.

SPECIFIC LIENS

A specific lien affects only designated property of a debtor. In almost all situations only one property is involved. The categories of specific liens include mortgage, tax, mechanic's, and other miscellaneous liens.

Mortgage Lien

A **mortgage (lien)** is a pledge of realty as security for a mortgage loan. The borrower-mortgagor remains in possession of the property. The lender-mortgagee has a basis for legal action on the mortgage only if the borrower defaults or fails to live up to the contract in any way. The most common default by borrowers, by far, is not meeting scheduled payments of principal and interest to the lender. A trust-deed-in-the-nature-of-a-mortgage is not a lien. The lender's remedy in the event of default is somewhat different from that of a mortgage, as explained in the chapter on mortgages and deeds of trust. A trust-deed has the same effect as a lien, however, in that if the note or debt is not paid, the pledged property may be sold to satisfy the terms of the note and trust-deed.

Tax Lien

Real estate taxes, special assessments, and charges for municipal services become liens against the affected property when levied. A *special assessment* is a charge to cover a proportional share of the cost of an improvement that benefits the property, such as street, sidewalk, sewer line or water line. Service charges by a municipal corporation are mainly for water, sewer, and electricity. Taxing bodies usually move slowly but steadily to enforce their lien claims.

Mechanic's Lien

A **mechanic's lien** is a claim in favor of those who performed work or provided materials toward the improvement of realty. The right to a lien is in addition to the right of action against the person who made the contract of employment or purchase of materials. If they are not paid, contractors, subcontractors, construction workers, material suppliers, architects, and others are entitled to a mechanic's lien. A mechanic's lien is effective against a homestead as well as against other types of property.

The law of mechanic's liens is highly technical. A mechanic's lien is based on state statute, and the law varies markedly from state to state. Anyone involved in business dealings or the improvement or alteration of realty is advised to ascertain the law, as it applies specifically, in his or her community. One unique characteristic of mechanic's liens, covered below, necessitates that buyers and lenders be specially cautious in dealing with newly constructed or recently altered property.

State statutes vary as to whether owner consent or contract is required in order to enforce a mechanic's lien. In states that have contract statutes, the claimant must show that the owner or the owner's agent expressly requested or contracted for the improvement. This prevents a claim against an owner's property when the improvement was not requested, although perhaps a tenant ordered the improvement. In states that have consent statutes, the claimant need only show that the owner or the owner's agent consented to the improvement; in these states a contract is implied.

Buyer and lender caution is extremely important relative to mechanic's liens. A mechanic's lien may be filed up to a year after the completion of construction with priority dating back to the beginning of construction. Therefore, where improvements are newly built or modified, a lien waiver signed by all parties contributing to the construction is desirable. Figure 5–1 shows a com-

FIGURE 5–1
Waiver of mechanic's lien

WAIVER OF LIEN—Material or Labor

STATE OF ILLINOIS

Rustic _____ County} ss.   September 18th _____ 19 80

TO ALL WHOM IT MAY CONCERN:
WHEREAS, we the undersigned _____ construction workers _____
_____ have been employed by THE CHAMPION _____
CONSTRUCTION COMPANY _____ to furnish
labor
for the building known as residence at 3611 - 34th Avenue _____
Situated on Lot—

in the city of Urbandale County of Rustic and State of Illinois

NOW THEREFORE, KNOW YE, That we the undersigned, for and in consideration of
Seven Hundred Eighteen ($718.00) Dollars, the receipt whereof is hereby
acknowledged, do hereby waive and release any and all lien, or claim, or right of lien on said above described building and premises under "An Act to Revise the Law in Relation to Mechanic's Liens," approved May 18, 1903, in force July 1, 1903, together with all amendments thereto and all the lien laws of the State of Illinois, on account of labor or materials, or both, furnished or which may be furnished by the undersigned to or on account of the said contractor _____
_____ for said building or premises.

Given under _____ hand _____ and seal _____ this _____ day
of _____ 19 _____

/s/ Harvey Lehr _____ (SEAL)

ALWAYS MAKE AND RETAIN AN EXACT COPY   /s/ Albert Johanson _____ (SEAL)

pleted lien waiver. By signing a waiver, mechanics or material suppliers renounce rights in the property of concern.

Miscellaneous Specific Liens

Several specific liens, while rare, need to be noted and defined for the reader's information. If a seller fails to deliver title to a property in fulfillment of a contract of sale, the buyer may obtain a *vendee's lien.* Conversely, if title was delivered but full payment not received, a seller may obtain a *vendor's lien.* And in a pending law suit, an **attachment lien** may be obtained on a property to ensure its availability to satisfy a claim for damages against its owner.

GENERAL LIENS

General liens affect all property of a debtor or a debtor's estate. Tax liens take priority over all nontax liens, as mentioned.

Tax

Unpaid income and inheritance taxes at the state and federal level are liens against real property. Until the taxes are paid, clear title cannot be delivered to the heirs of the deceased. A tax lien due to unpaid inheritance taxes becomes a lien immediately upon the death of the owner. A warrant stating the amount of unpaid income taxes must be filed with a local public recorder to create a lien for unpaid income taxes.

Judgments

A **judgment** is a court decree establishing indebtedness and fixing the amount, which becomes a lien against all property owned by the debtor. A judgment may originate in state or federal courts. A judgment becomes a lien in almost all states when properly docketed in a book or register kept by a county clerk or public recorder. A judgment continues as a lien until a *satisfaction piece* indicating that payment has been made is filed with the clerk or recorder. A judgment lien may also be removed by a reversal of the decree upon appeal to a higher court by the defendant.

A plaintiff (initiator of legal action) may wish to make known a claim against the property of a debtor before the judgment is rendered or at the initiation of the lawsuit. This can be done by filing a statutory notice of **lis pendens** or pendency of action. *Lis pendens* gives constructive notice of a claim against the defendant's real property to everyone subsequently acquiring an interest in the property. A notice of *lis pendens* should be filed in the county or community in which the property is located. A notice of *lis pendens* may also be filed to make known other legal actions, such as a mechanic's lien, so that anyone interested in the property may be made aware of an otherwise hidden claim against the property.

EASEMENTS

An *easement* is the right to use realty of another for a special or designated purpose. An easement is a real property right, but it is not regarded as an estate in real property in that it is nonpossessory. There are two kinds of easements: an easement appurtenant and an easement in gross.

Easement Appurtenant

An **easement appurtenant** requires at least two parcels of realty owned by different parties. The parcels are usually but not necessarily adjacent. The parcel benefited is known as the **dominant tenement.** The parcel subject to the easement is known as the **servient tenement.** Although the parcels need not be adjacent, the dominant tenement must be at the beginning or end of the easement. For example, a road or right-of-way easement could cross several servient parcels (A, B, C, and D) to serve a dominant parcel (E).

An easement appurtenant is said to "run with the land." *Appurtenant* means belonging to, or going with, another thing. An easement appurtenant therefore gives a slight gain or loss in real property rights that go with title to the real estate involved. The dominant parcel, of course, benefits from the transfer of rights while the servient tenement becomes less desirable. In turn, the value of the dominant tenement includes the value of the benefits derived from the easement. The servient parcel suffers a loss in value. Naturally enough, an easement resulting in a property's becoming a servient tenement is regarded as an encumbrance.

An access right of way across an adjacent property, a joint driveway, or the right to use a party wall are examples of an appurtenant easement. A party wall is an exterior building wall that straddles the property line and is used jointly by the adjacent property owners. Title is held to the part of the wall on one's own property, and an easement is held in the remainder. A written party-wall agreement should be used to create and control the use of this type of easement.

Easement in Gross

An **easement in gross** is a personal right to use the property of another. It does not belong to any ownership estate. Neither adjacent nor nearby property need be owned to possess the right. Examples of easements in gross are rights of way for pipelines, power lines, sewer lines, or roads used by public-service companies. A permanent right of an outdoor advertising company to place billboards and signs on a property is an easement in gross.

Creation

Easements may be created by any of the following ways:

1. Grant
2. Reservation

3. Necessity
4. Prescription
5. Condemnation

A property owner may create an easement by granting some non-possessory right to the owner of another property. The grant may be by deed or written agreement. Similarly, in splitting a tract of land, the owner may reserve an easement to the parcel retained. If the owner fails to specifically reserve an easement across the property transferred, and if the parcel retained is thereby "land-locked," or without access, an *easement by necessity* is created. It is implied that the owner retained a right of way across the transferred parcel.

An *easement by prescription* is created by open, exclusive, continued use of a servient parcel for a prescriptive period of time as required by state law. A prescriptive period is usually from ten to twenty years. The use must also have been under claim of right of use, without the approval of the owner of the encumbered parcel, and notorious to the point that the owner could learn of it. Prescriptive easements cannot be acquired in state or federally owned property or in property owned by legally incompetent persons, such as infants or mentally retarded individuals.

An *easement by condemnation* is sometimes created when railroads or utility companies acquire rights of way for their needs. Also, scenic easements are increasingly being created by condemnation or purchase to preserve open space.

Maintenance

The contract or agreement creating an easement controls the rights and duties of the parties to an easement, to the extent that the rights and duties are set forth. Beyond the agreement, the owner of the servient tenement may use the property in any way that does not unreasonably interfere with the use and enjoyment of the easement.

The beneficiary of the easement must keep the affected part of the servient parcel in repair relative to the easement. And the beneficiary may not enlarge or change the scope of the easement.

Termination

Easements may be terminated in any of the following ways:

1. Consolidation or merger, as when the dominant and servient parcels come under one ownership. The intention to terminate the easement must be made explicit, possibly by a statement entered into the public record.
2. Agreement, as when the owner of the dominant tenement releases the right of easement to the servient owner, possibly for a price.
3. Completion of purpose, as when the easement is no longer needed. A right-of-way easement of necessity ends if alternate access to the land-locked parcel is gained by its owner.

4. Abandonment, as when all parties recognize that the easement is to be used no longer.

5. Prescription, as when the owner of a servient parcel disregards the easement for a prescription period without objection by the benefiting owner of the easement.

DEED RESTRICTIONS

A **deed restriction** is a requirement, of public record, concerning the nature or intensity of use of realty. The requirement may be to do something, for example, to erect a structure of a certain minimum size or larger. Or the requirement may be not to do something, for example, not to erect a structure more than 28 feet in height or not to keep goats, chickens, or pigs on the premises. Restrictions have traditionally been entered into the public record on a deed at the time of conveyance of title to another; hence the term deed restrictions. Deed restrictions are increasingly being entered into the public record as a part of the plat at the time property is subdivided for development. A more appropriate term for deed restrictions would therefore be use restrictions, or title restrictions.

Courts distinguish between limitations on an owner's right to use and an owner's right to sell or otherwise dispose of a property. Reasonable restraints on use are generally upheld. Restraints on right of alienation or disposition are usually held to be illegal. Some courts do accept restraints on alienation for short or "reasonable" periods as valid. Any restrictions based on racial discrimination are also invalid.

A deed restriction is not an encumbrance to clear title if it is consistent with typical uses of properties in the neighborhood. If the restriction severely restricts use or the obtaining of financing, it is an encumbrance.

Typical Restrictions

The following restrictions are typical for a residential development:

Nuisances. Neither noxious nor offensive activity shall be carried on upon any lot, nor shall anything be done thereon which may be or may become an annoyance or nuisance to the neighborhood.

Animals. No animals, livestock, or poultry of any kind shall be raised, bred, or kept on any lot, except that dogs, cats, and other household pets may be kept provided that they are not kept, bred, or maintained for any commercial purpose.

Term. These covenants are to run with the land and shall be binding on all parties and all persons claiming under them for a period of thirty years from the date these covenants are recorded, after which time said covenants shall be automatically extended for successive periods of ten years unless an instrument signed by a majority of the then owners of the lots has been recorded agreeing to change said covenants in whole or in part.

Enforcement. Enforcement shall be by proceedings at law or in equity against any person or persons violating or attempting to violate any covenant either to restrain violation or to recover damages.

Severability. Invalidation of any one of these covenants by judgment or court order shall in no way affect any of the other provisions which shall remain in full force and effect.

Covenants versus Conditions

Deed restrictions take the form of covenants (promises) or conditions. These differ as to who may enforce them and as to the penalty for violation.

A **restrictive covenant** is a written promise to use or not to use property in a certain way. A grantee and the heirs and assignees of a grantee by accepting title subject to a covenant are bound by the promise or covenant. A covenant is enforced by an injunction whenever a violation occurs. An *injunction* is a court order requiring one to do or to stop doing a certain act. The injunction may be sought by the parties to the covenants or by beneficiaries of the covenants. Thus, restrictive covenants for a subdivision may be enforced by the subdivider or by residents of the subdivision. An owner of property adjacent to the subdivision, however, cannot obtain enforcement since the covenants were not imposed for his or her benefit.

A **restrictive condition** *with reverter* is a written statement providing that if a specified event occurs or if a certain use is made, or not made of property, title reverts to the grantor or heirs of the grantor. A qualified fee estate is created when a restrictive condition with reverter is placed against a property's ownership. The grantor or the grantor's heirs have a future conditional fee precedent interest in the property; that is, the condition must be violated for the interest to become active. See chapter 4 on ownership interests in real property.

The penalty for violation of a condition is reversion of title to the grantor or to heirs of the grantor who placed the limitation on the property. No remuneration need be paid, but legal action must be initiated to recover title. A mortgage interest is also wiped out by reversion. Only the grantor or heirs of the grantor may enforce a condition; that is, other beneficiaries of the condition may not enforce it. The penalty for violation of a condition is so harsh that courts prefer to interpret a restriction as a covenant. If, however, the language clearly indicates that a condition with reverter was intended, the condition prevails. Words like "on condition that" and "with right of reversion" must therefore be present for a restrictive condition to be created.

Termination

Deed restrictions may be terminated in the following ways:

1. *Lapse of time.* Restrictions are frequently placed on a subdivision for a specified period, often thirty years, subject to renewal or extension for from five- to ten-year periods unless two-thirds or three-quarters of the owners want the restrictions lifted. Renewal is often limited to another thirty years.

2. *Merger or consolidation.* An owner of all parcels affected by restrictive covenants may lift or remove some or all promises.

3. *Mutual agreement of parties.* All affected parties, primarily grantees, under a common scheme of restrictions may mutually agree to alter or terminate the restrictions.

4. *Material change in nature of neighborhood.* Courts may refuse to enforce restrictions that have outlived their usefulness because of substantial change in the nature of the neighborhood.

5. *Abandonment.* Frequent violations without enforcement by beneficiaries are interpreted by courts that the restrictions have been abandoned. Beneficiaries are later estopped from enforcement proceedings.

MISCELLANEOUS ENCUMBRANCES

Additional encumbrances that must be cleared up before clear title can be delivered include leases and encroachments. A written lease for years extending beyond the closing date in a sales transaction is an encumbrance. A leasehold with periodic tenancy, tenancy at will, and tenancy at sufferance is not usually considered an encumbrance unless time of occupancy and use is of the essence to the buyer. Encroachments of buildings or other improvements into or onto realty of another owner or the public also constitute an encumbrance to clear title until removed or otherwise cleared up.

Surprise encumbrances may be created by unwary acts of an owner. For example, an owner having an attorney-in-fact, with written authority, execute mortgages, deeds, or other real property instruments, is likely to create encumbrances. The sealed instrument granting power-of-attorney status, must be made a part of the public record to avoid creating an encumbrance in this situation. An *attorney-in-fact* is a person given written authority to perform certain acts as an agent of a principal. Also, violation of local police-power regulations may result in an encumbrance against a property, as when building, fire, or health codes are not obeyed.

SUMMARY

An encumbrance is a burden or limitation to full title to real estate. Examples are liens, certain easements and deed restrictions, encroachments, and leases. Easements or restrictions that benefit a property are generally not considered encumbrances.

A lien is a claim, enforceable at law, to have a debt or obligation satisfied out of a property belonging to another. Mortgage, tax, and mechanic's and/or material supplier's liens are the most usual specific liens. The most usual general lien is the judgment lien.

An easement is the right a party has to use the property of another without taking possession. Two types of easements exist: easement appurtenant and easement in gross. A deed restriction is a requirement of limitation concerning the nature or intensity of use of realty. Deed restrictions take the form of covenants or conditions. A covenant is a promise to use, or not use, property in a certain way that is enforced by an injunction. A condition is a statement that, upon violation of the limitation, allows the property to revert back to the grantor or the grantor's heirs. Easements and deed restrictions are terminated by merger, mutual agreement of parties, abandonment or nonuse.

KEY TERMS

Attachment lien	Lien
Deed restriction	*Lis pendens*
Dominant tenement	Mechanic's lien
Easement appurtenant	Mortgage lien
Easement in gross	Restrictive condition with reverter
Encumbrance	Restrictive covenant
General lien	Servient tenement
Judgment	Specific lien

QUESTIONS FOR REVIEW AND DISCUSSION

1. Distinguish between specific and general liens. Identify at least two of each type.

2. Distinguish between easement appurtenant and easement in gross. What is the usual purpose of each?

3. Distinguish between a covenant and a condition with reverter as a title restriction. Which is more commonly used?

4. Identify at least two encumbrances, not due to defects in title, in addition to liens, easements, and deed restrictions.

5. All mechanic's liens should have equal priority of claim, regardless of when work was performed or materials were supplied. Discuss.

6. Giving tax liens priority, by law, is unfair to other lienholders. Discuss.

7. It has been proposed that a statute of limitations is needed to remove encumbrances as clouds on title; thus liens, easements, and deed restrictions would become ineffective after some stipulated period, say fifteen years. Discuss. What implications?

8. Able, owner of 160 acres of land along a river, sold half to Baker. No frontage on the river was included, but an easement of access to use the river for rec-

reation was written into the deed. Baker later sold off five 10-acre parcels to other persons. Are these subsequent purchasers entitled to use the access easement to the river? Discuss.

9. When is a deed restriction not an encumbrance? Discuss.

REFERENCES

Corley, Robert N., and William J. Robert. *Principles of Business Law.* 11th ed. Englewood Cliffs, N.J.: Prentice-Hall, 1979. See chapter 43.

Kratovil, Robert, and Raymond J. Werner. *Real Estate Law.* 7th ed. Englewood Cliffs, N.J.: Prentice-Hall, 1979. See chapters 4, 18, 28, 32, and 39.

Governmental Limitations to Ownership

6

Society in every state is a blessing, but government, even in its best state, is but a necessary evil; in its worst state, an intolerable one.
Thomas Paine,
Common Sense, 1776

The governmental powers of regulation, condemnation, and taxation make ownership and control of real estate by private persons less than total or complete. These powers are reserved by governments to maintain themselves, to look after the public health, welfare, and safety, and to facilitate growth and adjustment of their communities in response to changing social and economic needs. The purpose of this chapter is to look at these three reservations of powers, and at how they impinge on the development and use of privately owned property by our rational investor. That is, only the limiting or restrictive aspects of these governmental powers, which an owner cannot avoid, are considered here. A secondary purpose is to give the reader the basic terminology of these limitations. Governmental powers and programs, which affect rights in real property, more or less at the option of an owner, are discussed at appropriate points farther on. Rent subsidy or mortgage-insurance programs are examples of optional involvement.

Topics are taken up in this chapter in the following order:

1. Police power
2. Eminent domain
3. Taxation
4. Trends in governmental regulation

POLICE POWER LIMITATIONS
Police power is a catchall or all-encompassing term for those regulations of property consistent with due process of law that courts consider necessary to protect public health, welfare, safety, and morals. Police power includes the operation of health and sanitation, police, fire, and planning departments, among others. Villages, cities, and counties all have rights of police power based on state enabling legislation or acts. An **enabling act** is the granting of express authority, by a state legislative body, to local governments to carry on certain activities. Police-power enabling legislation provides the basis for planning, zoning ordinances, subdivision regulations, building codes, and other land-use controls. Even rent controls are imposed under the police-power authority. No compensation need be paid for lowered property values resulting from the imposition of police power.

What does a rational investor need to know about the use of police power in regulating real estate? For one thing, it's helpful to know what each of its uses are, relative to real estate, and the purposes to be accomplished. For another, it is helpful to have a clear understanding of how it is applied. And for a third, it is helpful to know how to operate or respond, when police power is encountered, in order to maximize chances of achieving one's own investment objectives.

Planning

Communities thrive and grow and change because of physical, social, economic, and political interaction. Growth in population, commerce, manufacturing, and other activities results in demands that exceed the capabilities of physical facilities such as roads, sewers, water systems, schools, hospitals, and other public buildings. Depreciation and changes in technology also make changes necessary in these facilities. Designing and building such facilities require large amounts of money. One major purpose of planning is to avoid wasteful mistakes that are a result of poor coordination, duplication, and overbuilding. A second major purpose is to create and maintain a high-quality environment, one aspect of which is stabilized property values that result from orderly community growth and change. The emphasis is on land-use planning. To be effective, land-use planning must take the real estate market mechanism into account. That is, land-use planning that does not take account of locational economics is doomed to failure.

Properly done, planning is a systematic process involving data collection, classification, and analysis aimed at developing a comprehensive or master plan. A **master plan** is a comprehensive scheme setting forth ways and means by which a community can adjust its physical makeup to social and economic changes. The community may be a city, county, village, or metropolitan area. The plan or scheme concerns coordination of land uses with the provision of transportation, schools, parks, and other community services and facilities. To be effective, the comprehensive plan must be based on planning studies. The comprehensive plan, particularly the land-use portion, provides the underlying rationale for zoning, subdivision regulation, and building regulation. A master plan, to adequately fulfill its function, must at the very least be based on studies of (1) population, (2) economic base, (3) land use and (4) transportation of the area or community.

The master plan is a plan to project and provide for a community's future needs in an orderly manner. For a plan to effectively meet a community's needs, it must be

1. in scale with the population and economic outlook of the community;
2. in scale with the current and future financial resources of the community;
3. balanced and attractive in design in relation to the environment to be created and maintained;
4. in keeping with community sentiments on an attractive environment;
5. flexible and easily updated to accommodate changing conditions and projections.

The master plan really consists of several lesser coordinated plans for land use, transportation, schools, and other public facilities. The master plan is implemented primarily through the subdivision and zoning ordinances, which are examples of land-use controls. A **land-use control** is a public or private means used to regulate and guide the use of realty.

Zoning

Zoning is easily the most significant legal technique in land-use control. Zoning is dividing a community (city, village, or county) into districts for the regulation of land-use type (residential, commercial, and so forth) and intensity (one-family, multifamily, and so forth) and of height, bulk, and appearance of structures. Originally, the districts were geographic areas with only general land-use types specified. But increasingly, classes of uses, defined by performance standards, are permitted in the various districts. This is called performance zoning. *Performance,* as used here, means to meet the requirements or standards of the class. That is, **performance zoning** is establishing districts that allow or accept uses, regardless of type, if they meet certain standards relative to such things as density, appearance, traffic generation, and pollution origination. Thus, uses that do not adversely affect each other, and may, in fact, complement each other, are placed in the same class or district. This shift toward performance zoning is consistent with the general trend toward greater flexibility in zoning. Conventional zoning is considered too rigid to adequately accommodate community change over a long period. This greater flexibility is likely to increase in importance as our urban areas go through a redevelopment, rather than development, phase. This greater flexibility is likely to work to an owner-investor's advantage for the most part. Let us look at the following topics in this regard to see the impact of zoning on investors:

1. Content of the ordinance
2. Height, bulk, and area regulation

3. Multiple-use zoning
4. Negotiation and/or challenge
5. Inconsistent uses

ZONING-ORDINANCE CONTENT. A locally adopted set of laws or regulations that serve as controls on the use of land and space and on community appearance is a **zoning ordinance.** In addition to written regulations, a zoning ordinance usually includes a zoning map. These items are generally addressed:

1. The community is divided into districts in which the land uses are controlled; for example, residential versus commercial versus industrial versus agricultural.
2. Standards limiting the height and bulk of buildings are set for each district.
3. Standards regulating the proportion of a lot that can be built on, including detailed front-, side-, and back-yard requirements, are set for each district.
4. Limits are set on population density in the various districts of the community by regulation of the above factors; this procedure is called **density zoning.**

Thus zoning regulates land use, land coverage, height and bulk of buildings, and population. The zoning map should not be regarded as the land-use plan itself.

A properly drawn zoning ordinance is not legally concerned with the following:

1. Specifying building materials and construction methods. (Governed by construction or building codes.)
2. Setting minimum construction costs. (Not legally allowed by public ordinance but may be set by private deed restrictions.)
3. Regulation of street design and installation of utilities or reservation of land for park or school sites. (Governed primarily by subdivision regulations, along with street or public-works department, the park department, and the school board.)

HEIGHT, BULK, AND AREA REGULATIONS. Building height and bulk restrictions prevent the usurpation of air, ventilation, and sunlight by one parcel at the unreasonable expense of another parcel. The restrictions also limit fire risks as well as population density and street congestion in neighborhoods or districts. Building heights are generally limited to a certain number of stories, i.e., one and a half, two, two and a half, ten.

Floor-area ratio (FAR) zoning is gaining acceptance as a means of allowing greater design flexibility in a district while limiting population and development density. FAR is the relationship of building coverage to lot area. A FAR of 2.0 means that an owner is permitted to construct a two-story building over the entire lot, or a four-story over one-half of the lot, or an eight-story building over one-fourth of the lot. (See figure 6–1.) Proportion or fraction-of-lot coverage times the number of stories equals the allowed floor-area ratio of 2.0 in all cases. Bonuses are sometimes added to the FAR of a parcel if the parcel is adjacent to open space or if the owner agrees to provide adequate off-street parking. FAR zoning is used primarily in multifamily residential and commercial districts. Lot-coverage standards are not needed when FAR zoning is used. FAR zoning is a form of performance zoning.

FIGURE 6–1

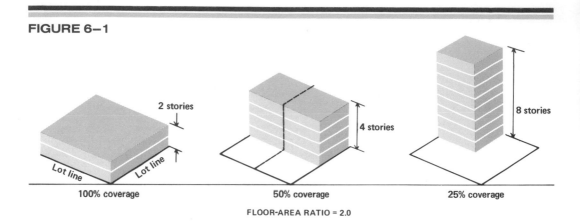

FLOOR-AREA RATIO = 2.0

Solar energy requires that adequate sunlight be available on a continuing basis. Thus, "right-to-light" zoning might modify FAR zoning, as shown in figure 6–2.

MULTIPLE-USE ZONING. Allowing several compatible, but different, uses in a district is called **multiple-use zoning.** Thus offices and small stores may be allowed in the same district as apartments or condominiums, an arrangement

FIGURE 6–2
"Right-to-Light" performance zoning

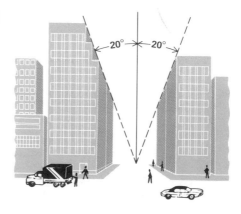

that may work to the benefit of all concerned. In fact, these uses may be combined into one project, termed a *planned-unit development,* as a result of a transfer of development rights. In a **planned-unit development** (PUD) improvements are added to realty at the same density as in conventional development, but the improvements may be clustered and surrounded by open, common areas. For example, assume a 10-acre parcel zoned for four dwelling units per acre. A developer is limited to forty one-family houses by conventional zoning. With PUD, the developer could construct four closely clustered ten-unit buildings, leaving the balance of the acreage for open space. PUD may be used in residential, commercial, or industrial development. PUD zoning is also termed *cluster zoning* or *density zoning.*

A transfer of development rights from one parcel to another is conceptually possible and becoming legally accepted. **Transferable Development Rights (TDRs)** also add flexibility to the development of a community. In the above PUD, if commercial development rights were acquired by the investor in developing the PUD, stores could be included in the project. This, of course, would be an extended form of multiple-use zoning.

ZONING CHALLENGE AND/OR NEGOTIATION. An owner, or potential owner, may petition for changes in, or relief from, the zoning ordinance. Initially, the key person to contact for information is the zoning-enforcement officer of the city or county. That may not be the exact title in every community, but zoning enforcement is the specific function of the job, regardless of title. In general, the officer is charged with literal enforcement of the zoning ordinance, with little or no authority to modify provisions in individual cases. A formal petition to a zoning board of adjustment or appeals may be necessary to obtain the desired change or relief.

In addition to a change in class, several ways of reaching a working arrangement with the zoning board are possible.

Under certain conditions, a zoning board may grant special-use permits or variances. A **special-use permit** gives the right to introduce a use into a zoning district where a definite need exists but where the use is normally not allowed. The introduction of a public-utility substation into a one-family residential district, under controlled conditions, is an example. A **zoning variance** is a deviation from the zoning ordinance granted because strict enforcement would result in undue hardship on a property owner. The usual rules are simply set aside, for example, where a lot is so steep that front-yard setback requirements cannot be met with reasonable expense. A variance must not violate the intent or spirit of the ordinance.

A technique known as contract zoning is sometimes used to fine tune a zoning ordinance. **Contract zoning** refers to an owner, who, by deed restriction or side agreement, limits a rezoned property to a more restrictive use than allowed by the new zoning classification. For example, a parcel is rezoned as commercial, and at the same time the owner records a deed restriction limiting use to one-story professional offices. Contract zoning is not a recognized legal concept.

An owner may circumvent the zoning board of appeals, though the process is costly. In such an effort, the zoning ordinance itself is challenged on legal grounds. That is, zoning ordinances must meet certain standards in order to be legal. The due-process rights of owners and other individuals are protected by the Fourteenth Amendment to the United States Constitution and must not be violated. This means that zoning ordinances must not be arbitrary, unreasonable, destructive, or confiscatory in application. The legal requirements of a valid ordinance may be summarized as follows:

1. Use districts must be provided for by enabling legislation; and applicable regulations must be uniform for each use classification and kind of building.
2. A reasonable basis for classifying districts differently must exist.
3. An entire jurisdiction (such as a city), and not just small, isolated areas, must be zoned.
4. Parcels must not be zoned for uses they cannot physically accommodate.

Effectively, a challenge on the above grounds means that the ordinance is not based on a well-conceived land-use or master plan.

Also, zoning may not be used to discriminate against minorities or low-income people. Zoning designed to keep low-income and moderately low income groups out of a residential district by setting an unreasonably large minimum lot size, floor-area requirement, or construction quality standard is **exclusionary zoning.**

INCONSISTENT USES. A parcel or small area may be zoned for a use or structure that is inconsistent with the rationale of the overall plan or ordinance; this is **spot zoning.** It is generally considered illegal for a zoning board to grant spot zoning. Therefore, an owner adversely affected by spot zoning of a neighboring parcel is likely to be able to successfully challenge such a rezoning in court.

On the other hand, existing uses or structures may be inconsistent with the applicable zoning; these are termed **nonconforming uses.** If they were created before and existed at the original adoption of the ordinance, they are legal, nonconforming uses. Nonconforming uses are allowed to continue, subject to several provisions, because to require their removal would inflict severe financial hardship on owners. Generally, the provisions regulating a nonconforming use prohibit the following:

1. Enlargement
2. Rebuilding or reconstruction after a specified percentage of damage or destruction, usually 50 percent
3. Changing to another nonconforming use
4. Resumption after a stated period of discontinuance, usually a year

New uses and structures must conform to the zoning ordinance. To introduce a use or to build a structure inconsistent with the ordinance is to create an illegal nonconforming use, which would be subject to immediate removal without compensation.

ZONING AND VALUE. Zoning does not create value in land or realty, and zoning does not prevent value declines. Market demand for a use is the basis of value, whether it involves an office building, a shopping center, or an apartment building. At the same time, the appropriate zoning must be obtained for the value, based on market demand, to be realized. If demand for a use is not present, commercial, industrial, or multifamily zoning does not enhance a property's value, except perhaps in the mind of the owner. Thus, inappropriate zoning may distort or alter the use to which a parcel is put, thereby limiting it to less than its highest and best use. Also, zoning cannot prevent the aging and depreciation of structures, factors that are likely to lead to lower values.

Subdivision Regulations

Subdivision regulations are locally adopted laws governing the conversion of raw land into building sites. The regulations work primarily through plat-approval procedures, under which a subdivider or developer is not permitted to split up land until the planning commission has approved a plat of the proposed project. A *plat* is a drawing, usually a map—for instance, of a subdivision—showing actual or proposed property lines, easements, setback lines, and so forth, that has been approved by the planning commission for entry into the public record. Approval is based on compliance with standards and requirements set forth in a subdivision regulation ordinance. A developer who attempts to record an unapproved drawing or map or attempts to sell lots by reference to such a map is usually subject to civil and criminal prosecution. For the most part, subdivision regulations apply at the fringe of communities where land is being converted from rural to urban uses.

In almost all states a comprehensive plan, a major street plan, or an official map must have been adopted prior to subdivision regulations to provide a legal basis for implementation. Either plan serves as evidence that the regulations are not arbitrary or discriminatory. That is, either plan coordinates the layout of a particular subdivision with others in the area and also ensures provision for rights of way for major thoroughfares, easements for utility lines, and school and park locations.

Major elements controlled by most subdivision regulations are as follows:

1. Rights of way for streets, alleys, cul-de-sacs, highways, and walkways—location, alignment, width, grade, surfacing material, and possible dedication to community
2. Lot and blocks—minimum dimensions and building setback lines
3. Utilities—easements for sewer, water, and power; assurance of pure water and ability to dispose of wastes without health problems.
4. Reserved areas for schools, parks, open space, and other public uses

Subdivision regulations vary greatly from community to community. The regulations in the jurisdiction where the land is located control its development. Development charges appear to be increasingly used by communities and incorporated into their subdivision ordinances and building regulations. A **devel-**

opment charge is a fee imposed against a subdivider or developer by the community to pay the costs of new waste-disposal facilities, roads, water storage tanks, and the like, necessitated by the new subdivision or structure. The intent is that the tenants of the subdivision or structure will pay the marginal costs of these community facilities rather than the citizenry in general.

Also, environmental-impact studies are increasingly being required of owners proposing large development projects. An **environmental-impact study (EIS)** is an investigation and analysis to determine the long-run physical effects of a proposed land use on its surroundings and the long-run economic and social effects on other people. The purpose of an EIS is to bring together in one report the likely costs and benefits of a project before the project is approved for development. For example, the EIS for a proposed shopping center would document the expected effects on auto traffic, air quality, the waste-disposal system, energy demand, employment, and vegetation. If costs are too substantial, the proposal may not obtain approval. Also, the project may be modified as a result of the study to avoid or ease expected problems.

Building Regulations

A **building code** is a local or state government ordinance, or series of ordinances, regulating the construction, alteration, and maintenance of structures within the jurisdiction. Almost all cities, towns, and counties have building or construction codes specifying structural requirements, material performance, and arrangement of buildings that must be met when erecting or repairing structures. The purpose of the codes is to protect public health and safety. Code requirements include or concern fireproof construction, means of emergency exit, windows, load and stress, size and location of rooms, adequacy of ventilation, sanitation facilities, electrical wiring and equipment, mechanical equipment, and the lighting of exits. Several separate codes as the electrical, plumbing, and fire code may make up the "building code."

The codes are particularly stringent for buildings likely to be occupied by large numbers of people, for example, apartment buildings, schools, churches, hospitals, and office buildings. Special provisions also usually apply to unique or potentially hazardous structures such as amusement parks, canopies, roof signs, grandstands, grain elevators, or cleaning plants.

Building codes effectively take up where subdivision regulations leave off. That is, subdivision regulations apply mainly to land, and building codes apply to improvements. Nevertheless, building codes and zoning ordinances tend to overlap.

Enforcement begins with the requirement that a building permit be obtained for new construction or alterations. Both the zoning and the building codes must be complied with. There must be an examination of the plans before a building permit is issued. The permit is only evidence of compliance with public regulations and does not exempt or cure a violation of deed restrictions. Construction work is inspected as it progresses. A certificate of occupancy must be obtained by an owner of a new or rehabilitated building before it can be put into use. A **certificate of occupancy** is an official notice that all code inspections were passed and that the structure is fit for use.

In many communities certain existing buildings are subject to annual inspections to detect code violations and changes in occupancy or use contrary to the certificate of occupancy. Violations must be corrected for continued use. Some communities also require a code inspection whenever ownership of a property changes. The seller is required to cure any violations. Owners may be fined or imprisoned if violations are not promptly remedied. Dangerous violations may result in forced vacating of a building, and possibly its demolition.

Miscellaneous Controls

Some communities maintain an *official map* which designates exact locations of existing and proposed street rights of way, of proposed street-widening projects, and of lands to be reserved for school sites, parks, and playgrounds. The official map is their equivalent of a master plan. Compensation will not be paid for any land improvements built in these proposed rights of way and reserved areas after they have been specifically designated or made a part of the map.

As a rule, fire and sanitation departments are empowered to make periodic inspections and to order compliance with directives to ensure safe and sanitary use and occupancy of buildings. Proper enforcement of fire-control and sanitation ordinances may go a long way toward retarding housing blight and the eventual elimination of unsightly and unsafe city slums. In almost all states there are health regulations for wells, septic tanks, and other waste-disposal installations.

EMINENT DOMAIN

The *right of eminent domain* is the power of government to take private property for public purposes without the owner's consent. This is sometimes called condemnation, or the right of expropriation. The right of eminent domain may be exercised by the local, state, and federal governments. In addition, semipublic organizations such as railroads and public-utility companies may exercise eminent domain for limited purposes. And private, nonprofit institutions, such as universities, also have a limited right of eminent domain.

Most agencies and organizations seek to acquire desired properties by negotiation before exercising their right of eminent domain. Great effort is exerted to explain to each owner both the proposed development and the owner's rights. The property is appraised and fair market value offered. If the offer is not considered acceptable, the owner may refuse it and hold out for a court hearing. At this point the governmental unit initiates condemnation proceedings.

Need

The right of eminent domain is needed because our society and economy are growing and changing. For example, in the 1930s sociologists predicted that the U.S. population would mature and stabilize at 150 million by 1950. Nearly half the population lived in rural areas at that time. Automobiles were still a relatively new mode of transportation. Air travel was only for the wealthy. Most intercity passenger and freight transportation was provided by the railroads. In the beginning of the 1980s, the U.S. population is actually about 225 million people, about three-fourths of whom live in urban areas. Almost everyone uses automobiles, and air travel is much more common than travel by rail. Trucks have taken over a large share of the task of intercity freight. Without the right of eminent domain, our society would be strangled for lack of adequate transportation and information-transmission networks. Our civilization depends on ready movement of people, goods, and natural resources, and the prompt exchange of information.

In a more specific sense, the power of eminent domain is exercised to acquire property for highway construction, public-building sites, flood-control projects, and airport expansion. The power has been legally exercised to acquire land for public parking lots to be operated by private concessionaires. The U.S. Supreme Court has even declared legal the acquisition of land in urban-renewal areas for later resale and redevelopment by profit-seeking individuals and corporations. Thus, the emphasis is on public purposes and not limited to public needs and uses per se.

Just Compensation

Just compensation is payment to an owner for property taken in condemnation proceedings. If an entire property is taken, just compensation is almost universally defined as the fair market value of the property. Many states provide for payment of **severance damages** to the owner if only part of the property is taken but the value of the remainder is lowered as a result of the taking. That is, fair market value is paid for the portion of the property taken, and severance damages are paid for any injury or reduction in value to the remainder. If, however, the remainder is increased in value as a result of the taking, payment for physical damages to the remainder is not likely to be made. The physical injury may involve interference with, or restriction on, access, or modification of the size and shape of the property so as to change its highest and best use.

The "before and after rule" is sometimes applied in cases involving partial takings. The entire property is valued under conditions that prevailed before the taking. The remaining land is then valued as if a part of the property had been taken and the proposed improvement built. The difference is the amount of the just compensation. If the value of the remainder exceeds the value of the entire property as appraised before the taking, no compensation need be paid. Of course, the owner would have no obligation to pay the governmental body for any excess enhancement in value of the remainder, in that the owner did not propose or initiate the change.

Usually, compensation is not paid for certain damages suffered by an owner. Examples are

1. Loss of business profits or good will
2. Moving costs (although the federal government and some states do pay these in some situations, independent of the court's decision)

3. Additional costs of securing replacement housing or facilities

4. Adverse effects of having the proposed improvement as a neighbor, such as in the case of an airport or a sewage-treatment plant

TAXATION AND SPECIAL ASSESSMENTS

The power to tax gives government a preferred-partner position in the ownership of real estate. The government always gets its taxes before the owner gets any profits.

The power to tax, if wisely used, may greatly benefit an owner. Taxes help provide police and fire protection, schools, parks, and a road system, all of which, if of high quality, enhance the value of a property. An investor's rights in owned property are also more secure because law and order are maintained through the government's legal system. Unwise use of the power to tax may distort locational choices in the real estate market and cause neighborhood deterioration and blight, and in turn lower property values. Both the community and the investor lose as a result. Both the Constitution and statutory law contain safeguards against unfair or unreasonable taxation. The purpose of this section is to make a clear statement about how taxes affect or impinge on an owner's rights and some idea about what these safeguards are. Ways to respond, when the power to tax is misused, are, more appropriately, discussed in the chapter on property management. Topics taken up in this section are

1. The basis for property taxation

2. Uniformity in assessment

3. Tax-exempt properties

4. Taxes and industrial location

5. Special assessments

The Basis for Property Taxation

Taxes are levied to pay the costs of governmental services. Equitable sharing of these costs is ever a problem. Two theories are accepted as guidelines in determining who should pay the costs. The *benefits-received theory* says that taxes should be imposed in proportion to benefits derived from governmental services. The benefits-received theory, while equitable, is generally not politically feasible; those people in greatest need of community aid and support are generally least able to pay. Thus, taxes are generally levied according to ability to pay. The result is "to each according to need and from each according to ability to pay," which translates into **ad valorem** taxation. Thus, property taxes are levied as a percentage or proportion of value. The percentage typically runs about 2½ percent of market value, generally being lower in rural areas and higher in urban areas. This reflects the higher level of public services provided in urban areas. The percentage is generally lowest in the southern part of the United States and highest in the eastern U.S. and California. A *Wall Street Jour-*

nal article reported that the property tax rate in Newark, New Jersey, equaled $8.44 per $100 of market value, undoubtedly one of the highest rates in the country.

Each parcel must be periodically appraised in ad valorem taxation and an assessed value determined. **Assessed value** means the worth or amount in dollars assigned a parcel by the tax administrator. Assessed value may equal or be a proportion of market value, and it varies directly with market value.

Uniformity in Assessment

The property tax burden in ad valorem taxation is fairly or equitably apportioned to real estate owners if all property is assessed at the same proportion of value. Thus, a store that sold for $100,000 and is assessed at $60,000 would be treated the same as a residence that sold for $40,000 and is assessed at $24,000. Each is assessed at 60 percent of its market price. The store stands to pay two and one-half times more in property taxes because its value is two and one-half times greater.

It would be unfair if the store and the house were both assessed at $24,000 because the store owner would not be paying a fair share of taxes. Lack of uniformity in assessing can and does occur from one taxing district to another and from one type of property to another. A market-value study sponsored by the Texas Legislature Property Tax Committee concluded that rural and industrial property were most often underassessed.[1] Similar studies in Oregon support this view.[2] It should be noted that the relative level of assessing makes no difference in the amount of taxes paid per property if the assessing is uniform and properly administered. The exception to this rule is in states such as Florida where home owners are given homestead exemptions by statute ($5,000 generally and $10,000 to owners age 65 and over). Thus, if a home is assessed at less than market value, the exemption provides a greater tax break than may have been intended by the law.

WHEN UNIFORMITY IS LACKING. Towns, cities, and counties tend to assess their properties at low levels in order to pay a lower share of taxes if the state levies taxes on local real estate. This assumes that the state would levy the tax as a fixed percent of assessed value. Some states, like Oregon and Florida, have passed laws requiring assessment at 100 percent of market value to offset this strategy. Another means to correct for differences in assessing levels is for the state to make assessed-value-sales-price-ratio studies. An **assessed-value-sales-price-ratio study** is the analysis of a sample of recently sold properties to determine the relationship between assessed values and "market value" in a taxing jurisdiction or district.

Based on these studies, a ratio by property type for each taxing juris-

[1]Legislative Property Tax Committee, *Market Value Study—Pilot Project, Phase II Summary Report* (Austin, Texas, February 1975), p. 25.

[2]Oregon Department of Revenue, *Ratio Study 1972: Locally Assessed Property* (Salem, Ore., 1973).

diction is determined. Thus, if a jurisdiction assesses properties at 80 percent of sales price, an adjustment factor of 1.25 may be applied to its assessed values to bring them to market value. Prorating state taxes to be collected to cities and counties based on the market value of properties in them gives equity or fairness in ad valorem taxation.

TAX CAPITALIZATION. A property can pay more or less taxes than its market value would justify because of over- or underassessment or because of being located in high or low tax-rate districts. This gives rise to tax capitalization. **Tax capitalization** is the converting of all future tax payments incurred or avoided into a lump-sum present value. For example, assume the assessed value of a property is higher by $8,000 than market value justifies. In turn, annual taxes at a 3 percent tax rate will be $240 higher. If the higher tax were capitalized into perpetuity or for all time at 10 percent, capitalized value would equal $2,400. The property, if sold, should then sell for $2,400 *less* than properties exactly comparable except for the property tax difference. Alternatively, tax rates that are too low represent advantages to owners and therefore justify sales prices above market value.

Tax-Exempt Property

A second item of major concern to property owners is the number of tax-exempt properties in their districts. Tax-exempt properties generally include all government property plus property owned by nonprofit institutions such as churches, hospitals, and private schools. The properties do require services like fire and police protection whether taxes are paid or not. Also, as in the case of military bases, the government property may house families who use local schools and public recreational facilities. In some cases, payments in lieu of taxes are made from one level of government to another in recognition of the extra burden placed on local facilities. In addition to the extra direct burden, however, large numbers of publicly owned properties mean that streets and sewer, water, and power lines must all extend greater distances to tie privately owned properties together. This constitutes an extra cost to private citizens of the community also. Thus, where other considerations are equal, a private citizen might well prefer to locate where the amount of tax-exempt property is not unduly great.

Industrial Location

Differences in levels of taxation apparently do not greatly influence locational choices for new industrial plants. A study by Helene A. Cameron concludes that factors like labor costs and nearness to materials and markets are more important than tax levels.[3] The study found that the differences in tax lev-

---

[3]"The Effects of the Property Tax on Location of Industrial Plants," *Bulletin of Business Research,* Center for Business and Economic Research, Ohio State University, April 1969.

els in a metropolitan area ranged from $27 per $1,000 of assessed valuation to $51 per $1,000. However, the net effect amounted to less than 1 percent of operating costs, not enough to be a significant factor in the choice of a plant site. The study concluded further that plants tend to cluster in low-tax areas for other reasons, with the low taxes in the area being an effect rather than a cause, and not vice versa.

Special Assessments

Special assessments are charges upon real property to pay all or part of the cost of a local improvement by which the property will be benefited. They do not recur regularly, as taxes do, and are not always apportioned according to the value of the property affected. For example, all lots fronting on a certain street are benefited by the paving of the street and are equally assessed for it, even though the corner lots may have a greater value than inside lots. Buildings are not considered in apportioning a special assessment, it being assumed that the land receives all the benefit. Sometimes special assessments are spread over a large area, the property nearest to the improvement being charged with a greater proportion of it than property more remote, the rate decreasing with the distance from the improvement.

Only where local improvements are beneficial—that is, where they increase the value of the affected properties—will courts sanction the levying of special assessments. That is especially true where construction of express highways or of other types of freeways limits access to and egress from the property of adjoining land owners. In a court case, some property owners in Miami Beach, Florida, challenged the right of the municipality to levy assessments for the widening of Indian Creek Drive in Miami Beach. The property owners contended that the widening of the drive from 25 to 40 feet was carried forth to relieve congested traffic on another street and that as a result of the widening the affected street had turned into a noisy, heavily traversed thoroughfare for the use of the public generally and that the effect on property was to lessen the value and desirability of the sites for homes. The state supreme court in a four to three decision held for the property owners, reversing the Dade County Circuit Court, which had ruled in favor of the city. In the majority opinion, Justice Glen Terrell said: "Before the days of the automobile and creation of zoning ordinances, paving and widening of streets invariably conferred additional benefits to the abutting property. But this may be far from true at present. Commercial property is increased in value by widening and paving of streets . . . but who ever heard of making a traffic count to locate a home!"

Special assessments become liens when they are definitely known and fixed. In some cities they become liens by statute ten or more days after being confirmed and entered. By provision of law in some states, a large assessment (usually 3 to 5 percent or more of the assessed value of the property) may be divided into installments payable over a period of five to ten years or more. Interest is charged on the deferred installments at 6 to 8 percent per annum; and on due and unpaid assessments, the interest rate is increased.

TRENDS IN GOVERNMENTAL
REGULATION

Real estate regulation was almost entirely a matter of local concern until the 1930s. But at that time slums were recognized as a national problem, as our stock of housing and other real estate facilities showed serious deterioration. The Federal Housing Administration (FHA) and the Public Housing Administration were created during that decade, in a first effort to solve the situation. In 1949 the first of many national housing acts was passed. Under the act, an urban-renewal program to assemble and clear slum lands for reuse was started. Also, city-, urban-, and regional-planning programs were initiated. These programs helped, but the need for additional effort became apparent.

In the early 1960s, federal legislation providing for condominiums and for real estate investment trusts, both new forms of ownership, was passed. By the late 1960s, consumer and environmental issues demanded attention. Consumer and environmental laws were soon passed, and the Environmental Protection Agency was created. In October 1973 the Organization of Petroleum Exporting Countries (OPEC) raised the price of oil from $2.25 to $11.00 per barrel to signal the world energy shortage. The federal Department of Energy was created shortly thereafter.

These issues and concerns have been slowly but surely changing the relationship between people and land. Part of this change is greater regulation of the use and the transfer of ownership of realty. On a positive note, part of the change involves incentives to use land more wisely. The purpose here is to look briefly at the trend toward tighter regulation, a trend that means loss of rights by individual owners. The trends in incentives, which are optional to the individual investor, are discussed at appropriate places later in this book, particularly in the chapters on finance and investment.

Most of the changes take the form of greater police power under the new legislation at the federal and state levels. Apparently the wise use of our land is considered too important to be left to chance regulation at the local levels of government. The legislation discussed here is representative of trends and not necessarily comprehensive in coverage. In addition to the name of each piece of legislation, we use an identifying number to more specifically indicate the law being discussed. For example, P.L. 93–533 means Public Law 533 passed by the 93rd session of Congress. A 94 in the identifier would refer to the 94th session of Congress.

Environmental Legislation

The National Environmental Policy Act (NEPA) of 1969 (P.L. 91–190) easily dominates all environmental laws passed to date. Among other things, the act requires a detailed environmental-impact statement on every major federal action that might significantly affect environmental quality. The statement must describe the environmental impact and the unavoidable adverse effects, set forth and discuss alternatives, and eventually resolve or reject the long-term, irreversible effects of the proposed action. The act established the Environmental Protection Agency (EPA) as an enforcement authority.

Several acts complement the National Environmental Policy Act. These are the Clean Air Act of 1970 (P.L. 91–604), the Water Pollution Control Act of 1972 (P.L. 92–240), the Energy Supply and Environmental Coordination Act (P.L. 93–319), and the Coastal Zone Management Act (P.L. 92–583).

The purpose of the Clean Air Act is to establish acceptable national standards of air quality. The Energy Supply and Environmental Coordination Act provides for a review, before construction or development, of new sources of air pollution, including indirect sources. The two laws directly affect all real estate, particularly those uses or parcels emitting large amounts or high concentrations of pollutants. Indirect sources of pollution include shopping centers and airports, which while not emitting pollutants directly, attract producers of pollution. The Energy Supply and Environmental Coordination Act provides for transportation controls, such as bans on parking and limits or stoppage of auto use in urban transportation patterns (central business districts) to reduce pollution.

The Water Pollution Control Act establishes water and sewage quality standards for citizen safety. The Coastal Zone Management Act calls for states to establish objectives, policies, and standards to guide public and private uses of land and waters in coastal areas. Salt-water and Great Lakes coasts are affected. The purpose is management, beneficial use, protection, and development of the land and waters of the nation's coastal zones.

One additional environmental regulation of concern to developers and lenders is the Office of Management and Budgets' (OMB) Circular A-95. Circular A-95 requires any real estate project using federal funds or guarantees to submit a project application to OMB-designated agencies for review and comment. The reviewing agencies are usually local councils of governments or regional-planning commissions. The purpose of A-95 reviews is to ascertain that the proposed project is consistent with the developmental and planning policies of the area. A-95 reviews apply to single-family subdivisions of twenty-five lots or more, or of multifamily projects of fifty dwelling units or more, in urban areas. In rural areas A-95 reviews apply to subdivisions of ten lots or more and to multifamily projects of twenty-five units or more. Detailed information about A-95 requirements may be obtained from the council of governments or planning commission for the area in which the proposed project is located.

Energy Legislation

To date, not much energy legislation has been passed that directly affects realty. But some obvious conflicts with environmental goals and with owners' rights are apparent. For example, the federal strip-mining bill requires that owners of grazing rights on federal lands must give written consent before any underlying coal can be mined. This of course means environmental quality has higher priority than lower-cost energy. On the other hand, Congress set aside portions of the Environmental Protection Act to facilitate the construction of the Alaskan Pipeline.

The energy shortage increases chances that private industry will get rights of eminent domain. By way of precedent, West Germany passed a Brown Coal Act in 1950 giving such right to mining firms. Under the act, a mining company must return land to its original condition, at its own expense, when the coal has been removed.

SUMMARY

Governmental limitations on real estate ownership are the powers to police, to condemn, and to tax. Police power is regulation to protect public health, welfare, safety, and morals. Eminent domain is exercised to enable community adjustment to changing social and economic needs. Taxation enables governments to provide needed public services and to maintain themselves.

Police power includes environmental planning, zoning, subdivision regulations, and building regulations. Zoning is the most significant of these controls, affecting land use, land coverage, height and bulk of buildings, and population density. Zoning must be based on a rational master plan to be legally enforceable. Performance zoning, based on accepted standards or requirements concerning things like density, traffic generation, or appearance, is increasingly being used to give greater flexibility in land-use control. Zoning does not regulate building materials, construction methods, or urban design.

The exercise of eminent domain requires a public purpose. Just compensation must be paid for property taken and for damages caused a remaining parcel in a partial taking. The power to tax makes the government a partner to the owner of real estate. Fairness requires that properties be assessed at a uniform proportion of their market value. Overassessment or underassessment results in a loss or gain in value through tax capitalization.

KEY TERMS

Ad valorem

Assessed value

Assessed-value-sales-price-ratio study

Building code

Certificate of occupancy

Contract zoning

Density zoning

Development charge

Enabling act

Environmental-impact study

Exclusionary zoning

Floor-area ratio (FAR) zoning

Just compensation

Land-use control

Master plan

Multiple-use zoning

Nonconforming use

Performance zoning

Planned-unit development

Severance damages

Special assessment

Special-use permit

Spot zoning

Subdivision regulations

Tax capitalization

Transferable development rights
  (TDRs)

Zoning

Zoning ordinance

Zoning variance

QUESTIONS FOR REVIEW AND DISCUSSION

1. Explain the need for land-use controls. Name and briefly explain four controls. Does an owner have any rights relative to these controls? Explain.

2. Explain the need for eminent domain. What are an owner's rights relative to eminent domain?

3. Explain the need for taxation. Does an owner have any rights relative to taxation? Explain.

4. What is a special assessment?

5. Indicate and discuss the purpose or purposes of urban planning. Do you agree with them?

6. Does zoning create value? Might zoning destroy value? Discuss.

7. Is the real property tax system equitable and fair? Discuss.

8. A ceiling on property taxes, as a percent of market value, is frequently proposed. What would be the effects of such a ceiling? Would a 3 percent ceiling affect your community? A 2 percent?

9. What are the trends in the use of police power? Eminent domain? Taxation? Discuss.

REFERENCES

Babcock, Richard F. *The Zoning Game: Municipal Practices and Policies.* Madison, Wis.: University of Wisconsin Press, 1969. A delightful discussion of the give and take in the zoning game, written by an experienced and active player.

Committee for Economic Development. *Guiding Metropolitan Growth.* New York: Committee for Economic Development, 1960. A short and to-the-point discussion of the interrelationships between economic development, urban problems, and government.

Goodman, William I., and Eric C. Freund. *Principles and Practices of Urban Planning.* Washington, D.C.: International City Managers Association, 1968. The basic text on planning, comprehensive in its coverage, with each chapter written by an expert in the subject matter of concern.

Haar, Charles M. *Land Use Planning: A Casebook on the Use, Misuse, and Re-use of Urban Land.* 3rd ed. Boston: Little, Brown and Co., 1977. A comprehensive and well-documented discussion of planning trends and issues. New issues include "the proliferation of environmental law," the financing of land-use controls, and the emergency of state planning as a force to break up the local-government monopoly on land-use planning.

Hinds, Dudley S.; Neil G. Carn; and Nicholas Ordway. *Winning at Zoning.* New York: McGraw-Hill, 1979. An interesting and current discussion of laws, rules, and examples pertaining to zoning problems and issues. Focuses on how to protect or enhance the value of realty through knowledge and use of community zoning regulations.

Kratovil, Robert, and Raymond J. Werner. *Real Estate Law,* 7th ed. Englewood Cliffs, N.J.: Prentice-Hall, 1979. Chapters 22–26, 31, and 32, and 39 are particularly pertinent.

TWO

CONVEYING OWNERSHIP RIGHTS

Contracts for the Sale of Real Estate

7

A verbal contract isn't worth the paper it's written on.
Samuel Goldwyn, movie executive

A **contract** is a voluntary and legally binding agreement between competent parties calling for them to do or not do some legal act, for consideration. A contract is also said to be a mutual set of promises to perform or not perform some legal act. In making a contract, the parties create for themselves a set of rights and duties that are interpreted and enforced according to the law of contracts. The *law of contracts* is a set of rules and customs concerned with the creation, transfer, and disposition of rights through mutual promises or agreements.

Contracts or agreements most commonly involved in the sale of ownership interests in real estate are as follows:

1. Contracts of sale between seller and buyer
2. Listing agreements
3. Escrow agreements

All are discussed, but the emphasis in this chapter is on contracts of sale between a seller and a buyer. First, however, a summary review of the essential elements of a legal contract is presented.

ESSENTIALS OF A VALID
REAL ESTATE CONTRACT

A contract for the sale or exchange of real estate must contain the elements of any legal contract. The five essentials of a valid real estate contract are

1. Competent parties
2. Bona fide offer and acceptance
3. Consideration
4. Legal object (including accurate property description)
5. Written and signed (some listing agreements are exceptions)

Competent Parties

A **competent party** is a person legally qualified or fit to enter into a binding contract. To be competent, a party to a contract must be of legal age, eighteen in most states. The parties must meet on the same legal level or plane and must reach a meeting of the minds as to the subject matter of the contract. A party must not be under some mental handicap that makes for incompetency, such as being mentally retarded or insane. Competence is also important when executors, administrators, trustees, people acting under a power of attorney, agents, and corporate officers are transacting real estate business. These persons must have legal authority to perform their duties. These persons have such rights and privileges only as contained in the legal instrument appointing them. For example, a corporation about to sell real estate must authorize its president or other officer, by resolution or bylaw, to execute the sales contract. Any real estate investor or practitioner dealing with such individuals is therefore strongly advised to demand evidence of their legal authority. Also, a contract with a minor is voidable; a **voidable contract** is one that may be either enforced or declared invalid, usually at the option of one of the parties, in this case, the minor.

Offer and Acceptance

The entire purpose of a real estate contract is to bind the buyer and seller to do something at a future time. Usually we do not make written contracts to buy things that we pay for and take away with us. But a real estate transaction is different. The seller claims ownership of the property, with good and marketable title, subject only to certain liens and encumbrances. None of these things can be verified by examining the property. The buyer must have the title searched and does not want to go to this expense unless the deal is relatively certain. The seller does not wish to remove the property from the market without a deposit and a commitment that binds the purchaser.

To safeguard the interests of both parties, a written contract is drawn. Each promises to do certain specific things in the future: the seller to give possession and title, the buyer to pay the price in accordance with specified terms.

The offer and acceptance of contract terms must relate, of course, to a specific property. No contract is created unless there is a meeting of the minds. A mutual mistake voids the agreement.

Consideration

Consideration is the promise made or price paid from each party to the other. Consideration is also what each party receives or gives up in the agreement. The amount paid for a property is consideration from a buyer. The conveying of title, evidenced by a deed, is consideration from a seller. Consideration must be given by both parties for an agreement to be a legally binding contract.

In other words, the promise of one party to the contract must be supported by an undertaking of the other. Each must undertake an obligation. Each must put some consideration into the agreement. A mere promise, even if made in writing, would not be binding upon its maker. A, seeing his good friend B, says to him, "B, I will give you my car tomorrow." B cannot enforce the delivery of the car. But if A offers to give B the car if B ceases to use tobacco for one week, and B accepts and agrees to cease use of tobacco for one week, then there is a mutual obligation or consideration. And if B performs, delivery of the car can be enforced.

Legal Object

An agreement, to be an enforceable contract, must contemplate the attainment of an object not expressly forbidden by law or contrary to public policy. An agreement for the sale of realty to be used expressly for an illegal purpose is void and unenforceable, for its object is contrary to law. An agreement that is legally unenforceable or invalid is called a **void contract.** An agreement by which A, a confirmed woman hater, promises B a house upon B's promise never to marry, is against public policy, for it discourages marriage and is therefore unenforceable.

Written and Signed

The **Statute of Frauds** is legislation requiring, among other things, that certain contracts must be in writing to be enforceable. The purpose is to avoid possible perjured testimony and fraudulent proofs in the transactions of concern. Thus, oral testimony is not admitted in court to alter the terms of the written agreement. **Fraud** itself means deceiving or using trickery to gain an advantage, as in business negotiations. Real estate contracts are governed by the Statute of Frauds of the state in which the subject property is located.

More specifically, in order to prevent enforcement of an oral contract that was fraudulently made up, the Statute of Frauds requires the following on all contracts:

1. Signature of buyer or buyers
2. Signature of any and all owners or sellers

3. Spouse's signature (if necessary to release marital rights such as dower, homestead, or community property)

4. Proper written authority, such as power of attorney, when an agent signs for a principal

Each real estate contract should include all points of agreements between the parties, so that the provisions may be carried out without difficulty. If a contract is not carefully written, disagreements may arise that will result in extended legal action and much loss of time to all parties.

A real estate contract may be written up by the parties themselves or by their attorneys. Almost all real estate contracts are actually drawn up by filling blanks on a printed-form contract. Blank printed-form contracts are available and are used because almost all transactions of any kind are similar in nature, and standard provisions apply. There are, however, three problems in using blank printed forms: (1) What goes in the blanks? (2) Which clauses or provisions are not applicable and should be crossed out? (3) Which clauses or provisions (sometimes termed *riders*) need to be added? Remember that according to the Statute of Frauds a real estate contract must be complete on its face.

The parties (usually buyer and seller) or their attorneys may prepare any contract or fill in the blanks on any printed forms. A property owner may prepare other legal documents connected with the handling of personal real estate affairs. If blank forms are used, the parties usually initial any additions or deletions in the margin.

A broker or salesperson may assist in completing a form contract only to the extent allowed by state law. Brokers and salespersons are forbidden by law to give legal advice. And usually brokers and salespersons are not allowed to prepare other legal documents, such as deeds and mortgages. The reader is urged to inquire about the rights of brokers and salespersons in his or her area. One of the best sources of information is the state real estate licensing authority.

TYPES OF SALES CONTRACTS

The purpose of a real estate sales contract is to hold the agreement together while the details are worked out. Neither the buyer nor the seller has assurance that the other can perform at the time the contract is drawn up. Time is needed to verify ownership, conditions of title, the accuracy of representations concerning the property to be transferred, and to arrange financing. Also, time is needed for working out the mechanics of closing. The buyer and seller do not want to undertake the effort and expense of preparing for a title closing without assurance that the other party is bound to the agreement.

A property transfer may be arranged without a formal contract, of course. Title by deed could be directly exchanged for cash or other consideration. Direct property transfers are most uncommon in practice, however, and are subject to many pitfalls, particularly from the buyer's viewpoint. The quantity and quality of an owner's interest in a property cannot be ascertained without a title search, which takes a certain minimum time. For example, Able conveys ownership of a house to Baker by warranty deed. In fact, Able is merely a tenant in the house. Baker, then, is also merely a tenant because Baker cannot get any rights that are greater than those possessed by Able, which in this case appear to be nothing. Baker could sue Able for damages and recovery of the money, of course—if Able can be found.

Contracts for the sale of real estate take the following forms:

1. Earnest money receipt, offer, and acceptance (for short-term transaction)
2. Binder
3. Installment land contract (for long-term transaction)
4. Option to buy

Of these, the first type of contract, calling for a relatively immediate transfer of title, is the most common and the most important.

Earnest Money Form Contract

An earnest money receipt, offer, and acceptance form is a special-purpose form contract. A form contract is used in almost all sales because many provisions are similar from one transaction to another. The earnest money receipt, offer, and acceptance form, explained in detail later in this chapter, is typical of form contracts in use.

A cash deposit, termed *earnest money,* is expected of buyers at the time an offer is made to purchase real estate. **Earnest money** is a down payment of money, or other consideration, made as evidence of good faith in offering to purchase real estate. An earnest-money deposit binds the prospective buyer to the offer and serves as evidence of an intent to live up to the terms of the proposed contract. Typically, from 5 to 10 percent of the total sale price is desirable as an earnest money deposit.

If earnest money is paid to a broker, in almost all states it must be held in a special trust, or **escrow,** account and not commingled with personal funds of the broker. A separate account is not needed for each earnest-money deposit received by a broker. One account for all funds is sufficient, but complete and accurate records that fully account for each deposit must be kept.

A copy of the earnest money receipt, offer, and acceptance form is left with the prospective buyer at the end of the first step of negotiations. Both the prospective buyer and the broker, or the broker's sales representative, must have signed the form. Legally, the form is only an earnest-money receipt and an offer at this point. In the second step of the negotiation process, a seller agreeing to the terms of the offer constitutes the acceptance.

Use of an earnest money receipt, offer, and acceptance form is usually limited to transactions on which closing is expected in the relatively near future, up to approximately three months. The purpose, with the standard terms, is to facilitate the transaction and to satisfy the Statute of Frauds, while holding the deal together.

Binder

Some sales transactions are very involved and are not suited to a standard form contract. Also, a buyer may insist that the contract be drawn up by an attorney so that particular provisions may be included. In either case, the deal is nearly ready for agreement, but time is needed to draw up a formal contract. The transaction must be "held together" until the detailed contract can be written up and agreed to by both buyer and seller.

The solution to holding a complex transaction together while a more formal contract is drawn up is the binder. A **binder** is a brief written agreement to enter into a longer written contract for the sale of real estate. The essential terms of the transaction and a brief description of the property are included in the binder along with a statement about the intention of the parties. A binder is therefore a valid contract, meeting the requirements of the Statute of Frauds. A binder is prepared in duplicate, with the buyer and seller each getting a copy. An attorney may then be contacted to prepare the more involved contract. If a broker is involved, a small earnest money deposit may be made by the buyer, for which a receipt is given. Also, if a broker is involved, a statement concerning the amount of a commission and who pays is usually included. A binder is shown in the documents appendix.

Installment Land Contract

An *installment land contract* is a written agreement for the purchase of real estate that calls for payments to be made over an extended period of time (often from two to five years) with title remaining in the seller until the terms of the arrangement are satisfied. An installment land contract is also known as a **land contract,** *real estate contract,* or a *contract for deed.* A land contract is used when the purchaser does not have sufficient cash to make an acceptable down payment to the seller, for example, in the sale of vacant lots. It is also used in an installment sale where a seller wishes to delay payment of taxes on capital gains realized in the sale. If title is transferred on a thin down payment, the cost to the seller of regaining clear title may exceed the initial down payment by the buyer. Yet the buyer would be willing to pay the price in installments. A contract is therefore drawn up specifying the amount and time of periodic payments. The payments usually apply first to hazard insurance, if needed, second to property taxes, third to interest, and fourth to reducing the unpaid balance due the seller. No deed is required until the amount due the seller has been paid down to a certain level. When the balance due the seller has been sufficiently reduced, the buyer arranges other financing and takes title. In some cases the seller may convey title and take back a purchase money mortgage.

For the seller's protection, the contract usually provides that in event of a default in payment by the purchaser, the contract be canceled and all sums paid by the purchaser be deemed rent for the period from the time he or she took possession up to the default. For the buyer's protection, assurance that the seller has clear title should be made immediately along with provision for the deed to be held in escrow (by a third party) until time for delivery comes. Thus in the event of death or other unforeseen happening to the seller, the buyer is able to get clear title without considerable litigation. Escrow is explained later in this chapter. A completed installment land contract is shown in the documents appendix.

Option

An **option** is an agreement whereby an owner agrees to sell property at a stipulated price to a certain buyer within a specified period of time. The tentative buyer pays a fee or price or gives some other consideration to obtain this right of purchase. An option is sometimes included as part of a lease, which combination is called a lease-option.

An option is used when a buyer is uncertain whether or not to buy but is willing to pay something to the owner for the right to buy. For example, the buyer may be trying to purchase two or three adjacent properties to gain plottage value. *Plottage value* is the increment of value realized by bringing together two or more parcels of real estate so that their combined value is greater than the sum of the values of the parcels when taken individually under separate owners. Each owner gets paid for holding his or her property off the market. If the last owner refuses to sell for a reasonable price, of course, the buyer may not want to purchase any of the optioned parcels. The buyer, in this instance, loses the cost of the options. Another common use of the option is to purchase a portion of a large tract for development, with the right to buy additional acreage if the development program on the first parcel goes well.

The option itself may contain all the terms of sale. Sometimes a proposed contract of sale is attached to the option, which includes important details in the event the option is exercised. A completed option is shown in the documents appendix.

COMPONENTS OF A FORM CONTRACT

The essential elements of a valid real estate contract are (1) competent parties, (2) bona fide offer and acceptance, (3) consideration, (4) legal object, including an adequate property description, and (5) a writing and signing. In addition, the type of deed to be used, the arrangement of financing, and the closing date and place are usually of crucial interest to the parties. All of these items show up in a form contract, although not necessarily in the order listed. The purpose of this section is to identify and explain these elements as they appear in a typical form contract. Buyers and sellers may agree, as a part of the negotiation, to other conditions and provisions. The Statute of Frauds states that these conditions and provisions must be written in to be included as parts of the contract.

A contract brought about by a broker or sales agent is also likely to include a receipt for earnest money put up by the buyer in making the offer to purchase. A broker's form contract also includes a seller's agreement to pay a commission. Form contracts are generally used by brokerage personnel in their sales work. These form contracts come in multiple copies so that, as the transaction develops and the form is filled in, a copy may be given to the appropriate party at the appropriate time. Figure 7–1 shows the completed earnest money receipt, offer, and acceptance form contract explained in this section.

The form contract is designed to go with the flow of a transaction as it develops. To illustrate, the form is divided into six parts, A–F, as follows:

A. Earnest money receipt
B. Agreement to purchase
C. Buyer's and seller's agreement regarding deposit of earnest money
D. Agreement to sell
E. Acknowledgment by buyer of seller's acceptance
F. Seller's closing instruction and agreement with broker regarding forfeited earnest money

The earnest money receipt (A) and agreement to purchase (B) start off the transaction. Part C covers how the earnest money is to be handled. Part D is the agreement to sell by the owner. In Part E, the buyer acknowledges being informed that the transaction is now binding. And Part F concerns payment of the commission and handling of the earnest-money deposit in the event of forfeiture.

Earnest Money Receipt

Part A of the form contract is the earnest-money receipt. The earnest money is paid to show seriousness of intent by the buyer. Before paying the money, however, the buyer wants the terms of the offer spelled out. Hence, the amount of consideration offered, the property description, the type of deed to be used, and the conditions related to financing are all stipulated.

The first five lines include the purchaser's name, the amount of the deposit, and the description of the property. In this case, the purchasers are Gerald and Nancy Investor. The amount of the earnest money is $32,000.

By signing at the bottom of Part A, Harvey Hustle acknowledges getting $32,000 from the Investors, as indicated by the opening words, "Received from." Harvey Hustle is a sales representative of the Everready Realty Co.

FINANCING. The source of monies to finance the purchase price follows the legal description. The price offered is $640,000. The earnest money deposit is $32,000. The minimum conditional loan is $500,000. This means the buyer may have to come up with an additional $108,000 in equity funds to see the transaction through. The offer is conditional on getting the $500,000 loan at 10 percent interest or less, with a life of twenty-five years or more, with monthly debt service. If any one of these conditions is not met, the buyer may withdraw from the transaction without penalty. On the other hand, if the seller can arrange financing within these conditions for the buyer, the buyer must continue with the transaction.

Conditional

FIGURE 7-1
Earnest money receipt

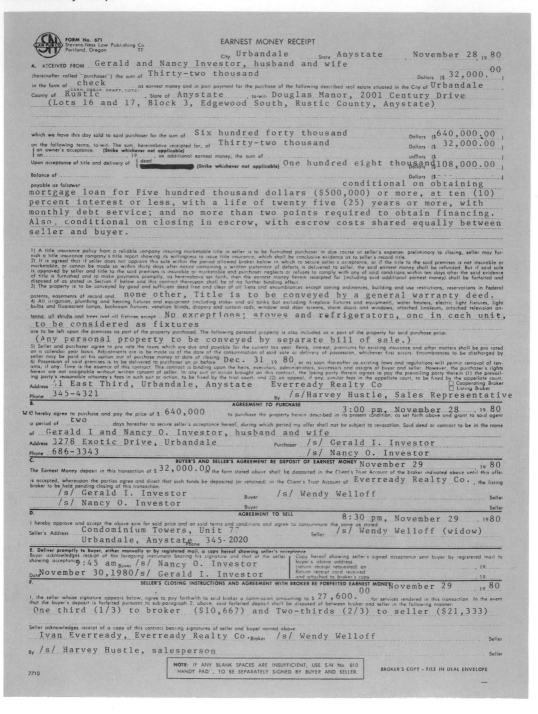

TITLE EVIDENCE AND DEED. The first three form clauses or paragraphs pertain to title assurance and deed requirements. Paragraph 1 calls for title assurance by a title insurance policy to be provided the buyer at seller's expense. Paragraph 2 says that the seller must provide for marketable title within thirty days of written notice, or the earnest money is to be refunded to the buyer. Also, if the seller does not accept the offer, the earnest money reverts to the buyer. If however, the seller accepts, and the buyer defaults, paragraph 2 says that the earnest money is to be forfeited by the buyer. Paragraph 3 specifies type of deed and types of acceptable loans. Paragraph 4 defines items borderline to being fixtures.

PRORATIONS, POSSESSION, AND ASSIGNMENT. Prorations of taxes, rents, interest, and so forth, are provided for in Paragraph 5. Also, the condition in the offer (written in above) says that the transaction must be closed in escrow, with the costs shared equally between buyer and seller.

Paragraph 6 calls for possession by the buyer on or before December 31, 1980. Prompt performance in accordance with the contract is required of the seller because the paragraph also states, **"Time is of the essence."** Finally, assignment of buyer's rights is allowed only with written consent of the seller. **Assignment** means a transfer of one's rights in a contract to another.

Agreement to Purchase

Part B of the form contract contains an agreement to purchase the property "in its present condition" or "as is" for the price and under the conditions stated above. By signing the contract at this point, the Investors make a two-day commitment to buy under the terms outlined in Part A. The binding words are "We hereby agree to purchase and pay the price of $640,000." The offer is made by Gerald and Nancy Investor at 3:00 p.m. on November 28, 1980. The owner has two days in which to respond before the offer is subject to revocation by the Investors.

Interim Disposition of Earnest Money

The earnest money check must be cashed to protect the seller's and the broker's interests. If the check does not clear, the deal doesn't hold together. But, once cashed, what happens to the money? In Part C of the contract, both the buyer and the seller agree that the $32,000 earnest money is to be held in the broker's client-trust account until the contract is fulfilled or otherwise terminated. Most states now require brokers to maintain trust accounts, which are periodically audited. If a buyer and seller enter into a contract without a broker, the contract is likely to require that the money be held by an escrow officer.

Agreement to Sell

Part D of the form contract provides for acceptance of the offer to purchase at the price, terms, and conditions stipulated by the buyer. The seller may refuse to accept if the price and terms are not satisfactory. Or the seller may counteroffer. If no major change from the initial offer is involved in the counteroffer, it may be written in on the same form. A major change from the price, terms, and conditions offered by the buyer is likely to necessitate the buyer's initiating a completely new offer to purchase. In this example, Wendy Welloff, the owner, accepts the offer of the Investors at 8:30 p.m. on the day after the offer was initially made.

The contract is now complete and binding. Both parties have agreed in writing and signed. A copy is given to the seller as a record of the price and terms of the agreement. The buyer is entitled to a copy of the contract promptly after the seller signs it. Good brokerage practice requires that the buyer sign, acknowledging receipt of a copy of the contract, as shown in Part E.

Forfeited Earnest Money

Part F shows the amount of commission ($27,600) due the broker, Everready Realty, for negotiating the sale. However, if a forfeiture of earnest money occurs, ($32,000) the split is to be one-third ($10,667) to the broker and two-thirds ($21,333) to the owner-seller. Forfeiture is *prima-facie* evidence that the buyer is not ready, willing, and able to complete the transaction. The split gives the broker some relief for effort and expenses incurred in arranging the transaction. In turn, the owner-seller is entitled to compensation as the principal party in the transaction and also for holding the property off the market. By signing Part F, the parties agree to the commission and also to the split. Needless to say, this signing takes place at the same time the agreement to sell, Part D, is signed.

From the broker's viewpoint the agreement by the seller to pay the sales commission makes the contract complete on its face. This completeness eliminates the need to refer back to the listing agreement in closing the sale, which means less paper shuffling for all concerned.

THE UNIFORM COMMERCIAL CODE

Investors and brokerage personnel increasingly need to be aware of the Uniform Commercial Code as it affects sales of commercial and industrial properties. The **Uniform Commercial Code (UCC)** is a set of laws governing the sale, financing, and security of personal property in commercial transactions. The code contains nine articles. Only two of the articles are of consequence in real estate. One concerns bulk transfers of personal property, and the other applies to secured transactions. The UCC simplifies, clarifies, and modernizes the law of contracts as it developed in individual states. The UCC therefore promotes consistency from state to state in the law of contracts applying to commercial transactions.

Bulk Transfers

Article 6 of the code concerns bulk transfers. A **bulk transfer** means sale of a major part of the materials, supplies, merchandise, and other inventory of an enterprise in bulk and not in the ordinary course of the transferer's business. Bulk itself means a large mass or a major portion of something.

A purchaser at a bulk sale does not get clear title to the equipment, inventory, furniture fixtures, and other goods until the requirements of the Bulk Transfer Act are satisfied. This means, among other things, that the seller's creditors must be given notice of the sale. This is important to the real estate investor or practitioner concerned with selling business properties. The purpose of the act is to prevent fraud, as, for example, when a businessman who has large debts sells all or almost all of his equipment, inventory, furniture, and fixtures and then disappears without paying his creditors.

A buyer, in a bulk sale, should demand and get a detailed list of the items purchased and a sworn list of the seller's creditors. The buyer is then expected to notify the creditors of the transaction. The seller is expected to provide the information to the buyer, of course. Any broker involved in the sale is obligated to see that the requirements of the law are fully met. The buyer is advised to see that the requirements are met, for self-protection.

Secured Transactions

A **secured transaction** is one in which a borrower or buyer pledges personal property to a lender or seller as collateral for a loan. Real estate owners and practitioners need to know about secured transactions because the personal property pledged as security for a loan may also be regarded as real property. Thus fixtures, growing crops, and standing timber have the possibility of being regarded as security on both personal and real property loans.

The UCC specifies the use of a security agreement in a secured transaction. A **security agreement** is a contract that provides that title to the pledged personal property remains in a seller or goes to a lender until a loan is repaid. A short form of a security agreement is called a **financing statement.** The financing statement, signifying the debt encumbrance on the personal property, is filed in the public record as evidence of the lender's interest or claim in the personal property. This recording serves as notice to subsequent purchasers and mortgagees of the debt encumbrance. Mortgagees sometimes require the signing and recording of a financing statement when lending money on a property that contains removable fixtures such as washers, dryers, hot-water heaters, and draperies.

REMEDIES FOR NONPERFORMANCE

Buyers and sellers sometimes fail to perform or live up to the terms of a contract. Failure to perform is variously called **breach of contract, nonperformance,** or *default.*

Buyer Remedies

A buyer has three alternative courses of action against a seller who is able but unwilling to fulfill a contract. First, the buyer may terminate the contract and *recover the earnest money deposit* plus any reasonable expense incurred in examination of the title. Second, the buyer may sue for *specific performance,* which means to bring legal action to force the seller to live up to the contract. Third, the buyer may sue the *seller for damages,* but this is not done very often. Damages would be the loss of the bargain or the difference between the market value of the property and the contract price. If market value is less than the contract price, no damages have been suffered, of course. If a seller has acted in good faith but is unable to perform, as by inability to convey clear title, the buyer's recovery in a suit for damages is likely to be minimal. Some contracts contain a liquidated-damages clause to be invoked on nonperformance. **Liquidated damages** is the penalty to be paid (usually a dollar amount) for nonperformance as agreed by the parties in making up the contract.

Seller Remedies

A seller has five alternative courses of action against a buyer who is able but unwilling to fulfill a contract. First, the seller may *rescind* or cancel the contract and *return the earnest money deposit* and all other payments received from the buyer. This, of course, is not very probable but would be highly acceptable to the buyer. Second, the seller may *cancel the contract* and keep the earnest money deposit and all payments received from the buyer. Third, the seller may tender a valid deed to the buyer, which, if refused, provides the basis for a *suit for the purchase price.* The deed must be offered to the buyer first to force the buyer to live up to the contract or to default. Fourth and fifth, the seller may sue the buyer for *specific performance* or for *damages.* Again liquidated damages may be stipulated in the contract.

LISTING AGREEMENTS

A **broker** arranges purchases, sales, leases, and/or exchanges of real estate for a commission. After successfully completing a buy-sell or leasing transaction, a broker must show that a listing agreement was made with the owner, or the owner's agent, to enforce his or her right to the commission. A **listing agreement** is an oral or written contract of employment of a broker by a principal to buy, sell, or lease real estate. A listing agreement creates a principal-agent relationship, the broker being the agent. A **principal** is a person who employs another (an agent) as a representative. In turn, an **agent** is a person who represents or acts for another (a principal) by the latter's authority. A principal, in this situation, is usually an owner-seller, but not necessarily; a broker may act as an agent for a buyer. The listing agreement is the foundation of the broker's business. Out of it arise the broker's relation of trust and confidence with his or her principal and the broker's rights for compensation. It is highly important, therefore, that any person engaging in the real estate business fully understand the rights and obligations underlying each of the listing contracts.

Strictly speaking, the typical "listing" is not a contract. At most, it may be classified as a unilateral contract that becomes an actual or bilateral contract upon performance by the broker. However, a listing agreement containing promises by a broker to make a diligent effort and by an owner to pay some minimum monetary consideration and a commission becomes a bilateral contract. Lacking consideration—until performance—a unilateral contract is revocable by either party at any time prior to performance, even though a definite time is stipulated in the listing agreement. Nevertheless, a principal owes certain duties to an agent, as explained in the chapter on the investor-broker relationship. Five listing agreements are in general use: (1) open, (2) exclusive agency, (3) exclusive right to sell, (4) multiple, and (5) net. Open and net listing agreements may be reached orally in some states. However, to better enforce a claim for the collection of a commission, brokers prefer written listings. In fact, most brokers refuse to handle or promote properties not subject to written listings.

Open Listing

An *open listing* occurs when an owner-principal offers several brokers an equal chance to sell realty. The broker who actually arranges a sale, receives compensation. The owner must remain neutral in the competition between the brokers in order to avoid obligation for a commission to more than one broker. The owner may reserve the right to personally sell the realty without becoming liable for a commission, and usually does so.

The sale of the property terminates the open listing. Usually, the owner need not notify the agents, since under the law effective in almost all states, the sale cancels all outstanding listings. This safeguards the owner against paying more than one commission.

Exclusive Agency Listing

An *exclusive agency listing* is the engaging of only one broker to sell realty for a commission, with a right retained by the owner to sell or rent the property without obligation for a commission. An exclusive agency listing contains the words "exclusive agency." Under this form of listing agreement, the commission is payable to the broker named in the contract. The purpose of the exclusive agency listing is to give the broker holding the listing an opportunity to apply "best efforts" without interference or competition from other brokers. In nearly every state the exclusive agency listing binds the owner to pay a commission to the listing broker in the event of a sale by the listing broker or any other broker.

An exclusive agency listing does not entitle the broker to a compensation when the property is sold by the owner to a prospect not procured by the broker. This listing is also revocable, unless a consideration was made. Further, the listing may be terminated if the broker has not performed, in which case the owner's liability is limited to the value of any services actually performed by the broker.

Exclusive Right to Sell Listing

An *exclusive right to sell listing* is the engagement of one broker to sell realty, with a commission to be paid the broker regardless of who sells the property, owner included. That is, the owner gives up the right to personally sell the realty and avoid paying a commission. An exclusive right to sell listing contains the words "exclusive right." This listing is similar in all respects to the exclusive agency listing except that under it a commission is due the broker named whether the property is sold by the listing broker, any other broker, or even the owner, within the time limit specified in the listing contract. An owner may reserve the right to sell to certain parties, who are or have been negotiating with the owner for the property, by including their names as exceptions in the contract. Figure 7–2 is an exclusive right to sell listing contract that may also serve as a multiple listing agreement.

Multiple Listing

A *multiple listing* is actually a special version of or a supplement to the exclusive right to sell listing whereby any member of a designated group of brokers may sell the realty and share in the commission. Each broker in the group brings listings to the attention of the other members. If a sale results, the commission is shared between the listing and the selling broker, with a small percentage going to the multiple-listing group or organization.

In a typical multiple listing organization, sales commissions may be divided as follows:

1. From 5 to 10 percent of the gross commission goes to the listing service to cover operating expenses and general overhead.
2. From 50 to 60 percent of the remainder goes to the selling broker.
3. From 40 to 50 percent, i.e., the balance, goes to the listing member.

Assume a $1,000 sale commission and a distribution of 5 percent, 50 percent, and 50 percent. The proceeds would be distributed as follows: $50 (5 percent of $1,000) to the listing bureau, $475 (50 percent of $950) to the broker effecting the sale, and $475 (50 percent of $950) to the broker who initiated the listing.

A multiple-listing agreement is generally an exclusive right to sell listing, with the broker being granted authority to make the property known to other brokers. A multiple-listing arrangement is advantageous to an owner-seller in that the property gets wider exposure, which tends to mean a higher price and shorter selling time.

Net Listing

A *net listing* is an agreement whereby an owner engages a broker to sell realty at a fixed or minimum price, with any excess to be considered as the broker's commission. A net listing is therefore a contract to obtain a minimum price for the owner. The broker usually adds the commission to the quoted net price. In some states the broker cannot lawfully obtain a compensation greater than the usual customary rate of compensation without the specific knowledge and consent of the owner. Because of the uncertainty of the agreed selling price, a net listing may give rise to a charge of fraud against the broker. This possibility is less when an experienced investor-owner is involved rather than a typical layperson homeowner.

FIGURE 7–2
Real estate broker's employment contract

REAL ESTATE BROKER'S EMPLOYMENT CONTRACT (involving lease and lessee's interest only; Use Form 676)

No. 678 © Rev. TT
Stevens-Ness L.P.Co.
Portland, Ore. 97204

APARTMENT, HOTEL, ROOMING HOUSE, MOTEL

Name of property __Douglas Manor__ Tel. ____
Location __2001 Century Drive, Urbandale, Anystate, 00000__ Legal Description __Lots 16 & 17,__
__Edgewood South Subdivision__
(If said property is incorrectly described, owner hereby expressly authorizes broker subsequently to write in hereon or attach hereto, the correct legal description thereof.)
City __Urbandale__ County __Rustic__ State and Zip __Anystate 00000__ for better description see owner's title deed on record, now made a part hereof.
No. of apts. __16__ No. of rms. __72__ No. of __4__ rm. apts __8__ No. of __5__ rm. apts. __8__ No. of __rm. apts.__ Does structure need remodeling or renovating? Yes ☐, No ☒
Selling price, free of encumbrances $ __680,000__ Terms: __Cash__

Is personal property included in this listing? Yes ☐, No ☐; if so, is signed inventory attached? Yes ☐, No ☐; to be attached? Yes ☐; No ☐

To __Ivan M. Everready, Realtor__ Broker, City __Urbandale__ State __Anystate__ __September 1st__ 80
FOR VALUE RECEIVED, you hereby are employed to sell or exchange the property described hereon at the selling price and on the terms noted. You hereby are authorized to accept a deposit on the purchase price. You may, if desired, secure the cooperation of any other broker, or group of brokers in procuring a sale of said property. In the event that you, or any other brokers cooperating with you, shall find a buyer ready and willing to enter into a deal for said price and terms, or such other terms and price as I may accept, or that during your employment you supply me with the name of or place me in contact with a buyer to or through whom, I may within 90 days after the termination of __6% on 1st $100,000; 4% on excess of $100,000 (see below__ or convey said property, I hereby agree to pay you in cash for your services a commission equal in amount to _____ of the above stated selling price. I agree to convey said real estate to the purchaser by a good and sufficient deed, to assign the outstanding lease(s), if any, to transfer and deliver said personal property, if any, by good and sufficient bill of sale and to furnish title insurance in an amount equal to the selling price insuring marketable title to said real estate and good right to convey. I hereby warrant that the information shown hereon below is true, that I am the owner of said property, that my title thereto is a good and marketable title, that the same is free of encumbrances except as shown hereafter under Financial Details and except taxes levied on said property for the current tax year which are to be pro rated between the seller and buyer. In case of an exchange, I have no objection to your representing and accepting compensation from the other party to the exchange as well as myself. I hereby authorize you and your customers to enter any part of said property at any reasonable time to show same. Also, I authorize you, at any time, to fill in and complete all or any part of the Information Data below, except financial details. The following items are to be left upon the premises as part of the property purchased. All irrigation, plumbing, ventilation, cooling and heating fixtures and equipment (including stoker and oil tanks but excluding fire place fixtures and equipment), water heaters, attached electric light and bathroom fixtures, light bulbs and fluorescent lamps, venetian blinds, wall-to-wall carpeting, awnings, window and door screens, storm doors and windows, attached floor coverings, attached television antenna, all plants, shrubs and trees and all fixtures except __stove and refrigerators to be regarded as fixtures also.__
The following personal property is also included as a __none__
part of the property to be offered for sale for said price ____
(or see signed inventory, if any attached) This agreement expires at midnight on __December 31__ 19__80__ but I further allow you a reasonable time thereafter to close any deal on which earnest money is then deposited. In case of suit or action on this contract, it is agreed between us that the court, whether trial or appellate, may allow the prevailing party therein that party's reasonable attorney's fees. It is further agreed that my signature affixed to the renewal clause below shall have the effect of renewing and extending your employment to a new date to be fixed by me on the same terms and all with the same effect as if the said new date had been fixed above as the expiration of your employment. Disposition of forfeited Earnest Money, if any, to be negotiated and set forth in the Earnest Money Receipt (Oregon only, delete if inapplicable). *THIS LISTING IS AN EXCLUSIVE LISTING and you hereby are granted the absolute, sole and exclusive right to sell or exchange the said described property in the event of any sale, by me or any other person, or of exchange or conveyance of said property, or any part thereof, during the term of your exclusive employment, or in case I withdraw the authority hereby given prior to said expiration date, I agree to pay you the said commission just the same as if a sale had actually been consummated by you.
I HEREBY CERTIFY THAT I HAVE READ AND RECEIVED A CARBON COPY OF THIS CONTRACT.

Accepted __September 1st__ 19__80__ Owner
__Ivan M. Everready, Realtor__ Broker __/s/ Wendy Welloff__ Owner
Owner's Address __Unit 77, Condominium Towers, Urbandale__ State __Anystate__ Zip __00000__ Phone __345-2020__

FOR VALUE RECEIVED, the above broker's employment hereby is renewed and extended to and including _____ 19__
Accepted _____ 19__ Owner
Broker Owner

-------FOLD ON DOTTED LINE FOR INSERTION IN RING BINDER-------

FINANCIAL DETAILS	APARTMENT ☒ HOTEL ☐ ROOMING HOUSE ☐ MOTEL ☐ ☐

FINANCIAL DETAILS
Selling price (free of encumbrances)
$ __680,000__ Terms __cash__
__Mortgage not assumable__

Payments include: Prin __X__ Int __X__ Taxes __X__ Ins __X__ (Check items to be included in payments)
Interest on deferred payments __none__ %

Fire ins $ _____ AHH I prem $ _____
Taxes last fiscal year $ _____

ENCUMBRANCES	PAYABLE
1st mtg. $ __481,647__	Int __9__ % __mo__
2nd mtg. $ _____	Int __—__ % __—__
Contr. bal $ _____	Int __—__ % __—__
Delinquent taxes $ __none__	
Municipal liens $ __none__	

OPERATION
Gross annual income $ __106,667__
Gross annual outgo $ __34,000__
Net annual income $ __72,667__

CHATTELS
What included in this sale (check items involved)
Outstanding lease _____ Furniture _____
Fixtures __X__ Equipment _____
Goodwill _____ Assumed Name _____
For details as to chattels included in sale
See above _____ See signed inventory _____
Are chattels fully paid for _____ Are chattels mtg'd _____
Possession may be had __at closing.__

7711

(REAL ESTATE INVOLVED - WITH OR WITHOUT OUTSTANDING LEASE)
INFORMATIVE DATA Office Listing No. ____
Name of property __Douglas Manor__
Location __2001 Century Drive, Urbandale, Anystate 00000__
Name of owner __Wendy Welloff__ Tel __345-2020__
Owner has: Abstract _____ Title Insurance _____ Cert. of Title _____ Contract _____ Deed _____
Type of construction: _____

LEASE		HOW MANY		UTILITIES - METERS			DISTANCES	
Is lease outstanding? Yes__ No__		Total No. of units __16__		Water	__1__ Pvt	__16__	City center __2-1/2 mls__	
Name of lessor _____			Furn Un-F	Elect	__1__ Pvt	__16__	Shopping center __1 mi__	
Name of lessee _____		1 bedrm apt _____		Gen			Bus stop __in front__	
Date of lease _____ 19__		2 bedrm apt _____	__8__	Gas	__1__ Pvt	__16__	Grade school __6 blks__	
Expiration date _____ 19__		3 bedrm. apt	__8__	Gen			High School __8 blks__	
Monthly rent $ _____		Rooms		Phone			__University-1 mi__	
Are rents paid to date? Yes__ No__				Pub __1__ Pvt __ Pay __X__			__waterfront-6 blk__	
Any option to renew? Yes__ No__		Baths	__16__ Pvt / __Pub__	Sewer __yes__				
If so, for how long _____		Showers	__24__	Heating __forced air__				
If so, for what rent $ _____		Toilets	__24__	Type __gas__				
Rent paid in advance? Yes__ No__		Elevator __yes__		Refrigerators __yes__				
If so, how much $ _____		Type __Otis-auto__		How Many __16__				
Is lease otherwise secured? _____		Garage __Under-adequate for 28 cars__		Type __various__			EMPLOYEES	
If so, how secured? _____				Ranges __yes__			Operating help _____	
				How Many __16__			Maids _____	
				Type __various__			Janitors _____	
Can lessee assign without lessor's				Garb. Dis __16__			Other _____	
consent? Yes__ No__				Laundry Fac __Coin op__				
				__4 washers__				
				__2 dryers__				

Remarks __commission 6% on 1st 100,000; 4% in excess of $100,000, payable only on closing__
Listed by __H. Ardent__
Signs permitted __yes__
Will consider exchange for __much larger property__
Inspected by _____

BROKER'S COPY

* TO MAKE NON EXCLUSIVE · Strike complete paragraph following asterisk * in Employment Contract and have owner initial deletion.

121

Termination of Listing Agreements

A listing agreement is terminated by any of the following: (1) mutual consent of the parties, (2) performance by the broker in selling the property, (3) expiration of agreed time, (4) revocation by the principal, (5) revocation or abandonment by the broker-agent, (6) destruction of the property, (7) death of the principal or agent, (8) insanity of the principal or agent, and (9) bankruptcy of the principal or agent. The first five represent termination by acts of the parties. The last four result from operation of the law.

ESCROW ARRANGEMENTS

Escrow is the depositing of money, legal documents (deeds, mortgages, options, and the like), other valuables, and instructions with a third party to be held until acts or conditions of a contractual agreement are performed or satisfied. Any real estate contract may be placed in escrow. The parties to the contract make up an escrow agreement (separate from the contract) that contains instructions for the escrow agent. The escrow agreement also states the duties and obligations of the parties to the contract and the overall requirements for completing the transaction. The escrow agent must perform his or her duties in a "neutral" or "impartial" manner. That is, the escrow agent must not be a party to the contract and must not be in a position to benefit in any way from the main contract, except for the escrow fee. Escrows are commonly used in the closing or settlement of a sale, an exchange, an installment sale, or a lease.

In a sale, the escrow agreement states all the terms to be performed by the seller and the buyer. The escrow holder is usually an attorney, a bank, or a title institution. Sometimes, at the signing of the escrow agreement, the buyer's cash and the seller's deed and the various other papers that are to be delivered by each are all turned over to the escrow holder, who, when the title search has been completed, makes the adjustments, records the title instruments, and remits the amount due to the seller. Other escrow agreements provide for initial payment of the deposit only and for the seller and buyer to later deliver the papers and monies needed to consummate the transaction. A completed "escrow instructions" form is shown as figure 7–3.

Requirements of the buyer and seller in closing of a sale in escrow are listed below.

The buyer provides:

1. The balance of the cash needed to close the transaction
2. Mortgage papers if a new mortgage is taken out
3. Other papers or documents as needed to complete the transaction

The seller usually provides:

1. Evidence of clear title (abstract, title insurance policy, or Torrens certificate)
2. Deed conveying title to the buyer

FIGURE 7-3
Escrow instructions

FORM No. 936
687 Stevens-Ness Law Publishing Co., Portland, Ore.

ESCROW INSTRUCTIONS

To: Hifidelity Escrow Services   Date December 1st, 1980

221 N. Main

Urbandale, Anystate 00000

Re: Wendy Welloff   Gerald & Nancy Investor

        Seller   Buyer

Gentlemen:

The following checked items are enclosed for your use in closing the above transaction:

1. (x) Earnest money receipt
2. (   ) Exchange agreement
3. (x) Deed showing subject property description
4. (x) Previous title insurance covering subject property
5. (x) Fire insurance policy covering subject property
6. (   ) List of personal property included in sale
7. (   ) Rental list
8. (   ) Earnest money note executed by buyer
9. (x) Our check in the amount of $ 32,000 ....earnest money paid
10. (   ) ....
11. (   ) ....
12. (   ) ....
13. (   ) ....
14. (   ) ....

You are directed to:

a. (x) Pay Multiple Listing Bureau   5   % of the commission
b. (   ) Pay ....% of the commission to ....
c. (   ) Pay ....% of the commission to ....
d. (x) Pay all commission (less MLB, if any), to I.M. Everready, Realtor

e. (   ) Have ....prepare contract of sale
f. (x) Order title insurance from Hifidelity Title Co.
g. (x) Pro-rate taxes, fire insurance, if any, and make necessary adjustments as of closing date
        Start interest on contract/trust deed or mortgage as of ....
h. (x) .split escrow fee evenly between buyer and seller.
i. (x) .payoff existing 1st mortgage w/ 1st National Bank of Rustic Co. and record release.
j. (x) .collect additional money from buyer as necessary to complete settlement.
k. (x) .take account of and adjust other fees and charges as appropriate.

Please call undersigned and/or Harvey Hustle   should you need further information.

                                Very truly yours,

                                /s/ Ivan Everready

Receipt of above mentioned items and   Everready Realty Co.
instructions acknowledged.   41 East Third
                                             Urbandale, Anystate 00000
By: /s/ Tom Barry

                                                    345-4321
                                Telephone

Form designed by
RUTH E. BEUTELL
MARION-POLK COUNTY ESCROW CO.
Salem, Oregon

3. Hazard insurance policies, as appropriate

4. Statement from the holder of the existing mortgage specifying the amount of money needed to clear or satisfy the mortgage

5. Any other documents or instruments needed to clear title and to complete the transaction

Instructions to the escrow agent contain authority to record the deed and the mortgage or deed of trust. When all conditions of the escrow agreement have been satisfied and clear title shows in the buyer's name, the escrow agent may disburse monies as provided in the instructions. The escrow agent has obligations to both the buyer and the seller for performance according to the instructions.

Advantages of an escrow closing include:

1. Neither buyer nor seller need be present at the closing of title.

2. The seller receives no money until the title is searched, found marketable, and is in the name of the buyer.

3. The seller has assurance that if the title is found marketable, the contract will be carried out, and monies will be forthcoming.

SUMMARY

A contract is a legally enforceable agreement to do (or not do) some legal act for consideration. The Statute of Frauds applies to real estate contracts. The five essentials of a valid real estate sales contract are (1) competent parties, (2) offer and acceptance, (3) legal object, including property description, (4) mutual consideration, and (5) a writing and signing. Additional items of import include (1) kind of title evidence and deed to be provided, (2) closing date and place, and (3) statement as to how the transaction is to be financed by the buyer. Real estate sales contracts are of four general types: (1) earnest money receipt, offer, and acceptance (form contract for immediate closing), (2) binder (for involved transaction), (3) installment land contract (for extended transaction), and (4) option (for flexible transaction).

Given nonperformance by a seller, a buyer may recover earnest money, sue for specific performance, or sue for damages. On the other hand, given buyer nonperformance, a seller may cancel the contract and keep the earnest money, sue for specific performance, sue for the purchase price, or sue for damages.

Listing agreements, creating a principal-agent relationship between an owner and a broker, are often used in selling property. The broker earns a commission upon selling the property. Five listing agreements are in use: (1) open, (2) exclusive agency, (3) exclusive right to sell, (4) multiple, and (5) net. Increasingly, real estate sales contracts are being closed in escrow. Title does not pass and funds are not disbursed in an escrow closing until all conditions are met.

KEY TERMS

Agent	Installment land contract
Assignment	Land contract
Binder	Liquidated damages
Breach of contract	Listing (agreement)
Broker	Nonperformance
Bulk transfer	Option
Competent party	Principal
Consideration	Secured transaction
Contract	Security agreement
Earnest money	"Time is of the essence."
Escrow	Uniform Commercial Code
Financing statement	Void contract
Fraud	Voidable contract

QUESTIONS FOR REVIEW AND DISCUSSION

1. List and briefly explain the five essentials of a real estate sales contract. What additional items are important in making up the contract?

2. List and explain briefly the four types of real estate sales contracts and explain the functions of each. How does a binder differ from a form contract?

3. In what way is the Uniform Commercial Code of importance in real estate sales contracts?

4. List and explain at least three alternative remedies for the buyer and the seller upon nonperformance by the other.

5. List and describe briefly at least four types of listing agreements, and explain their use.

6. Explain the nature and the advantages of closing in escrow.

7. Is there a legal requirement to have a written contract in the sale of realty?

8. May an owner and a buyer make up a valid real estate sales contract without a broker or an attorney?

125

9. Must fixtures be specifically mentioned in a sales contract? Is there any reason to do so?

10. Give at least four examples of persons not legally competent to make valid and binding contracts.

REFERENCES

Corley, Robert N., and William J. Robert. *Principles of Business Law.* 11th ed. Englewood Cliffs, N.J.: Prentice-Hall, 1979. Excellent coverage of business law, including entire sections on contracts and the Uniform Commercial Code. Widely used, easily understood, many examples.

Gray, Charles D., and Joseph L. Steinberg. *Real Estate Sales Contracts: From Preparation through Closing.* Englewood Cliffs, N.J.: Prentice-Hall, 1970. Comprehensive coverage of real estate sales contracts by two attorneys specializing in the area; includes many checklists and clauses.

Kratovil, Robert, and Raymond J. Werner. *Real Estate Law.* 7th ed. Englewood Cliffs, N.J.: Prentice-Hall, 1979. A basic coverage of real estate law in easily read form, many examples and cases given. See chapters 11 and 13.

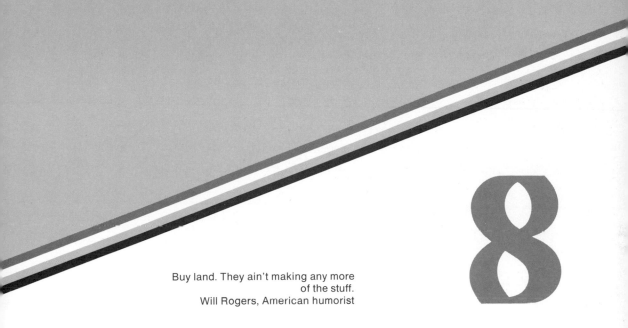

Title Closing

8

Buy land. They ain't making any more
of the stuff.
Will Rogers, American humorist

Knowledge of closing procedures and adjustments is advantageous to a real estate investor or sales agent, for several reasons. With an understanding of closing, an investor will have a better idea of "what's going on," in negotiations as well as in closing. Also, complete understanding will help both the investor and the agent in arranging financing or closing and even in holding a deal together. The need for certain documents or information becomes much more obvious to the involved parties. Further, knowledge of closing procedures is absolutely essential to passing a broker's exam as well as to operating as a broker. Finally, some states have questions on closing in their salesperson exams.

In Chapter 7, we covered contracts for the sale of real estate. This chapter concentrates on closing procedures and settlement statements. Necessary documents, typical closing costs, including prorations for the settlement statement, and recordation are all discussed. With the information in these two chapters, the reader will be ready to understand later chapters on title assurance and title transfer, investor-broker relationships, and brokerage operations. The Real Estate Settlement Procedures Act (RESPA) is also taken up, though it applies more to sales of one-family residences than of investment properties.

Major topics in this chapter are as follows:

1. Preliminary requirements
2. Elements of closing costs

3. Closing-statement entries and prorations
4. Escrow closing
5. RESPA closing

The most common closing involves the sale of property that is financed by a new mortgage loan. This is actually a double transaction: a sale and a financing. The costs and adjustments may be substantial for the buyer, totaling between 3 percent and 8 percent for the majority of properties. The sale-new-financing closing is explained in detail throughout this chapter.

Other common title closings are as follows:

1. Sale of property financed by an existing loan
2. Exchange of two or more properties
3. Refinancing of a property under a continuing owner
4. Sale of a leasehold

These closings are similar in procedures and details to the new-financing closing and are therefore not discussed separately.

PRELIMINARY REQUIREMENTS

Many details must be attended to between the signing of a sales contract and an actual closing. If an escrow closing is required, these details must be cleared through the escrow agent. Some of the more common and important details are shown in figure 8–1. Parties primarily concerned with each detail are indicated.

FIGURE 8–1
Reports/Documents/Actions in Preparing for a Title Closing

	PARTY PRIMARILY CONCERNED		
	Buyer	Seller	Lender
1. Survey	x		x
2. Inspection	x		x
3. Title search and report	x		x
4. RESPA disclosure			x
5. Encumbrances to be accepted by buyer	x		x
6. Encumbrances to be removed by seller		x	
7. Instruments			
Abstract of title or preliminary title report		x	
Deed	x		x
Mortgage or trust deed	x		x
Promissory note	x		x
Title insurance policy or certificate of title	x		x

The nature of these reports, actions, or documents are all discussed briefly in this section. The entire escrow closing process, within which these items must be processed, is shown in figure 8–2. Even if a closing is not in escrow, the same considerations or details must be handled by the broker, lender, buyer, or seller.

Survey and Inspection

A survey specifically identifies the property and brings to light any encroachments onto or from the property. Encroachments must almost always be corrected by the seller before the closing.

If the property is an income property, a detailed property inspection is usually necessary prior to a closing in order to ascertain that conditions are as represented in the contract. The inspection is to verify such matters as names of tenants, rents, space occupied, lengths of leases, and amounts of security deposits. The inspection is also to make sure that no one in possession of any part of the premises has or claims any rights of ownership or other interest in the property. The law is clear in almost all states that possession gives public notice of an interest just as strongly as does a recorded instrument. An inspection should be made shortly before the closing in conjunction with the title search and analyses.

Title Search and Report

Having the title searched and obtaining the title report are probably the most important requirements from the purchaser's viewpoint. The purpose of the search and report is for the purchaser to be sure that the seller's title is clear, or at least meets contract requirements. The seller usually provides title evidence in the form of a current abstract of title or title commitment from a title insurance company. If an abstract of title is provided, the buyer must obtain an opinion of title from an attorney. The title commitment or the title opinion sets forth liens, assessments, deed restrictions, and other encumbrances of record. The seller's title is subject to these limitations. The seller must remove any of these limitations that make the title unmarketable or otherwise do not meet the requirements of the sales contract.

An existing mortgage shows up as a claim against the seller's title. This mortgage is paid off at the closing and is released from the public record if the buyer is paying cash or obtaining a new mortgage. The sales contract usually provides that monies from the buyer's down payment and mortgage may be used to pay off the seller's mortgages and other liens.

The title opinion or commitment may be several days old at closing. Therefore, the seller is usually asked to sign an affidavit of title at closing to assure the buyer that no new encumbrances or claims have been placed against the title. An **affidavit of title** is a written statement of ownership signed and sworn to under oath by the person or persons purporting to be the owners. The affidavit usually contains a statement that no new claims have developed against the title as a result of divorces, judgments, or bankruptcies involving the seller or contracts made by the seller. Also, the seller warrants that repairs or improvements made to the property have been paid for. The affidavit may con-

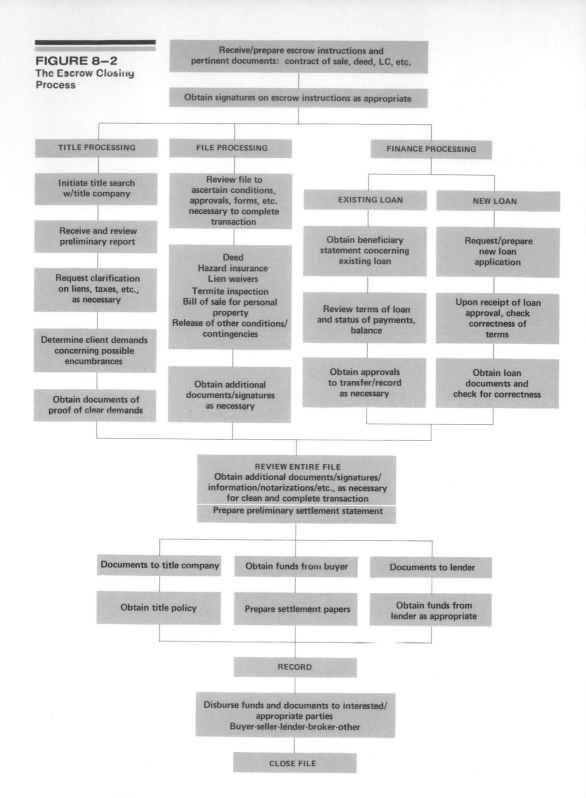

FIGURE 8–2
The Escrow Closing
Process

Receive/prepare escrow instructions and pertinent documents: contract of sale, deed, LC, etc.

Obtain signatures on escrow instructions as appropriate

TITLE PROCESSING

Initiate title search w/title company

Receive and review preliminary report

Request clarification on liens, taxes, etc., as necessary

Determine client demands concerning possible encumbrances

Obtain documents of proof of clear demands

FILE PROCESSING

Review file to ascertain conditions, approvals, forms, etc. necessary to complete transaction

Deed
Hazard insurance
Lien waivers
Termite inspection
Bill of sale for personal property
Release of other conditions/contingencies

Obtain additional documents/signatures as necessary

FINANCE PROCESSING

EXISTING LOAN

Obtain beneficiary statement concerning existing loan

Review terms of loan and status of payments, balance

Obtain approvals to transfer/record as necessary

NEW LOAN

Request/prepare new loan application

Upon receipt of loan approval, check correctness of terms

Obtain loan documents and check for correctness

REVIEW ENTIRE FILE
Obtain additional documents/signatures/information/notarizations/etc., as necessary for clean and complete transaction
Prepare preliminary settlement statement

Documents to title company

Obtain funds from buyer

Documents to lender

Obtain title policy

Prepare settlement papers

Obtain funds from lender as appropriate

RECORD

Disburse funds and documents to interested/appropriate parties
Buyer-seller-lender-broker-other

CLOSE FILE

tain a statement that the seller occupies the premises. In many states the title company may complete the title search just prior to closing so that there will be no need of an affidavit of title.

RESPA Disclosures

The **Real Estate Settlement Procedures Act (RESPA)** is a federal law that applies only to institutionally made first-mortgage loans on one-family homes. RESPA therefore affects lenders more than it does brokers. Even so, anyone involved with the buying or selling of homes is advised to be fully informed about the nature and implications of RESPA.

Under RESPA, the lender is at the heart of the closing process. When issuing a written loan commitment, lenders are required to give buyer-borrowers an approximation, or "good faith" estimate, of local closing costs. A special HUD informational booklet must also be given to the buyer along with the commitment. Actual settlement costs need not be given to the buyer-borrower until the time of settlement, and the RESPA requirements may be waived by the borrower. The borrower, however, upon request one business day before settlement, must be shown any settlement costs that are known and available.

Encumbrances: Acceptance or Removal

A marketable title must be delivered by the seller except for encumbrances specifically excepted in the sales contract. Customarily, the purchaser notifies the seller, shortly after receipt of the title report or opinion, of all encumbrances to be removed. The acceptability of encumbrances and other objections of title that show up on the title report or opinion must therefore be settled between the buyer and seller before the closing. If acceptable or waived by the buyer and the new lender, these limitations need not be removed or "cured."

Typical liens or encumbrances to be removed are mortgage liens, tax liens, clouds on title because of improperly signed deeds, and unexpected easements or deed restrictions.

A title report or opinion occasionally shows a title to be extremely unmarketable or clouded. After adequate opportunity has been given to the seller to remove clouds and encumbrances, the buyer may reject such a title and rescind the sales contract. Upon rejection and rescission, the buyer is entitled to recover reasonable expenses incurred because of the seller's inability to perform according to the contract of sale.

Instruments to be Delivered

The seller must sign and convey title either by a deed of the kind required by the sales contract or by one of higher quality. The new lender, in turn, provides a promissory note and a mortgage or trust deed to be signed by the buyer-borrower. If an existing loan is paid off as part of the closing, the old lender must sign and provide a mortgage satisfaction or deed of reconveyance. A **mortgage satisfaction** is a receipt from a mortgagee acknowledging payment of a loan, which when recorded, removes a mortgage lien from a property. When a **deed of reconveyance** is recorded, it cancels out a trust-deed. Finally, as mentioned earlier, the seller is often asked to sign an affidavit of title. If the sales contract calls for an escrow closing, all of the above instruments must be delivered to the escrow agent, along with escrow instructions.

ELEMENTS OF CLOSING COSTS

The main classes or types of closing costs and adjustments include: (1) title assurance charges and legal fees, (2) loan-related charges and fees, (3) commissions and fees, and (4) taxes and other buyer-seller adjustments. Typical buyer closing costs range from 4 to 8 percent, not including adjustments for property taxes and special assessments. Tax adjustments and special assessments may double or triple these percentages. Seller costs consist mainly of brokerage fees, legal fees, and extra charges to remove encumbrances that block conveying clear title.

Title Assurance Charges and Legal Fees

Title assurance means confidence or certainty in the quality of title. Title assurance is obtained thru title evidence or documentation. Title assurance charges include costs for the title search and examination and for title insurance. The cost of bringing an abstract of title up to date or the cost of title insurance is usually paid for by the seller. A buyer may incur fees for legal counsel to examine the title and otherwise look after the buyer's interests throughout the transaction.

Buyers and lenders both want assurances that the title to the property of concern has no hidden claims or liens filed against it. Therefore, a detailed search of various documents in the public record must be made to assure that hidden claims and liens do not exist. Title assurance evidence most generally consists of an attorney's certification of title or of a title insurance policy.

An attorney's search and a certification of title for a one-family house typically cost from $150 to $300. Title insurance typically costs from $2.50 to $3.50 per $1,000 of value over and above a base fee to cover the cost of a company title examination. The total cost of title insurance thus may run from $200 to $300 on a $45,000 house, with coverage or protection to both lender and owner. The charges might reach $1,000 for a $300,000 property.

Attorney's fees across the United States are in the following ranges. An attorney who provides legal counsel to a buyer in the negotiations and the sales contract, checks the title and deed, and handles the closing may charge from $150 to $800. In addition, the lender may need an attorney in making the loan, and that fee—from $100 to $250—is chargeable to the home buyer. A seller may engage an attorney to prepare the deed and provide miscellaneous legal advice at a cost ranging from $50 to $500 per transaction.

Loan-Related Charges and Fees

Major items of cost to a buyer in obtaining mortgage financing are for loan origination, discount points, property survey, appraisal, prepaid interest, hazard insurance, and the lender's attorney fee mentioned above. A seller may be required to pay a penalty to a lender for prepayment of a mortgage loan. Prepayment penalties typically run from 1 percent to 2 percent of the loan balance paid off. For example, a seller prepaying a loan with a balance of $200,000 might be required to pay a 1 percent charge of $2,000.

LENDER'S SERVICE CHARGE. Loan origination fees, payable by a borrower, typically amount to from 1 percent to 2 percent of the amount borrowed. The loan origination fee is also sometimes termed a lender's or a mortgage service charge. In addition, points must be paid by a seller on a FHA or VA loan because of below-market interest rates on these loans. Each discount point means 1 percent of the amount borrowed. In essence, the mortgage service charge is a mortgage brokerage fee to cover the expenses incurred in initiating a mortgage loan with a lending firm.

PROPERTY SURVEY. A property survey by a licensed land surveyor is sometimes required by lenders. Such a survey shows lot lines, dimensions, and the location of improvements with reference to lot lines. The costs for such surveys range from $100 to $250 for residential lots and are customarily borne by the purchaser.

APPRAISAL FEE. When the purchase funds are supplied by third parties or when the mortgage loan is guaranteed or insured by federal agencies, an appraisal report is generally required. The cost for the appraisal is charged to the purchaser. The appraisal fee varies with the distance to be traveled and the kind of appraisal required. For a residential property, the appraisal fee averages from $100 to $150.

PREPAID INTEREST. Another charge that sometimes has to be accounted for at the title closing is prepaid interest. When a new mortgage is negotiated to cover part of the purchase price, prepaid interest is customarily charged from date of settlement to the end of the month. The first regular payment of debt service then begins at the end of the following month. This prepayment makes it unnecessary to compute interest for periods of less than one month's time. Whenever outstanding mortgages are involved, an adjustment is made between the seller and the buyer, each bearing the respective obligation—the seller to the date of the closing and the buyer from the next day hence. Whenever interest on an existing mortgage has accrued, an appropriate credit is given to the buyer for interest charges due up to and including the day of the settlement.

HAZARD INSURANCE. At closing a prudent lender requires the purchaser-mortgagor to provide hazard insurance on the property in an amount sufficient to protect the loan. This insurance is to protect the lender against loss by fire, windstorm, and other specified hazards. It is customary at the time of closing for the buyer to pay the premium for one year if new insurance is obtained. If the policy of the seller is being taken over, it is necessary to make an adjustment to pay the seller for any premiums in the reserve account. The buyer must also reimburse the seller for prepaid premiums, representing the remaining term of the insurance being taken over.

Commissions and Escrow Fees

When a broker is used to bring about a transaction, sales commissions typically run from 4 percent to 7 percent of the price. The seller usually pays this sales commission because the broker is usually the agent of the seller. If the buyer employs the broker, the buyer pays the commission. Commissions on sales of lots and land may run up to 10 percent.

If an escrow agent is used to close the transaction, the cost is likely to run from $100 to $200, or more, depending on the complexity of the closing. Unless otherwise agreed, escrow charges are usually split evenly between the buyer and the seller.

Taxes and Other Buyer-Seller Adjustments

Real property taxes may constitute a lien prior to the mortgage lien. Therefore, provision is usually made at the closing to provide for prepayment into a reserve account to allow the lender or mortgage service agent to meet the tax payments as they fall due. As a rule, the estimated real property tax for the year is prorated on a monthly basis and is added to the payments due each month for the mortgage interest, principal, and hazard insurance. In addition to having a reserve account set up, there must be payments made to cover tax adjustments pursuant to contract agreements reached between the buyer and the seller.

There are a number of "other costs" or miscellaneous charges that the buyer must be prepared to meet at the time of the title closing. These costs, which may include any or all of the following, begin at about $100 per transaction and go up from there.

1. Tax on mortgage and on bond or note. A mortgage is classified as personal property, and some states levy a documentary stamp tax on the promissory note, an intangible tax on the amount of the mortgage debt, and a fee for recording the mortgage document. These fees and charges must be paid to the collector before the real estate mortgage may be recorded. Some states place the entire tax on the bond or note incorporated in the mortgage. The total mortgage and bond or notes taxes average approximately $3 to $5 per $1,000 of mortgage debt.

2. A credit report showing outstanding debts of the borrower, if any, and the borrower's credit relationship with various people and organizations with whom he or she has had financial dealings, required by almost all lending

agencies. The charge for this report is small and varies with the average credit report costing from $20 to $50, depending on location and custom.

3. Recording fees for deeds, mortgages, assignments, and mortgage satisfactions are customarily paid by the purchaser as part of the title closing costs. These recording fees vary with the length of the instrument and the recording fee customs. A charge of $2.50 to $3.50 per page recorded is typical.

4. Stamps on deeds required by state law are generally paid for by the seller and thus do not as a rule appear in the buyer's closing statement. However, if the purchaser under terms of the contract agreed to meet these charges, the costs involved are as follows: A surtax is charged in many states at the rate of 50¢ or 55¢ per $500, or fraction thereof, exclusive of the value of existing (old) mortgage obligations that are transferred to the purchaser as part of the purchase agreement. State documentary stamps, where applicable, average 20¢ to 30¢ per $100 of consideration stated, or fraction thereof.

In addition to the various costs and settlement charges enumerated above, adjustments are made for accrued or prepaid rentals if tenants are occupying the premises.

CLOSING-STATEMENT ENTRIES AND PRORATIONS

A written statement is needed at the closing to satisfy all parties involved, particularly the buyer and the seller. The statement shows the amount of money the buyer must pay to get title and possession. The statement also tells how much the seller will net after paying the broker's commission and other expenses. In this chapter, we show typical statements for the buyer and the seller. The settlement statement required by the Real Estate Settlement Procedures Act is also shown. To illustrate the use of that form, we use the same data used in the buyer's and seller's statements.

Prorations and adjustments are necessary in preparing closing statements. To **prorate** means to divide proportionately, as between a buyer and a seller. The seller typically owes property taxes, has prepaid insurance, and owns reserve deposits, all of which require adjustments. The buyer wants these and similar items cleared at or before the closing. Also, if an existing mortgage is taken over by the buyer, adjustments for accrued interest to date of the closing are necessary. These adjustments are representative of the many that may be necessary at the closing.

General Rules of Prorating

Closing-statement prorations divide financial responsibility for commissions, fees, fuel, interest, taxes, and other charges between the buyer and the seller. The rules or customs applicable to the prorations vary widely from state to state. In some states closing rules and procedures have been established by realty boards or bar associations. Rules most generally applicable are as follows:

1. The *seller* is generally responsible for the day of the closing. This means that prorations are usually made *to and including the day of closing.* (In a few states the buyer is responsible for the day of closing, and adjustments are made as of the day preceding the date of closing).

2. *A year is presumed to have 360 days,* with twelve 30-day months, for prorations of mortgage interest, real estate taxes, and insurance premiums. The actual number of days in a month may be used in prorations if specified in the sales contract. (Later in the chapter, figure 8–4 provides an easy way to calculate prorations.)

3. Accrued general real estate taxes that are not yet payable are prorated at the closing. The amount of the last tax bill is used in prorating if current taxes cannot be ascertained.

4. Special assessment taxes are usually assumed by the buyer and are not prorated at the closing. Special assessments are technically not taxes but are charges for improvements that benefit the property, such as sewers, sidewalks, streets, and water mains. Special assessments are usually paid in annual installments over several years. The seller usually pays the current installment, and the purchaser assumes all future intallments. Some purchasers demand that they get credit for the seller's share of the current year's interest on the remaining balance. Other arrangements may be stipulated in the sales contract.

5. *The proration of rents is usually based on the actual number of days in the month of the closing.* The buyer usually agrees in a separate statement to collect any unpaid rents for the current and previous periods, if any, and to forward the prorata share to the seller. (A buyer is advised against taking uncollected rents as an adjustment in the closing statement because the buyer should not accept the responsibility for rents that the seller cannot collect.)

6. Tenants' security deposits for the last month's rent or to cover possible damages to the property must be transferred to the buyer without any offsetting adjustment. The deposits belong to the tenants and not to the seller. And, as the new owner, the buyer will be responsible for them. In some instances, tenant consent to such transfers may be necessary.

7. If closing is between wage payment dates, unpaid wages of employees working on the property are prorated, including amounts for social security and other fringe benefits.

8. Adjustments for chattels and fixtures must be made according to local custom. Unless otherwise stipulated in the sales contract, the following items are usually regarded as fixtures: plumbing, heating, built-in appliances, oil tanks, water heaters, light fixtures, bathroom fixtures, blinds, shades, draperies and curtain rods, window and door screens, storm doors

and windows, wall-to-wall carpeting, shrubs, bulbs, plants, and trees. Hall carpets, refrigerators, stoves, and washers and dryers are also usually regarded as fixtures in apartment buildings.

Closing-Statement Entries

Several items on a closing statement are direct entries and do not require adjustments between the buyer and the seller. These items are commonly called credits. A **credit** is an entry in a person's favor, as, for example, the balance in a bank account is in the depositor's favor. We also speak of "giving credit to someone" for doing us a favor or showing honesty or otherwise being financially trustworthy. A credit, as used here, is recognition to the buyer or seller for a contribution made to the transaction. See figure 8–3 for a summary of closing-statement entries.

The obvious first entry on a closing statement is the sale price, which is credited to the seller. Crediting the seller with the sale price is recognition of the seller's contribution of the property to the transaction.

If the seller has on hand coal, oil, cleaning supplies, or other items that are being taken over by the buyer, a direct entry for their current market price is also credited to the seller. The items are over and above the sale price of the real estate, and they represent the seller's contribution to the transaction, for which credit should be given. In a similar vein, the seller's reserve deposits that are

FIGURE 8–3
Settlement Statement Items

CREDITS TO BUYER	CREDITS TO SELLER
Direct Entry; No Proration Necessary	
1. earnest money and down payments 2. remaining balance of outstanding mortgage loan, if taken over by buyer 3. purchase money mortgage 4. security deposits of tenants	1. sale price 2. fuel on hand (coal or fuel oil) or supplies at current market price 3. reserve deposits for taxes and hazard insurance (when existing mortgage is taken over by buyer)
Proration Necessary	
accrued general real estate taxes (seller's portion) accrued interest on loans (seller's portion) accrued wages of employees, including vacation allowance (seller's portion) prepaid rents or rents collected in advance by the seller (buyer's portion)	prepaid hazard-insurance premium (buyer's portion) prepaid water and sewer charges (buyer's portion) prepaid real estate taxes (buyer's portion)

being taken over by the buyer warrant a direct credit entry to the seller. Reserve deposits are commonly assumed by the buyer along with taking over an existing mortgage against the property.

The buyer is credited in the closing statement with any earnest money deposit or down payments made. In addition, if the buyer takes over an existing mortgage of the seller, a credit is due the buyer. The buyer is taking over the responsibility of a seller's obligation relative to the property and deserves recognition by a credit on the closing statement. A buyer's giving a purchase money mortgage to the seller as part of the sale price has a similar effect. A **purchase money mortgage** is a mortgage given to a seller by a buyer to cover all or a portion of the purchase price of a property.

Tenants' security deposits, if carried as an obligation of the property owner, must also be treated as a credit to the buyer. The buyer is relieving the seller of the obligation to repay the security deposits, which constitutes a contribution to the transaction. Alternatively, if the security deposits are carried in escrow accounts, the accounts may be transferred to the buyer's name, with no adjusting entry on the closing statement.

Buyer-Seller Prorations

Some items must be prorated between the buyer and seller rather than directly credited to one or to the other. A proration is necessary when a charge or a payment covers a time period for which both the buyer and seller are responsible. Real estate taxes, accrued interest, prepaid hazard insurance, and rents collected in advance are representative of items that must be prorated. See figure 8–4 on pages 140–141.

General real estate taxes, for example, are commonly levied and paid for an entire year. If a property is sold in the middle of the year, it stands to reason that the taxes should be shared equally by the buyer and the seller. Assume that the taxes accrued against the property during the seller's ownership are to be paid at a later time by the buyer. It follows that the buyer should get a credit in the closing statement for paying the seller's portion of the taxes.

A similar line of reasoning justifies a credit to the buyer for any mortgage interest accrued against the seller that the buyer will later pay. Accrued wages of employees, payable by the buyer, should also be credited to the buyer.

Prepaid rents or rents collected in advance by the seller mean that the seller collected money for a period in which the buyer will own the property. The buyer will not be able to collect rent again from the tenants for his or her period of ownership. Further, the seller has collected more rent than justified by his or her period of ownership. A credit to the buyer for the portion of rents applicable to the buyer's period of ownership is therefore in order.

The main pro rata credits due the seller are for prepaid hazard insurance and for prepaid water or sewer charges. The seller has paid for a period in which the buyer will be owner and able to get the benefits of the prepayments. Conceivably, the seller could get a refund for the prepayments. This would necessitate the buyer's having to make a later payment for the insurance protection or water service. A common alternative is to credit the seller on the closing statement for the amount of the prepayments.

Proration Calculations

Three considerations or steps are involved in prorating.

1. Identify the item to be prorated, (taxes, insurance premium, and so on.)
2. Determine whether a prepaid or accrued expense is involved.
3. Calculate the amount of the proration.

Figure 8–3 lists settlement statement items and indicates whether the buyer or seller gets a credit entry on the closing statement. Figure 8–3 also tells whether an item is an accrued expense or a prepaid expense. An **accrued expense** means accumulated charges, such as interest and taxes, owed but not yet paid. A **prepaid expense** is a charge, as rents or insurance paid in advance.

An accrued or prepaid expense, in turn, means a proration. For example, a hazard insurance premium prepaid by the seller means that the seller is due a credit for the portion of the premium that covers an ownership period of the buyer. Alternatively, accrued taxes of the seller, which the buyer eventually must pay, become a credit entry to the buyer on the closing statement. Some items do not require proration and are handled as direct credits, as the earnest money deposit for the buyer or the sale price for the seller.

ACCRUED-EXPENSE PRORATIONS. Real property taxes are a typical accrued expense. Assume a tax levied for a calendar year that is payable once a year, say in late October. Then, the accrued portion is for the portion of the year from January 1 to the date of closing, up to the time the tax is paid. Once the tax is paid, it becomes a prepaid expense. Of course, the whole cycle repeats beginning January 1 of the next year.

An example is in order. Assume a property is assessed at $640,000 with annual taxes of $12,000, or $1,000 per month. A closing on January 15 would mean accrued taxes for 15 days or ½ month. The amount of such taxes would be $500,

$$\$12,000 \times 15/360 = \$12,000 \times 1/24 = \$500$$

The $500 is credited to the buyer for assuming the seller's obligation to pay taxes.

A closing on September 18 (before the tax is paid for the year) would call for a buyer credit of $8,600, covering 8 months and 18 days. The calculation is as follows: Monthly taxes equal $1,000 ($12,000 ÷ 12 = $1,000). Eighteen days equals .6 month, for which taxes would be $600 ($1,000 x .6 = $600). Taxes for 8 months would amount to $8,000. Total taxes would then equal $8,600. Alternatively, a proration factor may be developed from figure 8–4 by using numbers from the "taxes or one-year insurance premium" column.

Factor for 8 months	.6667
Factor for 18 days	+ .0500
Factor for 8 months, 18 days	.7167
Times annual taxes of	× $12,000
Equals accrued taxes of	8,600

FIGURE 8–4
Proration Factors for Rents, Taxes, and Insurance Premiums

Number of Days, Months, or Years	RENTS — DAYS IN MONTH				TAXES OR ONE-YEAR INSURANCE PREMIUM		INSURANCE PREMIUMS — THREE-YEAR			FIVE-YEAR			Number of Days, Months, or Years
	28	29	30	31	Months	Days	Years	Months	Days	Years	Months	Days	
1	.0357	.0345	.0333	.0323	.0833	.0028	.3333	.0278	.0009	.2000	.0167	.0006	1
2	.0714	.0690	.0667	.0645	.1667	.0056	.6667	.0556	.0019	.4000	.0333	.0011	2
3	.1071	.1034	.1000	.0968	.2500	.0083	1.00000	.0833	.0028	.6000	.0500	.0017	3
4	.1429	.1379	.1333	.1290	.3333	.0111		.1111	.0037	.8000	.0667	.0022	4
5	.1786	.1724	.1667	.1613	.4167	.0139		.1389	.0046	1.0000	.0833	.0028	5
6	.2143	.2069	.2000	.1935	.5000	.0167		.1667	.0056		.1000	.0033	6
7	.2500	.2414	.2333	.2258	.5833	.0194		.1944	.0065		.1167	.0039	7
8	.2857	.2759	.2667	.2581	.6667	.0222		.2222	.0074		.1333	.0044	8
9	.3214	.3103	.3000	.2903	.7500	.0250		.2500	.0083		.1500	.0050	9
10	.3571	.3448	.3333	.3226	.8333	.0278		.2778	.0093		.1667	.0056	10
11	.3929	.3793	.3667	.3548	.9167	.0306		.3056	.0102		.1833	.0061	11
12	.4286	.4138	.4000	.3871	1.0000	.0333		.3333	.0111		.2000	.0067	12
13	.4643	.4483	.4333	.4194		.0361			.0120			.0072	13
14	.5000	.4828	.4667	.4516		.0389			.0130			.0078	14
15	.5357	.5172	.5000	.4839		.0417			.0139			.0083	15

Days								Days
16	.5714	.5517	.5333	.5161	.0444	.0148	.0089	16
17	.6071	.5862	.5667	.5484	.0472	.0157	.0094	17
18	.6429	.6209	.6000	.5806	.0500	.0167	.0100	18
19	.6786	.6552	.6333	.6129	.0528	.0176	.0106	19
20	.7143	.6897	.6667	.6452	.0556	.0185	.0111	20
21	.7500	.7241	.7000	.6774	.0583	.0194	.0117	21
22	.7857	.7586	.7333	.7087	.0611	.0204	.0122	22
23	.8214	.7931	.7667	.7419	.0639	.0213	.0128	23
24	.8571	.8276	.8000	.7742	.0667	.0222	.0133	24
25	.8929	.8621	.8333	.8065	.0694	.0231	.0139	25
26	.9286	.8966	.8667	.8387	.0722	.0241	.0144	26
27	.9643	.9310	.9000	.8710	.0750	.0250	.0150	27
28	1.0000	.9655	.9333	.9032	.0778	.0259	.0156	28
29		1.0000	.9667	.9355	.0806	.0269	.0161	29
30			1.0000	.9677	.0833	.0278	.0167	30
31				1.0000				31

Rent Example

Rent = $250 per month
To find amount of
17 days rent in
a 31-day month

17 days (from table) =	.5484
Times monthly rent	$ 250
Prorated amount	$ 137.10

Property Tax Example

Taxes = $1,080.24/year.
To find prorated amount
for 7 months, 23 days

7 months	.5833
23 days	.0639
7 months 23 days =	.6472
Times taxes	$1,080.24
Prorated amount	$ 699.13

Insurance Premium Example

Three year premium = $329.32
To find prorated value of
premiums with 1 year,
8 months, 13 days remaining:

1 year	.3333
8 months	.2222
13 days	.0120
1 year, 8 months	
13 days	.5675
Time premium	$329.32
Prorated amount	$186.89

In similar fashion, interest on a 9 percent, monthly payment loan of $300,000 for the first 20 days of a month would be $1,500, calculated as follows:

$$9\% \div 12 = \text{¾ percent } (.0075) \text{ per month}$$
$$\$300,000 \times \text{¾\% } (.0075) = \$2,250$$
$$\$2,250 \times \frac{20 \text{ days}}{30 \text{ days}} \text{ (⅔)} = \$1,500.$$

Assume a closing on the twentieth day of a month (a seller's day) with a buyer's assuming a seller's $300,000 mortgage as indicated. The buyer would be entitled to a $1,500 credit for assuming the seller's interest obligation. The buyer would also be entitled to a $300,000 credit for assuming the seller's mortgage loan obligation.

PREPAID-EXPENSE PRORATIONS. A typical adjustment of a **prepaid expense** involves the premium for hazard insurance. Hazard-insurance premiums are usually prepaid for 1, 3, or 5 years. A buyer frequently takes over the insurance coverage of a seller, as a matter of convenience. A careful check to correctly determine the period for which a premium has been paid is necessary prior to any prorating calculations. The number of future years, months, and days for which the premium has been prepaid must then be calculated. Two examples are given here to illustrate the usual methods of calculating the prepaid-insurance expense. The first example concerns a one-year prepayment, the second a 3-year prepayment.

Assume a seller's policy with an annual premium of $1,800 ($150 per month) that runs to November 30, 1981. A closing is on January 15, 1981. The buyer agrees to take over the seller's policy. What is the amount of the adjustment?

	Years	Months	Days
Premium paid to 11/30/81	1981	11	30
Closing date 1/15/81	1981	1	15
Remaining coverage available	0	10	15

The end date of the prepaid periods is compared to the closing date. Then, beginning with the *days* column, the closing date is subtracted from the end date. In this example, 10 months, 15 days of premium are prepaid as of the closing date. At $150 per month, this means a credit of $1,575 to the seller. ($150/month times 10.5 months equals $1,575.)

In a second, more complex example, assume a 3-year premium of $5,400 for a policy that ends on November 12, 1983. Closing is assumed to take place on September 15, 1981.

	Years	Months	Days
Premium paid to 11/12/83	1983	11	12
Closing date, 9/15/81	1981	9	15
Future years, months, and days for which premium is prepaid	?	?	?

Again, begin with the *days* column. When the days of the end time (12) are fewer than the days in the line for the closing date (15), a month must be borrowed from the *months* column. This increases the days column by 30, to 42. The 15 days on the lower line may now be subtracted from the upper line to give *27 future days* for which a premium has been paid. Next move to the *months* column. The months in the lower line in (9) may be directly subtracted from the months in the upper line (now 10 after 1 has been borrowed) to give one prepaid month. If the months in the upper line were less than the months in the lower line, 12 months (1 year) would have to be borrowed from the *years* column.

		10	42
Premium paid to 11/12/83	1983	~~11~~	~~12~~
Closing date, 9/15/81	1981	9	15
Future years, month, and day of prepaid premium	2	1	27

Finally, in the years column, 1981 is subtracted from 1983 to give 2 future years for which the premium is paid. In total, the premium has been prepared for 2 years, 1 month, 27 days.

The $5,400 premium breaks down to $1,800 per year or $150 per month. Two years times $1,800 equals $3,600. One month at $150 equals $150. And 27 days or .9 month (27 days/30 days) at $150 per month gives $135. The total credit due the seller for a prepaid insurance premium is $3,885.

Prepayment credit for 2 years	$3,600
Prepayment for 1 month	150
Prepayment for 27 days	135
Total prepayment credit due seller	$3,885

Alternatively, using the 3-year insurance premium factors from figure 8–4 gives the same answer of $3,885. This alternative calculation may serve as a convenient check on the first calculation. Slight differences may result due to rounding of factors in figure 8–4.

Factor for 2 years	.6667
Factor for 1 month	+ .0278
Factor for 27 days	+ .0250
Factor for 2 years, 1 month, 27 days	.7195
Times 3-year premium	× $5,400
Prepayment credit due seller	$3,885.30

ESCROW CLOSING

An illustrative example of a closing is appropriate at this point. A case problem, involving the sale of Douglas Manor, a 16-unit apartment building, for $640,000 is used in the example. The seller is Wendy Welloff, a widow. Gerald and Nancy Investor are the buyers. Calculations for two adjustments in the example (property taxes and hazard insurance) are shown earlier in this chapter. The closing is handled by Hifidelity Escrow Services.

Data Inputs

The basic information for our example is presented as the Douglas Manor Case Problem. The data involved are intended to be representative. Some detail is not included, for greater clarity of illustration.

DOUGLAS MANOR—CLOSING CASE PROBLEM

On November 28, 1980, Gerald and Nancy Investor deposit $32,000 of earnest money toward the purchase of Douglas Manor for $640,000. On November 29 the owner, Wendy Welloff, agrees to sell. The sale was negotiated by Harvey Hustle of Everready Realty Company. The parties subsequently agree to a January 15, 1981, closing date. Escrow closing costs are to be shared equally, as per contract. A 30-day month, 360-day banker's year is traditionally used for closing adjustments in the area. (See figure 7–1 for a copy of the Investor-Welloff contract.)

The offer is conditional on the Investor's obtaining a 25-year, monthly payment loan for $500,000 or more at 10 percent interest or less. The Urbandale Savings and Loan agrees to make a $500,000 loan, at 10 percent interest per year, with a 2 percent loan origination fee. Payments are to begin on March 1, so interest must be paid on the $500,000 to the end of January at the closing. The existing loan on Douglas Manor is $300,000 and is paid up to the end of December 1980.

Conditions in the transaction requiring noncash buyer-seller adjustments are as follows:

1. Cleaning supplies on hand worth $1,800 are taken over by the buyer.
2. Wendy Welloff holds $7,040 as security deposits of tenants. As the new

owners, the Investors will be liable for repayment of these deposits as tenants leave.

3. Property taxes of $12,000 were paid for 1980. This amount is not expected to change for 1981.

4. A payment of $1,800 was paid as a 1-year hazard-insurance premium for coverage to November 30, 1981. Buyer is agreeable to taking an assignment of the protection under the policy.

5. All rents for January 1981, totalling $8,400, are collected prior to closing.

6. Water and sewer charges run $288 per quarter for Douglas Manor, which amount is not payable until the end of the quarter.

Costs to the Investors in obtaining the loan include the following:

1. A lender's title policy from Hifidelity Title Company, costing $420 as a rider or addendum to the owners' title policy provided by the seller.

2. A fee of $700 payable to Allen Measure for a market-value appraisal of Douglas Manor.

3. A credit report, required by Urbandale S&L and costing $40, provided by the Rustic County Credit Bureau.

4. A $100 fee payable to Howard Light, attorney, for looking over the title and loan documents and drawing up the mortgage and note for the lender.

Other third-party costs payable by the buyer and/or seller in the closing are as follows:

1. Brokerage commission of $27,600, payable by the seller to Everready Realty Co.

2. Escrow closing costs of $420, to be shared equally.

3. Owner's title policy, provided by Hifidelity Title Co. for $1,680, payable by the seller.

4. Buyer has Michael Sharpe, of Sharpe and Brilliant, attorneys, look over the title and loan papers, at a fee of $180.

5. Rustic County charges $4 to record seller's mortgage satisfaction for paying off existing loan. The county charges buyer $16 for recording the deed and mortgage lien papers.

Explanation

Figure 8–5 shows a summary of the data inputs for our problem. Figure 8–6 is a settlement worksheet used by Hifidelity Escrow Services in handling a closing transaction. The worksheet serves as a summary of the entire transaction also. Figure 8–5 is related to 8–6 in the third column, worksheet line number. Each item in 8–5 is taken up in order in this explanation. The reader may also refer back to the case problem in following this explanation.

FIGURE 8–5
Douglas Manor Case Problem—Summary of Data Inputs

	PROPERTY	Douglas Manor, 2001 Century Drive, Urbandale
	BUYER	Gerald & Nancy Investor
	SELLER	Wendy Welloff
	BROKER	Everready Realty Co. (Ardent/Hustle)
	CLOSING DATE	January 15, 1981.

ITEM	AMOUNT	WORKSHEET LINE NUMBER	COMMENT	RESPA LINE NO.
Buyer-Seller Entries/Adjustments				
Contract sale price	$640,000	2	See contract, figure 7–1	101/401
Earnest money deposit	32,000	5		201
New mortgage loan	500,000	5	10%, mo. payments begin 3/1	202
Cleaning supplies on hand	1,800	11	Direct-entry adjustments	109/409
Tenant security deposits	7,040	13		209/509
Property tax	500	17		207/511
Prepaid hazard insurance	1,575	18	Prorata entry	110/410
Rental adjustment	4,200	19	adjustments	210/508
Water/sewer charges	48	20		211/513
Third-Party Entries/Payments				
Existing loan	300,000	28	Paid off by seller at settlement	
Accrued interest—existing loan	1,125	29	$300,000 x 9% x 1/24 (½ month)	501
New-loan interest to end of Jan.	2,083.33	30	$500,000 x 10% x 1/24 (½ month)	901
Loan origination fee (2%)	10,000	31		801
Lender's title policy	420	32		1108
Loan appraisal fee	700	33	Buyer costs in obtaining loan	803
Credit report	40	35		804
Lender's atty. fees	106	36		809
Brokerage Commission	27,600	38	Seller's expense	701
Escrow fee	420	39	Split equally	1303
Owner's title policy	1,680	41	Seller pays	1108
Buyer's atty. fees	180	42		1107
Seller's atty. fees	250	43		1107
Recording fees	20	44	Seller $4, Buyer $16	1201

Figure 8–6, the settlement worksheet, is based on a double-entry accounting system. Both the buyer and the seller have debit and credit columns. In the lower portion, debit and credit columns are also provided to take account of transactions with third parties that render support services such as title insurance, an appraisal, or a credit report. **Double-entry accounting** means that for every debit entry, there is a credit entry. In turn, total debits equal total credits for the entire worksheet.

A debit column is always on the left side of an account. And for our purposes, a **debit** is a debt, or what is owing to someone else. In a complete double-entry accounting system, a debit may also represent the worth of an asset.

A **credit,** for our purposes, is a bookkeeping entry in favor of a person or

FIGURE 8–6
Settlement Worksheet

HIFIDELITY ESCROW SERVICES
SETTLEMENT WORK SHEET AND TRANSACTION SUMMARY

Escrow Agent: Tom Barren   Gerald&Nancy Investor   Wendy Welloff   1/15/81

		BUYER		SELLER		
ENTRY ITEM		Debit	Credit	Debit	Credit	NOTES AND COMMENTS
1	BUYER-SELLER DIRECT ENTRIES					
2	Contract Sale Price................	$640,000			$640,000	
3	Earnest Money Deposit		32,000	32,000		Cash item
4	Additional Downpayment.............					
5	Loan: New _X_ Assumed _____......		500,000	500,000		Cash item, see line 37
6	Accrued Interest					
7	Second Loan					
8	Accrued Interest					
9	Purchasing Money Loan					
10	Fuel on Hand...................					
11	Supplies on Hand..................	$1,800			$1,800	
12	Lender Reserve Deposit					
13	Tenant Security Deposits		7,040	7,040		Buyer takes over seller's
14	Special Assessments					responsibility to tenants
15	_____					for security deposits
16	BUYER-SELLER PRORATA ENTRIES					
17	Property Taxes: from 1/1 to 1/15/81 .		500	500		
18	Prepaid Insurance: from 1/16 to 1/30/81	1,575			1,575	
19	Rental Adjustment..................		4,200	4,200		
20	Water/Sewer Charges...............		48	48		
21	Accrued Employee Wages					
22	_____					
23	_____					
24	Subtotals	643,375	543,788	543,788	643,375	
25	cash/check to balance		99,587	99,587		
26	TOTALS (must balance).............	$643,375	643,375	643,375	643,375	

27	COMMISSIONS, FEES, AND OTHER THIRD PARTY CHARGES					Party/Payee	Debit	Credit
						THIRD PARTY SUPPORT SERVICES		
28	Existing Loan — Payoff			300,000		1stNatl		300,000
29	Accrued Interest			1,125		"		1,125
30	New Loan Interest to EOM	2,083				UrbanS&L		2,083.33
31	Loan Origination Fee	10,000				"		10,000
32	Lender's Title Policy.............	420				HifiTitle		420
33	Appraisal Fee	700				AllenMeasure		700
34	Property Survey Fee							
35	Credit Report....................	40				Rustic Co		40
36	Lender's Attorney Fee..............	100				Howlight		100
37	New loan by buyer	500,000				Urbandale S&L		500,000
38	Brokerage Commission..............			27,600		Everredy Rlty		27,600
39	Escrow Fee	210		210		HifiEscrow		420
40	Property/Pest Inspection Fee							
41	Owner's Title Policy			1,680		HifiTitleCo		1,680
42	Buyer's Attorney Fee	180				Shrp&Brilliant		180
43	Seller's Attorney Fee..............			250		Tngl & Webb		250
44	Recording Fees...................	16		4		RusticCo		20
45	_____							
46	Subtotals	13,749.33		330,869				344,618.33
47	cash/check/note to balance		513,749.33		330,869		844,618.33	
48	TOTALS (must balance).............	$513,749.33	513,749.33	330,869	330,869		844,618.33	844,618.33

147

group; it is an acknowledgment of value attributable or due a person. The credit column is always on the right. In everyday parlance, we commonly give people credit for being honest and truthful or having a reputation for fair dealing. This, again, means something in their favor.

BUYER-SELLER ENTRIES. The upper portion of the settlement worksheet is limited to buyer-seller adjustments. Thus a debit entry to a buyer must be offset by a credit entry to a seller, and vice versa. Consequently, we start off the worksheet by entering the $640,000 sale price as a debit to the buyer and a credit to the seller. According to the contract, the buyer owes the seller $640,000 for Douglas Manor. In making an earnest money deposit, the buyer puts up cash for which credit is due. At the same time, the $32,000 earnest money deposit by the buyers is an offset to the $640,000 due the seller. Hence the $32,000 is a credit to the buyers and debit to the seller. It is assumed at this point that Everready Realty, the broker, advanced the $32,000 earnest money to Hifidelity Escrow Services.

In addition, the Investors, by pledging the property on a mortgage, obtain $500,000 from a lender in a third-party transaction (line 37). The $500,000 is put into the transaction as a credit to the Investors and a debit to Wendy Welloff (line 5), which directly parallels the $32,000 earnest money entries. In effect, at this point, the Investors have paid the seller $532,000 of the $640,000 and only owe $108,000 more. But a number of adjustment entries must be made to reach the net amount due the seller by the buyer in this transaction.

Direct-entry adjustment items involve cleaning supplies on hand and tenant security deposits. No proration is necessary. The cleaning supplies are worth $1,800 and contributed to the transaction by the seller, who deserves credit for them; hence a credit to the seller and a debit to the buyer on line 11 of the worksheet. With tenant security deposits, the buyers assume a liability, or debt of the seller, and deserve credit for them. The seller, Wendy Welloff, in turn is debited with $7,040 for security deposits on line 13 of the settlement sheet.

Several pro rata entries are included in our example and show up on lines 17–21 of the worksheet. First, we earlier calculated that property taxes of $500 would accrue as of January 15, the closing date. The investors are assuming this liability of the seller and merit the credit. On the other hand, we earlier calculated that the prepaid hazard insurance premium would have a residual value of $1,575 at closing. The prepayment was made by the seller, who should be credited, with an offsetting debit to the Investors, as shown on line 18.

Collection of all rents for the month by the seller means that the Investors won't receive payments for the last half of January from the tenants. Yet the Investors own the property for this period. The solution is to credit the buyers for $4,200, half the rents, and debit the seller (line 19). Finally, the Investors deserve credit for assuming accrued water and sewer charges of the seller from January 1 to 15 (line 20).

At this point the columns are subtotaled in working through the transaction. Note that total buyer debits ($643,375) equal total seller credits. Also, note that total buyer credits ($543,788) equal total seller debits. An additional payment of $99,587 is required of the Investors, as buyers, to balance the account.

Upon payment, they get a credit entry, while an offsetting debit entry is made to Wendy Welloff, the seller (line 25). At this point all buyer-seller accounts balance (line 26).

THIRD-PARTY ENTRIES. As a result of the buyer-seller settlement, Wendy Welloff has $631,587 in cash ($32,000 + $500,000 + $99,587). The Investors, as buyers, put in $131,587 of their own cash ($32,000 + $99,587) plus the $500,000 obtained through a mortgage loan. But the transaction is not over yet. Both the buyer and the seller must pay for support services obtained from third parties. These are shown on the lower portion of the worksheet, figure 8–6 (lines 27 to 48).

To begin with, the seller, to convey clear title, must pay off the existing mortgage of $300,000 against Douglas Manor, plus interest. The payment may be by the escrow agent as part of the closing. Accrued interest on the loan amounts to $1,125 for the first half of January.

The Investors initiate a new loan with Urbandale S&L to get $500,000 (line 37). On line 30, $2,083.33 interest on the new loan to the end of the month is charged the buyers as a debit. This charge means the first payment of debt service on the loan will be due on March 1, 1981. The Investors, as borrowers, are also charged with a $10,000 loan origination fee on line 31. Both payments must be made to the Urbandale Savings and Loan Association.

Wendy Welloff, as seller, must pay $1,680 for a title insurance policy. This charge is shown on line 41. A payment of $420 by the buyers extends the policy to give the lender protection up to the amount of the loan (line 32). Both charges are payable to the Hifidelity Title Company.

A market-value appraisal was required by the Urbandale Savings and Loan Association prior to making the mortgage loan. The appraisal was made by Allen Measure, for which a fee of $700 is due and payable by the Investors as borrowers (line 33). A credit report, costing $40, was also required by the Urbandale Savings and Loan Association prior to making the loan. The charge is payable by the buyer-borrowers (line 35). Finally, some legal work was performed for the Urbandale Savings and Loan Association by Howard Light at a cost of $100. Again, the Investors are charged (line 36).

The brokerage commission of $27,600 is charged against Wendy Welloff, as seller (line 38). This amount was noted earlier in discussing the contract for sale. This commission is payable to the Everready Realty Company. The sales contract calls for a closing in escrow, with fees to be shared equally between the buyer and seller. The Hifidelity Escrow Company fee is $420, with $210 each charged to Wendy Welloff and the Investors (line 39). The charge of $1,680 for the owner's title policy (line 41) is discussed above.

Sharp and Brilliant, attorneys, charged the Investors $180 for reviewing the deed, the title policy, the mortgage, and other miscellaneous legal work (line 42). At the same time, the seller had some difficulty in providing clear title. Tangle and Webb, attorneys, finally straightened things out, for a fee of $250 (line 43).

Finally, the Rustic County recorder charges the seller $4 for entering a mortgage satisfaction and a quitclaim deed into the public record. The charge to the buyer of recording a deed and a new mortgage is $16. Both entries show up on line 44.

At this point, subtotals show total third-party charges of $513,749.33 debited to the buyers and $330,869 to Wendy Welloff, the seller. The total of these two amounts exactly equal the $844,618.33 credited to the third parties for support services. Payment or notes for the respective amounts (line 47) result in all debits and all credits being in balance. The worksheet and transaction summary is complete on its face.

SUMMARY STATEMENTS. The settlement worksheet makes it relatively easy for the escrow agent to prepare separate summary statements for the buyer and seller. The entries are rearranged slightly to indicate the net amount of additional cash required of the buyer and of cash payout to the seller. Figures 8–7 and 8–8 show these summary statements.

FIGURE 8–7
Buyer's Closing Statement or Summary of Buyer's Transaction

Entry Item	Debits/Charges	Credits
Contract sales price	$640,000	
Earnest money deposit		$32,000
New first mortgage		500,000
Buyer-seller adjustments		
Supplies on hand by seller	1,800	
Tenant security deposits (owed by seller)		7,040
Accrued property taxes (1/1–1/15/81)		500
Hazard insurance prepaid (1/16–11/30/81)	1,575	
Rents prepaid to seller (1/16–1/31/81)		4,200
Accrued water/sewer charges		48
Settlement charges to third parties		
Interest on new loan to 1/31/81	2,083.33	
Loan origination fee	10,000	
Lender's title policy (Hifidelity Title Co.)	420	
Appraisal fee (Allen Measure)	700	
Credit report (Rustic Co. Credit Bureau)	40	
Lender's attorney fee (Howard Light)	100	
Escrow fee (one-half)	210	
Buyer-borrower attorney fee (Sharpe & Brilliant)	180	
Recording fees (Rustic Co. recorder)	16	
Subtotals	$657,124.33	$543,788.
Cash/check required of buyer to balance		113,336.33
TOTALS (must balance)	$657,124.33	$657,124.33

RESPA CLOSING

The Real Estate Settlement Procedures Act (RESPA) requires one settlement form to be used nationwide and therefore standardizes closing practices across the United States. RESPA applies to sales of residential property financed with institutionally made first mortgages. Spe-

FIGURE 8-8
Seller's Closing Statement or Summary of Seller's Transaction

	Debits/Charges	Credits
Contract sales price		$640,000
Buyer-seller adjustments		
Supplies on hand		1,800
Tenant security deposits	$7,040	
Property taxes (1/1–1/15/81)	500	
Prepaid insurance (1/16–11/30/81)		1,575
Prepaid rents	4,200	
Water/sewer charges	48	
Loan charges		
1st Nat'l., Rustic Co. payoff bal.	300,000	
accrued int.	1,125	
Other settlement charges		
Everready Realty—commission	27,600	
Hifidelity Escrow Co: fee	210	
Hifidelity Title Insurance: fee	1,680	
Tangle and Webb, attorney: fee	250	
Rustic Co.—recording fee	4	
Subtotals	$342,657	$643,375
Cash/check payout to seller	300,718	
TOTALS (must balance)	$643,375	$643,375

cifically, it applies only to the financing (and closing) of sales of one- to four-family homes, of individual condominium and cooperative units, and of mobile homes. RESPA was designed as consumer protection legislation to shield home-buyers from unnecessarily high closing costs. The burden of implementation is on lenders.

Because the act standardizes forms and terms, it facilitates communications among real estate practitioners. As indicated, it does not apply to investment property. However, to acquaint the reader with the RESPA settlement form, the case material just discussed is recast in figure 8–9 to fit the form. Line numbers of the RESPA form for each item for the case example are given in the summary of data inputs, figure 8–5. Effectively, buyer-seller adjustments appear on the first page while charges for third-party services appear on the second. Thus, the RESPA form is only slightly different from the settlement worksheet already discussed. A detailed explanation of the act is contained in *Settlement Costs and You: A HUD Guide for Homebuyers,* which may be obtained from any local financial institution.

Under RESPA, lenders have the following three obligations to borrowers:

1. Supply a special settlement-costs information booklet, written or approved by HUD, to anyone making a written loan application. The booklet explains the basics of settlement procedures, home financing, and the functions of the various parties in the sales transaction.

2. Supply a "good faith estimate" of the costs for settlement services likely to

FIGURE 8–9
RESPA Settlement Statement

ES (5 75) RESPA SETTLEMENT STATEMENT

Form Approved
OMB No. 63-R1501

U.S. DEPARTMENT OF HOUSING AND URBAN DEVELOPMENT	B. TYPE OF LOAN:

B. TYPE OF LOAN:
1. ☐ FHA 2. ☐ FMHA 3. ☒ CONV. UNINS.
4. ☐ VA 5. ☐ CONV. INS.
6. FILE NUMBER 7. LOAN NUMBER

DISCLOSURE/SETTLEMENT STATEMENT

8. MORTG. INS. CASE NO.

If the Truth-in-Lending Act applies to this transaction, a Truth-in-Lending statement is attached as page 3 of this form.

C. NOTE: This form is furnished to you prior to settlement to give you information about your settlement costs, and again after settlement to show the actual costs you have paid. The present copy of the form is:

☐ ADVANCE DISCLOSURE OF COSTS. Some items are estimated, and are marked "(e)". Some amounts may change if the settlement is held on a date other than the date estimated below. The preparer of this form is not responsible for errors or changes in amounts furnished by others.

☒ STATEMENT OF ACTUAL COSTS. Amounts paid to and by the settlement agent are shown. Items marked "(p.o.c.)" were paid outside the closing; they are shown here for informational purposes and are not included in totals.

D. NAME OF BORROWER	E. SELLER	F. LENDER
Gerald & Nancy Investor 3278 Exotic Drive Urbandale 00000	Wendy Welloff Condominium Towers, Unit 77 Urbandale, 00000	Urbandale Savings & Loan Assoc.

G. PROPERTY LOCATION	H. SETTLEMENT AGENT	I. DATES	
Douglas Manor 2001 Century Drive Urbandale 00000	Tom Barren	LOAN COMMITMENT	ADVANCE DISCLOSURE
	PLACE OF SETTLEMENT Hifidelity Escrow Services 221 N. Main, Urbandale 00000	SETTLEMENT	DATE OF PRORATIONS IF DIFFERENT FROM SETTLEMENT

J. SUMMARY OF BORROWER'S TRANSACTION		K. SUMMARY OF SELLER'S TRANSACTION	
100. GROSS AMOUNT DUE FROM BORROWER:		**400. GROSS AMOUNT DUE TO SELLER:**	
		401. Contract sales price	640,000
101. Contract sales price	640,000	402. Personal property	
102. Personal property		403.	
103. Settlement charges to borrower		404.	
(from line 1400, Section L)	13,749.33		
104.		Adjustments for items paid by seller in advance	
105.		405. City/town taxes to	
		406. County taxes to	
Adjustments for items paid by seller in advance		407. Assessments to	
		408. to	
106. City/town taxes to		409. Cleaning supplies to	1,800
107. County taxes to		410. Hazard insurance to	1,575
108. Assessments to		411. to	
109. Cleaning supplies to	1,800		
110. Hazard insurance to	1,575	**420. GROSS AMOUNT DUE TO SELLER**	643,375
111. to			
112. to		NOTE: The following 500 and 600 series sections are not required to be completed when this form is used for advance disclosure of settlement costs prior to settlement.	
120. GROSS AMOUNT DUE FROM BORROWER:	657,124.33		
200. AMOUNTS PAID BY OR IN BEHALF OF BORROWER:		**500. REDUCTIONS IN AMOUNT DUE TO SELLER:**	
		501. Payoff of first mortgage loan	300,000
201. Deposit or earnest money	32,000	502. Payoff of second mortgage loan	
202. Principal amount of new loan(s)	500,000	503. Settlement charges to seller	
203. Existing loan(s) taken subject to		(from line 1400, Section L)	29,744
204.			
205.		504. Existing loan(s) taken subject to	
		505. Accrued interest on existing loan	1,125
Credits to borrower for items unpaid by seller		506.	
206. City/town taxes to		507.	
207. County taxes to	500	508. Rents collected in advance	4,200
208. Assessments to		509. Tenant security deposits held	
209. Tenant security deposits	7,040	Credits to borrower for items unpaid by seller	
210. Rent prepaid 1/16 to 1/31	4,200		
211.	48	510. City/town taxes to	
212.		511. County taxes 1/1 to 1/15	500
220. TOTAL AMOUNTS PAID BY OR IN BEHALF OF BORROWER	543,788	512. Assessments to	48
		513. Water/sewer charge	
300. CASH AT SETTLEMENT REQUIRED FROM OR PAYABLE TO BORROWER:		514. to	
		515. to	
301. Gross amount due from borrower		**520. TOTAL REDUCTIONS IN AMOUNT DUE TO SELLER**	342,657
(from line 120)	657,124.33	**600. CASH TO SELLER FROM SETTLEMENT:**	
302. Less amounts paid by or in behalf of borrower		601. Gross amount due to seller	
(from line 220)	543,788	(from line 420)	643,375
		602. Less total reductions in amount due to seller	
303. CASH (☒ REQUIRED FROM) OR		(from line 520)	342,657
(☐ PAYABLE TO) BORROWER:	113,336.33	**603. CASH TO SELLER FROM SETTLEMENT**	300,718

HUD-1 (5-75)

Continued

FIGURE 8–9 (cont.)

L. SETTLEMENT CHARGES	PAID FROM BORROWER'S FUNDS	PAID FROM SELLER'S FUNDS
700. SALES/BROKER'S COMMISSION based on price $ @ %		
701. Total commission paid by seller (all payable to Everready Realty Co.)		$27,600
Division of commission as follows:		
702. $ to		
703. $ to		
704.		
800. ITEMS PAYABLE IN CONNECTION WITH LOAN.		
801. Loan Origination fee %	$10,000.	
802. Loan Discount %		
803. Appraisal Fee to Allen Measure	700.	
804. Credit Report to Rustic County Credit Bureau	40.	
805. Lender's inspection fee		
806. Mortgage Insurance application fee to		
807. Assumption/refinancing fee		
808.		
809. Attorney for lender, Howard Light	100.	
810.		
811.		
900. ITEMS REQUIRED BY LENDER TO BE PAID IN ADVANCE.		
901. Interest from 1/16 to 1/31 @ $ 138.89 /day (15 days)	2,083.33	
902. Mortgage insurance premium for mo. to		
903. Hazard insurance premium for yrs. to		
904. yrs. to		
905.		
1000. RESERVES DEPOSITED WITH LENDER FOR:		
1001. Hazard insurance mo. @$ /mo.		
1002. Mortgage insurance mo. @$ /mo.		
1003. City property taxes mo. @$ /mo.		
1004. County property taxes mo. @$ /mo.		
1005. Annual assessments mo. @$ /mo.		
1006. mo. @$ /mo.		
1007. mo. @$ /mo.		
1008. mo. @$ /mo.		
1100. TITLE CHARGES		
1101. Settlement or closing fee to		
1102. Abstract or title search to		
1103. Title examination to		
1104. Title insurance binder to		
1105. Document preparation to		
1106. Notary fees to		
1107. Attorney's Fees to Sharpe & Brilliant/ Tangle & Webb	180	750
(includes above items No.:)		
1108. Title insurance to Hifideltiy Title Company	420	1,680
(includes above items No.:)		
1109. Lender's coverage $		
1110. Owner's coverage $		
1111.		
1112.		
1113.		
1200. GOVERNMENT RECORDING AND TRANSFER CHARGES		
1201. Recording fees: Deed $ 4.00 ; Mortgage $ 12.00 Releases $ 4.00	16.00	4.00
1202. City/county tax/stamps: Deed $; Mortgage $		
1203. State tax/stamps: Deed $; Mortgage $		
1204.		
1300. ADDITIONAL SETTLEMENT CHARGES		
1301. Survey to		
1302. Pest inspection to		
1303. Escrow fee (shared equally)	210	210
1304.		
1305.		
1400. TOTAL SETTLEMENT CHARGES (entered on lines 103 and 503, Sections J and K)	13,749.33	29,744

NOTE: Under certain circumstances the borrower and seller may be permitted to waive the 12-day period which must normally occur between advance disclosure and settlement. In the event such a waiver is made, copies of the statements of waiver, executed as provided in the regulations of the Department of Housing and Urban Development, shall be attached to and made a part of this form when the form is used as a settlement statement.

HUD-1 (5-75)

be incurred in a closing. The intent is to indicate the approximate amount of cash likely to be needed by the buyer at closing.

3. Supply specific and actual costs of settlement to the buyer "at or before" actual settlement. Buyer may waive this requirement. At the same time, the buyer is entitled to see the settlement charges that have definitely been determined, upon request within one business day of closing.

Under RESPA, lenders are limited in making demands of buyers concerning escrow accounts. Lenders can only require deposits into escrow accounts up to amounts needed to make tax, insurance premium, and other payments at the time they should be made under prudent lending practice, plus one-sixth of the amount necessary for these payments over the first year of ownership.

In addition, RESPA prohibits kickbacks in connection with settlement-related services. Thus kickbacks in return for referrals related to title insurance or mortgage loan placements are illegal. But the act does not limit or restrict legitimate settlement fees. Thus cooperative brokerage and referral arrangements of brokers and sales agents are specifically exempt from RESPA. Finally, sellers, lenders, and brokers are prohibited from requiring the use of title insurance from a particular title company as a condition of sale.

TITLE CONVEYANCE

Delivery of the deed by the seller to the buyer conveys legal title. Date of delivery is not necessarily the date of execution. The deed may have been signed long before the day of delivery. Nevertheless, the law presumes the deed to have been delivered the day it was signed unless there is proof to the contrary. In an escrow closing, title passes upon performance of all conditions in the escrow agreement.

A grantor must be legally competent at the time of deed execution to legally convey title. Competency includes being of legal age and acting voluntarily and intentionally, with understanding.

All rights of the grantor cease upon delivery of the deed and conveyance of title. The closing or settlement statement becomes the buyer's and seller's permanent record of the transaction.

SUMMARY

Understanding closing procedures and settlement statements is advantageous for investors as well as for brokerage personnel. Preliminary requirements to an income-property closing may very likely include a property survey and inspection, a title search and report, with subsequent removal of encumbrances, and an arrangement of financing. Instruments likely to be required at closing include an abstract of title, a deed, a mortgage or trust deed and a promissory note, and a title insurance policy or certificate of title.

Major types of closing costs include (1) title assurance charges and fees, (2) loan-related charges and fees, (3) other third-party charges and fees, such as brokerage and escrow fees, and (4) buyer-seller charges and adjustments, such as property taxes, hazard insurance, and fuel on hand. Closing costs typically range from 4 to 8 percent of the sale price.

A seller is generally responsible for the day of closing insofar as proration of charges for such things as taxes, hazard insurance premiums, or interest on loans is concerned. Direct-entry buyer-seller adjustments require no proration; examples are sale price, earnest money deposits, remaining balance of mortgage, and fuel on hand.

An escrow closing means that a neutral third-party conducts the settlement to ensure that all acts or conditions of the contractual agreement are performed or satisfied. Costs of escrow are usually shared equally between a buyer and seller. Sales of residences financed by institutionally made loans must be closed according to RESPA (Real Estate Settlement Procedures Act) procedures. The burden of compliance with RESPA is primarily on the lender involved.

KEY TERMS

Accrued expense	Mortgage satisfaction
Affidavit	Prepaid expense
Affidavit of title	Proration
Credit	Purchase money mortgage
Debit	RESPA
Deed of reconveyance	Title assurance
Double-entry accounting	

QUESTIONS FOR REVIEW AND DISCUSSION

1. Explain the nature and importance of (1) survey and inspections, (2) title search and report, and (3) the acceptance or removal of encumbrances to the title-closing process.

2. List and briefly explain four classes of costs and adjustments in a title closing.

3. List and explain at least four rules of prorating.

4. Name two buyer and two seller closing-statement entries that do not involve proration.

5. Name two buyer and two seller closing-statement entries that involve proration and discuss the nature of each briefly.

6. Property taxes of $19,200 are payable for the current year. Closing is to be

on November 10. Calculate the amount of the adjustment and indicate whether the buyer or the seller gets the credit.

7. A one-year hazard-insurance premium of $660 provides coverage to April 15 of next year. Calculate the amount of the adjustment for a November 10th closing and indicate whether the buyer or the seller gets the credit.

8. All closings should be in escrow, by law. Discuss.

9. A standardized settlement form, such as the RESPA form, improves communications between brokerage personnel and lessens buyer-seller confusion in closings. Discuss.

10. An escrow agent is apparently an agent of both the buyer and the seller. What are the implications of such a role? Discuss.

11. Discuss the advantages of a closing's being handled by each of the following, from a buyer's point of view and from a seller's.
   (a) attorney
   (b) lender
   (c) broker
   (d) escrow agent

REFERENCES

Semenow, Robert W. *Questions and Answers on Real Estate.* 9th ed. Englewood Cliffs, N.J.: Prentice-Hall, 1978. See pages 679–87. A series of problems, with suggested solutions. Excellent practice set for anyone preparing to take a licensing examination.

U.S. Department of Housing and Urban Development. *Settlement Costs and You: A HUD Guide for Home Buyers.* Washington, D.C.: Government Printing Office, 1977. 31 pages. Explains home buyers' rights under RESPA, with excellent definition of terms and a detailed explanation of the RESPA settlement form. Available free from most institutional lenders.

Title Assurance and Title Transfer

A person about to get ownership of real estate wants the best possible title, even though getting the interest may be the result of inheritance, a gift, or some other event beyond the recipient's control. An investor about to purchase an interest in real estate wants marketable title; otherwise the investment may be very difficult to dispose of some time in the future. Also, when dealing with an owner, lenders and lessees want assurance that the owner has marketable title. **Marketable title** means an ownership interest that is readily salable to a reasonable, intelligent, prudent, and interested buyer at market value. Ultimately, it means title of adequate quality for courts to require its acceptance by a purchaser. The desire, of course, is for minimum risk of loss by an investor because of a superior claim during time of ownership. And as mentioned, the investor wants to avoid the possibility of loss upon disposition because the title has flaws or defects of some sort.

In addition, a prudent investor wants the deed through which title is received to include the best possible assurances of good title from the person conveying title. Finally, our investor wants the public records to be as current and clear as possible so that mistakes in title search and analysis are minimized or avoided.

The purpose of this chapter is to explain the ways and means by which marketable title is assured and transferred. The critical concerns in assurance of marketable title are as follows:

157

1. The tentative grantor must actually have an ownership interest in the property that can be conveyed. This means that the chain or history of ownership must run to the grantor.

2. The legal description must be accurate and complete.

3. Encumbrances against the property must not preclude its use for the desired purposes and must not preclude reconveyance of clear title at a later time.

4. Documentary evidence from experienced, competent, professional people must be provided that the above conditions are satisfied. Adequate public records are a substantial part of the means by which documentary evidence is provided.

5. The deed by which title is received gives the greatest possible assurances and protection to the recipient.

Aspects of title assurance and transfer are taken up under the following headings:

1. Methods of title transfer
2. Title evidence
3. Kinds of deeds
4. Essentials of a valid deed
5. Public records

Methods of legally describing real estate, as required for a valid conveyance, have already been explained in chapter 3.

METHODS OF TRANSFERRING TITLE

Transfer of title to real estate takes place in one of three general ways. Transfer, as used here, means the manner in which a change of ownership is directed, controlled, or brought about. For example, a will is a transfer arrangement to become effective at an owner's death, while a gift by deed may be effective immediately. Acquisition by an investor, of course, is usually through purchase and a sales contract. Other means of transferring title are covered here to make the reader fully aware of the alternatives open to an investor-owner, in acquiring and disposing of real estate. The actual conveyance of ownership from one person to another is by a deed. The three general ways title is transferred are by (1) public grant, (2) private grant, as a voluntary act of an owner, and (3) action of law.

Public Grant

The original public domain was transferred to states, corporations (primarily railroads), and individuals by public grants to open up the land. Transfers to individuals were made under homestead laws to make sure that the land was settled. Under homestead laws, several years of occupancy and the making of improvements were required to acquire title. The federal government used patents in making the original public grants of ownership. A **patent,** as used here, means a conveyance or grant of real estate from the United States government to a private citizen.

Subsequent transfers of ownership by grantees were expected to, and currently must, conform to the laws of the state in which the land is located. For all practical purposes, patents to the federal domain are no longer being issued.

Private Grant

An owner may voluntarily dispose of or transfer property by (1) sale or exchange for consideration, (2) gift, and (3) will. Technically, in some states, mortgaging also involves a voluntary title transfer. However, the owner retains possession and use of the property, and the transfer is effectively only a lien on the title. If the terms of the mortgage are met, title is recovered by the owner without incident.

TRANSFER FOR CONSIDERATION. An owner may sell or otherwise transfer an interest to another for consideration. A sales or exchange contract is usually used to arrange the transfer. A deed is used to convey the interest permanently. Some transfers or conveyances are intended to be only temporary, for example, when a property is mortgaged. Any ownership right or interest in real estate may be transferred for consideration.

TRANSFER BY GIFT. An owner may transfer title to an interest in real estate by gift to another at any time. The owner giving the gift is termed a **donor;** the recipient is the **donee.** The transfer is not void because of lack of consideration. The donee, however, cannot enforce any covenants against the donor because of the lack of consideration.

TRANSFER BY WILL. A **will,** legally termed a *last will and testament,* is a written instrument directing the voluntary conveyance of property upon the death of its owner, and not before. An owner may write a will, or have one drawn up, at any time before death. And after making a will, an owner is free to sell or give the property away or to draw up a new will. The owner who makes a will is a *testator.* If an owner who has a will dies, he or she is termed a **decedent** and is said to have died **testate.**

The law requires certain formalities for the execution or carrying out of the will. The testator must be of legal age and mentally competent. The will must be written and signed, usually at the end. The will cannot cut off rights of the surviving spouse. In many states, two witnesses who have no interest in the will must acknowledge the signing. Upon the testator's death, the will must be submitted to probate court for judicial determination that it is the last will and testament of the decedent. **Probate** means to prove or establish the validity of a will left, or presumably left, by a decedent. A *probate court* is a court for probating wills and, when necessary, administering estates. If no valid objection is raised, the will is accepted for probate and entered into the public record.

The person empowered to carry out the terms and provisions of the will is an **executor.** If a will does not name an executor, the probate court will appoint one. The executor settles the affairs of the decedent, which may involve selling off real property to raise cash for paying debts of the decedent or conveying property to designated persons, organizations, or causes. The giving of real property under a will is a **devise** and the recipient is a *devisee.* The giving of personal property under a will is a *bequest or* **legacy** and the recipient is a *legatee.* An *executor's deed* is used to convey title to real property in probating a will and settling an estate.

Action of Law

Ownership of real estate is transferred according to law under certain circumstances, by the following means:

1. Descent and/or escheat
2. Lien enforcement
3. Adverse possession
4. Condemnation or eminent domain
5. Confiscation
6. Erosion

TRANSFER BY DESCENT. Transfer of ownership by **descent** comes about when an owner dies without a will. One who dies without a will, or without a valid will, is said to have died **intestate.** Owned property passes to certain relatives, termed *heirs or distributees,* of the decedent according to specific state statutes of descent and distribution. The rights of the surviving spouse are always protected by dower, community property, or "intestate share" laws. A surviving spouse usually gets the entire estate in the absence of other surviving blood relatives. Children, or *lineal descendents* of the deceased, share first after the spouse. If no children exist, parents are next in line to inherit. Brothers and sisters, termed *collateral heirs,* are next in line to inherit. If no heirs exist, the property goes to the state, by escheat.

The affairs of a decedent who died intestate are settled by an **administrator,** who is appointed by a probate court. Generally, close relatives to the decedent are selected as administrators. The job of the administrator is essentially the same as that of an executor. Any real property sold is conveyed with an *administrator's deed,* which is exactly comparable to an executor's deed except for name.

TRANSFER BY LIEN ENFORCEMENT. Failure of an owner to meet the obligations of a lien gives the creditor the right to enforce the lien. Thus, properties are sold as a result of mortgage default, unpaid taxes, or not meeting other lien obligations.

TRANSFER BY ADVERSE POSSESSION. Title may be seized or taken from an owner of record who fails to maintain possession and control of the premises by a process known as **adverse possession.** Conditions of possession for gaining title by adverse occupancy vary from state to state but are generally as follows:

1. Open
2. Notorious
3. Hostile to the interest of the true owner
4. Exclusive of the true owner
5. Uninterrupted
6. Underwritten claim of title
7. For a prescriptive period as required by law

The prescriptive period varies, but it generally runs from ten to twenty years. It is long enough that a reasonably attentive owner has ample opportunity to defeat the developing claim. When the possessor pays taxes under "color of title," the prescriptive period may be as short as five years. Prescriptive, as used here, means according to legal precedent or established custom.

An occupant may acquire title by proving that all of the above circumstances exist. However, considerable proof of title is required of the claimant in selling the title; a buyer, in self-interest, wants marketable title or a reduced price to compensate for the additional risk involved. The purpose of allowing title to be acquired by adverse possession is to keep realty productive for society.

Squatters occupy property without written color of title and without any legal right of possession. Squatters may develop a "prescriptive claim" but unless "cured," such title is not marketable in the legal sense of the word.

TRANSFER BY CONDEMNATION. An exercise of right of eminent domain by a governmental or quasi-governmental agency may cause title to be transferred to the agency against the owner's will as discussed previously. Just compensation must be paid the owner. The use or purpose of taking must be public.

TRANSFER BY CONFISCATION. The taking of property by a government in time of emergency of war, without compensation, is **confiscation.** Generally, only property of enemies of the government is confiscated.

TRANSFER BY EROSION. **Erosion** means the wearing away of land through natural processes, for example, by wind and water. An owner gains title by erosion or accretion when additional soil is brought to his or her property by the natural causes. The owner of the property from which the soil is taken is said to be *losing title by erosion.* Title is gained by **reliction** when waters gradually recede, leaving dry land; this, however, is not considered a transfer of title.

TITLE EVIDENCE

A prudent investor buying property demands satisfactory proof that the seller holds title and that the title is marketable. Other new owners, as heirs or donees, also want marketable title because sale or financing of the property may be necessary in the future. Documentary proof, termed **title evidence,** must therefore be developed at some point. Title evidence takes three basic forms: (1) an attorney's opinion or certification, (2) a title insurance policy, and (3) a Torrens certificate. The first two are based on a proper legal description, a proper chain of title, and a search of the public records. A **chain of title** is the succession of all previous holders of title (owners) back to some accepted starting point. A deed is not evidence of title; it contains no proof concerning the kind or the conditions of the grantor's title.

Some judgment or interpretation may be required of an owner-seller, even after evidence of title is provided by one of the three forms. For example, certain easements or deed restrictions may or may not be acceptable to a buyer. Or, if an encroachment is suspected, a survey may be required, that is, an encroachment would not necessarily be brought to light by any of the three forms.

Opinion or Certificate of Title

A **certification of title** is an opinion that title is good. It is rendered by an attorney at law or other qualified person after examination of public records, an abstract of title, or other sources of information. Historically, the search and opinion were made by an attorney, who made up an informal abstract of title for personal use. But in recent decades other persons, working for or through abstract companies, have qualified as abstractors and title analysts. If flaws or encumbrances stand in the way of clear title, they are listed as exceptions. An attorney's opinion of title is primarily used in rural areas of the United States. The trend is away from using abstracts and attorney's opinions as evidence of title.

An **abstract of title** is a condensed history of the ownership of property. It has largely replaced the attorney's search of public records. That is, the attorney's opinion is based on the contents of the abstract only. Abstracting companies, which often maintain their own records, generally produce abstracts of title. An abstract contains a listing of documents bearing on title transactions, including summaries of important segments of the documents. That is, items like mortgages, wills, liens, deeds, foreclosure proceedings, tax sales, and other matters of record are noted. The information is arranged in chronological order, without any judgments made concerning the rights of the parties involved. A properly prepared abstract indicates the records examined, the period covered, and a certification that all matters of record indexed against the owners in the chain of title are included. An abstract does not guarantee title. An attorney's interpretation of the abstract is required for title to be certified as good or to point out significant flaws and/or encumbrances.

In practice, title and abstract companies, attorneys, and other title analysts assume title good at some early date. An irritating and expensive duplication of work in successive title examinations is involved, nevertheless. And some meticulous attorneys want the examination carried back to an unreasonable date, as shown by the following tale.

In a legal transaction involving transfer of property in New Orleans, a firm of New York lawyers retained a New Orleans attorney to search the title and perform other related duties. The New Orleans attorney sent his findings, which traced title back to 1803. The New York lawyers examined his opinion and wrote again to the New Orleans lawyer, saying in effect that the opinion rendered by him was all very well, as far as it went, but that title prior to 1803 had not been satisfactorily documented.

The New Orleans attorney replied to the New York firm as follows:

I acknowledge your letter inquiring as to the state of the title of the Canal Street property prior to 1803. Please be advised that in 1803 the United States of America acquired the territory of Louisiana from the Republic of France by purchase. The Republic of France acquired title from the Spanish Crown by conquest. The Spanish Crown had originally acquired title by virtue of the discoveries of one Christopher Columbus, sailor, who had been duly authorized to embark upon the voyage of discovery by Isabella, Queen of Spain. Isabella, before granting such authority, had obtained the sanction of His Holiness, the Pope; the Pope is the Vicar on Earth of Jesus Christ; Jesus Christ is the Son and Heir Apparent of God. God made Louisiana.

Title evidence by attorney's opinion has several limitations. If a claim against the property is missed and subsequently proven, the purchaser or lender suffers. For example, a forged deed does not wipe out a dower interest. Recovering damages from an attorney for an error or omission is extremely difficult and costly. In turn, lenders removed from the locality of the property are doubly reluctant to accept an attorney's opinion as evidence of title. The attorney's ability is uncertain. And recovering losses from the borrower or owner is difficult because of the difference in location. Lenders therefore increasingly prefer title insurance to a certification of title as evidence of marketable title.

Title Insurance Policy

Title insurance is protection against financial loss due to flaws, encumbrances, and other defects in the title of realty that existed but were not known at the time of purchase of the insurance policy. Title insurance is protection against events in the past rather than the future. The purchase of a policy simply shifts the risk of loss from a property owner or lender to the title insurance company. The premium or purchase price is paid only once, and the term is forever into the future. Title insurance, introduced in the late 1800s, currently provides ownership protection on more than one-half of all parcels of realty in the United States. Title insurance is used in almost all urban areas and in many rural areas.

THE INSURANCE CONTRACT. Title insurance policies are usually made between the company and an owner (usually a new or purchasing owner), a lender, or a lessee. In return for the premium, the company contracts to reimburse or compensate against all losses due to title defects other than those listed as exceptions in the policy. The company also agrees to finance the legal defense to protect an owner against a title lawsuit.

The main items insured against are as follows:

1. Flaws in the chain of title due to forged documents, improper delivery of a deed, incompetence or lack of capacity of a grantor, or lack of signature of a spouse.

2. Errors and omissions in the title search and examination due to negligence or fraud by a company employee or due to improper indexing of public records.

3. Possible lack of acceptability of title to a subsequent intelligent, prudent buyer, who may be unwilling to accept some minor encumbrance not listed as an exception in the title insurance policy; for example, a shared driveway easement.

Items usually not covered by the insurance are listed below. Newer title policies do cover these items, however. And even in the past, extended coverage as protection against these items could be purchased at some additional cost.

1. Defects disclosed by the title examination and listed as exceptions to the policy.

2. Defects that a survey or physical inspection of the property would disclose. Examples are encroachments, rights of an adverse possessor, unrecorded easements or leases, uncertain or incorrect boundary lines, and lack of access.

3. Defects known to the insured though not listed as an exception. Examples are (1) a recorded mortgage known to the insured but missed by the title analyst and (2) a violation of a covenant or condition.

4. Police power restrictions, which legally are not considered to make title unmarketable in any event.

5. Mechanic's liens not on record at time of policy issue.

In some states unrecorded mechanic's liens, encroachments, violation of zoning ordinance, and lack of access are covered. The coverage provided a mortgagee or lessee is the same as coverage provided an owner.

OBTAINING INSURANCE. Title insurance is most readily available from companies specializing in it. In a sales transaction the seller or the broker usually arranges for the insurance that is to serve as evidence of clear title. The title company frequently issues a preliminary title or informational report. The report lists the owner of record, unreleased liens, easements, restrictions of record, and other apparent encumbrances. The report indicates clouds that are likely to require removal. After completing an examination of title, the title company issues a commitment to issue a title policy.

The commitment (1) names all parties involved, (2) gives the legal description of the property, (3) defines the interest or estate covered, (4) lists exceptions, and (5) lists terms and stipulations including exceptions, of the policy. The policy is actually issued shortly after closing in a sale or refinancing transaction when all pertinent documents to the transaction have been recorded.

USE OF TITLE INSURANCE. Title insurance is ever more widely used for several reasons. Costs of defending title are absorbed by the title company. Claims of loss are usually settled promptly. Remote lenders prefer title insurance because of the reputation and corporate integrity of title insurance companies, which, to the lenders, means quick, easy claims settlements. The main limitation to title insurance, from an owner's point of view, is that the amount of coverage is fixed. Reimbursement is only to the face amount of the policy even though the property may have greatly appreciated in value after the policy was issued.

Torrens Certificate

The **Torrens system** is a method of title registration in which clear title is established with a governmental agency, which later issues title certificates to owners as evidence of their claim. The Torrens system of title registration operates inea fashion very similar to that used by states for automobiles. Title is initially cleared and registered into the system on a voluntary basis. A certificate is issued to the owner at this point. The certificate serves as proof of title. To be effective, sales, mortgages, and other claims against the property must be registered. Thus, the status of title may be determined at any time by checking with the register.

In theory, the Torrens system is considered ideal, but the high initial cost of registering a property in the system has worked against its wide acceptance. Also, because laws establishing Torren's registration vary from state to state, there is some uncertainty about its operation.

KINDS OF DEEDS

A **deed** is a legal instrument that, when properly executed and delivered, conveys title to, or ownership of an interest in, realty from a grantor to a grantee. By definition and in accordance with the Statute of Frauds, a deed must be written. *Proper execution* means signed by the grantor (or grantors), attested to by a witness or by witnesses, in nearly every state, acknowledged by a notary public or other qualified officer, and, in some states, sealed. A *seal* is a particular sign or mark to indicate the formal execution and nature of the instrument. The party conveying or giving title, as a seller, is the *grantor*. The party receiving title, as a buyer, is the *grantee*.

A deed is used to convey title to real property. The circumstances surrounding the conveyance vary greatly from one transaction to another. Generally, a grantor prefers to minimize the quality of title conveyed, consistent with the transaction, in order to avoid future obligation or liability to the grantee. Consequently, deeds take many forms to reflect the kind and quality of conveyance intended, as follows:

1. General warranty
2. Special warranty
3. Bargain and sale

4. Quitclaim
5. Trust (and release)
6. Other miscellaneous and/or special purpose

Deeds are sometimes classed as either statutory or nonstatutory. Statutory deeds are short forms of the deeds in which any covenants or warranties mentioned are implied by law, as though written out in full. Nonstatutory deeds are usually written for special purposes or situations; only covenants, warranties, and terms included in the deed apply. The main statutory deeds are the general warranty, the bargain and sale, and the quitclaim. These three types of deeds are included in this chapter as exhibits.

General Warranty Deed

A *general warranty deed* provides a grantee the most complete set of assurances of title possible from a grantor. The grantor covenants (or warrants) *good title, free of encumbrances* except as noted, which the grantee should be able to *quietly enjoy;* and if necessary, the grantor will *protect the grantee* against other claimants. A grantee cannot expect to receive a general warranty deed unless it is provided for in the sales agreement with the grantor. A general warranty deed is also known as a **warranty deed,** an illustration of which is shown in figure 9–1.

The grantor legally incurs a continuing future obligation by these covenants when certain words, stipulated by state law, appear in a statutory deed. The statutes of each state must be examined to determine the exact stipulated words. Typical stipulated words indicating a warranty of deed are "warrant generally" or "convey and warrant."

Five **covenants** or promises are actually made in a general warranty deed; these may be set forth in the deed itself. Even if the covenants are not stated in the deed, they are binding on the grantor because of the deed's statutory basis. In some states, if covenants are added to a statutory deed, the statutory nature of the deed may be destroyed and only the written in covenants or warranties apply.

1. *Covenant of Seizin.* The grantor claims and warrants that he or she holds, or is seized with, ownership of the property conveyed and the right to sell it. If this covenant is breached or broken, the grantee may recover from the grantor any losses or expense up to the amount or value of the consideration paid for the property.

2. *Covenant against Encumbrances.* The grantor claims and warrants that the property title is free of encumbrances except as stated specifically in the deed. If an encumbrance does exist against the property, the grantee may recover any expenses incurred to remove it from the grantor. Recovery is limited to the consideration given. Mortgage liens, easements, and deed restrictions are most likely to be noted as encumbrances.

3. *Covenant of Quiet Enjoyment.* The grantor claims and warrants that the grantee will be able to quietly enjoy or not be disturbed in the use of the

FIGURE 9–1
Warranty Deed (statutory form)

FORM No. 963—Stevens-Ness Law Publishing Co., Portland, Ore. 97204

TN

WARRANTY DEED—STATUTORY FORM
INDIVIDUAL GRANTOR

Wendy Welloff (widow)

Grantor,

conveys and warrants to Gerald & Nancy Investor, husband and wife

Grantee, the following described real property free of encumbrances except as specifically set forth herein situated in Rustic *County, Oregon, to-wit:*

Lots 16 & 17, Edgewood South Subdivision

(IF SPACE INSUFFICIENT, CONTINUE DESCRIPTION ON REVERSE SIDE)

The said property is free from encumbrances except

easements of record in subdivision plot

The true consideration for this conveyance is $ 640,000 *(Here comply with the requirements of ORS 93.030)*

Dated this 15th *day of* December *, 19* 80

/s/Wendy Welloff

STATE OF OREGON, County of Rustic) ss. December 15 *, 19* 80

Personally appeared the above named Wendy Welloff

and acknowledged the foregoing instrument to be *voluntary act and deed.*

Before me: /s/Alfred B. Culbertson

(OFFICIAL SEAL) *Notary Public for Oregon—My commission expires:* December 31, 1981 premises because the title conveyed is good and superior to that of any third person. If the grantee, or any subsequent grantee, is dispossessed by a superior title predating the conveyance, the grantor is legally liable for any damages or losses incurred. Threats and claims of superior title by outsiders do not constitute a breach of this covenant.

4. *Covenant of Further Assurance.* The grantor warrants that any other instrument needed to make the title good will be obtained and delivered to the grantee. Under this covenant, if a faulty legal description were given in the deed, the grantor would be obligated to have a new deed, containing the correct legal description, prepared and delivered to the grantee. Enforcement of this covenant is under a suit for specific performance rather than for damages.

5. *Covenant of Warranty of Title.* The grantor warrants forever the title to the premises, with monetary compensation to the grantee for any fault in the title, in whole or in part. This covenant is an absolute guarantee to the grantee of title and possession of the premises.

The first two of the above covenants relate to the past and apply only at the time of sale or conveyance. The last three relate to the future and run with the land.

Note that a warranty deed with covenants does not guarantee clear title. A seller-grantor may be a complete fraud and plan to leave town immediately after collecting money from the sale. Or valid claims against the title may be outstanding even though not pressed by legal action. Therefore, evidence of clear title, independent of a warranty deed, should be demanded of any grantor, even with the use of a general warranty deed.

Special Warranty Deed

A **special warranty deed** contains a single covenant that title has not been impaired, except as noted, by any acts of the grantor. That is, it contains a covenant against grantor's acts. This means that the grantor has liability only if the grantee is disturbed by a claim arising from or due to some act of the grantor. A special warranty deed gives a grantee less title protection than does a general warranty deed.

Bargain and Sale Deed

In effect, a **bargain and sale deed** is very similar to a special warranty deed. The grantor, in a bargain and sale deed, asserts ownership, by implication, of an interest in the property and makes no other covenants or claims, unless stated. The granting words are usually "grant, bargain, and sell," "grant and release," or simply "conveys." Thus, the grantee must demand or obtain good title evidence to be sure of receiving marketable title. Covenants against liens and other encumbrances may be inserted if agreeable to the grantor; the instrument is then called a *bargain and sale deed, with covenants.* Sellers prefer conveying on a bargain and sale deed to conveying on a warranty deed. A bargain and sale deed is shown in figure 9–2.

FIGURE 9–2
Bargain and Sale Deed (statutory form)

FORM No. 961—Stevens-Ness Law Publishing Co., Portland, Ore. 97204

TA

documents appendix

BARGAIN AND SALE DEED—STATUTORY FORM
INDIVIDUAL GRANTOR

Wendy Welloff (widow) .... Grantor,

conveys to Gerald & Nancy Investor, husband and wife .... Grantee,

the following described real property situated in   Rustic   County, Oregon, to-wit:

Lots 16 & 17, Edgewood South Subdivision

(IF SPACE INSUFFICIENT, CONTINUE DESCRIPTION ON REVERSE SIDE)

The true consideration for this conveyance is $ 640,000.   . (Here comply with the requirements of ORS 93.030)

Dated this 15th day of December , 19 80

/s/Wendy Welloff

STATE OF OREGON, County of Rustic   ) ss.   December 15th , 19 80
Personally appeared the above named Wendy Welloff

and acknowledged the foregoing instrument to be her   voluntary act and deed.

Before me: /s/Alfred B. Culbertson

(OFFICIAL SEAL)   Notary Public for Oregon—My commission expires: December 31, 1981.

169

Quitclaim Deed

A **quitclaim deed** conveys the rights of the grantor, if any, without any warranty, claim, or assertion of title by the grantor. A quitclaim deed is the simplest form of deed and gives the grantee the least possible amount of title protection. It only conveys an interest that a grantor *may* have when the deed is delivered. The operative words in a quitclaim deed are (the grantor) "does hereby remise, release, and quitclaim" (to the grantee). Title may be conveyed just as effectively and completely with a quitclaim deed as with a warranty deed, but without any warranties. The grantee has no recourse against the grantor, however, if no color of title is received.

Quitclaim deeds are widely used to clear up clouds on title. For example, a quitclaim deed is used whenever an heir might have a very weak title claim. Or whenever a long-ago common-law wife might have a dower claim. For a small consideration, the heir or "wife" gives up any claim held. A quitclaim deed to make right a legal description, names of parties, or some other error in a previously recorded deed is termed a *deed of confirmation* or a *deed of correction*. The purpose is to clear up or correct the defect so that it does not become, or continue to be, a cloud on title. A quitclaim deed is shown in figure 9–3.

Deeds of Trust and of Release

A deed conveying title to a third party (trustee) to be held as security for a debt owed a lender-beneficiary is known as a *trust-deed-in-the-nature-of-a-mortgage*. It is also known as a **trust deed** or a *deed of trust*. A deed of trust is a nonstatutory deed. When the terms of the deed of trust have been satisfied (the debt has been paid off), the trustee reconveys title to the former borrower on a **deed of release** or *of reconveyance*. A deed of release is also used to lift or remove a claim from a dower, remainder, or reversionary interest, or a mortgage lien.

A trust deed is not intended to convey all rights of ownership unless the borrower-grantor violates or fails to live up to the trust agreement, terms of which are stated in the instrument. The deed does give the trustee the power to sell the property (right of disposition) if the agreement is violated and to use the proceeds to satisfy the debt obligation. The trustee has no other interest in the property. The borrower-grantor retains what is called an *equitable title*. That is, right of possession is retained as well as the right to do anything else with the property that does not jeopardize the interest or position of the lender-beneficiary in the property.

Miscellaneous Deeds

Many other deeds are used from time to time for special purposes or situations, frequently by court order. For the most part, the name of the deed indicates the nature of the purpose or situation. Also, full consideration is usually stated. These are discussed only briefly because their use is largely removed from the market.

Some of these special-purpose deeds, when executed by individuals acting in a fiduciary capacity, contain covenants against the acts of the grantor. Ad-

FIGURE 9–3
A Quitclaim Deed (statutory form)

FORM No. 969 Stevens-Ness Law Publishing Co., Portland, Ore. 97204
TN

QUITCLAIM DEED—STATUTORY FORM
INDIVIDUAL GRANTOR

Wendy Welloff (widow)

.... *Grantor,*

releases and quitclaims to Gerald & Nancy Investor, husband & wife ....

.... *Grantee, all right, title and interest in and to the following described*

real property situated in Rustic .... *County, Oregon, to-wit:*

Lots 16 & 17, Edgewood South subdivision

(IF SPACE INSUFFICIENT, CONTINUE DESCRIPTION ON REVERSE SIDE)

The true consideration for this conveyance is $ 640,000 .... *(Here comply with the requirements of ORS 93.030)*

....

Dated this 15th day of December .... , 19 80

/s/Wendy Welloff

STATE OF OREGON, *County of* Rustic ....) ss.   December 15th .... , 19 80
Personally appeared the above named ....

.... *and acknowledged the foregoing instrument to be* her *voluntary act and deed.*

Before me: /s/Alfred B. Culbertson

(OFFICIAL SEAL)   *Notary Public for Oregon—My commission expires:* ....

ministrators, trustees, executors, and corporate officers are fiduciaries when they serve as grantors in a deed. As fiduciaries, they do not wish to assume any greater future obligation than necessary. They therefore include a *covenant against grantor's acts* in deeds they execute by stating that they "have not done or suffered anything whereby the said premises have been encumbered in any way whatever." The covenant means that the grantor has done nothing to harm or lessen the title and that neither encumbrances nor defects in title developed during the grantor's period of ownership or responsibility, except as noted. In most cases, the actions of fiduciaries affect title only briefly. The fiduciary usually has no personal interest in the realty.

ADMINISTRATOR'S DEED. An *administrator's deed* is a nonstatutory deed used to convey realty of a person who died intestate to an heir or to a purchaser. An *administrator* is a person appointed by the court to settle the decedent's estate. The administrator executes the deed, which should recite the proceeding under which the court authorizes the sale or conveyance. The deed contains a covenant against the acts of the grantor.

EXECUTOR'S DEED. An **executor** settles the affairs of a person who died leaving a will. An *executor's deed* conveys title to realty left by the decedent to a purchaser or to a devisee. It usually contains a covenant against grantor's acts. If more than one executor is designated in the will, all must sign the deed.

DEED OF CESSION. A *deed of cession* is a nonstatutory instrument to convey street rights of an abutting owner to a municipality. The purpose should be recited. A quitclaim deed may be used for this conveyance.

COMMITTEE'S DEED. A *committee's deed* is a nonstatutory instrument to convey property of infants, mentally retarded persons, and other incompetents whose affairs are managed by a court-appointed committee. Authority from the court must precede any such conveyance.

GIFT DEED. An instrument conveying title from a donor-grantor to a donee-grantee is a *gift deed.* The usual consideration is "love and affection." The grantee has no recourse against the grantor if title is defective because no monetary consideration was given by the grantee.

GUARDIAN'S DEED. A *guardian's deed* is an instrument used by a legal guardian to convey the realty interest of an infant or ward, upon permission of the court. Full consideration should be recited because the guardian is a fiduciary.

REFEREE'S DEED IN FORECLOSURE. An instrument used by an officer of the court to convey a mortgagor's title, following a foreclosure sale, is called a *referee's deed in foreclosure.* It is also called a *sheriff's deed* in some areas. It contains no other supporting covenants. The conditions surrounding the conveyance and the price paid by the purchaser should be cited in the deed.

REFEREE'S DEED IN PARTITION. Concurrent owners sometimes sue for partition or splitting up of jointly owned property. The instrument used following a partition judgment and sale is a *referee's deed in partition.* An officer of the court (the referee) conveys the interests of the former concurrent owners to purchasers with no other supporting covenants.

DEED OF SURRENDER. A *deed of surrender* is a nonstatutory instrument to convey a life estate to a remainderman or a qualified fee estate to the holder of the reversionary interest. These conveyances can also be accomplished with a quitclaim deed.

Other deeds are sometimes used in local areas. Examples are mining claim deeds and grant deeds. The most commonly and most widely used deeds are discussed above.

ESSENTIALS OF A VALID DEED

The formal requirements for a valid deed vary from state to state, but the following requirements are essential or basic to all states:

1. Name of grantor with legal capacity to execute the deed
2. Name of grantee, adequate for identification with reasonable certainty
3. A statement of some consideration
4. Granting clause or words of conveyance
5. Statement of the interest being conveyed
6. Description of realty in which interest is held
7. *Habendum* clause
8. Proper execution—signature of the grantor, notarized, with witnesses and seal when required
9. Voluntary delivery and acceptance

Grantor and Grantee

The conveyance must be from a competent grantor to a grantee capable of holding title. The rules of contracts usually apply in determining whether or not the grantor is competent to convey title to real property. Basically, the grantor must have reached the age of majority and be of sound mind. A deed signed by a minor is considered voidable (not void) at the option of the minor, until legal age of majority is reached.

The names of the grantor and grantee should be followed by their addresses to aid in their identification. The status of the parties should also be clearly indicated, for example, "John Jones and Mary Jones, husband and wife," or "brother and sister."

A deed conveying corporation property should be supported by a resolution properly passed by the *corporate board of directors*. The deed can be signed only be a corporate officer deriving authority from the corporate board of directors by resolution. Finally, the corporate seal must be affixed to the deed.

Consideration

Consideration is anything of value given in a contractual agreement—money, services, love and affection. Some consideration must always be stated in a deed. That shifts the burden of proving lack of consideration to anyone attacking the conveyance. Under the Statute of Frauds, the consideration cited in a deed cannot be disputed for purposes of defeating the deed. Dollar consideration is usually required except in a gift deed in which love and affection is sufficient. Even in gift deeds, a nominal consideration, such as "$12.00 and other good and valuable consideration," is customarily cited. Full dollar consideration is frequently not cited in a deed, except when the deed is executed by a fiduciary.

Words of Conveyance—Granting and Habendum Clauses

The granting clause includes words of conveyance such as "convey and warrant," "grant and release," "grant, bargain, and sell," or "remise, release, and quitclaim." Each of these words of conveyance carries a different connotation concerning the warranties and obligations of the grantor. The interest being conveyed, including appurtenances, should follow the granting clause. Only a present interest in realty can be conveyed; that is, a deed to convey at some future time, for example, at the grantor's death, is invalid.

The *habendum* clause defines or explains the ownership to be enjoyed by the grantee. The words "to have and to hold" introduce the clause. The description of the estate in the *habendum* clause should agree with the description in the granting clause. Deed restrictions and other encumbrances are usually stated after the *habendum* clause.

Unique Description

A description must be used that identifies the property clearly and uniquely. Street addresses are often inadequate because ambiguity and uncertainty might result. Any description that would enable a competent surveyor to locate the property is considered adequate. Legal descriptions of realty are fully discussed in chapter 3.

Proper Execution

Proper execution includes signatures, a seal, witnesses, in some states, and an acknowledgment of the signing before a public notary. Customarily, only the grantor or grantors sign a deed. If a mortgage is being assumed, the grantee must also sign. A grantor who is unable to write may sign with a mark in almost all states. A cross is usually used as a mark, with the grantor's name typed near the cross, thus:

---

		his		
John	(**X**)	mark	Brown	(seal)

The "X" must be made by the grantor. A signature by mark must generally be witnessed by two persons other than the public notary taking the acknowledgment. A signature by an attorney-in-fact is acceptable if power-of-attorney document has previously been properly filed in the public records.

The word "seal" printed or written behind a grantor's signature is required in some states to indicate the formal nature of the deed. The signature of an authorized officer, in a conveyance of corporate realty, must be followed by the corporate seal. In some states the signatures of witnesses to the signing are also required for proper execution.

An **acknowledgment** is a formal declaration, before a notary public or other authorized public official, by a person signing a legal document that the signing is a "free and voluntary act." A justice of the peace, a judge, or a commanding officer in one of the military services may also acknowledge a signature. An acknowledgment is required for recording in nearly every state. The public official is expected to require proper identification of parties involved in an acknowledgment. The purpose of the acknowledgment is to prevent the recording of forged instruments. A deed without an acknowledgment is not a satisfactory instrument for most conveyance purposes. Deeds should be recorded as soon as received to give notice to the world of grantee's rights in the property received.

Delivery and Acceptance

The final requirement for a valid deed is delivery and acceptance. **Delivery** means that the grantor, by some act or statement, signifies intent for the deed to be effective. The grantor handing the deed to the grantee is the most obvious form of delivery. Similarly, the grantor's directing an attorney or an escrow officer to give a signed deed to the grantee also constitutes delivery. Delivery must take place while the grantor is alive. If several people share ownership of a property, for delivery to occur, all must sign and in some way indicate that the deed is to be effective. A delivery in escrow does not occur until the conditions specified in the escrow instructions have been satisfied.

The grantee must accept the deed for title to pass. **Acceptance** is agreeing to the terms of a deed. Since most people desire to own property, acceptance is ordinarily assumed. Thus, if a grantor records a deed conveying title to a grantee, the grantee must object and dissent immediately in order to avoid an acceptance.

Fraudulent Conveyances

Courts will occasionally inquire into the consideration in a conveyance if there is a possibility of fraud. For example, if a grantor who is being crowded by creditors conveys for apparently insufficient consideration to a friend or relative, inquiry is justified. If the conveyance is proved fraudulent, the courts will require a reconveyance to the grantor, making the property available to satisfy creditor claims. If the indebtedness to creditors occurred after the conveyance, fraudulent intent must be proved in order to require a reconveyance to the grantor.

PUBLIC RECORDS

Anyone who has an interest in realty must give notice to the world in order to protect that interest. Notice may be actual or constructive. Possession of realty is legally considered **actual notice** to the world of an interest in the property. Entering a legal instrument that evidences an interest in real estate into the public records is considered **constructive notice** to the world of the interest. In turn, the public record serves as a source of information to anyone about to enter into a transaction concerning real estate, such as lenders, potential tenants, or interested buyers.

Public records are maintained by local governments in all states in accordance with recording acts. Public records provide a central repository or storehouse for certain kinds of information. Recording acts provide for the registration of every legal instrument creating, transferring, mortgaging, assigning, or otherwise affecting title to realty. Public records thus are designed to protect against fraud and to reinforce the Statute of Frauds. The records are maintained by city, town, and county officials under titles like clerk, recorder, treasurer, or tax collector. Public records include many documents affecting title to real and personal property, taxes, special assessments, ordinances, and building and zoning codes.

Historically, possession of realty served as actual notice of an interest in realty and was adequate for almost all purposes. Modern society is complex, however, and a more efficient and effective system of notice became necessary. For example, A, an owner, might sell property to B, conveying title with a deed. But, if B does not take possession, A might also sell to C, who upon moving into occupancy acquires a claim of title superior to that of B. Or A might obtain cash under a mortgage from D, after the sale to B, and subsequently leave the area. Either situation involves fraud and many legal problems. Recording deeds and mortgages gives constructive notice of the interest to all parties and is recognized as notice equal to actual possession. As a general rule, recording acts give legal priority to interests according to the sequence in which they are recorded. "First in time is first in line."

To be eligible for recording, instruments must be properly prepared and executed according to the specific state law. States are not uniform in this matter. General requirements include witnesses, acknowledgment before a notary public, names typed or printed below signatures, and the name of the person preparing the document. It is usually in the self-interest of mortgagees and other lien-creditors, lessees, buyers on installment land contracts, and others with a pending interest in real estate to be sure that the interest is properly entered into the public record.

Public records may be divided into the following five classes for convenience of discussion:

1. Real property title records
2. Mortgagor-mortgagee records
3. Recorded plats and architectural plans
4. Secured personal property records
5. Miscellaneous records

Real Property Title Records

Recording of a deed is highly recommended to give constructive notice to all of the grantee's interest in the property. The obligation and the benefit of recording both go to the grantee as the new owner. Recording is doubly important whenever vacant land is involved or whenever the grantee does not take immediate possession. Failure to record or to take occupancy leaves an opportunity for the grantor to sell and convey to a second grantee. If the second grantee records or moves into occupancy first, a claim of ownership superior to the first grantee's is realized. The first grantee's only recourse, for all practical purposes, is against the fraudulent grantor.

In recording a deed, many states require revenue stamps in the amount of a small fraction of the value conveyed. The stamps, usually available from the county clerk or recorder, must be affixed to the deed before it is recorded. In reality, this is a sales tax.

Some states also require a declaration, signed by buyer and seller, of the address, legal description, date and kind of deed, kind of improvements, and whether the conveyance is between friends or the result of a court order. The intent, in most cases, is to obtain sales information on market value of the property for assessment purposes.

Two systems are used in maintaining title records. The first is a grantor grantee index; the second is a tract or lot and block index.

GRANTOR-GRANTEE INDEX. In a grantor-grantee system, deeds are indexed according to the last name of the previous owner (grantor) and of the new owner (grantee). Thus, a title search can be initiated and a chain of title can be run if the name of either is known. In running a chain of title, the grantor is regarded as a grantee in a previous transaction. When located in the grantee index, the previous grantor's name then becomes immediately available.

TRACT INDEX (LOT AND BLOCK). In a tract system, deeds are indexed according to the legal description or the location of properties rather than by grantor-grantee. In urban areas the name of the subdivision in which the property is located will often serve as the key to entering the index. Alternatively, maps of the area will include a distinct number for each block. Transactions involving individual lots on the block can then be ascertained by looking in the index itself.

Entry into a tract index is more difficult in rural areas because the classification system is more involved in that property has a distinct legal description. The general system of the tract index in rural areas is based on identifying properties by township and by section. A chain of title can be run more easily with a tract index because all transactions involving a specific property are recorded on the same page. A tract index, however, is considered more difficult and more expensive to maintain than a grantor-grantee index.

Mortgagor-Mortgagee Records

In nearly every state mortgages are accepted for recording in, and constructive notice is given by, a mortgagor-mortgagee index. The index fucntions are in a manner very similar to a grantor-grantee index. That is, the index may be entered with either the name of the borrower-mortgagor or the lender-mortgagee. When a mortgage lien has been satisified, this also is entered in the index. In some states mortgages are filed and recorded in the same grantor-grantee index that is used for deeds.

Plat and Plan Records

Maps, restrictions, architectural plans, and other pertinent information on subdivision and condominium plats are maintained as a part of the public record. The plats are a particularly excellent source of information on easements and restrictions on a specific plat. Parcel and building dimensions and building layout can also be readily determined from this source.

Secured Personal-Property Records

Under the Uniform Commercial Code, discussed earlier, items of personal property may be purchased on a conditional sales contract, which is also termed a *security agreement*. Legally, purchase by a conditional sales contract means title does not pass until full payment is made. In the meantime, a short version of the security agreement, termed a *financing statement,* is entered into the public record to give public notice of a collateral lien on the property. For owners of real estate, this notice is of considerable importance when items like water heaters, boilers, appliances, draperies, and other equipment frequently classed as fixtures are involved. The items do not become fixtures, or part of the real estate until the security agreement is satisfied. That is, important components of a property may not actually be a part of the realty. Notice of the financing statement is usually entered in the mortgagor-mortgagee index.

Miscellaneous Records

Other records may contain information pertinent to clear title and deserve mention. Unpaid real estate taxes are automatically a lien against property of first priority. Also, liens for inheritance taxes and franchise taxes are of the highest priority even though not recorded. Income taxes become a lien upon the filing of a warrant of taxes due in the community where the real estate is located.

Notices of pending legal action or lawsuits are entered in the **lis pendens** index, which is set up alphabetically for plaintiffs and defendants. The listing of an owner as a defendant means that a potential claim stands against the property. Notices of other liens—judgments, attachments, mechanic's lien, and the like—are carried in files specific to each kind of lien. Each of these must be checked in a title search. *Lis pendens* means a pending list.

SUMMARY

A person owning, or about to own, real estate wants the best possible title. The legal term is marketable title. Marketable title means the quality is high enough that courts would require a buyer to accept the property at market value. Marketable title may be evidenced or documented by (1) title certification, (2) title insurance, or (3) a Torrens certificate. The most common methods of bringing about a transfer of title are private grant (sale for consideration, gift, or will) and action of law (descent, lien enforcement, adverse possession, or condemnation). Deeds most commonly used to actually convey title are the (1) general warranty, (2) special warranty, (3) bargain and sale, (4) quitclaim, and (5) trust. The essential parts of a valid deed are (1) names of grantor and grantee, (2) statement of consideration, (3) words of conveyance, (4) unique property description, (5) proper execution, including grantor's signature, and (6) delivery and acceptance. Recording gives constructive notice to all of the contents of a deed. In fact, any instrument showing an interest in real estate may be recorded to give constructive notice of the interest, which protects the owner of the interest. Thus, lien creditors, lessees, and owners not in possession find it advantageous to record their interests.

KEY TERMS

Abstract of title	Decedent
Acceptance	Deed
Acknowledgment	Deed of release
Actual notice	Delivery
Administrator	Descent
Adverse possession, title by	Devise
Bargain and sale deed	Donor/donee
Certification of title	Erosion
Chain of title	Executor
Confiscation	Grantor/grantee
Consideration	Intestate
Constructive notice	Legacy
Convenants	Lis pendens

Marketable title
Mortgagor-mortgagee index
Patent
Probate
Quitclaim deed
Reliction
Special warranty deed

Testate
Title evidence
Title insurance
Torrens system
Trust deed
Warranty deed
Will

QUESTIONS FOR REVIEW AND DISCUSSION

1. Briefly explain and distinguish among the following methods of transferring title:
   (a) Contract for consideration.
   (b) Gift
   (c) Will
   (d) Descent
   (e) Adverse possession
   (f) Lien enforcement
   (g) Erosion

2. Explain the use of an attorney's opinion of title, including any advantages or disadvantages from a potential owner's or lender's point of view.

3. Explain title insurance in detail, including any advantages or disadvantages from a potential owner's or lender's point of view.

4. Explain the nature of a general warranty deed, including the five accompanying convenants or warranties.

5. Explain the nature and uses of the following deeds:
   (a) Special warranty
   (b) Bargain and sale
   (c) Quitclaim
   (d) Trust

6. List and explain at least five essentials of a valid deed.

7. Explain briefly the nature and use of the following public record indexes:
   (a) Grantor-grantee
   (b) Tract
   (c) Mortgager-mortgagee
   (d) Secured personal property
   (e) *Lis pendens*

8. Title may be gained by adverse possession in ten to twenty years. Should this law not invalidate most claims of title more than twenty years old because most real estate is now held under color of title? Are laws needed to make this situation clear to everyone? Discuss.

9. The Torrens system should be adopted nationwide in the United States. Discuss. What major obstacles would have to be overcome? What probable effect on costs of title transfer?

10. What kind of deed would you prefer to use as a grantor of title? As a grantee? Why? How is the difference in attitude reconciled in practice?

11. Are deeds necessary? If not, what might be used instead?

12. Why should a deed be recorded from a grantee's viewpoint? A lender's? A leasee's?

REFERENCES

Gray, Charles D., and Joseph L. Steinberg. *Real Estate Sales Contracts: From Preparation through Closing.* Englewood Cliffs, N.J.: Prentice-Hall, 1970. The process of title transfer, through a sales contract, from negotiation to closing; includes check lists, forms, and sample clauses.

Kratovil, Robert, and Raymond J. Werner. *Real Estate Law.* 7th ed. Englewood Cliffs, N.J.: Prentice-Hall, 1979. See chapters 6–9, 14.

Lusk, Harold F., and William B. French. *Law of the Real Estate Business.* 3rd ed. Homewood, Ill.: Richard D. Irwin, 1975. Clear presentation of essential legal considerations in title transfer. Chapters 5–8.

The Investor-Broker Relationship

10

A real estate broker is anyone engaged to negotiate the sale, purchase, lease, or exchange of realty, or to arrange financing of realty, for a fee or commission. Brokerage specialization has now reached the stage where individuals—and entire organizations—limit operations to a single area, such as investment, commercial, industrial, land, or lease brokerage. Some organizations, however, do continue to provide a wide variety of functions and services, including appraising, brokerage, counseling, construction and development, financing, and insurance.

In looking at the investor-broker relationship, our concern is primarily with the buy-sell transaction. In this transaction, the broker is a negotiator and takes neither title nor possession of the realty. At the same time, the actions and success of the broker are of vital importance to the investor. The purpose of this chapter is to look at the real estate marketing process from the investor's viewpoint. The broker's viewpoint is given in the next chapter. Major topics of this chapter are as follows:

1. The law of agency—in general
2. Critical issues in the listing arrangement
3. More on commissions
4. Selecting a broker

THE LAW OF AGENCY—IN GENERAL

Agency is the fiduciary relationship created when one person acts on behalf of, or under the control of, another. In a **fiduciary relationship** trust and faith are expected and necessary, for instance, in financial matters such as the buying, selling, or leasing of property. The *law of agency* concerns the legal rights, duties, and liabilities of the principal, agent, and third parties based on contracts and/or relationships between them. The law of agency involves aspects of the law of contract and the law of torts. **A tort** is a wrongful or damaging act committed against another, for which a civil action may be brought. Causing personal injury to another, damaging another's property, fraud, and misrepresentation are examples of torts.

A person acting for or representing another, with the latter's authority, is an **agent.** Thus, a broker is an agent in selling property for an owner under a listing agreement. The person for whom an agent acts is a **principal.** An owner therefore becomes a principal when he or she signs a listing agreement with a broker.

Agency usually involves three parties: a principal (P), an agent (A), and a third party (T). A potential buyer, as an investor negotiating to purchase a property, is a **third party** in the typical real estate sales transaction.

A principal known or identified to a third party is a **disclosed principal.** A *partially disclosed principal* is one not known or identified to the third party, though the agent acknowledges that a principal is involved. Finally, an *undisclosed principal* is one who is secretly represented by an agent who appears to be acting in self-interest. Discussion here is mainly limited to situations involving disclosed principals.

Duties, Liabilities, and Rights of a Principal

A principal's main duty is to compensate an agent in accordance with the contract of employment. Thus, with the typical listing agreement, the owner must pay a commission to the broker when a "ready, willing, and able" buyer has been found. An owner also has a duty to give the broker-agent complete and accurate information when listing a property to be sold, leased, or exchanged.

A principal is liable on all agreements or contracts made by an agent within the authority given the agent. Unauthorized agreements also become a principal's liability, if subsequently affirmed or ratified by a principal with full knowledge of the pertinent facts. A principal, in turn, is not liable for unauthorized agreements of the agent that are not subsequently affirmed. Unauthorized agreements are agreements outside or beyond the authority given the agent. Most listing agreements clearly spell out the authority given a broker, and usually that authority does not include signing or accepting an offer to purchase the subject property.

In some cases, a principal becomes liable for torts committed by an agent. Thus, a tort committed by an agent within the scope of the employment agreement or under the direction of the principal, becomes a liability of the principal. At the same time, a principal is not generally liable if the agent is an independent contractor. An **independent contractor** is a person retaining personal

183

control over work details while performing a service or task for an employer. A broker engaged to sell property for an owner is almost certainly an independent contractor. A salesperson, engaged by a broker, may or may not be an independent contractor; the work relationship would be the primary determinant of whether the salesperson was an independent contractor. The greater the personal control exercised by the broker over the salesperson, the less the likelihood that the salesperson is an independent contractor.

A disclosed principal may enforce any contract made with a third party by an authorized agent for the principal's benefit. A real estate broker ordinarily does not enter contracts for a principal, but such is possible.

Duties, Liabilities, and Rights of An Agent

The duties of an agent to a principal are (1) to use reasonable care, (2) to obey reasonable instructions, (3) accountability, (4) loyalty, and (5) to give notice. Using reasonable care means that the agent must be diligent and must act in good faith in representing the principal. And the agent is expected to follow or obey all reasonable instructions of a principal, assuming they pertain to the purpose of the principal-agent relationship. Following instructions includes keeping within the authority given by the principal. Instructions creating a tort or criminal situation would not be reasonable. An agent also has a legal duty of **accountability**—to account for all money or property to the principal, including keeping adequate records concerning such money or property. In addition, it is illegal for a broker to *commingle* or mix personal funds and funds of a principal.

Loyalty means that the agent must not benefit from the relationship except through compensation from the principal, unless otherwise agreed. Faithful performance is another term for loyalty. A broker therefore may not represent both parties in a buy-sell transaction without the knowledge and consent of both. Representing two principals is called **dual agency,** or **divided agency.** Contracts involving agent disloyalty are voidable at the option of the principal. The reasoning behind this right to void is that the broker cannot get the highest possible price for the seller and at the same time get the lowest possible price for the buyer. It follows that the broker cannot collect a commission for arranging a voided contract. If the broker acts for both buyer and seller, with both having full knowledge of the double agency, the double-agency rule does not apply. In this situation the broker is often termed a **middleman.**

"Giving notice" to a principal means that any information given the agent must be communicated immediately to the principal. Any knowledge given the agent legally binds the principal. Therefore, it follows that the agent is bound to keep the principal informed of any important facts concerning the object of the agency arrangement.

An agent is generally not personally liable on contracts entered into for the benefit of a principal. However, an agent exceeding his or her authority does incur personal liability, unless such act is affirmed or ratified by the principal. A broker is usually engaged only to find a buyer and not to make a sales contract for an owner. Therefore, a broker's operations usually do not provide a situation where the authority of the agency agreement might be exceeded. However, if a principal lacks legal competence to make a valid agency contract (because of insanity or being too young), the agent incurs personal liability for any resulting contract.

In the matter of torts, agents and independent contractors are personally liable for their own acts. At the same time, agents and independent contractors are not liable for torts committed by their principals.

An agent has a right to enforce a contract of a principal against a third party in which an interest is held. Thus a broker may enforce a sales contract of an owner with a buyer because of an anticipated commission. Finally, a broker derives authority from an owner through the listing agreement. And in order to enforce collection of a commission, a broker must have the agreement in writing. Ordinarily, the broker is authorized only to negotiate for the principal under a listing agreement. Most listing agreements provide that a broker may engage salespersons to help conduct the negotiations. The salespersons also operate under the law of agency, with the broker as the principal.

CRITICAL ISSUES IN
THE LISTING ARRANGEMENT

The agreement in which a broker is engaged to sell a property for an owner in return for a fee or commission is a listing contract. In most situations the listing agreement must be in writing for a broker to collect a commission. And as in any real estate transaction, legal rights and obligations are involved. These rights and obligations are discussed, in general terms, in the previous section. Several critical and rather specific issues of a listing agreement are discussed in this section. These issues are (1) the property listing price, (2) owner reservation of the right to sell, (3) broker compensation, (4) duration or termination, and (5) point at which commission is payable.

Property Listing Price

In self-interest, an owner wants the highest possible price in selling a property. A broker ordinarily prefers to list a property at a price that is low enough to make it likely for the property to sell quickly. A broker, however, as an agent in a fiduciary relationship, has a duty of keeping the principal informed of all material facts affecting the subject matter of the agency relationship. This means keeping the owner informed of the market value of the property. Increasingly, the broker, as a real estate practitioner, has an obligation to document that any suggested listing price is not too low. Information from sales of comparable properties is one generally accepted way of documenting value. An owner is generally advised to list at a price above indicated market value, to take account of possible inflation in values and to retain room for bargaining. A property that sells too quickly may very well have been listed at too low a price.

Reservation of Right to Sell

Several types of listing agreements are explained in chapter 7. Three of these types differ mainly in the designation of who has a right to sell the property. The three types are the (1) open contract, (2) exclusive agency contract, and (3) exclusive right to sell contract. The broker's control increases sharply in going from an open to an exclusive agency to an exclusive right to sell. And with greater control, the broker is likely to expend greater effort or go to more expense to bring about a sale.

In an open listing, any broker selling the property is entitled to a commission; of course, the owner may personally sell the property and pay no commission. In the exclusive agency, the listing broker is the only person legally entitled to a commission if someone other than the owner sells the property. That is, the owner may still sell the property and avoid paying a commission.

In an exclusive right to sell agreement, the listing broker is entitled to a commission if the property is sold by anyone. In making an exclusive right to sell agreement, the owner may list exceptions to the agreement. Including as exceptions the names of parties with whom negotiations have been or are being conducted means that the owner may arrange a sale with one of them and avoid paying a commission.

Broker Compensation

The usual arrangement is for a broker to get some percentage of the selling price for a commission. And commission rates are largely set by local area custom. However, brokers are prohibited from collusion in setting commission rates, according to the Sherman and Clayton Antitrust Acts, which prohibits monopoly and agreements in restraint of trade. Collusion to fix commission rates is in restraint of trade and lessens competition. The anticollusion law means brokers may charge what the traffic will bear; and owners are free to negotiate the amount of commission to be paid with the broker. Brokers may not, in turn, cite local agreement or custom as reasons for not cutting a commission.

The amount of commission, or a method of determining the amount of commission, is best included in the listing agreement. The situation is not too different from leasing. It follows that flat and percentage commissions are possible, individually or in combination. Also, a net listing may be used.

FLAT COMMISSION. Certain basic costs are almost certain to be incurred in selling any property. These costs include advertising, office expenses, broker's time, and overhead in general. Thus some flat amount, say $1,000, might be justified, whether a small lot or a large house is sold. An owner may quickly determine the net amount to be realized from a sale when a flat commission is to be paid. For example:

Sale price	$100,000
Less broker's commission	−1,000
Seller's net	$99,000

PERCENTAGE COMMISSION. Brokers typically get 5 to 7 percent of the sales price as commission. Thus, a sale for $100,000 with a 6 percent commission would net a seller $94,000.

Sale price	$100,000
Less brokerage commission	−6,000
Seller's net	$94,000

If a seller wanted to net $100,000 from a sale, the $100,000 would be 94 percent of the necessary gross sale price. To calculate the necessary sale price, the net amount would be divided by .94.

$$\frac{\$100,000}{.94} = \$106,383$$

Six percent of $106,383 equals $6,383, when rounded to the nearest dollar.

SPLIT COMMISSION. A brokerage fee might also be negotiated on larger properties that would give a higher rate of commission up to a certain base amount, with a lower rate for any amount of sale price above the base amount. A flat fee plus a percentage might also be negotiated. For example, a commission of 6 percent on the first $100,000 plus 4 percent of any price in excess of $100,000 might be agreed to in listing a property. A sale for $640,000 would result in a commission of $27,600 under this scheme.

Sale price		$640,000
Commission on first $100,000	$6,000	
Commission on price in excess of $100,000:		
Sale price	$640,000	
Less base	100,000	
excess	$540,000	
at 4% gives commission of		$21,600
Total commission		$27,600
Seller's net		$612,400

The selling price, assuming the owner wants to net $640,000 from a property, would be calculated as follows:

Net plus commission = 100,000		$94,000 + $6000 =	100,000
Necessary sale price to net additional $546,000			
at 4% rate : $\dfrac{546,000}{.96}$ = 568,750			$568,750
Gross required sale price			$668,750
Proof			
568,750 x 4% =		22,750	
Commission on first $100,000 =		6,000	
Total commission		$28,750	
Gross sale price		$668,750	
Net sale price			
($668,750 − $28,750)		$640,000	

Not allowed
N.Y.S.

NET LISTING/RESIDUAL COMMISSION. A net listing means that the broker gets anything above the asking price stipulated by an owner. However, a sale of a property for $750,000 for which the owner expected $640,000 would be almost prima-facie evidence of disloyalty by the broker. The duties of loyalty and of keeping a principal informed would require the broker to make an owner aware that $640,000 was too low an asking price. An owner would have a strong case for avoiding the payment of a $110,000 commission on a $750,000 sale, which calculates to a 14.7 percent commission rate, far above the more usual 5 to 7 percent rates.

Duration/Termination of Agreement

A listing agreement may be terminated by action of the parties or operation of the law. Actions of the parties that end the agreement include (1) mutual consent of the parties, (2) completion of the agreement as by sale of the property, (3) time expiration or running out, (4) revocation by the principal, and (5) revocation or abandonment by the agent. Operation of the law ends the agreement upon (1) destruction of the property, as by fire, (2) death of the principal or agent, (3) insanity of principal or agent, and (4) bankruptcy of the principal or agent.

A listing agreement is, of course, terminated by sale of the subject property and payment of a commission. And an agreement for a fixed period terminates at the end of the period unless an extension is arranged. Termination by completion of purpose or time expiration are the two most common ways listing agreements are ended. Some agreements contain a *clause for automatic renewal* or *extension*, meaning that the listing continues until terminated by written notice. Automatic extensions are generally deemed to be unfair to an owner and are actually illegal in some states.

If no time limit is specified, a listing agreement expires after a "reasonable time." A reasonable time might be three months for a one-family residence and from six months to a year for a large office building. An owner may terminate any time up to the start of performance by the broker. Effectively, beginning performance converts the agreement from a unilateral contract to a bilateral contract. The broker is showing good faith toward consideration by making the effort to sell. Performance, of course, also terminates the agreement.

Broker Proof of Performance

An agent must complete the assigned task to earn compensation. A broker must also perform according to the listing agreement to earn a commission. Generally the broker's obligation is to produce a **"ready, willing, and able" buyer.** A purchaser acceptable to the seller or capable of meeting the seller's terms is such a buyer. The owner is not obligated to accept the offer of a third party even though the property is listed for sale. However, failure to complete a sale though the fault of the owner does not cancel a commission. Such failure might result because of title defects, refusal of a spouse to sign a deed, fraud, inability to deliver possession within a reasonable time, owner change of mind, buyer-seller agreement to cancel, or owner insisting on terms not included in listing agreement. In all these situations a broker is entitled to a commission, whether or not the owner completes the sale to the aspiring purchaser.

An owner may include a "no closing, no commission" clause on a listing agreement. Such a clause means that unless the transaction results in a conveyance of title, no commission need be paid. Also, courts are increasingly saying that a broker is better able to judge the ability of a buyer to obtain financing than an owner. And therefore, a buyer is not "ready, willing, and able," until adequate financing has been obtained.

In open and exclusive agency listing agreements, the broker must be the "procuring cause" of sale to earn a commission. **Procuring cause of sale** means that the broker's actions resulted in a series of related and continuous events leading to a completed transaction for the principal. The broker does not have to introduce the parties or bring them together personally. If the parties get together and come to an agreement through the broker's efforts, the broker must be recognized. For example, suppose a purchaser comes to the broker's office, is furnished with information, and is sent to a property. If the purchaser then goes directly to the owner and a deal is made between them (without the broker's name being mentioned) the broker has an enforceable claim for a commission. If a broker advertises property and receives and transmits an offer, even if the sale is finally consummated directly between owner and purchaser, the broker is entitled to a commission.

MORE ON COMMISSIONS

Compensation paid a real estate broker by a principal is called a commission or brokerage fee. The amount of the fee is usually proportional to the size of the transaction and is paid only on success in finding a ready, willing, and able buyer, or in bringing about a transaction. Usually no salary or advance fee is paid the broker to bring about a sale. Also, special rules apply in brokerage involving percentage leases and installment land contracts. The purpose of this section is to discuss more specifically the collection of commissions.

General Rules on Earning Commissions

In order to recover commissions, the broker must (1) show an agreement or contract of employment, (2) be the procuring cause of the sale, (3) bring about the deal on the terms of his or her employer, (4) act in good faith, (5) produce an available purchaser who under the general rule is ready and willing to purchase and also legally able to do so, and (6) bring about a completed transaction. We have already seen that double employment or secret sharing in profits violates the requirement that the broker act in good faith. The purchaser obtained by the broker must meet all of the terms as stated by the seller, unless the seller is willing to modify them. The broker must successfully complete the agreement. He or she cannot abandon the negotiations and expect that if the parties, later and in good faith, get together and make a deal, a commission can be claimed. The employer must give the broker a fair chance to complete the transaction once it is commenced. But having done so, the owner may refuse to negtotiate further through the broker and may take up the matter directly or through another broker. Mere introduction of the parties by a broker or commencement of negotiations does not commit the owner to dealing forever with the aspiring purchaser through the broker.

Employment and Commission

Employment contracts were discussed earlier in this chapter. A broker has earned a commission when that for which he or she was employed has been accomplished. If the broker is employed to sell, a sale must result. Payment is not made for making impressions, interesting people in the property, or an unsuccessful effort. The rule, supported by many judicial decisions, is that the broker is entitled to commission when he or she produces a purchaser ready, willing, and able to purchase either on terms offered by the seller or on terms that the seller is willing to accept. If a contract of sale has been signed, the broker has good evidence of a successful effort. A purchaser truly answering the description of ready, willing, and able would without question be the best person to have sign such a contract. The principal, of course, does not have to sell at this point, but, nevertheless, is liable to the broker for a commission. The broker has performed the service for which he or she was employed even though no actual sale resulted. The broker should, however, be prepared to prove that the customer answered the required description.

The principal may make a special arrangement with the broker whereby the broker limits himself or herself to recovery of commission only in the event that a sale is actually consummated by delivery of the deed and payment of the purchase price. Such an arrangement, to be binding upon the broker, must be made prior to the time the commission is earned. If the broker made it after rendering the service for which he or she was employed, it would probably not be enforceable by reason of lack of consideration. Any special agreement of this kind should contain a distinct provision that commission on the sale shall be due and payable only if and when the title passes to the purchaser. It should be remembered that the ordinary obligation of the broker is to bring the principals to an agreement so that there is "a meeting of minds" as to the terms.

Who Pays the Commission?

The employer is liable for the commission in every case. The broker's employer is usually the owner of the property or the owner's representative. In some cases the purchaser employs the broker to obtain the property for him or her. The rule on double employment has already been noted. It is no violation of this rule for a purchaser to employ a broker to procure the property with the understanding that whatever commission the broker is to receive shall be paid by the seller. But in such a case the broker should advise the seller to that effect. Persons not owning the property, or those acting in a representative capacity, are personally liable for commission if they employ the broker to sell the property. It sometimes happens that a purchaser assumes, in the contract, the seller's obligation to pay the broker's commission. This agreement is good between vendor and vendee, but it has no effect upon the right of the broker to recover from his or her employer. Subagents and salespersons look to the broker, as their employer, for their commissions.

Deferring or Reducing a Commission

In almost all states the broker engaged "to sell" has completed the agreement when the parties are brought together and they have agreed on terms. The commission is earned when the work is done. In some cases, in order to make a deal, an owner may modify the terms on condition that the commission be deferred or reduced. If modification of terms can be shown to be a consideration for the promise of deferral or reduction, the broker is bound by it. Another situation that often arises is that the buyer is willing to pay only a small deposit on the contract. In such a case the seller may be unwilling to pay the broker until title closes because (1) the owner wants to be able to retain the entire deposit if the buyer defaults and (2) the broker will work harder to keep the buyer from backing out. Hence the seller, before agreeing to the terms, will often make it a condition that the broker agree to defer payment of his commission until title closing.

Unless there is some agreement by the broker such as that mentioned above, or unless the very listing itself has stated that no commission is to be paid "unless and until title closes," the broker is entitled to a commission when a qualified buyer has been procured. The broker therefore is likely to hasten the signing of a contract, as the best evidence of agreement, and then promptly request the fee or commission.

Commission on an Installment Sale

An installment land contract provides that a purchaser shall pay the seller for a property in installments extending over a period of years. Installment sales are intended to minimize as well as to defer payments of capital gain taxes. Brokers, as a condition of employment, often agree to receive commission payments in proportion to the amounts of principal cash payments made by the purchaser to the seller or his or her agent. Thus when the purchase agreement calls for 25 percent cash at the time of closing and the balance in equal installments over a three-year period with interest on the purchase money mortgage debt at 10 percent on unpaid balances, the broker under the commission agreement may receive only 25 percent of the total commission at the time of closing and the balance in installments over the ensuing three years. The seller should expect that the deferred commission agreement will provide for interest payments on the commission balances at the same rate and in proportion to the amounts received under terms of the installment sales agreement. Deferred commission payments are still the exception rather than the rule, and when agreed upon rarely extend beyond a contract period of five years.

Commissions on Exchanges, Loans, and Leases

The rules that apply to recovery of commission on sales apply also to exchanges. It is customary, however, for both parties to an exchange to pay a commission based on the value or price of their respective properties. A statement in the contract that each party shall pay the broker is sufficient notice to each that the broker is receiving a double commission. The broker has no right to make a double commission secretly. It often happens that two or more brokers are interested in an exchange representing opposite sides, and they sometimes pool their commissions and take an equal division of them.

The broker is usually entitled to commission for procuring a mortgage loan only if the loan is actually made. The commission is also earned if the broker procured an acceptance of the loan and it failed to close through a defect in the title to the property or through a fault of the borrower. The reason for this is that there is rarely an enforceable agreement on the part of the lender to make a loan. The lender may agree to accept it, but this does not constitute a contract. In many jurisdictions the rule is that a broker has earned a commission when a lender who is willing, ready, and able to make the loan on the terms offered has been produced.

The rule on making commissions on leases is similar to that for procuring loans. The broker is not entitled to compensation unless a lease or a complete agreement on its terms is obtained. The broker would, however, be entitled to a commission if the owner tried to impose new and unreasonable terms upon a prospective tenant and the lease was not made for that reason. When a lease has been made, the broker is entitled to full commission, and this is so regardless of the tenant's subsequent default, unless, of course, the broker has made a binding agreement to the contrary.

Percentage leases are sometimes entered into with lessees of business property with a minimum rent required. In addition, an agreed percentage of the lessee's gross income from the business conducted on the leased premises must be paid for rent. In this lease the broker is paid a commission at the time the lease is signed, based on the minimum rental. The broker receives a further commission on the accrual of the additional rental computed on the percentage basis set forth in the lease. Such further commission is usually payable at the end of each year.

SELECTING A BROKER

Experienced investors often buy properties through one broker and sell through another. In buying, these investors know that selecting the proper broker and/or agent may result in a price that is relatively low. They know that some brokers bargain/counsel their principal down rather than negotiating harder with a buyer making a high offer. Hence, a better buy may be made through them. Other brokers work very hard to get the highest possible price for their principals and hence provide a strong advantage to an owner in selling. The higher price may more than pay the broker's commission. Great care should therefore be exercised in selecting a broker. The decision is too important for a sophisticated investor to leave it to chance, as by casually listing with a friend or relative.

Important considerations in selecting a broker are (1) office and agent specialization, (2) office location and procedures, (3) firm's attitude and reputation, (4) a track record as evidenced by satisfied clients. Names of promising firms and agents may be obtained from fellow property owners. Also, names of firms specializing in the types of property of concern may be obtained from classified ads and MLS listing books. Given several firm names, a survey to collect information necessary to making an informed selection is suggested. The first phase of the survey may be made by telephone. Later phases require personal contact.

Much background knowledge is obtained in making a survey. Such knowledge becomes useful in the immediate selection as well as for long-term purposes. Thus, while the investor may have one type of property in mind at the moment, another type may be of concern later on. Also, once a survey has been made, the broker selection process may be short-circuited in later selling situations.

The process of selecting a broker suggested here involves going from the general to the specific, from the firm to the individual. This process is intended to maximize chances of selecting the best broker-agent combination for an investor's needs. A number of ideas from John T. Reed's article on broker selection in the September 1978 *Real Estate Investment Letter* are incorporated in this suggested process. The ideal firm and agent are frist briefly described so that the object of the survey is clear. Then firms and agents are interviewed. Then the selection is made.

An owner should not expect legal advice as part of the services provided by brokerage personnel. The law says that only licensed attorneys may give legal advice. At the same time, an owner is advised to get financial and real estate advice from brokers rather than attorneys. Unfortunately, no law prohibits attorneys from giving financial and real estate advice, two areas in which most attorneys are not qualified. A broker may fill in blanks on a listing agreement or sales contract, however.

Finally, an investor, when buying property, should remember that sales representatives are agents of the owner. This means that brokerage personnel owe care, obedience, accountability, and loyalty to the owner-seller and not to a buyer. The investor, in buying, is a third party.

The Ideal Firm / Agent

The ideal brokerage firm is a leader in its community in the type of property and the location of concern to the investor. Its owner and/or sales manager has a can-do attitude backed up by a strong performance record. It has a reputation for fair dealing while getting the job done. Its office is well located and attractive, and has adequate parking for clients and employees. Its hours of operation are adequate to accommodate all potential buyers of the property type under consideration. For commercial-investment property, weekdays may be adequate. For residences, weekend and evening operating hours are desirable. Finally, the ideal firm has enough lender connections that it can arrange financing even during periods of tight money. The ideal salesperson specializes on the property type and the area of interest to the owner. Also the agent works full time with this property type. The agent is competent as evidenced by professional preparation, designations, and performance. Inexperienced personnel are seldom effective. The agent is also knowledgeable about financing. Satisfied clients provide clear evidence of professional competence, experience, and an ability to get the job done. Ultimately, an investor wants an agent able to do the best possible job in selling the subject property, particularly if it might be a problem property.

Firm Survey

The brokers or sales managers of firms likely to serve an owner's need are best interviewed first. This approach avoids the chance of an investor's getting locked in with a particular agent in a firm before it is clear that that agent will suit the investor's need best. The following questions should be asked:

1. Does your firm specialize in any particular property type? If so, what type?

2. Does your firm specialize in any particular areas or locations? If so, which locations?

3. What properties of _____ type were sold by your firm in the last twelve months?

4. I'd like to contact some of the former owners of properties sold through your office. Would you give me the names of several?

5. How long has your office/firm been in operation?

6. During what hours does your office/firm operate?

7. Are your phones covered during off hours? If so, how?

8. What are your commission rates? Are they open to negotiation?

9. What listings do you currently have in _____ type of properties? What is their age? For how long are they?

10. Is your office affiliated with the Multiple Listing Service?

11. Where does your office rank in its sales of _____ type properties relative to other firms/offices in this area/community? (Firm preferably is among the leaders.)

12. Do you personally own any properties of _____ type? If so, which are they?

13. Does your firm have a continuing arrangement with any financial institutions that might facilitate obtaining loans in times of tight money? If so, what institutions? Whom might I talk with at these institutions about you?

14. Who are your leading salespersons for _____ type properties? Does anyone clearly stand out above the others?

15. Is there anything else about your office/firm that you would like me to know?

This interview may be by telephone and terminated at any time if it is obvious that the firm is not suited to the owner's needs. After several such interviews, it's likely that two or three firms will stand out. Follow-up interviews with former clients, lenders, and agents of these two or three firms then becomes a logical next step.

Agent Survey

At some point during an office survey, it usually becomes apparent that the choice is really among two, three, or four offices. It is at this point that the investor's emphasis shifts to selecting an agent or salesperson. The emphasis should continue to be on specialization and performance. Information from the salesperson may be obtained by asking the following questions, again by phone if desired:

1. Do you specialize in any particular type of property?

2. If so, in what type? In what locations?

3. How long have you specialized in these types of property?

4. What properties of this type have you sold in the past twelve months?

5. What are the names of the former owners of these sold properties. I'd like to contact them for reference purposes.

6. Are you full time in real estate sales?

7. How long have you been licensed?

8. To what real estate organizations do you belong?

9. What real estate courses have you taken in the last four years?

10. Do you have any real estate designations? If so, what are they?

11. What real estate publications do you usually read?

12. Where do you rank in sales in your company? In sales of this type of property in the area?

13. What listings of property do you currently have?

14. Do you own any investment property? If so, of what type?

15. Do you have any other comments or information that I should be aware of about yourself or your firm?

Personal Interviews and Selection

Owner and lender references of firms and agents still under consideration may be checked out. And, visits may be arranged to the firm offices to interview the agents, and possibly the sales managers, personally. Agents best measuring up to the "ideal agent" concept may be invited to the property. Each agent under consideration may then be asked to research the market as to the value of the property, how long a sale is likely to take, and so on. The way the agent responds in this situation is likely to tell a great deal about his or her professional competence.

The responses may be compared as to probable sales value, consistency, and depth of analysis. Sales of comparable properties may be inspected as indicators of value. Conditions of sale may also be indicated by the agent, along with a marketing and advertising program. At some point, an owner-investor should be able to make an informed decision as to which agent-broker combination to select. An exclusive right to sell listing is probably in order at this point, considering that the agent is highly qualified and has undergone considerable review. Of course, specific reservations of possible buyers may be included as a part of the listing.

SUMMARY

The investor-broker relationship becomes that of principal and agent when a property is listed for sale with the broker. The law of agency therefore applies. A principal's main duties in this relationship is to provide accurate information and to compensate the broker upon the completion of a sale. A principal is liable on all agreements or contracts made by the agent within instructions or the authority given the agent. A principal is not liable for contracts made outside the agent's instructions or authority or for torts committed by the agent. An agent's main duties are care, obedience, accountability, loyalty, and giving notice. An agent is not responsible for torts committed by a principal.

Important considerations in the listing agreement from an owner's point of view are (1) the price, (2) reservation of the right to sell, (3) broker compensation, (4) length of listing period, and (5) point at which commission is payable. Owners may make the commission payable at closing or on transfer of title rather than upon the finding of a "ready, willing, and able" buyer. Commissions on installment sales, leases, and exchanges are often deferred in a manner consistent with the unfolding of the transaction.

Informed selection of a broker-agent may benefit an owner by more than the amount of a commission. Some investors buy through one broker and sell through another for greatest advantage. Important criteria in selecting a broker are (1) specialization, (2) office suitability as to location and appearance, (3) attitude and reputation, (4) successful experience. In short, an owner seeks an experienced professional. A selection process of interviewing brokers, agents, and former clients is recommended.

KEY TERMS

Accountability

Agency

Agent

Disclosed principal

Dual/Divided agency

Fiduciary relationship

Independent contractor

Loyalty

Middleman

Principal

Procuring cause of sale

Ready, willing, and able buyer

Third Party

Tort

Undisclosed principal

QUESTIONS FOR REVIEW AND DISCUSSION

1. What is the law of agency? What does a fiduciary relationship mean?

2. What duties does a principal owe an agent?

3. What duties does an agent owe a principal?

4. List and discuss at least four critical issues in listing a property from an owner's point of view.

5. Calculate the commission on a $320,000 sale at 5 percent. At a split rate of 6 percent on the first $100,000 and 4 percent of anything in excess of $100,000.

6. List and discuss from an owner's point of view at least four important considerations in selecting a broker.

7. Outline and discuss the process suggested in this chapter for the selection of a broker.

8. Selecting the right broker may result in a benefit greater than the amount of a commission. Do you agree? Discuss.

9. How might a sophisticated investor best select a broker or agent through whom to buy?

10. Are there any advantages, from an investor's point of view, in entering into a principal-agency relationship with a broker or agent for buying property? (A buyer's agent)

REFERENCES

Corley, Robert N., and William J. Robert. *Principles of Business Law.* 11th ed. Englewood Cliffs, N.J.: Prentice-Hall, 1979. Chapters 29–32 are devoted specifically to agency law. Not real estate oriented, but certainly applicable.

Gaines, Kenneth S. *How to Sell (and Buy) Your Home Without a Broker.* New York: Coward, McCann & Geoghegan, 1975. Pricing, advertising, showing, negotiating, and closing a sale for the do-it-yourselfer.

Henszey, Benjamin N. "Broker's Liability: Cause for Concern." *Real Estate Review,* fall 1978. Guidelines for the broker that are also guidelines for the investor. Shows trends in court cases. Well documented. Easy to understand.

Kratovil, Robert, and Raymond J. Werner. *Real Estate Law.* 7th ed. Englewood Cliffs, N.J.: Prentice-Hall, 1979. Old standby on real estate law. Interesting. To the point. See chapters 10, 11, and 33.

Lee, Jack. "Representing Buyers." *Real Estate Today,* January 1972. Discusses means by which an investor can work through a broker in buying property.

Reed, John T. "How to Select a Real Estate Agent When You Sell Property." *Real Estate Investing Letter,* September 1978. Brief, clearly written, easily understood approach to selecting a broker-agent, written from owner's point of view.

Brokerage Operations and Practices

11

Nature magically suits a man to his fortunes, by
making them the fruit of his character.
Emerson,
Conduct of Life: Fate

Thus far we have discussed the nature of real property as a product, sales contracts, closing statements, title evidence, deeds, public records, and investor-broker relations, including the laws of agency. We have examined all of these topics from the viewpoint of the investor. It now seems appropriate to devote one chapter to a look at brokerage operations and practices from a broker's viewpoint. This overview of brokerage is intended to provide our investor with a basis for judgment in dealing with brokerage personnel.

Brokerage operations require a knowledge of everything covered thus far; successful brokerage operations mean "putting it all together." Professional training and experience are therefore needed for a successful career in real estate brokerage and sales. Brokerage personnel serve as catalysts or lubricants in the purchase and sale transactions. Brokers and sales people make things happen in the world of real estate.

Topics taken up in this overview of brokerage operations are as follows:

1. Fair housing laws
2. The broker's function
3. The listing process
4. Selling the listed property
5. Advertising real estate

199

FAIR HOUSING LAWS

Real estate is a "public interest" commodity and real estate brokerage is a "public service" industry. The average citizen uses the services of a real estate broker only every five or ten years and consequently is usually not knowledgeable about the services of brokers and the treatment to be expected from brokers. The federal government and some state governments, therefore, have laws, known as open or **fair housing laws,** to ensure equality of treatment of the public by brokers and, in some cases, by owners. Title VIII of the Civil Rights Act of 1968 is of greatest concern to brokerage personnel. Owners are subject to both the Civil Rights Act of 1968 and the Civil Rights Act of 1866, as upheld by the United States Supreme Court. *Brokers and owners are expected to know and to comply with these laws.*

The Civil Rights Act of 1968

The Civil Rights Act of 1968 with its amendments requires that real estate agents (brokers) in their business dealings on behalf of principals (clients) must consider their product (real estate) as "open" and for sale, lease, mortgage, and so forth, to all legally competent persons. The 1968 act therefore prohibits discrimination because of an individual's sex, race, color, religion, or national origin in real estate transactions. This act applies particularly to housing transactions. That is, one-family dwellings, apartment buildings, and even vacant residential parcels are covered.

The following acts are specifically prohibited or unlawful if they are based on an individual's sex, race, color, religion, or national origin:

1. Refusal to sell, rent, or negotiate, or otherwise make a dwelling unavailable to any person
2. Using terms, conditions, or privileges of sale or rental to deny or to discriminate against any person
3. Discriminating in the provision of services or facilities against any person
4. Using advertising or oral statements to limit the sale or rental of any dwelling
5. Falsely representing, as a means of discrimination, that a dwelling is not available for inspection, sale, or rental
6. Inducing for profit, or attempting to induce for profit, the sale or rental of housing because of entry, or prospective entry, into a neighborhood of persons of a particular sex, race, color, religion, or national origin

In addition, denying access to, membership in, or participation in any multiple listing service, real estate brokers' organization, or other service or organization relating to the sale or rental of dwellings as a means of discrimination is unlawful.

Almost all of the unlawful acts listed above relate specifically to discrimination in the sale or rental transaction. Steering and blockbusting are also prohibited. **Blockbusting** means using scare tactics (of neighborhood invasion by a minority group) to induce panic sales of houses by owners at prices below market value. The blockbuster buys the homes at reduced prices and later resells them at inflated prices to minority persons. **Steering** is channeling home seekers to specific areas in order to create a blockbusting situation or to maintain the homogeneous makeup (all white, for example) of a neighborhood.

Individual owners are exempt from the 1968 Civil Rights Act if

1. A sale or lease is arranged without the aid of real estate agents
2. A sale or lease is arranged without discriminating advertising
3. Fewer than three houses or fewer than four apartment units (one of which is owner occupied) are owned by the seller.

For enforcement of the law, violations of, and complaints about, the 1968 Civil Rights Act must be reported to the Fair Housing section of any HUD office within 180 days of an infraction.

The Civil Rights Act of 1866

Fair housing had a banner year in 1968. A United States Supreme Court decision in June 1968 upheld the constitutionality of the Civil Rights Act of 1866. Under the 1866 act, owners of property are barred from discriminating in the sale or rental of real or personal property to anyone on racial grounds. This 1968 landmark decision culminated a lawsuit brought by a Mr. Jones against Mayer Company, the builder of a community near St. Louis, Missouri. Mayer Company had refused to sell Jones a home solely because he was black. Jones's attorney centered his case on the almost forgotten Civil Rights Act of 1866. The district court dismissed the complaint and the court of appeals affirmed. The Supreme Court, however, reversed, holding that the statute does cover discrimination on racial grounds and that the statute is constitutional under the Thirteenth Amendment to the Constitution.

In effect, this decision voids the exemptions given individual property owners, under the open housing law of 1968, who sell their homes without assistance from real estate brokers. A person seeking protection under the reaffirmed Civil Rights Act of 1866, however, must bring legal action personally. Support from government agencies is not provided for in the law. Aside from an injunction ordering sale, when a lawsuit is successful, the property owner faces no statutory penalty for damages and no fine under the Civil Rights Act of 1866.

THE BROKER'S FUNCTION IN MARKETING REAL ESTATE

A broker must play many roles to successfully market real estate on a continuing basis. Among the more important of these roles are (1) negotiator and (2) manager.

The Broker as a Negotiator

A broker's primary function is negotiating sales. Listing a property at a reasonable asking price is a greater challenge, in some ways, than selling the property. Both tasks involve sales or negotiating ability. The objective in either case is to persuade another person (or other persons) to make a major decision about property ownership.

Basic qualifications for negotiations include being clean and neat in appearance, being reasonably well dressed, and conducting oneself with self-confidence. Tact, good judgment, and reasonable knowledge of property and laws are equally important qualifications.

Important points that brokerage personnel should keep in mind as they seek to list or to sell property are as follows:

1. Never offer a property without having looked at it personally. An agent cannot sell what he or she does not know. And a person cannot know improved real estate without having inspected it thoroughly.

2. Analyze the property. Never offer anything without having thought it out clearly. Get your thoughts down on paper because almost everyone reads better than he or she listens.

3. Try to know enough about the property to answer almost any question about it.

4. Talk to the prospect in his or her own language. Never talk down to a prospect.

5. Always try to please the prospect. The prospect does not have to deal with a broker or salesperson, and will not if irritated.

6. Remember that a prospect will not buy or sell unless he or she thinks it is advantageous. A prospect must be convinced that there is some good reason to act. Do not try to sell a property unless in your judgment the prospect ought to buy it.

7. Never lie. Do not misstate. Almost all prospects are on the lookout for misstatements. And the salesperson is finished the instant he or she is detected making misstatements.

8. Never argue. A salesperson may be right and still lose the sale.

9. Get the prospect to the property as soon as possible. If there is more than one prospect, for instance, a husband and wife, get them all there. Do not handle them separately.

10. Concentrate on a few sales rather than putting in a little work on many and closing none.

11. Speak with discretion. Give your client ample opportunity to ask questions. Know when to stop; it is possible to talk oneself out of a sale.

12. Use the telephone to save time and steps. But bear in mind that if an issue is critical, a personal interview is better.

13. Never fail to submit an offer. It is not an agent's function to turn down an offer. Ridiculous offers are sometimes accepted. An agent cannot be absolutely sure of what a principal has in mind.

14. Look for business at all times. It is surprising how many listings may be picked up while working on something else.

15. Bear in mind that a prospect is a busy person. Do not waste his or her time.

16. Do not worry about competitors. Salespeople get their share of business if they work intelligently and diligently.

17. Never take anything for granted. Overconfidence has lost many a sale.

The Broker as a Manager

A broker must first organize his or her own time. In addition, a broker must set up and operate an organization for sales personnel and other employees. Attending to all the details involved requires considerable managerial ability. The functions involved include the following:

1. Setting up and maintaining an office
2. Setting up and maintaining an organization
3. Seeing that decisions are made and that details are attended to at appropriate times

THE REAL ESTATE OFFICE. Real estate offices are of many kinds and sizes. A few specialize in distinct kinds of work. Almost all of them transact all kinds of real estate business. Larger, well-rounded offices, with separate departments, each comprised of an executive and various subordinates, are found in larger cities. Some of the larger firms provide several, or all, of the following functions:

1. Appraising
2. Brokerage (property, mortgage, and exchange)
3. Counseling
4. Development and construction
5. Insurance
6. Management and leasing

THE REAL ESTATE ORGANIZATION. Each department has its own functions, but all are basically engaged in selling ownership, equity, or space. The small office consists of the "chief" and one or more sales personnel. The large office expands this organization. Naturally, the ambition of nearly every salesperson is to work up to an executive position and possibly to branch out into the operation of his or her own office. The broker-manager must obtain business, retain and train personnel, and maintain the organization.

FOLLOWING THROUGH. The broker is the originator or source of drive in almost every organization. Sales and other office personnel attend to details, but the ultimate responsibility for the details falls back on the broker. The broker, through his or her organizational ability, must see that the details are taken care of for each transaction of the business. The broker's skill and persistence in following through on matters of listing, finance, insurance, accounting, property management, and closings provide the key to customer satisfaction and to success.

THE LISTING PROCESS

Listing is the general term for the process that real estate brokers go through to obtain authority to sell a piece of property. Property listings are necessary to a brokerage operation. No one can sell what he or she does not have. Kinds of listing agreements are (1) open, (2) exclusive agency, (3) exclusive right to sell, (4) multiple, and (5) net, as discussed previously.

The three following basic steps must be satisfied for a successful and continuing brokerage program:

1. Obtaining the listing
2. Servicing the listing
3. Selling the listing

The first two are discussed in this section. The third is discussed in the next section of this chapter.

Listings may be secured by brokers and sales personnel from many sources. The most usual sources are (1) repeat business or referrals from satisfied customers; (2) friends and acquaintances, for example, fellow members of clubs and organizations; (3) "for sale by owner" leads; (4) expiring listings of competing brokers, noted through a multiple listing pool; (5) leads based on births, deaths, marriages, promotions, or corporate transfers picked up from newspapers; (6) solicited office drop-ins of owners desiring to sell; and (7) **canvassing,** or contacting property owners by telephone or in person without a prior appointment. Leads to a possible listing opportunity must be followed up promptly. In making an effort to list a property, a broker or salesperson should be clean and neat in appearance and professional in attitude in order to realize the greatest chance of success.

Obtaining the Listing

An owner must make at least the following four decisions in listing a property for sale:

1. The advantages of listing (hiring a broker) are worth the brokerage fee or commission to be paid upon sale of the property.

2. The advantages of listing with one particular broker (your firm) are greater than the advantages of listing with any other broker.

3. Setting the listing price.

4. The length of time to be allowed the broker to find a buyer.

ADVANTAGES OF LISTING. To an owner the main advantages of listing a property for sale are (1) obtaining an objective negotiator, (2) professional assistance and service, (3) technical knowledge, and (4) broker cooperation.

A broker or a sales agent can negotiate the sale without personal involvement. In any sale, and particularly in the sale of a home, the seller has strong feelings about the property and its worth. These feelings make direct negotiations with a buyer very difficult. In addition, very few people are skilled negotiators. Many owners try to sell their own homes and fail because they are unable to negotiate effectively with potential buyers. Personal selling efforts of owners often create a deep-rooted, negative feeling in the prospect. Eventually these owners give up and list their properties with a real estate broker.

Owners also recognize that a broker can render professional assistance and service in the sale of properties. Professional assistance includes several items. One is advice on preparing the property to get a higher price and quicker sale. Another is advertising. Items of service include screening out unqualified prospects, showing the property to its best advantage, and always being present when a prospect visits the listed property. Brokerage service also includes looking after the property if the owner or owners move to another community.

Brokerage personnel generally have better technical knowledge than owners do. Brokers know the real estate market better. They also know financing better. A broker's knowledge of sources of mortgage money is particularly useful to sellers.

Another major reason that owners engage brokers to sell properties is that there is greater market exposure through broker cooperation. Increasing the number of brokers, and people, who know about the property increases the likely sale price and shortens the time required for sale. Brokers who belong to multiple listing services offer an especially strong advantage to owners.

SPECIFIC BROKER ADVANTAGES. Owners must decide whether or not the advantages of listing with one specific broker outweigh the advantages of listing with other brokers. The advantages of listing with a specific broker may be greater knowledge, better service, or more effective promotion and sales ability. A broker's reputation for professional, competent handling of listings helps greatly in obtaining listings. The broker's, or sales agent's, task in obtaining a listing is to convince the owner that the broker's firm can do a better job of selling the property than anyone else can.

THE LISTING PRICE. It is critical that a property be listed at a price not greatly in excess of its market value. Every owner wants to sell his or her property for as much as possible. At the same time, almost all owners recognize that they are limited by market competition as to how much they will actually realize from their property. Very few owners know the market value of their properties. And, usually, if they do have any value in mind, it is well above the property's actual value. Prudent brokers require that a property be listed at a price reasonably close to its market value and will not spend the time and effort promoting a property that is listed at too high a price.

A broker should have a fair idea of what a property will sell for when the listing is originally obtained. The most probable selling price of a property is its market value. The principles of market-value appraising are explained in chapter 22. Professional brokerage people use these principles to advise owners on a reasonable listing price for their properties. These brokers do not accept the owner's statement, "Let's list at my price, and I can always come down." The broker should make a strong effort to persuade the owner to list at a price at which a sale can be made. "A property well listed is half sold." Calculations of commission amounts and net sale prices to owners are discussed in an earlier chapter.

THE LISTING TERM. A listing agreement may be written to run from one day to one year or more. Brokers prefer that a house listing run for a minimum of three or four months to allow time for a reasonable promotion and sales effort. Usually, the larger and the more valuable the property, the longer the desired listing time is. Some multiple listing boards have minimum listing periods.

OBTAIN ACCURATE LISTING INFORMATION. All information likely to help sell a property should be obtained when the property is listed. Information taken at time of listing must be accurate and complete. The listing contact is often the first contact with an owner. The broker or salesperson should make a good impression. Thorough inspection and accurate measurement of a property at time of listing are excellent ways to impress an owner of professional competence.

Specific information, as appropriate, should be recorded in listing a property. The listing form usually provides space for specific items, like the following:

1. Lot dimensions (frontage and depth) and area
2. Building dimensions and area or volume
3. Number and sizes of rooms
4. Kind of construction
5. Age and condition of structures
6. Equipment data (heat, water, electricity, etc.)
7. Financing offered by owner
8. Neighborhood data
9. Zoning (very important for vacant land)
10. Tax data

Additional items should be noted if they pertain directly to the sale of the property.

Servicing the Listing

Owners select brokers more on the basis of their sales results and of service offered than for any other reason. A reputation for sales and service performance must be earned.

Clear communication at the following times greatly helps to establish a reputation for service.

1. *Initial communication.* Upon taking a listing, a broker should advise the owner-seller specifically *what* services are to be provided, *who* will provide each service, and *why* the services are necessary.

2. *Continuing communication.* Owner-sellers should be advised as to what services are rendered and where results are to be expected. Personal contact (setting up showings of the listed property and explaining the results of a showing) are particularly important.

3. *Periodic review and recommendation.* A listed property that does not sell in a reasonable time requires a discussion between the owner and the broker. The history of the listing and selling prices of comparable properties or houses should be reviewed. The broker or sales agent should have recommendations in mind before the review. This review often takes place just before the expiration of the listing. If initial and continuing communications have been clear, and if all services have been performed, the owner should be receptive to extending the listing and following other suggestions. Both the owner and the broker are interested in getting the best price and terms as quickly as possible.

SELLING THE LISTED PROPERTY

Successful selling of real estate involves three essential steps: (1) prospecting, (2) presenting and negotiating, and (3) closing. The broker or sales agent must sell himself or herself and the property throughout the process.

Prospecting

The broker's task is to sell properties once they have been listed. A sale cannot be made until someone is located who might be interested in the property. Locating potential buyers is called prospecting.

Several methods are used to locate prospects. The most widely used method is by advertising the property. Advertising is so important to locating prospects that the last major section of this chapter is devoted to the classes, methods, and principles of advertising. The main purpose of specific advertising of properties is to locate potential buyers for the properties.

Other methods of locating prospects include the following:

1. Using a file of properties wanted
2. Contacting tenants in the property offered for sale
3. Personal contacts

A well-run brokerage office maintains a file of properties wanted in addition to the listings of properties for sale. Every time an inquiry comes in for property that the office cannot supply, a memorandum of that fact and the details of the location, kind, and so on, of the property desired should be noted. Whenever a listing of property for sale comes into the office, a check can at once be made against the property-wanted file, and possibly a sale may be made in a short time.

A most likely source of prospects for any property is the tenants in a building. They usually do not want to move, and there is always the chance that the new owner may wish to occupy their unit. This is particularly true of business property. The broker or salesperson should therefore interview the tenant or tenants at once. If the tenant does not want to buy, the other storekeepers on the street should be canvassed. One of them may be persuaded to stop paying rent and to become an owner.

Personal contacts are always important and helpful. Friends who know that a broker is capable are likely to refer prospects to him or her. The same is true of old customers if they know that a broker is reliable and industrious. Thus, brokers and sales agents are wise to verbally promote their listings among friends and old customers.

Presenting and Negotiating

Prospecting leads to negotiations. Negotiations begin once the initial contact has been made. The contact may be the result of an advertisement and come in the way of a telephone call or an office drop-in.

A prospect must be carefully studied to determine whether he or she is serious or is merely a "looker." An experienced salesperson can usually determine whether the prospect is serious or not early in the interview. Considerations such as urgency to move, newness to the community, or a recent birth in a family indicate a serious intent. Time should not be wasted on a looker.

The broker must be a keen student of human nature. The first contact is usually brief; in many instances the first impressions and analysis must be made in a few minutes. An older and more experienced broker sometimes seems to have a sixth sense. In reality, it is merely the ability to judge the prospect quickly and with a minimum of error.

Some prospects harbor an inner fear of real estate brokers and their sales associates. This fear is an internal defense against the power of persuasion or salesmanship that may lead the prospect to a premature decision or a disadvantageous position in the negotiations. This fear is generally no longer warranted, or justified, because of prevailing real estate practices. Almost all established brokers are conscious of the benefits that arise from "satisfied" customers and community good will. Thus, efforts are made not to *sell* the customer but to *guide* him or her in the purchase of what is needed and affordable. The broker is foolish to allow a customer to contract to purchase a home beyond the customer's means. It only results in the customer's failing to qualify for a mortgage loan. Or if the customer does get title, he or she later becomes unable to carry the property and loses it, creating ill will. A considerate philosophy of negotiating is beneficially reflected in the increasing number of services that the broker is called upon to render for the property owner. Negotiating, when carried forth in a spirit of *service,* not only wins friends but aids in building a professional reputation that is essential to sound business growth and continued success for the broker.

Having classified the prospect, the salesperson next shows the property or properties. The initial presentation is to a large extent oral, but it must always be borne in mind that most people learn more by seeing than by hearing. Ordinarily, the sales agent should tell his or her story simply and truthfully, never dressing up the truth and never exaggerating.

The sales representative should use the prospect's language. Few prospects are familiar with real estate terms and some may be buying for the first time. The prospect should be taken out to the property as soon as possible. The salesperson should always make it a point to be familiar with a house before showing it to anyone. Thorough knowledge of the property inspires confidence in the prospect.

Sales personnel may legally engage in "puffing," or building up a property. **Puffing** is making positive statements and opinions about a property without misrepresenting facts and without an intent to deceive. The intent, of course, is to induce a purchase. Misstating facts is misrepresentation and the basis of fraud. Also, making superficial or inaccurate statements may cost the sale and injure the reputation of the real estate firm. A salesperson should go into detail, describing structural or property site weaknesses or faults in their true perspective. Good points, especially those that fit the prospect's needs or wants, should be stressed, with similar honesty.

It is usually helpful to have something in writing to show the prospective buyer. This often takes the form of a property brief. The property brief may be simple or complicated. If the subject of the transaction is an apartment house or office building, the brief will take the form of a pamphlet of several pages, including a description of the property, diagrams of the lot and the building, floor plans, elevations, information on nearness of mass transit, and a detailed financial setup of the operating expenses and income. If it is a home, the property brief should give a diagram of the lot and of the house, photographs of the building, and a financial statement showing the operating expenses reduced to an average monthly carrying charge. Almost all realty boards have a special form for this purpose. Placing the brief in the hands of the prospect during the interview gives him or her something to look at that will probably be absorbed more readily than the sales associate's words. In addition, the prospect can take the property brief with him or her to study before making a decision.

The temperament of the prospect requires that the salesperson fit the general scope of the presentation to the prospect. In addition, the sales associate should find out various facts about the prospect's business as early as possible in the negotiations; for example, approximate family income, marital status, number and ages of children, if any, interests outside his or her business, where and how he or she has previously lived, and church and club connections, if any. Obviously, the sales associate who has these facts in mind can more readily appeal to the prospect's situation. For example, if there are any children, he or she could say, "This is a safe, healthy place in which to bring up children," adding, if the children are of school age and the prospect is in the average income group, "The public schools are convenient and very good, and the trip to and from schools is safe."

Closing

Closing is the stage in the negotiations at which the prospect is finally persuaded to purchase a property; that is, when negotiations are brought to a conclusion. Much has been written on this subject, but as far as the salesperson is concerned, there are no set rules. Experience will teach him or her when to bring the matter to a head.

Rarely does the psychological moment to close arrive at the first interview. The deal may be closed while the salesperson and the prospect are standing in the living room of the home that the prospect is about to buy. More often, however, there are several interviews, but there comes a time when the sales agent must frankly and tactfully bring the prospect to a decision. The trend of negotiations will usually indicate when the time is ripe.

The sales agent can learn to judge when to try to close by noting when the prospect has made the following key buying determinations: (1) recognition of the *need* for a new dwelling unit; (2) recognition of the house, condominium, or cooperative unit to *fill the need;* (3) acceptance, based on analysis, that the *price* is manageable; and (4) recognition that the *time to decide* is now. The sales agent, in continuing conversation with the prospect, must determine when the first three decisions have been made. When they have been made, then the sales agent's task is to persuade the prospect to make an offer to purchase the property.

ADVERTISING REAL ESTATE

Real estate transactions are usually brought about by the combination of direct personal sales effort, and **advertising.** Occasionally, a sales representative carries through an entire transaction without aid, but even here advertising almost always preceded the effort. Advertising is therefore an essential element to successful real estate brokerage operations.

Important aspects of real estate advertising are taken up here as follows:

1. Classes of advertising
2. Advertising media
3. Advertising principles
4. Advertising agencies

Classes of Advertising

Real estate advertising falls into three general classes: (1) general or name, (2) institutional, and (3) specific. These are discussed as follows:

NAME ADVERTISING. General or **name advertising** places the broker's name and business before the public; the purpose is to establish identity and location in the minds of potential clients or customers. When these people need real estate services, they are likely to recall the broker who advertised. Name advertising is not intended to sell or lease a specific piece of property or to obtain a mortgage loan on a certain house.

Name advertising very often takes the form of "professional cards" in various places in newspapers. Occasionally, general advertising is used to indicate some specific field or kind of real estate in which the dealer is engaged. Examples would be a small box advertisement reading "JOHN JONES, real estate, factory sites," or "HELEN SMITH, real estate mortgage financing." Advertisements like these often appear in real estate trade journals. Their function is largely to solicit cooperation with other brokers. Good examples are the advertisements of lists of brokers and appraisers appearing in nationally known real estate magazines. It is through these ads that brokers in one area seek out alert brokers in another area when one of their prospects desires to reside there or to purchase property in that community for investment purposes.

INSTITUTIONAL ADVERTISING. Advertising to create good will and confidence in real estate organizations or groups is known as **institutional advertising.** Such advertising is carried out by the National Association of Realtors,® by local real estate boards, or by other groups seeking to inspire interest in a district, city, or mode of real estate transaction and to direct business to member firms. It seems reasonable to assume that the general public has greater confidence in an individual or firm governed by, and holding to, a code of ethics and business rules designed to protect its clients.

SPECIFIC ADVERTISING. **Specific advertising** pertains to the promotion of a particular property or article. It may take the form of a display or a classified ad. A publicity release is another means for a firm to get such information published. In any event, the purpose of such an ad or release, whether large or small, no matter where placed or how arranged, is to sell a specific piece of real estate, to secure a mortgage loan on a definite property, or to lease a particular location. The greatest individual effort is expended in direct or specific advertising. It is in this form of advertising and in news releases that the enterprising brokerage firm can use its ingenuity and creative ability to draw attention to the offering of a specific good or service.

Advertising Media

A survey to determine the effectiveness of the various methods of advertising and promotions that motivate home buyers was conducted by the Association of Newspaper Classified Advertising Managers and covered ten cities in all parts of the country. This survey disclosed the following:

1. Seventy-three percent of home buyers were motivated by newspaper advertisements.

2. Over 51 percent initially consulted real estate brokers.
3. Eight percent found the house through friends and neighbors.
4. Nine percent were motivated by open house signs, billboards, and other advertising sources.

Brokerage activities have already been discussed. The various classes of advertising media obviously merit attention by anyone engaged in real estate brokerage and sales work.

The general field of advertising media may be divided into the following four general classes, which are taken up in the order indicated:

1. Newspapers
2. Billboards, signs, and posters, mainly outdoor
3. Direct mail, including pamphlets and circular letters
4. Miscellaneous

NEWSPAPERS. The bulk of real estate advertising undoubtedly is done in newspapers. Newspapers get the message to the public quickly. Their life is short, often only a few hours. Although it is true that a newspaper advertisement ordinarily lives less than a day, it sometimes happens that a month or more after a builder has advertised a certain style of house that he or she is building, prospects come into the office with a neat little bundle of advertising that they have been clipping for a month or more. Having finally decided on the style of house they want, the prospects have come to this particular builder because the plan, layout, and location best suit their needs.

Two kinds of advertisements are commonly used in newspapers: display and classified. In display advertising the real estate broker prepares copy for a specific property and runs it in the real estate section for a day or two. The broker buys as much space as desirable and lays out the advertisement with the proper white space, capitals, headline, and argument. Display advertising is expensive because it usually involves a large amount of space. One of the greatest difficulties with this form of advertising is to know the amount of space to use. Brokers occasionally persuade owners to pay for the advertising, but generally the broker advertises on his or her own responsibility. The broker must therefore use skill, wisdom, and experience in wording the display advertising and in allowing the correct amount of space.

The second kind of newspaper advertising, the classified ad, is used extensively for the sale of real estate. It is fairly inexpensive because it takes up little space. Although it is not as attractive as display advertising, it nevertheless has proved to be a good means of reaching a specific person who is seeking a specific kind of property. It is said that a person who reads the classified ads is already half sold because he or she is scanning the market to fill a need.

As for publicity releases, they are an ideal way for the real estate broker to keep in the public's eye. He or she should, even in the smallest community, build a reputation for "knowing real estate." To this end, whenever possible, the broker can write articles and try to have them published in newspapers. In the larger communities the papers that carry real estate sections always want articles of general interest around which to group their real estate advertisements. These articles, though often written up as interviews, in nine cases out of ten are prepared by real estate operators for the purpose of drawing attention to themselves and to some particular venture in which they are engaged. Although they give the impression of being general news stories dealing with real estate, nevertheless their particular virtue is that they give the broker the appearance of being an expert. In addition, they draw the public's attention to the particular line of real estate activity in which the broker-author is interested.

BILLBOARDS, SIGNS, AND POSTERS. Billboard advertising is expensive but lasting. It seldom pays to advertise a single piece of property unless the property is a large building or tract. Billboards are used mainly for institutional and name advertising. Billboards are often found on the main highways leading into a community, so that visitors who may be interested in purchasing or leasing in the town may be led or enticed to a broker's office.

Posters and signs in railroad stations and bus terminals are less expensive outdoor advertising. These are often used because of their small expense and because the many people who are forced to wait for their trains and buses almost unconsciously read everything in sight. Since these signs are likely to become soiled, the broker should be careful to see that signs are replaced periodically. The signs must be clean in order to avoid giving the reader the impression that the property itself is unattractive and that the broker is slipshod.

On-site signs advertising property for sale or to let are very widely used. They are simple and effective. They need not tell much of a story since they are placed on the property to which they refer. For instance, a "for sale" sign in the middle of a vacant lot need not tell anything about the lot; the lot is there, in plain sight. Such a sign does not even give the dimensions of the lot unless the lot varies from the normal size. A "to let" sign in a store window usually need not tell anything about the store because passersby, if interested, can stop, look through the window, and decide then and there whether or not they are interested. The sign need only indicate whether the property is for sale or for rent and simply give the broker's name, address, and telephone number. Sometimes additional information may be given on a sign, for example, "zoned for duplex" on a lot or "swimming pool" for an apartment building.

Almost all local and suburban transits carry advertising cards and posters. The great bulk of these cards and posters advertise products that may be used anywhere. Very little space is devoted to real estate. A certain amount of real estate advertising, however, can be very satisfactorily placed in these vehicles, because many of the riders are commuters and the real estate that may appeal to them will be sales of homes or rental property.

DIRECT MAIL. A great deal of real estate selling is done through circular letters. Since this is a very important aspect of the business, care should be taken to observe a number of points. The first point involves the careful selection of a prospect list. Although there are many companies throughout the country that sell lists of almost every kind of prospect, these lists are of little use in the real estate business. The most satisfactory lists the broker can use are those he or she prepares personally. Names may be obtained from various sources. Telephone directories will give a general list. Also available are lists of the members of churches, clubs, and civic associations, of civil service employees, and of others. These, of course, should be used with selective care and with due regard to the kind of property to be sold.

The second point involves the material to be sent out. In cities in which people receive a great deal of mail, such material gets scant attention, and therefore the keynote of direct mail is, "Make it short." The broker cannot do much more than stir interest, get a reply, and then finish the work through sales associates.

Maps and pamphlets are ordinarily used when a number of properties are to be sold, for example, lots or homes in a development. Here the seller can afford to include the cost of the maps and pamphlets in the advertising budget. The maps must be attractively prepared, and the pamphlet must be well written and on paper of good quality. The first impression should not be one of cheapness, whether because of a poor map, a mediocre pamphlet, or a shoddily dressed salesman. It is always important to have the map show not only the development itself but also the main highways leading to it. Otherwise, the average buyer who looks at the map does not know just where the property is situated.

MISCELLANEOUS MEDIA. Stationery can be very useful in creating a good impression, even though business stationery is not usually thought of in an advertising sense. Writing paper should always be neat. The printed matter should be readable and reasonably conservative in its makeup. Avoid putting too much in the letterhead. For example, if the office handles insurance, it would probably be better to list only two or three kinds than to have a long list of twenty-five or thirty kinds of insurance in the margin of the letterhead. The symbol used by the real estate broker should always be a part of the letterhead.

Business cards should attract attention. If possible, every salesperson should have his or her own business card. Nothing hurts a sales associate so much as to have to present a business card that gives the impression the associate is either a new employee or on trial because his or her name is hand printed in ink or pencil on an engraved card or does not even appear on the card; that is, the business card presented is only engraved with the name, address, and telephone number of the employing broker.

Motion picture advertising is used very little in real estate, but when it is used, it is almost always as a selling stimulus. Motion picture theaters have very little data on which to estimate the response to real estate advertising; consequently, their charges are more or less a matter of guess and may be entirely too high. In addition, there are very likely only a few people in the audience who are interested in the advertisement. Most of the audience would feel that it is an intrusion on time for which they have paid; they came to see a movie, not advertising. If motion picture advertising is used at all, it must be very short. If possible, it should not only show the property, but it should also be artistically appealing.

Radio is still an uncertain medium for advertising as far as specific real estate is concerned. Time costs are very high compared with space costs in other forms of advertising. The message must be short, and since it is heard rather than seen, it does not make nearly so great an impression as a newspaper ad, a pamphlet, or a circular. Radio is useful in connection with the sale of a large number of buildings or lots.

Television, although a more expensive medium of advertising than radio, has been successfully used by real estate firms, particularly in large urban centers. Television broadcasts provide the opportunity to bring a model house directly into the homes of the television audience. Showing the many features of a new house is considerably more effective than describing them by spoken or written words. A number of real estate men now sponsor weekly television shows to bring to their viewers the "buy of the week" coupled with an informative discussion of why this home and others in similar settings are considered sound investments. When these television programs are sponsored and narrated by sales personnel known to the viewers, the advertising effects are doubly effective. They are known to have produced gratifying commercial results, in fact.

Advertising Principles

Advertising is absorbed primarily through the eye. Newspapers, billboards, signs, window displays, and direct mail circulars must all produce a reaction when they are seen. Television and movie advertising are absorbed through the ear as well, and of course radio ads have to catch the listener's ears. In either case, the intended effects of advertising are (1) attention, (2) interest, (3) desire, and (4) action. The four effects are coded AIDA.

The first intended effect is to catch the eye or to get attention. No matter how good the property offered may be, no matter how much care may have been taken in preparing the copy, no matter how important the message, unless the eye of the prospect is caught, the advertising is ineffective.

Second, the advertisement must arouse interest. The readers' emotions or curiosity must be stimulated enough so that the entire message is read. The copy, letter, or other advertising vehicle must be interesting and human.

Third, the advertisement must arouse desire. The desire for the property or service must be strong enough to cause the reader to take the fourth step, action. Action, by way of actual contact between the prospect and a sales representative of the broker, is the goal of successful advertising. Once contact has been brought about, sales ability must take over where advertising left off.

Successful advertising depends on two elements: (1) proper appeals and (2) compliance with established rules or guidelines.

ADVERTISING APPEALS. An advertisement must be aimed at some human instinct or personal interest. Every property has some feature that can be made the basis of an appeal to one of these motives. Common appeals in real estate advertising may be made to any one or more of the following:

1. Pride of ownership
2. Security and protection

3. Saving impulse
4. Parental appeal
5. Prestige
6. Comfort instinct
7. Investment and speculation

In stressing "pride of ownership," appeal is made to buyers who yearn for the satisfaction of owning a home or who would like to live among the more successful citizens of the community. These ads should stress the spaciousness of the rooms, the quality of the neighborhood, the beauty of the landscaped grounds, and the joy of the owner when showing this home to friends and visitors.

Security and protection of property ownership are also strong buying motives. People past middle age look upon home ownership as a way to build a nest egg for retirement. A well-located house may give its owner a feeling that he or she will be protected from street crime; a brick residence with heavy doors may provide a feeling of safety from fire and from violent crimes.

Groups of buyers who are frugal minded, and to whom the "saving impulse" appeals, can be successfully reached by pointing out prevailing low carrying charges (payable like rent) that lead to ownership of a home and not to a bundle of rent receipts. Mortgage debt-service payments for principal, interest, taxes, and insurance are usually less than rental payments would be for a given dwelling unit. The saving impulse is instinctive in almost everyone. This appeal, if honestly presented, will not only produce effective sales but will also result in long-term benefits through increased customer good will, upon which business success depends.

Attention, too, can be called to the windfall capital gains that accrue to real estate owners during years of abnormal monetary inflation. A home, like a ship upon the seas, will ride the rising crest of inflationary levels of prices and maintain its relative purchasing power as compared with other capital goods and services. This fact was driven home by one active developer who effectively advertised that residences built by his corporation "do not depreciate." To back up this claim, his corporation offered to buy back any home purchased by an occupant and owned for a period of five years or more at the full price paid at the time of acquisition. With inflation causing an average loss of 7 percent per year during the 1970–1974 period, it is no wonder that the builder reported "no takers" to his offer. Nevertheless, this method of advertising attracted attention and proved promotionally effective.

Use of "parental appeal" can be successfully made to young married couples and, of course, to families with school-age children who keep uppermost in mind the healthy family life and sound growth of their youngsters. Since, under current purchase practices, a home can be acquired on the "pay-as-you-live" plan, parental appeal is one of the strongest incentives that stimulate home buying. This appeal can be convincingly used by stressing the following: Here is a better place in which to bring up children; a home conducive to health and happiness for all the family; a place where happy childhood memories are instilled; a setting where good schools, good neighbors, and a clean and healthy environment contribute to sound character development and strong family ties.

In advertising costlier homes and those in finer settings, effective use can be made of the "prestige" appeal. Who doesn't dream of a country home or a city home in a garden setting? Well-to-do prospects often seek a home in an atmosphere of social elegance or near the homes of the town's outstanding personalities. In developing this appeal, reference should be made to fine architectural style, beautifully landscaped gardens, spacious living quarters, fireplaces in bedrooms and sitting rooms, and surrounding homes occupied by leading citizens.

A home as a place of rest and comfort, away from the busy everyday world, is gaining increasing appeal. Those who seek "comfort" in home life can be convincingly reached by highlighting such selling points as enjoyable and restful living in a quiet atmosphere; nearness to transportation and other public and recreational conveniences; outdoor living; labor- and time-saving devices, playrooms, large living porches, guest room, extra bathrooms; and adequate storage and utility facilities.

For properties other than homes, the "investment" interests of the buyer generally should be stressed. Investment appeal can be successfully developed by presenting factual data on the safety of investment, attractiveness of rate or amount of return, ease of ownership and managerial operation, adequacy of demand for space facilities, effect of growth of community on appreciation of the investment, adequacy of utility facilities, especially rail, water, and highway transportation, and available opportunities for financing and income employment. When the investment opportunity offers special incentives for buyers of vision and quick action, the appeal should be broadened to attract buyers who are motivated by speculative capital rather than investment-income gains.

ADVERTISING GUIDELINES. Experience with real estate advertising has led to the recognition of a number of truisms or rules that apply to many advertising media.

Symbols used as trademarks play an important role in attracting the reader's attention; every real estate man is urged to make use of this means of identification. Symbols, however, must be designed with care. A flashy symbol, or one of colorful and unusual design, may attract attention but fail to associate the product or services offered with a *specific* real estate office. It is for this reason that symbols that partially incorporate a broker's name have proved so successful. Once a symbol or trademark has been adopted, it should be used on letterheads and all advertising copy in order to popularize the broker's name and services. The symbol should arouse and strengthen the power of suggestion that motivates a prospect to select that particular broker as agent in the real estate transaction. Many brokers use slogans in addition to or as a substitute for symbols. Some slogans have proven advantageous, but if they are trite or juvenile, the broker is advised not to use them.

Always frame an advertisement from the buyer's point of view. You know all the reasons that the seller wants to sell, but they are not what make a buyer show an interest. Before you sit down to prepare any copy, decide what kind of person would want to buy the property and write your message to him or her.

Every advertisement should be honest. This sounds axiomatic, but it is important. Often an advertisement that almost condemns the property does more to sell it than an advertisement written in glowing terms. Many real estate men have discovered this, and specimens of such advertising are reproduced from time to time in different real estate magazines.

To attract the reader's eye, every advertisement should display a good headline that caters to the prospect's wants or needs. Headlines such as "Why pay rent if you can own?" or "Own a home, not rent receipts" appeal to every tenant interested in purchasing a home. Since rent money may, in fact, be applied toward the purchase of a home, headlines could call attention to this in a number of ways, each intended to keep the desire for home ownership uppermost in the minds of interested prospects.

To attract and interest the reader, an advertisement should be simple and easy to read. The wording of the advertisement should be carefully chosen and, whenever possible, augmented by photographs or sketches that tell a story. No essential facts should be omitted. The wants or needs of the reader must be kept in mind and the phraseology used should be suited to the level of thinking of the reader. Of course, every advertisement should be written for the purpose of getting the reader to contact a sales agent or the broker.

Advertising Agencies

Many real estate firms engage advertising agencies to handle their account. The use of agencies is successful in connection with large campaigns, such as a development or an auction of valuable properties. Ordinarily, however, the expense is far too great for the average parcel of real estate.

SUMMARY

Real estate is a "public interest" commodity, which makes real estate brokerage a "public service" industry. Therefore, real estate brokerage is subject to federal fair housing laws, notably the Civil Rights Act of 1968. The 1968 act prohibits discrimination in housing because of an individual's sex, race, color, religion, or national origin. The 1866 Civil Rights Act extends nondiscrimination in housing to owners.

Two important roles of a broker in real estate marketing are as a negotiator and a manager. A broker must organize and manage sales personnel as well as himself or herself. Negotiating a transaction usually means getting a buyer and a seller to agree to terms.

Brokerage involves both listing and selling properties. Listing involves getting an owner to grant authority to sell a property and later keeping the owner informed on selling efforts. The sales process involves prospecting or locating potential buyers, presenting and negotiating, and closing. Closing is persuading a prospect to make an offer to purchase the listed property.

Advertising is critical to successful brokerage operations. Three classes of advertising are (1) name, (2) institutional, and (3) specific. The main advertising media are (1) newspapers, (2) billboards and signs, and (3) direct mail. Advertising appeals are usually made to motives of (1) pride of ownership, (2) security and protection, (3) parental satisfaction, and (4) investment or gain.

trade journals

KEY TERMS

Advertising
AIDA
Blockbusting
Canvassing
Closing
Fair housing laws

Institutional advertising
Name advertising
Puffing
Specific advertising
Steering

QUESTIONS FOR REVIEW AND DISCUSSION

1. Explain the effect of the 1968 Civil Rights Act on real estate brokerage operations.

2. Explain the broker's function as a manager and as a negotiator.

3. Identify at least three key decisions an owner must make in listing a property.

4. Explain the real estate sales process from the viewpoint of a salesperson.

5. What are the three main advertising media used by brokers? In what ways are they used most effectively?

6. What steps or decisions must be made in making a purchase?

7. What is AIDA?

8. Name and explain at least four motives for buying real estate.

9. An owner wants to list a service station with a broker for $330,000, which is about $80,000 more than its market value. Should the broker accept the listing? If not, how might the broker best proceed? What about an interested buyer?

10. What advantages does selling through a broker offer an owner? What disadvantages? Should an owner always sell through a broker?

REFERENCES

Burch, Charles G. "Why Merrill Lynch Wants to Sell You a House." *Fortune,* January 29, 1979. An overview of efforts by America's largest securities broker to break into residential real estate brokerage. Perhaps a preview of things to come.

McMahan, John. "The Future of the Real Estate Industry: New Directions and New Roles." *Real Estate Review,* summer 1977. Another view of things to come in the industry; must reading for the beginner and the veteran.

Miller, Norman G. "The Changing Structure of Residential Brokerage." *Real Estate Review,* fall 1978. A look into the future, when economies of scale and operating efficiency are likely to be increasingly important. The small broker will have to be flexible to coexist with giant conglomerates. Very readable and intriguing.

Realtors National Marketing Institute. *Real Estate Office Management: People, Functions, Systems.* Chicago: RNMI, 1975. An organizational manual for the broker.

Messner, Stephen D.; Irving Schreiber; and Victor L. Lyon. *Marketing Investment Real Estate: Finance Taxation Techniques.* Chicago: Realtors National Marketing Institute, 1975. A technical approach to a total investment program suited to a client's goals. Aimed primarily at the commercial-investment broker. Includes case problems of brokerage applications of principles.

Woodward, Lynn N. "A Cause for Brokerage Failure." *Real Estate Today,* May/June 1978. A brief look at broker personality and its relation to the success or failure of a small brokerage office.

THREE

FINANCING REAL ESTATE

Mortgage Financing

The house was more covered
with mortgages than paint.
George Ade

Real estate is pledged as security for a loan in much the same manner as other commodities of economic value. For example, many of us in buying a car pledge the vehicle to a financial institution to get enough money to make the purchase. Likewise, most of us pledge real estate to obtain money to buy it. However, the legal instruments involved differ somewhat because of the high value, long life, fixed location, and lack of liquidity of real estate. Our purpose in these next few chapters is to look more closely at the financing of real estate.

In this chapter, we look at the mortgage, which is the traditional instrument of real estate finance. In the next chapter, we look at several alternatives to mortgage financing, namely trust deeds, land contracts, and long-term leases. Next we look at sources of credit. And finally, we look at the financial calculations involved in arranging a loan.

The general topics of this chapter are as follows:

1. The mortgaging process
2. The promissory note
3. Typical mortgage clauses
4. Types of mortgages
5. Other mortgage instruments

THE MORTGAGING PROCESS

Two separate legal instruments must be executed in obtaining an enforceable loan on real estate. The first is either a mortgage or a trust deed. The second is a promissory note or, in some states, a personal bond.

A **mortgage** is a pledge of real property as security for a debt or other obligation. The borrower in a mortgage contract is the **mortgagor;** the lender is the **mortgagee.** A **promissory note** is a written promise to repay the debt, and it serves as evidence of the debt. A *personal bond* is an interest-bearing certificate containing a promise to pay a certain sum on a specified date, and thus is similar to a note. Usually only the mortgage, pledging the property, is recorded.

A mortgage is a lien against the property pledged as security until cleared or satisfied. Though usually fee ownership of realty is pledged as security, any real property interest that is a proper and legal subject of a sale, grant, or assignment may be pledged. Thus, a leasehold, a life estate, rights of a remainder-man, or improvements apart from the land all provide a legal basis for a mortgage.

Increasingly, a trust deed is being used in place of a mortgage. The reason is time and convenience to the lender. A mortgage is a lien on the pledged property. Foreclosure proceedings in mortgage default require from several months to two or three years to complete. **Default** is failure of the borrower to meet the debt obligation. A **trust deed,** instead of being a lien, conveys title to the pledged property to a third party (trustee) to be held as security for the debt owed the lender-beneficiary. A promissory note still evidences the debt. Upon default, the trustee has automatic right of sale, which considerably shortens the time required to get satisfaction by the lender. Thus, after three or four payments are missed, the lender may request sale, with satisfaction realized in six to seven months. A trust deed is also referred to as a *deed of trust* or a *trust-deed-in-the-nature-of-a-mortgage.*

A promissory note or bond, as mentioned, serves as evidence of the debt and makes the debt the personal obligation of the borrower, which expands the lender's rights in case of default. If only a mortgage or trust deed were used, the borrower might abandon the property, move elsewhere, and have no further personal obligation or liability regarding the loan. The note or bond, as a personal obligation, is enforceable wherever the borrower might take up residence.

The emphasis in this chapter is on the mortgage and promissory note. Similarities between the content of the mortgage and the trust deed are also pointed up. Differences between the mortgage and trust deed are delayed to the next chapter.

The mortgage and promissory note used as illustrations in this chapter were developed jointly by the Federal National Mortgage Association (FNMA) and the Federal Home Loan Mortgage Corporation (FHLMC). These instruments are representative of financing forms used throughout the country. These instruments are as uniform as possible from state to state to make the buying and selling of existing mortgages easier. Because the wording is standardized, buyers do not have to study each document in detail before accepting it. Borrowers still need to read each note and mortgage document, however, in obtaining a loan. Additional completed FNMA/FHLMC instruments are included as exhibits in the forms and documents appendix.

The mortgaging process breaks down into three basic phases: (1) Initiation, (2) interim or servicing, and (3) termination. These phases apply, regardless of the type of mortgage involved.

Loan Initiation

Following application for a loan, several basic considerations enter into the decision to make the loan, from a lender's point of view. The borrower must have an acceptable credit rating and adequate income to justify making the loan, especially for a owner-occupied residence. Also, the loan is likely to be limited to 90 to 95 percent of market value. For an income property, the loan may be limited to from 60 to 80 percent of market value. Also, with an income property, the net operating income must be great enough to meet debt service requirements of the loan, with some excess to serve as a buffer. For example, annual net operating income may have to be 1.25 times annual debt service. Thus even though operating revenues dipped for a short while, the owner would still be able to make the necessary payments. Assuming the lender's criteria are met, the loan is made, typically at a closing similar to that discussed in the chapter on title closing. The borrower signs the mortgage and note and meets other settlement cost requirements, and the contract is made.

Interim or Servicing Phase

A borrower-owner is expected to make agreed payments of principal and interest to the lender during the life of the mortgage. It is also expected that the property will be maintained in a reasonable condition. A borrower-owner may sometimes sell the property without paying off the loan, thereby continuing the life of the loan.

Title to property may be conveyed from one person to another without paying off the mortgage lien against the property. The buyer may take title "subject to" the mortgage or the buyer may take title and "assume and promise to pay" the mortgage. The distinction between the two alternatives is very important to both the buyer and the seller. Increasingly, lenders are not allowing mortgages to be taken over by buyers without prior consent from the lender.

TAKING SUBJECT TO A MORTGAGE. A buyer, taking title subject to a mortgage, does not take over legal responsibility for repayment of the mortgage debt. If unable to make mortgage debt service payments, the buyer may simply walk away from the property without further obligation to the lender. That is, in case of default, the lender has no recourse or basis for action for debt satisfaction against the buyer-owner.

It is in the buyer-owner's interest to continue making payments of debt service as long as the buyer-owner has an equity interest in the property. The seller remains liable for the debt should the buyer default in making the payments.

A statement, such as the following, is inserted in the deed when title is conveyed subject to a mortgage:

This deed is subject to a first mortgage in the amount of $37,000, plus any accumulated interest, made between Albert Long, borrower-mortgager, and the Urbandale Savings and Loan Association, lender-mortgagee, on April 5th, 1976, and recorded as document 3,317,916 in Rustic County, Any State, in Book 512 of the mortgager-mortgagee records.

ASSUMING AND PROMISING TO PAY A MORTGAGE. Agreement by a grantee (usually a buyer) to accept responsibility for and become liable for payment of an existing mortgage against a property is termed **mortgage assumption.** The buyer agrees to pay debt service and to pay any deficiency should a default occur. Unless released, the seller continues to be liable to the lender for payment of the loan. Both the seller and the buyer usually sign the deed when a loan is being assumed. Without the buyer's signature, the contract for assumption would not be binding on the buyer.

Loan Termination

In early times, when real estate was used as security for a loan, the borrower deeded the property outright to the lender, who thereafter was its legal owner. The borrower usually retained possession, but upon default, the lender immediately took possession. The borrower only retained an equitable right for return of the property if the loan and interest were fully paid. This right is now called the *equitable right of redemption.* Today, the transaction is still basically the same, although the property is now mortgaged instead of deeded, to the lender. Also, the law surrounding the transaction is more fully developed.

THEORIES OF MORTGAGE LAW. The two basic theories of mortgage law in the United States are title theory and lien theory.

In some states, termed *title theory states,* a limited form of legal title is considered to be conveyed to the lender when a property is mortgaged. The lender-mortgagee's ownership claim may be defeated upon full performance on the mortgage agreement, which is usually payment of the mortgage debt plus interest. In the event of nonpayment or default, the borrower retains possession unless the mortgage contract states otherwise. Foreclosure proceedings must be initiated and completed by the mortgagee even though the mortgagee is legally regarded as the owner of the property.

In most states, known as *lien theory states,* a mortgage creates a lien on property and does not convey title. Title remains with the borrower. The property is still pledged as security for the debt or obligation. The mortgagor may remain in possession even in default; and as in the title theory states, the mortgagee must initiate and complete foreclosure proceedings to get benefit from the pledged property.

Over the years the line of distinction between title theory and lien theory states has become blurred. In both classes of states, an interest held through a mortgage lien is legally, personal property and must be accompanied by the note, as evidence of the debt, if sold or otherwise transferred. Some differences exist; for example, rents from, and possession of, income properties are more readily realized by the lender in title theory states. Also, the foreclosure process may be slightly faster in title theory states. In both classes of states, however, foreclosure means eventually offering the pledged property for sale and reducing or paying off the debt with the proceeds. Excess proceeds from the sale go to the borrower-mortgagor. For all practical purposes, therefore, the differences between title theory and lien theory states tend to be almost nonexistent.

TERMINATION BY MUTUAL AGREEMENT. Payment in full is the most common way of terminating a mortgage loan. The payment may be amortized over a number of years until the balance is reduced to zero. A borrower may decide to refinance or recast a loan, which means paying off and clearing an existing mortgage. **Refinancing** is usually taken to mean obtaining a new and larger loan, usually at new terms. **Recasting** means keeping the same-size loan but changing the interest rate or the amortization period, which directly affects the amount of debt service required. Finally, the mortgage loan may be prepaid, for example, when a property is sold and the buyer obtains new financing.

Upon full repayment of the mortgage loan, the borrower is entitled to a statement of mortgage satisfaction from the lender. A **mortgage satisfaction** is a receipt acknowledging payment of the loan, which when recorded, cancels the mortgage lien against the property. Almost all mortgages contain a defeasance clause to protect the borrower in the event that the lender refuses to give a mortgage satisfaction statement upon complete repayment of the loan. A **defeasance clause** states that if the loan and interest are paid in due course, the rights and interests of the lender in the property cease. Thus, without a debt, a mortgage has no life and is not enforceable.

A **deed in lieu of foreclosure** is sometimes "voluntarily" given to lenders by borrowers in default to avoid foreclosure, problems and procedures. Such a deed is generally given when the owner's equity in the property is less than the expected costs of foreclosure proceedings.

TERMINATION BY DEFAULT AND FORECLOSURE. The failure of a borrower to pay debt service or otherwise fulfill the terms of the mortgage contract constitutes *default*. If the lapse or failure to perform is of short duration, a lender is unlikely to take any corrective action. Lenders recognize that financial distress causes borrowers to miss debt-service payments occasionally and that most borrowers live up to their obligations if given an opportunity.

If default is more extended, a lender must eventually file a foreclosure suit. **Foreclosure** is a legal process initiated by a mortgagee, upon default by an owner-debtor, to force immediate payment of the debt. The foreclosure process may require from one to three years to run its course. Foreclosure may involve the mortgagee-lender in taking over the property as satisfaction of the debt, which is termed **strict foreclosure.** Alternatively, and more commonly, the property is disposed of at a judicial or foreclosure sale to raise money to pay the debt.

Nearly every mortgage contains an acceleration clause to facilitate foreclosure in the event of default. An **acceleration clause** gives the lender the right to declare the remaining balance of a loan due and payable immediately because of a violation of one of the covenants in the loan contract. If there is no acceleration clause, a lender must sue for each payment of debt service as it becomes due and payable.

A borrower may exercise an equitable right of redemption, up until the foreclosure sale, to recover or redeem the property. This right is also called the *equity of redemption.* The **equitable right of redemption** is the right of a borrower to recover mortgaged property by paying the debt plus any costs of foreclosure incurred by the lender. The equitable right of redemption is intended to protect the borrower and cannot be cut off except by foreclosure.

After the foreclosure sale, some states give the borrower a statutory right of redemption. The **statutory right of redemption** is the right of a borrower to recover foreclosed property for a limited time after the foreclosure sale by payment of the sale price plus foreclosure costs plus any other costs or losses incurred by the lender. Figure 12–1 illustrates the foreclosure process.

FIGURE 12–1
The Mortgage Foreclosure Process

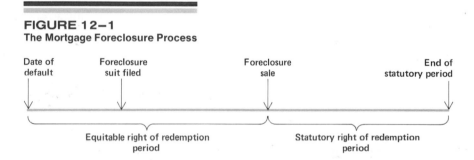

If the price in a foreclosure sale exceeds all claims against the borrower plus foreclosure costs, the surplus usually goes to the borrower-mortgagor. If the price is less thanethe debt plus interest plus foreclosure costs, a lender may obtain a deficiency judgment against the borrower in some states. A **deficiency judgment** is a judicial decree in favor of a lender for that portion of a mortgage debt that remains unsatisfied after the foreclosure sale of the property pledged as security. A deficiency judgment is an unsecured claim against the borrower. Some states do not recognize or have deficiency judgments. A deficiency judgment also applies to endorsers and guarantors of the note and to any persons who agreed in writing to assume the mortgage debt.

A lender may include provisions in a mortgage contract for management and collection of rents on a pledged income property, if it goes into default. A *management agreement* merely allows the lender to appoint someone to look after the property. Alternatively, a lender may take possession of a property in default under an assignment of rents. This alternative is rather unattractive to most lenders because items of income and expense must be accounted for very closely. If, however, the mortgagor is not using the rents properly or is allowing the property to waste, a lender may need to exercise this alternative. Lenders prefer not to take over foreclosed properties. As one bank vice president said about taking over foreclosed real estate: "We are in property management involuntarily."[1]

THE PROMISSORY NOTE

The debt gives life to a mortgage or trust deed. The debt is evidenced by a promissory note or a personal bond. If the debt is unenforceable for any reason, the mortgage or trust deed is also unenforceable. A personal bond is not widely used, and in fact, its use may be decreasing.

A valid promissory note acknowledges the debt and contains a promise to pay the debt. It also provides security to the lender, in case of borrower default, by reference to a mortgage or trust deed. A note approved for use in the state of Texas by the FHLMC is explained below, paragraph by paragraph, to give the reader greater insight into the nature of notes. This note is substantially the same as notes used in other states. The complete note is included as figure 12–2.

In summary form and based on the law of contracts, the essential elements of a valid promissory note are as follows:

1. A written instrument
2. A borrower (obligor) with contractual capacity
3. A lender (obligee) with contractual capacity
4. A promise or covenant by a borrower to pay a specific sum
5. Terms of payment
6. A default clause, including reference to the mortgage or trust deed
7. Proper execution
8. Voluntary delivery and acceptance

We discussed the need for a written contract and contractual capacity in chapter 7, on real estate contracts.

Indebtedness, Promise to Pay, and Terms of Payment

The first paragraph of the sample note shows indebtedness of $500,000. The interest rate is 10 percent per annum. Monthly debt service of $4,543.50 over twenty-five years is called for to pay interest on and to amortize the debt. This is a fixed-rate mortgage note. These payments are to be made on the first day of each month at the main office of the lending institution, which in our example is the Urbandale Savings and Loan Association. In summary, this para-

---

[1] "Holding the Bag: Sour Real Estate Loans Turn Big Bank Lenders into Uneasy Landlords," *Wall Street Journal,* August 18, 1977.

FIGURE 12–2
Note

NOTE

(Multifamily)

US $ .....500,000.....

Urbandale
City ...., Texas

January 15 , 19 81

1. For Value Received, the undersigned promise to pay .....Urbandale Savings and Loan Association..... ...., or order, the principal sum of .....Five Hundred Thousand..... .....and no/100 ($500,000.00)..................................... Dollars, with interest on the unpaid principal balance from the date of this Note, until paid, at the rate of .....10..... percent per annum. The principal and interest shall be payable at .....Urbandale Savings and Loan Association, 300 North..... .....Main, Urbandale............................... in consecutive monthly installments of .....Four Thousand Five Hundred Forty Three and fifty/100..... Dollars (US $.....4,543.50..... .....) on the .....1st..... day of each month beginning .....March 1st....., 19 81 , (herein "amortization commencement date"), until the entire indebtedness evidenced hereby is fully paid, except that any remaining indebtedness, if not sooner paid, shall be due and payable on the .....1st..... day of .....February....., ...2006..... .

2. If the amortization commencement date is more than .....30..... calendar days from the date of this Note, the undersigned shall pay the holder hereof interest only on the outstanding principal balance of this Note at the rate of .....10..... percent per annum in .....one..... installments beginning .....15 January..... 19 81 , and on .....no other..................................... thereafter until the amortization commencement date, at which time any remaining interest payable pursuant to this paragraph (and not paid as a part of the first monthly installment of principal and interest) shall be paid.

3. If any installment under this Note is not paid when due, the unpaid principal balance of this Note shall bear interest during the period of delinquency at a rate of .....10..... percent per annum, or, if such increased rate of interest may not be collected from the undersigned under applicable law, then at the maximum increased rate of interest, if any, which may be collected from the undersigned under applicable law; and, at the option of the holder hereof, the entire principal amount outstanding hereunder and accrued interest thereon shall at once become due and payable. Failure to exercise such option shall not constitute a waiver of the right to exercise such option if the undersigned is in default hereunder. In the event of any default in the payment of this Note, and if the same is referred to an attorney at law for collection or suit is brought hereon, the undersigned shall pay the holder hereof, in either case, all expenses and costs of collection, including, but not limited to, attorney's fees.

4. The undersigned shall pay to the holder hereof on demand a late charge of .....2..... percent of any installment not received by the holder hereof within .....15..... calendar days after the day the installment is due.

5. The undersigned shall have the right to prepay the principal amount outstanding hereunder in whole or in part at any time after the amortization commencement date, provided that the holder hereof may require that any partial prepayments shall be made on the date monthly installments are due and shall be in the amount of that part of one or more monthly installments which would be applicable to principal and further provided that the undersigned has given the holder hereof written notice of the amount intended to be prepaid at least .....five (5)..... days prior to such prepayment. The undersigned shall pay the holder hereof together with any prepayments (including prepayments occurring as a result of the acceleration by the holder hereof of the principal amount of this Note, but excluding prepayments occurring because of the application by the holder hereof of insurance or condemnation awards or proceeds pursuant to a Deed of Trust securing this Note) a percentage of the amount prepaid in excess of any amount upon which a charge is not permitted by applicable law as follows: .....4..... percent of the sums prepaid in the first year from the amortization commencement date, the percentage payable declining by the number one (1) each year thereafter until the percentage payable is .....0..... percent, which percentage shall be payable for the remaining term of the Note. Prepayments shall be applied against the outstanding principal balance of this Note and shall not extend or postpone the due date of any subsequent monthly installments or change the amount of such installments, unless the holder hereof shall otherwise agree in writing.

6. From time to time, without affecting the obligation of the undersigned or the successors or assigns of the undersigned to pay the outstanding principal balance of this Note and observe the covenants of the undersigned contained herein, without affecting the guaranty of any person, corporation, partnership or other entity for payment of the outstanding principal balance of this Note, without giving notice to or obtaining the consent of the undersigned, the successors or assigns of the undersigned or guarantors, and without liability on the part of the holder hereof, the holder hereof may, at the option of the holder hereof, extend the time for payment of said outstanding principal balance or any part thereof, reduce the payments thereon, release anyone liable on any of said outstanding principal balance, accept a renewal of this Note, modify the terms and time of payment of said outstanding principal balance or join in any extension or subordination agreement, and agree in writing with the undersigned to modify the rate of interest or period of amortization of this Note or change the amount of the monthly installments payable hereunder.

7. Presentment, notice of dishonor, and protest are hereby waived by all makers, sureties, guarantors and endorsers hereof. This Note shall be the joint and several obligation of all makers, sureties, guarantors and endorsers, and shall be binding upon them and their heirs, personal representatives, successors and assigns.

8. The indebtedness evidenced by this Note is secured by a Deed of Trust, dated of even date herewith, and reference is made thereto for rights as to acceleration of the indebtedness evidenced by this Note.

.....Douglas Manor.....
.....2001 Century Drive.....
.....Urbandale, Texas 00000.....
.....(property address).....

/s/Gerald I. Investor

/s/Nancy O. Investor

graph states the amount of the debt, the promise to pay, the rate of interest, and the time and place at which payments are to be made.

1. For Value Received, the undersigned promise to pay ......Urbandale Savings and Loan Association.................., or order, the principal sum of ..Five Hundred Thousand ...and..no/100..($500,000.00)........................... Dollars, with interest on the unpaid principal balance from the date of this Note, until paid, at the rate of ...10.... percent per annum. The principal and interest shall be payable at ..Urbandale..Savings..and..Loan..Association,..300..North.. ...Main,..Urbandale....................................... in consecutive monthly installments of ...Four Thousand Five Hundred Forty Three and Fifty/100...... Dollars (US $...4,543.50.. ....) on the ...1st........ day of each month beginning ..March..1st.........., 19..81.. (herein "amortization commencement date"), until the entire indebtedness evidenced hereby is fully paid, except that any remaining indebtedness, if not sooner paid, shall be due and payable on the ..1st.. day of ...February......................., ..2006..... .

Paragraph 2 simply provides that interest for an odd (other than thirty days) period be paid without any amortization to get payments on a regular basis. In our example, this means interest to the end of January 1981, which amount shows up on the closing statement. With this adjustment, regular payments are shifted to the beginning of each month even though the closing occurs on January 15.

2. If the amortization commencement date is more than ..30.... calendar days from the date of this Note, the undersigned shall pay the holder hereof interest only on the outstanding principal balance of this Note at the rate of ..10.... percent per annum in ......one....... installments beginning ..15 January......., 19..81, and on ..no other.................... thereafter until the amortization commencement date, at which time any remaining interest payable pursuant to this paragraph (and not paid as a part of the first monthly installment of principal and interest) shall be paid.

Default and Late-Payment Provisions

Paragraph 3 contains the default provision, including the noteholder's right to accelerate or call for immediate payment of the entire outstanding principal plus accrued interest. This is the **acceleration clause.** Reasonable costs and expenses, including attorney's fees, may be collected by the noteholder under this paragraph if a foreclosure suit is filed. A specific point is also made that the right of acceleration is not lost if not exercised previously under conditions of default.

3. If any installment under this Note is not paid when due, the unpaid principal balance of this Note shall bear interest during the period of delinquency at a rate of ....10...... percent per annum, or, if such increased rate of interest may not be collected from the undersigned under applicable law, then at the maximum increased rate of interest, if any, which may be collected from the undersigned under applicable law; and, at the option of the holder hereof, the entire principal amount outstanding hereunder and accrued interest thereon shall at once become due and payable. Failure to exercise such option shall not constitute a waiver of the right to exercise such option if the undersigned is in default hereunder. In the event of any default in the payment of this Note, and if the same is referred to an attorney at law for collection or suit is brought hereon, the undersigned shall pay the holder hereof, in either case, all expenses and costs of collection, including, but not limited to, attorney's fees.

4. The undersigned shall pay to the holder hereof on demand a late charge of ....percent of any installment not received by the holder hereof within .....15................. calendar days after the day the installment is due.

Paragraph 4 provides for a late-payment penalty on any past due install-ment. In our example, the late penalty is 2 percent of the installment or $90.87 ($4,543.50 times 2 percent) if the payment is not made on or before the fif-teenth of the month. The intent, of course, is to give the borrower reason to make payments on time.

Prepayment Provision

Paragraph 5 is the **prepayment clause** and explains the prepayment pro-visions of the note. Accordingly the noteholder in our example may require that prepayments be made on the date monthly payments are due and in an amount of the portion of one or more monthly installments that would be ap-plicable to principal. Five days' advance notice of prepayment must also be given. The main purpose is to simplify record keeping for the transaction. The treatment of prepayments against the principal is also stipulated. And it is made clear that a prepayment does not change the size of subsequent monthly payments or automatically allow the borrower to miss making subsequent in-stallments. Thus, prepayments reduce the number of payments required but do not give the borrower the right to skip making any payments until the principal has been completely repaid.

A 4 percent penalty may be required by our noteholder of any amounts prepaid in the first year. This percentage drops 1 percent per year; thus no pen-alty may be charged in the fifth year. A charge of this type is called a *prepayment penalty.*

> 5. The undersigned shall have the right to prepay the principal amount outstanding hereunder in whole or in part at any time after the amortization commencement date, provided that the holder hereof may require that any partial prepayments shall be made on the date monthly installments are due and shall be in the amount of that part of one or more monthly installments which would be applicable to principal and further provided that the undersigned has given the holder hereof written notice of the amount intended to be prepaid at least five..(5).......... days prior to such prepayment. The undersigned shall pay the holder hereof together with any prepayments (including prepayments occurring as a result of the acceleration by the holder hereof of the principal amount of this Note, but excluding prepayments occurring because of the application by the holder hereof of insurance or condemnation awards or proceeds pursuant to a Deed of Trust securing this Note) a percentage of the amount prepaid in excess of any amount upon which a charge is not permitted by applicable law as follows: ...4..... percent of the sums prepaid in the first year from the amortization commencement date, the percentage payable declining by the number one (1) each year thereafter until the percentage payable is ....0.... percent, which percentage shall be payable for the remaining term of the Note. Prepayments shall be applied against the outstanding principal balance of this Note and shall not extend or postpone the due date of any subsequent monthly installments or change the amount of such installments, unless the holder hereof shall otherwise agree in writing.

Notes are sometimes drawn up to allow the borrower to prepay any amount at any time; this is termed a *prepayment privilege.* If nothing is said about payment, the borrower cannot prepay except at the noteholder's option. In this case, the right to prepay must be negotiated with the noteholder. In our ex-ample, the borrower has a prepayment privilege, subject to a declining pre-payment penalty in the first four years.

Negotiability

A prudent lender wants the greatest possible security and negotiability in accepting or holding a note. Paragraph 6 protects the security and negotiability of this note by stating that any modification to the terms shall not affect the obligation of the borrowers to abide by the terms and to repay the principal of the note. Then, in paragraph 7, the note is made the "joint and several obligation of all makers, sureties, guarantors, and endorsers, . . ." Finally, in paragraph 7, makers, endorsers, and others waive the right to protect or to deny the note as their obligation. The net effect of these provisions is to make the note more negotiable or liquid for its holder.

6. From time to time, without affecting the obligation of the undersigned or the successors or assigns of the undersigned to pay the outstanding principal balance of this Note and observe the covenants of the undersigned contained herein, without affecting the guaranty of any person, corporation, partnership or other entity for payment of the outstanding principal balance of this Note, without giving notice to or obtaining the consent of the undersigned, the successors or assigns of the undersigned or guarantors, and without liability on the part of the holder hereof, the holder hereof may, at the option of the holder hereof, extend the time for payment of said outstanding principal balance or any part thereof, reduce the payments thereon, release anyone liable on any of said outstanding principal balance, accept a renewal of this Note, modify the terms and time of payment of said outstanding principal balance or join in any extension or subordination agreement, and agree in writing with the undersigned to modify the rate of interest or period of amortization of this Note or change the amount of the monthly installments payable hereunder.

7. Presentment, notice of dishonor, and protest are hereby waived by all makers, sureties, guarantors and endorsers hereof. This Note shall be the joint and several obligation of all makers, sureties, guarantors and endorsers, and shall be binding upon them and their heirs, personal representatives, successors and assigns.

8. The indebtedness evidenced by this Note is secured by a Deed of Trust, dated of even date herewith, and reference is made thereto for rights as to acceleration of the indebtedness evidenced by this Note.

Douglas Manor
2001 Century Drive
Urbandale, Texas 00000
(property address)

/s/Gerald I. Investor

/s/Nancy O. Investor

Reference to Security Instrument

The eighth and last paragraph of the note refers to the security instrument, which might be a mortgage or trust deed. The security instrument sets forth the rights and obligations of the borrower and lender in much more detail.

To be properly executed, the note must be voluntarily signed by all parties with an interest in the property, in this case Gerald and Nancy Investor. Finally the note must be voluntarily delivered and accepted to complete the transaction. And at this point, all the essential requirements of a valid contract have been met in our example.

Usury

Nearly all states have a maximum legal rate of interest. A lender who charges and collects at a higher rate is committing **usury.** Some states limit the lender to the legal rate when a usurious loan has been made. In other states the lender loses all interest and can recover principal only. In a few states the entire amount loaned is lost, along with the interest.

Corporations are exempt from usury laws in nearly every state. That is, if a borrower is a corporation, the lender may charge any rate of interest the corporation agrees to pay. Many lenders therefore prefer to make loans to corporations and get a higher rate of interest.

Real property loans are usually made at fixed interest rates. Variable-rate mortgages, where the interest rate can go up or down based on money market conditions, are becoming more popular, however, and give some cause for concern about usury. Conceivably, if interest rates were to go up too high, the rate on a property loan would become usurious, but a ceiling on the interest rate that could be charged, in the mortgage contract, would prevent the rate from becoming usurious.

TYPICAL PROVISIONS
OF MORTGAGES AND TRUST DEEDS

Mortgages and deeds of trust are two very different and distinct ways of pledging real property as security for a loan. Yet they have many similar provisions. Each clearly establishes that the realty is to secure the debt. Each refers to a promissory note as evidence of the debt. Each identifies the borrower and the lender. Each contains an accurate legal description of the pledged property. Each should be signed by all parties with an interest in the realty, although the lender usually signs neither. And on an overall basis, a mortgage or a trust deed defines the rights and obligations of the borrower relative to the lender.

The following are generally considered important borrower obligations and hence are consistently provided for in a mortgage or trust deed:

1. Meeting debt-service payments in accordance with the promissory note
2. Paying all real estate taxes on the property pledged as security
3. Providing adequate hazard insurance to protect the lender against loss if the property is damaged or destroyed by fire, wind, or other peril
4. Maintaining the property in good repair at all times
5. Obtaining authorization from the lender before substantially altering the property

The following items are frequently but not necessarily provided for in a mortgage or trust deed:

1. Reservation of right of lender or noteholder to inspect the property and to protect the property as security if the borrower fails to do so
2. Stipulation that debt-service payments of the borrower apply to taxes first, insurance second, interest third, and principal reduction fourth
3. Stipulation that proceeds from insurance or condemnation go to protect the lender first, with any excess going to the borrower
4. Reservation of right of lender to approve transfer of ownership of secured property and assumption of the loan, including a change in the interest rate

The lender may declare the mortgage or trust deed in default upon violation of any of the above provisions or obligations by a borrower-mortgagor, when such provisions are included in the instrument.

The first twenty-six clauses or provisions of the FNMA/FHLMC uniform instrument for multifamily residential mortgages are discussed here. These provisions are typical for mortgages on business and investment properties. These provisions, uniform for mortgages and trust deeds from state to state, are intended to facilitate buying and selling of existing loans among lenders. The FNMA/FHLMC mortgage for one-family residences contains only seventeen clauses, which are generally less stringent than the clauses discussed here.

The purpose or content of each of the twenty-six clauses is discussed here only briefly. The clauses are taken up in the same order as they appear in the instrument. The clauses themselves are not restated because of their length and complexity. The reader is encouraged to look over and compare the specific wording in the document itself, which is presented in figure 12–3. The reader should keep in mind that the document is typical only. In a real-life situation, documents differ and must be individually read for specific content.

Payments of Principal and Interest

Clause 1 obligates the borrower to make payments of debt service promptly and otherwise to live up to making payments as agreed, as for example, for a late charge or prepayment penalty.

Deposits for Taxes and Insurance

Clause 2 obligates the borrower to make deposits with the lender for property taxes, hazard insurance, mortgage insurance, if any, water and sewer charges, if any, and rents or ground rents, if any. Also, if the deposits exceed the charges, the borrower may get a reduction in required charges for the next year. On the other hand, if the deposits are less than the charges, the borrower agrees to make up the deficiency. Finally, the noteholder agrees to refund the deposits at such time as the borrower pays the note in full.

Application of Payments

Clause 3 gives the notcholder wide discretion in applying payments to taxes, insurance, interest, and rents. The uniform instrument for a one-family residence states payments shall first apply to insurance and taxes as necessary, second to interest on the principal, and third to reduction of the principal. With a higher value, income property, both borrower and lender are deemed more knowledgeable. In turn greater latitude is given the notcholder concerning application of payments, unless an agreement is otherwise negotiated.

In clause 4, the borrower agrees to pay any charges or liens against the property promptly. Also, the borrower agrees not to allow inferior or lower-priority liens to be perfected against the property.

Hazard Insurance

Hazard insurance is intended to provide protection for the lender and borrower from loss should the property be damaged or destroyed. The lender wants assurance that this insurance is maintained. In clause 5, the borrower is

FIGURE 12–3
FNMA/FHLMC Uniform Instrument

FNMA/FHLMC UNIFORM INSTRUMENT

WHEN RECORDED MAIL TO

Urbandale Savings and Loan
300 North Main
Urbandale, Anystate   00000

SPACE ABOVE THIS LINE FOR RECORDER'S USE

This instrument was prepared by:

....

....

MULTIFAMILY MORTGAGE,
ASSIGNMENT OF RENTS AND SECURITY AGREEMENT
~~- (Security for Construction Loan Agreement) - -~~

THIS MORTGAGE (herein "Instrument") is made this ......15th...... day of ....January.........,
19 ...., between the Mortgagor/Grantor, ...Gerald and Nancy Investor, H & W....................
....
whose address is ....
(herein "Borrower"), and the Mortgagee, ...Urbandale Savings and Loan Association..............
...., a ....corporation........... organized and existing under the laws of
......Florida.................., whose address is ..300.North.Main,.Urbandale,.Florida.....00000..
.... (herein "Lender").

WHEREAS, Borrower is indebted to Lender in the principal sum of ....Five.Hundred.Thousand..........
.............($500,000).. Dollars, which indebtedness is
evidenced by Borrower's note dated ...January.15,.1981................... (herein "Note"), providing for
monthly installments of principal and interest, with the balance of the indebtedness, if not sooner paid, due and
payable on ....1.February,.2006........................;

To Secure to Lender (a) the repayment of the indebtedness evidenced by the Note, with interest thereon, and
all renewals, extensions and modifications thereof; (b) the repayment of any future advances, with interest thereon,
made by Lender to Borrower pursuant to paragraph 30 hereof (herein "Future Advances"); (c) the performance of
the covenants and agreements of Borrower contained in a Construction Loan Agreement between Lender and
Borrower dated ....None.............., 19.........; if any, as provided in paragraph 25 hereof; (d) the payment of
all other sums, with interest thereon, advanced in accordance herewith to protect the security of this Instrument; and
(e) the performance of the covenants and agreements of Borrower herein contained, Borrower does hereby mortgage,
grant, convey and assign to Lender [the leasehold estate pursuant to a lease (herein "ground lease") dated
...........................,. between ....(Apartment.lease.only)...
.... and
.................., recorded in ....
....
.... in and to*]
the following described property located in ......Rustic.County..., State of Florida:
* *Delete bracketed material if not completed.*

       Lots 16 and 17, Block 3, Edgewood South,
       Rustic County, Florida
       (Douglas Manor; 2001 Century Drive, Urbandale, Florida, 00000)

FLORIDA—Multifamily—1/77—FNMA/FHLMC Uniform Instrument   *(page 1 of 8 pages)*

FIGURE 12–3 (cont.)

TOGETHER with all buildings, improvements, and tenements now or hereafter erected on the property, and all heretofore or hereafter vacated alleys and streets abutting the property, and all easements, rights, appurtenances, rents, royalties, mineral, oil and gas rights and profits, water, water rights, and water stock appurtenant to the property, and all fixtures, machinery, equipment, engines, boilers, incinerators, building materials, appliances and goods of every nature whatsoever now or hereafter located in, or on, or used, or intended to be used in connection with the property, including, but not limited to, those for the purposes of supplying or distributing heating, cooling, electricity, gas, water, air and light; and all elevators, and related machinery and equipment, fire prevention and extinguishing apparatus, security and access control apparatus, plumbing, bath tubs, water heaters, water closets, sinks, ranges, stoves, refrigerators, dishwashers, disposals, washers, dryers, awnings, storm windows, storm doors, screens, blinds, shades, curtains and curtain rods, mirrors, cabinets, panelling, rugs, attached floor coverings, furniture, pictures, antennas, trees and plants, and ....

....; all of which, including replacements and additions thereto, shall be deemed to be and remain a part of the real property covered by this Instrument; and all of the foregoing, together with said property (or the leasehold estate in the event this Instrument is on a leasehold) are herein referred to as the "Property".

Borrower covenants that Borrower is lawfully seised of the estate hereby conveyed and has the right to mortgage, grant, convey and assign the Property (and, if this Instrument is on a leasehold, that the ground lease is in full force and effect without modification except as noted above and without default on the part of either lessor or lessee thereunder), that the Property is unencumbered, and that Borrower will warrant and defend generally the title to the Property against all claims and demands, subject to any easements and restrictions listed in a schedule of exceptions to coverage in any title insurance policy insuring Lender's interest in the Property.

(page 2 of 8 pages)

FIGURE 12–3 (cont.)

Uniform Covenants. Borrower and Lender covenant and agree as follows:

1. PAYMENT OF PRINCIPAL AND INTEREST. Borrower shall promptly pay when due the principal of and interest on the indebtedness evidenced by the Note, any prepayment and late charges provided in the Note and all other sums secured by this Instrument.

2. FUNDS FOR TAXES, INSURANCE AND OTHER CHARGES. Subject to applicable law or to a written waiver by Lender, Borrower shall pay to Lender on the day monthly installments of principal or interest are payable under the Note (or on another day designated in writing by Lender), until the Note is paid in full, a sum (herein "Funds") equal to one-twelfth of (a) the yearly water and sewer rates and taxes and assessments which may be levied on the Property, (b) the yearly ground rents, if any, (c) the yearly premium installments for fire and other hazard insurance, rent loss insurance and such other insurance covering the Property as Lender may require pursuant to paragraph 5 hereof, (d) the yearly premium installments for mortgage insurance, if any, and (e) if this Instrument is on a leasehold, the yearly fixed rents, if any, under the ground lease, all as reasonably estimated initially and from time to time by Lender on the basis of assessments and bills and reasonable estimates thereof. Any waiver by Lender of a requirement that Borrower pay such Funds may be revoked by Lender, in Lender's sole discretion, at any time upon notice in writing to Borrower. Lender may require Borrower to pay to Lender, in advance, such other Funds for other taxes, charges, premiums, assessments and impositions in connection with Borrower or the Property which Lender shall reasonably deem necessary to protect Lender's interests (herein "Other Impositions"). Unless otherwise provided by applicable law, Lender may require Funds for Other Impositions to be paid by Borrower in a lump sum or in periodic installments, at Lender's option.

The Funds shall be held in an institution(s) the deposits or accounts of which are insured or guaranteed by a Federal or state agency (including Lender if Lender is such an institution). Lender shall apply the Funds to pay said rates, rents, taxes, assessments, insurance premiums and Other Impositions so long as Borrower is not in breach of any covenant or agreement of Borrower in this Instrument. Lender shall make no charge for so holding and applying the Funds, analyzing said account or for verifying and compiling said assessments and bills, unless Lender pays Borrower interest, earnings or profits on the Funds and applicable law permits Lender to make such a charge. Borrower and Lender may agree in writing at the time of execution of this Instrument that interest on the Funds shall be paid to Borrower, and unless such agreement is made or applicable law requires interest, earnings or profits to be paid, Lender shall not be required to pay Borrower any interest, earnings or profits on the Funds. Lender shall give to Borrower, without charge, an annual accounting of the Funds in Lender's normal format showing credits and debits to the Funds and the purpose for which each debit to the Funds was made. The Funds are pledged as additional security for the sums secured by this Instrument.

If the amount of the Funds held by Lender at the time of the annual accounting thereof shall exceed the amount deemed necessary by Lender to provide for the payment of water and sewer rates, taxes, assessments, insurance premiums, rents and Other Impositions, as they fall due, such excess shall be credited to Borrower on the next monthly installment or installments of Funds due. If at any time the amount of the Funds held by Lender shall be less than the amount deemed necessary by Lender to pay water and sewer rates, taxes, assessments, insurance premiums, rents and Other Impositions, as they fall due, Borrower shall pay to Lender any amount necessary to make up the deficiency within thirty days after notice from Lender to Borrower requesting payment thereof.

Upon Borrower's breach of any covenant or agreement of Borrower in this Instrument, Lender may apply, in any amount and in any order as Lender shall determine in Lender's sole discretion, any Funds held by Lender at the time of application (i) to pay rates, rents, taxes, assessments, insurance premiums and Other Impositions which are now or will hereafter become due, or (ii) as a credit against sums secured by this Instrument. Upon payment in full of all sums secured by this Instrument, Lender shall promptly refund to Borrower any Funds held by Lender.

3. APPLICATION OF PAYMENTS. Unless applicable law provides otherwise, all payments received by Lender from Borrower under the Note or this Instrument shall be applied by Lender in the following order of priority: (i) amounts payable to Lender by Borrower under paragraph 2 hereof; (ii) interest payable on the Note; (iii) principal of the Note; (iv) interest payable on advances made pursuant to paragraph 8 hereof; (v) principal of advances made pursuant to paragraph 8 hereof; (vi) interest payable on any Future Advance, provided that if more than one Future Advance is outstanding, Lender may apply payments received among the amounts of interest payable on the Future Advances in such order as Lender, in Lender's sole discretion, may determine; (vii) principal of any Future Advance, provided that if more than one Future Advance is outstanding, Lender may apply payments received among the principal balances of the Future Advances in such order as Lender, in Lender's sole discretion, may determine; and (viii) any other sums secured by this Instrument in such order as Lender, at Lender's option, may determine; provided, however, that Lender may, at Lender's option, apply any sums payable pursuant to paragraph 8 hereof prior to interest on and principal of the Note, but such application shall not otherwise affect the order of priority of application specified in this paragraph 3.

4. CHARGES; LIENS. Borrower shall pay all water and sewer rates, rents, taxes, assessments, premiums, and Other Impositions attributable to the Property at Lender's option in the manner provided under paragraph 2 hereof or, if not paid in such manner, by Borrower making payment, when due, directly to the payee thereof, or in such other manner as Lender may designate in writing. Borrower shall promptly furnish to Lender all notices of amounts due under this paragraph 4, and in the event Borrower shall make payment directly, Borrower shall promptly furnish to Lender receipts evidencing such payments. Borrower shall promptly discharge any lien which has, or may have, priority over or equality with, the lien of this Instrument, and Borrower shall pay, when due, the claims of all persons supplying labor or materials to or in connection with the Property. Without Lender's prior written permission, Borrower shall not allow any lien inferior to this Instrument to be perfected against the Property.

5. HAZARD INSURANCE. Borrower shall keep the improvements now existing or hereafter erected on the Property insured by carriers at all times satisfactory to Lender against loss by fire, hazards included within the term "extended coverage", rent loss and such other hazards, casualties, liabilities and contingencies as Lender (and, if this Instrument is on a leasehold, the ground lease) shall require and in such amounts and for such periods as Lender shall require. All premiums on insurance policies shall be paid, at Lender's option, in the manner provided under paragraph 2 hereof, or by Borrower making payment, when due, directly to the carrier, or in such other manner as Lender may designate in writing.

All insurance policies and renewals thereof shall be in a form acceptable to Lender and shall include a standard mortgage clause in favor of and in form acceptable to Lender. Lender shall have the right to hold the policies, and Borrower shall promptly furnish to Lender all renewal notices and all receipts of paid premiums. At least thirty days prior to the expiration date of a policy, Borrower shall deliver to Lender a renewal policy in form satisfactory to Lender. If this Instrument is on a leasehold, Borrower shall furnish Lender a duplicate of all policies, renewal notices, renewal policies and receipts of paid premiums if, by virtue of the ground lease, the originals thereof may not be supplied by Borrower to Lender.

In the event of loss, Borrower shall give immediate written notice to the insurance carrier and to Lender. Borrower hereby authorizes and empowers Lender as attorney-in-fact for Borrower to make proof of loss, to adjust and compromise any claim under insurance policies, to appear in and prosecute any action arising from such insurance policies, to collect and receive insurance proceeds, and to deduct therefrom Lender's expenses incurred in the collection of such proceeds; provided however, that nothing contained in this paragraph 5 shall require Lender to incur any expense or take any action hereunder. Borrower further authorizes Lender, at Lender's option, (a) to hold the balance of such proceeds to be used to reimburse Borrower for the cost of reconstruction or repair of the Property or (b) to apply the balance of such proceeds to the payment of the sums secured by this Instrument, whether or not then due, in the order of application set forth in paragraph 3 hereof (subject, however, to the rights of the lessor under the ground lease if this Instrument is on a leasehold).

If the insurance proceeds are held by Lender to reimburse Borrower for the cost of restoration and repair of the Property, the Property shall be restored to the equivalent of its original condition or such other condition as Lender may approve in writing. Lender may, at Lender's option, condition disbursement of said proceeds on Lender's approval of such plans and specifications of an architect satisfactory to Lender, contractor's cost estimates, architect's certificates, waivers of liens, sworn statements of mechanics and materialmen and such other evidence of costs, percentage completion of construction, application of payments, and satisfaction of liens as Lender may reasonably require. If the insurance proceeds are applied to the payment of the sums secured by this Instrument, any such application of proceeds to principal shall not extend or postpone the due dates of the monthly installments referred to in paragraphs 1 and 2 hereof or change the amounts of such installments. If the Property is sold pursuant to paragraph 27 hereof or if Lender acquires title to the Property, Lender shall have all of the right, title and interest of Borrower in and to any insurance policies and unearned premiums thereon and in and to the proceeds resulting from any damage to the Property prior to such sale or acquisition.

6. PRESERVATION AND MAINTENANCE OF PROPERTY; LEASEHOLDS. Borrower (a) shall not commit waste or permit impairment or deterioration of the Property, (b) shall not abandon the Property, (c) shall restore or repair promptly and in a good and workmanlike manner all

Uniform Covenants—Multifamily—1/77—FNMA/FHLMC Uniform Instrument *(page 3 of 8 pages)*

FIGURE 12–3 (cont.)

or any part of the Property to the equivalent of its original condition, or such other condition as Lender may approve in writing, in the event of any damage, injury or loss thereto, whether or not insurance proceeds are available to cover in whole or in part the costs of such restoration or repair, (d) shall keep the Property, including improvements, fixtures, equipment, machinery and appliances thereon in good repair and shall replace fixtures, equipment, machinery and appliances on the Property when necessary to keep such items in good repair, (e) shall comply with all laws, ordinances, regulations and requirements of any governmental body applicable to the Property, (f) shall provide for professional management of the Property by a residential rental property manager satisfactory to Lender pursuant to a contract approved by Lender in writing, unless such requirement shall be waived by Lender in writing, (g) shall generally operate and maintain the Property in a manner to ensure maximum rentals, and (h) shall give notice in writing to Lender of and, unless otherwise directed in writing by Lender, appear in and defend any action or proceeding purporting to affect the Property, the security of this Instrument or the rights or powers of Lender. Neither Borrower nor any tenant or other person shall remove, demolish or alter any improvement now existing or hereafter erected on the Property or any fixture, equipment, machinery or appliance in or on the Property except when incident to the replacement of fixtures, equipment, machinery and appliances with items of like kind.

If this Instrument is on a leasehold, Borrower (i) shall comply with the provisions of the ground lease, (ii) shall give immediate written notice to Lender of any default by lessor under the ground lease or of any notice received by Borrower from such lessor of any default under the ground lease by Borrower, (iii) shall exercise any option to renew or extend the ground lease and give written confirmation thereof to Lender within thirty days after such option becomes exercisable, (iv) shall give immediate written notice to Lender of the commencement of any remedial proceedings under the ground lease by any party thereto and, if required by Lender, shall permit Lender as Borrower's attorney-in-fact to control and act for Borrower in any such remedial proceedings and (v) shall within thirty days after request by Lender obtain from the lessor under the ground lease and deliver to Lender the lessor's estoppel certificate required thereunder, if any. Borrower hereby expressly transfers and assigns to Lender the benefit of all covenants contained in the ground lease, whether or not such covenants run with the land, but Lender shall have no liability with respect to such covenants nor any other covenants contained in the ground lease.

Borrower shall not surrender the leasehold estate and interests herein conveyed nor terminate or cancel the ground lease creating said estate and interests, and Borrower shall not, without the express written consent of Lender, alter or amend said ground lease. Borrower covenants and agrees that there shall not be a merger of the ground lease, or of the leasehold estate created thereby, with the fee estate covered by the ground lease by reason of said leasehold estate or said fee estate, or any part of either, coming into common ownership, unless Lender shall consent in writing to such merger; if Borrower shall acquire such fee estate, then this Instrument shall simultaneously and without further action be spread so as to become a lien on such fee estate.

7. USE OF PROPERTY. Unless required by applicable law or unless Lender has otherwise agreed in writing, Borrower shall not allow changes in the use for which all or any part of the Property was intended at the time this Instrument was executed. Borrower shall not initiate or acquiesce in a change in the zoning classification of the Property without Lender's prior written consent.

8. PROTECTION OF LENDER'S SECURITY. If Borrower fails to perform the covenants and agreements contained in this Instrument, or if any action or proceeding is commenced which affects the Property or title thereto or the interest of Lender therein, including, but not limited to, eminent domain, insolvency, code enforcement, or arrangements or proceedings involving a bankrupt or decedent, then Lender at Lender's option may make such appearances, disburse such sums and take such action as Lender deems necessary, in its sole discretion, to protect Lender's interest, including, but not limited to, (i) disbursement of attorney's fees, (ii) entry upon the Property to make repairs, (iii) procurement of satisfactory insurance as provided in paragraph 5 hereof, and (iv) if this Instrument is on a leasehold, exercise of any option to renew or extend the ground lease on behalf of Borrower and the curing of any default of Borrower in the terms and conditions of the ground lease.

Any amounts disbursed by Lender pursuant to this paragraph 8, with interest thereon, shall become additional indebtedness of Borrower secured by this Instrument. Unless Borrower and Lender agree to other terms of payment, such amounts shall be immediately due and payable and shall bear interest from the date of disbursement at the rate stated in the Note unless collection from Borrower of interest at such rate would be contrary to applicable law, in which event such amounts shall bear interest at the highest rate which may be collected from Borrower under applicable law. Borrower hereby covenants and agrees that Lender shall be subrogated to the lien of any mortgage or other lien discharged, in whole or in part, by the indebtedness secured hereby. Nothing contained in this paragraph 8 shall require Lender to incur any expense or take any action hereunder.

9. INSPECTION. Lender may make or cause to be made reasonable entries upon and inspections of the Property.

10. BOOKS AND RECORDS. Borrower shall keep and maintain at all times at Borrower's address stated below, or such other place as Lender may approve in writing, complete and accurate books of accounts and records adequate to reflect correctly the results of the operation of the Property and copies of all written contracts, leases and other instruments which affect the Property. Such books, records, contracts, leases and other instruments shall be subject to examination and inspection at any reasonable time by Lender. Upon Lender's request, Borrower shall furnish to Lender, within one hundred and twenty days after the end of each fiscal year of Borrower, a balance sheet, a statement of income and expenses of the Property and a statement of changes in financial position, each in reasonable detail and certified by Borrower and, if Lender shall require, by an independent certified public accountant. Borrower shall furnish, together with the foregoing financial statements and at any other time upon Lender's request, a rent schedule for the Property, certified by Borrower, showing the name of each tenant, and for each tenant, the space occupied, the lease expiration date, the rent payable and the rent paid.

11. CONDEMNATION. Borrower shall promptly notify Lender of any action or proceeding relating to any condemnation or other taking, whether direct or indirect, of the Property, or part thereof, and Borrower shall appear in and prosecute any such action or proceeding unless otherwise directed by Lender in writing. Borrower authorizes Lender, at Lender's option, as attorney-in-fact for Borrower, to commence, appear in and prosecute, in Lender's or Borrower's name, any action or proceeding relating to any condemnation or other taking of the Property, whether direct or indirect, and to settle or compromise any claim in connection with such condemnation or other taking. The proceeds of any award, payment or claim for damages, direct or consequential, in connection with any condemnation or other taking, whether direct or indirect, of the Property, or part thereof, or for conveyances in lieu of condemnation, are hereby assigned to and shall be paid to Lender subject, if this Instrument is on a leasehold, to the rights of lessor under the ground lease.

Borrower authorizes Lender to apply such awards, payments, proceeds or damages, after the deduction of Lender's expenses incurred in the collection of such amounts, at Lender's option, to restoration or repair of the Property or to payment of the sums secured by this Instrument, whether or not then due, in the order of application set forth in paragraph 3 hereof, with the balance, if any, to Borrower. Unless Borrower and Lender otherwise agree in writing, any application of proceeds to principal shall not extend or postpone the due date of the monthly installments referred to in paragraphs 1 and 2 hereof or change the amount of such installments. Borrower agrees to execute such further evidence of assignment of any awards, proceeds, damages or claims arising in connection with such condemnation or taking as Lender may require.

12. BORROWER AND LIEN NOT RELEASED. From time to time, Lender may, at Lender's option, without giving notice to or obtaining the consent of Borrower, Borrower's successors or assigns or of any junior lienholder or guarantors, without liability on Lender's part and notwithstanding Borrower's breach of any covenant or agreement of Borrower in this Instrument, extend the time for payment of said indebtedness or any part thereof, reduce the payments thereon, release anyone liable on any of said indebtedness, accept a renewal note or notes therefor, modify the terms and time of payment of said indebtedness, release from the lien of this Instrument any part of the Property, take or release other or additional security, reconvey any part of the Property, consent to any map or plan of the Property, consent to the granting of any easement, join in any extension or subordination agreement, and agree in writing with Borrower to modify the rate of interest or period of amortization of the Note or change the amount of the monthly installments payable thereunder. Any actions taken by Lender pursuant to the terms of this paragraph 12 shall not affect the obligation of Borrower or Borrower's successors or assigns to pay the sums secured by this Instrument and to observe the covenants of Borrower contained herein, shall not affect the guaranty of any person, corporation, partnership or other entity for payment of the indebtedness secured hereby, and shall not affect the lien or priority of lien hereof on the Property. Borrower shall pay Lender a reasonable service charge, together with such title insurance premiums and attorney's fees as may be incurred at Lender's option, for any such action if taken at Borrower's request.

13. FORBEARANCE BY LENDER NOT A WAIVER. Any forbearance by Lender in exercising any right or remedy hereunder, or otherwise afforded by applicable law, shall not be a waiver of or preclude the exercise of any right or remedy. The acceptance by Lender of payment of any sum secured by this Instrument after the due date of such payment shall not be a waiver of Lender's right to either require prompt payment when due of all other sums so secured or to declare a default for failure to make prompt payment. The procurement of insurance or the payment of taxes or other liens or charges by Lender shall not be a waiver of Lender's right to accelerate the maturity of the indebtedness secured by this Instrument, nor shall Lender's receipt of any awards, proceeds or damages under paragraphs 5 and 11 hereof operate to cure or waive Borrower's default in payment of sums secured by this Instrument.

(page 4 of 8 pages)

FIGURE 12–3 (cont.)

14. ESTOPPEL CERTIFICATE. Borrower shall within ten days of a written request from Lender furnish Lender with a written statement, duly acknowledged, setting forth the sums secured by this Instrument and any right of set-off, counterclaim or other defense which exists against such sums and the obligations of this Instrument.

15. UNIFORM COMMERCIAL CODE SECURITY AGREEMENT. This Instrument is intended to be a security agreement pursuant to the Uniform Commercial Code for any of the items specified above as part of the Property which, under applicable law, may be subject to a security interest pursuant to the Uniform Commercial Code, and Borrower hereby grants Lender a security interest in said items. Borrower agrees that Lender may file this Instrument, or a reproduction thereof, in the real estate records or other appropriate index, as a financing statement for any of the items specified above as part of the Property. Any reproduction of this Instrument or of any other security agreement or financing statement shall be sufficient as a financing statement. In addition, Borrower agrees to execute and deliver to Lender, upon Lender's request, any financing statements, as well as extensions, renewals and amendments thereof, and reproductions of this Instrument in such form as Lender may require to perfect a security interest with respect to said items. Borrower shall pay all costs of filing such financing statements and any extensions, renewals, amendments and releases thereof, and shall pay all reasonable costs and expenses of any record searches for financing statements Lender may reasonably require. Without the prior written consent of Lender, Borrower shall not create or suffer to be created pursuant to the Uniform Commercial Code any other security interest in said items, including replacements and additions thereto. Upon Borrower's breach of any covenant or agreement of Borrower contained in this Instrument, including the covenants to pay when due all sums secured by this Instrument, Lender shall have the remedies of a secured party under the Uniform Commercial Code and, at Lender's option, may also invoke the remedies provided in paragraph 27 of this Instrument as to such items. In exercising any of said remedies, Lender may proceed against the items of real property and any items of personal property specified above as part of the Property separately or together and in any order whatsoever, without in any way affecting the availability of Lender's remedies under the Uniform Commercial Code or of the remedies provided in paragraph 27 of this Instrument.

16. LEASES OF THE PROPERTY. As used in this paragraph 16, the word "lease" shall mean "sublease" if this Instrument is on a leasehold. Borrower shall comply with and observe Borrower's obligations as landlord under all leases of the Property or any part thereof. Borrower will not lease any portion of the Property for non-residential use except with the prior written approval of Lender. Borrower, at Lender's request, shall furnish Lender with executed copies of all leases now existing or hereafter made of all or any part of the Property, and all leases now or hereafter entered into will be in form and substance subject to the approval of Lender. All leases of the Property shall specifically provide that such leases are subordinate to this Instrument; that the tenant attorns to Lender, such attornment to be effective upon Lender's acquisition of title to the Property; that the tenant agrees to execute such further evidences of attornment as Lender may from time to time request; that the attornment of the tenant shall not be terminated by foreclosure; and that Lender may, at Lender's option, accept or reject such attornments. Borrower shall not, without Lender's written consent, execute, modify, surrender or terminate, either orally or in writing, any lease now existing or hereafter made of all or any part of the Property providing for a term of three years or more, permit an assignment or sublease of such a lease without Lender's written consent, or request or consent to the subordination of any lease of all or any part of the Property to any lien subordinate to this Instrument. If Borrower becomes aware that any tenant proposes to do, or is doing, any act or thing which may give rise to any right of set-off against rent, Borrower shall (i) take such steps as shall be reasonably calculated to prevent the accrual of any right to a set-off against rent, (ii) notify Lender thereof and of the amount of said set-offs, and (iii) within ten days after such accrual, reimburse the tenant who shall have acquired such right to set-off or take such other steps as shall effectively discharge such set-off and as shall assure that rents thereafter due shall continue to be payable without set-off or deduction.

Upon Lender's request, Borrower shall assign to Lender, by written instrument satisfactory to Lender, all leases now existing or hereafter made of all or any part of the Property and all security deposits made by tenants in connection with such leases of the Property. Upon assignment by Borrower to Lender of any leases of the Property, Lender shall have all of the rights and powers possessed by Borrower prior to such assignment and Lender shall have the right to modify, extend or terminate such existing leases and to execute new leases, in Lender's sole discretion.

17. REMEDIES CUMULATIVE. Each remedy provided in this Instrument is distinct and cumulative to all other rights or remedies under this Instrument or afforded by law or equity, and may be exercised concurrently, independently, or successively, in any order whatsoever.

18. ACCELERATION IN CASE OF BORROWER'S INSOLVENCY. If Borrower shall voluntarily file a petition under the Federal Bankruptcy Act, as such Act may from time to time be amended, or under any similar or successor Federal statute relating to bankruptcy, insolvency, arrangements or reorganizations, or under any state bankruptcy or insolvency act, or file an answer in an involuntary proceeding admitting insolvency or inability to pay debts, or if Borrower shall fail to obtain a vacation or stay of involuntary proceedings brought for the reorganization, dissolution or liquidation of Borrower, or if Borrower shall be adjudged a bankrupt, or if a trustee or receiver shall be appointed for Borrower or Borrower's property, or if the Property shall become subject to the jurisdiction of a Federal bankruptcy court or similar state court, or if Borrower shall make an assignment for the benefit of Borrower's creditors, or if there is an attachment, execution or other judicial seizure of any portion of Borrower's assets and such seizure is not discharged within ten days, then Lender may, at Lender's option, declare all of the sums secured by this Instrument to be immediately due and payable without prior notice to Borrower, and Lender may invoke any remedies permitted by paragraph 27 of this Instrument. Any attorney's fees and other expenses incurred by Lender in connection with Borrower's bankruptcy or any of the other aforesaid events shall be additional indebtedness of Borrower secured by this Instrument pursuant to paragraph 8 hereof.

19. TRANSFERS OF THE PROPERTY OR BENEFICIAL INTERESTS IN BORROWER; ASSUMPTION. On sale or transfer of (i) all or any part of the Property, or any interest therein, or (ii) beneficial interests in Borrower (if Borrower is not a natural person or persons but is a corporation, partnership, trust or other legal entity), Lender may, at Lender's option, declare all of the sums secured by this Instrument to be immediately due and payable, and Lender may invoke any remedies permitted by paragraph 27 of this Instrument. This option shall not apply in case of

(a) transfers by devise or descent or by operation of law upon the death of a joint tenant or a partner;

(b) sales or transfers when the transferee's creditworthiness and management ability are satisfactory to Lender and the transferee has executed, prior to the sale or transfer, a written assumption agreement containing such terms as Lender may require, including, if required by Lender, an increase in the rate of interest payable under the Note;

(c) the grant of a leasehold interest in a part of the Property of three years or less (or such longer lease term as Lender may permit by prior written approval) not containing an option to purchase (except any interest in the ground lease, if this Instrument is on a leasehold);

(d) sales or transfers of beneficial interests in Borrower provided that such sales or transfers, together with any prior sales or transfers of beneficial interests in Borrower, but excluding sales or transfers under subparagraphs (a) and (b) above, do not result in more than 49% of the beneficial interests in Borrower having been sold or transferred since commencement of amortization of the Note; and

(e) sales or transfers of fixtures or any personal property pursuant to the first paragraph of paragraph 6 hereof.

20. NOTICE. Except for any notice required under applicable law to be given in another manner, (a) any notice to Borrower provided for in this Instrument or in the Note shall be given by mailing such notice by certified mail addressed to Borrower at Borrower's address stated below or at such other address as Borrower may designate by notice to Lender as provided herein, and (b) any notice to Lender shall be given by certified mail, return receipt requested, to Lender's address stated herein or to such other address as Lender may designate by notice to Borrower as provided herein. Any notice provided for in this Instrument or in the Note shall be deemed to have been given to Borrower or Lender when given in the manner designated herein.

21. SUCCESSORS AND ASSIGNS BOUND; JOINT AND SEVERAL LIABILITY; AGENTS; CAPTIONS. The covenants and agreements herein contained shall bind, and the rights hereunder shall inure to, the respective successors and assigns of Lender and Borrower, subject to the provisions of paragraph 19 hereof. All covenants and agreements of Borrower shall be joint and several. In exercising any rights hereunder or taking any actions provided for herein, Lender may act through its employees, agents or independent contractors as authorized by Lender. The captions and headings of the paragraphs of this Instrument are for convenience only and are not to be used to interpret or define the provisions hereof.

22. UNIFORM MULTIFAMILY INSTRUMENT; GOVERNING LAW; SEVERABILITY. This form of multifamily instrument combines uniform covenants for national use and non-uniform covenants with limited variations by jurisdiction to constitute a uniform security instrument covering real property and related fixtures and personal property. This Instrument shall be governed by the law of the jurisdiction in which the Property is located. In the event that any provision of this Instrument or the Note conflicts with applicable law, such conflict shall not affect other provisions of this Instrument or the Note which can be given effect without the conflicting provisions, and to this end the provisions of this

(page 5 of 8 pages)

FIGURE 12–3 (cont.)

Instrument and the Note are declared to be severable. In the event that any applicable law limiting the amount of interest or other charges permitted to be collected from Borrower is interpreted so that any charge provided for in this Instrument or in the Note, whether considered separately or together with other charges levied in connection with this Instrument and the Note, violates such law, and Borrower is entitled to the benefit of such law, such charge is hereby reduced to the extent necessary to eliminate such violation. The amounts, if any, previously paid to Lender in excess of the amounts payable to Lender pursuant to such charges as reduced shall be applied by Lender to reduce the principal of the indebtedness evidenced by the Note. For the purpose of determining whether any applicable law limiting the amount of interest or other charges permitted to be collected from Borrower has been violated, all indebtedness which is secured by this Instrument or evidenced by the Note and which constitutes interest, as well as all other charges levied in connection with such indebtedness which constitute interest, shall be deemed to be allocated and spread over the stated term of the Note. Unless otherwise required by applicable law, such allocation and spreading shall be effected in such a manner that the rate of interest computed thereby is uniform throughout the stated term of the Note.

23. WAIVER OF STATUTE OF LIMITATIONS. Borrower hereby waives the right to assert any statute of limitations as a bar to the enforcement of the lien of this Instrument or to any action brought to enforce the Note or any other obligation secured by this Instrument.

24. WAIVER OF MARSHALLING. Notwithstanding the existence of any other security interests in the Property held by Lender or by any other party, Lender shall have the right to determine the order in which any or all of the Property shall be subjected to the remedies provided herein. Lender shall have the right to determine the order in which any or all portions of the indebtedness secured hereby are satisfied from the proceeds realized upon the exercise of the remedies provided herein. Borrower, any party who consents to this Instrument and any party who now or hereafter acquires a security interest in the Property and who has actual or constructive notice hereof hereby waives any and all right to require the marshalling of assets in connection with the exercise of any of the remedies permitted by applicable law or provided herein.

25. CONSTRUCTION LOAN PROVISIONS. Borrower agrees to comply with the covenants and conditions of the Construction Loan Agreement, if any, which is hereby incorporated by reference in and made a part of this Instrument. All advances made by Lender pursuant to the Construction Loan Agreement shall be indebtedness of Borrower secured by this Instrument, and such advances may be obligatory as provided in the Construction Loan Agreement. All sums disbursed by Lender prior to completion of the improvements to protect the security of this Instrument up to the principal amount of the Note shall be treated as disbursements pursuant to the Construction Loan Agreement. All such sums shall bear interest from the date of disbursement at the rate stated in the Note, unless collection from Borrower of interest at such rate would be contrary to applicable law in which event such amounts shall bear interest at the highest rate which may be collected from Borrower under applicable law and shall be payable upon notice from Lender to Borrower requesting payment therefor.

From time to time as Lender deems necessary to protect Lender's interests, Borrower shall, upon request of Lender, execute and deliver to Lender, in such form as Lender shall direct, assignments of any and all rights or claims which relate to the construction of the Property and which Borrower may have against any party supplying or who has supplied labor, materials or services in connection with construction of the Property. In case of breach by Borrower of the covenants and conditions of the Construction Loan Agreement, Lender, at Lender's option, with or without entry upon the Property, (i) may invoke any of the rights or remedies provided in the Construction Loan Agreement, (ii) may accelerate the sums secured by this Instrument and invoke those remedies provided in paragraph 27 hereof, or (iii) may do both. If, after the commencement of amortization of the Note, the Note and this Instrument are sold by Lender, from and after such sale the Construction Loan Agreement shall cease to be a part of this Instrument and Borrower shall not assert any right of set-off, counterclaim or other claim or defense arising out of or in connection with the Construction Loan Agreement against the obligations of the Note and this Instrument.

26. ASSIGNMENT OF RENTS; APPOINTMENT OF RECEIVER; LENDER IN POSSESSION. As part of the consideration for the indebtedness evidenced by the Note, Borrower hereby absolutely and unconditionally assigns and transfers to Lender all the rents and revenues of the Property, including those now due, past due, or to become due by virtue of any lease or other agreement for the occupancy or use of all or any part of the Property, regardless of to whom the rents and revenues of the Property are payable. Borrower hereby authorizes Lender or Lender's agents to collect the aforesaid rents and revenues and hereby directs each tenant of the Property to pay such rents to Lender or Lender's agents; provided, however, that prior to written notice given by Lender to Borrower of the breach by Borrower of any covenant or agreement of Borrower in this Instrument, Borrower shall collect and receive all rents and revenues of the Property as trustee for the benefit of Lender and Borrower, to apply the rents and revenues so collected to the sums secured by this Instrument in the order provided in paragraph 3 hereof with the balance, so long as no such breach has occurred, to the account of Borrower, it being intended by Borrower and Lender that this assignment of rents constitutes an absolute assignment and not an assignment for additional security only. Upon delivery of written notice by Lender to Borrower of the breach by Borrower of any covenant or agreement of Borrower in this Instrument, and without the necessity of Lender entering upon and taking and maintaining full control of the Property in person, by agent or by a court-appointed receiver, Lender shall immediately be entitled to possession of all rents and revenues of the Property as specified in this paragraph 26 as the same become due and payable, including but not limited to rents then due and unpaid, and all such rents shall immediately upon delivery of such notice be held by Borrower as trustee for the benefit of Lender only; provided, however, that the written notice by Lender to Borrower of the breach by Borrower shall contain a statement that Lender exercises its rights to such rents. Borrower agrees that commencing upon delivery of such written notice of Borrower's breach by Lender to Borrower, each tenant of the Property shall make such rents payable to and pay such rents to Lender or Lender's agents on Lender's written demand to each tenant therefor, delivered to each tenant personally, by mail or by delivering such demand to each rental unit, without any liability on the part of said tenant to inquire further as to the existence of a default by Borrower.

Borrower hereby covenants that Borrower has not executed any prior assignment of said rents, that Borrower has not performed, and will not perform, any acts or has not executed, and will not execute, any instrument which would prevent Lender from exercising its rights under this paragraph 26, and that at the time of execution of this Instrument there has been no anticipation or prepayment of any of the rents of the Property for more than two months prior to the due dates of such rents. Borrower covenants that Borrower will not hereafter collect or accept payment of any rents of the Property more than two months prior to the due dates of such rents. Borrower further covenants that Borrower will execute and deliver to Lender such further assignments of rents and revenues of the Property as Lender may from time to time request.

Upon Borrower's breach of any covenant or agreement of Borrower in this Instrument, Lender may in person, by agent or by a court-appointed receiver, regardless of the adequacy of Lender's security, enter upon and take and maintain full control of the Property in order to perform all acts necessary and appropriate for the operation and maintenance thereof including, but not limited to, the execution, cancellation or modification of leases, the collection of all rents and revenues of the Property, the making of repairs to the Property and the execution or termination of contracts providing for the management or maintenance of the Property, all on such terms as are deemed best to protect the security of this Instrument. In the event Lender elects to seek the appointment of a receiver for the Property upon Borrower's breach of any covenant or agreement of Borrower in this Instrument, Borrower hereby expressly consents to the appointment of such receiver. Lender or the receiver shall be entitled to receive a reasonable fee for so managing the Property.

All rents and revenues collected subsequent to delivery of written notice by Lender to Borrower of the breach by Borrower of any covenant or agreement of Borrower in this Instrument shall be applied first to the costs, if any, of taking control of and managing the Property and collecting the rents, including, but not limited to, attorney's fees, receiver's fees, premiums on receiver's bonds, costs of repairs to the Property, premiums on insurance policies, taxes, assessments and other charges on the Property, and the costs of discharging any obligation or liability of Borrower as lessor or landlord of the Property and then to the sums secured by this Instrument. Lender or the receiver shall have access to the books and records used in the operation and maintenance of the Property and shall be liable to account only for those rents actually received. Lender shall not be liable to Borrower, anyone claiming under or through Borrower or anyone having an interest in the Property by reason of anything done or left undone by Lender under this paragraph 26.

If the rents of the Property are not sufficient to meet the costs, if any, of taking control of and managing the Property and collecting the rents, any funds expended by Lender for such purposes shall become indebtedness of Borrower to Lender secured by this Instrument pursuant to paragraph 8 hereof. Unless Lender and Borrower agree in writing to other terms of payment, such amounts shall be payable upon notice from Lender to Borrower requesting payment thereof and shall bear interest from the date of disbursement at the rate stated in the Note unless payment of interest at such rate would be contrary to applicable law, in which event such amounts shall bear interest at the highest rate which may be collected from Borrower under applicable law.

Any entering upon and taking and maintaining of control of the Property by Lender or the receiver and any application of rents as provided herein shall not cure or waive any default hereunder or invalidate any other right or remedy of Lender under applicable law or provided herein. This assignment of rents of the Property shall terminate at such time as this Instrument ceases to secure indebtedness held by Lender.

FIGURE 12-3 (cont.)

Non-Uniform Covenants. Borrower and Lender further covenant and agree as follows:

27. ACCELERATION; REMEDIES. Upon Borrower's breach of any covenant or agreement of Borrower in this Instrument, including, but not limited to, the covenants to pay when due any sums secured by this Instrument, Lender at Lender's option may declare all of the sums secured by this Instrument to be immediately due and payable without further demand and may foreclose this Instrument by judicial proceeding and may invoke any other remedies permitted by applicable law or provided herein. Lender shall be entitled to collect all costs and expenses incurred in pursuing such remedies, including, but not limited to, attorney's fees, costs of documentary evidence, abstracts and title reports.

28. RELEASE. Upon payment of all sums secured by this Instrument, Lender shall release this Instrument. Borrower shall pay Lender's reasonable costs incurred in releasing this Instrument.

29. ATTORNEY'S FEES. As used in this Instrument and in the Note, "attorney's fees" shall include attorney's fees, if any, which may be awarded by an appellate court.

30. FUTURE ADVANCES. Upon request of Borrower, Lender, at Lender's option within twenty years from the date of this Instrument, may make Future Advances to Borrower. Such Future Advances, with interest thereon, shall be secured by this Instrument when evidenced by promissory notes stating that said notes are secured hereby. At no time shall the principal amount of the indebtedness secured by this Instrument, not including sums advanced in accordance herewith to protect the security of this Instrument, exceed the original amount of the Note (US $ ....) plus the additional sum of US $................................. .

IN WITNESS WHEREOF, Borrower has executed this Instrument or has caused the same to be executed by its representatives thereunto duly authorized.

.............../S/ Nancy O. Investor........................ ....(Seal)

.............../S/ Gerald I. Investor........................ ....(Seal)

....(Seal)

....(Seal)

Signed, sealed and delivered in the presence of: Borrower's Address:

....

....

241

required to keep the property insured against fire and other hazards up to the amount of the loan balance, and against rent losses. The borrower, in self-interest, is advised to insure the property for a larger amount, up to market value. The clause requires the insurance to be payable to the noteholder. In the event of loss, the insurance proceeds may be used to restore the property, if financially feasible, or to repay the debt. Any excess must be paid the borrower. The borrower must promptly notify the noteholder of any damage or destruction.

Property Maintenance and Use

Clause 6 obligates the borrower to maintain the property in good repair and not permit its waste or deterioration. The borrower further agrees to operate and maintain the property for continuing rental income. It is also agreed that fixtures, buildings, equipment, and other improvements shall not be removed or demolished without prior written consent from the noteholder.

In clause 7, the borrower agrees not to change the use of the property unless otherwise agreed or required by law. Even a change in zoning is subject to review by the noteholder.

Protection of Lender's Security

Clause 8 states that the lender reserves the right to protect the secured property if the borrower fails to do so. Thus, any actions necessary to look after the noteholder's interest, such as paying taxes and insurance premiums, having the property maintained and repaired, or appearing for an eminent-domain or bankruptcy proceeding may be taken over by the noteholder. Any amounts disbursed for these and similar reasons may be added to the borrower's indebtedness and be subject to interest at the loan rate. The lender, however, is not required to make disbursements for the borrower. If payments are made, the lender obtains subrogation rights. *Subrogation* means taking the place of another as the possessor of legal rights. Thus, in paying a claim against a borrower, the lender obtains all rights and remedies of the borrower. For example, a lender may conduct eminent-domain negotiations with the same rights and remedies as possessed by an owner-borrower who may be sick or incapacitated.

Clause 9 gives the noteholder reasonable entry to the property for inspections to assure its maintenance, safety, and proper operation, among other things. In addition, clause 10 gives the lender reasonable access to the borrower's books and other financial records concerning the property. Again, the objective is assurance and protection of the lender's interests in the property.

Condemnation

Properties are taken from time to time for public uses or purposes through eminent domain. Clause 11 states that proceeds from condemnation shall first go to pay lender expenses and the debt, with any excess going to the borrower-owner.

Borrower Not Released by Lender Forbearance

Clause 12 states that a lender or noteholder does not release the lien or forgive any of the borrower's obligations by extending time for payment or by failure to press for payment. That is, the lender loses no rights by being courteous and considerate in dealing with the borrower or debtor. Clause 13 makes it even more clear that forbearance by a noteholder—postponing action to a later time—does not waive or preclude exercise of a right or remedy. Thus, if the contract is in default, payments may be accelerated or made due immediately or at a later time, without damage to the noteholder.

Additional Legal Documentation

Clause 14 states that borrower will provide lender an estoppel certificate on demand. An **estoppel certificate** is a written statement that, when signed and given to another person, legally prevents the signer from saying subsequently that the facts are different from those set forth. An estoppel certificate might, then, be used to establish agreement on the principal balance, on sums secured, or on legal rights of the parties at some specific time. Subsequently, the borrower would not be legally able to deny the facts stated in the certificate.

Clause 15 requires the borrower to provide statements and to pay recording charges necessary to bring the mortgage into compliance with the Uniform Commercial Code. And clause 16 requires the borrower to continue the property in residential use and to provide the lender with copies of leases and side agreements with tenants, upon request.

Remedies Cumulative

Clause 17 makes clear that lender remedies are distinct and cumulative. The remedies may therefore be exercised one at a time, all at one time, or in various in-between combinations, according to the noteholder's preferences.

Acceleration

The lender may accelerate payments on the borrower's insolvency or sale of ownership under clauses 18 and 19. Filing bankruptcy proceedings evidences insolvency. An assumption of the loan obligation by another party, meaning that payments have been taken over by the other party, constitutes a sale. As long as the transfers are relatively minor (less than 49 percent of the borrower's interest) the acceleration clause may not be invoked. And as long as an acceptable borrower continues to be responsible for the loan, in many states acceleration may not be initiated. Thus, sale to a credit-worthy buyer is allowed with a written assumption agreement, which may increase the interest rate. In addition, transfer by "devise or descent" (death of borrower) is not a violation. Also, the borrower is allowed to grant a leasehold for up to three years.

Notice

Certified mail must be used by the lender or borrower to give notice to the other party, according to clause 20. The mail is to be sent to the address of record in the mortgage. Sending notices is important in situations involving (1) changes of name or address, (2) default and foreclosure, (3) sale of the property, or (4) damage or destruction to the property.

Catch-all Clauses

A mortgage is a complex instrument. Lots of legal detail must be included even though the intent is to write in clear and easy-to-understand language. Clauses 21–25 include necessary detail.

Clause 21 says that successors and assigns of lender and/or borrower, (people taking over the legal positions of the lender and/or borrower at a later time) are equally bound by the contracts provisions. If more than one borrower is involved, all are bound jointly and severally. Thus, the borrowers may have any arrangement they wish among themselves, but the lender-mortgagee is not burdened to treat them equally or to collect proportionately from them, in case of default particularly.

According to clause 22, conflicts between the uniform instrument and local law are to be resolved according to the law of the jurisdiction in which the property is located. Further, any such conflict shall not invalidate the remaining provisions of the instrument. This division of the instrument into distinct, independent obligations or agreements, any one of which may be removed without affecting the others, is termed **severability.**

Any applicable statute of limitations to provisions in the instrument is waived by paragraph 23. And in paragraph 24, the right to the marshalling of assets (arranging in a certain order) in connection with default remedies in the contract is waived. These provisions have the effect of giving the lender greater freedom in pursuing remedies under the instrument. And according to paragraph 25, a construction loan agreement may be made and tied into the instrument.

Assignment of Rents

With an income property, possession and control, including collection of rents, are critical concerns in default. Without control by a lender, a borrower may collect rents and otherwise "milk" the property until the foreclosure suit is substantially completed. Clause 26 provides that upon breach of a condition, and proper notice, the rents are to be paid to a *receiver*. A **receiver** is an officer of the court appointed to take possession and control of the property of concern in a suit. Having a receiver take control of the property serves to keep all remedies open to the lender, while at the same time protecting the lender's immediate interests. As long as no covenants or agreements are broken, and no notice given, the borrower continues to have the right to manage the property and to collect rents.

TYPES OF MORTGAGES

Mortgages may be classified in many ways. The most common mortgages are discussed here according to three grouping systems. The systems are not unique or distinct; that is, some overlap occurs from one system to another. The first system is based on the activity or parties to the contract and is a general classification system. The second is a repayment plan. The third is based on a special provision, clause, or arrangement.

General Kinds of Mortgage Loans

The general kinds of mortgage loans include the following:

1. Construction
2. Conventional
3. FHA insured
4. VA guaranteed
5. Privately insured
6. Purchase money
7. Second or junior
8. Participation

CONSTRUCTION LOAN. A loan to aid an owner, a builder, or a developer to finance the erection of a structure or the addition of other improvements to a property is called a **construction mortgage.** The loan is made for from six to twelve months or until the completion of the proposed structure in accordance with plans and specifications included as part of the arrangement. Construction loans to builders usually extend to the sale of the property, which may be several months after completion.

A construction loan is distinct in that the total of the loan is not initially fully paid out to the borrower. Instead, funds are paid out in installments at agreed stages as construction progresses. A lender representative usually inspects and certifies satisfactory progress prior to each payout. Depending on local custom, interest is payable either on the entire amount from date of agreement or only on the amounts of the installments as advanced. The latter arrangement is more common.

Upon completion of construction or sale, permanent financing must be arranged. Some lenders allow land owners to convert their construction loans directly into permanent loans. They also make conditional commitments to builders that if a financially responsible and capable buyer is found, the loan may be converted into long-term or permanent financing. In any event, sometime after completion of construction, permanent financing must be arranged.

CONVENTIONAL LOAN. A **conventional mortgage loan** is a loan not insured by the Federal Housing Administration (FHA) or guaranteed by the Veterans' Administration (VA). A conventional loan, although not FHA insured or VA guaranteed, must be consistent with accepted standards of mortgage lending, modified within legal bounds by mutual consent of the borrower and the lender. Traditionally, conventional loans are made at lower loan-to-value ratios than FHA or VA loans. The interest rate is the market rate at the time the loan is made. Also, conventional loans are more subject to the policies and regulations of individual institutions. Conventional loans account for approximately 70 percent of "permanent" or long-term mortgage loans on properties containing one to four dwelling units.

FHA-INSURED LOAN. The Federal Housing Administration (FHA) insures lenders against loss on mortgage loans in return for fees or premiums paid by borrowers. These insured loans are known as **FHA loans.** The FHA, as an agency of the United States government, only insures loans made by approved lenders under regulated conditions and terms. That is, the FHA does not lend money. The conditions and terms include minimum standards of property location and construction and fixed mortgage terms. Dollarwise, FHA insures approximately one-sixth of all the mortgage loans made on from one- to four-family structures. In recent years, the much wider acceptance of private mortgage insurance has led to a decline in popularity of FHA loans.

FHA-insured loans may be made for up to 97 percent of value of newly built, low-cost homes. With this high loan-to-value ratio, the lender would be exposed to great risk if not covered by FHA insurance. The borrower therefore agrees to pay a premium of 0.5 percent of the outstanding loan balance, to protect the lender.

VA-GUARANTEED LOAN. A mortgage loan to an eligible veteran and certain others that is partially guaranteed against loss by the Veterans' Administration of the United States is termed a **VA or "GI" mortgage.** The borrower pays no charge or premium for the guarantee. The terms and interest rate of the loan, however, are fixed by law. The VA sets no maximum amount for the loan.

The loan must initially be made to a qualified veteran or the dependent of a qualified veteran, usually a surviving spouse. The lending institution simply makes the loan from its own monies and gets the guarantee from the VA. The Veterans' Administration makes no loans. The loan may later be taken over by a nonveteran.

VA-guaranteed loans account for nearly one-sixth of all United States mortgage loans outstanding on from one- to four-family structures. This figure does not include loans made by or guaranteed by the Veterans' Administration at the state level, which are known as state "GI" or VA loans.

PRIVATELY INSURED LOAN. A conventional mortgage loan, on which the lender is partially protected against loss by a private mortgage insurance company in return for a fee or premium, is termed a *privately insured loan.* The insurance companies and the financial institutions that do business with them make up the private mortgage insurance (PMI) industry. From a lender's point of view, the PMI industry is in direct competition with the Federal Housing Administraton and the Veterans' Administration.

Basically, PMI covers the top 20 to 25 percent of the initial amount of a loan, which is the portion most exposed to risk and loss. Almost all states allow lenders to make loans up to 95 percent of value with private mortgage insurance. The insurance coverage runs out or is not needed after several years because the mortgage balance and the loan-to-value ratio are reduced.

Private mortgage insurance gives lenders more flexibility in their lending policies because it applies to loans made on conventional terms. The standardized terms of FHA and VA loans are therefore avoided. Loans can also be processed more quickly because much of the bureaucratic red tape associated with FHA and VA is avoided. Finally, like existing FHA and VA loans, PMI loans are bought and sold among banks, savings and loan associations, insurance companies, and others, in what is called the secondary mortgage market.

PURCHASE MONEY MORTGAGE LOAN. A **purchase money mortgage** is a mortgage given by a buyer to a seller to secure all, or a portion, of the purchase price of a property. The seller is therefore financing or partially financing the transaction. The seller therefore becomes the lender-mortgagee and the buyer becomes the borrower-mortgagor. A purchase money mortgage becomes a lien simultaneously with the passing of title. The lien is prior to any lien that might develop against the property due to the purchaser's actions, provided the deed and the mortgage are recorded together. The words "purchase money mortgage" are commonly included when the mortgage is drawn up, to give notice of its special character. In foreclosure, a purchase money mortgage or trust deed takes priority, as a lien, over judgment liens against the borrower, over the homestead exemption of the borrower and his or her spouse, and over dower or curtesy rights of the spouse of the borrower-buyer. The legal presumption is that since the mortgage became a lien at the same time title passed, no other party could have developed a prior claim.

At the same time, in some states a deficiency judgment is not permitted on a purchase money mortgage. The law presumes that the seller-lender may recover the original property and therefore is no worse off after foreclosure than if no sale had occurred and no mortgage made. Hence, no deficiency judgment is justified.

SECOND OR JUNIOR MORTGAGE LOAN. A mortgage with priority as a lien over all other mortgages against a property is a *first mortgage*. A mortgage second in priority to another mortgage is a *second mortgage*. And a mortgage with two mortgages of higher priority is a *third mortgage*. Mortgages sometimes get stacked six and seven deep as to priority. The collective name for mortgages lower in priority than the first mortgage is *junior mortgages*. It follows that the lower the priority of a mortgage, the greater the risk of loss to the lender-mortgagee.

The second or junior mortgage was commonly used in real estate financing prior to the depression of the early 1930s. Relatively few second mortgages are now made in connection with acquisition of newer single-family residences. Lenders are usually able to meet the requirements of borrowers by means of a single, high loan-to-value mortgage on a long-term amortizing basis, repayment of which is geared to the financial ability of individual borrowers. Second mortgages are mainly used in financing older properties. A key clause in junior mortgages provides for possible default in the prior mortgage, and another clause usually included is a subordination provision. Both clauses are described below.

A *default-in-the-prior-mortgage* clause provides that if the mortgagor defaults in payment of interest, principal, or taxes on any prior mortgage, such interest, principal, or taxes may be paid by the junior mortgagee and added to the amount of the junior loan. Furthermore, the junior lender may forthwith declare a default and proceed to foreclose. This clause is for the protection of the mortgagee. The implications are a very important matter to the junior mortgagee. Should the prior mortgage be foreclosed, the junior mortgagee may be compelled either to abandon the lien or to purchase the property and replace the prior mortgage. This clause permits the secondary lender to prevent a default in the prior mortgage while foreclosing the junior mortgage.

Another clause usually found in junior mortgages in the **subordination** clause, which is designed for the protection of the mortgagor. When the junior mortgagee made the loan, a property, already subject to a mortgage, was taken as security to secure the sum or sums advanced the borrower. Presumably, the second mortgage should continue in the same subordinated position. But without any provision to cover the situation, the junior mortagee's mortgage would automatically become a first lien upon payment of the prior mortgage claims. Hence, it is customary to insert a clause by which the junior mortgagee's position is fixed. The following is an example of a subordination clause:

This mortgage shall be and remain subordinate to the present first mortgage or any renewal thereof, or in event of its payment, to any new mortgage provided the excess (if any) of said mortgage over the amount of the present first mortgage be applied in reduction of the principal of this mortgage.

PARTICIPATION MORTGAGE LOAN. A *participation mortgage* is one owned by two or more lenders. These persons do not own the entire mortgage jointly, but rather each owns a specified interest in it. A mortgage may be made to a trustee, who issues a certificate of ownership to each person or party having an interest in it. As payments of interest and principal are made, each participant receives a pro rata share. An arrangement of this kind usually means that each ownership in the mortgage is coordinate or equal in standing.

In some participation mortgages the ownerships are not coordinate; but rather, one ranks ahead of another. For example, an owner may wish to secure a mortgage of a certain amount but, upon application to a lender, finds the lender willing to advance a smaller amount. Another lender, however, might wish to make a loan for the difference, subject to the first lender's amount. Thus the mortgage is made for the total amount and is usually made to the first or largest lender, and the securing lien is placed in the first lender's possession or name. An agreement is then made between the two lenders, called a *participation agreement,* or *ownership agreement,* in which the mortgage is owned by the first lender to the extent of a certain amount of principal and interest only, with the second party owning the balance of the mortgage note. The ownership of the first party is agreed to be superior to that of the second party, as though one held a first mortgage for a portion and the other a second mortgage for the remainder. The share of one lender in a participation mortgage of this kind is called a *prior participation, or senior participation,* and that of the other lender a *subordinate participation, or junior participation.*

Mortgages Classified by Repayment Plan

Mortgage contracts may be negotiated with a wide variety of repayment plans. The various plans are based on some combination of the term loan and the amortizing loan concepts.

A *term or straight-term mortgage loan* is one in which the principal amount of the loan is not reduced during the life of the contract. Interest payments are usually made quarterly, semiannually, or annually. The life is usually from three to five years. At the end of the contract the entire balance plus the interest for the last period is due and payable.

A mortgage loan contract in which the periodic debt service pays interest on the loan and systematically repays the principal of the loan over the life of the agreement is termed an *amortizing mortgage loan.* Nearly all mortgages with an extended life include a periodic-amortization provision. Home loans are usually amortized on a monthly basis while farm loans typically call for annual payments in late fall after the harvest has been marketed. Commercial loans may call for monthly, quarterly, semi-annual, or annual debt service.

An amortizing loan assures a lender of a constant, or even improving, loan-to-value ratio because in almost every case the payments for mortgage amortization exceed property value losses due to property wear, tear, and obsolescence. At the same time, an amortizing mortgage reduces a borrower's fear of inability to meet repayment or replacement of a large maturing debt under uncertain future conditions.

With these concepts in mind, we may now discuss the alternative repayment plans, of which there are the following general types:

1. Fixed-rate mortgage (FRM)
2. Canadian rollover mortgage
3. Variable-rate mortgage (VRM)
4. Graduated-payment mortgage (GPM)
5. Partially amortizing mortgage

FIXED-RATE MORTGAGE. A **fixed-rate mortgage (FRM)** loan means that the interest rate remains unchanged over the life of the loan, and debt service payments are equal or uniform in size. Debt service payments during the early part of the life go mostly to interest with a small portion to principal reduction. As the loan ages, the portion going to principal reduction increases while the portion to interest decreases. With the last payment, both principal and interest requirements are fully satisfied. The FRM loan was born during the depression through federal government efforts. FRM loans are traditionally for twenty to thirty years.

CANADIAN ROLLOVER MORTGAGE. Prior to the introduction of the FRM loan, with its built-in provision for amortization, most lending was on three-to-five-year straight term loans. Only interest payments were required during the five years. Borrowers faced a large "balloon" payment at the end of the five years, which led to refinancing at extra costs or default; many lenders refused to refinance during the depression because of the uncertain times. Lenders have now gone back to the straight term loans to gain greater interest rate flexibility in managing their loans. Effectively, they now willingly refinance or "roll over" a maturing loan, but at the current interest rate. This plan, reintroduced in Canada when interest rates advanced sharply in the early 1970s, is called the **Canadian rollover mortgage.** Borrowers benefit from this plan because debt-service payments are smaller relative to amortizing plans.

VARIABLE-RATE MORTGAGE. A mortgage loan agreement that allows the interest rate to increase or decrease directly with fluctuations in an index beyond the control of the lender is called a **variable-rate mortgage (VRM).** The fluctuating index may be the prime rate charged by banks or the interest rate quoted for long-term government or industrial bonds. A VRM loan is amortizing, and debt-service payments usually remain level. If the interest rate increases, the life of the loan is simply extended, and vice versa.

VRM lending shifts the risk of increasing interest rates to borrowers; at the same time, any decrease in interest rates benefits the borrower. Unless money is extremely tight or relatively unavailable, VRM loans are often made at slightly lower rates than FRM loans. This flexible rate allows lenders to continue making loans in the face of increasing interest rates without fear of being locked in at a low fixed rate. Hence, VRM lending maintains a more even flow of funds into real estate. VRM lending appears to be spreading rapidly.

GRADUATED-PAYMENT MORTGAGES. A **graduated-payment mortgage (GPM)** *loan* provides for low initial debt-service payments with regular increases for a stated period, usually five or ten years. The interest rate may be fixed or variable. Sometimes payments in the early years won't cover all interest due on the loan, and the principal owed actually increases. A GPM loan is also sometimes called a young people's loan because it seems to best suit the needs of people who are just forming households but have increasing incomes. GPM loans are best suited to situations where the borrower expects steady increases in income at about the same rate as the scheduled increases in debt-service requirements. Thus, young families are able to afford better housing than they otherwise would.

PARTIALLY AMORTIZING MORTGAGE. A loan contract calling for systematic, periodic repayment of a portion of the original principal over the life of an agreement and repayment of the balance in a single lump-sum payment at the end of the agreement is a **partially amortizing mortgage.** It is a combination of a fully amortizing loan for a portion of the original principal and of a term loan for the balance. The lump-sum payment of the principal balance at the end of the agreement is commonly called a **balloon payment.** An example of a partially amortizing mortgage is one set up on a thirty-year amortization schedule with a balloon payment required at the end of the twentieth year.

Mortgages Classified by Miscellaneous Provisions or Arrangements

Mortgages frequently contain unique clauses or arrangements for special situations or purposes, and get special names: (1) blanket, (2) package, (3) open-end, and (4) wraparound.

BLANKET LOAN. One mortgage with two or more houses or other parcels of property pledged as security for the debt is called a *blanket mortgage.* The most common use of a blanket mortgage is in subdividing land, where a lender makes an initial mortgage loan with raw acreage as security. The acreage, after being split up into lots, remains subject to the mortgage. Blanket mortgages usually include a provision to release lots on an individual basis in return for payments of specified size when used for subdivisions. If a release provision is not included in the mortgage, the amount paid as each parcel is removed from the mortgage must be negotiated. Customarily, the release price on each lot is slightly higher than the lot's proportional share of the loan based on its value because better lots are usually sold first. The lender therefore ensures that the remaining parcels adequately secure the loan.

PACKAGE LOAN. A mortgage contract that includes fixtures and building equipment as collateral is termed a *package mortgage.* Equipment, widely accepted as security in a residential package mortgage, includes refrigerators, ranges, washing machines and dryers, dishwasher, and garbage disposal units. Including fixtures and equipment as security for mortgage loans is becoming so commonplace that the term *package mortgage* is dropping into disuse.

The acceptance of fixtures and building equipment as collateral in a package mortgage requires mutual agreement of borrower and lender. Acceptance of the fixtures and equipment in a mortgage loan requires that (1) the article be considered realty by expressed intent of the parties, (2) the equipment be paid for with mortgage money, (3) the article be appropriate for use in the home, and (4) the article be actually annexed to the realty to some degree. Package mortgages strengthen the credit position of the home buyer by reducing monthly payments for household equipment in the years immediately following purchase. The home buyer is therefore in a better position to meet an emergency and in turn is less likely to become delinquent on mortgage payments. This reduction in delinquencies pleases lenders, of course.

OPEN-END LOAN. A mortgage contract providing for later advances from a lender, up to but not exceeding the original amount of the loan, is defined as an *open-end mortgage.* The interest rate on the loan may be renegotiated in the process. An open-end provision in a loan simplifies an owner's problem of financing additions or major repairs to a home in the years following the original purchase. Thus, the home owner may readily borrow funds to add a fireplace, garage, or extra room, or to replace a roof.

The open-end mortgage strengthens the investment portfolio of lenders. Seasoned loans can be restored to original amounts at interest rates more in line with current market rates. Also, property improvement loans advantageously improve the loan-to-value ratio of mortgages in the portfolio. Borrowers benefit from lower overall interest rates.

WRAPAROUND LOAN. A wraparound mortgage is used when a mortgagee refuses to refinance a property at reasonable terms. A precondition of a wraparound mortgage is current market interest rates exceeding the interest rate on the existing mortgage.

The existing first mortgage remains outstanding and unsatisfied in a wraparound mortgage arrangement. A second lender simply makes a new, larger loan to the borrower at an interest rate between that on the first mortgage and that in the market. The amount of money actually advanced by the second lender equals the amount of the new loan less the amount of the existing first mortgage. The face amount of the wraparound loan therefore overstates the borrower's indebtedness to the second lender. In turn, the second lender realizes leverage by wraping a high-interest-rate second mortgage around a low-interest-rate first mortgage.

The borrower pays debt service to the second lender for the wraparound mortgage only. The second lender assumes responsibility for debt service or repayment of the original loan.

OTHER MORTGAGE INSTRUMENTS

A number of other instruments are used in the mortgaging process in conjunction with the note and the mortgage. Many of these instruments are special purpose in nature. The more common of these instruments are as follows:

1. Satisfaction of mortgage
2. Extension of mortgage
3. Assignment of mortgage
4. Release of mortgage
5. Subordination of mortgage
6. Certificate of reduction of mortgage
7. Estoppel certificate
8. Mortgage consolidation agreement
9. Mortgage spreading agreement
10. Collateral bond

Satisfaction of Mortgage

The word *satisfaction* when used legally means receipt, and the expression *satisfaction piece* simply means a formal written receipt. Thus *satisfaction of lien, satisfaction of judgment,* and *satisfaction of mortgage* are each names of a particular type of formal acknowledgment of payment. When a mortgage is paid off, the property owner should insist on having the original mortgage and bond or note returned to him or her. If the owner has these, it is of course impossible for anyone to substantiate a claim on the mortgage. A very important point to be borne in mind, however, is that mortgages are nearly always recorded and the mere payment of the amount of the mortgage debt and the surrender of the bond or note and mortgage by the mortgagee to the property owner do not change the fact of the records in the recording office where the mortgage was originally filed. It is therefore very important that some procedure be followed that will not only close the door against a suit on the note or bond and mortgage but also secure the cancellation of the mortgage of record. For this purpose the mortgagee, upon receiving payment, should be required to sign a formal receipt or satisfaction piece, which is then recorded. The recording officer, upon receiving it, marks the mortgage on the records as being canceled or satisfied. In that way the lien of the mortgage is removed, and the mortgage no longer continues to affect the property in any way.

The satisfaction piece recites a detailed description of the mortgage, giving its date, the amount, and the date and place where it was recorded, as well as the names of the parties to the mortgage. If the bond or note and mortgage have been assigned, the satisfaction piece should recite the details of each assignment. If any assignments have not been recorded, they should be recorded, so that there is a clear chain of ownership of the mortgage from the original lender down to the person executing the satisfaction piece. The instrument should further state that the mortgage debt has been paid and that the mortgage may be discharged on the records. When this satisfaction piece is filed and the necessary fees paid, it is customary to stamp or write across the face of the mortgage as copied in the recording books a statement to the effect that the mortgage has been "canceled or satisfied by satisfaction piece filed on [the date when filed]."

Much trouble is constantly arising through the failure of property owners to record the satisfaction piece of a mortgage when they pay it off. They seem to feel that, since they have repossessed the bond or note and the mortgage, nothing concerns them any longer. Often they destroy the mortgage instruments. This gives rise to considerable difficulty when, possibly, many years later, they seek to sell the property and then discover that, although the mortgage has long since been paid off, it is still "open on the record" and constitutes a flaw or cloud on the title. The only safe procedure is for the owner to record the satisfaction piece as soon as he or she receives it. In some places it is required that the original mortgage be recorded with the satisfaction piece, as an additional check against forgery. One of the most common crimes in connection with real estate has been the filing of a forged satisfaction of mortgage by someone who has decided to turn criminal and who then, posing as the owner, negotiates a new mortgage loan, keeping the holder of the old mortgage quiescent by continuing regular payments on the mortgage. There have been instances of criminals doing this thirty or forty times before being discovered. Requiring the filing of the original mortgage with the satisfaction piece is at least something of a safeguard.

The satisfaction piece should, or course, be signed by the present holder of the mortgage. His or her signature must be formally proved, either by self-acknowledgment or by the deposition of a subscribing witness. If the mortgage is held by several people, each one must sign the satisfaction piece. If it is held by executors, it is customary to endeavor to secure the signatures of all, although legally any one of the executors may satisfy a mortgage if the original holder was the testator. If a mortgage is held by trustees, each of them should be required to sign. If a mortgage is held by a guardian for an infant, signature by the guardian is sufficient until such time as the ward becomes of age. Then it is advisable to have the satisfaction piece executed by both the guardian and the ward.

In some jurisdictions, the county clerk will arrange, upon request by the rightful holder of the mortgage, for direct cancellation of the mortgage on the county records. Where this is permissible, the mortgagee presents the original mortgage to the recording clerk who will stamp the record mortgage page and the original mortgage instruments as follows:

For and in consideration of the full payment of the sum of money secured to be paid by this mortgage, I hereby cancel and discharge the same from record.
This .... day of .... 19..........
Attested ....
Clerk of .... Court

....
Mortgagee

This direct cancellation procedure, for which a nominal charge is made, obviates the necessity to prepare a satisfaction of mortgage instrument and thus saves related acknowledgment and recording fees.

Extension of Mortgage

A mortgage always states a certain time when the principal shall be paid. It may be payable on demand, in which event the holder of the mortgage may require its payment at any time, or it may be payable at some date in the future—either in installments or in full at some set time, possibly three to five years after the loan is made. After the due date has passed, if the mortgage is not paid, a situation arises in which the lender may demand payment at any time, possibly to the great inconvenience of the property owner, who may have difficulty in refinancing on sudden call. So, also, the lender may be inconvenienced by having his or her investment suddenly paid off when he or she finds it inopportune to get a new investment. This inconvenience is very likely to arise, because the lender naturally will demand his or her money when mortgage money is scarce and interest rates high and he or she wishes the funds for some other form of investment, or because real estate at the time is unattractive. Thus, in either case it is difficult for the property owner to secure other financing except at considerable expense. On the other hand, if the property owner pays off the mortgage, he or she will probably do so at a time when money is plentiful and interest rates are low, and the lender will be unable to secure any other investment at so attractive an interest rate. It is therefore advantageous for the mortgagor and the mortgagee alike not to let the mortgage run open or past due.

Many mortgages are so arranged, at the time they are first placed on the property, that they continue during a considerable part of the useful life of the building. Such are the mortgages that amortize themselves at from 3 to 5 percent per year and consequently run twenty or more years. As to these mortgages, there is no concern over their becoming past due. They do not become past due until finally paid off.

It is important, however, that mortgages running without any reduction provisions be extended periodically. Many investors do not wish their mortgages to be reduced. They feel they are safe and desire the fixed income arising from a mortgage running for a period of three to five years without reduction in principal and consequent change in the amount of interest coming in. When this is the case, the holder of the mortgage, shortly prior to its due date, should inspect and reappraise the property and decide whether he or she wishes the mortgage to continue for the same amount or wishes it reduced and, if so, to what extent. It is then a matter of negotiation between the property owner and the mortgagee as to the amount of the mortgage to be extended, the period of time, and the interest rate. Naturally, if the holder of the mortgage desires the mortgage reduced below an amount that the property owner feels he or she can secure elsewhere, a new mortgage will be arranged; but if the parties agree, a written agreement should embody terms of the extension.

Such an extension agreement is dated. The first party is the holder of the mortgage; the second is the owner of the property. There follows a brief description of the mortgage, giving sufficient facts to identify it, such as its date, amount, parties, date of record, the office in which recorded, and a statement of the book or *liber* and page of record. The instrument states the date to which payment has been extended, the interest rate, and the times when interest shall be paid. If any arrangement is made for amortization, that fact also will be stated. There should also be stated the present amount or balance of principal and the date to which interest has been paid. In this way any possible dispute between the parties as to past payments is settled. Following in the form are a number of clauses that conform in a general way to the clauses appearing in a mortgage. It may be noted that by the use of an extension agreement old mortgages that omit clauses that have since become important may be cured of this deficiency, and wherever the mortgage is extended, the extension agreement should be looked upon not as a perfunctory paper but as one of only slightly less importance than the original mortgage instruments that underlie the extension agreement.

Under the extension agreement, the present property owner agrees to pay the mortgage debt and the interest. This makes him or her the primary debtor, and in some instances, when the property owner wishes to avoid this responsibility, he or she may prefer to let the mortgage run open rather than become liable for a deficiency in the event of foreclosure. It is also the general impression that the making of an extension agreement releases from liability the person liable on the note or bond; but this is not true in most states. The law governing is a phase of the law or suretyship. Applied to extension agreements, it works as follows: on an open or past-due mortgage, and up to the time the mortgage is extended, the holder of the mortgage can enforce payment at any time, and even though the property passes into the hands of a third party, the original bondsman can demand that the mortgage be collected and force the holder of the mortgage to foreclose. If the original bondsman fails to do this, he permits himself to continue liable and risks having the property decline in value; but (and this is the important thing) the minute the holder of the mortgage by a written extension agreement puts it out of his means to enforce collection, he releases the old bondsman to the extent of any value the property may lose, after the extension agreement is made. Quite possibly at the time the extension agreement was made, the property was worth more than enough to satisfy the mortgage. It would therefore be unfair to hold the old bondsman for any loss that might thereafter accrue by reason of subsequent shrinkage in the value of the property.

The extension agreement is prepared in duplicate, and both copies are executed by both parties. Usually extension agreements are not recorded, but since the agreements may need to be offered in evidence of foreclosure, it is generally customary to have the signatures of the parties proved either by acknowledgment or by deposition of a subscribing witness.

Assignment of Mortgage

A bond or note and mortgage are personal property, and hence their ownership may be transferred by mere delivery. It is not necessary, technically, to have any instrument executed for the purpose of transferring the mortgage instruments. However, it is always customary to use what is known as an *assignment of mortgage*. The use of such a written instrument accomplishes two purposes: (1) it may be recorded, so that the records show the transfer of ownership; (2) it negates any possibility that possession by the transferee is the result of fraud or theft. The instrument is always dated, although often at the end. The assignor, naturally, is the person transferring the note and mortgage. Sometimes the assignor is called the party of the first part. The transferee is the assignee, or party of the second part. The consideration stated may be nominal, unless the transfer is made by or to a fiduciary, when the full consideration should be stated. Next follows a description of the mortgage assigned, which normally consists of a statement of the date of the mortgage, the names of the parties, the amount of the mortgage, and the date, place, book or *liber,* and page of recording. The instrument technically also assigns the bond or note, because in legal theory the bond or note is the principal indebtedness and the mortgage merely the security. It is customary to include in an assignment what is spoken of as *the covenant,* a paragraph that recites the amount of unpaid principal, the interest rate, and the date to which interest has been paid. It should always be the purpose of the transferee to have this clause used, for it is at least to some extent an assurance that he or she is not purchasing a mortgage that actually represents less than the amount he or she has been told. To be sure, the covenant is binding only on the assignor, and usually the assignee will insist on a written statement or estoppel certificate from the property owner as well.

In many cases in which a mortgage is being assigned at the instance of the owner of the property, the assignor insists on using a *no recourse clause.* This is a short paragraph that says, substantially, "This assignment is given and received upon the express understanding that no recourse whatever shall ever be had to the assignor, his or its heirs, assigns, successors, or personal representatives." The effect of this clause is to transfer the bond or note and mortgage without any obligation on the part of the assignor. It is nearly always used by banks, trust companies, and fiduciaries.

The assignment must be signed by the assignor, but the assignor's wife or husband need not join. If the mortgage is held by more than one person, all should sign, even if they are executors and trustees, although technically, in many states, if the mortgage was part of the testator's estate, the assignment may be executed by just one of the executors. If a mortgage is held by the guardian of an infant or a committee for an incompetent, an assignment should be executed by the guardian or the committee. If the infant has reached his or her majority, however, the assignment should be executed by the former infant also.

Because the assignment should be recorded, its execution must be duly attested by proof of the signature of the assignor either by acknowledgment or by deposition of the subscribing witness.

Release of Mortgage

The meaning of the term *release of mortgage* varies in some of the states. When a mortgage is paid off, in some states the instrument given to evidence that fact is spoken of as a release of mortgage, and where that is the case, its form and functions are the same as has been discussed earlier in this chapter under *satisfaction of mortgage.* Release of mortgage, as used here, refers to what might technically be called *release of part of mortgaged premises.* In other words, the instrument now under discussion is used for the purpose of removing from the lien of the mortgage a part of the real estate pledged by the mortgage as security for the bond or note.

The situation requiring the use of this instrument arises generally in connection with *blanket mortgages;* that is, mortgages that cover a large, usually vacant, tract of land. At the time the mortgage loan is negotiated, the tract may have been subdivided into lots, and in some instances no subdivision may as yet have been made; but in any event there will come a time when the land is ripe for sale in "retail" lots, and the property owner is then faced with the problem of transferring title to the lots as he or she sells them free and clear of the lien of the mortgage. Seldom does the owner wish to pay off the entire amount before selling the lots; usually he or she is financially unable to do so. More often than not he or she intends to pay out of the price of each lot a fair amount toward reduction of the mortgage, so that it may remain on the balance of the lots for the lessened amount.

If the tract owner expects to sell the lots reasonably soon after placing the mortgage, he or she usually seeks an agreement with the holder of the mortgage, which is either embodied in a separate instrument or included as a schedule in the mortgage itself. The agreement designates the lots and specifies the amount that must be paid to release each one. It also states the charge for preparation of releases and usually that no releases may be had if there are delinquencies of any sort under the mortgage. Experience indicates the wisdom of having such an agreement. The mortgagee naturally wishes to protect his or her mortgage and, unless some previous agreement has been made, quite possibly may insist on being paid more than a fair amount for the earlier lots as they are released. This may place an embarrassing financial burden on the subdivider or developer. As the lots are released, the release price for each should be somewhat more than the pro rata of the mortgage loan on each lot, usually 125 percent. Such a price is reasonable in view of the fact that the most desirable lots usually are the first sold. Also, it must be realized that as lots are sold the tract is being broken up. The preparation of such a schedule or agreement made at the time the mortgage is placed, or before the developer or subdivider starts a selling campaign, obviates any disputes.

When the time does come for lots to be released, the instrument accomplishing that purpose is spoken of as the release of mortgage. This instrument recites the holder of the mortgage as the party of the first part and the owner of the land as the party of the second part. There follows a reference to the mortgage, giving the names of the parties and date and where recorded, so that it may be identified. Next appears a recital of the consideration paid for the release, which naturally reduces the amount of the mortgage, and a description of that part of the mortgaged premises that is released. The instrument ends with words confirming the fact of the release and that the portion so released is free and clear of the mortgage debt, but stating that the remaining premises are still a pledge to secure the balance of the mortgage. The party of the first part executes the release, and the property owner or lot buyer should immediately record the release so that the county records may show that this particular part of the mortgaged property is no longer subject to the mortgage.

Subordination of Mortgage

Mortgages normally have priority according to the order in which they are recorded; that is, if two mortgages are recorded against a piece of property, the first or prior mortgage is the one that was first recorded. Occasionally it is desired to change this order of priority, and that can be accomplished by means of a subordination agreement. Usually this will occur when a piece of property is already mortgaged and it is desired to obtain a new first mortgage, the holder of the present mortgage agreeing that his or her mortgage shall become a second mortgage. For instance, often a lot is sold to a builder for part cash, with the rest a purchase money mortgage taken back by the seller. An agreement is made at the time of the sale that the builder may obtain a first mortgage for the purpose of erecting a building on the lot, and the lot owner agrees to subordinate all or part of his or her purchase money mortgage to the new mortgage. This is not an extraordinary arrangement; many owners of lots do prefer, in order to sell them, to take back a mortgage behind a first mortgage on an improved, income-producing piece of property rather than to continue to own unimproved, nonincome-producing land or to have a mortgage on such land.

The subordination agreement is sometimes made between two parties and sometimes between three. In a two-part agreement, the owner of the mortgage to be subordinated is the party of the first part and the new mortgagee, the party of the second part. As is usual in real estate agreements, the instrument opens with a statement of the names of the parties; then comes a brief reference to the property, followed by a statement that the party of the first part is the owner of the existing mortgage, the particulars of which are fully stated. Next is a statement that the present owner of the property is about to make a mortgage to the party of the second part covering the premises to secure a stated amount. When the agreement is in three parts, there will also be a statement that the third party is the owner of the premises involved. The instrument recites the consideration of the subordination, which normally is that the new lender will not make the loan unless the present mortgage is subordinated. Then follows the declaration by the party of the first part to the effect that the mortgage held by him or her is and shall continue to be subject and subordinate in lien to the new mortgage. This agreement is usually prepared in duplicate, and the new lender, after it has been executed by all parties, will record one copy either at or before the time he or she records the mortgage. In this way the new mortgage, even though recorded after the existing one, becomes a first lien, and the existing mortgage a subordinate lien.

Certificate of Reduction of Mortgage

When a mortgage loan is negotiated, the mortgage states the amount of the lien. As the mortgage is reduced in amount, nothing normally appears of record to show the reduction of the mortgage. Occasionally it is desirable, or possibly even necessary, to have the records show the reduction. This is accomplished by a certificate of reduction of mortgage. The most usual circumstances under which this instrument is needed arise when a purchaser is buying a piece of property subject to an existing mortgage that is represented by the seller as having been reduced. The purchaser naturally should have some definite and distinct proof of that reduction. Most contracts of sale contain a provision for the seller to obtain and deliver such a certificate on the closing of title. The certificate is executed by the holder of the mortgage. It describes the mortgage fully, so that there may be no question as to the mortgage referred to. It further recites that the person executing the certificate is the holder of the mortgage. The certificate then goes on to state the exact balance of principal, the current interest rate, and the date to which interest has been paid. If the terms of the mortgage have been changed, it may further recite at what future date the mortgage is due and the details of any agreement for its payment in installments. Usually the certificate further states that it is made by the holder of the mortgage, who knows that the property is being sold and that the purchaser relies on the statement in the certificate in paying for the property. This statement constitutes what is called in law an **estoppel certificate,** by which the holder of the mortgage, having given such a certificate upon which the purchaser of the property relied, is thereafter *estopped,* or legally prevented from urging that the balance of the mortgage and other terms are different from those stated in the certificate. The certificate, naturally, must be signed by the holder of the mortgage. Usually the holder acknowledges it; this must be done if it is to be recorded. Occasionally he or she simply verifies it—that is, swears to its truth before a notary public or other officer authorized to take affidavits.

Estoppel Certificate

In the preceding paragraph concerning the certificate of reduction of mortgage, the use of the word *estoppel* was explained. There are various certificates of this nature, but all of them have the same basic purpose; namely, to provide a written statement signed by one, which, when acted upon by another, cannot be denied. In the previous illustration in connection with the reduction of a mortgage, the certificate was obtained from the holder of a mortgage for the benefit of a person purchasing the property. There are other instances in which estoppel certificates may be sought. For example, assume that M holds a mortgage on a piece of property. He desires to sell it to P. P, naturally, has been told by M that a certain amount of principal on the mortgage is unpaid and that it bears interest at a certain rate, which interest has been paid to a stated time. That is all right as far as it goes, but suppose that P pays for and takes an assignment of the mortgage and then finds, upon sending out the first interest notice, that the owner of the property insists that the mortgage is a lien for a lesser amount, that the interest rate is lower, or that the interest has been paid to a later date. This makes a very embarrassing situation for P, which may result in loss. To avoid controversy, P, before taking the assignment, should insist that M obtain an estoppel certificate from the owner.

Then, too, if there is a second mortgage on the property, P, if he or she is wise, will insist on an estoppel certificate from the holder of that mortgage to prevent the holder later, possibly in the event of foreclosure, from insisting and perhaps proving that the prior mortgage is a lien for a lesser amount than P has been told.

Mortgage Consolidation Agreement

Two or more mortgages may be consolidated into one single lien, and the terms of payment and interest may be stated and made applicable to the combined mortgages. A consolidation agreement is signed by the owner of the property involved and the holder of the mortgages involved. It is recorded on the mortgage records.

Mortgage Spreading Agreement

A *mortgage spreading agreement* extends the lien of a mortgage over property other than that already covered by the mortgage. It is signed by the owner of the property and the holder of the mortgage. Spreading agreements are usually resorted to when a mortgagee requires additional security as a condition to continuing the loan. Such agreements are also filed in the mortgage records.

Collateral Bond

This type of bond is signed by a party other than the primary bondsman. The primary bondsman is the mortgagor of the real estate. A collateral bondsman is required usually when the mortgagee wishes to strengthen the security of his or her loan. The collateral bondsman may be resorted to in the event the primary bondsman fails to make good on his or her obligation.

SUMMARY

A mortgage is a pledge of real property as security for a debt or other obligation. The debt, evidenced by a promissory note, gives life to the mortgage. The mortgaging process involves the initiation, servicing, and termination stages. Terms are negotiated and agreed to in the initiation phase. A mortgage may be terminated by mutual agreement (paying off) or by default and foreclosure.

A promissory note summarizes the terms of the loan and is a contract. Typical provisions of a mortgage include agreements to: (1) make debt-service payments, (2) make deposits for taxes and insurance, (3) maintain the property in good repair, and (4) obtain lender authorization before alteration or demolition of property improvements. In addition, control and assignment of rents are extremely important considerations in the financing of income properties.

Mortgages are commonly classified as conventional, FHA, VA, purchase money, or construction. Five payment-plan classes of mortgages are (1) fixed rate, (2) Canadian rollover, (3) variable rate, (4) graduated payment, and (5) partially amortizing. A number of other mortgage instruments of importance are mortgage satisfaction, assignment, release, and subordination.

KEY TERMS

Acceleration clause	Conventional mortgage loan
Balloon payment	Deed in lieu of foreclosure
Canadian rollover mortgage	Default
Construction mortgage loan	Defeasance clause

Deficiency judgment

Estoppel certificate

Equitable right of redemption

FHA loan

Fixed-rate mortgage (FRM)

Foreclosure

Graduated-payment mortgage (GPM)

Mortgage

Mortgage, subject to a

Mortgage assignment

Mortgage, assumption

Mortgagee/mortgagor

Mortgage satisfaction

Partially amortizing mortgage

Prepayment clause

Promissory note

Purchase money mortgage

Recast

Receiver

Redemption, statutory right of

Refinance

Severability

Strict foreclosure

Subordination

Trust deed

Usury

VA mortgage loan

Variable-rate mortgage (VRM)

QUESTIONS FOR REVIEW AND DISCUSSION

1. Explain the mortgage-financing process, including the documents involved, the parties involved, and the foreclosure process.

2. What purpose is served by the promissory note?

3. State at least four provisions that are typical for both mortgages and trust deeds. In what other ways are mortgages and trust deeds similar?

4. List and explain mortgages by classification as follows:
   (a) At least five mortgages by general type
   (b) At least four mortgages by payment plan
   (c) At least three mortgages by special provision

5. What are the purposes or functions of the following:
   (a) Satisfaction of mortgage
   (b) Assignment of mortgage
   (c) Subordination of mortgage
   (d) Estoppel certificate
   (e) Certificate of reduction

6. Does a prepayment privilege provide an advantage to the borrower or the lender?

7. What is a deed in lieu of a mortgage, and when might it be used?

8. Distinguish between the equitable right of redemption and the statutory right of redemption.

9. Distinguish between a deficiency judgment and a defeasance clause. When is each applicable?

10. A first, second, and third mortgage are placed against a new apartment building. Which of these are junior mortgages? Which are senior?

11. Does the lender or the borrower have the greater power in mortgage loan negotiations? Discuss.

REFERENCES

Bagby, Joseph R. *Real Estate Financing Desk Book,* 2nd ed. Englewood Cliffs, N.J.: Institute for Business Planning, 1977. A handbook for individuals aspiring to property ownership and development, written in three parts. Part one emphasizes methods of financing, part two sources of money, and part three is a glossary of financing terms. Generally easy to read and follow.

Hoagland, Henry E.; Leo D. Stone; and William B. Brueggeman. *Real Estate Finance.* 6th ed. Homewood, Ill.: Richard D. Irwin, 1977. Comprehensive coverage of real estate finance; instruments, techniques, sources, and government programs. A must sourcebook for the beginner or the professional. Generally readable.

Kratovil, Robert, and Raymond J. Werner. *Real Estate Law.* 7th ed. Englewood Cliffs, N.J.: Prentice-Hall, 1979. Chapters 19–21 focus on mortgage law. Easy to read and understand, with many case examples.

Trust Deed. Land Contract. and Lease Financing

13

If you want to know the value of money,
go and try to borrow some.
Benjamin Franklin

The purpose of this chapter is to extend our discussion of alternative ways to finance real estate. Certainly mortgaging property is the most traditional means to finance real estate. But trust deeds, land contracts, and leases are also commonly used and have their place.

Our discussion begins with an overview of real estate financing. Then, trust deeds, land contracts, and leases are taken up. Finally, some brief attention is given equity financing.

OVERVIEW OF REAL ESTATE FINANCING

The total value of a parcel of real estate is financed by someone at all times and in many different ways. The owner may finance the entire property without borrowing, which is known as 100 percent equity financing. **Equity** is, therefore, the owner's interest in the property. Alternatively, the owner may pledge the property as security for a loan, as on a mortgage. The loan may be desired or needed to help finance ownership of the property. Borrowing money or taking out a loan to finance a property is termed **debt financing** from the owner's point of view. Making loans to help finance properties is termed **credit financing** from a lender's point of view.

For purposes of this chapter, the combination of the equity and debt financing equals the total value of a property. Thus, an owner's equity in a property equals the market value of a property less any debt against the property. The value of an owner's equity may be zero if the amount borrowed against a property equals or exceeds the value of the property. Later, we will see that miscellaneous charges against the property, such as property taxes, unpaid assessments, and liens, must also be deducted from the property value to get the owner's equity.

Loan Terminology

Lenders and borrowers need common terminology in order to communicate effectively in negotiating a loan. For the most part, the terms or concepts are the same, whether a mortgage, a trust deed, a land contract, or some other instrument is involved because the terms relate to the loan and not to the legal instrument. The key terms of borrowing are

1. Loan-to-value ratio
2. Principal or amount of the loan
3. Interest rate
4. Duration of the loan
5. Loan amortization
6. Debt service

An $800,000 loan on a one-million-dollar commercial property provides a convenient example to illustrate these terms and concepts.

LOAN-TO-VALUE RATIO. The proportion of a property's appraised market value is usually expressed as a percentage, called the **loan-to-value ratio.** In the above example the loan-to-value ratio is 80 percent.

$$\frac{\text{Loan}}{\text{Market value}} = \frac{\$800,000}{\$1,000,000} = 80\% = \text{LVR}$$

The maximum LVR is set by law for almost all financial institutions, including all banks and savings and loan associations. The LVR is extremely important to borrowers who have limited savings for a down payment. If lenders are subject to a maximum LVR of 75 percent, a borrower with $10,000 of savings for a down payment is not able to bid for a property with a value in excess of $40,000. This is in contrast to a $100,000 property where a 90 percent LVR controls. The higher the loan-to-value ratio, the smaller the amount of down payment required for a given property. Also, the higher the loan-to-value ratio, the higher the risk to the borrower and to the lender.

PRINCIPAL OF THE LOAN. The **principal of a loan** is the number of dollars actually borrowed or the remaining balance of the loan. Almost all homeowners derive their income from wages or salaries, of which approximately 25 percent is typically used for housing. The amount home buyers can afford to borrow therefore depends directly on their income and directly affects the quality of housing they can command. Also, lenders generally have a maximum amount they lend in a given situation or for a kind of property; the amount is based on law or policy.

INTEREST RATE. **Interest** is the rent or charge paid for the use of money. The *interest rate* is the amount paid to borrow money, usually calculated as a percent per year of the amount borrowed. The higher the interest rate, the greater the cost of borrowing money and the higher loan payments must be. For example, at 6 percent, annual interest on $800,000 equals $48,000. At 9 percent, annual interest equals $72,000. From a lender's point of view, the interest rate charged borrowers reflects several factors: (1) the yields available on competitive investments such as stocks and bonds, (2) the lender's cost of money, (3) the interest rates of other lenders, and (4) the risks in the loan based on the characteristics of the property and the borrower.

DURATION OF THE LOAN. The maturity date of the loan contract determines the duration or loan period. That is, the **duration of a loan** is the period of time given the borrower to repay the loan. Laws govern the maximum loan period for almost all lenders. However, the lenders may have shorter loan periods based on management policy. A loan duration of from twenty to thirty years is typical for residential properties of reasonable quality. The loan period on commercial properties tends to be between ten and twenty years.

LOAN AMORTIZATION. *Amortization* means regular periodic repayment of the principal amount of borrowed money. The periodic repayment is usually made at the same time interest payments are made. The longer the amortization period, the smaller the required payments to repay the principal. If amortization is not required, interest must usually be paid periodically, with repayment of the total amount of the loan on the last day of the contract.

DEBT SERVICE. The periodic payment required on a loan for interest, and usually principal reduction, is termed **debt service.** If amortization or principal reduction is not called for, debt service is made up of interest only. Debt service reflects the amount, the interest rate, the duration, and the amortization schedule of a loan. The larger the principal amount, the greater the required debt service. The higher the interest rate, the greater the debt service. The longer the duration, the smaller the debt service. The more frequent the payments (monthly versus annual, for example), the smaller the debt service.

Reasons for Borrowing

The two major reasons for borrowing are necessity and leverage.

NECESSITY. Families need to borrow to buy homes because houses typically cost two to three times the home buyer's annual income. That is, the average family only has savings that equal approximately 10 to 20 percent of its annual income, or from 5 to 10 percent of the purchase price of the desired house. Home buyers usually prefer to buy and borrow the balance and make payments on a loan rather than to make rental payments. In a similar manner, most investors find they must borrow in buying real estate.

LEVERAGE. **Leverage** is the use of borrowed monies to magnify or increase the rate of return earned from an equity investment. This definition presumes that the property earns income at a higher rate than is charged for the borrowed money. An increased rate of return is, of course, advantageous to the investor. The term *leverage* is an economic analogy to the physical use of a lever to gain a mechanical advantage. Leverage is also known as **trading on the equity,** meaning exploiting or taking the best possible advantage of an equity position in an investment. Leverage provides an advantage to an equity investor through an increase in the rate of return. Two examples illustrate the point.

Assume an investor owns a $1 million property with an $800,000 mortgage loan against it. The investor's equity in the property is $200,000. An increase of $200,000 in the market value of the property, to $1,200,000, accrues entirely to the owner-investor. Thus, the value of the equity position doubles from $200,000 to $400,000. The debt, $800,000, remains unchanged.

Interest in Property	Initial Financing	Financing after Increase in Property Value
Market value	$1,000,000	$1,200,000
Debt (fixed)	− 800,000	− 800,000
Owner's equity	$ 200,000	$ 400,000

Our second example shows leverage on a rate of return basis. The facts are simplified to make the principle of leverage stand out. Assume that a commercial lot worth $1 million is under a long-term net lease for $100,000 per year. The tenant pays taxes, insurance, and all other costs of operation. Without debt financing, the rate of return to the owner is 10 percent. Suppose however that the owner obtains a long-term loan of $900,000 at 9 percent interest against the property, with no amortization required. That is, only interest payments of $81,000 need be paid each year ($900,000 x 9% = $81,000). The difference in income of $19,000 ($100,000 − $81,000 = $19,000) goes entirely to the equity position, which now is $100,000 ($1,000,000 − $900,000 = $100,000). The rate of return to equity has been leveraged up to 19 percent.

Total annual net income from lease	$100,000
Less interest on fixed debt ($900,000 x 9% = $81,000)	− 81,000
Equals net cash flow to equity	$19,000
Divided by value of equity position	÷ $100,000
Equals equity rate of return	19%

The advantages of leverage are not received without a cost. The borrower incurs increased risk of loss of income or of the property. Suppose, in the above examples, that the property value declined by $100,000 or annual net income decreased by $10,000. The equity position would be cut 50 percent in the first case. The rate of return would be reduced to 9 percent in the second. Under worse circumstances, the equity position might become a liability, as a result of what is termed *negative leverage*. Use of leverage always increases the risk of loss to the equity position.

TRUST DEED FINANCING

A **trust deed** is a legal instrument conveying title of realty to a third party (trustee) to be held as security for a debt owed a lender-beneficiary. A trust deed is also known as a *deed of trust* or a *trust-deed-in-the-nature-of-a-mortgage*. Note that a trust deed arrangement is a three-party transaction even though it is used in place of a mortgage loan arrangement in many areas. The owner-borrower-trustor receives money and conveys title to the trustee and at the same time gives a promissory note to the lender-beneficiary. The lender therefore becomes the legal owner and holder of the promissory note. The trustee holds title to the property as security for the lender in case of default by the borrower on the note. A trust deed arrangement is increasingly used in place of a mortgage loan arrangement. Figure 13–1 shows the structure of the transaction.

The arrangement provides the lender with security for the loan. A trust deed arrangement shows up as different from a mortgage loan arrangement only when default occurs. The wording of the trust deed makes explicit the rights of the parties. Upon default, the trustee has authority in almost every state to promptly carry out the terms of the arrangement, which usually means selling the property. The requirements of mortgage foreclosure by the courts are therefore avoided, which means a speedier and less costly "foreclosure." At the

FIGURE 13–1
Trust Deed Financing

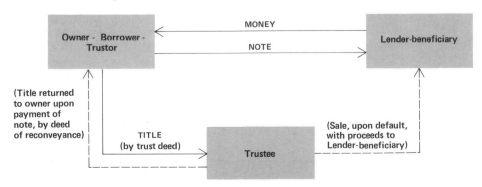

same time, the borrower is not entitled to any redemption rights after the fore-closure sale. In some states the lender also has the right to foreclose upon default as if the trust deed actually were a mortgage.

The method of clearing a trust-deed-in-the-nature-of-a-mortgage from the public record differs from that for clearing a mortgage. Upon payment of the debt, a mortgage is cleared by recording a mortgage release or satisfaction piece. A trust deed is cleared by a **deed of reconveyance,** also called a **deed of release.** The borrower has the same rights to pay on schedule, to prepay, to refinance, or to recast the loan under a trust deed as under a mortgage.

To be valid, the deed of release must be signed by the trustee of record. If the trustee arbitrarily refuses to sign a deed of release, a court order requiring the trustee to act may have to be obtained. If the trustee of record has died, a replacement must be appointed to execute the required deed of reconveyance. Ordinarily the lender, as beneficiary, has the right to appoint a substitute trustee upon resignation, dismissal, or death of the incumbent trustee.

In many states, upon default, a trustee has the power of sale. **Power of sale** is the right to sell the property without any court proceedings being necessary. The trustee, at the request of the lender-beneficiary, simply records a notice of default, gives notice of sale, and sells the property to the highest bidder. Each state has a minimum statutory period that must pass between default and sale. This period varies from three months to one year. The trustee generally is not permitted to buy the real estate at such a sale, although the lender is permitted to do so. As a rule, a deficiency judgment is not recognized when a trustee has a right of power of sale.

In other states, court action to foreclose a trust deed may be required for lender satisfaction on a trust deed in default. And in a few states the lender has the option to request the trustee to exercise power of sale or to foreclose by court action. A deficiency judgment, in favor of the lender, may be involved when foreclosure is through court action. A right of redemption to time of sale applies, whether foreclosure is through power of sale or through court action. Almost all states allow a borrower merely to make up missed payments to stop the trustee sale. This is a significant advantage for a borrower on a trust deed in comparison to a borrower on a mortgage. If a borrower has a mortgage, he or she must generally repay the entire debt to recover the property under an equitable right of redemption, unless the lender voluntarily agrees to reinstate the loan upon the borrower's making up missed payments. This borrower advantage is offset somewhat by a generally shorter period of time from default to sale under a trust deed.

LAND CONTRACT FINANCING

A **land contract** is a written agreement between a buyer and a seller for the sale and payment of real property over an extended time, with title remaining in the seller until the terms of the arrangement are met. A land contract is also known as a *contract for deed,* an *installment land contract,* or a *real estate contract.*

As indicated, title remains in the seller's name during the life of the contract. The buyer receives no deed until the terms have been met and the full purchase price paid. The buyer normally takes possession when the contract is made. Payments are credited toward purchase.

Example

Assume a forty-unit residential complex is being sold on a land contract for $1 million. The seller has an existing mortgage of $700,000 against the property at an interest rate of 8 percent. The owner's equity in the property is therefore $300,000.

Contract sale price	$1,000,000
Less seller's mortgage	700,000 @ 8%
Equals owner's equity	$ 300,000

The buyer makes a $50,000 down payment and agrees to make payments sufficient to cover interest and to reduce the balance due the seller from $950,000 to $800,000 by the end of five years. The buyer may refinance at any time and must refinance before the end of the sixth year. The interest rate on the unpaid land contract balance is 10 percent. Thus, from the buyer's viewpoint, the land contract is similar to a partially amortizing loan. Buyer payments go for interest and principal reduction. In addition, the buyer gets equitable title in entering the land contract but doesn't get legal title until all conditions of the land contract are satisfied and a deed is obtained. The seller retains and continues to pay debt service on the existing mortgage against the property. In so doing, the seller gains a highly leveraged position. The transaction now looks like this:

Item	Value Allocation
Contract sale price	$1,000,000
Less buyer's down payment	50,000
Equals amount of contract balance	$ 950,000 @ 10%
Less seller's mortgage loan	700,000 @ 8%
Equals owner-seller's equity	$ 250,000

Amortization aside, seller receives approximately $95,000 in interest in the first year (10% x $950,000), while paying approximately $56,000 interest on the mortgage loan (8% x $700,000). The difference is $39,000, while the owner-seller's equity equals $250,000. This calculates to an approximate rate of return to the owner-seller of 15.6 percent ($39,000 divided by $250,000).

In net, buyer gets a 95 percent loan-to-value ratio loan, and the seller both disposes of the property and stands to earn over 15 percent on the $250,000 loan to buyer.

Use of Land Contracts

A land contract is extremely useful because it serves as a sales, a financing, and a tax-avoidance instrument. Generally, in a land contract, the buyer makes a nominal or thin down payment and agrees to make regular payments (usually monthly) over a number of years. The buyer also agrees to pay the seller interest on the unpaid balance of the purchase price. Further, the buyer agrees to pay the annual taxes and insurance premiums on the property and to maintain the property properly. In other words, the land contract spells out the rights and obligations of the buyer and seller over the years until the sale is consummated. The thin down payment, less than 30 percent in the year of sale, also enables the seller to defer taxes on capital gains involved in the transaction.

Traditionally, land contracts are written to protect the seller. The property involved may be difficult to finance from another source, possibly because of its run-down condition or its location in a blighted area. Or alternative financing may be difficult to arrange because of the buyer's thin down payment and relatively weak credit rating. In these situations, the seller wants to be able to recover the property in case of buyer default with a minimum of time and expense. Use of a purchase money mortgage might create a situation where the time and expense of recovering title would exceed the value of the buyer's thin down payment. Hence, the land contract makes possible the sale and financing of properties that would be very difficult to arrange in other ways.

A land contract may also be used to benefit both a seller and a buyer, as in preserving a favorable mortgage loan. Assume a loan at 8 percent with an acceleration clause on sale, also termed an alienation clause or "all-due-on-sale" clause. In a money market of 11 or 12 percent interest, it would be highly advantageous to preserve the loan. A land contract sale may or may not violate the alienation clause of the uniform instrument discussed in the previous chapter. But, according to *Tucker* v. *Lassen,* a case recently decided by the California Supreme Court, an acceleration provision is not enforceable unless the lender can demonstrate damage from a transfer of possession. As long as the original borrower remains liable on the note, the lender's security position is good or even improved, as a result of a land contract.

Seller Considerations

One of the main advantages of financing a sale with a land contract rather than a purchase money mortgage, from a seller's viewpoint, is less litigation and more rapid recovery of the property in case of default by the buyer. The time of conveyance of title may also be delayed to gain a benefit for tax purposes. Further, transactions can be set up quickly, as with subdivision lots, to avoid any delay in financing that might allow a hot prospect to cool off.

The seller or vendor is advised to coordinate any prepayment privileges in the land contract with comparable privileges in any mortgage against the property. Failure to do so might mean that the buyer or vendee has the right to prepay the land contract, while the vendor is not able to prepay the mortgage. The vendor is then liable for a heavy prepayment penalty from the mortgagee or a breach of contract suit from the vendee for failure to deliver clear title.

Buyer Considerations

One buyer advantage in a land contract is the need for only a small down payment in order to control a property. Of course, a small down payment means that the property and the financing are both being purchased. A land contract also gives a buyer time to build up equity in the property until more traditional financing is possible and title can be transferred to the buyer. Vacant lots and marginal properties, in many cases, can be purchased only with the aid of a land contract arrangement.

Several cautions should be exercised by a buyer in a land contract. First, the seller should be required to provide evidence of clear and marketable title when the land contract is drawn up. Failure to insure the seller's clear title might mean that the buyer would make payments for several years only to find that the seller can't deliver clear title.

Second, the land contract transaction should be handled in escrow. A deed conveying title to the buyer and signed by the seller should be placed in escrow immediately. Failure to have a deed in escrow could mean delay and added cost to the buyer if the seller died or became incapacitated before signing a deed or conveying title.

Third, if the vendee does not move into possession immediately, as with a vacant lot, the land contract or notice of the land contract should be recorded. Recording gives public notice of the buyer's interest in the property, of course. Without recording or possession, the seller could conceivably sell the lot several times, giving all the buyers a serious and expensive litigation problem.

Fourth, a provision limiting the seller in refinancing the property is desirable in a land contract. The seller should not be permitted to obtain financing with the vendee's equity put up as collateral. To illustrate the problem, let us take the example of a land contract given earlier. Assume it is five years later and the balance of the land contract has been paid down to $800,000. Meanwhile, the value of the property increased to $1,300,000. The buyer's equity should therefore be $500,000. But suppose the seller refinanced the property with a $1,100,000 mortgage six months ago and left the area for whereabouts unknown. The vendee's equity has been reduced to $200,000 ($1,300,000 less $1,100,000). Of course, the vendee also has a legal claim for $300,000 against the seller, assuming the seller could be found.

Recording the land contract, placing the transaction in escrow, and placing the vendee in possession all serve as protection against fraudulent activity by the seller. Some buyers even make their periodic payments to escrow agents in order to ensure that mortgage debt-service payments are made on schedule.

Default

Several options are open to the vendor if a buyer defaults in a land contract transaction. These options include forfeiture, specific performance, foreclosure suit, or a suit for damages.

The vendor may take the option of declaring forfeiture of rights by the buyer and retaining as damages any amounts paid or any improvements made by the vendee. In some states experienced buyers may recover payments made less a reasonable charge for use of the property. Alternatively, the vendor may exercise the option requiring specific performance by the vendee. **Specific performance** is a court order compelling a defendant to carry out, or live up to, the terms of an agreement or contract. This option would probably be exercised if the unpaid balance of the land contract exceeds the value of the property and if the vendee is financially capable.

The seller may also file a foreclosure suit upon buyer default and seek to have the property sold. If foreclosed the buyer may be allowed a statutory period of redemption after the sale. Finally, the seller may file suit for damages against the buyer if none of the above options seems satisfactory.

LEASE FINANCING

Controlling real estate by long-term lease rather than by purchase is often done to realize financial advantages and to avoid ownership problems. Insurance companies, pension funds, universities, and other private investors own and finance the properties that are leased. Oil companies, motel chains, retail chains, supermarket chains, trucking companies, and public utilities all frequently lease rather than buy facilities to conserve working capital while expanding activities and services. Even the federal government leases rather than building new post offices.

A sale-leaseback arrangement may be used to convert an existing property into working capital while retaining control of the premises. Alternatively, a firm may buy vacant land, erect a new structure to its own specific purposes, and enter a sale-leaseback arrangement with an investor. This technique enables a firm that has limited working capital to expand very rapidly without tying up large amounts of money in real estate.

Common Considerations in Lease Financing

The most immediate consideration in lease negotiations is the amount of rent to be paid. The rent should be adequate to cover expected depreciation of the leased property and to give the owner a competitive rate of return on the investment. Rental payments in a sale-leaseback are usually net to the lessor-owner. That is, the tenant pays property taxes, insurance, and operating and maintenance expenses.

Long-term leases run from ten to ninety-nine years, and sometimes longer. The length of the lease, and any renewal option, must also be specified, including a means of setting rents for any extensions. In addition to renewal options, many leases contain an option to purchase or, in a sale-leaseback, to repurchase.

Mortgages enter into lease negotiations by way of subordination and the right of the lessee to make payments of debt service. *Subordination* means that a party who has an interest in real estate, such as a lessee, grants a subsequent right of prior claim in a property to another, such as a lender-mortgagee. Subordination of a lease to a mortgage means that in default the lessee's interest could be completely wiped out by default and foreclosure. Lease subordination is frequently requested by an owner-lessor to obtain better financing terms on the property. In accepting subordination, the lessee should expect better rental terms and may even reserve the right to pay debt service directly to the mortgagee to prevent default.

The tenant receives the use of the premises and the right to sell the leasehold. Also, the owner-lessor may sell or assign rights to rents from a leasehold unless otherwise agreed.

Almost all long-term leases are terminated because the contract runs out, the property is purchased by the lessee, or the tenant defaults and is evicted.

Sale-Leaseback Arrangement

A **sale-leaseback transaction** is the transfer of title for consideration (sale) with the simultaneous renting back to the seller (leaseback) for a specified time at an agreed-upon rent. A sale-leaseback might come about in the following manner. A supermarket chain has owned a store with high sales production for some fourteen years. The improvements have been largely written off or depreciated for tax purposes. Also, the property has tripled in value. The chain wishes to retain the store and also to raise more working capital. A mortgage could be placed against the store for two-thirds of its value, but the mortgage debt would show up on the chain's balance sheet as a liability. A sale-leaseback arrangement with a private investor may be a better alternative. A sale-leaseback is also likely to show up on the chain's balance sheet but as both a capital asset and a liability, according to statement 13 of the Financial Accounting Standards Board.

The store is therefore simultaneously sold to the private investor and rented back to the supermarket chain. The rent is set high enough to allow the investor a reasonable profit on the investment while writing off the improvements over the life of the lease. By treating the property as an income property and taking out a mortgage against it, the investment position is leveraged to gain a higher rate of profit. Both the supermarket chain and the investor gain from the transaction.

BENEFITS TO THE LESSEE. Following are several advantages that accrue to the lessee from the transaction:

1. Working capital is increased by liquidating a capital investment, that is, selling the store at a profit. The money can usually be used to better advantage by the firm.

2. All of the rent can be written off as a business expense. Effectively, this means that 100 percent of the property value can be written off for tax purposes in rents paid over the life of the lease, much of it for a second time.

3. Problems of real estate ownership are passed on to the investor. For example, a decline in the neighborhood around the store merely means that an option for extension in the lease will not be exercised. Instead, the chain simply opens another store in a new location.

4. In net, the chain ends up using its assets in the business activity it knows best: operating as a supermarket.

BENEFITS TO THE LESSOR. Advantages to the buyer-lessor in a sale-leaseback or other long-term lease are as follows:

1. A long-term investment is made with a strong client at a known minimum rate of return.
2. The investment is usually large in size and requires only limited attention for many years.
3. For financial institutions such as insurance companies, a long-term lease represents long-term financing to a client, with no prepayment, and with more control than is generally available with a mortgage.
4. At the end of the lease the remaining value of the property reverts to the owner-lessor; this may substantially increase the rate of return from the investment.
5. If the lease is extended, the rate of return is increased.
6. Tax depreciation may be taken on the investment to shelter income.

Buy-Build-Sell Lease

Some rapidly expanding business firms use a buy-build-sell lease. The purpose is to get facilities designed and built specifically to the needs of the business but financed by someone else. For example, a restaurant chain may buy land in a desired location, build a structure, sell the improved property to an interested investor, and simultaneously lease it back. Sometimes, after a working relationship has been established, the investor buys and improves the land for subsequent lease to the business firm; hence, the firm never does take title. A buy-build-sell lease arrangement is a variation of the sale-leaseback arrangement.

Ground Lease with a Mortgaged Leasehold

A third major option of a business firm is to use leasing and mortgage financing in combination. A desired parcel of vacant land is rented on a long-term lease, which is termed a *ground lease*. Improvements are added and financed with a leasehold mortgage, which means that only the lessee's interest in the property is mortgaged. This arrangement allows the lessee to depreciate the improvements completely for tax purposes over the life of the lease. Thus, the firm keeps depreciation as a tax shelter rather than passing it on to an investor. In addition, rental payments for the land are tax deductible. And, over everything else, the firm is able to minimize its investment in real estate.

Default

A breach of rental terms, most likely nonpayment of rent, constitutes lease default. With default, the owner-landlord has a range of options from evicting the tenant and rerenting to suing the tenant for specific performance. Default by nonpayment of rent puts the owner-lender in a real crunch if the property has an underlying mortgage as the debt service on the mortgage continues to be paid. The pressure from the crunch may be reduced through the use of rent insurance. In any event, the solution to default depends directly on the relative amount of pressure on the owner-lessor as a result of the default.

EQUITY FINANCING

We have now discussed the major alternative techniques for debt financing of real estate. Those techniques are summarized in figure 13–2 on pp. 278–79. We have not discussed equity financing however. And, as stated earlier, the total value of a parcel must be financed. Let us therefore look briefly at equity financing.

The equity position is the interest of the owner or owners in property. The equity position may be owned by one individual or by two or more individuals and/or business organizations working together as a group. Thus, funds to acquire and control an equity position must be provided by an individual or a group.

Equity funds, for acquisition or development of a property, come primarily from the personal resources of individuals or from monies accumulated by institutional investors. Some aspiring home owners provide "sweat equity" or work in kind: painting, labor, and so forth, in new construction. Institutional investors include insurance companies, banks, pension funds, business corporations, trusts, and savings and loan associations. Institutional investors buying an equity position are not lending money to the venture; they share in the profits and the risks of property operations the same as other equity investors. Thus, institutional investors are in a significantly different position relative to the property from institutional lenders.

The value of an equity position may be increased through debt amortization or property appreciation.

The following discussion is intended as a brief review to link the legal concepts of ownership, explained in an earlier chapter, to the equity position described in this chapter. The central concern or focus is the financing of the equity position in realty.

Individual Equity Financing

Sole ownership of real property by one individual is termed an *estate in severalty*. Typically, the individual uses personal savings as equity funds to purchase or develop the property. Debt financing, e.g., a mortgage, may be used by the sole owner to help in acquiring and holding the property. A condominium interest in real property is also owned by an individual as an estate in severalty, even though debt financing is used to acquire the interest.

Group Equity Financing

An equity interest in real property may be owned and financed by a group, through a tenancy or a business organizational arrangement. Under either arrangement, individual members must supply or provide equity funds in proportion to the partial interest desired or held, unless an agreement is made to the contrary. A major distinction between the arrangements is real property versus personal property. If property is held by a group as tenants, the laws of real property apply between and among the members of the group. If the property is held under a business organizational arrangement, the laws of personal property apply. Ownership of corporate stock (personal property) backed up by real property is thus treated differently under the law from direct ownership of real property under a tenancy arrangement.

BY TENANCY ARRANGEMENT. *Tenancy by the entirety* and *community property* are two forms of concurrent ownership of realty that are reserved exclusively to a husband and wife. Each of the two spouses is regarded as owning the entire property under both arrangements. The couple is considered as jointly putting up the equity funds to finance the property under either form of tenancy, except when the property is received as a gift or inherited by them. At the same time, the couple usually borrows against the property to be able to purchase the property.

In some states two or more persons may acquire and finance an equity interest in real property under a joint-tenancy arrangement. Partnerships sometimes use joint-tenancy arrangements to hold and finance property to ensure continuity of the enterprise should one of the partners die. That is, the right of survivorship means that ownership goes to the remaining partners instantaneously. In return, life insurance is usually carried on each partner, and paid for by the partnership, with the insurance benefits going to the deceased partner's spouse or estate. Again, debt financing may be used to help finance the purchase of the property.

The equity position may be split into equal or unequal shares under tenancy in common ownership. Each tenant owns an undivided interest in the property. Debt financing, if obtained, would require that all tenants in common sign the note and mortgage or other security agreement.

Finally, many people may own a large, complex property under a condominium arrangement. Each condominium unit must be financed by its individual owner, however. In turn, default by one condominium owner does not obligate other owners to pick up the payments to protect themselves. The unit in default simply goes through foreclosure proceedings the same as any other property owned in fee simple.

BY BUSINESS ORGANIZATIONAL ARRANGEMENT The main *business organizational arrangements* for owning and financing an equity position in property are the corporation, trust, and cooperative. Property owned by a partnership is really held by the partners as tenants in common. In the case of a limited partnership, only the general partners hold as tenants in common. A syndicate may be a partnership, corporation, or trust, depending on which is most advantageous.

The financial structure of a corporation is usually made up of bonds and stocks. The bonds represent debt financing of the organization; the shares of stock represent equity ownership. Corporations have the right to engage in various business activities, including real estate investment. The stockholders enjoy limited liability but are subject to double taxation on income earned by the

FIGURE 13–2
Real Estate Debt Financing Techniques

Alternative	Lender	Maximum LVR	BUYER	
			Advantages	
MORTGAGE	Usually financial institution, sometimes other.	90%; higher with FHA or private mortgage insurance or with VA guarantee.	a. Required appraisal serves as check on property value and quality. b. Strong redemption rights in default. c. FHA & VA—no deficiency judgment.	
TRUST DEED	(same as above)	(same as above)	(same as for mortgage except deficiency judgment not generally recognized)	
LAND CONTRACT	Seller	100%	a. Equitable terms. b. Low closing costs. c. Quick closing. d. No deficiency judgment. e. Usually low payment.	
LONG-TERM LEASE (as from sale and leaseback)	Lessor	100%	a. Long-term investment at known rate of return. b. Limited investment management required. c. Little loan servicing required if strong tenant. d. Opportunity for value appreciation. e. Tax depreciation.	

BUYER	SELLER		Settlement Procedure in Default
Disadvantages	Advantages	Disadvantages	
a. Closing costs and fees sometimes very high. b. Contract clauses not standardized if conventional.	a. LVR usually high enough to keep buyer's down payment relatively low.	a. Loan amount may be inadequate if appraised value too far below sales contract price. b. Points sometimes required with FHA and VA loans.	a. Default declared by lender. b. Foreclosure suit filed. c. Equitable right of redemption. d. Foreclosure sale/deficiency judgment. e. Statutory right of redemption. f. End redemption and foreclosure period, after 15–36 months.
a. Equitable right of redemption period cut short. b. No statutory period of redemption.	(same as above)	(same as above)	a. Default declared by lender-beneficiary. b. Notice of default recorded. c. Notice of sale. d. Redemption period to sale. e. Trustee's sale. f. End of process after 4–6 months.
a. No appraisal check on value or quality of property. b. Price and interest rate usually higher. c. Contract not standardized. d. Short redemption period in default.	a. Price frequently higher. b. Quick sale and closing facilitated. c. Low closing costs. d. Easy property recovery upon default.	a. Care required to coordinate prepayment privileges in contract and mortgage.	a. Default declared by seller. b. Court decree obtained (1) to terminate buyer's rights (2) to require specific performance of buyer (3) to get liquidated damages from buyer
a. Crunch in default if financing against property.	a. Capital released for better use. b. All rent is business expense. c. Ownership problems avoided.	a. Opportunity for value appreciation lost. b. No tax depreciation.	a. Default declared by owner-lesser. b. Court decree obtained for (1) eviction (2) damages (3) specific performance

corporation—once at the corporate level and once at the personal level when dividends are received. The corporation may own an equity interest in real property against which debt financing has been obtained.

A trust operates much in the manner of a corporation except that profits or proceeds go to specific beneficiaries rather than to stockholders. Cooperatives are either corporations or trusts. The corporation or trust owns the real estate. Shareholders get a proprietary lease to a specified unit of space upon purchase of stock. The cooperative pays taxes and obtains needed debt financing on the property. If shareholder-proprietary tenants fail to pay their pro rata share of taxes and debt service, the burden of keeping the cooperative solvent falls on the remaining shareholder-tenants, who make up the group owning the equity interest in the property.

SUMMARY

Key terms relative to loan financing are (1) loan-to-value rates (LVR), (2) principal, (3) interest rate, (4) duration, (5) amortization provisions, and (6) debt service. These terms apply whether real estate is being financed by a mortgage, trust deed, or land contract.

Trust deed financing is very similar to mortgage financing except in default. With power of sale, the trustee may market the secured property rather soon after default under a trust deed to satisfy the lender-beneficiary's claim. Upon payment of the loan, the trustee returns title to the owner-borrower by a deed of reconveyance.

A land contract is sale of real estate with payments spread over an extended time, though the buyer usually goes into immediate possession. The buyer gets only equitable title until the contract is satisfied. The arrangement generally favors the seller. Important buyer considerations are to (1) obtain immediate evidence of clear title, (2) have deed placed in immediately, (3) record if possession not immediately taken, and (4) prohibit seller from pledging buyer's equity in any refinancing.

Lease financing covers 100 percent of a property's value, and therefore conserves working capital for the lessee. Leasing to a strong tenant gives the owner-lesser a large, high-quality investment at a known rate of return. Chains of supermarkets, motels, and restaurants commonly use sale and leaseback financing to conserve working capital and make faster expansion possible.

KEY TERMS

Credit financing
Debt financing
Debt service

Deed of reconveyance
Deed of release
Duration of loan

Equity	Power of sale
Interest	Principal of loan
Land contract	Sale-leaseback
Leverage	Specific performance
Loan-to-value ratio (LVR)	Trading on the equity

QUESTIONS FOR REVIEW AND DISCUSSION

1. Explain fully the relationship between equity financing and debt financing as they pertain to a property's value.

2. What are the six key terms in loan terminology? Define or explain each briefly.

3. Compare the trust deed financing as to parties, documents, and the legal process in default to mortgage financing.

4. How does a land contract work as a financing device? Give two key considerations in its use for a buyer and a seller.

5. Discuss long-term leases as financing devices, with emphasis on the sale-leaseback arrangement.

6. Is a land contract more a sales or a financing device? Discuss. What circumstances might influence your answer?

7. Is a land contract likely to have provisions pertaining to the applicability of payments to taxes, insurance, interest, and principal reduction? If not, should it? Why?

8. Does the trustee, in trust deed financing, need the right of entry and inspection prior to default? If not, who does?

9. Does the lessor or the lessee have the greater power in negotiating a long-term lease? Explain. Would your response be different if a sale and lease-back were being negotiated?

10. Does the buyer or the seller have the greater power in negotiating a land contract sale? Explain. What considerations enter into your answer?

REFERENCES

Kratovil, Robert, and Raymond J. Werner. *Real Estate Law,* 7th ed. Englewood Cliffs, N.J.: Prentice-Hall, 1979. See chapter 11 on contracts, and chapter 19, on mortgages. Installment contracts and trust deeds are also discussed in these chapters.

Reed, John T. "How and When to Use a Land Contract." *Real Estate Investing Letter,* October 1978. Short but excellent discussion of the use of land contracts, including a reasonably involved example. Easy to read and understand.

Real Estate Credit and Our Financial System

14

Bankers are just like anybody else, except richer.
Ogden Nash

Money or credit is the lifeblood of real estate construction and sales activity. Money forms a very strong and a very direct link between national economic conditions and real estate market activity. With adequate money, termed **easy money,** interest rates fall or remain low, and, in turn construction and sales activity tend to be brisk. With a scarcity of money in the economy, termed **tight money,** interest rates go up or remain up. Loans for building properties or refinancing old ones become difficult to obtain. And in turn, when money is tight, construction and sales activity lag, and incomes of builders, brokers, and salespeople fall. Obviously, money is important to real estate.

Money generally comes to real estate through mortgage and trust deed arrangements, which are both commonly used to secure realty loans. To simplify discussion, the term *mortgages* is used in this chapter to mean both kinds of loans. In addition to knowing the importance of money to real estate, a borrower or a real estate professional, in self-interest, needs to know how to obtain a loan locally and needs to be aware of the federal laws that apply to obtaining a loan. A sound knowledge of financial institutions and governmental agencies that make up mortgage markets is also helpful.

The purpose of this chapter therefore is to explain briefly the relationship of mortgage markets and interest rates to the general economy. The purpose is also to explain the lending laws, procedures, and institutions that an investor-borrower is likely to encounter in obtaining real estate credit. Major sections are as follows:

1. Monetary policy and interest rates
2. Mortgage market overview
3. Primary lenders
4. Secondary lenders
5. Lending laws
6. Lending procedures and commitments

MONETARY POLICY AND INTEREST RATES

The President, the Treasury Department, and the Federal Reserve Banking System usually work together to achieve the economic goals of the country. The main goals are full employment, economic growth, and price stability. One of the major ways to achieve full employment and economic growth is to have an adequate supply of money in the economic system. Too much money in the system, however, causes interest rates to drop and may lead to inflation. Too much money puts more purchasing power (demand) in the system than can be satisfied by the available goods and services (supply) at existing price levels. The excess purchasing power competes for the available goods and services, driving prices upward. This increase in prices, of course, is not consistent with the third goal, price stability. Too little money in the economic system causes interest rates to go up, and the result is a recession. Adjustments in the money supply, termed *monetary policy,* are thus made to maintain a reasonable interest rate and to provide an acceptable balance in the economic goals. Monetary policy is usually implemented through the Federal Reserve Banking System. The Federal Reserve Banking System, often called the Fed, is the most dominant financial institution in the United States. The Fed, in managing the nation's money supply, directly affects most of our private financial institutions. The main financial institutions (also called financial intermediaries) affected are commercial banks, savings and loan associations, and mutual savings banks. In addition, the Fed directly regulates commercial banks.

Intermediary means to act as a go-between. Thus, a *financial intermediary* is a go-between in money matters, taking deposits from savers and lending to borrowers for investment. The process is called **intermediation.** Sometimes savers withdraw the monies and lend them directly to investors, which process is called **disintermediation.**

In addition to private financial institutions, a number of public and semipublic agencies exist to buy and sell mortgage and to promote housing policies of the federal government. Taken together, these institutions and agencies financially tie construction and real estate activity to the national economy.

Therefore, the investor, builder, developer, finance officer, and broker must know and watch these public agencies as well as the private financial intermediaries.

Costs and Availability of Mortgage Money

The availability of money and the level of interest rates greatly affect lending or borrowing terms. As money gets tighter, lenders raise interest rates; they may also shorten the term of life of loans made. The result can be a substantial increase in debt service for borrowers. For example, suppose that tighter money conditions cause a lender to raise the interest rate from 9 to 12 percent and to decrease the life from thirty years to twenty-five years. On a $100,000 mortgage these changes would increase monthly debt service from $804.62 to $1,053.22, or by more than 30 percent. See figure 14-1.

FIGURE 14-1
Monthly Debt Service on a $100,000 Loan with Varying Life and Interest Rates

Life (years)	INTEREST RATE			
	6%	9%	12%	15%
15	$843.86	$1,014.27	$1,200.17	$1,399.59
20	716.43	899.72	1,101.09	1,316.79
25	644.30	839.20	1,053.22	1,280.83
30	599.55	804.62	1,028.61	1,264.44
35	570.19	783.99	1,015.55	1,256.81

What does this 30 percent increase mean for an investor, a tenant, or a home buyer? For income properties, debt service often runs to 80 percent of net operating income, or more. If cost of borrowed money goes up, an equity investor is also likely to want a proportionally higher rate of return because of greater risk. Thus, net operating income must go up by 30 percent, and rents to tenants must be raised accordingly.

As for home ownership, assume that a typical family spends 20 percent of its income for PITI (principal, interest, taxes, and insurance) payments. Of this 20 percent, three-fourths, or 15 percent, goes to loan debt service, principal and interest, and the remaining 5 percent to taxes and insurance. The shift in borrowing terms means the annual income needed to borrow $60,000 would also increase by more than 30 percent, from $38,622 to $50,555.

Obviously an increase of this amount would sharply reduce the number of buyers able to meet the demand of a $60,000 mortgage. This reduction in potential buyers would be true at all income levels and, if sustained, would reduce the number of units demanded and would eventually result in an across-the-board reduction in the quality of housing for the population.

The Lender's Viewpoint

The long-term upward trend in interest rates during the past two decades has severely squeezed profits of financial institutions with large mortgage portfolios. Normally, such institutions need a 1½ to 2 percent spread or differential between the interest rate they pay on savings deposited with them and the interest rate they charge on mortgage loans. Mortgage loans have traditionally been long-term commitments with fixed terms. Interest rates paid on all deposits, however, tend to go up periodically with increasing interest rates in the economy. The result is a squeeze on profits. This pattern is changing with increasing use of VRMs and rollover mortgages.

As an illustration of the squeeze on profits, assume the following institutional assets in mortgage loans and cash. Thirty percent of the loans—in dollar terms—were made over ten years ago at an average of 6 percent, 30 percent were made from five to ten years ago at an average of 8 percent, and 30 percent were made in the last five years at an average of 10 percent. The balance of the firm's assets are held as cash, buildings, or equipment, and hence earn no income. The average interest rate paid by the institution on savings is expected to increase from 5.5 percent to 6.0 percent because of money market conditions. What effect on profits?

30% x 6% =	1.8%
30% x 8% =	2.4
30% x 10% =	3.0
10% x 0% =	0.0
Weighted rate of return	7.2%

The margin or differential equals 1.7 percent currently (7.2% − 5.5%). The expected increase in the rate paid on savings deposits will drop the differential to 1.2%, not enough to cover operating costs and leave a profit.

It is this squeeze on profits that is causing financial institutions to turn to the variable-rate mortgage (VRM). Under a typical VRM, an interest rate is agreed upon when the loan is made, to be increased or decreased in accordance with fluctuations in an index beyond the control of the lender. The index might be either the interest rates paid on corporate or treasury securities or the average interest rates of new mortgages made. Usually, VRM terms provide that rate changes can be made only twice a year, at a maximum of ½ percent per change. The change may fluctuate a maximum of from 2 percent to 3 percent above or below the original loan rate. If the interest rate increases, the term increases while the debt service is held constant. If too large an increase occurs, an increase in debt service might become necessary.

The benefit of the variable-rate mortgage to the lender is, of course, that an acceptable differential is maintained between the interest rate paid on savings deposits and the interest rate earned on mortgage loans. Also, with variable-rate terms, lenders may make loans more readily in a time of rising interest rates because they avoid running the risk of being locked in on long-term fixed interest rate mortgages.

VRM lending is not widely accepted and, in fact, is strongly opposed by consumer-interest groups. A more detailed discussion of primary and secondary mortgage lenders is necessary before we can take up other ways that lenders can operate to function effectively under tight money conditions.

Shifting Interest Rates

The two main methods used by the Fed in implementing monetary policy are (1) open-market operations and (2) changing reserve requirements of member banks. Secondary methods are (1) changing the discount rate, (2) imposing selective controls when authorized by Congress, and (3) moral suasion. The process and effects of tightening or easing the money supply is summarized in figure 14–2.

OPEN-MARKET OPERATIONS. Government bonds and notes may be bought and sold in the open market by the Fed through its **open-market** committee. Offering and selling large numbers of bonds drive bond prices down, as the supply exceeds demand. Individuals, banks, insurance companies, and other investors buy the bonds and pay by checks drawn on commercial banks, which reduces the number of dollars in the banks for loan purposes. This process makes money tight or scarce. Bankers ration out the scarce money by being more selective in making loans and by raising the interest rates charged on the loans. If the bankers cannot make sound loans at reasonable rates, they buy government bonds that are risk free and involve very low handling costs. Thus, the interest rate is pushed up and held up by the Fed's selling bonds on the open market. The Fed may buy bonds on the open market and lower the interest rate if easy monetary policy is the goal.

CHANGING RESERVE REQUIREMENTS. The Fed has the authority, within limits set by Congress, to raise or lower the **reserve requirements** of member banks. Reserve requirements are increased to make money tight or scarce. Since increasing requirements means that banks have less money to lend, the banks raise interest rates and credit requirements in making loans. For easy money, requirements are lowered so that banks have more money to lend. The banks, in turn, lower interest rates and act less selectively in making loans.

Monetary policy is usually not implemented by changing reserve requirements of banks because a small change in requirements results in a large change in the money supply. Changing reserve requirements is too crude a tool for day-to-day monetary policy purposes.

SECONDARY TOOLS OF THE FED. Member banks may borrow from a federal reserve bank by pledging customers' promissory notes as collateral. The interest rate the banks pay when borrowing is termed the *discount rate.* By raising the rate of interest that member banks are charged for borrowing, the Fed can signal a desire for tighter money. Lowering the interest rate signals easy money.

FIGURE 14-2
Generalized Sequence of Effects of Change in Money Supply

As Money Tightens	As Money Eases
1. Federal Reserve System raises reserve requirements of member banks or sells bonds in open market to cause relative decrease in money supply.	1. Federal Reserve System lowers reserve requirements of member banks or buys bonds in open market to increase money supply.
2. Reserves of member banks are decreased on relative basis. Money for new loans becomes limited.	2. Reserves of member banks are increased on relative basis. The reserves earn interest and produce profit only if put to work.
3. Member banks sell bonds and short-term notes to obtain money to meet demand of customers for new loans.	3. Member banks extend loans to customers more readily and buy bonds and notes with excess reserves.
4. As supply of bonds and notes offered for sale exceeds demand, prices drop; rate of return to buyers therefore increases.	4. As more bonds are purchased, demand exceeds supply offered for sale, and prices go up; rate of return to buyers decreases.
5. As rate of return increases, money is withdrawn from time and savings deposits to buy the bonds and notes. Also, bonds and notes are bought by savers in preference to putting new savings into time and savings accounts, which is *disintermediation*. Thus money is lost by banks and savings and loan associations.	5. As rate of return on bonds falls, more money is deposited in time and savings accounts in preference to more bond purchases. Therefore, *intermediation* increases as banks and savings and loan associations get more money to invest.
6. With less money to lend, banks and savings and loan associations raise lending standards and interest rates. Marginal borrowers are therefore unable to obtain credit.	6. With more money to lend, banks and savings and loan associations lower lending standards and interest rates. Marginal borrowers are therefore able to obtain credit.
7. Prepayment of mortgage loans and other low-interest debt drops off.	7. Prepayment of mortgage loans and other debt picks up as costs of refinancing drop.
8. Refinancing and new financing activity are slow because of higher interest rates and credit standards. Investment opportunities decline. Net result is reduced financial activity until money gets easier. Economy is slowed down, and inflation is brought under control.	8. Refinancing and new financing activity is brisk because of lower interest rates and credit standards. More investment opportunities become possible. Net result is increased financial activity as long as economy remains healthy and inflation remains under control.

Banks usually do not borrow heavily from the Fed. Consequently, changing the discount rate does not greatly affect the interest rate that banks charge their customers.

Selective financial controls are sometimes authorized by Congress and administered by the Fed. For example, the Fed was authorized to raise down payments on houses during the Korean War. Selective controls, in the past, have been used only in times of emergency. **Moral suasion** is the effort by federal officials to convince banks to tighten or ease credit without any direct regulation.

287

Importance of Interest Rates to Real Estate Activity

In times of tight money, interest rates go up. Monetary policy is therefore related directly to the availability and cost of mortgage money. If inflation is a national problem, monetary theory calls for a cutback in the money supply in order to decrease the purchasing power or effective demand for goods and services in the hands of the public. This, in turn, is meant to check further price increases. A limited or reduced money supply means that the available money will be directed to those users able to pay the highest interest rates. Thus, interest rates on mortgage loans must go up to attract money. If potential borrowers cannot or will not pay the higher rates, money is not channeled to them.

Alternatively, if unemployment and recession are national problems, one solution is to increase the money supply. With increased supply, funds begin to build up in financial institutions and must be lent out if interest is to be earned. The interest rate is lowered and more business and individuals can afford the price. Hence more mortgage money is available and interest rates drop.

An investor or builder is therefore advised to key in on stated monetary policy in making decisions regarding the buying or selling of property or arranging to ensure future mortgage money availability. Of course, other considerations may complicate the decision-making process. For example, in 1979–80 the nation simultaneously experienced high unemployment, recession, and double-digit inflation. Economists and politicians were sharply divided on what goals to emphasize and what methods or policies to apply. No clear-cut indicator of policy was evident.

MORTGAGE MARKET OVERVIEW

The objective of this section is to provide a basic perspective and understanding of mortgage market operations. Such an understanding should aid our investor in obtaining real estate credit to maximum advantage. In order to provide perspective, we relate the mortgage market to the larger, more general, financial market. In this section, we also look briefly at agencies of the federal government that are intended to stabilize mortgage market activity. Further, we look at how monies are channeled into real estate. In addition, we look at the risks or broad considerations of lenders in making mortgage loans. In general, these considerations are borrower risks, property risks, and portfolio risks. Decisions and actions by the various lenders in making loans largely determine the flow of funds into mortgages as well as who gets the funds, and why.

Financial Markets and Money Flows

Mortgage lending represents only a portion of the total money flows in our economy. Before looking closely at mortgage markets, let us take a brief look at overall flows of money in our economy. Money flows are also often referred to as flow of funds by economists.

In the overall scheme of economics, payments must be made by our business sector to the factors of production in generating the gross national product,

GNP. The factors of production are land, labor, capital, and management. **Gross national product** is the total value of all goods and services produced by our economy, valued at market prices.

GNP is made up of all goods and services produced plus gross domestic private investment. See figure 14–3, which shows major money flows in our economy.

At the same time, the consuming sector of our economy, made up of the owner/managers of the factors of production, use the goods and services produced. These owner/managers get rents from land or realty, wages for labor, interest from money, and profits from ownership and management of businesses.

FIGURE 14–3
Simplified Flow of Funds in Our Economy, with Emphasis on Monies Flowing through Financial Markets

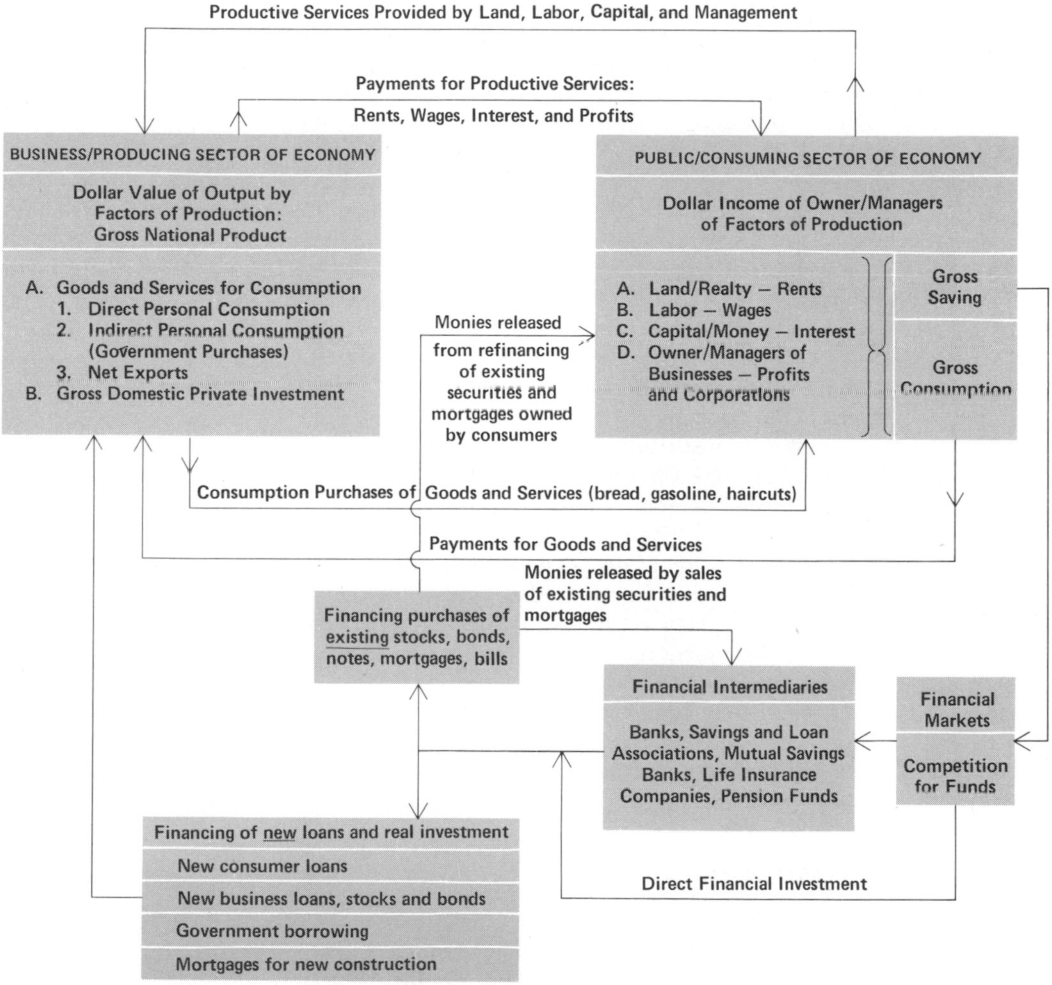

The monies received go mostly to pay for the goods and services consumed. But some excess, or saving, is also realized by the consuming sector. This excess goes to the financial markets for investment. **Financial markets** are the places or the processes whereby those with funds lend to those wishing to borrow; money is exchanged for financial claims, such as bonds, bills, or mortgages.

In financial markets, a distinction is usually made between money markets and capital markets. **Money markets** involve the exchange of money for short-term money instruments, and the subsequent buying and selling of these short-term instruments. Examples are notes and treasury bills. Short term means the instruments have one year or less to maturity. Financial institutions, and others, continually create and trade short-term instruments to adjust and maintain liquidity positions. **Capital markets** refer to the creation and exchanges of long-term debt instruments (bonds, mortgages, commercial paper) and stocks for money. It follows that long term means the instruments have a maturity of longer than one year. Using one year as a dividing line is arbitrary but useful. And of course, stocks generally have no maturity date at all. The mortgage market is basically a capital or long-term market.

Competition for funds is implicit in a financial market. The function of the market is to channel the nation's savings to its highest and best use, usually meaning that use able and willing to pay the highest rate of return. As indicated by figure 14–3, the competition for funds is between and among financial institutions as well as investment alternatives. The main institutions of concern are commercial banks (CBs), savings and loan associations (S&Ls), mutual savings banks (MSBs) and life insurance companies (LICs). In general, the alternatives open to lenders are consumer loans, business loans, corporate stocks and bonds, government bonds, and mortgages.

A distinction needs to be noted between the buying and selling of existing financial instruments and the creation of new ones. The purchase of an existing stock, bond, or mortgage from another holder simply channels money to another financial institution or returns money to the public or consuming sector of the economy. The seller may save the money or spend it for consumption goods. Sales between financial institutions, on the other hand, *releases* money for the selling institution. The released money may go to maintain liquidity or another investment. The creation of new financial instruments (bonds, loans, mortgages), on the other hand, feeds money into the productive sector. This new money stimulates the economy and, if used for investment, creates new wealth.

In 1976, mortgage loans accounted for nearly one-fourth (23.6 percent) of all public and private debt in the U.S. See figure 14–4. Federal, state, and local government debt also accounted for nearly one-fourth (24.8 percent). Corporation borrowing, at 42.2 percent, easily accounted for the largest share of domestic debt. Consumer borrowing, at 9.4 percent, accounted for the smallest share of debt. All four of these areas compete for funds on a continuing basis.

The Secondary Mortgage Market

Broadly speaking, mortgage market participants may be divided into primary and secondary lenders. **Primary lenders** invest in mortgages but generally are neither equipped nor willing to originate and service mortgage loans for sec-

FIGURE 14–4
Net Public and Private Debt: 1976 (in billions of dollars)

Item	Dollar	Percent
PUBLIC		
Federal and federally sponsored credit agencies	$597	17.8
State and local government	236	7.0
PRIVATE		
Corporate	1,415	42.2
Mortgage	792	23.6
Consumer	314	9.4
TOTAL	$3,354	100.0

Source: *Statistical Abstract of the U.S.*, 1977, Table 854.

ondary lenders. Secondary lenders buy existing mortgage loans in competition with other types of debt instruments, such as corporate or government bonds through mortgage bankers and brokers, or mortgage companies. Many federal government agencies are active as secondary lenders. The aggregate buying and selling of existing mortgage loans is the **secondary mortgage market.**

Home buyers, builders and developers, investors, and businesses all pledge property and borrow by way of mortgage loans. The most common primary lenders are savings and loan associations (S&Ls), commercial banks (CBs), mutual savings banks (MSBs), life insurance companies (LICs), and mortgage companies. Pension funds, LICs, and private mortgage corporations are the main private secondary lenders. The Federal Home Loan Mortgage Corporation (FHLMC), Federal National Mortgage Association (FNMA), and the Government National Mortgage Association (GNMA), are the main secondary lenders from the federal government. The Federal Home Loan Bank (FHLB) System, and the Department of Housing and Urban Development (HUD) serve as back-up institutions to FHLMC, FNMA, and GNMA. Figure 14–5 gives an overview of mortgage market operations. Most of these agencies and institutions are discussed in more detail in the later sections of this chapter. These agencies and institutions provide most real estate credit. If left to themselves, primary lenders would soon run out of money for loans in periods of tight money. The federal government therefore created the Home Loan Bank System, FNMA, GNMA, and the Home Loan Mortgage Corporation to add liquidity to mortgage markets. These agencies either advance monies to primary lenders or buy mortgages from them. In either event, monies of primary lenders are released to make more mortgages.

In addition, financial institutions frequently buy and sell mortgages among themselves. For example, a New York MSB with excess funds may buy mortgages from an S&L in Colorado where funds are scarce. Or a life insurance company may buy loans from mortage bankers in several states. FHA-insured and VA-guaranteed loans facilitate this buying and selling of mortgages because of their standardized terms. Privately insured conventional loans on uniform FNMA/FHLMC instruments also give lenders protection and stand-

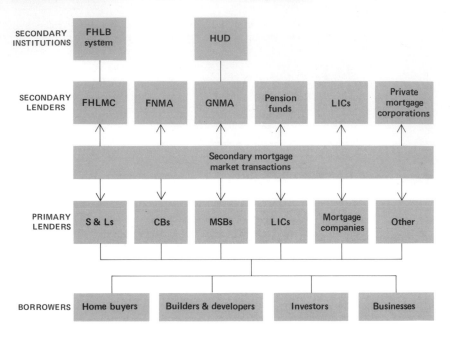

FIGURE 14-5
Borrowers, Institutions, and Agencies of the Mortgage Market

ardized terms. The result of this buying and selling activity among lenders is higher liquidity for mortgages and a broadening of the mortgage market. In addition, with commercial banks and life insurance being active in mortgage markets, mortgages must be directly competitive with other investments—stocks and bonds—in competing for excess funds. This competition means that mortgages and home construction are increasingly tied to the supply and demand for money in our entire economy. This buying and selling activity makes up the secondary mortgage market.

Lender Risks

An investor or home buyer can almost always obtain real estate credit if he or she is willing to pay the price by way of interest rate and other terms of borrowing. Savings and loan associations, banks, and insurance companies are in business to lend money and to make a profit. A knowledgeable investor or home owner makes it a point to know the procedures of borrowing and, in addition, to borrow in the most opportune way and at the most advantageous terms.

Advantageous borrowing begins by understanding money market conditions. For example, the inverse relationship between money market supply and interest rates is an economic fact of life. The time required for a change in monetary conditions to be reflected in a changed level of residential construction is uncertain and depends on several complex factors. Nevertheless, the basic relationship continues; when plenty of money is available, interest rates drop, and vice versa.

A further consideration for the potential borrower is approaching the right institutions for the kind of loan desired. Savings and loan associations and mutual savings banks lend much more readily on one-family houses than do life insurance companies or commercial banks. Commercial banks and life insurance companies, however, are more likely to make loans on farms and commercial properties. And of course individual lenders must be approached for purchase money mortgages and land contracts, as on undeveloped land.

A third major consideration in borrowing money is risks of lenders. The potential borrower must be aware of those. Lenders continually balance opportunities for profit against chances of loss of profit and principal. Lenders operate on the principle that as risk increases, profits should also increase. Mortgage lenders have three major types of **risk:** (1) borrower, (2) property, and (3) portfolio.

BORROWER RISK. A lender's analysis of **borrower risk** in making a loan begins with the borrower. The borrower's situation must not possess undue risks that cause it to be screened out by lenders if a loan is to be obtained. The categories of concern in the analysis generally are (a) credit rating, (b) assets, (c) earning capacity or income, and (d) motivation. A lender is likely to have accept-reject guidelines for each category.

A credit rating may be obtained simply by ordering a credit report on the prospective borrower. The borrower's credit experience and reputation must show an acceptably stable performance, including job and income patterns and family life. The credit report and the borrower's application provide information on assets owned or net worth, including savings and checking account balances. Third, the borrower's monthly or annual income must show a capability of meeting the principal, interest, taxes, and insurance (PITI) requirements of the proposed loan. For a home owner's loan, the usual rule is that PITI must not exceed one-fourth or 25 percent of the borrower's gross monthly income. In addition, PITI and other debt obligations must not exceed one-third of the borrower's gross monthly income. The lender looks more to the property for security in making a loan on an investment property, and these rules do not necessarily apply.

The borrower's motivation is the final, and perhaps the most important, of the four categories. *Motivation* means the borrower has sufficient incentive and desire to meet the requirements of the loan. A young family wishing to own their own home is usually considered to have high incentive. An ambitious investor might also be considered highly motivated. Motivation may be judged in several ways. A strong credit report, a steady accumulation of assets, and rising income all indicate strong motivation, for example.

PROPERTY RISKS. In analyzing property risks, three categories of concern must be addressed: (a) on-site characteristics, (b) location, and (c) marketability. Borrower risks are generally more important than property risks for owner-occupied dwellings. But for investment properties, where the value may be many, many times the borrower's income, the property must be looked to more strongly for security. Property risks are largely evaluated in a market-value appraisal.

The size, shape, and topography of a site are the first considerations in judging on-site characteristics. These characteristics must be complementary to the improvements and the use. Next, the size, condition, functional capability, mechanical equipment, and appearance of any improvements are taken into account.

Relative ease of accessibility to the property is an important consideration in location. A property that can be easily reached by major roads from work and shopping areas is preferable to one reached only with great effort by narrow, bumpy roads, for example. Easy access to schools is also usually important for houses with several bedrooms. And for a commercial property, location on a major thoroughfare becomes a must. The exposure or environment of a property is also important to the location of a property. By way of example, a house with a pleasing view in a well-kept neighborhood is preferable to a house opposite a junkyard in a blighted neighborhood.

Marketability risks pertain largely to the economic makeup of the community. A growing community with diversified industries seems likely to provide greater marketability, for example, than a community with one industry that is declining. Also, stable employment and economic patterns are preferable to cyclical patterns.

A lender in a given community may exercise greatest control over on-site and locational risks. That is, properties with better improvements or locations are subject to fewer risks than properties with obsolete improvements in out-of-the-way locations. A local lender must often live with the economic or marketability risks inherent to the community. This means the competition for loans may turn largely on condition and location.

PORTFOLIO RISKS. A portfolio, in finance, is all the securities or investments owned or managed. Owning and managing a large number of investments includes many risks, termed **portfolio risks.** For a mortgage lender, these risks may be categorized as (a) administrative, (b) investment, and (c) mix and turn-over, or diversification, perils.

Administrative risks are perils inherent in making and servicing loans that might lead to losses. The chance of error in the property file and in keeping records of payments is ever present. At the time a loan is closed, a chance of error in the contract terms is possible. The property requires periodic inspections to insure upkeep and maintenance. Fortunately for lenders, most administrative risks are under their direct control. Unanticipated costs or risks may develop, but over a period of time, control usually becomes routine.

Investment risks are chances that an adequate rate of return will not be realized on loans. Lenders are in business to make a profit. After the borrower and property are found acceptable, the lender must be concerned with yields realized on loans made, individually and collectively. Once loans are extended, they may go sour for two reasons. First, the borrower might not be able to keep up with increasing costs of operation, in which event, abandonment or foreclosure would result. Second, the property's value may decline faster than the loan is amortized. This decline would mean an increasing loan-to-value ratio, with the possibility, in foreclosure, that the unamortized principal plus foreclosure expenses would exceed the disposition value of the property. Either of these events would decrease profitability of the investment.

Earlier, we briefly discussed mix and turnover of loans risk. Financial intermediaries need a spread between costs of money, usually interest paid on deposits, and earnings from loans extended. If an adequate portion of the lender's loans do not earn more than the lender's cost of money, the lender's profits are squeezed. In addition, lenders limit risk by diversifying their portfolio by location, by loan-to-value ratios, and by time to maturity. Further, funds are not always available from depositors, as when disintermediation occurs. At such times, the lender needs the run-off from monthly payments of debt service and prepayments to meet possible net withdrawals of funds by depositors.

CONCLUSIONS ON RISKS. Lenders must continually keep their money working. This means continually reviewing and balancing borrower risk, property risks, and portfolio risks. A motivated investor improves his or her chances for obtaining loans at reasonable terms by maintaining a strong credit reputation and by understanding and responding to the risks that concern a lender.

Mortgage Market Summary

Mortgages are in competition with stocks, bonds, and consumer loans in the financial markets. Money is channeled to mortgages through financial intermediaries such as banks, S&Ls, and LICs. Primary lenders originate loans, which are frequently sold to secondary lenders to maintain liquidity and lending power. Major categories of lenders' risks concern borrowers, properties, and portfolio management. Thus in this section we have had an overview of the process and the considerations involved in getting money from capital markets into mortgage loans.

PRIMARY LENDERS

The mortgage market is made up of primary and secondary lenders. *Primary lenders* originate loans or supply funds directly to borrowers. Savings and loan associations, mutual savings banks, commercial banks, mortgage bankers, and life insurance companies make up the bulk of primary lenders. Others, including individuals, also sometimes act as primary lenders. *Secondary lenders* buy loans from, or originate loans through, someone else. Federally supported agencies, pension funds, and some life insurance companies are the major secondary lenders. Some financial organizations act as both primary and secondary lenders.

As a class, other lenders account for approximately one-eighth of all mortgage loans outstanding (see figure 14–7). The classification *other lenders* includes individuals, endowment and pension funds, trustees of individual trusts, estates, and other miscellaneous organizations seeking an investment outlet for accumulated monies. Other lenders generally have much more freedom and flexibility in making loans than established financial institutions. Consequently, other lenders are the main source of funds for land contracts and junior mortgages.

Primary lending institutions exert great influence in mortgage markets. In dollar terms, they originate nearly seven-eighths of all mortgage debt. These institutions, for the most part, act as financial intermediaries, accepting deposits from savers and making loans to borrowers. The laws and regulations governing them are taken up in the order of their relative importance in mortgage lending.

1. Savings and loan associations (S&Ls)
2. Commercial banks (CBs)
3. Mutual savings banks (MSBs)
4. Life insurance companies (LICs)
5. Mortgage bankers (MBs)

Figures 14–6 and 14–7 show the relative importance of all lenders based on loans outstanding. Lending by property type is also depicted. The total of mortgage loans, $1,169.3 billions, was over 40 percent greater than the federal interest-bearing debt of $822.9 billions at the end of 1978. Thrift institutions— savings and loan associations and mutual savings banks—accounted for nearly one-half of the mortgage loans.

FIGURE 14–6
Mortgage Loans Outstanding, by Type of Lender and Type of Property, Year-End 1978* (in billions of dollars)

Lender	RESIDENTIAL PROPERTIES			Commercial Properties	Farm Properties	Total Mortgage Loans	%
	One- to Four-family	Multi-family	Total				
Savings associations	$354.6	$ 36.4	$391.0	$ 41.9	†	$ 432.9	37.0
Commercial banks	126.4	10.9	137.3	67.0	$ 9.1	213.4	18.3
Mutual savings banks	62.1	16.5	78.6	16.3	0.1	95.0	8.1
Life insurance companies	14.5	19.3	33.8	60.8	10.3	105.0	9.0
All others	200.8	38.8	239.6	27.0	56.5	323.1	27.6
Total	$758.4	$121.9	$880.3	$213.0	$76.0	$1,169.3	100.0
%	64.9	10.4	75.3	18.2	6.5	100.0	—

Note: Components may not add to totals due to rounding.
* Preliminary.
† Less than $50 million.
Sources: Federal Home Loan Bank Board; Federal Reserve Board.

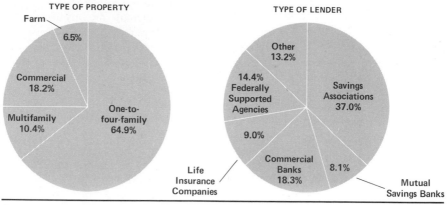

FIGURE 14-7
Mortgage Loans Outstanding, by Type of Property and Type of Lender, Year-end 1978

TYPE OF PROPERTY

Farm 6.5%

Commercial 18.2%

Multifamily 10.4%

One-to-four-family 64.9%

TYPE OF LENDER

Other 13.2%

14.4% Federally Supported Agencies

Savings Associations 37.0%

9.0%

Life Insurance Companies

Commercial Banks 18.3%

8.1%

Mutual Savings Banks

Source: Federal Reserve Board.

Savings and Loan Associations

At the end of 1978 there were 4,723 savings and loan associations in the United States. They receive over one-third of all savings deposits in the United States. These associations accounted for more than one-third of all mortgage loans outstanding, in dollar terms, and nearly one-half of all home mortgage loans.

Savings and loan associations have been active for over 100 years. Yet regulation of their lending activities on a regional and national scale did not begin until 1932 when Congress created the Federal Home Loan Bank (FHLB) System. Today, all federally chartered S&Ls are supervised by the FHLB System. In addition, almost all state chartered S&Ls choose to be members of the system and subject to its regulations. A major reason for this is that members may borrow on short notice from a district home loan bank whenever funds are needed to pay off accounts of withdrawing depositors or to finance additional mortgage loans.

Almost all savings and loan associations, if qualified, also belong to the Federal Savings and Loan Insurance Corporation (FSLIC), which was created by Congress in 1934. FSLIC insures public deposits with member institutions for up to $100,000 per account. Depositor confidence in S&Ls is very high because of this FSLIC insurance and because of FSLIC's uniform lending policies and accounting supervision. As a result, S&Ls have grown rapidly in total assets and in mortgage loans outstanding.

S&Ls may make conventional installment loans for up to 95 percent of either the purchase price or approved market value of any home offered as security, whichever is less. The loans must be amortized on a monthly basis and have a maximum life of thirty years. Almost all high loan-to-value ratio loans are made on an insured or guaranteed basis. According to FHLB System regulations, the loan must be secured by first-mortgage liens on residences within

297

the state of the home office of the association making the loan or within 100 miles of the office making the loan if outside the home office state. FHA and VA loans may be made up to any loan-to-value limits acceptable to the Federal Housing Administration or the Veterans Administration.

First-mortgage loans may also be made on business and income properties, churches, and other improved properties up to a maximum loan-to-value ratio of 75 percent. Monthly loan amortization payments and a maximum term of twenty-five years, apply to these loans. Not more than 20 percent of an association's assets may be placed in "business property" loans. Savings and loan associations may also make loans for property improvement, alteration, repair, and equipment. Finally, mobile homes may be financed by S&Ls.

Commercial Banks

Commercial banks are required by law to maintain relatively greater liquidity in their assets than other financial institutions. The reason is that they are more subject to immediate withdrawal of deposits by the nature of their operation. Thus, although some 14,000 commercial banks control approximately one-half of Americans' savings, their role in mortgage lending continues to be, for them, a secondary activity. Even so, CB's account for almost one-fifth of all mortgage loans outstanding. Making short-term commercial loans to local business firms is their primary lending activity. Short-term loans enable the banks to meet their liquidity requirements and at the same time to maximize their profits.

Commercial banks may make uninsured conventional loans on homes for up to 80 percent of the lesser of purchase price or appraised market value. The loans may be made, if fully amortized, for up to thirty years. Insured conventional loans may be made for up to 95 percent loan-to-value ratio. FHA insured and VA guaranteed loans may be made to any loan-to-value limits and terms allowed by the federal government. Commercial banks may also make construction loans for up to twenty-four months.

Commercial banks generally increase their mortgage lending activity when demand for local business loans is slow. They decrease mortgage lending activity when business loan demand is strong. That is, they tend to invest in real estate loans only when funds on hand exceed local business needs. Recent improvements in secondary mortgage market operations has lessened the pressure on commercial banks to avoid mortgage lending activity. With an active secondary mortgage market, mortgages may be sold off at almost any time by a bank in order to increase cash on hand. Thus mortgage loans are now reasonably liquid assets.

Mutual Savings Banks

Mutual savings banks accept savings from individuals and channel them into productive investments. MSBs account for approximately one-eighth of all savings in the United States. Approximately three-fourths of the savings are invested in mortgage loans. MSBs account for approximately 10 percent of all mortgage loans outstanding.

All of the approximately 475 mutual savings banks in the United States are state chartered. Nearly all of them are located in the Middle Atlantic States and in New England, with nearly seven-eighths in the states of New York, Massachusetts, Connecticut, Pennsylvania, and New Jersey. Over 90 percent of MSB deposits are concentrated in these five states, with New York accounting for over one-half of the total. Mutual savings banks tend to be strong when savings and loan associations are weak, and vice versa. From the viewpoint of mortgage borrowers, the difference between S&Ls and MSBs is slight.

In almost all states MSBs may make insured conventional loans up to 95 percent of value with a life of up to thirty years. Conventional, uninsured loans may generally be made up to 80 percent of value, also with an amortization period of up to thirty years. In a few states, uninsured conventional loans may be made up to 90 percent of value. FHA and VA loans may be made up to any loan-to-value rates acceptable to the federal government.

Life Insurance Companies

Life insurance companies have shifted their mortgage lending emphasis since 1965 from one-family residences to multifamily and commercial properties. Larger loans and higher interest rates on loans for these properties make lending on them more profitable. Also, a share of the equity action, including participation in the income generated by these properties, is frequently possible in multifamily and commercial lending. Investing in mortgage loans is particularly advantageous to LICs because of the long-term nature of their insurance policy obligations. Actuaries are able to forecast dollar requirements of their policy obligations and match them up with mortgages of appropriate terms.

Larger insurance companies make mortgages on a national scale. Some loans are made through branch offices, but many are made through mortgage bankers and brokers. Extremely large loans are usually arranged from the home office. LICs have considerable flexibility in their mortgage lending, but they generally limit loans to two-thirds of appraised value with amortization periods up to thirty years. FHA insured and VA guaranteed loans are purchased in the secondary mortgage market from time to time when excess reserves pile up and investment opportunities are limited.

Mortgage Companies

Mortgage bankers and mortgage brokers hold little long-term mortgage debt. Instead, they serve secondary lenders, such as life insurance companies and governmental agencies, that wish to invest in mortgages. **Mortgage bankers** originate and service loans for these secondary lenders for a fee. *Mortgage brokers* originate loans for the fee but do not provide any servicing. The secondary lenders must then arrange for servicing elsewhere, often through mortgage bankers. Mortgage bankers sometimes originate loans first and look for a buyer later if the loan presents a profit opportunity.

Eastern and Midwestern banks and savings and loan associations sometimes become secondary lenders when they accumulate surplus funds that cannot otherwise be placed profitably; they use the surplus funds to buy loans, secured by properties in other regions, through mortgage bankers and brokers. The operations of mortgage firms become large in capital-scarce areas of the South and West where dependence on out-of-state funds is great.

Mortgage bankers generally charge three-eighths of 1 percent of outstanding loan balances as a servicing fee. Thus an outstanding loan balance of $10,000 yields $37.50 per year to a mortgage banker. This $37.50 must cover the cost of accounting, filing, making monthly statements, correspondence, and office overhead. This effectively means that the mortgage banker must service a high volume of loans to have a profitable operation.

SECONDARY LENDERS

The main **secondary lenders** are agencies of the federal government and life insurance companies. Banks and S&Ls also sometimes act as secondary lenders if profit opportunities elsewhere exceed local profit opportunities. Pension funds also increasingly invest in mortgages. The combined activities of all of these lenders link the nation's capital and mortgage markets.

The major organizations involved in secondary mortgage market activity and their relation to primary lenders and borrowers are shown in figure 14–5. The order in which these organizations are taken up is as follows:

1. Federal Home Loan Bank System (FHLBS)
2. Federal Home Loan Mortgage Corporation (FHLMC)
3. Federal National Mortgage Association (FNMA)
4. Government National Mortgage Association (GNMA)
5. Private mortgage corporations

A number of organizations promote loan safety, thus facilitating the purchase and sale of loans in the secondary mortgage market. These organizations offering protection to holders of mortgage loans include private mortgage insurance corporations, the Federal Housing Administration, the Veterans' Administration, and the Farmers' Home Administration.

Federal Home Loan Bank System

The Federal Home Loan Bank System (FHLBS) was created by Congress during the financial crisis of the 1930s. The purpose was to establish a source of central credit for the nation's home financing institutions. This initial purpose has expanded into five functions as follows:

1. To link mortgage lending institutions to the nation's capital markets
2. To serve as a source of secondary credit for member institutions during periods of heavy withdrawal demand

3. To smooth out seasonal differences between saving flows and loan changes

4. To smooth flow of funds from capital surplus areas to capital deficit areas

5. To generally stabilize residential construction and financing

The FHLB System advances funds to members in need, consistent with the above functions. The system does not operate as a secondary mortgage market facility per se.

The Federal Home Loan Bank System is made up of twelve regional banks and member institutions. Membership is open to savings and loan associations, mutual savings banks, and life insurance companies. By law, all federally chartered savings and loan associations must belong to the FHLB System. At the end of 1978 the system had 4,242 members: 4,158 S&Ls, 86 MSBs, and 2 life insurance companies. The system is governed by a three-member board appointed by the President of the United States.

Federal Home Loan Mortgage Corporation

The Federal Home Loan Mortgage Corporation (FHLMC) was created by Congress in 1970. The trade name for FHLMC is **Freddie Mac.** Freddie Mac functions as a secondary mortgage market facility under the supervision of the FHLB Board. It buys and sells conventional, FHA insured, and VA guaranteed mortgages. The declared goal of the FHLMC is to make mortgages as highly liquid, and equally as attractive, as other securities to investors. In the past, mortgages have been considered a relatively illiquid investment.

Liquidity refers to the ease of quickness with which an investment can be converted into cash and to the cash-to-value ratio realized. The easier the conversion into cash and the higher the cash-to-value ratio, the more liquid the investment. An active secondary mortgage market would give mortgages liquidity equal to that of stocks and bonds.

The FHLMC seeks to accomplish its goal in several ways:

1. Development, in conjunction with the Federal National Mortgage Association (FNMA), of uniform conventional mortgage instruments so that a lack of standardized terms would no longer be a major deterrent to the ready buying and selling of conventional mortgages.

2. Purchase and sale of conventional mortgage loans on a whole and a participation basis. *Participation* means that two or more investors or lenders share or participate in the ownership of the loan.

3. Purchase and sale of FHA insured and VA guaranteed loans on a continuing basis.

Federal National Mortgage Association

The Federal National Mortgage Association (FNMA) was created by Congress in 1938. FNMA carries the nickname of **Fannie Mae.** Fannie Mae is a government-sponsored corporation, but its stock is privately owned. This unique combination of interest makes FNMA a private corporation with a public purpose.

The basic purpose of FNMA is to provide a secondary market for residential loans. FNMA buys, services, and sells loans to fulfill this purpose. It deals in conventional, FHA insured, and VA guaranteed loans. Operationally, FNMA buys mortgages when loanable funds are in short supply and sells them when funds are plentiful. FNMA and FHLMC developed uniform instruments for conventional mortgage loans to facilitate their use in the secondary mortgage market.

Government National Mortgage Association

The Government National Mortgage Association (GNMA) was created by Congress in 1968. GNMA is referred to in the trade as **Ginnie Mae.** Ginnie Mae is entirely owned by the federal government, and its financial activities are supported by borrowings from the federal government. In fact, Ginnie Mae is an agency of the Department of Housing and Urban Development and has its operating policies set by the HUD secretary. The Government National Mortgage Association has three main functions: (1) special assistance for disadvantaged residential borrowers, (2) raising additional funds for residential lending, and (3) mortgage portfolio management and liquidation.

The special assistance function involves providing funds for low-cost housing and for residential mortgages in underdeveloped, capital-scarce areas. The fund-raising function is to stabilize mortgage lending and home construction activities. Techniques to accomplish these two functions are the Tandem Plan and government-guaranteed securities.

The Tandem Plan is so named because GNMA and FNMA work together in implementing it. The plan works as follows. A lending institution obtains a firm commitment from GNMA to purchase, at a fixed price, a mortgage loan on low-income housing. The interest rate is fixed on the loan so that if interest rates rise, the value of the loan falls. Without the commitment, the lender would not make the loan. With the commitment, the loan is made by a local lending institution and sold to GNMA at the fixed price. GNMA, in turn, sells the loan to FNMA at the discounted or reduced value and absorbs the discount as a loss.

GNMA raises funds through guarantees of securities backed by government-insured or guaranteed mortgages, namely FHA and VA loans. The loans underlying the guarantee are pooled, a covering security is issued, and repayments from the pool are used to pay off the security. Two basic types of securities are issued—the pass through and the bond. The pass through provides for monthly payments to the security holder. The bond provides for semiannual payments of principal and interest. Debt service from the pool of mortgages is used to make payments on the securities. The funds raised from sale of the security are used to purchase additional mortgages.

The above programs, of course, result in GNMA's carrying a very large portfolio of mortgages which requires continuing management. GNMA may buy, service, and sell mortgages in an orderly manner that will have a minimum adverse effect on the residential mortgage market and cause a minimum loss to the federal government.

Private Mortgage Corporations

Some private mortgage insurance corporations organize subsidiary mortgage corporations to invest reserves in mortgages. Prepayments and monthly debt service on the mortgages are used to pay claims on insured mortgages on which lenders lost money. These companies therefore constitute a private, secondary mortgage lender or investor. The largest of these firms is the MGIC Mortgage Corporation. The trade nickname for the MGIC Mortgage Corporation is Maggy Mae.

LENDING LAWS

Several federal laws have been passed in recent years to protect consumers. Three laws of particular importance in mortgage lending are (1) the Consumer Credit Protection Act (Regulation Z), (2) the Real Estate Settlement Procedures Act (RESPA), and (3) the National Flood Insurance Act. The essence of each act as it relates to truth in lending is set forth here. However, the reader should consult current and personal sources of information before entering into or making a transaction involving truth in lending.

Regulation Z

The Consumer Credit Protection Act authorizes and requires the Board of Governors of the Federal Reserve System to develop and distribute regulations concerning consumer loans. The Board of Governors publishes the required regulations as Federal Reserve **Regulation Z** or truth-in-lending (TIL) laws. The purpose of Regulation Z is to let borrowers and consumers know and compare the costs of credit from alternative sources, and, in turn, make informed credit decisions. Regulation Z does not set minimum, maximum, or any, charges for credit.

APPLICABILITY OF REGULATION Z. Regulation Z applies to consumer credit loans, to individuals, where a finance charge is or may be made. Also, such loans appear to be covered by the Consumer Credit Protection Act where the proceeds are to be for consumer needs—personal, family, or household. On the other hand, loans to organizations (corporations, trusts, partnerships, corporations, associations, governments, and estates) are not covered. TIL laws affect banks, savings and loan associations, insurance companies, residential mortgage brokers and bankers, and any other organizations, extending consumer credit requiring five or more repayment installments.

TIL laws do not cover loans to individuals made for business or commercial purposes. Loans and advances to individuals under the following circumstances therefore appear to be exempt:

1. Loans on one-family houses where the house is to produce profit or rental income. Loans to builders and landlords are therefore not covered.

2. Loans on property where the proceeds are to be used for business purposes.

3. Loans on property with two or more dwellings, one of which is to be rented or sold as a condominium.

FINANCE CHARGE AND APR. The two most important concepts to bear in mind about Regulation Z are "finance charge" and "annual percentage rate." Knowledge of these two concepts enables a consumer to tell at a glance how much is being paid for credit as well as the relative costs of the credit in percentage terms.

The **finance charge** is the total of all costs a consumer or borrower must pay, directly or indirectly, to obtain credit. The finance charge must be clearly identified to the consumer as a dollars and cents amount. Cost items included in the finance charge are interest, loan fees, finder's fees, mortgage insurance fees, discounts or points, and service or carrying charges. Cost items exempt as finance charges are as follows:

1. Payments for title search and examination, title insurance, and the like

2. Fees for appraisals, surveys, and credit reports

3. Fees for preparation of deeds, settlement statements, and other documents

4. Escrow fees relative to taxes, insurances, and rents

The **Annual Percentage Rate (APR)** is the yearly cost of credit in percentage terms. The APR must be stated to the nearest one-quarter of 1 percent. Calculation of the APR is extremely complex and not taken up here. An example may be helpful in explaining APR relative to truth in lending, however. A loan is made for $10,000, with a "nominal," or contract, rate of interest of 7½ percent. If the loan were scheduled to be repaid over twenty-five years, the monthly payment including interest and principal would be $73.90. However, if a required service charge of 2 percent, or $200, is subtracted, the net loan amount is $9,800 instead of $10,000. And the true interest rate is 7¾ percent and not 7½ percent, as stated on the face of the note or mortgage. In cases involving improvement loans where interest at a stipulated rate is charged on the original amount of the loan rather than on the remaining periodic balances of the amortized loan, the "true" interest could be nearly double the "stated" rate where the loan extends over a period of two years or more.

Required disclosures must be made before a transaction is consummated. "Consummated" means the time a contractual relationship between a lender and a borrower is created, regardless of when performance is required. State law governs the specific point at which a contractual relationship is created. The disclosures must be made in a clear, conspicuous, and meaningful sequence.

DISCLOSURE SPECIFICS. Disclosure must be made for any new loan transaction, including refinancing, consolidation, or increase in an existing obligation.

Advances to protect a security, as for taxes and hazard insurance, do not require additional disclosure. Also, assumption of a loan by a "new borrower" does not constitute a new transaction.

The following information must be disclosed to the consumer. (Several lesser items, which must also be disclosed, are omitted.)

1. The amount financed (loan amount), including a breakdown of its separate components
2. The amount and items of the finance charges
3. The finance charge expressed as an annual percentage rate
4. Property encumbered as security for the loan—this must be described in detail
5. The type of security interest involved in the transaction (mortgage or deed of trust, land contract)
6. The amount or method of computing any default, delinquency, or late payment charges
7. Prepayment penalty provisions, including method of computation

BORROWER'S RIGHT OF RESCISSION. A borrower has the right to rescind (cancel or repeal) a loan transaction involving an interest in a home already occupied as his or her personal residence. This **right of rescission** also applies to most open-end mortgage advances. It also applies when the borrower's personal residence is used as security to finance such other consumer needs as home equipment, autos, debt consolidation, or home improvements. This right does not apply to the typical real estate transaction in which the loan is obtained to finance the purchase of a dwelling unit as a personal residence by the borrower.

The borrower has the right to cancel the transaction for three business days following the date of consummation of the transaction, or the delivery of the disclosures, whichever is later. A business day is any day except Sunday, New Year's Day, Washington's Birthday, Memorial Day, Independence Day, Labor Day, Veterans' Day, Thanksgiving, and Christmas. The borrower must be given notice of his or her right to rescind before the three-day waiting period can begin. Regulation Z also stipulates the specific language of the notice.

The lender cannot disburse funds, perform any work, or make any deliveries to the property during the three-day waiting period, except in case of any emergency. Section 226.9(E) of Regulation Z provides that in a personal financial emergency, a borrower may waive or modify the right of rescission. The need to replace an oil furnace in midwinter is an example of a personal consumer emergency. If a borrower exercises the right of rescission in a "normal" transaction, finance charges and any lien interests against the borrower become void.

VIOLATIONS. Penalties for violation of Regulation Z are both criminal and civil. Willful and knowing failure to comply with the act is punishable by a fine of up to $5,000 and a year in jail. Civil penalties may be invoked if a lender cannot show that the violation was unintentional.

RESPA Disclosures

Originally the Real Estate Settlement Procedures Act of 1975 required a Federal Truth in Lending statement be given to borrowers on one- to four-family properties that involved a new loan. The statement tended to duplicate disclosures required by Regulation Z. Also, much delay and difficulty was experienced by buyers as a result of strict compliance with RESPA by lenders. Consequently, an amendment to the Real Estate Settlement Procedures Act, signed into law in early 1976, dropped all such disclosure requirements. Thus, all truth in lending disclosures are now made in accordance with Regulation Z.

RESPA continues to require a lender to give the borrower-buyer full disclosure about closing costs however, and the lender is the primary party responsible for implementing RESPA.

National Flood Insurance Act

The National Flood Insurance Act provides for protection from economic losses resulting from physical damage to or loss of real or personal property due to floods. The flood insurance program is meant to be a joint venture, insofar as possible, between the federal government and the private insurance industry, with the industry participating on a risk-sharing basis. The insurance must be obtained by the community in which the property is located. The community must develop a land-use plan and provide for flood plain zoning. Any community that has developed a flood protection system, as determined by the Department of Housing and Urban Development, is eligible for coverage under the National Flood Insurance program. Communities that do not comply are subject to the loss of federal backing in mortgage financing.

The act discourages development of flood-prone areas by imposing restrictive regulations on lenders for properties in flood-prone areas. Many real estate practitioners regard the restrictions as too stringent. At the time of this writing, the flood insurance program is being modified, and detailed procedures are being developed. Harley W. Snyder, chairman of the National Association of Realtors Subcommittee on Environment, considers that several major changes in the act are needed.

1. Existing homes in flood plains should be exempt from the act because their owners were not aware of the flood danger at the time they bought or built them.

2. Owners should be able to participate in the insurance program on an individual basis. Actions of a community to participate or not participate in the program are beyond the control of the individuals.

3. Maximum coverage limits should be removed as long as the owner is paying actuarially sound rates. A maximum coverage limit discriminates against owners of high-priced homes.

LENDING PROCEDURES
AND COMMITMENTS

The first step in obtaining a loan is making an application with a lender. Information required by lenders includes: (1) the amount of the loan desired, (2) identification of the property to be pledged as security, and (3) annual income, kind of employment, and other financial information on the applicant. If the property and the applicant look acceptable to the lender, a loan commitment is given the borrower. A lender usually requires and reviews an appraisal of the property and a credit report on the applicant before issuing the commitment.

A **loan commitment** is a written pledge, promise, or letter of agreement to lend or advance money under specified terms and conditions. The amount, the interest rate, and the life of the loan are stated along with any other terms demanded by the lender. In most cases the applicant has the right to shop with other lenders if the amount and terms of the commitment are unacceptable. At the same time, the lender is likely to include a termination date on the commitment, after which the offer to make the loan is withdrawn.

The four commonly used loan commitments are (1) firm, (2) conditional, (3) takeout, and (4) standby. The first two commitments, firm and conditional, are most applicable to consumer loans on residential properties. Takeout and standby commitments are important to builder-lender transactions as well as to transactions between lending agencies themselves.

VA, FHA, and private mortgage insurers make commitments to guarantee or insure loans. The terminology of these commitments is comparable to that of commitments by lenders.

Firm Commitment

A **firm commitment** is a definite offer to make a loan at stated terms and conditions. For all practical purposes, the borrower-applicant need only accept the offer and prepare for the loan closing. Nearly all commitments to home buyers and small investors are firm commitments.

Conditional Commitment

An agreement to make a loan, subject to certain limitations or provisions, is a **conditional commitment.** The provision may be completion of construction or development of a property. The Federal Housing Administration commonly issues conditional commitments for loan insurance to builders which depend on the builder's finding an acceptable buyer-borrower for the speculative house. The builder therefore accepts the risk of finding an acceptable buyer. Because the property is already approved, the conditional commitment facilitates the sale of the house and closing of the loan.

Takeout Commitment

A **takeout commitment** is an agreement by one lender to make a permanent loan to take another lender out of a temporary or construction loan. A

307

takeout commitment is also a firm agreement to buy a loan from an originating lender at a definite price.

A takeout commitment is commonly used between financial institutions and governmental agencies. For example, a takeout commitment may be given by a governmental agency, such as the Government National Mortgage Association, to a local lender, such as a bank. The governmental agency agrees to buy and take over a mortgage loan from a local lender as soon as the loan is closed and all contingencies surrounding the loan are satisfied. The local lender is usually considered contractually bound to sell the loan at the stipulated price. The price to be paid for the loan is included in the written commitment. Takeout commitments usually involve properties under construction or development.

Standby Commitment

A **standby commitment** is the promise to buy a loan from a second lender, without the second lender's being obligated to sell the loan. That is, a standby commitment gives the owner of a loan the option to sell or not to sell the loan at a stipulated price. The option to sell is obtained for a fee payable in advance, and the price may be lower than the market value of the loan.

A standby commitment is usually issued by a large institutional lender, such as a life insurance company, to a local bank or mortgage banker. An owner or developer may pay the fee for the local lender to obtain construction financing. With a standby commitment, the local lender is able to make the construction loan with assurance of being able to sell it promptly at a definite price instead of keeping it as a large loan on the books. If a higher price can be obtained elsewhere, the local lender has the right to take advantage of it and to realize a larger profit.

SUMMARY

Monetary policy to achieve national economic goals directly affects and ties real estate construction and sales activity to the general economy. Monetary policy is intended to achieve national economic goals. Easy money and low interest rates help to realize the goals of economic growth and full employment. The combination of tight money and high interest rates slows inflation, to achieve the goal of price stability. In periods of tight monetary policy and high interest rates, real estate activity tends to decline. On the other hand, easy money tends to stimulate real estate activity. The main financial institution for implementing monetary policy is "the Fed."

Real estate competes for money or credit in our capital markets. Financial intermediaries or go-betweens, mainly S&Ls and banks, channel money or savings from the public to real estate. Real estate credit accounts for about one-fourth of all public and private debt in the U.S. In times of tightening money conditions disintermediation, or direct investment by the public, sometimes occurs and traditional financial intermediaries are by-passed.

Our mortgage markets are made up of primary and secondary lenders. Primary lenders originate loans with home buyers, builders and developers, investors, and businesses. Secondary lenders buy loans. S&Ls, CBs, MSBs, and LICs make up the bulk of our primary lenders. LICs, pension funds, private mortgage companies, and governmental agencies make up our secondary lenders. The buying and selling of existing first mortgages is termed the secondary mortgage market. "Fannie Mae," "Ginnie Mae," and "Freddie Mac" are the main governmental agencies involved in secondary lending. Mortgage lending risks may be divided into three categories: (1) borrower risks, (2) property risks, and (3) portfolio risks. The main concerns in analyzing borrower risks are credit rating, assets, income, and motivation. Market value relative to loan amount and potential marketability are the main property risks of a lender. Portfolio risks include administration, investment or rate of return, and diversification considerations. Mortgage lenders must know and take account of the Consumer Credit Protection Act (Regulation Z), RESPA, and the National Flood Insurance Act in their operations. Four types of commitments used in mortgage markets are the (1) firm, (2) conditional, (3) takeout, and (4) standby.

KEY TERMS

Annual percentage rate (APR)	Money markets
Borrower risk	Moral suasion
Capital markets	Mortgage banker
Commitment	Open-market operations
Conditional commitment	Portfolio risks
Disintermediation	Primary lender
Easy money	Property risks
Fannie Mae (FNMA)	Regulation Z
Finance charge	Reserve requirements
Financial markets	Right of rescission
Firm commitment	Risk
Freddie Mac (FHLMC)	Secondary lender
Ginnie Mae (GNMA)	Secondary mortgage market
Gross national product (GNP)	Standby commitment
Intermediation	Takeout commitment
Loan commitment	Tight money

QUESTIONS FOR REVIEW AND DISCUSSION

1. Identify our national economic goals. Explain how monetary policy helps to achieve these goals. How is monetary policy carried out?

2. Define or explain intermediation and disintermediation. When are these concepts important?

3. What is the relationship of monetary policy and conditions to real estate construction and sales activity? What does this mean to a sophisticated investor?

4. Is the mortgage market a money or capital market? Why? What happens in capital markets?

5. What is the secondary mortgage market?

6. Identify and explain the three major classes of lender risk.

7. What is a primary lender? What financial institutions are most likely to be primary lenders?

8. What is a secondary lender? What institutions make up the bulk of secondary lenders?

9. Summarize Regulation Z.

10. Distinguish among conditional, takeout, and standby loan commitments.

11. Does real estate get its fair share of public savings? Explain how our various financial institutions affect the allocation to real estate. What other considerations influence the portion of public savings channeled into real estate?

12. A federal law lowering the maximum mortgage interest rate would benefit consumers. Discuss.

13. Real estate construction and sales activity are causes rather than effects of changing monetary conditions. Discuss.

REFERENCES

Cargill, Thomas F. *Money, The Financial System, and Monetary Policy.* Englewood Cliffs, N.J.: Prentice-Hall, 1979. Excellent overview of the nature and operation of our financial system. Moderately technical but still easy to read and understand. Recommended for the serious reader.

Case, Frederick E., and John M. Clapp. *Real Estate Financing.* New York: John Wiley, 1978. Comprehensive discussion of real estate finance; generally easy reading. Emphasis on perspective and decision making in real estate finance.

Henning, Charles N.; William Pigott; and Robert Haney Scott. *Financial Markets and the Economy.* 2nd ed. Englewood Cliffs, N.J.: Prentice-Hall, 1978. Overview of our financial system relative to the economy. Includes discussion of mortgage markets. Easy to read and understand.

Hoagland, Henry E.; Leo D. Stone; and William B. Brueggeman. *Real Estate Finance.* 6th ed. Homewood, Ill.: Richard D. Irwin, 1977. A basic source for anyone interested in real estate finance. Has considerable institutional content with a strong thrust toward decision making in the financing of real estate. Generally easy to read and understand.

Schwartz, Arthur L., Jr. "The Mortgage Market: A Basic Primer." *Real Estate Today,* August 1979. An excellent overview or summary of important considerations in the operation of the mortgage market. Easy to read and understand. Presents the material covered in this chapter in a slightly different way.

Savings and Loan Fact Book '79. Chicago: U.S. League of Savings Associations, 1979. Succinct and up-to-date presentation of facts and current trends in real estate finance. Coverage is comprehensive and not limited to S&Ls. Easy to read and understand. Updated each year. Copies may be obtained by writing the League at 111 E. Wacker Drive, Chicago, Ill. 60601.

Siegelaub, Harold, and Herbert A. Meistrich. "How the Professional Shopping Center Developer Obtains a Mortgage." *Real Estate Review,* Spring 1979, pp. 50–58. A step-by-step example of negotiation for a large mortgage loan from initial submission to final closing. Easy to follow. Many practical comments and insights concerning clauses included and documents required.

Time Value of Money in Real Estate

Seven percent has no rest, nor no religion; it
works nights, and Sundays, and even wet days.
Josh Billings, American humorist and lecturer

Financial management of real estate means using and administering realty to maximize self-interest, which is usually taken as maximizing wealth. Financial management of real estate generally involves decisions based on comparisons of cash flows through time. The key concerns of an investor are interest, or the price paid for borrowed money, and equity-rate-of-return or the rate of earnings on money invested. Thus, this chapter deals with the mathematics of compound interest and discounting, or **time value of money,** as applied in real estate to compare cash flows. This material may be new and difficult for some readers, but it must be addressed to maintain and complete the financial management framework for real estate decision making.

Money has time value for at least three reasons. Individuals prefer current consumption over future consumption and therefore must be compensated if they are to forego current consumption or expenditures. Second, individuals have alternative investment opportunities and, being rational, allocate money to the opportunities on the basis of comparative rates of return, the highest rates of return usually being preferred. Third, inflation causes people to demand a return on money held as cash to maintain purchasing power. In addition, interest rates are a reality in our economy providing a very pragmatic reason for their recognition; we cannot borrow money without paying interest.

This material is introductory in nature and covers only the basic ideas and applications of time value of money. A few essential formulas are taken up.

Any reader interested in greater depth is referred to books on financial management and capital budgeting or the mathematics of finance, some of which are listed at the end of this chapter. The problems discussed are difficult to work by hand; therefore the reader is encouraged to use a calculator to follow and verify the examples. Tables of time value of money (TVM) factors are given in the appendix. Calculators increasingly are designed and built to perform TVM calculations without need to refer to outside tables. Calculators produced by Hewlett-Packard and Texas Instruments are the largest sellers in this respect.

TVM topics are taken up in the following sequence in this chapter:

1. Future value or compounding
2. Present value or discounting
3. TVM factors
4. Interest calculations
5. Mortgage points—discounts and premiums
6. Investor equity value calculations
7. Selecting among alternative investments

FUTURE VALUE, OR COMPOUNDING

Understanding compound interest is essential to understanding the mathematics of finance. Compound means to mix or combine. **Compound interest** means to compute additional interest on both principal and accumulated, unpaid interest. That is, interest on a loan or an investment is added to or mixed with the principal, and consequently, interest is earned or paid on interest as well as on the principal.

Let us look at a few problems or examples to illustrate the concept. First, consider an individual paying or depositing $100 into a savings account to earn 5 percent interest, compounded annually. What amount or future value will the account contain at the end of one year? A simple equation showing the relationship solves the problem. Incidentally, **EOY** means end of year.

$$\text{Future value (EOY1)} = \text{amount of deposit (1 plus the interest rate)}$$
$$\text{F V (EOY1)} = \text{deposit } (1 + i)$$
$$\text{F V (EOY1)} = \$100 \, (1 + .05) = \$105$$

At the end of two years, the future value equals $110.25.

$$\text{Future value (EOY2)} = \text{amount of deposit } (1 + i)(1 + i)$$
$$\text{F V (EOY2)} = \text{deposit } (1 + i)^2$$
$$\text{F V (EOY2)} = \$100 \, (1 + .05)^2 = \$110.25$$

Thus, in the second year, interest at 5 percent is earned on the interest accumulated in the first year. That is, $5 is earned on the initial $100 deposit, and 25¢ is earned on the $5 interest earned in the first year.

At the end of three years, the value of the account is $115.76, calculated as follows:

$$\text{F V (EOY3)} = \text{deposit} \, (1 + i) \, (1 + i) \, (1 + i)$$
$$\text{F V (EOY3)} = \text{deposit} \, (1 + i)^3$$
$$\text{F V (EOY3)} = \$100 \, (1 + .05)^3 = \$115.76$$

And generalizing, the future value of a deposit at the end of *n* years may be calculated by the formula.

$$\text{F V (EOY}n) = \text{deposit} \, (1 + i)^n$$

where:

n equals the number of years and
i equals the interest rate.

The accumulation of interest for ten years at 10 percent is shown in figure 15–1. Interest being earned on interest shows up clearly in the interest-earned column. **BOY** means beginning of year in the figure.

FIGURE 15–1
Ten Years of Compound Interest at 10 Percent on an Initial Investment or Deposit of $1,000

Year	BOY Value	Interest Earned During Year at 10 Percent	Future or EOY Value
1	$1,000	$100	$1,100
2	1,100	110	1,210
3	1,210	121	1,331
4	1,331	133.10	1,464.10
5	1,464.10	146.41	1,610.51
6	1,610.51	161.05	1,771.56
7	1,771.56	177.16	1,948.72
8	1,948.72	194.87	2,143.59
9	2,143.59	214.36	2,357.95
10	2,357.95	235.79	2,593.74

The higher the interest rate, the faster the rate of increase in the deposit or investment. Also, the greater the number of periods, the greater the future value. Figure 15–2 shows the relative rates of compounding at interest rates of 5, 10, and 20 percent.

PRESENT VALUE, OR DISCOUNTING

We are now ready to take up present values, having discussed compounding, or future values. As mentioned earlier, time value of money calculations are a means of standardizing or comparing cash flows through time, with interest taken into account. TVM calculations

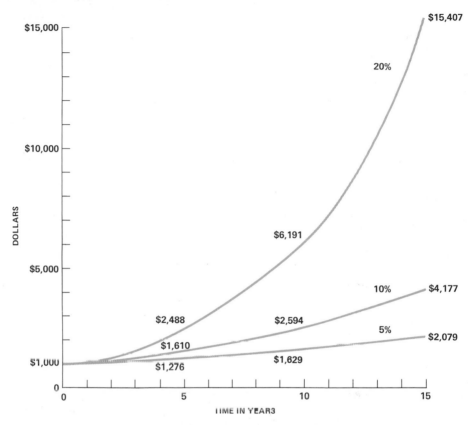

are necessary because a dollar in hand is worth more than a dollar received next year or at the end of the decade. Calculating the present values of future cash flows enables us to analyze and compare differences in time of receipt or payment of these cash flows. And this analysis and comparison is necessary for making optimum decisions between financial alternatives.

To illustrate present-value calculations, assume an investor expecting to receive $1,000 at the end of each of the next two years, wishing to sell the right. Other investors earn 10 percent per year on comparable investments. So, what is the value of our investor's position? What might other investors pay for the right to receive $1,000 at the end of each of the next two years? By comparing this to our earlier compounding example, we can ask, What amounts invested today at 10 percent would grow to $1,000 at the end of each of the next two years? In calculating the future value of an immediate deposit, we multiplied the initial deposit by $(1 + i)$, where i equaled the interest rate. Here, we have the future values and the interest rate. We must solve for the initial or present value; consequently, we must divide the future value by $1 + i$, a process called **discounting.** For our example, the payment to be received at the end of year 1 has a present value of $909.09.

$$\text{Present value (BOY1)} = \frac{\text{future payment (EOY1)}}{(1 + i)^1}$$

$$\text{PV (BOY1)} = \frac{\$1,000}{1.10} = \$909.09$$

In like fashion, the present value of the $1,000 to be received at the end of year 2 is $826.45.

$$\text{PV (BOY1)} = \frac{\text{future payment (EOY2)}}{(1 + i)^2}$$

$$\text{PV (BOY1)} = \frac{\$1,000}{(1.10)^2} = \frac{\$1,000}{(1.21)} = 826.45$$

Thus, the investor's position is worth $1,735.54 ($909.09 + 826.45).

The general formula for finding the present value of a future payment to be received at the end of year n, discounted at rate i, is

$$\text{Present value (BOY1)} = \frac{\text{future payment (EOY}n)}{(1 + i)^n}$$

The interest rate is usually called the **discount rate** in present-value calculations.

Application of the equation results in the present value getting smaller and smaller as the time of receipt extends further in the future. Figure 15–3 il-

FIGURE 15–3
Present, or Discounted-Value, Schedules of $1,000 at Interest Rates of 5, 10, and 20 Percent

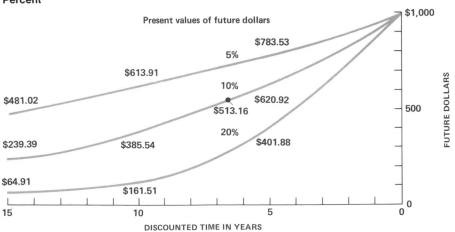

lustrates the decreasing value of the future payments at discount rates of 5, 10, and 20 percent. According to figure 15–3, for example, $1,000 discounted at 10 percent for seven years is worth only $513.16, or about half the amount of the payment.

TVM CALCULATIONS

Tables of precalculated factors or multipliers are available, so we do not need to calculate the appropriate $(1 + i)^n$ for common problems. Calculators are best used to solve problems involving atypical interest rates or terms. In calculating tables, $(1 + i)$ is defined as the *base* of each table. Thus for a 5 percent table, $(1 + .05)$ is the base. For a 10 percent table, $(1 + .10)$ is the base. Almost all TVM calculations in real estate involve only present-value factors; therefore only present-value factors are given in the appendix.

To illustrate the construction of a TVM table, let us develop a few factors using a discount rate of 10 percent. Let us calculate present-value factors for payments to be received at the end of one, two, and three years. The general equation is

$$PV = \frac{1}{(1 + i)^n}$$

one-year factor ($n = 1$):

$$PV = \frac{1}{(1.10)^1} = 0.090901$$

two-year factor ($n = 2$):

$$PV = \frac{1}{(1 + .10)^2} = \frac{1}{1.21} = 0.826446$$

three-year factor ($n = 3$):

$$PV = \frac{1}{(1 + .10)^3} = \frac{1}{1.331} = .751315$$

In TVM terminology, the present-value factors we have just calculated are present value of one (PV1) factors. The PV1 factor provides the means to calculate two other commonly used factors: the present value of one-per-period factor (PV1/P) and the principal recovery factor (PR). Let us take up each of these in order.

PV1 Factor

The PV1 factors we have just calculated are shown in the PV1 column of the 10 percent *annual* TVM table in the appendix, along with factors for other years. The **PV1 factor** converts a single payment to be received in the future into a present, lump-sum value. See figure 15–4.

FIGURE 15–4

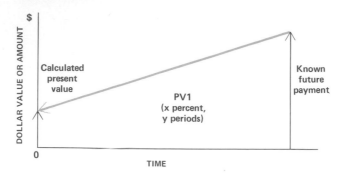

The PV1 may be used several times in solving a single problem. Suppose we expected to receive $10 one year from now, $20 two years from now, and $30 three years from now. What is the present value of this series of payments using a discount rate of 10 percent? The answer is $48.16, rounded.

Time	Payment Expected		PV1 Factor		Present Value
EOY1	$10	x	0.909091	=	$ 9.09091
EOY2	20	x	0.826446	=	16.52892
EOY3	30	x	0.751315	=	22.53945
			Total present value		$48.15928

PV1 / P Factor

Given a PV1 table, we may calculate the present value of any series of future cash flows in a similar manner. However, if the future cash flows are equal in size, the procedure may be simplified for faster calculation. Suppose that a series of $10 payments are to be received at the end of each of the next three years. What is the present value of the series at a 10 percent discount rate? Using the above procedure, the value of the series is $24.87, rounded.

Time	Payment Expected		PV1 Factor	Present Value
EOY1	$10	x	0.090901	$9.09091
EOY2	10	x	0.826446	8.26446
EOY3	10	x	0.751315	7.51315
	Total of factors and values		2.486852	$24.86852

Note however, the total of the PV1 factors equals 2.486852. And multiplying the equal payment, $10, times this 2.486852 also gives us $24.87. Thus,

318

totaling PV1 factors gives us a new, short-cut factor, which is termed the present value of one-per-period factor (PV1/P). The **PV1/P factor** is used as a multiplier to convert a series of equal or level payments, to be received in the future, into a single, lump-sum present value. See figure 15–5.

FIGURE 15–5

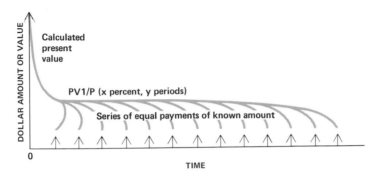

A further example seems in order. Suppose we wish to know the present value of a series of $20 payments to be received at the end of each of the next four years. The discount rate is 12 percent.

$$\text{Payment} \times \frac{\text{PV1/P factor}}{(12\%, 4 \text{ years})} = \text{present value}$$

$$\$20 \quad \times 3.037349 \quad = \$60.74698$$

The factor is obtained from the PV1/P column of the 12 percent, annual table in the appendix. The present value equals $60.75, rounded.

Present-value factors may be used in combination. One common use is in finding the value of a leased property. Suppose a vacant lot with a net lease paying $12,000 to a lessor at the end of each of the next eight years is to be sold. The reversion value (market value, EOY8) of the lot is $100,000. At a 12 percent discount rate, what is the value of the parcel, disregarding tax considerations? The cash flows look as follows:

$$\text{Payments x } \frac{\text{PV1/P factor}}{(12\%, 8 \text{ years})} = \text{present value of lease payments}$$

$$12{,}000 \quad \text{x} \quad 4.967639 \quad = \$59{,}612$$

$$\text{Reversion value x } \frac{\text{PV1 factor}}{(12\%, 8 \text{ years})} = \text{present value of reversion}$$

$$100{,}000 \quad \text{x} \quad .403883 \quad = \$40{,}388$$

Total indicated value of leased parcel equals $100,000 ($59.612 + $40,388). We look at this problem again later in the chapter.

PR Factor

In making a mortgage loan, the lender exchanges cash for the right to receive a series of cash flows from the borrower. Of course, the lender charges interest. Is there a definite relationship between the amount of the loan and the amount of the payments? Is there an easy way to calculate the necessary payments? The answer to both questions is yes.

A **principal recovery factor** (PR) acts in exactly the inverse way from the PV1/P factor. The PV1/P converts a series of equal cash flows into a present lump-sum value. The PR factor converts a present lump-sum amount (the loan) into a series of future cash flows (payments). In fact, the PR factor is 1 divided by the PV1/P factor. See figure 15–6.

FIGURE 15–6

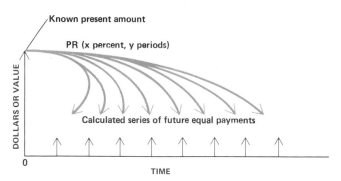

As an example, suppose a lender makes a $4,000 fixed-rate mortgage loan at 10 percent to be repaid by equal end-of-year payments over four years. How much is each payment?

$$\begin{array}{ccc} \text{Present value} & \text{PR} & \\ \text{or loan principal} \ ^{\text{x}} \ (10\%, 4 \text{ years}) & = \text{required payment} \end{array}$$

$$\$4,000 \quad \text{x} \quad 0.315471 \quad = \$1,261.88$$

The PR factor allows us to quickly calculate the size of each payment. Let us take a brief look at the amortization of the loan, so we can feel assured that the arithmetic works out. See figure 15–7.

FIGURE 15–7
Annual Amortization of a 10 Percent, 4-Year, $4,000
Loan on a Level or Fixed-Payment Plan

Principal balance, BOY1		$4,000.00
Year 1 debt service	$1,261.88	
Interest (10% x $4,000)	400.00	
Principal reduction	861.88	−861.88
Principal balance, EOY1, BOY2		3,138.12
Year 2 debt service	1,261.88	
Interest (10% x $3,138.12)	313.81	
Principal reduction	948.07	−948.07
Principal balance, EOY2, BOY3		2,190.05
Year 3 debt service	1,261.88	
Interest (10% x $2,190.05)	219.00	
Principal reduction	1,042.88	−1,042.88
Principal balance, EOY3, BOY4		1,147.17
Year 4 debt service	1,261.89	
Interest (10% x $1,147.17)	114.72	
	1,147.17	−1,147.17
Principal balance, EOY4		$ 000.00

Compounding / Discounting More Than Once a Year

The equations for compounding and discounting must be modified when compounding periods of less than a year are used. The conventional adjustments in the United States are as follows. The interest rate must be *divided* by the number of periods per year. And the number of years must be *multiplied* by the number of periods per year to get the total number of compounding periods. Thus, with monthly compounding, a 9 percent annual or nominal interest rate becomes a three quarters of 1 percent per month effective interest rate.

$$9\% / 12 \text{ months} = \text{¾}\% / \text{month}$$

And a 25-year loan becomes a 300-month loan with monthly compounding. Finally, annual payments become monthly payments, of 1/12th the size. Thus $2,400-per-year payments become $200-per-month payments.

Most mortgages call for monthly payments. Therefore, let us take one more quick illustration. Suppose a $500,000 loan for 25 years is obtained at 10 percent interest and monthly payments are called for. How much is monthly debt service?

We must refer to the 10 percent, *monthly,* TVM table in the appendix. The principal recovery factor for 25 years or 300 months is .009087. Monthly debt service equals $4,543.50 ($500,000 x .009087).

Rule of 72

A useful guide when one is frequently working with real estate values is the rule of 72. The **rule of 72** is: Divide 72 by the interest rate to get the number of years required to double a value by compounding. Thus, an investment at 12 percent may be expected to double in value in 6 years. An investment at 20 percent may be expected to double in value in slightly over 3½ years. The rule of 72 goes back to our earlier discussion of compounding. Study figure 15–2 to see if it holds true for other interest rates.

For an application, suppose an investor wants an 18 percent rate of return from any money invested. Ten acres of vacant land may be bought for $60,000. In what time period must the parcel's value increase to $120,000 for the rate of return to be earned? Four years; 72/18 = 4. If this rate of increase doesn't seem realistic, a lower price should be negotiated or the investment avoided.

Of course, the rule of 72 works in discounting also. That is, dividing 72 by the interest rate gives the time in which a future value should halve. Suppose our investor expects the above 10 acres to be worth only $100,000 in four years. At an 18 percent required rate of return, the acreage is then only worth $50,000 to our investor. Study figure 15–3 relative to the rule of 72 in discounting.

Elements of TVM Calculations

Present-value factors may be used in TVM calculations to solve a wide variety of problems in real estate financing, leasing, and equity investment, a process that is often called **present-value analysis** or **discounted cash flow analysis.** Several relatively simple applications are shown here. It is important for the reader to understand what each factor does and to have confidence that the arithmetic works out in any application. For this reason, in several examples, the arithmetic is worked out. Once convinced that the arithmetic works, the reader is encouraged to place emphasis on use of the factors as tools or aids, rather than on the arithmetic itself. Each problem needs to be studied and broken down into segments or components prior to applying TVM factors or techniques. TVM factors just express mathematical relationships. It is up to the reader to apply the tool properly.

In any TVM application, four elements are involved: (1) payment, (2) interest rate, (3) time, and (4) the lump-sum value. The equation simply expresses the relationship.

$$\text{Payment x } \frac{\text{factor}}{(x\%, \, y \text{ time})} = \text{value}$$

If any three of the elements are known, the fourth may be determined, though the process may be involved. It is this ability to determine unknown information, along with aiding judgment, that makes TVM analysis so useful in the financial management of real estate.

INTEREST CALCULATIONS

Interest is often a deductible item for income tax purposes. Also, interest must be deducted from any loan payment to determine the amount of principal reduction from any loan payment. Interest is usually due and charged at the end of each month or payment period. Mortgage debt-service payments are customarily made at the beginning of each month. The payment therefore includes interest due for the previous month plus the principal reduction amount for the current period. Interest payable at the end of each month is termed **interest in arrears.** Interest is sometimes payable at the beginning of a payment period and is termed **interest due** or **interest due in advance.**

Several ways of making calculations for interest in arrears are used, depending on the situation. Of course, the easiest way of determining the amount of an interest payment is to refer to a loan amortization table, an example of which is shown in Appendix A–4.

For individual periods, when the loan balance is known, interest may be calculated by taking the rate per period times the remaining principal. For example, let's take our 10 percent, monthly payment, 25-year loan of $500,000. Monthly debt service is $4,543.50 ($500,000 x .009087).

METHOD A		METHOD B	
Loan balance, BOM1	$500,000	Interest rate	10%
Times annual interest rate	10%	Divided by number of months	÷ 12
Equals interest/year	$ 50,000	Equals monthly interest rate	.8333%
Divided by number of months		Times loan balance	$500,000
in a year	÷ 12	Equals interest for month 1	$ 4,166.67
Equals interest for month 1	$ 4,166.67		

Period 1 (heading above table)

Monthly debt service of $4,543.50 less interest of $4,166.67 means $376.83 principal reduction at the end of period 1. Thus, at the beginning of period 1, the principal balance is $499,623.17 ($500,000 less $376.83).

Period 2

Loan balance, EOM1, BOM2	$499,612.17	Loan balance	$499,623.17
Times annual interest rate	x 10%	Times monthly interest rate	.83333%
Equals interest or annual basis	$ 49,962.23	Equals interest for	
Divided by number of months		month 2	$ 4,163.53
in a year	÷ 12		
Equals interest for month 2	$ 4,163.53		

Monthly calculation of interest has two major difficulties. It is tedious. And the exact beginning-of-month balance must be known, which is not a usual situation.

Interest payments are usually needed on an annual basis for income tax purposes. And the principal balance of a loan may be calculated with TVM factors at any point. A loan progress charge may therefore be developed to summarize the annual principal balance and the interest paid during the year. The methodology is shown here using our $500,000, 10 percent, 25-year, monthly payment loan.

We know debt service is $4,543.50 per month or $54,522 per year (12 x $4,543.50).

At the end of year 1, 24 years of debt service remain to be paid. The loan balance equals the present value of these payments, discounted at 10 percent, or $495,264.

$$\text{Monthly debt service x} \quad \underset{(10\%, \text{ monthly, 24 years})}{\text{PV1/P}} \quad = \underset{(\text{EOY1, BOY2})}{\text{principal balance}}$$

$$4,543.50 \text{ x} \qquad 109.005031 \qquad = \$495,264.36$$

At the end of year 2, with 23 years of debt service remaining, the loan balance calculates to $490,033.

$$\text{Monthly DS x} \quad \underset{(10\%, \text{ monthly, 23 years})}{\text{PV1/P}} \quad = \underset{(\text{EOY2, BOY3})}{\text{principal balance}}$$

$$\$4,543.50 \text{ x} \qquad 107.853716 \qquad = \$490,033.36$$

Given the initial loan balances and the loan balances at the end of years 1 and 2, taking the differences gives the amount of principal reduction or loan amortization in each year.

$$\$500,000 - \$495,264.36 = \$4,735.64 = \text{principal reduction.}$$

And deducting principal reduction from total debt service for each of the two years gives us the amount of interest paid in each year.

$$\$54,522 - \$4,735.64 = \$49,786.36 = \text{interest paid.}$$

The process for the first two years is summarized in figure 15–8.

FIGURE 15–8
Principal Reduction and Interest Paid for First Two Years of a $500,000, 25-Year 10 Percent Monthly Pay Loan

Time	Principal Balance	Principal Reduction During Year	Interest Paid During Year
BOY1	$500,000.00	—	—
EOY1	495,264.36	$4,735.64	$49,786.36
EOY2	490,033.36	5,231.00	49,291.00

Figure 15–9 summarizes the amortization progress for the first 11 years of the loan. We use these balances later in case problems.

FIGURE 15–9
Eleven-Year Amortization Summary for a $500,000 10 Percent, 25-Year, Monthly Pay Loan (Annual Debt Service Equals $54,522)

Time	Principal Balance	Principal Reduction During Year	Interest Paid During Year
BOY1	$500,000	$ 4,735.64	$49,786.36
EOY1	495,264	5,231.00	49,291.00
EOY2	490,033	5,778.00	48,744.00
EOY3	484,255	6,384.00	48,138.00
EOY4	477,871	7,052.00	47,470.00
EOY5	470,819	7,791.00	46,731.00
EOY6	463,028	8,607.00	45,915.00
EOY7	454,421	9,507.00	45,015.00
EOY8	444,914	10,504.00	44,018.00
EOY9	434,410	11,603.00	42,919.00
EOY10	422,807	12,818.00	41,704.00
EOY11	409,989		

MORTGAGE POINTS— DISCOUNTS AND PREMIUMS

At times we are told to "discount" a statement or rumor made by a commonly known gossip or liar; that is, to take the statement at less than face value. Merchants run sales at discounted prices, meaning reductions from regular or list prices. *Discounting* therefore means to buy or sell, or offer to buy or sell, at a price less than face value. A *premium* is the opposite of a discount; a premium means to buy or sell, or offer to buy or sell, at a price above face value.

A **loan discount** is an amount off of or a reduction from the unamortized balance or face amount, as of a mortgage loan. A **loan premium** is an amount in addition to the unamortized balance. A discount or premium is calculated on the basis of the loan balance at the time the loan is originated, a sale is made, or an offer to buy or sell is made.

Mortgage discount and premiums are expressed in terms of dollars and of percentages or points. For example, a $10,000 loan that sells for $9,000 carries a dollar discount of $1,000 ($10,000 less $9,000). A sale price of $12,000 would mean a dollar premium of $2,000 ($12,000 less $10,000). A dollar discount of $1,000 on a $10,000 loan is a 10 percent discount, or a discount of 10 points.

$$\frac{\text{Dollar discount}}{\substack{\text{face value} \\ \text{(unamortized} \\ \text{balance)}}} = \frac{\$1,000}{\$10,000} = 10 \text{ points (or a 10\% discount)}$$

A dollar premium of $2,000 on the same loan is equal to a 20-point premium.

Mortgage discounts and premiums come about because the market interest rate differs from the contract or face interest rate on the loan. The **market interest rate** is the rate currently being charged by lenders. The **contract interest rate** is the rate agreed to in a specific note or loan. A person or institution in this situation has the option of making new loans at market interest rates or buying existing loans at prices that give an interest yield equal to that offered by the market. The following rules always apply. When the market interest rate is higher than the face or contract interest rate, the market value of loans is always less than the unamortized loan balances or face values, and loans sell at a discount. When the market interest rate is lower than contract rates, loans sell at premiums because the market value exceeds the face value.

Long-term mortgages are historically prepaid in from 8 to 12 years on the average. Prepayment comes about because a borrower (1) inherits money or otherwise suddenly becomes wealthy; (2) refinances; (3) sells to a buyer who obtains new financing; or (4) defaults and the loan is foreclosed. The 1966 FHA Annual Statistical Summary shows the average life of loans as follows:

Original Term	Average Life
18 through 22 years	9.5 years
23 through 25 years	11.8 years
26 through 30 years	14.1 years (estimated)
All loans	10.35 years

The life of a loan tends to increase when interest rates go up and to decrease when rates go down. Refinancing and sales occur much less frequently when interest rates are high or going up.

Suppose the Urbandale Savings and Loan Association made a $500,000, 10 percent, monthly payment loan for 25 years a year ago. Now the association needs money and decides to sell the loan. The market interest rate, in the meantime, has increased to 11 percent. At what price is the loan likely to sell, assuming prepayment at the end of the eleventh year of the loan, or 10 years from the time of sale? The unpaid principal at the end of year one is $495,264; see figure 15–9.

We know monthly debt service is $4,543.50 from previous calculations. We also know that at the end of year 11, the principal balance could be $409,989. See figure 15–6. Thus a buyer would be looking at cash flows of $4,543.50 per month for 10 years and a single lump-sum payment of $409,989 at the end of the tenth year, as shown in figure 15–10.

The present value of the $4,543.50 for 10 years discounted at 11 percent equals $329,837.

$$\text{Mo. debt service} \times \genfrac{}{}{0pt}{}{\text{PV1/P factor}}{\text{(10 years, monthly, 11\%)}} = \text{present value}$$

$$\$4,543.50 \times 72.595270 = \$329,837$$

FIGURE 15–10

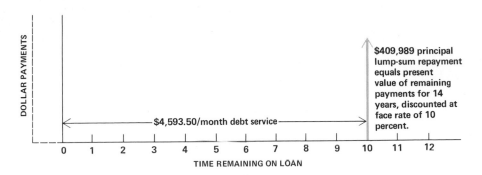

The present value of the $409,989 discounted at 11 percent equals $137,159.

$$\text{Single payment} \times \frac{\text{PV1 factor}}{(10 \text{ years, monthly, } 11\%)} = \text{present value}$$

$$\$409,989 \times .334543 = \$137,159$$

And the total discounted value of all payments equals $466,996 ($329,837 + $137,159). That is, the value of the 10 percent loan in an 11 percent market is $466,996, or about $467,000.

The dollar discount on the loan therefore amounts to $28,268 ($495,264 − 466,996). The percent discount off the face value equals 5.71%.

$$\frac{28,268}{495,264} = \frac{\text{dollar discount}}{\text{face value}} = 5.71\% = \text{percent discount}$$

Loan Premium

As an alternative, suppose the market interest rate dropped to slightly below 10 percent and $505,170 were offered for the loan. What is the premium for the loan?

The dollar premium amounts to $505,170 − $495,264, or $9,906, which converts to a 2 percent premium.

$$\frac{\text{Dollar premium}}{\text{Face amount}} = \frac{\$9,906}{\$495,264} = 2.0\% = \text{percent premium}$$

INVESTOR EQUITY ANALYSIS

An investor, in self-interest, seeks to maximize return on any venture while keeping risk under control. One major way to increase return is to use leverage. *Leverage,* again, when positive, is borrowing money at a rate of interest lower than the rate of return earned by the property or investment. Considerable analysis of financing alternatives is necessary to select that one offering the most advantageous leverage. TVM techniques are central to this analysis. Let us look at an investment situation offering an opportunity to exercise leverage.

Earlier in this chapter we valued a vacant lot renting for $12,000 per year net for 8 years and a reversion value of $100,000 at EOY 8. At $100,000, the investor expected to earn 12 percent on money ventured. Suppose, at this point, the investor contacts several lenders and negotiates an 8-year straight term mortgage loan of $80,000, calling for 10 percent interest, payable at the end of each year. Is the investor's rate of return on equity improved? Note that now the investor's equity in the lot is only $20,000.

The property earns $12,000 per year in rents, $8,000 of which must be paid for loan interest. At the end of 8 years, the loan may be repaid out of the $100,000 proceeds from sale of the vacant lot. We'll call this property investment alternative A. The cash flows look as follows. We may disregard the interest payments on the loan and the repayment of the loan in our analysis as we are only interested in the equity rate of return, which must be higher than 12 percent in that the leverage is positive. Also, note that the straight term mortgage is used to simplify the discussion; that is, the same principle of leverage applies with amortizing mortgages but the arithmetic is much more complicated. See figure 15–11.

FIGURE 15–11

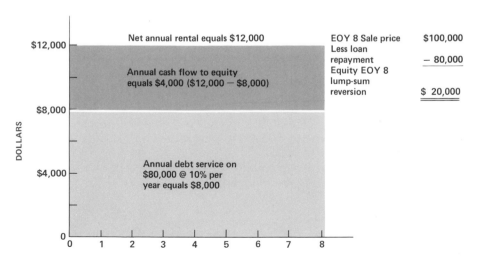

Let us discount the cash flows from alternative A at 15, 20, and 25 percent. See figure 15–12.

FIGURE 15–12
Present Value of Cash Flows from Alternative A, Discounted at 15, 20, and 25 Percent

	15%	20%	25%
Annual cash flow to equity	$ 4,000	$ 4,000	$ 4,000
PV1/P factor (8 years, annual)	4.487321	3.837159	3.328911
PV of annual CF to equity	$17,949	$15,349	$13,316
Equity reversion (EOY8)	$20,000	$20,000	$20,000
PV1 factor (8 years, annual)	.326902	.232568	.167772
PV of equity reversion	$ 6,538	$ 4,651	$ 3,355
Indicated value of equity	$24,487	$20,000	$16,671

The cash flows to equity have a present value of $20,000 when discounted at 20 percent. This means the investor increased the annual rate of return on equity investment from 12 percent to 20 percent by leveraging, a substantial improvement. Of course, the investor's risk has increased also by the use of the $80,000 debt financing.

Our concern here is with leverage and maximizing rate of return to equity. Not all financing alternatives need be analyzed in detail in seeking the one offering greatest advantage. The following rules or guidelines apply to the positive use of leverage. Knowledge and application of these guidelines can help the investor avoid unnecessary calculations and therefore proceed more quickly and efficiently to the "best solution" for his or her financing problem.

1. Debt service is a function of interest rate and loan life, varying directly with the interest rate and inversely with loan life. Thus, a higher interest rate may be offset with a longer loan term if a property's earnings effectively serve as an upper limit on debt service.

2. The higher the loan-to-value ratio, the greater the leverage, other things equal. Faster amortization on a high LVR loan will reduce this advantage. The lower the debt service, the longer the high leverage is likely to be maintained, other things equal.

3. The greater the use of positive leverage, the higher the likely rate of return to the equity position.

4. The greater the use of leverage, the greater the number of properties that can be controlled with a given amount of money. And the more properties controlled, the greater the spreading of risks.

5. Limited liability should be established for each property, or group of properties, to avoid having risks and losses of problem properties offsetting gains on profitable properties.

6. Alternative financing methods that carry undue risks, or are otherwise unacceptable to the investor, should be dropped from consideration before detailed financial calculations and analyses are performed. For example, if a land-sale contract is unacceptable to an investor for some reason, it should be dropped from consideration immediately.

By application of these guidelines, several alternatives may be dropped from the analysis because they are unacceptable or because they obviously provide less advantage to the investor. For example, detailed analysis of a 20-year, 8 percent loan on an 80 percent LVR ratio need not be made if a 90 percent, 25-year, 8 percent loan is available. The assumption is that these loans would be available from different lenders. Obviously the investor must shop lenders to generate alternatives for comparison and analysis.

SELECTING AMONG ALTERNATIVE INVESTMENTS

An investor, to maximize wealth, seeks to maximize rate of return on investments, after adjustments for risk or assuming risk held constant. In addition, most investors have limited money or capital to invest. Limited capital means the investor must ration the capital to those investments promising the highest rates of return.

Capital-budgeting theory is well developed insofar as capital rationing is concerned. **Capital budgeting** means making decisions about long-term investments, ordinarily meaning for more than one year. **Capital rationing** is allocating or budgeting financial resources to the alternative projects or investments, when more acceptable alternatives are available than the investor has funds to finance—in other words, given limited capital and a set of alternative investments, deciding which investment or group of investments should be selected. The alternative investments are generally considered to be independent of one another; that is, acceptance of one alternative does not depend on, or imply the acceptance of another.

Three methods for evaluating alternative investment opportunities are generally recognized in finance and real estate: (1) payback period, (2) internal rate of return, and (3) net present value. These methods culminate in indices, rates of return, and relative values by which competing investment alternatives may be ranked and compared. Let us look at the calculation, and the merits and limitations, of each.

We'll use our earlier example of an initial cash investment of $20,000 in a lot purchased for $100,000, with the aid of an $80,000 straight term loan at 10 percent for 8 years. The property rents for $12,000 per year net. Interest on the loan is $8,000, leaving $4,000 per year cash flow to equity. At the end of year 8, the property is presumably sold for $100,000, the mortgage is repaid, and an equity reversion of $20,000 realized. Therefore the cash flows are as follows:

BOY1	−$20,000
EOY 1	4,000
EOY 2	4,000
EOY 3	4,000
EOY 4	4,000
EOY 5	4,000
EOY 6	4,000
EOY 7	4,000
EOY 8	24,000 ($4,000 CF to equity plus $20,000 equity reversion)

Payback Period

Financial managers sometimes use the payback-period method to rank investments. The **payback-period** method concerns the number of years required to recover the initial cash investment. Payback period may be calculated by dividing the initial investment by the expected cash flow per year, when the cash flows are level. In our example, the payback period is 5 years. With uneven flows, the payback period is the number of years required for cash receipts to accumulate to an amount equal to the initial cash investment.

$$\frac{\text{Initial cash investment}}{\text{Annual cash flow}} = \frac{\text{payback period}}{\text{(in years)}}$$

$$\frac{\$20,000}{\$4,000} = 5 \text{ years}$$

The payback-period method is the rough equivalent of the real estate investor's rate of return method. Effectively, the **investor's rate of return** is 100 percent divided by the payback period; or average annual cash flow divided by the initial cash investment. In our example, the investor's rate of return is 20 percent.

$$\frac{\text{Average annual cash flow to equity}}{\text{Initial cash investment}} \times 100 = \frac{\text{investor's rate}}{\text{of return}}$$

$$\frac{\$4,000}{\$20,000} \times 100 = 20\%$$

Presumably if the payback period is less than an acceptable maximum, say 5 years, a project is accepted. Alternatively, if the investor's rate of return exceeds some minimum, say 20 percent, the project is also accepted.

Either method is easily and quickly applied, and either method may serve as a "quick and dirty" screen. Alternatively, the methods give little attention to timing of cash flows and completely ignore post-payment cash flows. In short, the methods are not as suitable as internal rate of return or net present value in pursuing the objective of maximizing wealth. Further, the investor's rate of return is not suitable in a period of rapid inflation as a ranking technique for real estate projects. Sometimes the annual cash flow to equity of property may be negative in the early years, with profits to be realized from rapid value appreciation.

331

Internal Rate of Return

Internal rate of return (IRR) is that rate of interest or discount that equates the present value of cash outflows to the present value of cash inflows or receipts. As shown earlier in this chapter, the IRR for our example is 20 percent. Fifteen percent, being too low a rate, gives a discounted value of $24,487 to the cash flows, which greatly exceeds the initial equity investment of $20,000, and 25 percent being too high a rate, gives too low a present value to the cash flows.

Discount Rate	Present Value of Cash Flows
15%	$24,487
20	20,000
25	16,671

The usual acceptance criterion for the internal-rate-of-return method of selecting an investment is that the IRR exceed some minimum or required rate of return. If several investment alternatives are being considered, those with the highest internal rates are usually selected first in a capital-rationing situation.

However, the internal-rate-of-return method has two major limitations. First, there may be multiple internal rates of return that equate the same series of future cash flows to the initial investment; in fact, it is conceivable that a negative rate of return might equate the cash flows. Second, use of the IRR method implies that funds recovered from the present investment will be reinvested at the internal rate of return. This reinvestment rate may not be realistic or valid. Also, a high reinvestment rate means that cash flows must be received early to offset the large initial cash investment.

Net Present Value

The net-present-value (NPV) method of evaluating investments means discounting all cash flows at a required rate of return, with acceptance of an alternative depending on the present value of the cash flows exceeding zero. The required rate of return is, at a minimum, the cost of capital, that is, the rate of return equity investors may reasonably expect to earn from other investment alternatives. Thus, if the net present value of an investment exceeds the initial cash investment, the investor's wealth is increased. Or, stated in other terms, the rate of return to be realized exceeds the rate of return the investor might otherwise expect to realize.

The NPV acceptance criterion is that the present value of the cash flows exceed the initial cash investment, or that the present value of all cash flows exceed zero. For example, suppose the required rate of return for our alternative A is 15 percent. At 15 percent, the discounted value of the future cash flows equals $24,487, which exceeds the initial equity investment of $20,000. That is, the net present value of all cash flows equals $4,487. Thus, our investment would be accepted in that it increases the investor's wealth above what it would

332

otherwise be. And wealth maximization is the usual goal in the financial management of real estate.

With several investment alternatives, a profitability index may be used with the NPV method to rank the alternatives. A **profitability index** equals the present value of future cash flows divided by the initial cash investment. In example A, the profitability index equals 1.22.

$$\text{Profitability index} = \frac{\text{present value of future cash flows}}{\text{initial cash investment}}$$

$$= \frac{\$24{,}487}{\$20{,}000} = 1.22$$

As long as the profitability index equals or exceeds 1.00, an investment proposal is acceptable. But, for purposes of rationing limited capital, it is generally considered that the higher the profitability index, the higher the rate of return, and the better the investment.

For accept-reject alternatives, the net-present-value-method always provides theoretically correct choices or decisions for wealth maximization regarding alternative investments. NPV is easily calculated. In addition, the NPV method implies reinvestment of recovered capital at the required rate of return. The main limitation of the NPV method is that it is not easily understood.

IRR versus NPV versus Payback Period

The net-present-value and internal-rate-of-return methods generally lead to the same accept-reject decision for investments. The payback method is much less reliable. But, let us look at a more involved and therefore a less clear-cut situation. Consider two alternative investments with projected cash flows as follows:

Time	Alternative A	Alternative B
BOY 1	−20,000	−20,000
EOY 1	4,000	1,000
EOY 2	4,000	1,000
EOY 3	4,000	− 2,000
EOY 4	4,000	6,000
EOY 5	4,000	8,000
EOY 6	4,000	10,000
EOY 7	4,000	10,000
EOY 8	24,000	30,000

In each case, the initial cash investment is $20,000, which is a cash outflow. Project A is the example at which we have been looking. We have calculated that project A has a payback period of 5 years, an IRR of 20 percent, a net present value of $4,487, and a profitability index of 1.22.

To make a comparison, we must first calculate the present value of the cash flows in alternative B at 15 percent, our required rate of return, and at 20 percent. The calculations are shown in figure 15–13.

FIGURE 15–13
Present Value of Cash Flows from Alternative B, Discounted at 15 and 20 Percent

Time EOY	B Future Cash Flows	15% PV1 Factor	15% PV	20% PV1 Factor	20% PV
1	$ 1,000	0.8696	$ 870	0.8333	$ 833
2	1,000	0.7561	756	0.6944	694
3	−2,000	0.6575	−1,315	0.5787	−1,157
4	6,000	0.5718	3,431	0.4823	2,894
5	8,000	0.4972	3,977	0.4019	3,215
6	10,000	0.4323	4,323	0.3349	3,349
7	10,000	0.3759	3,759	0.2791	2,791
8	30,000	0.3269	9,807	0.2326	6,977
TOTAL	—	—	$25,608	—	$19,596

Based on these calculations, the NPV of project B's cash flows is $5,608 ($25,608 − $20,000). The profitability index is 1.28 ($25,608/20,000 = 1.28). The internal rate of return is slightly below 20 percent in that the discounted value of the cash flows at 20 percent is slightly below $20,000. The actual internal rate of return is 19.6 percent, and the payback period is 5.6 years. On a comparative basis, the projects look as follows:

	A	B
Payback Period	5 years	5.6 years
IRR	20%	19.6%
NPV @ 15%	$4,487	$5,608
Profitability Index	1.22	1.28

Project A would be selected by both the payback-period method and the IRR method. On the other hand, project B would be selected by the NPV method. Financial theory says NPV is the preferred method, and project B should be selected. Is there any way to clearly show that project B should be selected. Yes, based on our criterion of wealth maximization, there is.

Let us calculate the EOY8 compounded values of all cash flows, including the initial cash investment, at 15 percent, the required rate of return, and at the respective internal rate of return, 20 and 19.6 percent. See figures 15–14 and 15–15.

FIGURE 15–14
Future or Compounded Values, EOY8, Alternative A

Time	Cash Flows	RRR(15%)	IRR(20%)
BOY1(8)	$—20,000	$—61,180	$—85,996
EOY1(7)	4,000	10,640	14,333
EOY2(6)	4,000	9,252	11,944
EOY3(5)	4,000	8,045	9,953
EOY4(4)	4,000	6,996	8,294
EOY5(3)	4,000	6,083	6,912
EOY6(2)	4,000	5,290	5,760
EOY7(1)	4,000	4,600	4,800
EOY8(0)	24,000	24,000	24,000
TOTAL (FV)		$13,726	–0–

FIGURE 15–15
Future or Compounded Values, EOY8, Alternative B

Time	Cash Flows	RRR(15%)	IRR(19.6%)
BOY1(8)	$—20,000	$—61,180	$—83,730
EOY1(7)	1,000	2,660	3,500
EOY2(6)	1,000	2,313	2,927
EOY3(5)	—2,000	—4,023	—4,894
EOY4(4)	6,000	10,494	12,277
EOY5(3)	8,000	12,167	13,686
EOY6(2)	10,000	13,225	14,304
EOY7(1)	10,000	11,500	11,960
EOY8(0)	30,000	30,000	30,000
TOTAL (FV)		$ 17,156	–0–

Summarizing the results from figures 15–14 and 15–15, the EOY8 values of the cash flows from the two alternative projects are as follows:

	PROJECT	
Method	A	B
Internal rate of return	–0–	–0–
NPV @ 15%	$13,726	$17,156

And, discounted at the respective rates, the present values (BOY1) of the above amounts are as follows:

Method	A	B
Internal rate of return	–0–	–0–
NPV @ 15%	$4,487	$5,608

The BOY1 present values of $4,487 for A and $5,608 for B coincide exactly with our earlier accept-reject criterion. That is, accepting project B would increase the investor's wealth by $1,121 more than accepting project A, ($5,608 − $4,487 = $1,121). Thus, the NPV method indicated the proper project for selection. The IRR method requires further analysis to provide the correct answer.

The higher IRR of A applies to the initial cash investment, a capital outflow, as well as to later cash inflows, in calculating future values, or wealth maximization. This higher rate means later receipts count for less. Also, the IRR method may have multiple rates of return for some alternatives, casting uncertainty over the method. Further, the assumption of reinvestment of cash flows at the higher IRRs is more speculative than an assumption of reinvestment at a lower 15 percent required rate of return. Finally, IRR varies from project to project, while the required rate of return is the same from project to project. Therefore the required rate of return serves as a single standard for all alternatives.

One other item regarding real estate investing deserves mention. Alternative real estate investments are often separated by time. That is, an investor or developer may look at only one project at a time. Real estate has high value, and sales or developments occur only infrequently. Also, costs of collecting and processing information are quite high. Thus, when an alternative satisfies the investor's required rate of return by having a positive net present value, it is, and ordinarily should be, made. Thus, net present value makes for an easy prompt decision. If several alternatives are posed at one time, the profitability index may then be used as a second ranking and selection technique.

SUMMARY

Financial management of real estate is administering realty to maximize self-interest, which usually means maximizing wealth. TVM calculations provide a means of comparing cash flows through time to achieve this end. Time value of money involves both compounding and discounting. Compounding means computing interest on principal and on accumulated, unpaid interest to get a future value. Discounting is deducting interest in advance, as in converting a future value into a present value. Discounting is the opposite of compounding. Tables of precalculated factors are commonly available for making TVM calculations; also electronic calculators increasingly have TVM equations built in.

TVM factors frequently used in real estate are the present value of one (PV1), the present value of one per period (PV1/P), and the principal recovery factor (PR). TVM calculations may be used to determine the amount of interest paid in a year, the discount or premium on a mortgage note because the market interest rate differs from the face rate, and the rate of return earned on an investment.

Three methods of ranking alternative investment opportunities for acceptance are generally recognized: (1) payback period, (2) internal rate of return (IRR) and (3) net present value (NPV). Payback period is the time required to recover the original investment. IRR is the rate of discount that equates the present value of future cash flows to the original investment. NPV is that amount by which the present value of future cash flows, discounted at a required rate of return, exceeds the original investment. The NPV method is theoretically most correct and preferred. Ranking alternatives by a profitability index may be used to supplement the NPV method. The index is computed by dividing the present values of future cash flows by the original cash investment.

KEY TERMS

BOY	Investor's rate of return
Capital budgeting	Loan discount
Capital rationing	Loan premium
Compound interest	Market interest rate
Contract interest rate	Net present value (NPV)
Discounting	Payback period
Discount rate	Present-value analysis
Discounted cash flow (DCF)	Profitability index
EOY	PV1 factor (present value of one)
Financial management of real estate	PV1/P factor (present value of one per period)
Interest due (in advance)	Principal recovery factor
Interest in arrears	Rule of 72
Internal rate of return (IRR)	Time value of money (TVM)

QUESTIONS FOR REVIEW AND DISCUSSION

1. What is compound interest? What is the importance of compound interest?
2. Explain the relation of compounding to discounting.
3. Explain the interrelation between the principal recovery factor and the present value of one-per-period factor.

4. What is the rule of 72?

5. How may the amount of interest paid on a monthly payment loan be determined for any one year?

6. Distinguish between buying a loan at a 5-point discount and a discount rate of 5 percent.

7. What is the internal rate of return? Net present value? Payback period? Explain the use of each in selecting among alternative investments.

8. At an annual growth rate of 8 percent, how long would it take a lot worth $10,000 to double in value?

9. Calculate the present value of $6,000, to be received at the end of 5 years, assuming discount rates of 5, 10, and 20 percent. Which discount rate gives the highest value?

10. Calculate the present values of the following, using a discount rate of 10 percent:
    a. $1,200 to be received at the end of each of 5 years.
    b. $100 to be received at the end of each of 60 months.
    Which value is greater? In that $1,200 per year is received in each case, why?

11. Three income streams are to be received as follows. Calculate the present value and the profitability index of each using a discount rate of 12 percent and assuming an initial investment of $450.

	A	B	C
EOY1	$100	$200	$300
EOY2	200	200	200
EOY3	300	200	100

12. Calculate the payback period and internal rate of return for the income streams in question 11, assuming an original investment of $450.

13. Rank the income streams (investment alternatives) in question 11 by payback period, internal rate of return, net present value, and profitability index. Are the selection methods consistent in indicating the relative desirabilities of the alternatives?

REFERENCES

Clettenberg, Karel J., and Charles O. Kroncke. "How to Calculate Real Estate Return on Investment." *Real Estate Review,* winter 1973. A succinct, easily read and understood comparison of payback period, internal rate of return, and net present value as applied in comparing real estate investment alternatives. A specific investment proposal is used to illustrate the techniques.

Messner, Stephen D., and M. Chapman Findlay, II. "Real Estate Investment Analysis: IRR Versus FMRR." *The Real Estate Appraiser,* July–August 1975. A technical treatment of the problem of selecting among mutually exclusive investment alternatives with a limited budget.

Pyhrr, Stephen A. "Chapter 28: Mathematics of Real Estate Finance." In *Financing Income Producing Real Estate* by James A. Britten, Jr. and Lewis O. Kerwood. New York: McGraw-Hill, 1977. An alternative development of time value of money applications in real estate. Covers much material presented in this chapter. Generally easy to read and understand. Very worthwhile reading for a newcomer to time value of money and real estate.

Real Estate Appraiser and Analyst, November–December 1978. Contains seven excellent articles written around the theme, real estate values and money markets. Articles were prepared for the eleventh annual manuscript competition sponsored by the Society of Real Estate Appraisers. They all extend the line of thought developed in this chapter. Authors are Mike Miles and Michael Rice, Stanley F. Miller, Jr., George W. Gau and Daniel B. Kohlhepp, C. F. Sirmans and James R. Webb, Walter H. Chudleigh, III and Lawrence E. Brown, Larry E. Wofford and Edward A. Moses, and Stephen E. Roulac.

Schall, Lawrence D., and Charles W. Haley. *Introduction to Financial Management.* New York: McGraw-Hill, 1977. A basic text in financial management with a technical orientation. Chapter 4, "The Time Value of Money," and chapter 7, "Fundamentals of Capital Budgeting," provide additional depth to material covered in this chapter.

Van Horne, James C. *Fundamentals of Financial Management.* 3rd ed. Englewood Cliffs, N.J.: Prentice-Hall, 1977. A well-written, easy to understand text on financial management. Chapter 12, "Mathematics of Finance," and chapter 13, "Capital Budgeting," provide additional depth to material covered in this chapter.

Weston, J. Fred, and Eugene F. Brigham. *Essentials of Managerial Finance.* 5th ed. Hinsdale, Ill.: Dryden Press, 1978. A basic text in managerial finance. Chapter 11, "The Interest Factor in Financial Decisions," and chapter 12, "Capital Budgeting Techniques," provide additional depth to material covered in this chapter.

FOUR

REAL ESTATE MARKETS AND THE INVESTMENT CLIMATE

Long-Run Trends Affecting the Climate for Real Estate Investment

You won't have any trouble in your country
as long as you have few people and much land,
but when you have many people and little land, your
trials will begin.
Thomas Carlyle, 1851

16

Each parcel of real estate is fixed in location. This fixity means demand must come to the parcel. Fixity also means that the environment around each parcel greatly influences its use and value. It is in an investor's self-interest to be aware of and to understand the many considerations or forces affecting real estate, its use, and its value. The main purpose of this chapter is to delineate and discuss these many forces that make up the setting in which real estate is developed and used, that make the setting of local real estate markets, and that make up the real estate investment climate. The relative importance of the many forces affecting real estate is not easily determined; yet knowing about them and their trends should definitely give an investor a better basis for making decisions. Specific sections of this chapter are therefore as follows:

1. Three categories of forces
2. Physical and biological forces
3. Economic forces
4. Institutional forces

THREE CATEGORIES OF FORCES

A **force** is an influence for change. It involves a certain magnitude of energy, or power, and direction. Gravity is a physical force pulling us toward the center of the earth, for example. Because forces involve both magnitude and direction, they may complement or offset each other. When forces complement each other, they increase the influence or energy for change in a certain direction. When forces offset each other, a situation of stability, or no change, may result.

Forces causing change in the use and value of real estate are traditionally classified as (1) physical and biological, (2) economic, and (3) institutional. This classification is convenient for purposes of discussion and analysis. In everyday life, however, considerable interaction takes place between and among these forces, whereby they sometimes complement each other and sometimes offset each other. The net result of all these forces determines the direction and extent of change. These forces are summarized in figure 16–1.

The category of **physical and biological forces** includes the natural environment in which we live, the nature and characteristics of the various resources with which we work, and living organisms, including humankind. Land provides the physical support, the site, for the activities of humans and animals. The earth, land, and water, provide the raw materials (minerals, fuels, soil, climate, and so on) for humankind's activities. The earth is therefore the physical setting or stage. Living organisms (humans, animals, plants, bacteria) are the players that interact on this stage. The knowledge and activities of these players, particularly humans, greatly affect the supply of, and demand for, raw materials and urban real estate.

The category of **economic forces** includes the market and pricing system that allocates resources to various uses. Price usually means dollars, or some other monetary unit, paid or bid for something, such as the price of a house. But price also has a broader meaning, namely opportunity cost. **Opportunity cost** is the value of what is given up in making a choice, as in trading a one-family house for a condominium.

Rational people seek to maximize benefits and minimize costs in making choices. It follows that opportunity costs are also minimized by rational decision makers. Consider then, that raw materials, goods, and services, can be used in only one way at any one time. For example, lumber to build a house cannot also serve as kindling wood. A person cannot simultaneously be a medical doctor, an airline pilot, and a professional clown. Likewise, raw materials of a country may be left in the ground, used to produce tractors and cars, or used to produce tanks for war. Thus even in a warlike nation, which decrees production of tanks, or in a primitive country, which leaves resources in the earth, costs or foregone opportunities are incurred. Thus economics or a pricing system operates explicitly or implicitly.

Living in a country with an open-market economy, we in the United States are rich in such terms as profit, loss, cost, rate of return, and value, that indicate how well we are doing in maximizing benefits and minimizing costs. Much of our thinking and decision analysis takes place in an economic framework.

Our third category of forces is the institutional. **Institutional forces** in-

FIGURE 16-1
Factors and Forces Influencing the Development and Use of Realty

Category of Influence	LEVEL OF INFLUENCE		
	National and International	Regional	Local
Physical and biological	Population	Population (natural increase and migration)	Population (natural increase and migration) Age-sex distribution
	Natural resources (minerals, soils, climate, water, topography)	Resource distribution	Specific natural resources (soils, minerals, terrain)
	World locations for trade and commerce	Location relative to raw materials and markets	Location relative to raw materials and markets. Manmade structures/constraints
Economic	Gross national product		
	Personal income		Personal income
	Employment and unemployment		Employment and unemployment
	Price levels (CPI)		Price levels (CPI)
	Money and credit (financial systems)		
Institutional Political	Federal powers and legislation	State powers and legislation	Local governmental powers and legislation
Religious Tradition, custom, and beliefs	Work ethnic Attitude toward education		Attitude toward education Attitude toward architecture Chance

clude our culture, beliefs, religion, educational system, organizations, technology, and politics. Tradition, laws, governmental systems, and habitual ways of thinking are also included. In effect, institutional forces reflect the collective conditioning and ways of acting of people in a society. Thus our use of land in the United States, with our emphasis on manufacturing and trade, on wide use of the automobile, and on living in single-family dwelling units differs appreciably from the use of land in India, Hong Kong, or Ethiopia. All factors or in-

344

fluences affecting real estate are included in these three categories. The forces involved continually interact and affect our use of land. All must be understood and taken into account to achieve optimum decisions relative to the use of realty.

The interaction of all of these forces and their impact on property values are well illustrated by conflict and war. Aggression and conflict result from the desire for such things as more living space, a higher standard of living, and sheer power. Wars break out when these desires or forces are exerted at the national and international level. The outbreak of a shooting war immediately and adversely affects the value of property developed and employed for recreational use. Travel restrictions, gas rationing, and possible food shortages compel ocean, lake, and mountain vacation resorts to restrict or close their operations, with resultant losses in income and value. Hotels, motels, restaurants, and places of amusement serving resort cities also feel the negative impact of a war economy immediately. Cities that are university centers usually are also adversely affected. Students and faculty may be drafted for war purposes, and community-service facilities surrounding a campus area suffer as a consequence. A big segment of the economy, however, may experience an acceleration of activity essential to, and associated with, the war effort. Manufacturing centers, iron and coal mines, oil, and public utilities increase production; and property employed in these activities therefore benefits immediately from the increased efforts to win the war.

These many forces—physical, economic, and institutional—vary in the level at which their influence is exerted. Some are strongest at the national level, some at the local level. The approach taken here is to go from the general, or national, level to the specific, or local, level in discussing the forces and their influence. Note that the real estate market, with money as a least-common denominator, is the arena in which the influence on value of the many forces is exerted and reflected. We introduce the concept of the real estate market briefly in this chapter. Chapter 18 discusses the market in detail.

Nationally, factors and forces of change affect real estate in only a general or nonspecific way. That is, we have national population, resources, production, income, and traditions. But these are seldom tied or linked directly to a specific parcel of land, except for federal government decisions pertaining to dams, military bases, national parks, and the like. In fact, national data may be viewed as the aggregate of many local events or activities. U.S. population, oil reserves, or gross national product are examples. Even so, national data are important for a real estate analyst or investor. The data reflect the use or potential use of realty. Let us now look in more detail at the forces in our three categories.

PHYSICAL AND BIOLOGICAL FORCES

Population is the basic biological statistic at the national, regional, and local levels. The relative abundance and availability of natural resources constitute the major physical concern of most countries and communities. Population is more easily defined and interpreted than are resources and is therefore taken up first.

Population

The study of population characteristics and patterns is called **demography.** People—the population—serve as the interpreters and carriers of physical, economic, and institutional forces. In other words, the attitudes, motivations, and actions of people give life to the forces. Population forces and trends are therefore important. Local population forces and trends cannot be fully understood without national data as background. Let us, then, look first at U.S. population trends and characteristics.

U.S. DEMOGRAPHIC TRENDS. The U.S. population was 76.0 million in 1900. By 1950 our population had nearly doubled, having reached 151.7 million, and by 1980, our population is expected to have nearly tripled, to 220 million, according to the most likely projection of the U.S. Census Bureau. Further, by the end of this century, in the year 2000, the U.S. is projected to have a population of nearly 250 million. Finally, our population is expected to top out and level off at about 270 million by the year 2050.

The annual rate of increase to the end of the century, based on the above projection, is about 0.6 percent. The annual rate of increase to the year 2030 is about 0.5 percent. From 1900 to 1970, our historical rate of increase was about 1.4 percent per year. The reason for the decline rate is the zero-population-growth (ZPG) attitude of many people. Among the reasons for the ZPG attitude are the concern about overcrowding, concern about running out of resources necessary to maintain our standard of living, and desire by individuals for freedom of personal choice in selecting a life style.

Life expectancy at birth in the U.S. in 1976 was 72.8 years. This breaks down to 69 years for males and 76.7 for females. In 1900, life expectancy at birth equaled 47.3 years. By 1920, life expectancy at birth had increased to 54.1, with little difference between males and females. Life expectancy increased rapidly to 68.2 years by 1950 but since has increased only by about one year per decade. The result of greater life expectancy is an increase in the median age of our population. *Median* means the middle, as 30 is the middle value in the sequence of numbers 9, 23, 30, 38, and 50. In 1900, the median age was 22.9 years and in 1950, 29.6 years. The baby boom following World War II caused this median age to dip to 28.0 years in 1970. But as these people mature, the median age is again expected to advance, reaching 30.1 in 1980 and 35.4 by 2000.

The greater longevity of females shows up in the changing sex distribution of the population. In 1900, males outnumbered females 104.4 to 100. By 1950, there were 98.6 males per 100 females, and by 1975, the number of males per 100 females had dropped to 95.3. The Census Bureau Series II projection is 94.6 males per 100 females in the year 2000. Figures 16–2 and 16–3 show the changing age sex distribution of our population.

A direct relationship exists between population trends and real estate values. An increasing population means increased demand for real estate services and, in turn, higher values, other things being equal. A declining population has the opposite effect, other things equal. Of course, other things usually are not equal. For example, on a national level, the thrust toward ZPG has several

FIGURE 16–2
U.S. Male-Female Population by Selected Years, 1900–2000

	ABSOLUTE NUMBERS (000)			RATIO	
Year	Males	Females	Total	Males	Females
1900	38,816	37,178	75,994	104.4	100
1950	74,833	75,864	150,697	98.6	100
1975	104,202	109,338	213,540	95.3	100
2000	126,588	133,790	260,378	94.6	100

FIGURE 16–3
Percent Distribution of the Population of the United States for the Year 1940 and Forecast for the Year 2000 by Age and Sex

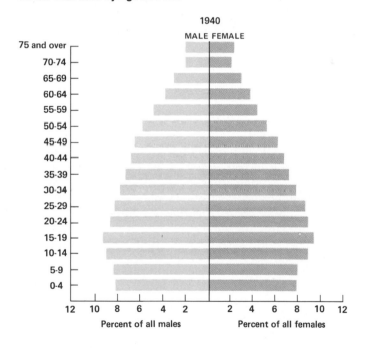

implications for real estate. First, even though population stabilizes, per capita income is likely to continue increasing. Therefore, higher-quality space is likely to be demanded. With a stable population, pressures on resources and the environment will probably ease, meaning less air, water, and noise pollution. With an older and less venturesome population, beaches, lakes, waterways, hiking

FIGURE 16–3 (cont.)

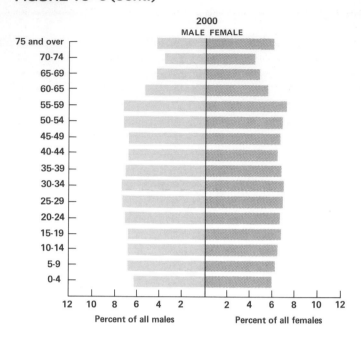

trails, ski slopes, and wilderness areas are likely to be less congested. Less new urban development of real estate will be necessary; rather, rehabilitation and redevelopment of existing urban areas will become more important.

Extending the above line of reasoning to housing one can see that a stable population primarily needs replacement housing, not expansive developments of new housing. Thus, the number of housing units in the nation seems likely to stabilize. As shown in figure 16–4, dwelling units increased from 15.96 million in 1900 to 63.45 million in 1970, almost a fourfold increase. With a projected population of 250 million people, and assuming a continued decrease in the number of persons per dwelling unit to 3, we'll need only 83 million dwelling units in 2000, an increase of about 20 million from 1970. With capability to build 2 to 3 million housing units per year, this increase will not tax our economy. In turn, the housing stock will be aging and will increasingly need repair and replacement. Figure 16–5 shows U.S. population projections to the year 2050.

POPULATION DISTRIBUTION. In 1970, 73.5 percent of the U.S. population lived in urban areas. This was up sharply from 64 percent in 1950 and 39.7 percent in 1900. Currently, 75 percent of the U.S. population is estimated to live in urban areas.

FIGURE 16–4
Total Dwelling Units in the United States, 1900–1970

Year	Population (millions)	Dwelling Units (millions)	Population Per Dwelling Unit
1900	76.2	15,964	4.77
1910	92.2	20,256	4.55
1920	106.0	24,352	4.35
1930	123.2	29,905	4.12
1940	132.2	34,855	3.79
1950	151.3	42,826	3.53
1960	179.3	53,024	3.38
1970	203.2	63,450	3.20

Source: U.S. Department of Commerce, Bureau of the Census, Population Series Reports, 1960 and 1970.

Figure 16–5
United States Population Projections 1976 to 2050

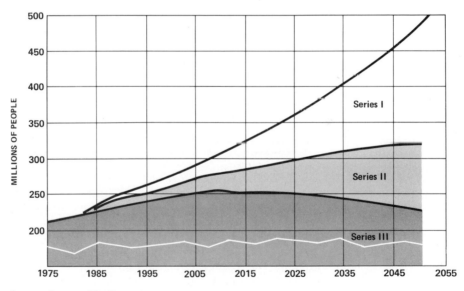

Source: Bureau of the Census.

By way of comparison, 79 percent of the population of England and 82.2 percent of the population of West Germany was urbanized in 1970, while Russia was only 62.3 percent urbanized. Australia, a large country relative to its population, was the most highly urbanized country in 1970 at 88.5 percent.

349

China, on the other hand, with an estimated population of 750 million people in 1970, was only 23.5 percent urbanized; and India, with 544 million people, was only 18.8 percent urbanized. While some differences in the definition of urban may be involved in these figures, it is clear that high population count does not translate directly into a high percentage of urbanization.

In regional terms, the distribution of our population shows a steady shifting toward the West. See figure 16–6. The Pacific states grew at a much more rapid rate than other areas, for a much larger share of total U.S. population. A less obvious tendency has been for the south Atlantic states to grow at a steady rate. These shifts are the result of people following the sun for economic opportunity and for life style. Also, the increasing median age of our population has migrational implications. Elderly people increasingly demand retirement areas where mild climate keeps housing and clothing costs at a minimum. During the past decades, states such as California, Arizona, New Mexico, and Florida experienced extraordinary population gains and increasing activity in real estate market transactions. Figure 16–3, showing the estimated distribution of total population by age and sex for the year 2000 as compared with the year 1940, was prepared from special reports of the Bureau of the Census. Close inspection of this chart discloses that whereas only 20.2 percent of the total population were 50 years or over in 1940, 33.0 percent are expected to exceed that age in the year 2000.

FIGURE 16–6
Regional Population as Percentage of Total U.S. Population: 1900, 1950, and Projection to 1980*

Region	1900 Population (thousands)	Percent	1950 Population (thousands)	Percent	1980 (projected) Population (thousands)	Percent
United States	76,212	100.0	151,326	100.0	220,000	100.0
NORTHEAST	21,047	27.6	39,478	26.1	51,863	23.6
New England	5,592	7.3	9,314	6.2	12,847	5.8
Middle Atlantic	15,455	20.3	30,164	19.9	39,016	17.7
NORTH CENTRAL	26,333	34.6	44,461	29.4	60,163	27.3
East N. Central	15,986	21.0	30,399	20.1	43,309	19.7
West N. Central	10,347	13.6	14,061	9.3	16,854	7.7
SOUTH	24,524	32.2	47,197	31.2	67,990	30.9
South Atlantic	10,443	13.7	21,182	14.0	33,995	15.5
East S. Central	7,548	9.9	11,477	7.6	13,029	5.9
West S. Central	6,533	8.6	14,538	9.6	20,966	9.5
WEST	4,309	5.7	20,190	13.3	40,182	18.3
Mountain	1,675	2.2	5,075	3.4	9,323	4.2
Pacific	2,634	3.5	15,115	10.0	30,859	14.0

* Numbers are sometimes slightly inconsistent because of rounding.
Sources: 1970 Census of Population: Number of Inhabitants: United States Summary, tables 8 and 10; and the *Statistical Abstract of the United States,* 1976, tables 3 and 13.

Natural Resources

Natural resources, or the lack of them, greatly influence the nature and extent of a country's development. Population, minerals, oil, water, location, and complementary soils, terrain, and climate are all natural resources and are all needed for balanced development of a country. Large countries, which are more likely to have all of these basic ingredients, are therefore more likely to be world powers. The United States, Russia, and China are examples. Brazil, Canada, and Australia, while roughly equal in area, lack friendly climates and population and hence do not qualify as world powers. Japan and England are excellent examples of countries that exploited advantageous location for trade to have considerable influence in world affairs. OPEC countries have exploited oil reserves to achieve power. And, of course, the inadequacy of oil reserves has hurt the U.S. position of leadership in the world.

The lack of a balance of resources in some parts of the United States results in an uneven pattern of development. Thus, the prairie states and the mountain states of the West are less densely populated than our eastern states. This means that resources become forces affecting the development and value of real estate only through the decisions and actions of people. On the other hand, little happens in an area unless resources are present. Resources enter into our discussion, in this sense, numerous times throughout this chapter.

ECONOMIC FORCES

Economics is often defined as the allocation of limited resources to satisfy human needs and wants. Economic forces or adjustments are generated by humankind's efforts to maximize benefits while allocating and utilizing limited resources to satisfy human needs and wants. The resources may be water, oil, minerals, or land. A large portion of our daily work effort is devoted to economic activity.

Real estate prices and values, real estate sales activity, and construction and developmental activity are directly influenced by the pace of economic activity and the sense of economic well-being at both the local and national levels. However, economic forces leading to this economic activity and sense of well-being cannot be observed or measured directly. Thus, an analyst or investor must look to economic statistics that measure the results of these economic forces. In addition, our prudent investor looks to the future. This section therefore has three divisions. The first identifies and discusses several of the more important and more enduring economic forces. The second concerns common and important measures of our national economic activity. The third takes up national economic indicators. Even so, not all measures of economic activity or all economic forces are covered in this discussion.

Economic Forces Identified

An *economic force* is an influence for change growing out of man's efforts to use and allocate limited resources to satisfy needs and wants. The basic economic force, self-interest, motivates people to try to achieve the highest possible standard of living in the process. Self-interest is also reflected in business decisions to maximize profits or wealth. It follows that both individuals and businesses tend to minimize transportation costs in the movement of people and goods. That is, transportation costs, which per se are unproductive (do not increase profits or raise the standard of living), are rationally avoided. In more direct terms, transportation costs are rationally incurred only when a benefit is likely to result.

Self-interest and a tendency to minimize transportation costs are assumed, or given, in discussing economic forces. Resources are generally considered gifts of nature and are important assets in our economic system. With this introductory statement, we now discuss several of the most basic economic forces as follows:

> Technological change
> Resources and their changing availability
> Organizational change
> Shifting consumer choices

TECHNOLOGICAL CHANGE. New technology has probably caused more change than any other social, economic, or political force over the centuries. New technology accounts for "advances" in the art of war from sticks and stones to spears and arrows to rifle and cannon to tanks and planes to rockets and nuclear bombs. The impact of new technology has been equally significant in the peacetime pursuits of man. Since 1900, the tractor has replaced the horse in agriculture. In addition, fertilizers are now widely used. The result is that whereas perhaps 5 or 10 percent of our population once lived in urban areas, now over 75 percent live in urban areas. Likewise, in transportation, the progression has been from walking to horse-drawn carriages to autos, trains, and trucks to airplanes. In communications, the progression includes the telephone, radio, and television. Similarly, computers and calculators are strongly influencing information processing and analysis.

Many other technological advances have been overlooked in this brief review. For example, microfiche for information storage, steel and elevators for skyscrapers, and nuclear power plants for instant energy to drive machines and light offices are commonplace today. Technological change goes on around us continually.

RESOURCES AND THEIR DISTRIBUTION. Resource availability goes hand in hand with technological change in determining where and how people live. Initially, humans lived by hunting, fishing, and foraging for fruit and berries. A cave or hut provided shelter. Life was simple. There was no particular use for land or a specific location. Man moved from place to place as game or climate required.

Domesticated animals, and later agriculture, gave humans more control over their destiny. But new tools were required to handle the animals and to dig the soils, such as ropes, harnesses, and plows. Eventually it became more advantageous to have fixed settlements and farms. Humans became dependent on the land and ownership rights developed.

With each effort to improve life, people improved their tools and expanded their need for resources. With the industrial revolution, energy sources—water power, wood, coal, oil and gas, and eventually uranium for nuclear power—became critical to maintaining a desired standard of living. Likewise, minerals and other raw materials—iron, copper, gold, diamonds, salt, sulphur, phosphorus, and rare metals—were needed to achieve the standard of living. The pattern became established. More resources and better technology meant more freedom and easier living. More freedom and easier living permitted more time to seek new resources and create new inventions. The result of this circular process is that people can live almost anywhere in the world they wish, at a standard of living well above any known in the past; and people go almost anywhere in the world to obtain new resources to increase this freedom of choice and opportunity.

ORGANIZATIONAL CHANGE. Organizational change, like technological change, helps increase man's economic output. The cost for any one person to manufacture a car or dishwasher or book would be extremely high, if indeed, one person could do the job. Yet, with **labor specialization** and mass production, these and many other products are available at relatively low cost to most people in our society. Other examples of organizational change include supermarkets in place of corner groceries, corporations in place of sole proprietorships for businesses, and freeways in place of many local streets.

SHIFTING CONSUMER CHOICES. Change in what people eat and wear, where they live, and how they travel affect economic output and the regional distribution of economic opportunity. For example, people can eat and wear only so much. Consequently, as a family's income increases, an increasing proportion of its income is spent on autos, recreation, and travel, while a smaller proportion is spent on food and clothing. Also, higher family income usually means more meat and fewer potatoes eaten. That is, high-quality foods replace lower-quality foods. Further, an increasing proportion of our population prefers to work in Sun Belt states; hence Florida, California, and the Southwest experienced rapid in-migration since World War II. Higher incomes also mean people prefer to travel by auto and plane rather than by train or bus. Each shift in **consumer choice,** with higher incomes, means a higher level of social and economic well-being. Self-interest does indeed drive our economy.

Changing consumer choices, in turn, influence the use of our land resources. More autos mean more land devoted to roads. More meat and fewer potatoes mean more land devoted to raising grain and livestock, with less acreage in potatoes. A preference for more space gives rise to urban sprawl. And the recent resurgence of demand for natural fibers means more land devoted to raising cotton and sheep.

Measures of Economic Activity

Economic forces are difficult, if not impossible, to measure directly, even though they exert their influence anywhere people live. Thus, we resort to measures of economic activity. The most common and most important measures at the national level are (1) gross national product (GNP), (2) personal income per capita, (3) consumer price index (CPI), and (4) employment and unemployment. Statistics for these measures may be compared from one time period to another and, except for GNP, from one community or area to another at both regional and local levels. Figure 16–7 contains these statistics for the U.S. Each of these statistics may be integrated into the analysis for a specific community and/or property.

The *Statistical Abstract of the United States,* the *Survey of Current Business,* and the *Economic Report of the President* are reliable sources of national economic statistics. All should be available at local libraries. The *Statistical Abstract* contains an extensive appendix, "Guide to Sources of Statistics," which an analyst/investor might use to compile regional and local social and economic data. One section of this appendix, "Guide to State Statistical Abstracts," is a valuable source of state and local statistical data. Finally, most Standard Metropolitan Statistical Areas (SMSAs) have branch offices of the U.S. Department of Labor. These branch offices, which are listed in local telephone directories, readily provide local data on employment and unemployment.

GROSS NATIONAL PRODUCT. The **gross national product** (GNP) is *the grand measure* of economic activity. *GNP* aggregates, in dollars, the value of all goods and services produced in the United States for a year at current market prices. Thus, GNP measures the output attributable to the factors of production (land, labor, capital, and management) provided by residents of the U.S. during each year. GNP includes the imputed rental value of owner-occupied dwellings plus allowances for depreciation. Using 1950 as a base, GNP increased fivefold during the twenty-five years to 1975. This steep surge includes rising prices caused by inflation or decreased purchasing power of the dollar as well as increased output.

Among other things, GNP tells us how well we are doing as a country, in economic terms, relative to our potential. Figure 16–8 shows this relationship in terms of 1972, constant, dollars. The closer we operate to our potential, the higher our standard of living and the greater our sense of economic well-being are likely to be.

A gross product figure is sometimes calculated and published for states and local areas. The state statistical abstracts, mentioned earlier, contain this information. Local economic conditions may also be judged by levels of employment and per capita income as well.

PER CAPITA PERSONAL INCOME. **Personal income,** as defined for national income-accounting purposes, is the current income received by persons from all sources with contributions for social insurance (primarily social security) taken out. Total personal income is an aggregate figure that is not very useful for comparative purposes because communities vary in size. Thus, to say that community A, with 10,200 people, had total personal income of $61.2 million in 1975 has limited meaning when compared with community B, with a population of 78,600, and total personal income of $393 million. But to say that in 1975 per capita income in community A was $6,000 and in community B was $5,000 is a useful comparison. Also, to say that per capita income in community

FIGURE 16–7
Selected Social and Economic Statistics for the United States, 1950–78

Year*	Population (millions)	Gross National Product (billions)	Per Capita Personal Income*	Per Capita Disposable Personal Income	Consumer Price Index (1967 = 100)	Employed (millions)	Unemployed (millions)	Percent Unemployed
1950	151.7	$ 286.2	$1,491	$1,355	72.1	58.9	3.3	5.3
1955		399.3	1,868	1,654	80.2	62.2	2.9	4.4
1960	179.3	506.0	2,212	1,934	88.7	65.8	3.9	5.5
1965		688.1	2,764	2,430	94.5	71.1	3.4	5.5
1970	203.2	982.4	3,911	3,348	116.3	78.6	4.1	4.9
1975	213.6	1,578.8	5,832	5,088	161.2	84.8	7.8	8.5
1978†	213.5	2,106.6	7,840	6,640	181.5	94.4	6.0	6.0

* Unadjusted dollars.

† Data for 1978 estimated or based on latest figures available.

Source: 1979 Economic Report of the President and Statistical Abstract of the United States, 1978.

FIGURE 16–8
Gross National Product, Actual and Potential, 1968–78

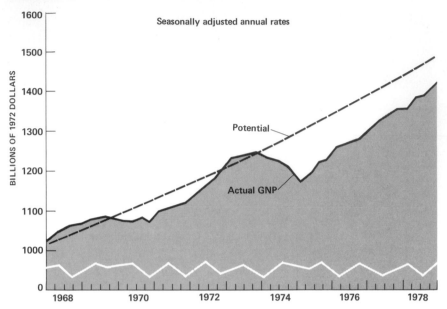

Sources: Department of Commerce and Council of Economic Advisers, as presented in the *1979 Economic Report of the President*, Chart 7, p. 75, with some editing by the authors.

A increased from $1,500 in 1950 to $6,000 in 1975 provides useful information. Per capita personal income in the United States in 1978 was $7,840. Figure 16–9 shows regional per capita income for selected years from 1950. Disposable per capita income is an alternative measure of per capita income, adjusted for payments to governments, primarily taxes. *Disposable personal income* (DPI) is money that people may either spend or save, at their discretion. Per capita disposable income increased almost five times between 1950 and 1978, going from $1,355 to $6,640.

CONSUMER PRICE INDEX. The **Consumer Price Index (CPI)** measures changes in the cost of living. Over the last few decades, it has therefore been a measure of inflation. The Consumer Price Index *does not* measure changes in the total amount spent for living.

The Consumer Price Index is based on the average change in prices of approximately four hundred items of consumer goods and services purchased in urban areas. The index has several components: food, shelter, fuel oil and coal, apparel, transportation, and medical care. It is also broken down to all commodities and all services. An analyst would find it useful to compare the index for shelter from one time period to another for a community under analysis, where data are available, to determine trends of housing costs in the area. The CPI given in figure 16–7 is for all items.

FIGURE 16–9
Per Capita Income and Ratio to U.S. Per Capita Income by Census Region: 1950, 1960, 1970, and 1978

Region	1950 Dollars	1950 Ratio to U.S. per capita income	1960 Dollars	1960 Ratio to U.S. per capita income	1970 Dollars	1970 Ratio to U.S. per capita income	1978 Dollars	1978 Ratio to U.S. per capita income
United States	$1,496	100.0	$2,201	100.0	$3,893	100.0	$7,836	100.0
NORTHEAST								
New England	$1,601	107.0	$2,419	109.9	$4,245	109.0	$7,900	100.8
Middle Atlantic	1,751	117.0	2,549	115.8	4,390	112.8	8,179	104.4
NORTH CENTRAL								
East N. Central	1,666	111.3	2,367	107.5	4,050	104.0	8,224	105.0
West N. Central	1,428	95.4	2,022	91.9	3,657	93.9	7,650	97.6
SOUTH								
South Atlantic	1,211	80.9	1,838	83.5	3,562	91.5	7,296	93.1
East S. Central	915	61.2	1,490	67.7	2,936	75.4	6,396	81.6
West S. Central	1,207	80.7	1,785	81.1	3,323	85.4	7,296	93.1
WEST								
Mountain	1,418	94.8	2,054	93.3	3,557	91.4	7,473	95.4
Pacific	1,798	120.2	2,608	118.5	4,317	110.9	8,816	112.5

Source: Statistical Abstract of the United States, 1972, table 519; and 1976, table 644; and Survey of Current Business, part II, August 1979, table 2.

The Consumer Price Index may be used to determine changes from one time to another in real or constant terms. For example, U.S. per capita disposable personal income was $1,355 in 1950 and $5,088 in 1975. Dividing both figures by their respective consumer price indexes gives $1,879 in 1950 and $3,127 in 1975. Thus, per capita DPI increased only by 66 percent during the twenty-five years in real terms. Alternatively, it might be said that the standard of living improved by 66 percent during this period.

EMPLOYMENT AND UNEMPLOYMENT. Another, more sensitive measure of economic well-being is employment and unemployment. Unemployment is directly related to mortgage foreclosures and property tax delinquencies, as might be expected. People without jobs and earnings probably use any income they get (unemployment compensation, welfare) for food and clothing first, just to survive. Outlays for shelter have a lower priority, hence the higher foreclosures and delinquency rates.

Employed persons and unemployed persons, taken together, make up the labor force. *Employed* includes all persons working for pay or profit, and all persons temporarily not working for pay or profit for noneconomic reasons (illness, bad weather, vacation, and labor-management disputes). *Unemployed* means all persons not working who made specific efforts to find a job in the previous month (such as applying for work with an employer or a public employment service) and who are currently available for work.

The number of employed gives hard evidence of growth trends and the health of an area or economy. For example, in 1975, 84.8 million people were employed in the U.S. and another 7.8 million were unemployed. The unemployment rate of 8.5 percent is high compared with a rate more commonly around 5 to 5½ percent in the 1960s and early 1970s. The economic health of the U.S. was not very good in 1975. Thus it is no surprise that figure 16–8 shows our actual GNP in 1975 to have been well below our potential GNP.

Local employment trends and projections also closely affect population and potential demand for realty. For instance, in 1970, 38.7 percent of the total population in the U.S. was employed ($78.6/203.2 = 38.7\%$). Assuming a comparable ratio in 1975, the total population in 1975 is estimated at 219.1 million; and 219.1 million people, at the 1970 figure of 3.2 persons per dwelling unit, means that 68.475 million dwelling units were demanded in 1975, an increase of 5,025 million. And with greater demand, values go up and new construction is warranted.

These figures may be slightly high because of shifts in the age distribution of the U.S. population. At the local level, employment data are much more easily obtained than population data. In turn, a gross figure of total demand for housing units is easily developed. This type of analysis may be extended to estimate demand for other kinds of real estate.

REGIONAL PER CAPITA INCOME. The Census Bureau publishes data on regional shifts in population annually, as shown in figure 16–6. In a similar manner, the Bureau of Economic Analysis estimates and publishes data on regional shifts in personal income per capita; see figures 16–9 and 16–10. The combination of population and personal-income trends tells much, in a general way, about what is likely to be happening in real estate. That is, an area with

FIGURE 16–10
U.S. per capita personal income, 1978, by state

Source: U.S. Department of Commerce, Bureau of Economic Analysis, Survey of Current Business, August 1979, Part II, p. 27

sharp increases in population and personal income has greatly increased effective demand for real estate. For example, figures 16–6 and 16–9 show that the Pacific states (Washington, Oregon, California, Alaska, and Hawaii) have increased rapidly in both statistics since 1950. And these states have been growth areas for many years. Conversely, the west north central states (Minnesota, Iowa, Missouri, North and South Dakota, Nebraska, and Kansas) increased only slightly in population and lag behind the U.S. in per capita personal income. On a relative basis, these are slow-growth states. In turn, construction and real estate activity are probably not as strong as in many other states. Even so, urbanization trends may make real estate development and investment very attractive in some communities in the west north central states. The regional data are intended to show only broad trends, or the big picture.

National Economic Indicators

Our intent here is to relate local real estate activity to national economic activity. The data presented thus far are historical in nature. The serious investor or analyst might find it advantageous to go an extra step—to consider na-

359

tional economic indicators and look into the future. It is the future that determines the success, or lack of success, of a real estate investment or development.

Figure 16–11 summarizes the national economic indicators by economic process and cyclical timing. Studies by the National Bureau of Economic Research (NBER) show that business and economic cycles vary in length and intensity. That is, they are not regular or rhythmic. The cyclical indicators in figure 16–11 have been singled out by the NBER as leaders, coinciders, or laggers, based on the general conformance to cyclical movements in general economic activity. The indicators are reported monthly in *Business Conditions Digest,* a publication of the U.S. Bureau of Economic Analysis. These indicators have proven useful in forecasting, measuring, and interpreting short-term fluctuations in aggregate economic activity.

INSTITUTIONAL FORCES

An **institution** is an established principle, law, organization, custom, or belief. An institution may then also be considered as an established arrangement or way of doing things. Being established, an institution may also be regarded as the influence of the past, and of other people, in defining "acceptable" action for individuals. Thus, institutions provide structure for human activity.

An *institutional force* is the energy generated through the acceptance by people of certain principles, laws, or beliefs. Our use of realty takes place in an environment containing numerous institutional forces, such as the law of property, land-use controls, property taxation, accepted architectural styles, and the established use of the automobile for transportation. Institutional forces modify economic behavior, making it at one time more stable and more changeable or unpredictable. Institutional forces cannot be ignored in making rational decisions about the use of realty.

Institutional forces may be generally subclassified as social or political/legal. Institutional forces do not lend themselves to statistical measurement or presentation. Hence, our discussion must be of a slightly different nature than for economic forces.

Social Forces

A **social force** is the influence generated by the physical and psychological needs and desires of human beings. Beliefs, customs, and religion are social forces. Some examples of these forces in action seem appropriate.

Many of our cities were initially laid out on a rectangular grid system; this customary way of laying out streets persisted for many decades even though other street systems would have been more suitable to the hills, winding river valleys, and soil conditions encountered. Only since World War II have curvilinear streets, planned unit developments, and superblocks become acceptable. Our belief in individual freedom goes far to rationalize the common use of the auto in preference to mass transit or bicycles.

Religion has been, and continues to be, a strong social force. The effect is through ownership or operation of land-use activities and through beliefs that

FIGURE 16-11
Cross-Classification of U.S. Indicators (1966 List Modified) By Economic Process and Cyclical Timing

ECONOMIC PROCESS	CYCLICAL TIMING		
	Leading	Roughly Coincident	Lagging
Employment and unemployment	Average work week, mfg. New unemployment insurance claims, inverted	Nonfarm employment Unemployment, inverted	Long-duration unemployment, inverted
Production, income, consumption, and trade	New orders, consumer goods, and materials*	Gross national product* Industrial production Personal income* Manufacturing and trade sales*	
Fixed capital investment	Formation of business enterprises Contracts and orders, plant and equipment* Building permits, housing		Investment expenditures, plant, and equipment*
Inventories and inventory investment	Change in business inventories*		Business inventories*
Prices, costs, and profits	Industrial-materials price index Stock price index Profits* Ratio, price-to-unit labor cost, nonfarm		Change in output per manhour, mfg. inverted
Money and credit	Change, consumer installment debt*		Commercial and industrial loans outstanding Bank interest rates, business loans

* In constant prices.

Source: National Bureau of Economic Research.

affect land-use practices. The Crusades of the Middle Ages are an excellent example of the power of religious beliefs to influence people's actions, even to lead some to their death.

Development and operation of real estate by religious bodies provided a focus for cities in Europe during the Middle Ages. Cathedrals and monasteries formed the nucleus of numerous communities. Prestige neighborhoods developed around the bishop's residence in the process, and the diocese was generally a stronger administrative unit at the time than were local and regional governments. Today, because of the separation of church and state, churches and most other religious facilities are exempt from property taxes. This tax-exempt status discourages the development and redevelopment of church-owned properties to what many people would consider their highest and best economic uses. The intrusion of church-owned properties into commercial areas often limits the development and growth of such areas also.

Religious beliefs affect the use of land indirectly also. The Hindu belief in India results in large local "sacred" populations of monkeys and cattle, which require space for living and feed. Lest we point too quickly, Christmas trees are raised in the U.S. to help celebrate a religious season. Further, in some communities, taverns and nightclubs may not be located within certain distances, say, 300 feet, of a church, by local zoning ordinance.

Social forces tend to be more local and more informal in their operation than political forces. Even so, social forces must sometimes be reckoned with by an investor. Neighborhood resistance to change has killed many an application for rezoning that appeared economically justified.

Political Forces

Political forces, including laws, are the most obvious and probably the most significant of the institutional forces influencing our use of realty. A **political force** is an influence for change generated out of our efforts to organize and manage ourselves and others through government and laws. Political forces sometimes grow out of social and economic needs and wants (forces) and therefore represent the interaction of biological, economic, and institutional forces. For example, federal, state, and local elections reflect the competition for political power to write and/or enforce the rules or laws of our society. The winning party takes the lead in passing laws concerning energy, the environment, birth control, welfare programs, income taxes, and other current issues.

Political forces establish conditions, usually a stable environment, that social or economic forces cannot provide. For example, political forces bring about and maintain government and laws, thereby providing a setting of order and continuity for social and economic activities. Our system of private ownership of property, as opposed to state or federal ownership and control, is another example of political/legal forces at work. Even so, these ownership rights are continually modified by legislative, executive, and judicial decisions and actions. And at the same time, these rights are enforced by our governmental system, which makes women and men, the black, white, and yellow, the big and the not so big, equally able to have and enforce ownership positions.

Governmental actions also constitute political forces. We've already seen that monetary policy and open-market operations of the federal government affect real estate credit. Governmental tax policies—at the local, state, and federal levels—also have an impact upon real estate. On the other side, governmental-expenditure decisions also affect real estate. Expenditures for a new highway, school, sanitary sewer line, urban renewal project, or dam definitely affect decisions by private investors. And of course, expenditures plus encouraging legislation or incentives increase the potential and likelihood of private investment.

At the national level, political forces in the form of federal laws are rapidly becoming more important in their effect on real estate. Real estate regulation was almost entirely a matter of local concern until the 1930s. In 1934, Congress created the Federal Housing Administration to encourage the construction and ownership of homes. The Public Housing Administration was established in 1937 to provide decent, safe, and sanitary dwellings for lower-income families who could not afford such housing on their own. In the 1930s, also, slums were recognized as a national problem, as our stock of housing and other real estate facilities began showing their age. Our physical facilities were out of adjustment with the social and economic demands placed on them.

World War II intervened, and finally in 1949 a national housing act was passed that started an urban renewal program to assemble and clear slum lands for reuse. Also, city, urban, and regional-planning programs were initiated about this time. All of these programs helped, but urban and community and other real estate problems increased at a faster rate than they were solved by these acts and programs. During the fifties, need for further federal legislation became apparent.

In the early 1960s new forms of real estate ownership were needed, and federal legislation was passed providing for condominium ownership and for real estate investment trusts. In 1966, the Model Cities program was begun, putting emphasis on rehabilitating rather than clearing slum areas. By the late 1960s, consumer and environmental problems became more apparent. The 1968 Housing and Community Development Act provided for rent supplements, flood insurance, regulation of interstate land sales, new community development, and urban planning and facilities, among other things. In more recent years, Congress has passed acts relating to environmental protection, energy conservation, settlement procedures, truth in lending, and emergency mortgage relief.

Three of the more significant categories of federal legislation are briefly taken up as follows:

1. Consumer protection and welfare
2. Environment, energy, and land use
3. Housing and community development

An identifier, in addition to the short name given each piece of legislation, is given to indicate more specifically the law being discussed. For instance, the identifier, P.L. 93–533, means Public Law 533 passed by the 93rd session of Congress. A 94 in the identifier would mean the 94th session of Congress.

CONSUMER PROTECTION AND WELFARE. Considerable federal consumer protection and welfare legislation has been passed in recent years, a fact that has obvious long-run implications for real estate. The Real Estate Settlement Procedures Act (RESPA) is intended to ensure consumers greater and more timely information on the nature and costs of the settlement process. RESPA is explained in somewhat more detail in the chapter on title closing. Two other examples of important federal consumer legislation of importance to real estate are the Interstate Land Sales Full Disclosure Act and the Emergency Mortgage Relief Act.

The Interstate Land Sales Full Disclosure Act (P.L. 90–448) makes it unlawful for any developer to sell or lease, by the use of the mail or by any means in interstate commerce, any lot in any subdivision (defined as fifty or more lots for sale as part of a common promotional plan) unless the following items have been satisfied:

1. A *statement of record* listing certain required information about the ownership of the land, the state of its title, its physical nature, the availability of roads and utilities, and other matters must be filed with the secretary of HUD.

2. A printed *property report,* containing pertinent extracts from the statement of record, must be furnished to the purchaser in advance of the signing of an agreement for purchase or lease.

Any contract for the purchase or lease of a lot covered by this act is voidable at the option of the purchaser if a property report was not furnished at least three business days before the contract signing. The sale or lease of lots in bona fide industrial or commercial development is exempt from the requirement of the Interstate Land Sales Full Disclosure Act in those cases where certain stringent requirements are met.

The Emergency Mortgage Relief Act (P.L. 94–50) gives aid to homeowners threatened with foreclosure because of unemployment. Federal loans of up to $250 per month for as long as two years may be made to jobless homeowners. HUD is also authorized to ask mortgage lenders to delay foreclosures, with the understanding that the federal government will guarantee any mortgages that eventually prove uncollectable. From a national point of view, the act is desirable. With emergency relief available, families are more willing to undertake home ownership. This willingness is particularly important in the middle of a recession because it maintains the construction industry, the lumber industry, and eventually the economy. Without such willingness, these industries might sag to lower and lower levels as a result of a depression psychology, and that might mean an ever-worsening economic situation.

ENVIRONMENT, ENERGY, AND LAND USE. Environmental quality, energy usage, land use, and transportation modes are all closely interrelated and are therefore discussed here as one topic. Environmental quality—air, water, and land—is of ever-greater concern as population and energy usage continue to increase. The legislation in this area is generally for single-purpose, functional programs even though coordination is greatly needed. In 1979 comprehensive land-use planning legislation was proposed several times without success, to coordinate these programs.

A federal comprehensive land-use planning act would obviously stimulate land-use planning. However, it is generally agreed that the federal government has no constitutional power to regulate land use per se. Therefore, actual planning would have to be done at the state and local levels, stimulated by federal financial incentives.

Environmental legislation is of critical importance to real estate developers, investors, and lenders. They must know that any proposed real estate project meets all federal environmental regulations. Enforcement of the regulations is the responsibility of several agencies including HUD, FHA, VA, the Department of Agriculture, the Office of Management and Budget, the Coastal Zone Management Agency, and the Environmental Protection Agency. For the most part, the regulations do not affect existing projects or construction. Failure of a project to comply with the regulations results in costly delays, litigation, and modifications that could eventually lead to failure of the undertaking. Large developers, investors, and lenders are therefore establishing systematic evaluation procedures to determine the probable impact of proposed projects on the environment.

The National Environmental Policy Act (NEPA) of 1969 (P.L. 91–190) easily dominates all environmental laws passed to date. Among other things, the act requires a detailed environmental-impact statement on every major federal action that might significantly affect environmental quality. The statement must describe the environmental impact and the unavoidable adverse effects, set forth and discuss alternatives, and eventually resolve or reject the long-term, irreversible effects of the proposed action. Environmental-impact studies are required of major private real estate developments as well. The act established the Environmental Protection Agency (EPA) as an enforcement authority.

Several acts complement the National Environmental Policy Act. These are the Clean Air Act of 1970 (P.L. 91–604), the Water Pollution Control Act of 1972 (P.L. 93–240), the Energy Supply and Environmental Coordination Act (P.L. 93–319), and the Coastal Zone Management Act (P.L. 92–583).

The Federal Energy Administration Act, as amended, (P.L. 93–275) establishes and authorizes the Department of Energy (DOE) to evaluate the nation's energy supplies and to take a wide range of actions to cope with energy shortages and pricing problems. The DOE's actions will have many significant implications for growth and location of economic activities in this country. Duties of the DOE include: (1) administration of petroleum and gas distribution and consumption programs, (2) efforts to reduce demand for fuels and to increase fuel efficiency, 3) development of plans and programs to handle shortages in energy production, (4) promotion of stability in energy prices, and (5) development of a strategy to reduce U.S. dependence on imported fuels (Project Independence). The impact of the act on real estate is likely to be mainly through locational economic effects. As of 1980, DOE had not been particularly effective.

Federal legislation concerning highways and mass transportation have great implications for real estate. Federal legislation provided for the planning, financing, and development of the Interstate Highway System. It also provided substantial financial support for the development and maintenance of a system of state roads and highways. Major items in the 1974 highway legislation (P.L. 93–643) include a uniform national speed limit of 55 miles per hour, bikeway demonstration programs, and stimulants for the organization of car pools.

A National Mass Transportation Act was also passed in 1974 (P.L. 93–503). The act increased financial assistance to urban mass transportation systems and provided for fare-free mass transportation demonstration projects. The act stipulates that "society depends on the provisions of efficient, economical, and convenient transportation within and between urban areas." With energy shortages imminent, revitalization of mass transportation systems seems critical to save fuel and to move people and goods rapidly and smoothly.

Most recently enacted transportation legislation concerns either energy conservation or preservation of environmental quality. Land-use patterns of the future will reflect this shift in emphasis from "the auto is king" to "make way for mass transportation and car pools." Greater density of development should occur along main arteries where buses run or around stations on mass transit systems as a result of the shift. Also, the central business district should become more of a focal point for the community because most mass transportation lines run to, or through, the central area, making it the most accessible of all points in the community. The likely result, as usual, will be continued change in the pattern of land use.

HOUSING AND COMMUNITY DEVELOPMENT. In 1949 Congress established as a national goal "a decent home and a suitable living environment for every American family." This goal has been the central theme of housing and community-development legislation ever since. Housing and community-development legislation calls for many changes and affects many areas at once. It is therefore the most important and the most wide-ranging of all federal laws affecting real estate and is often referred to as a form of omnibus legislation.

Seven specific objectives of housing and community-development legislation are as follows:

1. Conserving and expanding the nation's housing stock
2. Using land and other national resources more rationally, including better arrangements of residential, commercial, industrial, recreational, and other land-use activities
3. Eliminating slums and blight, and preventing the deterioration of property and facilities important to communities
4. Eliminating conditions detrimental to the public health, safety, and welfare through code enforcement, demolition, rehabilitation, and related activities
5. Expanding and improving the quantity and quality of community services that are designed principally for persons of low and moderate income
6. Reducing the isolation of various income groups within communities and geographical areas
7. Restoring and preserving properties of special value for historic, architectural, or aesthetic reasons

Typically, new or additional housing and community-development legislation, in the form of a new federal act, is passed every two or three years. Specific information about these acts may be obtained from HUD field offices, which are located in most large metropolitan areas.

Political forces are usually not powerful at the regional level in that our political system is not organized on a regional basis. So, regional political forces exert energy at the national level or the state level. Political/legal forces may be extemely potent in their influence on real estate, however. We see this in property taxation, planning and zoning, rent controls, and eminent domain.

SUMMARY

Natural endowment and demand largely determine the use and value of real estate. A threefold framework, concerned with (1) physical and biological, (2) economic, and (3) institutional forces, is traditionally used in land economics to facilitate analysis of this demand and endowment. Physical and biological forces include land, land resources, and people. Economic forces are those created by our efforts to allocate limited resources for social and economic ends. An institutional force is created through people's acceptance of certain laws, principles, customs, or beliefs. Institutional forces may be subclassified as social or political/legal. A social force is generated by the physical and psychological needs of people. A political force is an influence generated out of people's efforts to organize and manage themselves, and others, through government and laws. These forces operate in the real estate market and are seldom found in their "pure" form.

KEY TERMS

Consumer choices	Institution
Consumer Price Index (CPI)	Institutional forces
Demography	Labor specialization
Economic forces	Opportunity cost
Economics	Personal income
Force	Political force
Gross national product (GNP)	Social force

QUESTIONS FOR REVIEW AND DISCUSSION

1. Identify and explain briefly the three components of the framework traditionally used for discussion and analysis in land economics.

2. What demographic characteristics are most important in relating population to real estate? Give examples.

3. Define economics. Give at least two examples of economic forces, and relate them to your definition of economics.

4. What is an institution? What are the two main categories of institutional forces? Give at least one example of each.

5. Define gross national product. What is the importance of GNP as a measure of economic activity?

6. Explain why personal income per capita is a better measure of local economic activity than total personal income of the area.

7. Are levels of employment and unemployment related to GNP? How or why not?

8. We identified basic economic forces as (1) technological change, (2) changing availability of resources, (3) organizational change, and (4) shifting consumer choices. Are these forces likely to increase or decrease in strength in the years ahead? In what direction are they moving? Discuss.

9. The forces discussed in this chapter are said to make up the investment climate. Yet, the forces cannot be directly related to any specific property. So how and why are they important? Or are they? Discuss.

REFERENCES

Kapplin, Steven D. "Economic Forecasting for Real Estate Appraising." *The Real Estate Appraiser,* March–April 1978, pp. 47–55. A discussion of the structure of, and impact of changes in the national economy, on local real estate markets and values. Techniques for interpreting national economic change, by way of indicators, are also presented. For the serious student or investor.

Ratcliff, Richard U. *Real Estate Analysis.* New York: McGraw-Hill, 1961. A classic in the literature of real estate analysis and decision making. Relates real estate investing to forces of change in the urban environment. Moderately easy reading, chapters 1, 2, and 12 in particular.

Shafer, Thomas W. *Urban Growth and Economics.* Reston; Va.: Reston, 1977. A very readable presentation on economic growth and urban development. One of the best and most readable explanations of the forces making up the urban environment.

Smith, Wallace F. *Urban Development: The Process and the Problems.* Berkeley: University of California Press, 1975. A generalized overview of decisions and actions involved in urbanization, including a look at their implications. Relates urban economics to urban real estate, using real estate concepts. For the advanced student. Chapters 2–5 particularly relevant.

Urban-Area Structure and Neighborhood Dynamics

17

The test of a civilization is the power of drawing
the most benefits out of its cities.
Emerson, *Journals,* 1864

Urban areas are the result of social, economic, and political forces. These forces and local physical characteristics interact to create functional areas, which are major components or building blocks of our urban areas. A **functional area** is a place where some specialized activity, for instance, manufacturing, is performed. Residential neighborhoods, commercial districts, and industrial districts are the most obvious examples of functional areas. Streets and other parts of our transportation system tie urban areas together by facilitating movement of people and/or goods between land uses and functional areas.

Social, economic, and political forces change constantly. Natural resources are used up, and new technology is developed to compensate. In turn, people and economic activities migrate from one part of the country to another and from one community to another. Movement also occurs from central city to suburb and back again.

All of these forces and events affect the nature of our urban areas. As a consequence, our urban areas are in a constant state of flux. The purpose of this chapter is to look at the effect of long-run trends on the nature and structure of our urban areas and on urban real estate. With this perspective, an investor is better able to judge local real estate trends and, in turn, able to make better decisions about local real estate values. In the final analysis, real estate is an immobile physical asset that serves social, economic, and political needs.

The physical, biological, economic, social, and political forces discussed in the previous chapter are therefore reconsidered here in regard to their influence on land-use decisions at the local level. That is, intangible national and regional forces must be interpreted according to the effects on tangible local real estate activity and change to benefit our rational investor.

Social, economic, and political forces influence where people live, play, work, and die. An influence toward concentration of people, buildings, and machines, is an **urbanizing force.** Manufacturing, trade, education, and government are prime examples of activities that are more advantageously carried on with people concentrated in one place. An influence toward scatteration of people and activities is a **dispersing force.** Desire for isolation (e.g., a hermit) and the scatteration of Minuteman missiles for national defense are examples of dispersing forces. Most economic, social, and political forces are urbanizing in their effect, hence the long-term trend toward larger and larger cities.

Understanding the dynamics of urban areas is extremely important to a real estate investor. Real estate is a fixed physical asset that is highly dependent on its environment for value. Real estate is expensive to modify. Neighborhoods change very slowly in their makeup. Thus, an understanding of urban-area dynamics increases an investor's chances for investing in the right type of property in the right area. In turn, our investor increases chances for the highest possible rate of return.

Major topics in this chapter are

1. Urbanizing forces
2. Theories of urbanization
3. Rent theory and urban structure
4. Residential-neighborhood dynamics
5. Value analysis of commercial districts
6. Value analysis of industrial districts

URBANIZING FORCES

Most long-run forces in our society are also urbanizing forces in that they encourage concentration rather than dispersion of resources. In that we are primarily interested in urban real estate, let us begin by identifying several prominent urbanizing forces. We can then go on to discuss their influence on the location and nature of urban areas and of urban real estate. A brief look at the urbanization process concludes this section.

Components of Urbanizing Forces

Self-interest, often in the way of competitive or personal advantage, is the key to urbanizing forces. Manufacturing, trade, education, and government all benefit from a concentration of people and facilities. History is filled with evidence of humankind's march toward urbanization, as more and more benefits or forces of urbanization were identified.

Our early ancestors were hunters and nomads. They wandered about in response to the seasons, often with annual migrations. Gradually, they learned to harvest grains, berries, nuts, and other vegetation. With this shift to tilling the soil, they built permanent dwellings. Small villages developed as they banded together to share tools and benefit from mutual defense. Use of force to conquer and loot remained a way of life for many of the nomadic tribes.

Exchange, based on territorial specialization, soon became recognized as advantageous. Some areas had gold or silver to trade, others furs, others salt, others grain, and so forth. With trade, convenient transportation became advantageous. Settlements located in good harbors or on inland waterways tended to prosper most. Merchants found it more convenient to live near transport nodes, as did sailors. Inns or hotels and livery stables for traveling merchants prospered at these nodes. These strategic locations soon became important as military bases, particularly for the navy, and as political capitals. Specialization of labor, in manufacturing as well as in trade, soon developed, so productivity greatly increased. Individual skills increased as did the variety of manufactured products.

With modern modes of transportation (trains, automobiles, and airplanes) urban concentration soon became advantageous at other points. In addition, advances in technology increased the use of, and need for, raw materials like oil, copper, steel, coal, electricity, and rubber. Also, tractors replaced horses and oxen in agriculture, with a twofold benefit: tractors made greater productivity possible, and they didn't require part of the crop as feed. In turn, this meant that a smaller proportion of the population had to remain on the farm to grow food and fiber for those living in urban areas.

As a result of the above changes, the United States has gone from 5 percent urban in 1800 to 40 percent urban in 1900, to 64 percent urban in 1950, to about 75 percent urban currently. Urbanizing forces continue stronger than dispersal forces, but the rate of change is slowing.

A number of urban analysts have studied the above forces and broken them down into several elements. Professor Wallace F. Smith of the University of California lists six benefits or elements that make up the basis of urbanizing forces. In brief, these benefits are as follows:

1. Savings in costs of social interaction
2. Internal economies of scale to the firm
3. External economies of scale to the firm
4. Labor mobility or labor specialization
5. Greater consumer choice
6. Fostering of innovation[1]

SAVINGS IN COSTS OF SOCIAL INTERACTION. Most of us like social interaction, preferably on a face-to-face basis. The closer we live together, and the better the transportation technology, the lower the cost of this interaction. Thus, cars, streetcars, buses, and bicycles and the supporting road systems, en-

---

[1] *Urban Development,* (Berkeley: University of California Press, 1975). Chapter 2, pp. 21–47.

able us to see friends and relatives with a minimum of effort. In addition, we are able to join in more exchanges and get greater personal satisfaction by living close together in urban areas with good transportation facilities.

INTERNAL ECONOMIES OF SCALE. Using specialized labor and machinery producing large numbers of units of output for one firm reduces the cost per unit and is termed **internal economies of scale.** Lower costs per unit mean lower costs to users and consumers, and a larger market. Henry Ford capitalized on the idea of mass production or economies of scale in producing automobiles, for example. A firm, using this principle, must concentrate large numbers of people in one place, and urbanization results.

EXTERNAL ECONOMIES OF SCALE. Firms realize lower costs by locating in a larger community where adequate support services and supplies are readily available at reasonable costs. The term for such action is **external economies of scale.** For example, large inventories are maintained by suppliers with several local customers, meaning that each firm can buy on a hand-to-mouth basis. Also, subcontractors are nearby to take over small jobs. In addition, law firms, accounting firms, machinery-repair firms, and an adequate labor pool are readily available. Finally, users or consumers of the firm's product may be in the urban area, saving transportation costs on finished goods.

In *The Economy of Cities,* Jane Jacobs provides a vivid example of the importance of external economies of scale to a manufacturing effort.

The Rockefellers, early in the 1960's, decided to build a factory in India to produce plastic intrauterine loops for birth control. At the same time they were undertaking to combat the Indian birth rate, they also wanted to curb the migration of rural Indians to cities. A way to do this, they thought, was to set an example of village industry, placing new industry in small settlements instead of cities. The location they chose for the factory, then, was a small town named Etawah in highly rural Uttar state. It seemed plausible that the factory could as well be located one place in India as another. The machinery had to be imported anyway and the loops were to be exported throughout India. The factory was to be small, for with modern machinery even a small factory could begin by turning out 14,000 loops a day. The work had been rationalized into simple, easily taught tasks; no pre-existing, trained labor pool was required. The problem of hooking up to electric power had been explored and judged feasible. Capital was sufficient, and the scheme enjoyed the cooperation of the government of Uttar.

But as soon as the project was started everything went wrong, culminating in what the *New York Times* called "a fiasco." No single problem seems to have been horrendous. Instead, endless small difficulties arose: delays in getting the right tools, in repairing things that broke, in collecting work that had not been done to specifications, in sending off for a bit of missing material. Hooking up to the power did not go as smoothly as expected, and when it was accomplished the power was insufficient. Worse, the difficulties did not diminish as the work progressed. New ones cropped up. It became clear that—even in the increasingly doubtful event the plant could get into operation—keeping it in operating condition thereafter would probably be impractical. So after most of a year and considerable money had been wasted, Etawah was abandoned and a new site was chosen at Kanpur, a city of some 1,200,000 persons, the largest in Uttar, where industry and commerce had, by Indian standards, been growing rapidly. Space in two unused rooms in an electroplating plant was quickly found. The machinery was installed, the workers hired, and the plant was producing within six weeks. Kanpur possessed not only the space and the electric power, but also repairmen, tools, electricians, bits of needed material, and relatively swift and direct transportation service to other major Indian cities if what was required was not to be found in Kanpur.[2]

LABOR SPECIALIZATION. The larger an urban area, the greater is the feasibility of labor specialization. As individuals, we seek the work we are best at or that we get the greatest satisfaction out of. At the same time, businesses want those workers who give greatest productivity or lowest costs per unit of output. An electrical engineer or a machinist has far fewer opportunities to specialize in a small town than in a large metropolitan area. And in the event of a layoff, the chances of a specialist's finding a satisfactory job locally are much higher in a metropolitan area.

GREATER CONSUMER CHOICE. Economies of scale and labor specialization are limited by the size of the market. For example, unless the market can absorb one million cases of beer a day, it does little good to amass the facilities and people to produce one million cases of beer a day. But as a community grows larger, more and more firms find a market large enough for them to survive. Conversely, the greater the number of auto dealers, restaurants, law firms, schools, hardware stores, and shoe stores, the greater the choices available to citizens of a community.

FOSTERING INNOVATION. An innovator or investor generally finds it easier to find needed equipment and services in a larger metropolitan area. This makes it easier to translate creative ideas into reality, though a determined innovator might succeed anywhere. The availability of supplies and services for an innovator is essentially an extension of the idea of external economies of scale, labor specialization, and wider consumer choice. Fostering innovation may be a small force relative to some of the earlier components of urbanizing forces, yet it does exert influence in the same direction.

COSTS OF URBANIZATION. In fairness, some costs are also associated with urbanization. Urban life increases our exposure to contacts that are involuntary and often undesirable. Panhandlers, drug pushers, gamblers, and high-pressure sales people are all more likely to be encountered in metropolitan areas. We are also more tied into the "system" in urban areas. Thus, a strike of garbage handlers, of transportation workers, or of teachers is more likely in a city and tends to have a greater debilitating affect on us than it would in a rural area. In a similar vein, we are committed to a greater support of things we may not use or believe in. For example, we pay taxes to support municipal parks, schools, and hospitals even though we may not use them. Air and water pollution, con-

---

[2] *The Economy of Cities* (New York: Random House, 1969), pp. 183–84.

gestion, and costs of commuting tend to be higher in urban areas. Hence, these items decrease the quality of life in cities and act toward decentralization or dispersal. Finally, anonymity is sometimes considered a cost of urbanization, though many people consider it a benefit.

Functional Basis of Urban Areas

All cities or urban areas exist for a reason. It follows that the investor or analyst who understands the forces that brought his or her community into existence is in a much stronger position to judge its future. Thus, a brief look at the functional basis of cities seems warranted.

Cities, broadly speaking, may be classified as primary and secondary urban centers. A primary community is one that has its own economic base; that is, its existence is not dependent on the operations or well-being of other communities within the state or metropolitan region. A secondary community, on the other hand, is a satellite whose size and strength of orbit depends on the principal city to which it owes its existence. These satellite communities are better known as "bedroom" cities, where commuters (people who work where they would rather not live) reside. The economic strength of a satellite community is entirely dependent on the strength of the primary community, of which it is a part.

Primary communities may be divided into classes, which in a general sense reflect their cause of urbanization, as follows:

	Example
Industrial cities	Detroit, Pittsburgh
Commercial cities	Chicago, San Francisco
Mining cities	Scranton, Pennsylvania; Wheeling, West Virginia; Butte, Montana
Resort cities	Miami; Atlantic City; Scottsdale, Arizona
Political cities	Tallahassee, Florida; Washington, D.C.; Springfield, Illinois; Salem, Oregon
Educational cities	Chapel Hill, North Carolina; Ann Arbor, Michigan; Champaign-Urbana, Illinois; Corvallis, Oregon

Many communities have assumed a diverse economic base and may fall with nearly equal importance into two or more subclassifications. Thus New York City is industrial and commercial in character as well as a tourist Mecca. Miami, Florida, which started as a resort city, is presently one of the most important commercial centers in the South with one of the largest international airports in the country. New Orleans, which served as the fishing and commercial center of Louisiana, is important today as an international shipping center second only to New York in harbor facilities and shipping tonnage, as well as a fun city for tourists.

Urban Location

Land is a resource necessary for almost all social and economic activities. But the characteristics of land vary from place to place. Topography and soil characteristics are both important for urban development, although soil fertility is generally not important per se. Beyond these basic observations, what can we say about the location and growth patterns of cities?

Initially, defense considerations were important in the location of cities because invasion and conflict were common realities. Hence, Rome was founded on seven hills, Paris on an island, and London and Moscow in swamps. Walled cities were common in the Middle Ages.

As trade developed, those settlements with the greatest comparative advantage for transportation and communication between producers and their markets prospered most. The principle of **comparative advantage** is that communities benefit most by specializing in producing goods or services providing the greatest advantage relative to other communities.

Locations of greatest advantage for trade were as follows:

1. At points on oceans or lakes with the greatest convenience between the hinterland and markets, e.g., San Francisco, Seattle, and Chicago

2. At or near mouths of rivers, e.g., New York City, New Orleans, Philadelphia, and Portland, Oregon

3. At branches of rivers or near other inland water transportation, e.g., Pittsburgh, St. Louis, Cincinnati, Omaha, and Syracuse

4. At obstructions on the river requiring unloading and transshipment by another mode, e.g., St. Paul, Minnesota; and Albany, New York

5. At river crossings, e.g., Rockford, Illinois, and Harrisburg, Pennsylvania

6. At breaks in mountain chains, or where mountain meets plain or intersections of land trade routes, e.g., Denver, Salt Lake City, and Albuquerque, New Mexico

7. At points where modes of transportation require servicing, even temporary, e.g., Atlanta.

Note the importance of water transportation in the early development of the United States.

The emphasis in urban location and prosperity shifted to other factors with the coming of the industrial revolution. Comparative advantage continued to be important relative to these factors. The most significant factors were availability of raw materials, skilled labor, adequate power, and suitable climate. Nearness to market also tended to be important with weight-gaining or losing processes. Some examples seem appropriate.

1. *Raw materials*
    (a) Relative availability of coal and iron ore were important in the development of Pittsburgh; Birmingham, Alabama; and Gary, Indiana.

375

(b) Lumber mills are built near forests and at one time were prominent in the Midwest. Tacoma, Washington, and Eugene, Oregon are leading mill towns now. But faster second growth of timber is causing the industry to move to the southeast.

2. *Power:*   Fall River, Massachusetts; Minneapolis; and Spokane all owe much of their early growth to ready availability of low-cost water or hydroelectric power.

3. *Skilled labor:*   The auto industry is concentrated largely in Ohio and Michigan because of the huge reservoir of skilled labor in these areas. Likewise Seattle and Los Angeles have large reserves of skilled labor for airplane manufacture.

4. *Suitable climate:*   Tucson, Phoenix, San Diego, and Miami owe much of their growth to their pleasant climates. A general shift of economic activity to the Sun Belt is a current trend.

5. *Weight gain/loss:*   A manufacturing process involving considerable weight gain is best located near the market for the product because the manufacturer avoids paying transportation costs on the weight gain. Examples are soda pop, beer, and bread. Bulk, fragility, and perishability also increase market orientation. With considerable weight loss, the manufacturer avoids unnecessary transportation costs by processing nearer the raw materials. Examples are copper mining and processing and lumber manufacture. Some products, like grains, may be processed anywhere between producer and the market, because little weight is gained or lost.

Manufacturing and trade, as leading economic activities in our society, locate for the reasons mentioned. Political capitals and educational centers, while having some economies of scale, are best located to serve with maximum convenience to the citizens or students. Madison, Wisconsin; Albany, New York; and Austin, Texas are clear examples of well-located governmental/educational centers. Ann Arbor, Michigan; Champaign-Urbana, Illinois; and Gainesville, Florida owe their existence largely to the state universities located in each. Washington, D.C., is very definitely a governmental center and at one time was centrally located for all the states. Communities may also be founded as resort or health centers, as religious centers, or as military bases, with climate often a determining factor.

The Urbanizing Process

Most urban real estate is manmade space. This space is created in response to physical, social, economic, and political forces. People locate to maximize satisfactions; businesses locate to maximize profits. The space needs of people and businesses are negotiated in the real estate market, in what may best be described as the urbanizing process.

Initially, an urban area is raw land, which may or may not grow vegetation. Natural resources, such as oil, minerals, fertile soil, or abundant snow (for skiing), or advantageous location may provide reason for a settlement. A community develops based on the beliefs, laws, political and financial systems, and other institutional considerations of the citizens. Buildings and other improvements are added to the land, based on need or perceived demand. These improvements constitute the supply of urban real estate. Opportunities for businesses, employment, or pleasure create the demand. Credit is usually needed to help create the supply as well as to help buyers in financing acquired realty. As time moves on, people buy and sell the existing supply of real estate, and new space may be built. The combined activities of these buyers, sellers, and builders and others make up the real estate market. Their investment and development activity results in the cities we see today. And with each passing year, the existing supply of space tends to become more dominant relative to new space added during the year. New construction typically adds only 2 or 3 percent to a community's supply of space in any one year. The market tends to be more stable and predictable as a result. A sound knowledge of real estate markets is therefore important to our rational investor; therefore our next chapter focuses on real estate markets. However, we must complete our discussion of urban growth and change before taking up markets.

THEORIES OF URBAN GROWTH

Cities or urban areas are built by people and are not gifts of nature. They are established and grow in response to need. The place of origin may be by design or historical accident. But to fill a need, an area grows in spite of rugged topography and unfriendly climate. Problems of water supply, waste disposal, transport, and schools are overcome as the occasion demands. Are there any theories to explain the growth and change of urban areas? Yes, many theories have been proposed, of which three have considerable applicability to our cities. These theories are (1) **concentric circle**, (2) **direction of least resistance**, and (3) **multiple nuclei.**

Concentric Circle

In 1826, Johann Heinrich von Thunen, an owner of a German estate, wrote *Der Isalierte Staat* (*The Isolated State*) to explain the allocation of land to various land-use activities. Von Thunen began by assuming a walled city or village in the middle of a level, productive, and isolated field or plain. Climate, soils, topography, and transportation and other factors were all held constant or uniform so as not to influence or distort the analysis. Autos and railroads were not yet known, so goods to be moved had to be hauled by wagons, hand carried, or driven, in the case of livestock. Differences in land use could therefore be attributed entirely to differences in transportation costs or location. (See figure 17–1.)

Von Thunen identified five zones or concentric circles outside the village or central city. Zone 1, immediately outside the walls of the city, would be used primarily for growing vegetables, milk cattle, and egg-laying hens. These activities are intensive, involving many trips from the village, with the products often hand carried into the city. Forest-products production turned out to be the best

FIGURE 17–1
Concentric-Circle Allocation of Space in an Isolated State

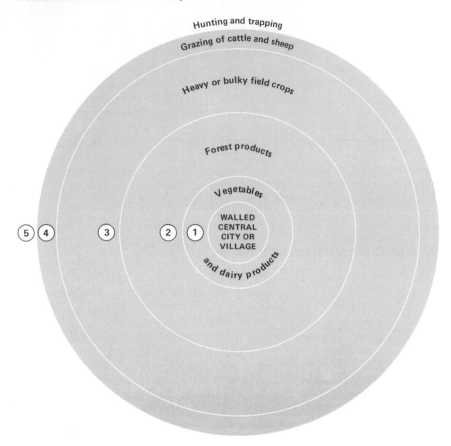

use for zone 2. Forest products are both bulky and heavy and were used for fuel and for construction in Von Thunen's day. Hence, production near the city saved time and energy.

Heavy or bulky field-crop production—potatoes, grain, hay—would be the main use in zone 3. Grazing of cattle and sheep was the appropriate use for zone 4, in that the livestock could be driven to zone 1 for slaughter or milking. The surrounding wilderness, zone 5, was appropriate for hunting and trapping.

Von Thunen's allocation of space was based on the net value of the product from the land after delivery in the city. Thus, both production and transportation costs were taken into account. Also, it was based entirely on the operation of an open market. Government control or intervention was not considered. Of course, it was a steady state rather than a dynamic society. And land-use conflicts were not considered.

In the 1920s, about a hundred years after Von Thunen, Ernest W. Burgess updated the concentric-circle theory to fit urban areas. According to Burgess, urban areas expand outward from the central business district of retail stores, office buildings, and factories. The next area was a zone of transaction containing low-income people and light-manufacturing plants. Zone 3 housed workers for zones 1 and 2. High-income residences were in zone 4. Zone 5 consisted of suburbs or semirural-type properties. At the time Burgess was writing, planning and zoning were still relatively unknown.

Direction of Least Resistance

Richard M. Hurd, a mortgage banker, compiled information on the expansion and growth of more than fifty American cities. In 1903, Hurd wrote that cities grow in the direction of least resistance or greatest attraction, or their resultants. He continues:

The point of contact differs according to the methods of transportation, whether by water, by turnpike or by railroad. The forces of attraction and resistance include topography, the underlying material on which city builders work; external influences, projected into the city by trade routes; internal influences derived from located utilities, and finally the reactions and readjustments due to the continual harmonizing of conflicting elements. The influence of topography, all-powerful when cities start, is constantly modified by human labor, hills being cut down, waterfronts extended, and swamps, creeks and low-lands filled in, this, however, not taking place until the new building sites are worth more than the cost of filling and cutting. The measure of resistance to the city's growth is here changed from terms of land elevation or depression, and hence income cost, to terms of investment or capital cost. The most direct results of topography come from its control of transportation, the water fronts locating exchange points for water commerce, and the water grade normally determining the location of the railroads entering the city.

Growth in cities consists of movement away from the point of origin in all directions, except as topographically hindered, this movement being due both to aggregation at the edges and pressure from the centre. Central growth takes place both from the heart of the city and from each subcentre of attraction, and axial growth pushes into the outlying territory by means of railroads, turnpikes and street railroads. All cities are built up from these two influences, which vary in quantity, intensity and quality, the resulting districts overlapping, interpenetrating, neutralizing and harmonizing as the pressure of the city's growth brings them in contact with each other. The fact of vital interest is that, despite confusion from the intermingling of utilities, the order of dependence of each definite district on the other is always the same. Residences are early driven to the circumference, while business remains at the centre, and as residences divide into various social grades, retail shops of corresponding grades follow them, and wholesale shops in turn follow the retailers, while institutions and various mixed utilities irregularly fill in the intermediate zone, and the banking and office section remains at the main business centre. Complicating this broad outward movement of zones, axes of traffic project shops through residence areas, create business subcentres, where they intersect, and change circular cities into star-shaped cities. Central growth, due to proximity, and axial growth, due to accessibility, are summed up in the static power of established sections and the dynamic power of their chief lines of intercommunication.[3]

Considerable research and writing have been done since Hurd made his statement. Yet, no simpler, clearer, or comprehensive statement about urban-growth dynamics has since been made. Also, direction of least resistance is an extension or modification of the concentric-circle theory. Concentric-circle theory assumes no barriers to growth; direction of least resistance does.

Multiple Nuclei

In the 1930s, Homer Hoyt developed the sector theory, based on wedge-shaped neighborhoods surrounding the central business district. New, high-income residential areas were seen as developing along highways and next to other fast-transportation facilities. In this sense, the theory is not too different from the route, or axial, theory, which says that an urban area tends to grow along its lines of transportation, owing to the economic advantage of convenience, such as easy, low-cost movement. Both theories tend to be a restatement of Hurd's line-of-least-resistance theory, and the power of these theories to explain urban growth and change, over and above Hurd's theory, seems limited.

Frederick Babcock, an appraiser studying urban growth and change in the 1930s, characterized urban areas as *sliding, jumping,* and *bursting* in their growth.[4] One district expands by gradually encroaching or moving into neighboring districts in a sliding manner. *Jumping* means that a district will sometimes leap over a barrier, such as another well-established district, in its expansion. Thus, an expanding business district will jump a river, a civic center, or a university. *Bursting* means the scatteration of a district to several new subdistricts. Thus, the pre-World War II central business districts of large metropolitan areas burst, and the suburban shopping center resulted. In like fashion, manufacturing areas scattered from the central city to the suburbs, taking the form of industrial parks and districts.

Ullman and Harris advanced the idea of multiple nuclei, or clusters of development, in 1945.[5] Essentially, this theory is an extension of Babcock's bursting explanation, with economic and social considerations taken into account as well as physical. It is also an extension of the ideas that cities are functional areas. Four reasons suggested by Harris and Ullman for the development of clusters or nuclei are

1. Some activities require specialized facilities.
2. Like activities tend to group together because they mutually benefit from cohesion.

---

[3] *Principles of City Land Values* (New York: The Record and Guide, 1903, 1924), pp. 13–15.

[4] *The Valuation of Real Estate* (New York: McGraw-Hill, 1932), p. 59.

[5] Chauncey D. Harms and Edward L. Ullman, "The Nature of Cities," in *Building the Future City, Annals of the American Academy of Political and Social Sciences,* November 1945, pp. 7–17.

3.   Unlike activities sometimes are adverse or detrimental to each other.

4.   Some activities can afford the high rents of the most desirable sites, others cannot and must take less desirable sites.

The multiple-nuclei theory of land-use arrangements is based strongly on the rent-paying ability of the various uses. The use able to pay the highest rent gets the most desirable site for its purposes. The worth of a specific site or location depends on transportation and communication possibilities and the surrounding environment. Thus, business and industrial centers developed outside the central business district. Currently, these nuclei take the form of shopping centers, industrial parks, convention centers (often near major airports), and resort communities.

It should be noted that major changes occurred in transport as these theories developed. Until about 1900, trains, street cars, and buggies or wagons were the main modes of transport. The automobile gave everyone greater flexibility and faster movement. It seems unlikely that central cities would have declined so sharply in the absence of widespread use of cars. But with increasing costs of energy, central cities seem to be getting new life. Figure 17–2 is a generalized illustration of how modern urban areas are made up of multiple nuclei or functional areas. The emphasis, as with the concentric-circle and direction-of-least-resistance theories, is on keeping costs of movement of people and goods to a minimum.

RENT THEORY
AND URBAN STRUCTURE

Urban-growth theory may be restated as rent theory, to reflect the many decisions by individual owners about the use of their properties. In fact, it is the decisions by the individual owner-investors that make up urban-growth theory. Also, rent theory, or value theory, is the means by which local economic activity is related to real estate. The key for rent theory is maximization of self-interest, usually in monetary terms. Note that we are *not* talking of maximizing revenues. And we are not talking of minimizing costs. Maximizing self-interest means maximizing net profits, rents, satisfaction or benefits, or, in some cases, minimization of net losses. In the immediate context, we are talking of maximizing net rents to land.

We begin our discussion of rent theory by looking at the allocation of space in a large hotel. We move then to space allocation in rural areas, followed by a longer look at land-use allocation in urban areas. We continue by discussing hills, rivers, and limited travel time, to show how these constraints affect urban form and structure. Finally, a general statement of rent theory is presented.

Space Allocation in a Large Hotel

Which of all the uses in a large hotel gets its choice of location? Remember that owners and operators of hotels are rational and want to maximize the profitability and the value of the space under their control. In effect, once the

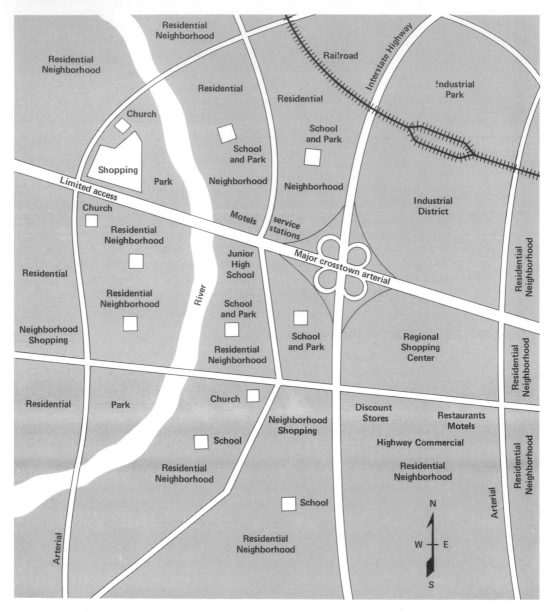

hotel use has been decided on and approval obtained, there are few limits on the use of space within the structure.

In most tall structures, the premium location is the top floor, followed by space at the street level. Brief reflection or observation shows that a bar or cocktail lounge is usually found in both these locations. Very large hotels often have four or five bars in the most accessible or desirable locations. Restaurants follow closely behind bars in this respect. From experience, owners know that these two uses are most profitable and able to pay the highest rents.

Other common uses in slightly less-advantageous locations are typically barber and beauty shops, drug stores, liquor stores, and newsstands. High-fashion clothing stores may also be included here. The second-to-fourth floors are often devoted to ballrooms, meeting rooms, swimming pools, and health facilities. Auto parking is typically below ground or on the back side of the building away from the main thoroughfare. Guest rooms then occupy the space from about the fifth floor to just under the top floor. One must look carefully to find the lobby and registration desk in our newer hotels. The owner knows that guests will come to the hotel and will not be turned away by a slight delay in finding the registration desk.

The above hierarchy of uses is illustrated by rent triangles in figure 17–3.

FIGURE 17–3
Hierarchy of Space Uses in a Large Hotel Based on Profitability or Rent-Paying Ability

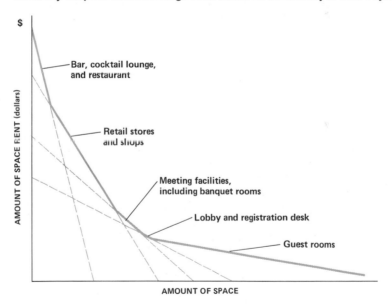

A **rent triangle** is a schedule showing the amount of rent a use or business activity can pay as an increasing amount of space is devoted to the use. Thus, the cocktail bar in the Top of the Mark in the Mark Hopkins Hotel in San Francisco may be able to pay a rent of $1,000 per square foot each year. But as more space is allocated to serving liquor (more bars and restaurants are opened in the building), the rent paying-ability per square foot decreases. At some point, other uses—drug stores, news stands, guest rooms—offer a higher rate of return and therefore command the space. Each type of use has its own triangle or schedule of payments it can afford. That use paying the highest rent gets its choice of space.

An important exception to the hierarchy described above occurs in areas allowing gambling. The exception reinforces rent theory as a basis for space allocation. In Las Vegas, hotels devote much of their prime space at street level to slot machines and other gaming activities. This space is the most easily accessible to potential gamblers.

Rural Land Allocation

Fertile land in an area with a friendly climate is more productive than land not so well endowed. That is, more bushels of corn, soybeans, wheat, and so on, may be grown per acre on the more productive land for a given amount of effort. In turn, each acre of the most productive land is more profitable and more valuable than less productive lands, assuming markets are available to use the crops grown.

An owner-operator of the more favorably endowed land, in self-interest, would use it to produce that crop giving the highest return per acre. A tenant-operator would also grow the crop or product giving the highest return. And an owner-landlord would charge a rent based on the profitability of the crop giving the highest returns per acre. Thus, self-interest pushes the use of land to that use giving the greatest return or value, or the highest and best use. In the Midwest, known for its productive lands, owners concentrate on growing corn and soybeans. The two crops reinforce each other in maintaining soil productivity and are about equally profitable. Moving West, the lands of Kansas and the Dakotas get less rain and are farther from the markets of the East. These areas concentrate on growing wheat rather than corn or soybean. Grazing cattle and sheep is the most common use of lands in the drier areas of our Western states. Alternatively, rugged or inaccessible lands with abundant rainfall, as in the Southeast and the Northwest, are devoted to growing timber. Thus, we have lumber and wood-products companies named Georgia-Pacific and Boise-Cascade. Finally, some lands (swamps, mountain tops, and deserts) yield no profit to human efforts and remain in their natural state. Lands yielding no margin of profit to an owner-operator are termed **submarginal.** Figure 17–4 depicts broad uses of land in the United States.

There are exceptions to the above generalizations. Almost every state has some land better suited to growing vegetables than to field crops, because of the nearness of markets. Also, climate in California, Hawaii, and Florida favors the growing of oranges, grapefruit, pineapple, grapes, nuts, and produce over corn, wheat, or soybeans.

Space Allocation in an Urban Area

What land uses pay the highest rent or give the highest value to sites in urban areas? Location theory says that the most accessible site is likely to be most productive or profitable. And unless rivers or hills intervene, the most cen-

FIGURE 17–4
Allocation of Land to Alternative Rural Uses Based on Profitability or Rent-Paying Ability

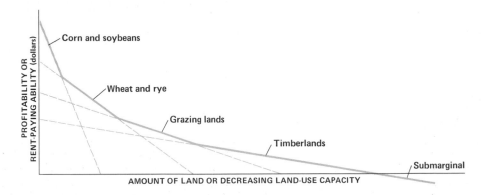

tral location is the most accessible in an urban area. And what uses dominate in our central business districts?

Early in this century, large department stores and other retail outlets occupied the prime sites in our major cities. Office buildings, hotels, apartment buildings, and manufacturing plants were usually located nearby. Moving out from the central city, one-family homes became a dominant land use. Individual commercial and industrial districts sometimes developed along major arteries as wedges or sectors. Lot sizes increased as the edge of the city blended into the countryside. That hierarchy of land uses is diagrammed in figure 17–5.

With wide use of autos and trucks, industry moved to the suburbs after World War II. People and residential neighborhoods followed, pulling commercial districts with them. Satellite villages were often engulfed by the rapid urban expansion. Industrial parks, shopping centers, recreation centers and residential neighborhoods combined to make up the community fabric. The land-use structure became a pattern of more or less distinct functional neighborhoods or districts superimposed on a network of streets and highways. The value pattern that developed is shown, in cross section, in figure 17–6. Thus, land-use patterns took on a structure that tended to minimize the costs of moving people and goods in the area and which is best described by the multiple-nuclei concept, discussed earlier. Space was being allocated to uses on rent-paying ability.

Rivers, lakes, marshes, and hills all act as barriers to the "normal" expansion of urban areas. In accordance with Hurd's direction-of-least-resistance principle, expansion takes place in directions away from these barriers because the cost is less relative to the benefits realized. However, with time and growth, the time costs of travel to the urban fringe in other directions steadily increase. At some point it becomes feasible to incur the costs to bridge rivers and lakes, to fill in marshes, and to expand into hilly areas. The Golden Gate Bridge of San Francisco, the Lake Pontchartrain Bridge near New Orleans, and the recent filling in of the tidal marshes near Newark, New Jersey, for industrial devel-

385

FIGURE 17–5
Hierarchy of Urban Land Uses Based on Profitability or Rent-Paying Ability

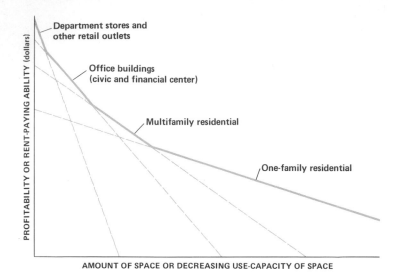

FIGURE 17–6
Schematic Cross-section of Land Uses and Their Rent-Paying Ability in a Large Metropolitan Area

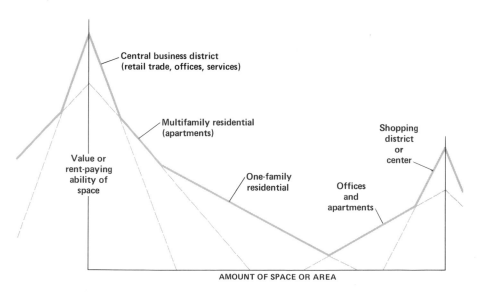

opment are examples of "delayed" development outward from an urban center.

Existing realty improvements tend to lag behind social and economic needs of a community. That is, several one-family houses or a church may be moved or torn down to make way for a discount store. Likewise, the existing urban infrastructure may retard or constrain urban adjustment. **Urban infrastructure** is the basic installations and facilities of a community, such as schools, sewer and water systems, power and communications systems, and transportation systems, including streets, freeways, and subways. In either of these two situations, additional costs must be incurred for the immediate site or area to be used more intensely. At some point, the potential benefits may justify the additional costs.

Rent Theory Restated

Let us now summarize our discussion and restate rent theory as an explanation of urban growth and change. With this restatement, we should be able to better understand urban growth and change as a process.

First, land-use activities tend to locate at the point of greatest comparative advantage. If the site or location is not owned, it must be bought or rented. Land-use competition is based on rent-paying ability. Over a period of time, those uses able to pay the highest rents or prices get the most choice locations. In addition, a hierarchy of land uses develops. Department stores, office buildings, and apartment buildings therefore tend to get the choice or central urban sites. Moving out from the center, the hierarchy goes to one-family residences to field crops to grazing and forestry to submarginal deserts and mountaintops. Subcenters of value, for example, shopping centers and industrial parks, intervene into urban areas as businessmen and other citizens strive to minimize transportation costs relative to benefits received in accepting a location.

At any given time, an urban area may be expanding or contracting. Most of our experience is with growth and expansion. Growth usually begins with an expansion of the economic base of the community. An urban area may grow outward or upward.

Outward expansion, such as the urbanization and development of new lands, is growth at the extensive margin. The **extensive margin** is that point at which rents or values make it just barely financially feasible to convert land to urban uses and to add urban improvements. The extensive margin is symbolized by land subdivision and development at the urban fringe. The building of bridges and roads and the filling in of marshes are also activities associated with the extensive margin.

Urban areas also expand upward or at the intensive margin. The **intensive margin** is that point at which rents or values make it just barely financially feasible to use urban land more intensely with the addition of more capital and labor. Replacing old houses with a discount store is an example. Alternatively, converting an old factory or cannery into a shopping center is another.

Note that intensity of use and rent are related but not identical concepts. **Rent** is the payment for the use of land, in an economic sense, and in the sense

FIGURE 17–7
Intensive and Extensive Margins of Urban Land Uses

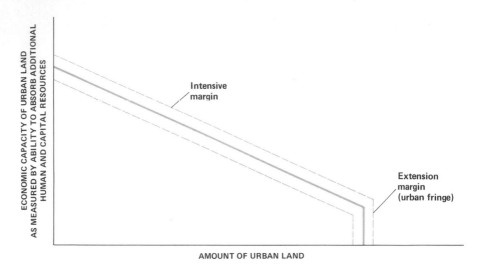

used here. Rent is also the payment for the use of realty, in its more general meaning. **Intensity of use** refers to the relative amount of human and capital resources added in the use of land. Generally, the higher the value of a site, the higher its rent and the greater its intensity of use. Intensity of use, rent, and value are all closely related to highest and best uses of land.

Intensity of use is the key to understanding why urban areas may grow upward as well as outward. Land, urban or rural, is not productive in and of itself. Corn, wheat, office space, or residential units all require labor, capital, and management in addition to land. These factors of production (land, labor, capital, and management) must be combined according to the principle of proportionality for each factor to get its greatest return. The **principle of proportionality** is that real estate reaches its maximum productivity, or highest and best use, when the factors of production are in balance with one another. This is also known as the principle of balance, the principle of variable proportions, or the principle of increasing and decreasing returns. The ability of a site to absorb additional human and capital resources, under the principle of proportionality, is the **economic capacity** of land.

Stated another way, the factors of production must be used in optimum balance to achieve the highest and best use of realty. How is the optimum determined? In the construction or modification of a property, expenditures should be made for those items adding the most to value, as judged by the market. Thus, $2,000 might be used for a fireplace, a third bathroom, or a patio.

388

	Fireplace	3rd Bathroom	Patio
Marginal contribution to market value of property	$4,000	$2,500	$3,000

Adding the fireplace gives $2.00 of market value for every dollar expended and the patio gives $1.50 of market value while the third bathroom gives only $1.25 of market value. Clearly, the addition of a fireplace is a better choice. And if another $2,000 is available, the addition of the patio would be a second choice with its $1.50 return for every dollar invested.

Obviously, the more money that is spent on improvements to the land, the more intensely the land is used. Intense development of land requires high rents, to be justified. Thus, land must have high value or high economic capacity to warrant intense development. Urban uses are generally much more intense than rural uses. And urban land values are generally higher than rural land values. The highest and best use of a site is reached when no further value can be gained by the addition of resources. And in fact, the value may be decreased with more additions, in accordance with the principle of increasing and decreasing returns. At the urban fringe or extensive margin, this point means that conversion of additional rural land to urban uses is just barely financially or economically feasible. That is, a developer would earn either no profit at all or only a minimally acceptable one after paying costs of subdividing and construction. At the intensive margin, this point means that an owner of a developed property adding resources (to rehabilitate or convert to another use) realizes no value advantage or only a small increment of value in excess of costs incurred. In either case, any lower returns would result in a decision not to develop the land or rehabilitate the property.

We are now ready to look at the dynamics and value-creating characteristics of residential, commercial, and industrial neighborhoods. That is, we need to look at specific characteristics of these districts to identify where properties in them might be, relative to the intensive and extensive margins of urban areas.

DYNAMICS OF RESIDENTIAL NEIGHBORHOODS

Residential neighborhoods change constantly in terms of physical, social, economic, locational, and public-service characteristics. And property values in the neighborhood go up, remain stable, or go down as a result of these changes. Therefore, in predicting value changes of a neighborhood, many judgments must be made. Categories of key characteristics to be considered are (1) physical, (2) social, (3) economic, and (4) public service. The stages of neighborhood change are shown graphically in figure 17–8.

Decisions by owners, lenders, investors, school boards, real estate brokers, public-utility districts, and others affect these variables or characteristics. Kenneth Boulding, a renowned economist, said:

FIGURE 17–8
Stages of Neighborhood Change

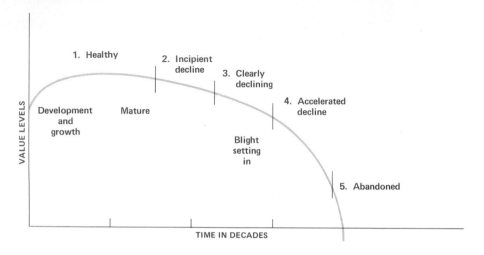

The world moves into the future as a result of decisions, not as a result of plans. Plans are significant only insofar as they affect decisions. Planning may be defined in such a way that it is part of the decision-making process; but if it is not, it is a bag of wind, a piece of paper, or a worthless diagram.

Stages and events of neighborhood change are described here so the reader may better know and understand what to look for in analyzing residential neighborhoods. These stages and events are identified in a HUD report, *The Dynamics of Neighborhood Change*. (See figure 17–9.) Major concerns in this discussion are (1) stages of neighborhood change, (2) value dynamics, and (3) decisions underlying neighborhood change.

Determining a neighborhood *age-cycle* position is an important first step in valuing residential properties. All neighborhoods have a beginning, and most go through stages that reflect changes in their physical, social, and economic makeup. These stages are

1. Healthy
2. Incipient or pending decline
3. Clearly declining
4. Accelerated decline
5. Abandoned

Efforts by neighborhood residents and local governments may stop and actually reverse progression through these stages. Examples are the Georgetown district in Washington, D.C., and Old Town in Chicago. Basic decisions by residents and others, and value changes, accompany each stage.

Stage 1: Healthy

Buildings in a healthy neighborhood are usually harmonious to each other and in sound condition, reflecting good maintenance. The buildings may be mostly one-family residences or mostly apartment houses. Property values are stable or rising at a pace consistent with the income of residents. The residents in turn are generally homogeneous or similar in race, income, social status, education, and jobs. A neighborhood may be healthy in the developing stage as well as in the mature stage. A healthy neighborhood enjoys good location, social cohesiveness, and good reputation as a pleasant and safe place to live.

The attitudes of various citizens toward a healthy neighborhood are positive. Owners are conscientious in maintaining properties. Real estate brokers generally show the properties only to clients with characteristics similar to those of the residents. Home insurance and financing are readily available at reasonable terms. Public services are sufficient, efficient, and suited to the needs of the neighborhood; and schools are in good condition and well regarded. Finally, the economic activity on which the residents depend is stable, so that fluctuations in employment and income are not likely to adversely affect the neighborhood.

Stage 2: Incipient Decline

A primary characteristic of a neighborhood in the incipient-decline stage is its aging housing stock that shows signs of wear and physical deterioration. Functional obsolescence appears. Maintenance costs go up. In areas dominated by apartments, investor-owners become aware of the changed conditions and of the likelihood of reduced profits and lower values.

As a neighborhood ages, residents who leave are increasingly replaced by people of lower income levels, educational attainment, and social status. Sometimes the new residents are racially or ethnically different from the former residents as well. The change may be barely noticeable at first but becomes general knowledge after a while. In effect, the neighborhood is rejected by households similar to those that had made up its population.

Real estate brokers are probably the first to recognize a change in a neighborhood's appeal. They may steer clients similar to the former residents away from the neighborhood. Some brokers may even begin blockbusting to realize quick large profits. Lenders may become reluctant to make mortgages or home improvement loans to residents. Insurance companies may raise their rates.

More general factors and events also sometimes affect a neighborhood's relative appeal. Its locational advantage may be reduced by new roads or freeways or by new shopping facilities. New housing construction may reduce the competitive position of the old neighborhood. Rapidly rising incomes may stimulate families to relocate to upgrade their housing. Or reduced job opportunities may force residents to relocate to obtain employment. Finally, home values and rents may decline, or at least not rise. Some houses may even be converted into neighborhood businesses. At this point, the neighborhood may be entering the clearly declining stage.

FIGURE 17–9
Stages in the Neighborhood Life Cycle

1. Healthy	2. Incipient Decline	3. Clearly Declining	4. Accelerated Decline	5. Abandoned
PHYSICAL	PHYSICAL	PHYSICAL	PHYSICAL	PHYSICAL
Good Property Upkeep	Spot Maintenance Neglect	General Minor, Many Major Deficiencies	Major Deficiencies, Deterioration Prevalent	Severe Dilapidation
Sound Structural Condition	Aging Housing Stock	Larger Capital Improvements Needed	Old Buildings Predominate	Adjacent Abandoned Buildings
Homogeneous Housing Type	Some New Nonresidential Uses	Higher Density Leads to Visible Wear	Increasing Vandalized Property	Voluntary/Involuntary Demolition
Good Location	Less Desirable Location	Relatively Poor Location	Undesirable Location	Noise, Abandoned Cars
Neighborhood Well Maintained	SOCIAL	Visible Deterioration in Public Areas	Incompatible Land Uses Allowed	Vacant Littered Lots
SOCIAL	Decline in Social Status	Commercial Vacancies	Increasing Residential Vacancies	General Area Decay
Middle to High Social Status	Declining Household Income	SOCIAL	Some Abandonment	Widespread Abandonment
Moderate-to-Upper-Income Levels	Influx of Middle-Income Minorities	Major Decline in Social Status	SOCIAL	SOCIAL
Ethnic Homogeneity	Decline in Education Level	Lower Incomes, More Welfare Households	Low Social Status	Lowest Social Status
High School Graduates and Above	Smaller Families (Widowed, Elderly)	Decrease in White In-Movers	Predominantly Low Income/Minority Tenants	Poverty Level Incomes
Family Oriented or Childless Adults	More Semiskilled, Underemployed	Large Families, Often Female Headed	Elderly Ethnics	Squatter Population
White Collar and/or Skilled Blue Collar Workers	Often Fear of Racial Transition	Increasing Unskilled Workers and Unemployed	Increasing Multiproblem Families	Multiproblem Welfare Families Prevalent
Pride in Neighborhood and House	Decline in Neighborhood Reputation	Lack of Social Cohesion	Mostly Unskilled Workers: High Unemployment	Bad Neighborhood Reputation
Good Neighborhood Reputation	ECONOMIC	Fair to Poor Neighborhood Reputation	Poor Tenant-Landlord Relations	Households With Options Leave
Neighborhood Perceived as Safe	Some Cutback in Maintenance	Lack of Pride in House and Neighborhood	Poor Neighborhood Reputation	Fear, Apathy
Socially Cohesive	No Rise, Some Decline in Property Values	Increasing Fear for Safety	Absolute Decline in Population	High Crime and Fire Incidence
	Increasing Insurance Costs		Fear for Personal Safety	ECONOMIC
				Collapsed Rental Market
				Serious Rent Collection Problems
				Negative cashflows

FIGURE 17–9 (cont.)

1. Healthy	2. Incipient Decline	3. Clearly Declining	4. Accelerated Decline	5. Abandoned
ECONOMIC High Owner Investment Good Property Values Insurance Available Conventional Financing Available High Confidence in Future Value PUBLIC SERVICES Services Efficient and Appropriate Some Reliance or Private Services	ECONOMIC Some Difficulty in Getting Financing Waning Confidence in Future Value Property Tax Burden Increases More Renters, in Single-Family Areas PUBLIC SERVICES Mismatch Between Needs and Service Provision	SOCIAL More Minority Children in Schools ECONOMIC Further Cutback on Maintenance and Repairs Definite Decline in Property Values Insurance Prohibitive Serious Problems in Getting Financing Fear for Future Value of Investment Predominantly Renters Revenue at Breakeven Point Increasing Operating Costs Small Scale Investor Owners PUBLIC SERVICES Perceived Decline in Service Responsiveness Increasing Dependence on Public/Social Services	SOCIAL Predominantly Minority Children in Schools Increasing Fire and Crime ECONOMIC Almost No Maintenance or Repairs Lack of Buyers Insurance Denied Costly Noninstitutional Financing Only Extreme Pessimism Toward Present and Future Frequent Overassessment Increasing Cashflow Problems Skyrocketing Operating Costs High Proportion of Absentee Owners PUBLIC SERVICES Absolute Decline in Services	PUBLIC SERVICES Inadequate, Unresponsive to Need

Source: *The Dynamics of Neighborhood Change* (Washington, D.C.: Office of Policy Development and Change, U.S. Department of Housing and Urban Development, 1976).

Stage 3: Clearly Declining

As a neighborhood enters the clearly declining stage, many owners convert one-family houses into several small apartments or business places. Owners also tend to reduce maintenance in accordance with the lower rent levels. Wear and tear of the houses increases with the greater intensity of use. More physical deficiencies become apparent.

The residents of a clearly declining neighborhood have ever-lower incomes. Many may be unemployed. Social status and education levels may also be declining. Financial institutions may refuse to make loans to residents. Insurance companies may refuse coverage. Public agencies may place welfare recipients and sponsor low-income housing in the neighborhood. Continued shifts in commercial facilities, employment opportunities, and transportation facilities reinforce the decline.

The net result of a neighborhood's being in a clearly declining stage is an undesirable location, a fair-to-poor reputation, and lower property values. Toward the latter part of the clearly declining stage, the incidence of crime and fire increases, and commercial buildings are frequently obsolete and vacant.

Stage 4: Accelerating Decline

In an accelerating-decline neighborhood, buildings are old, crowded, and poorly maintained, and have major deficiencies. Most residents are tenants, meaning much absentee ownership. Some properties have been vandalized. Operating and maintenance costs are extremely high relative to the low-rent levels. Consequently, investor owners "milk" the properties, making only utility and mortgage payments. Incompatible land uses often appear, while many houses and apartments are vacant. Services are inadequate, particularly garbage pickup, street cleaning, and security.

The only people moving into the neighborhood are welfare recipients, the poor, and the unskilled. Many residents have behavioral problems, including drug addiction. Residents fear for personal safety. Lenders increasingly grant mortgage extensions and delays to avoid foreclosures. For all practical purposes, conditions in the neighborhood are so bad that the neighborhood can no longer be saved, even with considerable public assistance.

Stage 5: Abandoned

Squatters, transients, and people in the lowest rung of the social ladder are the only residents of an abandoned neighborhood. These few residents are marked by futility, apathy, and fear. They refuse to pay rent, and most owners no longer make mortgage or utility payments. Crime, fires, and abandoned cars are common. City services are totally lacking or inadequate, with garbage and trash piled everywhere.

Buildings are severely dilapidated and often entirely abandoned. Vacant, littered lots are common as a result of demolitions. Over all, the area is completely decayed and has a bad reputation. The neighborhood is almost of no value to anyone. If it is located in a community that is growing and prospering, the neighborhood is likely to be cleared eventually and turned to a different use, possibly a commercial center or an office building.

Summary Conclusions About Stages of Change

Figure 17–8 shows graphically the five stages of neighborhood change. The figure clearly shows that change is a process and not a series of unrelated events. The growth-and-development period varies, but fifteen to twenty years is considered typical. Peak values are reached during the period of maturity when improvement shows to their best advantage. A neighborhood is likely to appear healthy and mature for twenty to twenty-five years; some overlap with the development stage may be included here. Unless checked, the process moves through the three declining stages in a matter of a decade or two. The abandonment stage lasts until circumstances or outside forces cause a clearing or rehabilitation of the area.

VALUE ANALYSIS
OF COMMERCIAL DISTRICTS

Analyzing commercial districts is a more complex undertaking than analyzing residential neighborhoods. Commercial districts are usually more diverse and unique in their makeup. In addition, there are far fewer commercial properties, thus far less background and experience is available concerning their appraisal. The discussion here is intended only to provide basic insights into, or guidelines for, analyzing commercial districts and shopping centers. That is, considerably more background than provided here is needed to do an adequate job of analyzing commercial districts and properties.

Key considerations in analyzing commercial districts are as follows:

1. Location—accessibility and environment
2. Physical characteristics, including parking adequacy
3. Architecture
4. Mix of activities

Location

The location of commercial districts, as with residential neighborhoods, divides into accessibility and environment. The inward orientation of location for commercial districts is particularly important. That is, easy access for customers to a commercial district is critical to its success. The lower the costs of travel (out-of-pocket expenses, time required to travel, and aggravation involved in travel) for customers in moving to the district, therefore, the better is the relative location of the district. Shoppers continue to depend on the auto for mobility, despite the energy shortage. Therefore, the easier and safer the roads leading to and from the district are, the better is the location. Traffic congestion, if heavy and persistent, is of course a negative locational factor.

Location near a cloverleaf of a limited-access highway is almost always considered desirable. Likewise, location near the intersection of two arterials means easy accessibility. A downtown or central business district is especially advantaged if easily reached by bus and mass transit as well as by auto. In that commercial districts, other than the downtown, are not usually centrally located, they are not likely to enjoy the convergence of bus, mass transit, and auto. Even so, service by bus and/or mass transit is desirable to a district's accessibility.

In terms of environment, the desirability of a district is improved if it is oriented to a pleasing physical feature, such as a river, lake, or mountain. Also, being located near upper-income residential neighborhoods is generally considered a plus. On the other hand, being located in a blighted area or being subject to heavy and persistent air pollution or other adverse influences detracts from a district's location for value purposes. Finally, vacant land near a commercial district or shopping center may provide opportunity for competing activities, such as discount stores and drive-ins, to draw off or intercept business from the district.

Physical Characteristics

A commercial district should be large enough to provide all the activities needed by customers in its tributary or drawing area without undue crowding. Movement from one store or service outlet to another should be easy and natural. In addition, the size should be large enough to provide adequate parking for all customers or clientele as well as for employees. Five to six parking spaces per thousand square feet of gross sales area is considered acceptable.

Level terrain is desirable for a commercial district. Uneven terrain makes movement by people and cars awkward and difficult, particularly when there is snow and ice. In addition, it is costly and difficult to make building fronts conform to sloping sidewalks and streets. The soil or ground should be stable, not marshy or subject to shifting.

Needless to say, public services are vital to the operation of a commercial district. Lack of, or inadequacy of, water, electricity, telephone sevice, sanitary sewer, or storm sewer would seriously hamper a commercial center's activity.

Architecture

Most shopping centers, having been developed under one owner with the aid of an architect, are pleasing and harmonious in appearance. However, other commercial districts have usually developed over a period of time with diverse ownership and architecture. Through cooperation, merchants in a district have sometimes been able to bring a variety of building designs into reasonable harmony. That has been particularly true in central business districts, redeveloped into malls, under urban renewal. In addition, through traffic has been eliminated from downtowns under redevelopment programs, reducing congestion. The result is business districts that are competitive with shopping centers in appearance as well as in economic activity. It is increasingly apparent that shoppers take appearance into account in choosing where to do business.

Activities Mix

The number and variety of activities in a commercial district are important to its success. That is, the principle of balance applies to the proper makeup of activities in a commercial district. The kind and number depends, among other things, on community custom, climate, and general characteristics of the clientele. Figure 17–10 shows approximate personal consumption expenditures, by product, since 1970.

FIGURE 17–10
Personal Consumption Expenditures: By Product or Service

Class of Expenditure (nature of item purchased)	Percent of Income Spent for Each Category*
Food, beverages, and tobacco	22.5
Clothing, accessories and jewelry	8.5
Personal care	1.5
Housing	15.5
Household operations	14.5
Medical care	8.5
Personal business	5.0
Transportation	13.5
Recreation	7.0
Other	3.5
TOTAL	100.0

* Percentages rounded by authors
Source: *The Statistical Abstract of the United States,* 1976, table 635

The list is highly generalized, of course. In order to provide more specific guidelines for the makeup of a commercial district, we show in figure 17–11 tenant classifications generally found in neighborhood, community, and regional centers. The relationship isn't exact, but it is expected that commercial districts would have a comparable tenant mix, depending on their size.

The centers are classified as follows. A **neighborhood center** provides "convenience goods" (food, drugs, hardware) for daily living needs. A supermarket is the principal tenant. The site may cover from 5 to 15 acres; and a trade area of one to two thousand families is served. A **community center** ranges from 10 to 30 acres in area, serves from five to ten thousand families, and is usually anchored by a variety of junior department stores. A community center provides a limited line of shopping goods, such as apparel and furniture, in

FIGURE 17–11
Shopping Center Composition (Percent) by Tenant Classification Group

Tenant Group	SIZE OF CENTER		
	Neighborhood	Community	Regional
Food	13.0	10.4	9.5
Food service	10.4	8.5	9.3
General merchandise	5.5	9.9	9.5
Clothing and shoes	8.0	9.6	9.3
Dry goods	4.3	6.6	8.5
Furniture	6.0	6.9	8.2
Other retail	14.1	10.8	9.7
Financial	7.4	9.2	8.7
Offices	6.7	6.0	5.1
Services	14.2	10.1	9.3
Other	4.9	5.8	6.8
Vacant Space	5.5	6.2	6.1
TOTAL	100.0	100.0	100.0

Source: *Dollar and Cents of Shopping Centers: 1975* (Washington, D.C.: Urban Land Institute, 1975), pp. 297–98.

addition to convenience goods. A **regional center** has a minimum of 35 acres and has at least one large department store, and carries a wide variety of shopping goods. At least one hundred thousand people are needed to support a regional center. A regional center is the equivalent of a central business district (CBD), except for the largest metropolitan areas. However, a CBD has many owners and is likely to offer a much greater diversity of goods and services. Buildings are likely to have a greater diversity in age and design also. This diversity, if properly merchandised, makes the CBD more interesting and therefore more competitive.

VALUE ANALYSIS
OF INDUSTRIAL DISTRICTS

Industrial districts are even more diverse in makeup than commercial districts, and frequently unique. Department stores, shoe stores, clothing stores, gasoline service stations, motels, hotels, and office buildings involve similar functions and accommodations as property types, regardless of where they are located. And with some exceptions, the buildings or space for the activities may be modified and used for some other activity without undue cost of conversion. Further, most commercial activities do not involve waste products.

An industrial district or park is likely to have occupants involved in everything from warehousing to tire manufacture to cracking crude oil to processing trees into lumber to producing fertilizers. This diversity means that manufacturing plants tend to be unique to the type of product made. In turn, it is not financially feasible to convert a crude-oil cracking plant into a lumber mill or automobile assembly plant. Also, industrial activities often produce waste products, which if not controlled, cause air and water pollution. Important considerations in evaluating industrial districts are

1. Location
2. Physical characteristics
3. Building design and flexibility

As for location, the critical transportation relationships or linkages of an industrial area, are to raw materials, labor, and markets. Easy street or highway access is therefore almost always important; rail or water access may be important. Environmental considerations that may be of concern, depending on the type of industry, include smoke, odors, and noxious gases, noise, fire hazards, and chemicals. For example, a slaughter house or a dynamite plant would be an undesirable neighbor for most industrial activities. Further, as was pointed out earlier, weight-losing processes are best located near raw materials while weight-gaining processes gain advantage by being located near markets.

In physical terms, the streets and utilities must serve the district adequately. Sufficient space for employee parking, storage, and possible expansion of buildings is desirable. Level but well-drained terrain is desirable because most modern plants are one level for continuous flow of materials in process.

Pleasing architectural design is desirable in buildings. But further, buildings with large free spans allow greater flexibility in the internal use of space and the setting up of assembly lines.

The activities mix in an industrial district is not of great importance except that linkages may be involved. Thus, it may be desirable to have laundries, machine-repair shops, material suppliers, and delivery services close by if these are important to the operation of the main manufacturing operation carried on in the district.

SUMMARY

Urban areas come about because of social, economic, and political forces requiring a concentration of people, buildings, and machines. Six major benefits of urbanization are (1) savings in costs of social interaction, (2) internal economies of scale to a firm, (3) external economies of scale to a firm, (4) labor specialization, (5) greater consumer choice, and (6) fostering of innovation.

Three major theories of urban growth are (1) concentric circle, (2) direction of least resistance, and (3) multiple nuclei. Rent theory is an alternative explanation of urban growth and change, and is consistent with the above three theories. According to rent theory, urban areas grow outward at the extensive margin and upward at the intensive margin. Ability to pay rents is the basis of competition among various uses; that use able to pay the highest rent or price gets its choice of location; that use able to pay the next highest rent gets second choice, and so on. Rent-paying ability is also the link between the local economy and local property values.

Land must be combined with other factors of production (labor, capital, and management) for most urban purposes. When these factors are combined in an optimal balance or proportion for a given site, the highest and best use is realized. Land that does not warrant the application of other factors of production is submarginal.

Rent theory must be related to the dynamics of residential, commercial, and industrial districts to make the theory useful for investment purposes. Residential neighborhoods go through five stages in their life cycle: (1) healthy, (2) incipient decline, (3) clearly declining, (4) accelerating decline, and (5) abandoned. Important value characteristics of commercial districts are (1) location, (2) physical adequacy, (3) architectural design and appearance, and (4) mix of activities. Location, physical adequacy, and building design and flexibility are key value characteristics of industrial districts.

KEY TERMS

Community shopping center	Intensive margin
Comparative advantage	Internal economies of scale
Concentric-circle theory	Multiple-nuclei theory
Direction of least resistance	Neighborhood shopping center
Dispersing force	Proportionality, principle of
Economic capacity of land	Regional shopping center
Extensive margin	Rent
Economies of scale	Rent triangle
External economies of scale	Submarginal land
Functional area	Urban infrastructure
Intensity of use	Urbanizing force

QUESTIONS FOR REVIEW AND DISCUSSION

1. List and explain briefly four benefits and three costs of urbanization.
2. Explain concentric circle, direction of least resistance, and multiple nuclei as theories of urban growth. Are these theories related?
3. Relate rent theory to each of the theories in question 2. Do these theories fit your community?
4. Illustrate with rent triangles the allocation of space in a large hotel. In a department store.

400

5. Define the intensive margin and extensive margin of rent for urban land uses. What is submarginal land?

6. Explain the interrelationships, if any, between intensity of use, rent levels, value, and highest and best use for a specific site.

7. List and describe the five stages in the life cycle of a residential neighborhood. Explain briefly the characteristics of the incipient-decline stage.

8. What might be done to slow down or reverse the stages in the neighborhood life cycle? Discuss.

9. List and discuss briefly the value characteristics of commercial districts.

10. Survey your community and note where development and redevelopment is taking place. Can you identify where development is most likely to occur in the next five years? Are there any by-passed hills or marshes that look ripe for development?

11. Is anonymity a cost or a benefit of urbanization? Discuss.

REFERENCES

Barlowe, Raleigh. *Land Resource Economics.* 3rd ed. Englewood Cliffs, N.J.: Prentice-Hall, 1978. The economics of real property, presented in a technical and theoretically sound framework. Somewhat difficult to read. For the advanced student.

The Dynamics of Neighborhood Change. Washington, D.C.: U.S. Department of Housing and Urban Development, 1976. A monograph detailing neighborhood change, including decisions by participants that lead to the decline of neighborhoods. Easy to read and understand A must for appraisers, sales people, and others concerned with residential real estate.

Jacobs, Jane. *The Economy of Cities.* New York: Random House, 1969. Easy to read and an engaging account of the growth and development of business activities benefiting from or causing urbanization. Many philosophical insights and observations included.

Ratcliff, Richard U. *Real Estate Analysis.* New York: McGraw-Hill, 1961. One of the earliest efforts to relate real estate activity and urban-growth theory. Most of Professor Ratcliff's observations are still valid today. Easy to read and understand. Chapters 1, 2, and 12 are most pertinent to urban dynamics.

Wendt, Paul F. *Real Estate Appraisal: Review and Outlook.* Athens: University of Georgia Press, 1974. An overview relating property values, urban development and growth, and appraisal analysis. Chapter 4, analyzing the internal structure of cities, is particularly pertinent to the content of this chapter. Easy to read and understand, for the most part.

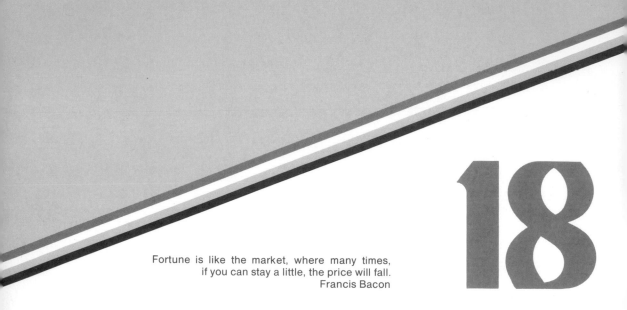

Real Estate Markets

Fortune is like the market, where many times,
if you can stay a little, the price will fall.
Francis Bacon

The term *market* has many meanings. As commonly defined, a market may be

1. A meeting of people (buyers and sellers) who wish to exchange goods and money
2. A public place (as in a town) or a large building where a market is held
3. The region in which any commodity can be sold
4. The course of commercial activity by which the exchange of commodities within a market area is affected; as, "the market is active"
5. A body of goods—"the stock market," "the beef market"

The term **market** as applied to real estate transactions is a title conferred by general usage rather than one of precise economic meaning or measurement. Of the market definitions enumerated above, only the fourth one can be applied with any assurance to real estate and then only because of the broad and all-inclusive conception that a market is a "course of commercial activity by which the exchange of commodities within a market area is affected."

The market for real estate thus cannot be described accurately as a meeting of buyers and sellers who truck and barter for commodities that are readily measurable as to quality and quantity, nor can it be described as a public or trading place for commodities such as produce, cattle, stocks, or bond securities. The commodity in the real estate market is the elusive "property rights."

In the early history of land development and community settlement, it was a practice to sell through voluntary auction entire farms, estates or parts of them, and even building sites in areas under planned development. These voluntary auctions, which were local in character, did not prove satisfactory as marketing methods. The discontinuance of the voluntary land-auction practice has severed the weak link by which real estate as a commodity was traded at a given place in terms of "bargain and sale," which the average person has in mind when speaking of a market.

Real estate markets may therefore be regarded as different and relatively distinct, and further discussion is in order. The following topics are addressed in our discussion:

1. Types of real estate markets
2. Characteristics of real estate markets
3. Supply-and-demand forces
4. Market operation
5. Local market indicators
6. Market functions

MARKET TYPES

In practice, real estate market operations are classified according to type of property traded. The kinds of real estate markets recognized as specialized fields of operation include the following:

1. Residential
2. Commercial
3. Industrial
4. Agricultural
5. Special-purpose properties

Each of these broad fields of market operations is further subdivided into smaller and more specialized market areas as follows:

Residential market—(1) urban, (2) suburban, and (3) rural housing
Commercial market—(1) office buildings, (2) store properties, (3) loft buildings, (4) theaters, (5) garages, and (6) hotels and motels
Industrial market—(1) factories, (2) utilities, (3) mining, and (4) warehouses
Agricultural market—(1) timberland, (2) pasture land, (3) ranches, (4) orchards, and (5) open farm land (for produce, tobacco, cotton, and so on)
Special-purpose properties—(1) cemeteries, (2) churches, (3) clubs, (4) golf courses, (5) parks, and (6) public properties (buildings, highways, streets, and the like)

Each of these specialized areas of the real estate market may be further classified as to rights of ownership or use. Thus, it is in order to speak of (1) a rental market involving transfer of space and (2) an equity market involving transfer of real estate ownership. The interrelationships of these markets are discussed in the chapters on real estate business, management, and valuation.

We might also note two additional types of markets termed *buyer's market* and *seller's market.* A **buyer's market** occurs when the supply of goods and services greatly exceeds demand, thereby enabling purchasers to bargain for lower prices and get them. Conversely, a **seller's market** occurs when demand greatly exceeds supply, thereby enabling sellers to bargain for higher prices and get them. We discuss these concepts further later in this chapter.

MARKET CHARACTERISTICS

Real estate as a commodity has distinct and peculiar characteristics that affect its ownership and transfer by sale. Because of these characteristics, the real estate market differs from other markets in the following ways:

1. Market is local in character.
2. Transactions are private in nature.
3. Commodity is not standardized.
4. Market is unorganized and lacks central control.
5. Absence of short selling.
6. Poor adjustment of market supply and demand.

Local in Character

Fixity of location causes the market for real estate to be *local* in character. As a commodity, real estate cannot be moved from place to place. Demand must come to the parcel or property. An oversupply of land or land improvements in a midwestern state is of no avail to fill a market demand for like land or improvements in another region or metropolitan center. Real estate must be employed where it is, and because of its fixity in geographic location it is extremely vulnerable to shifts in local demand.

Fixity in location, too, creates the need for a real estate specialist who is familiar with local and environmental market conditions and with the applicable physical, economic, and legal characteristics of real estate as a commodity. A real estate broker in Los Angeles, California, cannot well advise a home owner or business executive seeking a site in Atlanta, Georgia. It's possible, of course, that the California broker is familiar with real estate market conditions in Georgia, but absence from the scene of local market operations, if only for a few days' time, may leave a broker uninformed about significant changes that may have taken place in the supply-demand relationship.

Transactions Private in Nature

Real estate transactions are principally private in nature. Buyers and sellers meet in confidence, and their bid and offering prices are rarely publicized. Even to this date the practice of not disclosing the transaction price is generally followed. Deeds of record do not specify the actual dollar exchange, and secrecy is attempted by the legal phrase that the transfer of real estate was "in consideration of one dollar and other good and valuable considerations." Documentary stamps, required by law in many states and based on dollar value of the transaction, do give a clue to the transaction price. However, the possibility of understating or overstating the stamp requirements must be considered in weighing documentary tax data as evidence of market prices. Privacy in transaction is directly attributable to the specialized nature of real estate as a commodity, which requires personal business meetings between the seller and buyer, or agents authorized to act on their behalf. Potential buyers and sellers do seek out sales information to guide them in their efforts, however.

Commodity Not Standardized

Lack of similarity in kind is another real estate characteristic that imposes special marketing conditions. No two parcels of real estate are geographically alike. In respect to location, each parcel of real estate is unique. Even where physical similarity seems apparent, legal and situs characteristics may affect the relative value of each. On the other hand, physically different parcels of real estate may serve economically identical purposes and be almost exactly exchangeable in value. To illustrate, two residential sites equal in width and depth may support identical buildings, similar not only in floor plan and building material but also as to details of building construction and time of completion. Still, these two real estate properties, equal as far as inspection may disclose, may warrant different values or permit different uses because of intangible legal or economic limitations. One property may be zoned residence A and the other B, permitting different site utilization for one but not the other. One property may be subject to deed restrictions limiting its use for high-class residential purposes; the other may be free of any contractual limitations and thus subject to any legal use. Easements, utility rights of way, or any of many legal encumbrances may affect the title of one and not the other property.

Market Not Organized or Centrally Controlled

Attempts to centralize or organize real estate activities on a large scale have failed because of the nature of the commodity traded. Fixity in location and lack of standardization of real estate as a commodity account for the wide fluctuations in value and number of transactions that characterize the real estate market. Such fluctuations are notable not only in different regions throughout the nation but also within a state or single community. The market for U.S. farmland, for instance, may be judged good or active when based on number of sales and increase in overall and relative values. But this overall "favorable" average may be a composite derived from an extraordinary demand and increase in value of farm land in the wheat, corn, tobacco, or cattle-raising regions, as well as from substantial softening in demand and decrease in value of farm land traded in the cotton belt region. Similar divergent real estate activity is experienced in urban areas. Whereas average national real estate activity may favorably advance, individual cities may show increases in varying degrees or even record notable decreases in real estate business activity. Thus real estate activity in Phoenix, Los Angeles, or Miami Beach may record index sales 200 percent or more above the national average while sales in Tacoma, Washington, and Portland, Maine, may experience notable declines in real estate activity over the same period. The fixity of real estate as a commodity thus not only prevents the transfer of real estate from an area of low demand to one of high demand but makes centralized control of market transactions or the equalization of supply and demand beyond the limits of a local market area inoperative.

Absence of Short Selling

Dissimilarity of real estate as a commodity and the legal right to specific performance discourage speculation and prevent the market operations known as short selling. Short selling is the practice of selling, when prices are high, securities or commodities that the speculator does not own. Anticipating a drop in market prices, the speculator hopes to cover these short sales by purchasing at lower prices the quantities previously sold. This he expects to do at the time when delivery of the securities or commodities is due—as a rule, days or weeks later. The speculator hopes that the time interval will create a market favorable to him. The practice of short selling can, however, apply only to articles or goods that are legally fungible or substitutable, such as grain, corn, or shares of stock. The practice of short selling in the grain or security markets, for instance, not only is legally permissible but is welcomed as a stabilizing trading influence by necessitating the placing of purchase orders, to fill short-selling commitments, when market activity normally might be low or even panicky. Because real estate as a commodity is nonfungible or nonsubstitutable, it is not subject to the market-stabilizing practice of short selling. Lack of centralized control as well as absence of short selling causes wide price fluctuations in real estate transactions and also "sticky" market operations that may lead to a freeze, or suspension, of real estate sales and related market activities.

Poor Adjustment of Supply and Demand

The fixity in real estate location prevents equalization of supply and demand on a regional or national level. The durability of real estate causes maladjustments in supply and demand on a local market level. Land itself is indestructible and physically will exist forever. Improvements, if properly maintained, will last a hundred years or more. Thus, where demand suddenly falls, for any reason, inability to adjust (withdraw) supply will cause real estate to become a drug on the market. An oversupply of real estate creates a buyer's market, which readily results in lower purchase-price offerings and keenly competitive trade practices.

On the other hand, a sudden increase in demand for real estate is also difficult to meet. The housing problem caused by shifting of population due to defense or war efforts is an illustration in kind. It takes weeks or even months to construct a single home; construction conditions must be favorable for the entire building industry to supply in excess of two million dwelling units during a given year. Even at an anticipated favorable rate of home construction, averaging two million starts per year, it would require thirty-five years just to replace the nation's housing stock. Based on conservative estimates, another ten years of construction time are required to provide replacement for housing destroyed in interim years by wear and tear, action of the elements, and circumstances causing functional and economic obsolescence. The time required to bring the forces of supply and demand into reasonable balance, as well as the uncertainty of keeping these price-determining forces in equilibrium, makes real estate market transactions a calculated business venture. The risks involved are reflected in high interest rates, especially those applicable to the equity part of a real estate investment.

SUPPLY-AND-DEMAND FORCES

A local real estate market is sensitive to changes in the balance of biological, economic, political, and social forces. Changes in these forces, in turn, influence the supply of real estate and the demand for it. Among the more important forces to be considered in local real estate markets are the following:

1. Population—number, age-sex mix, and family composition
2. Employment and wage levels and stability of incomes
3. Personal savings, availability of mortgage funds, and levels of interest rates
4. Sales prices, rent levels, and vacancy percentage
5. Taxation rates and land-use controls, including rent controls
6. Availability and costs of land, labor, and building materials
7. Relative quality of existing structures, and changes in construction technology

Population, employment, incomes, savings, and availability of credit combine to provide effective demand. **Effective demand** is desire backed up by purchasing power.

Population

Population is a prerequisite of demand for most types of real estate. An increase in numbers of people means increased potential demand. And a decrease in population means declining demand. To become effective demand, the population must have wealth or income.

Given population and purchasing power, demand then depends on characteristics of the population. For example, an elderly population means fewer children per household and therefore translates into demand for dwelling units with only one and two bedrooms. Alternatively, a community with many young people under eighteen years old means strong demand for three- and four-bedroom, two-bath, dwelling units. More schools and playgrounds are also likely to be needed. A largely middle-aged population, most of whom work, is likely to translate into demand for two- and three-bedroom housing units of moderate-to-high value. With higher incomes, couples generally want larger and more attractive places to live.

Wage Levels and Income Stability

The real estate market is sensitive to changes in wage levels, employment opportunities, and stability of income. Rental payments and housing costs are closely geared to ability to pay. In fact, there are definite rules of thumb accepted by mortgage lenders and federal housing agencies under which total housing costs should not exceed 20 to 30 percent of the wage earner's income. Homes, too, may now be purchased on time-payment plans, as can other consumer goods, and payments are made out of income on a monthly basis. The introduction of the amortization mortgage that made home purchases possible "on time" has in fact revolutionized the residential real estate market and, since World War II, proven a bonanza to the home-building industry. Since 1940 home ownership increased from 43.6 percent of total occupied dwelling units to about 65 percent currently.

Personal Savings, Credit Availability, and Levels of Interest Rates

Higher wage and salary payments are significantly reflected in the increase of total disposable personal income, which—after correction for changes in purchasing power—rose from $155 billion in 1929 to approximately $900 billion in 1978. Estimated savings of individuals rose in excess of 600 percent during the same period. These personal savings and investments by financial institutions provide a great reservoir of mortgage funds. The mortgage loan insurance and guarantee policies underwritten by the Federal Housing Administration and the Veterans' Administration have also proven important in making mortgage credit generally available.

Mortgage credit policy may be called the barometer of the residential real estate market. A tightening or liberalization of mortgage lending policy has a direct and immediate influence on home construction and real estate market activity. Most homes are bought on credit. Terms, therefore, are an important part of a purchase transaction and often influence the transaction price. Real estate brokers are well aware of the role that terms play in bringing about a sale. It is not uncommon, therefore, to see new homes advertised for XX dollars of down payment and YY dollars of payment per month, without reference to the total transaction price. To most buyers who enter the market with small equity down payments, price undoubtedly means size of monthly payments. With mortgage payments on single residential homes now extending over twenty-five- and thirty-year periods, the home-ownership market for real estate continues to expand.

Rent and Vacancy Levels

Rental activity, particularly in metropolitan areas, still forms an important part of the total real estate market. Currently, about 22 million dwelling units are renter-occupied, and the owners of these units are much concerned in securing a fair return on, and adequate return of, their investment. The rental market is highly competitive; in areas not subject to rent control, rent levels are in direct relation to costs of housing and contractual service requirements. If rents are set too high in relation to servicing costs, tenants will economize on space, and vacancies will result. Housing supply cannot be withdrawn from the market, for all practical purposes. Competition to maintain full occupancy therefore forces prices into line. In the analysis of the real estate market, a study of prevailing vacancy ratios to total rental supply should prove of interest. Ratios exceeding 3 to 5 percent are indicative of either an oversupply in rental space or overpricing. In either case, downward adjustments in rents are necessary to stimulate demand. The importance of vacancy ratios as a measure of the economic health of rental housing has caused real estate boards in the larger communities to maintain occupancy records as an index of real estate market activity and guide to broker members.

Taxation and Land-Use Controls

Taxation is one of the more important forces that influence the supply and demand for real estate. This force may be positive or negative and is often used as a governmental tool to compel or deter real estate development or to direct employment of land for particular uses. In many urban areas, particularly those of high population concentration, vacant land is sometimes assessed and taxed in excess of its contribution to overall real estate market value to stimulate its use and thus indirectly discourage the holding of vacant urban land for speculative purposes. In states where homestead laws are operative and where owner occupants are given tax exemptions up to certain limits of the assessed value of their property, the burden of municipal costs is shifted largely to owners of business and tenant-occupied properties. Such tax policy is directly designed to encourage home ownership and the use of land for residential owner occupancy. Homestead laws have proven popular with states that seek to develop land with the aid of migrant settlers. As a market device, the laws are also popular with real estate brokers, builders, and suppliers of home furnishings.

Other land-use controls, whether of private or public nature, also affect real estate market operations. Controls, generally, are designed to direct real estate use and development in the interest of the community at large and to protect the investment of real estate owners from exploitation or misuse of neighboring lands. Increased land-use controls and permit requirements have driven real estate prices sharply upward in recent years.

Costs of Land, Labor, and Building Materials

The availability of land and the cost of land, labor, and building materials affect the supply side of the real estate market. Though physically abundant, land that is economically usable is often in short supply. Improvements in the form of access roads, drainage facilities, water, and other community utilities must ordinarily be added to "raw" land before it can be subdivided and offered for sale through marketing channels. Because such improvements are costly and can be successfully carried out only with community sanction and on a relatively large scale, a scarcity of economic land often occurs. Scarcity of building sites in turn causes upward pricing of real estate holdings to a point where community development and real estate market activities may be adversely affected. On the other hand, speculative optimism, unchecked by community foresight and planning, may cause economic land to be produced in quantities too great to be absorbed by prevailing demand, creating an oversupply that may depress the market for real estate for many months or even years.

Cost of labor and building materials also affects importantly the market supply of real estate. Where labor and material prices rise faster than the "lagging" prices of existing real estate improvements, new construction activity will be slowed until demand prices and costs of improvement again attain an equilibrium. This "spurt and coast" cycle of building activity is particularly evident during and immediately following periods of war or defense emergencies.

Construction Technology and Building Quality

More buildings are torn down than fall down. This destruction of often physically sound improvements is caused by changes in the arts and by building obsolescence. Rapid advance in building design and methods of construction have sparked the demand for modern homes that offer greater conveniences and, hence, greater amenities of living. Improvements in home heating, lighting, insulation, soundproofing, air conditioning, and interior design have brought about an active demand for home modernization and replacement that is estimated to sustain a high level of real estate market activities for many years to come. Based on surveys of the Federal Housing Agency, more than 600,000 dwelling units—40 percent of anticipated new construction—are required each year to meet replacement demands caused by physical deterioration, changes in the arts, and building obsolescence.

MARKET OPERATION

Supply-and-demand forces interact constantly in the real estate market. The market adjusts on a short-run and on a long-run basis. Some analysts claim that cycles can be discerned as an adjustment in the long-run market.

Supply-and-Demand Dynamics

The real estate market acts much like the market of economic theory in response to changes in supply-and-demand forces. Imperfections, such as lack of product standardization and long lead time for production of new supply, cause some deviations from the theory. The basic rules of market dynamics, as applied in real estate, are as follows:

1. Units or types of real estate that are comparable in size and quality tend to sell at similar prices.

2. If supply-and-demand forces are in balance, price tends to be stable.

3. If demand exceeds existing supply, a seller's market is created and the price advances. The increased price cuts back on the number of units demanded and also stimulates construction of new units. Several weeks, and often several months, are required for new supply to be produced after the need is recognized. New construction will continue until supply and demand are again in balance and price is stabilized.

4. If supply exceeds demand, as in a declining community or region, a buyer's market exists and price declines. A decline in price stimulates demand but discourages new construction. Price will decline to the level at which supply and demand are again in balance.

Short-Run Adjustments

Demand is much more dynamic than supply in the short run. If demand suddenly declines, the excess supply cannot quickly be removed from the market area. If demand suddenly increases, additional supply cannot be provided on short notice.

For illustrative purposes, consider the housing market in a medium-sized community that is not tied to a large metropolitan area by commuters and is therefore independent of outside influences. An assumption of standardized housing units is made to simplify the discussion. In fact, this assumption is extremely unrealistic. However, any one housing unit can be substituted for another of nearly equal quality. With many market adjustments possible, no great distortion in the operation of the market therefore needs to result from making this assumption. The short-run interaction between supply, demand, and price is shown in figure 18–1.

In figure 18–1, curve D_o represents the demand schedule for housing as of a given time. Curve S represents the supply schedule. The vertical axis can represent either the rental or sale price per housing unit. The horizontal axis indicates the number of housing units demanded or supplied.

The demand curve means that fewer housing units will be demanded at a higher price than at a lower price. The supply curve, on the other hand, says that at a low price fewer housing units will be supplied than at a higher price.

The supply and demand forces are in balance at the point where curves D_o and S intersect. The price at this point is P_o, at which level X units of hous-

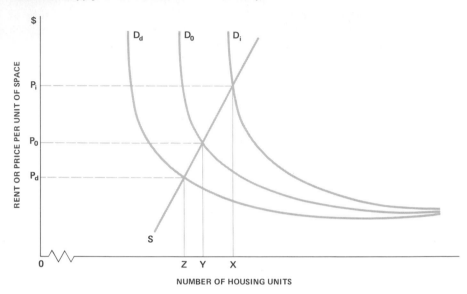

FIGURE 18–1
Short-run Supply, Demand, and Price Relationships

ing are demanded. A sudden increase in population or income would shift the demand schedule to the right, curve D_i. Because new units cannot be readily produced, the price rises sharply to P_i. At this price, Y units are demanded and supplied. Alternatively, a decline in demand, curve D_d, would cause the price to drop to P_d, with fewer units, Z, being supplied.

A sudden increase in demand cannot greatly increase the number of housing units supplied in the short run. Several weeks would be required as a minimum to increase supply, even though the price had increased to P_i. The additional amount of supply equals $Y - X$. This would come about by vacancies being absorbed first. Purchase and rental prices would then increase as demand pressed on supply. Some people would use their living space more intensely by doubling up—that is, by crowding more people into their dwelling. The motives might be to earn a profit or to help out friends and relatives who were forced out of other units by higher prices. Low-income people would be forced to double up because they could not afford the higher prices. Some families would find housing in the country or in the surrounding villages, with the workers commuting greater distances. Trailers, mobile homes, and seasonal housing would also be brought in and occupied to increase the housing supply.

Long-Run Adjustments

The cost of building new housing units enters into the long-run determination of a new equilibrium. For example, assume that several new industries moved to our middle-sized community over a period of years. This is realistic.

Most urban areas have steadily increased in population since World War II. The successive increases in demand are represented by curves D_1 and D_2 in figure 18–2. A long-run cost curve is also introduced in figure 18–2 to show the cost of building an additional housing unit.

FIGURE 18–2
Long-run Supply, Demand, Price, and Cost Relationships

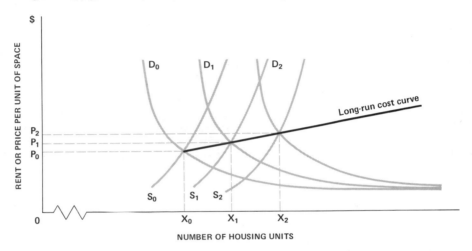

In figure 18–2, an increase in demand, from curve D_0 to curve D_1, increases the price above the cost to produce a unit. This is represented by the intersection of curves S_0 and D_1. New housing units would be built and eventually a new balance reached at the intersection of curves S_1 and D_1. Because the price at the intersection equals the cost of production, builders would not find it profitable to continue new construction beyond this point.

A second increase in demand, to curve D_2 (more new industry moving into town), would start the process again. With demand exceeding supply, prices advance. Under conditions of steadily increasing demand, costs of land, labor, and building materials all tend to increase rapidly. That is, owners and workers can hold out for higher prices and wages, and they almost always get the increase. Hence, the long-run cost curve slopes upward. Eventually a new equilibrium is reached where the long-run cost curve and curves D_2 and S_2 intersect. The new price level is P_2, while the number of housing units in the community has increased to X_2. The net increase in the number of units equals $X_2 - X_0$.

Little or no new construction would occur if demand decreased—that is, if the demand curve shifted to the left. The price would quickly drop below the cost curve, and no profit incentive would be present to justify starting construction of new housing units.

Real Estate Cycles

Some analysts and authors assert that over time, population, income, and the economy interact to produce a real estate cycle. A **real estate cycle** is a regular rise and fall in real estate sales and construction activity. Variations do occur in the level of these activities, as seasons and as economic conditions change. Seasonal changes or fluctuations are regular, with higher levels of activity occurring in the summertime in most communities. But business and real estate fluctuations are not regular in that they occur over periods of from three to seven or more years. Expansions and contractions of business and real estate activity therefore have little regularity or rhythm as to either intensity or time. Each period of expansion and interaction seems to be unique with its own characteristics.

Real estate construction and sales activity seem more closely related to the cost and availability of financing than to any regular cycle. For example, shortages of credit in 1966, 1969–70, 1973–74, and 1979 caused sharp cutbacks in housing starts across the United States. Thus, an investor or developer might better look to current and likely monetary policy than to a regular real estate cycle in deciding whether to take on a new project. On an overall basis, real estate construction and sales activities have been more stable since World War II because of better fiscal and monetary policies by our federal government.

Real Estate Market Efficiency

A market is a mechanism for allocation of resources. Supply-and-demand forces and past prices interact in a real estate market to influence the allocation of land and space to alternative uses. In a free and perfect market, space or land is allocated to alternative uses based on relative rent or price paying ability, with those uses able to pay the highest prices getting preferred sites or locations.

Markets range from perfect to imperfect in operation. A **perfect market** is one in which all information concerning future risks and benefits for each property is available to all participants. Full information is generally not readily available to participants, particularly in real estate markets, which are generally considered to be imperfect. Real estate information costs considerable money, time, and effort to collect and analyze. Therefore less wealthy investors find it relatively more expensive than wealthy investors to acquire information. Effectively this means that not all investors operate from comparable levels of information. In turn, this means market participants have differing expectations of returns and risks from real estate, and differing values for a given parcel of realty.

Perfect or not, what is the efficiency of the real estate market? An **efficient market** is one in which changes in the information about the outlook for a given property are quickly reflected in the property's probable selling price or value. That is, favorable information about a parcel causes an immediate increase in its value while negative or unfavorable information pushes its value down. In an inefficient market, participants with greater knowledge or skill can exploit other participants and thereby rapidly increase their wealth. Research has not provided a clear answer to the question. One thing is sure, information

414

is generally captured and disseminated rather slowly in real estate markets. But once information is known, the value expectations of participants is influenced. This suggests that real estate markets are relatively inefficient in that those able to gain the greatest knowledge are also able to gain the greatest advantage in the market. This conclusion provides an extremely strong reason to study cause-and-effect relationships and market indicators in investment real estate.

LOCAL MARKET INDICATORS

Market outlook is extremely important to an investor considering the development or purchase of a property. Levels of prices and values are uncertain and risky; they do not rise and fall in regular cycles. Uncertainty and risk may be reduced, however, by monitoring and interpreting local market indicators. Key market indicators for housing are discussed here. These same indicators may aid in interpreting change in other submarkets as well. The housing market is used as an example here because it is larger and more familiar and has more transactions.

Supply-and-demand forces and the theory of markets, already discussed, must be understood to interpret these indicators. Self-interest plays a large part in the theory and in the interpretation of markets. As buyers and sellers, most of us are opportunists. We like to buy low and sell high. Reading indicators enables us to better follow this maximizing strategy, insofar as it is possible. In short, market indicators help us identify "buyers' " and "sellers' " markets. But buyers must sometimes purchase in a seller's market, and sellers must sometimes sell in a buyer's market. The result is that prices advance or decline according to the relative strengths of the supply-and-demand forces.

Four groups or categories of indicators are identified and discussed here. The basis of these groups are (1) demand, (2) supply-demand interaction, (3) financing, and (4) construction or new supply. See figure 18–3. Supply indicators are conspicuous by their absence as a group, even though 95 to 97 percent of the space that influences market activity in any year already exists at the beginning of the year. That is, supply changes only very slowly. Demand is the dynamic force in real estate markets. Trends, rates of change, and direction of change in these various indicators provide the most important information.

Demand Indicators

The four key demand indicators are (1) population, (2) employment, (3) unemployment, and (4) per capita personal income. Population represents raw or **potential demand** only. Potential demand must be armed with purchasing power to become **effective demand.** Trends and fluctuations in these four variables tell a great deal about likely changes in effective demand.

Obviously, increases in population mean increased demand for housing. And an increase in employment, along with low levels of unemployment, indicates economic growth and is likely to result in immigration of additional workers and population. Per capita personal income tells how much purchasing power is available for housing in the population. Declines in population and income obviously mean decreased effective demand for housing.

FIGURE 18–3
Local Real Estate Market Indicators

Category and Items	Sources
1. DEMAND	
(a) Population	Population center, Chamber of Commerce
(b) Employment	Local U.S. Dept. of Labor office
(c) Unemployment	Local U.S. Dept. of Labor office
(d) Personal income per capita (wage levels)	Census data, Local U.S. Dept. of Labor office
2. SUPPLY-DEMAND INTERACTION	
(a) Sales prices	Comparison of standard house with local sales prices
(b) Rent levels	
(c) Vacancy rate/utilization rate	Comparison in market
(d) Sales volume	Surveys, personal observation
3. FINANCE	MLS reports, want ads
(a) Relative availability of money	Survey of local lenders
(b) Costs of money; interest rates	Survey of local lenders
(c) Prime rate	News reports, local lenders
(d) Foreclosure rates	Lenders, courthouse records
4. NEW SUPPLY	
(a) Subdivision activity	Plat records, court house
(b) Building permits	Local housing office/dodge reports
(c) Construction volume	Contractors, news reports
(d) Construction costs	Contractors

Many states have population centers, usually at a major university, from which population data may be obtained. The U.S. Department of Labor provides employment, unemployment, and wage (income) information for most communities. Planning commissions and chambers of commerce often publish reports containing population and labor-force information. And most newspapers periodically publish reviews and comments on the economic outlook for an area or region.

Indicators of Supply-and-Demand Interaction

Price levels, vacancy rates, sales volume, and rent levels tell what is happening in regard to supply-demand interaction in local real estate. For the most part, information on these variables must be captured on a personal basis. That is, data are not regularly published concerning the variables.

Price-level information may be obtained by comparing prices for certain "standard" houses through time. That is, a typical two-, three-, and four- bedroom house might be priced on a comparative basis every few months. In like manner, rent levels for one-, two-, and three- bedroom apartments might be checked. The checking might involve asking prices in want ads, or specific visits to dwelling units offered for sale or rent. Also a summary of completed transactions published monthly by a multiple listing service might serve as a service of

416

price information. Sales volume may also be estimated from this summary. A further indication of sales activity is volume of deeds recorded by a county recorder. Again, trends and rates of change are vital information.

Vacancy rates tell what portion of the existing supply of space is not being utilized. Thus, the rate of property utilization in a community is the complement or flip side of the vacancy rate. Post office surveys are sometimes made to determine vacancy rates. Checks with property managers and monitoring want ads may also indicate vacancy levels. New, unsold houses must also be classified as vacancies. An increasing vacancy rate foretells a weakening in prices or rents. A declining rate suggests that rents and prices are likely to advance.

Financing Indicators

Key financing indicators are the relative availability of money, the interest rates being charged, the prime rate, and mortgage foreclosure rate. Credit is a prerequisite to real estate sales and construction activity. Limited money shackles market activity and is likely to lead to higher interest rates. As interest rates advance, time is required for buyers to accept the higher cost of money. Easier money is a necessary precondition to higher levels of activity, but it does not ensure them. Money availability and interest-rate levels may best be determined by a direct survey of lenders.

The **prime rate** is the rate that major commercial banks typically charge large, well-established, financially sound companies on business loans. The rate tends to be uniform across the country and, in a sense, ties all financial markets together. The prime rate tends to vary with conditions in the money and financial markets. An increase in the prime rate indicates a tightening in the money markets, while a decrease indicates easier money. Changes in the prime rate are widely quoted in the financial news. A change in the prime rate is usually followed by a comparable shift in mortgage interest rates.

Mortgage foreclosure rates tell of failures of borrowers to live up to their mortgage contracts. Major causes are deaths, divorces, and unemployment. Deaths and divorces tend to be relatively stable through time in their incidence. Thus, a sudden increase in foreclosures evidences layoffs and declining economic conditions. A decrease in the rate, in turn, means improving conditions. Foreclosures translate into a decline in demand, at least in the short run.

New-Supply Indicators

Development and construction mean increases in the supply of real estate. Developers and builders generally add to supply only if they expect sales prices or market values to exceed costs. Starting construction of a new building means that an aspiring home owner or investor has decided that value exceeds cost. In the short run, construction may continue as a builder strives to keep a crew going, in spite of a discouraging market outlook. Key statistics in this area are subdivision-activity, building permits, construction volume, and construction costs.

Subdivision requires several months to a year from plat approvals to market availability of sites. Housing construction may take only from two to three months. And construction does not always follow immediately after the taking out of a building permit. Thus, lags must be taken into account in interpreting development and construction indicators.

Building permits and dollar construction volume tell of short-term increases in supply. These increases must be related to the indicated effective demand. Subdivision activity indicates the long-run outlook is more promising. And increasing costs of construction result in higher costs of space. In turn, the cost of new space is at the margin; any increases tend to spread over the entire existing supply, given time. Eventually, higher costs mean less space is likely to be demanded and used.

Interrelatedness of Indicators

Real estate supply-and-demand forces exert pressures in many directions. Increasing births or incomes translate into greater demand. At the same time, outmigration to better opportunities elsewhere decreases demand. Thus, supply-and-demand forces are interrelated in their effects. And market prices and sales volume are the result of these and many other conditions. Likewise, market indicators may not all point in the same direction. The investor-analyst must read and interpret the signs provided by indicators on a continuing basis.

MARKET FUNCTIONS

The primary functions performed by the real estate market encompass the following three points:

1. Exchange and the reallocation of land and existing space to alternative uses based on their rent-paying ability
2. Price and value establishment, thereby providing information to other market participants for their use in making decisions
3. Adjustment in the quality and quantity of space in response to changing social and economic needs of the community or area

The result of the market's operation is a physical pattern of land uses that reflects the social and economic tastes and needs of the community or area.

Exchange

A sale of property occurs in a free market only when it is mutually advantageous to both buyer and seller. The buyer would rather have the property than the money. The seller prefers the money. The real estate market therefore reallocates property and redistributes space according to the preferences of property users with financial capability.

Most sellers have been buyers at one time, preferring the property to the money. Through time, conditions may have changed to the point where the owner now prefers to give up control of the property. New roads, new stores, and new factories may have been built. The tax shelter provided by the property may have been largely used up. A related business may have gone bankrupt. A spouse may have died or children married and left home. Any one of these would be reason for an owner to want to sell out and relocate.

The sale of property is the most common way in which owners change their position. The value of each property, as well as how it might best be used, depends on its physical characteristics and its location. The owner wishes the property exposed to the greatest number of possible buyers to get the highest price possible. The expectation is that the buyer best able to use the property will pay the highest price. Each buyer, in turn, shops the many properties available, seeking the best possible property for his or her needs with price taken into account. The highest and best use for each site is expected to win out in the competition. The result of many transactions of this type is a continuing redistribution of land and space in a community.

The exchange function includes rentals and tax-deferred exchanges in addition to outright sales. Attention here is focused on the sales transaction because it is most common. The concerns of a renter are essentially the same as those of a buyer, except that control of the property is gained by leasing rather than by purchase. A separate chapter, later, is devoted entirely to leases and leasing. The tax-deferred exchange is such an involved and advanced transaction that it is not taken up in detail in this text.

The transfer of real estate, primarily by sale, is in itself quite an involved transaction. Many legal, financial, and market factors enter into it. Part II of this book, in fact, is devoted entirely to the mechanics of the sale and transfer process.

Price and Value Establishment

The real estate sales transaction is private in nature. Yet investors, lenders, managers, assessors, and brokers want and need information about the sale for judgments and decisions that turn on value. An investor wishes to pay no more for a property than the amount for which a comparable property sold. On the other hand, an owner wishes to sell for no less. A lender does not want to make a loan on a property for more than it can be sold for. The broker wants the information to show a client that the transaction being proposed is sound.

Price and value information are important to the continuing operation and stability of the real estate market as well as to the individual participants. Careful research and analysis of several transactions can yield a considerable amount of information about value and value trends in the market. The strong need for this information has brought into being specialists, appraisers, and counselors, who provide the information for a fee. These specialists are needed because of the complexity of real estate, which makes value generalization from one property to another very difficult. These specialists are also needed to provide estimates of the investment values of properties.

Value considerations in addition to price include property productivity, the availability of financing, tax laws, and the amount of cash equity in the hands of the investors. Part III of this book is devoted to the processing of market information as it might be analyzed by an investor considering the purchase or sale of a property.

Quantity and Quality Adjustments

Owners, managers, developers, and builders constantly seek to maximize the value of real estate under their control. Proper attention to property taxes, insurance, financing, and leasing can aid in this effort. Being responsive to the real estate market and to changes therein can also help. For example, a new bridge and freeway may change a neighborhood so that old houses promise higher profits if they are used as offices rather than as residential space. At the same time, the eviction of tenants from the old houses, along with increased population and income in the community, creates demand for new apartments. Also, blight creeping into a high-income residential area might signal that a change to middle-income tenancy is imminent.

Owners therefore change the nature of use of properties they own in response to market pressures and opportunities. Remodeling and renovation may be necessary to adjust to the changing need of the market. If demand is increased, raw land must be subdivided and vacant sites developed to increase the quantity of space in the community. Part IV of this book is devoted to adjusting the quantity and quality of space, in addition to considerations of property ownership and management.

SUMMARY

Property rights make up the commodity of the real estate market. Real estate markets are often classified as (1) residential, (2) commercial, (3) industrial, (4) agricultural, and (5) special purpose. Real estate markets are also sometimes termed as a "buyer's market" or a "seller's market." In a buyer's market, purchasers bargain for and get lower prices. In a seller's market, owners bargain for and get higher prices.

Several relatively distinct characteristics of real estate markets are (1) local in character, (2) private transactions, (3) nonstandard commodity, (4) noncentralized and unorganized, and (5) slow adjustment of supply and demand. Some of the more important supply-and-demand forces are population, income levels, wealth, interest rates, rent and vacancy levels, government powers or controls, and construction technology. These forces interact to bring forth new space as long as the value of additional supply exceeds its cost. These forces result in fluctuations in real estate sales and construction fluctuations that vary in intensity and frequency; therefore investors, lenders, builders, and brokers find market indicators extremely important. Indicators may be grouped into four categories: (1) demand, (2) supply-demand interaction, (3) financing, and (4) construction or new supply.

Three important functions of real estate markets are (1) exchange, (2) price and value establishment, and (3) supply adjustment in quantity and quality.

KEY TERMS

Buyer's market
Effective demand
Efficient market
Market
Perfect market

Potential demand
Prime rate
Real estate cycle
Seller's market

QUESTIONS FOR REVIEW AND DISCUSSION

1. Name at least two submarkets for each of the following market types (1) residential, (2) commercial, (3) industrial, (4) agricultural, and (5) special purpose.

2. List and describe briefly at least four characteristics that make real estate markets relatively unique.

3. List and describe briefly four demand and four supply forces of local real estate markets.

4. Describe briefly short-run and long-run adjustments in real estate markets. Illustrate with supply-demand diagrams.

5. Explain why market indicators are needed if real estate activity is cycled.

6. Name and briefly discuss the nature of two market indicators in each of these four categories: (1) demand, (2) supply-demand interaction, (3) finance, and (4) new supply.

7. Identify and briefly describe three functions of real estate markets.

8. Would we need an urban real estate market if we did not have private ownership rights in real property? Discuss.

9. Property owners sometimes oppose community growth even though values generally go up as a result of growth. Is this rational? Explain.

10. In earlier chapters we noted that real estate has characteristics of heterogeneity, durability, and interdependence. What implications do these characteristics have relative to stability in the real estate market? (Think hard, this is a tough one.)

REFERENCES

Case, Fred E. *Real Estate Economics: A Systematic Introduction.* Los Angeles: California Association of Realtors, 1974. This is a systematic treatment of the relationships between real estate, income and wealth, finance, and city growth as reflected in urban real estate markets. Terms are well defined. Must reading for anyone likely to be in real estate on a continuing basis. The first five chapters particularly relate to real estate markets.

McClellan, W. M. "Inflation/Monetary Policy/Real Estate Market." *The Appraisal Journal,* October 1978, pp. 547–50. A brief discussion of the interactions of inflation, monetary policy, and real estate values. McClellan suggests that a basic knowledge of the real estate market and market indicators would help an investor or analyst to anticipate market change. Easy to read and understand.

Ratcliff, Richard A. *Real Estate Analysis.* New York: McGraw-Hill, 1961. Previously cited as a classic in real estate literature. Chapters 2, 10, and 12 focus on real estate market considerations. Generally easy to read; gives excellent perspective.

Redman, Arnold L., and C. F. Sirmans. "Regional/Local Economic Analysis: A Discussion of Data Sources." *The Appraisal Journal,* April 1977, pp. 261–72. An annotated summary of data sources for real estate analysts and investors, with an emphasis on government publications. Easy to read, comprehensive.

Smith, Wallace F. *Urban Development: The Process and the Problems.* Berkeley: University of California Press, 1975. Excellent overview of real estate markets as they relate to urban development. See chapters 6, 7, and 9. For the advanced undergraduate and the graduate student.

Real Estate Market and Feasibility Analysis

Real estate **market analysis** is a study to predict changes in the amount and types of real estate facilities needed in a community or area. The emphasis is usually on urban space needs—that is, on residential, retail trade, office, and industrial space needs. The time horizon used on a study varies from one or two years to ten years or more, depending on the type of real estate being considered and on the financial size and stability of the party requesting and paying for the study. The larger the size and the greater the stability, the longer the study horizon is likely to be.

A real estate market study is a management tool for decision making as well as for planning and budgeting. An investor may wish a market study before purchasing a large apartment complex. The study results could give assurance that the outlook for the property is sound. The study could also provide a basis for judging the amount to be bid for the property. Owners might want a market study to ascertain whether their property is being put to its highest and best use and is being merchandised to its best advantage.

A developer would use a study to judge whether a new shopping center is needed and where. Assuming a new center is justified, the study helps a lender decide how large a loan to make to finance its development. Tenants are induced to the center on the basis of the market analysis results. The study might also be useful in obtaining approvals from planning officials for the construction of the center. Finally, the study can provide the developer a basis for planning and budgeting finances until the center is a going operation.

Real estate market analysis is in the early stages of development; years will probably be required before the concepts, methodology, and applications are refined. In the meantime, much judgment will be required of the analyst and the decision maker. Also, the discussion in this chapter assumes that the decision maker wants accurate, realistic information, not a report to justify an action or development that he or she has already decided to undertake or promote. Topics covered in this chapter are as follows:

1. Urban change and market analysis
2. Market area delineation
3. Economic base analysis
4. Supply-and-demand analysis
5. Current market conditions
6. Market study conclusions
7. Feasibility analysis

URBAN CHANGE AND MARKET ANALYSIS

Urban areas are made up of many types of land uses serving a wide variety of people. Urban areas constantly change, usually expanding as a result of economic growth. In some cases, decline and contraction do set in, however. And all sectors of expanding areas do not share equally in the growth. The important considerations are when and where change will take place; and what types of change.

Economic Change and Land Use

Urban areas grow and expand because their economic base grows and expands. An economic base involves the activity that exports goods and services outside the community in return for money or income to the community. The economic base provides employment and income on which the rest of the local economy depends. Employment and income in the rest of the local economy, often called service activities, expand and contract in direct relation to changes in base activities.

A local economy that is expanding attracts additional workers and population. With increased economic activity and population, the space needs of the area or community also increase. There are two major ways in which such change takes place. One is essentially growth outward; the other is growth upward.

LAND DEVELOPMENT. Raw or vacant land is constantly converted from nonurban use to sites for productive urban space. Examples are the construction of shopping centers, industrial plants, or stadiums in previously open fields. A further example is the subdivision of open land with subsequent construction of houses. This type of growth and change usually occurs at the urban fringe, thus is growth outward.

LAND-USE SUCCESSION. Because urban areas are dynamic, the use of land and the improvements to the land tend to be in a constant state of flux. The changes came about in one or more of the following ways:

1. *Change in type of use.* A large old house being converted into an office building represents a change in type of use. So also is the tearing down of a gasoline service station to make way for an apartment house. A change in the type of use involves the modification of an existing structure, or its replacement by new improvements. The new use must be able to absorb the cost of conversion or replacement to be profitable and feasible.

2. *Change in intensity of use.* Adding another story to increase display and sales area is an intensity of use change. Converting a larger, old, single-family residence into several small apartment units is, also. Although the type of use is not changed, the amount of economic or social activity on the site is modified. If the intensity is increased, the additional benefits must be great enough to justify the costs of structural change usually involved in such a change.

3. *Change in quality of use.* The nature of the benefits of use of a property may be upgraded or downgraded. Creeping blight can lead to the gradual deterioration in the benefits generated by a residential neighborhood or a commercial area. The rehabilitation of the Georgetown area in Washington, D.C., on the other hand, is an excellent example of improving the quality of use. Upgrading the quality of use depends on an explicit act of a manager or owner plus a favorable set of environmental conditions for the property.

Urban areas tend to grow and expand along the lines of least economic resistance. That is, they grow in the direction in which costs are lowest for the additional space gained. For an economist, this is another way of saying that marginal growth occurs where the marginal cost, including cost of movement, is lowest.

For an area with an expanding economy, the path of least economic resistance may be outward, and hence raw land at the edge of the urban area is developed. This is essentially what happened in most American cities in the forties and fifties as suburban growth surged. The direction might also be upward, resulting in substantial changes in types and intensities of land uses.

The task of real estate market analysis is to detect when and where growth should take place and what type of growth is needed in a community or area. The task may involve only a cursory survey of current market conditions, or it may include everything from an economic base analysis to an intense feasibility study.

The Study Framework

Several distinct phases are involved in making a market study. A decison concerning the type of real estate of concern—office space, warehousing, or apartments—is presumed to have been made before entry into these steps. An awareness of the relation of the national and regional economy to the local economy is also taken as a given.

1. *Market area delineation.* The market area is largely determined by the range of influence or competitiveness of the type of real estate under consideration. A housing study might cover one community, for example. On the other hand, a study for a regional shopping center might extend for fifty to seventy-five miles from a study site.

2. *Analysis of the area's economy.* Analysis of an area's basic resources, employment, income, population, and economic trends provides a setting for later detailed consideration of real estate needs. This is commonly called an **economic base analysis.**

3. *Supply-and-demand analysis.* Real estate supply-and-demand factors are identified, followed by data collection and evaluation. Supply factors ordinarily include an inventory of space, plus current new construction, conversion, and demolition activity. Common demand factors are age-sex distribution of the population, per capita disposable income levels, and family size.

4. *Analysis of current market conditions.* Current market conditions reflect the interaction of the supply-and-demand factors. Thus, items like prices and construction costs, rent levels and vacancies, and the availability and costs of financing must be considered as they relate to the specific type of real estate under study.

5. *Projections and conclusions.* Conclusions about the relative strength of market demand currently and into the future must be reached. The types of space needed at various prices or rent levels must be identified. Finally, a judgment on the share of the market that can be captured must be reached.

6. *Feasibility analysis.* The market study can be made more specific by a feasibility analysis. A feasibility analysis is a study of the profit potential in a proposed real estate project. The study must take account of market, physical, locational, legal, social, governmental, and financial factors.

A market study is usually conducted by an experienced analyst. Identifying and measuring the significant variables is sometimes almost impossible. Even collecting existing data on important factors for a complete market and feasibility analysis is difficult, time consuming, and expensive. The decision maker's research budget is usually quite limited. Therefore the intensity of emphasis given to each of the phases depends on the availability of data and on the size and type of decision to be made.

In interpreting a report, the decision maker should recognize data limitations as well as the sometimes loose interrelationships among the factors stud-

426

ied. In other words, judgment must be exercised. A theoretical framework is needed to exercise this judgment. The major phases of a real estate market study are expanded on in the following sections to provide this framework.

MARKET AREA DELINEATION

The range of competition of the type of real estate under study determines the market area. Criteria for defining a market area include physical, social, legal, and economic elements. These change from one type of use to another. And the importance given to each depends on the situation. Several brief examples illustrate the difficulty of the problem and how judgment must be used in delineating an area for study purposes. These examples are only suggestive of the considerations that can enter into the delineation of a market area.

Competition is communitywide for housing, except possibly in the largest metropolitan areas. People working in the central business district may live by themselves or with their families in a downtown apartment or a one-family suburban house. Workers in suburban factories, shopping centers, and offices are somewhat more likely to live near the urban fringe than in the central city. The analysis of demand must therefore be communitywide. The analyst can make some judgments about needs for apartments versus one-family homes and about needs for middle-income housing verus high-income housing to narrow the scope of the study. Even so, the market area continues to be communitywide.

By way of contrast, the market study area for a supermarket might be limited to a trade area or neighborhood. Groceries tend to be convenience goods; that is, people buy them on their way home from work. Or if they begin the shopping trip from their home, they usually go to one of the two or three nearest stores. Knowing this, the analyst can establish a trade area based on several considerations:

1. *Neighborhood boundaries.* Major streets and highways, freeways, railroad tracks, large parks, reservoirs, rivers, lakes, and steep hills all tend to serve as boundaries between neighborhoods.

2. *Social and economic groupings.* Neighborhoods tend to be made up of people of similar tastes and income levels. Observation of people's dress, cars, and housing gives a clue as to the extent of the similarity. Similar information can be obtained from census tract data.

3. *Travel patterns.* The mode of travel affects where people buy groceries. Street and traffic patterns for motor vehicles and public transit therefore become important in delineating the trade area.

A third example would be the market area for a regional shopping center. It is generally known that people will drive a hundred miles, and sometimes further, to shop. Hence, this is the trade area and the area of competition.

Finally, competition for office and industrial space occurs on a regional and national basis. In locating a new plant or relocating its main office, a major corporation may weigh the relative merits of several cities like New York, Chicago, Houston, Los Angeles, and Atlanta.

ECONOMIC BASE ANALYSIS

Communities, areas, or regions tend to grow or decline in direct proportion to some particular economic advantage they possess relative to the rest of the country and world. This is termed their **comparative economic advantage.** The activities providing this advantage, which results in exports of goods and services in return for money, are collectively called the **economic base** of a community or area. The economic base is sometimes considered the product for which a community is famous, as cars in Detroit or beer in Milwaukee.

Specialization in the economic activity having the greatest comparative advantage takes place over time because the benefits or returns are maximized. For example, Western Oregon and Washington excel in producing quality lumber, primarily Douglas fir, for export to the other parts of the United States and to other countries. Iowa farmers grow corn and soybeans rather than wheat or rice because the net returns per acre are greatest. And Florida, Arizona, and Southern California have built recreation and retirement into major industries because they have better climate than most other states. The activity or activities of specialization make up the economic base of the area or community.

Identifying the Economic Base

Economic activity is generally identified and measured in terms of employment, income, or business earnings. If census data is used as a source, employment is most often used because it is more easily available and is more easily translated into population and demand for real estate. However, the Bureau of Economic Analysis of the U.S. Department of Commerce publishes reports that provide personal income, business earnings, and employment data, including projections. Data used in the examples of this chapter are taken from one of these publications, *Area Economic Projections 1990,* cited in the references for this chapter.

In a base study, economic activity is divided into two categories: base and service or base and nonbase. **Base activity** produces goods or services that are exported to the outside world in return for money, which in turn is used to buy other goods and services. The exchange enables the community or area to survive and to continue as an independent entity. Naturally enough, nonbasic or **service activity** produces goods or services for local consumption or use. That is, they are not exported. Base activity is also sometimes termed primary activity. In this event, service activity becomes secondary activity.

But how can base activity be identified? Frequently people "know what the base is" and presumably can easily identify base activity. In fact, the problem is not so simple. For example, should a department store, a bakery, a service station, and a university be classified as base or service activities? The answer depends considerably on the size of the community or area being studied. Almost all economic activity in the United States is service in that less than 5 percent of our production is exported. If the study unit is a relatively small city of 32,000 people, the answer is more difficult. To the extent that an activity satisfies the needs of a portion of one of the 32,000, it is service. But to the extent that the department store draws farmers as customers or bakery goods are trucked to neighboring communities, the store and the bakery are basic. Likewise, a service station, located on a highway and catering to through traffic, is basic. And if the university draws students and funds from outside the city, it contributes to the economic base of the city.

A **locational quotient (LQ)** is commonly used to distinguish between base and service portions of economic activity. An LQ is the percentage of total *local* activity in an industry relative to the percentage of total *national* activity in the same industry. For example, using business or industry earnings as the measure, the locational quotient of the Oregon lumber and wood products industry is calculated as follows. Data from figure 19–1 for 1971 are used.

$$
\begin{aligned}
&\begin{array}{l}\text{Percentage of industry}\\\text{earnings for Oregon}\\\text{from the lumber and wood-}\\\text{products industry}\end{array} = \frac{\$617{,}824{,}000}{\$5{,}631{,}836{,}000} \times 100 = 10.970\%
\end{aligned}
$$

$$
\begin{aligned}
&\begin{array}{l}\text{Percentage of industry earnings}\\\text{for the United States}\\\text{from the lumber and wood-}\\\text{products industry}\end{array} = \frac{\$6{,}719{,}090{,}000}{\$575{,}459{,}943{,}000} \times 100 = 1.167\%
\end{aligned}
$$

$$
LQ = \frac{\begin{array}{c}\text{percentage of Oregon business earnings}\\\text{from the lumber and wood-products industry}\end{array}}{\begin{array}{c}\text{percentage of U.S. business earnings}\\\text{from the lumber and wood-products industry}\end{array}} = \frac{10.970\%}{1.167\%} = 9.4
$$

An LQ of 1 would mean that Oregon generated business earnings from the lumber and wood products industry at the same rate as the U.S. in general. Hence, the industry, in net, would be service only. A location quotient of less than 1 would mean that Oregon did not meet its needs from this industry and hence had to import lumber and wood products. In actuality, the LQ is 9.4, meaning that Oregon produces over nine times its needs in lumber and wood products. Obviously the industry is very important to the economic base of Oregon. In fact, Oregon produces about 10 percent of the total lumber and wood products used in the United States.

Base Projections

As shown in figure 19–1, the Bureau of Economic Analysis (BEA) report contains projections to 1990 for population, personal income, employment, and business earnings. An analyst, working with employment data only, might project employment to 1990 based on trends and other information available. The

FIGURE 19–1
Population, Employment, Personal Income, and Earnings by Industry for the United States, Oregon, and Eugene-Springfield, Oregon

			UNITED STATES		
Item	1950	1969*	1971	1980	1990
Population, midyear	151,871,000	201,298,000	206,188,080	223,532,000	246,039,000
Per capita income (1967 $)	2,065	3,435	3,544	4,780	6,166
Per capita income relative (U.S. = 1.00)	1.00	1.00	1.00	1.00	1.00
Total employment	57,474,912	79,306,527		96,114,000	106,388,000
Total personal income	313,545,612	691,450,638	730,630,679	1,068,496,000	1,517,173,000
Total earnings	258,747,759	556,542,319	575,459,943	837,490,000	1,176,711,000
Agriculture, forestry and fisheries	23,597,263	20,086,323	19,563,957	21,264,000	23,016,000
Agriculture		19,826,212	19,267,216	20,897,000	22,562,000
Forestry and fisheries		260,111	296,741	367,000	454,000
Mining	5,145,232	5,418,046	5,602,367	6,498,000	7,319,000
Metal		806,825	819,214	972,000	1,115,000
Coal		1,257,943	1,484,985	1,814,000	2,150,000
Crude petroleum and natural gas		2,452,895	2,340,855	2,528,000	2,651,000
Nonmetallic, except fuels		900,383	957,313	1,184,000	1,403,000
Contract construction	15,483,087	34,359,988	35,967,845	51,910,000	71,347,000
Manufacturing	74,817,598	161,773,451	154,042,932	219,486,000	291,595,000
Food and kindred products		12,835,090	13,195,228	16,016,000	19,000,000
Textile mill products		5,498,636	5,297,186	6,721,000	8,109,000
Apparel and other fabric products		6,788,999	6,422,434	8,736,000	11,048,000
Lumber products and furniture		6,881,631	6,719,090	8,925,000	11,286,000
Paper and allied products		5,670,931	5,667,154	8,378,000	11,311,000
Printing and publishing		8,727,787	8,770,961	13,015,000	17,945,000
Chemicals and allied products		10,112,635	10,218,438	15,632,000	22,549,000
Petroleum refining		2,488,096	2,725,315	3,385,000	4,188,000
Primary metals		12,879,553	11,876,473	14,302,000	16,404,000
Fabricated metals and ordnance		14,577,868	13,047,412	19,479,000	26,112,000
Machinery, excluding electrical		18,521,768	16,789,200	24,539,000	32,198,000
Electrical machinery and supplies		16,060,536	14,733,066	25,078,000	37,166,000
Motor vehicles and equipment		10,908,344	11,438,308	15,523,000	20,902,000
Transportation equip., excl. mtr. vehs.		10,885,742	8,603,367	11,634,000	14,184,000
Other manufacturing		18,935,833	18,539,300	28,123,000	39,193,000
Trans., comm. and public utilities	21,131,028	38,611,797	41,690,409	58,672,000	81,233,000
Railroad transportation		5,789,500	5,833,384	5,612,000	5,396,000
Trucking and warehousing		9,302,105	10,105,061	14,784,000	21,063,000
Other transportation and services		8,576,797	8,783,748	12,408,000	16,432,000
Communications		8,542,523	9,846,765	15,785,000	24,398,000
Utilities (elec., gas, sanitary)		6,400,871	7,121,451	10,083,000	13,944,000
Wholesale and retail trade	48,939,614	91,431,489	95,825,881	133,912,000	179,102,000
Finance, insurance and real estate	10,911,234	28,875,247	30,917,872	48,461,000	72,377,000
Services	28,904,344	81,997,846	88,250,069	150,270,000	234,589,000
Lodging places and personal services		9,329,895	9,064,207	11,433,000	13,888,000
Business and repair services		15,472,323	15,837,854	28,786,000	46,980,000
Amusement and recreation services		3,605,237	3,807,939	5,345,000	7,187,000
Private households		4,261,998	4,145,513	4,488,000	4,746,000
Professional services		49,328,393	55,394,556	100,218,000	161,788,000
Government	29,818,358	93,988,132	103,598,611	147,017,000	216,133,000
Federal government	9,500,679	28,831,435	26,155,178	36,388,000	52,201,000
State and local government	14,430,204	54,685,301	62,578,236	95,158,000	144,239,000
Federal military	5,887,475	15,471,397	14,865,197	15,471,000	19,693,000

* Employment is for 1970.

Source: Area Economic Projections 1990, U.S. Department of Commerce Bureau of Economic Analysis (Washington, D.C.: Government Printing Office, 1974).

| OREGON | | | | | EUGENE—SPRINGFIELD, OREG. | | | | |
1950	1969*	1971	1980	1990	1950	1969*	1971	1980	1990
1,532,000	2,062,000	2,139,000	2,334,600	2,537,200	126,657	208,936	222,432	247,200	263,100
2,229	3,242	3,350	4,483	5,815	2,221	2,800	2,902	3,807	4,959
1.08	.94	.95	.94	.94	1.08	.82	.82	.80	.80
579,372	792,602		971,600	1,063,600	45,339	78,452		98,200	104,400
	in thousands of 1967 dollars								
3,414,543	6,685,523	7,166,098	10,466,100	14,754,000	281,319	584,960	645,525	941,100	1,305,000
2,882,424	5,387,183	5,631,836	8,178,700	11,412,200	237,050	465,437	504,559	731,500	1,004,300
309,204	230,023	203,518	216,600	223,800	12,212	4,773	3,380	3,400	3,300
	225,013	197,139	209,300	215,400				2,800	2,600
	5,010	6,376	7,200	8,400				(S)	(S)
10,516	11,572	12,622	16,300	19,500	1,428	2,255	2,823	3,200	3,900
	(D)	618	(S)	(S)				(S)	(S)
	(L)	(D)	(S)	(S)					
	(D)	(D)	(S)	(S)					
	10,570	11,890	15,500	18,600				3,500	4,200
207,608	344,329	337,497	491,200	671,200	25,552	31,911	31,624	46,600	61,100
777,756	1,424,070	1,437,384	2,033,800	2,731,100	83,207	150,986	160,108	225,700	295,600
	159,405	164,277	205,900	248,600				14,100	16,600
	13,744	14,074	17,700	21,500				(S)	(S)
	15,393	16,000	24,300	34,500				(S)	(S)
	589,972	617,824	801,200	979,300				165,700	209,900
	84,291	88,632	124,500	164,300				5,900	7,400
	49,209	51,593	83,200	119,100				7,200	9,900
	20,244	19,986	32,700	45,100				3,100	5,000
	5,044	5,698	8,000	10,700					
	76,128	73,291	103,000	131,600				1,000	1,200
	(D)	(D)	111,300	161,200				11,300	18,800
	95,125	89,659	144,500	230,900				8,000	12,100
	80,755	69,093	137,400	234,100				800	1,500
	38,985	37,644	57,300	84,300				1,200	1,600
	58,407	51,951	72,000	98,300				(S)	(S)
	(D)	(D)	110,000	167,000				6,800	10,900
261,083	436,252	462,781	631,400	852,900	21,495	34,513	37,754	47,300	60,500
	83,505	86,090	85,600	85,800				15,000	16,000
	126,865	135,626	188,800	256,400				13,600	18,400
	72,283	65,114	91,700	124,300				2,600	3,700
	85,414	99,718	158,100	240,100				12,900	18,500
	68,180	76,232	107,000	146,100				3,000	3,600
601,861	1,035,197	1,074,964	1,473,800	1,934,600	44,441	82,974	91,020	122,700	159,200
118,078	261,337	270,679	450,900	679,700	6,189	14,667	15,892	25,800	38,900
319,513	759,188	828,171	1,420,900	2,208,100	24,364	65,361	71,901	121,000	186,700
	92,021	92,614	113,900	134,200				9,900	11,300
	111,216	116,257	212,800	352,500				20,700	35,300
	20,963	24,287	34,600	47,400				2,900	4,300
	31,839	30,964	33,400	35,400				2,900	2,900
	503,145	564,049	1,026,000	1,638,400				84,400	132,700
276,798	885,200	1,004,229	1,443,300	2,091,000	18,162	77,997	90,058	135,300	194,700
89,803	211,740	241,876	330,400	460,600	2,662	11,257	13,464	16,800	22,200
165,155	623,645	718,170	1,067,700	1,572,900	14,502	63,906	73,572	115,200	168,300
21,843	49,819	44,186	45,100	57,300	998	2,835	3,023	3,200	4,100

D—deleted to avoid disclosure of data pertaining to an individual establishment.

L—less than $50,000.

S—too small to project.

employment projection would then be converted into population by dividing by the expected proportion of employment to population for the projection year. Typically, the proportion is about 42 percent, and is rising because of an increasing percentage of women working. Thus a 1980 projection of 15,000 workers for a community would mean an expected population of about 36,000 people.

The projections of the BEA report are quickly available at low cost. Also, many local planning commissions make economic base analysis studies and projections. Thus, unless an investor has a specific need and is willing to pay for information, the data sources mentioned should be satisfactory.

SUPPLY-AND-DEMAND ANALYSIS

Each type of land use has its own unique determinants of supply and demand. Supply determinants tend to be physical and economic in nature, while demand determinants tend to be more social and economic. The discussion here is only meant to indicate the basic supply and demand factors to be considered in a market analysis.

Supply Factors

The existing inventory of space for the use or need under study marks the point of beginning in considering determinants of supply. The supply of real estate (manmade space), on an overall basis, is highly inflexible. That is, at best, new construction can increase the total supply of space less than 2 or 3 percent prices one year. With strong demand, the amount of space for a specific use, other than housing, can be doubled or tripled in one year, however, by the conversion of space from alternative uses in less demand.

An example will make the point clearer. In 1970, the United States had about 75 million dwelling units. The construction industry, operating near peak capacity, can add about 2.5 million units in one year. During this same year, about 300,000 units will be removed from the housing supply because of fire, flood, urban renewal, street and highway projects, and miscellaneous factors. The net added to the supply is 2.2 million units, or just slightly less than a 3 percent increase. Thus, supply of housing increases only slowly, even with considerable demand. Generally this is acceptable because of the long life of real estate.

To extend the example, assume that housing represents 50 percent of the total supply of space. Assume further that commercial office space represents 10 percent of the total supply of space. This means that the supply of office space could be increased approximately five times faster than the supply of housing, assuming the same input of resources. This assumes that all housing construction activities would be redirected toward creating new office space. In fact, if the demand were strong enough, apartment buildings, houses, warehouses, and garages might be modified to increase the supply of office space. Although the example is highly unlikely, the net result might be to double the amount of office space in one year. The example can be extended even further by narrowing the use. It is conceivable that the supply of space for real estate brokerage offices could be increased several times without seriously affecting the supply of space for other needs.

In a similar sense, the supply of space in Madison, Wisconsin, can be increased sharply by shifting contractors, workers, and materials from surrounding communities. Milwaukee, Chicago, and Rockford, Illinois, the nearby communities, might grow at a slightly lower rate as a result because resources are removed from them.

To summarize, the primary determinant of supply is the existing inventory of space for a given use. The existing inventory can be increased by new construction and by alteration of the nature of existing space. Removals, whether by destruction or by alteration for another use, would decrease the inventory of space. As in any market, the value of space must exceed the costs of producing it if increases are to occur.

The principal considerations involved in increasing the supply of space are as follows:

1. The availability and costs of land and utilities
2. The availability and costs of materials and labor
3. The availability and costs of financing
4. The availability and willingness of a contractor, developer, or other decision maker to organize the above factors to produce new space

Demand Factors

The economic base is the primary determinant of space needs in a community. The essential variables are employment, population, and income. The function of the real estate market analysis is to relate the type and amount of economic activity to the specific type of space or use under study. The spending pattern of the population provides a means of relating population, income, and land use.

The recent spending pattern of the U.S. population, by product service, was shown in figure 17–10. Each of the items purchased represents some type of real estate improvement. Food, beverages, clothing, and furniture are distributed through stores, for example. Housing is purchased directly, or rented. Medical and other services are dispensed through doctors' offices, clinics, and hospitals. By applying these percentages to a community's income, as determined in the base analysis, an estimate of the amount of money available to each land use is reached. This money is spent according to the tastes, desires, and values of the population.

The effective demand must still be related to each land use. The market area becomes important here. The income for housing can be spent anywhere in the community, which is the market area for housing. The income for groceries is spent largely in the neighborhood, which is roughly the trade area for a supermarket. A regional shopping center draws from a very broad area. The income earned by the inhabitants of the area must be ascertained and a judgment made as to how much of it the center can hope to draw.

The purchasing power in the hands of the population is therefore the primary determinant of the demand for space. The values, tastes, attitudes, and demographic makeup of the population determine the type of space to be demanded. For example, if the population is young and families are small, demand for living units in multifamily structures is likely to be relatively stronger. A few figures show the importance of age distribution in the population. In 1960, 22.8 percent of new housing starts were in multifamily structures. By 1970, this proportion had doubled to 45.2 percent as a result of changes in the age distribution of the population. And by 1977, the percentage had declined to 27. In a similar fashion, autos and parts accounted for about 5 percent of personal income expenditures in 1960, and for about 7.5 percent in 1970. The land-use reflection of this upward shift was more auto sales agencies, auto parts stores, and gasoline service stations. With the energy crisis, a tendency toward smaller cars and fewer service stations is reversing this trend.

CURRENT MARKET CONDITIONS

Current market conditions are the result of the interaction of supply and demand in the past. The important indicators of current market conditions are unsold inventory and rental vacancies, prices and construction costs, and mortgage defaults and foreclosures. With strong demand, unsold inventory, rental vacancies, and mortgage defaults should be down. Prices and construction costs are likely to be up or increasing. With weak demand, the indications are likely to point in the opposite directions.

Unsold Inventory, Prices, and Construction Costs

Prices must exceed total construction costs for new construction to be justified. Thus, if new houses sell for $25 per square foot, and costs are $23, a contractor will continue to build new units. However, if not all units sell, an inventory of unsold units develops. The increasing inventory should eventually drive prices down and signal the contractor to slow the rate of construction. Of course, units selling quickly and very low inventory signal strong demand and the need for faster construction. The shorter the time horizon of the study, the more important these signals become.

Vacancies and Rent Levels

Vacancies are the equivalent of unsold inventory. If the amount of vacant space builds up, rent levels should fall, and construction of new space should be slowed, or stopped. Thus, for example, an office building developer might note an increase in the amount of unused office space and lower or not increase his asking rental prices. On the other hand, an apartment house manager might note low vacancies and use the occasion to raise rents. Projected demand for an area must be reduced to the extent that vacancies exist because the vacant space is the equivalent of newly constructed space for market purposes.

Mortgage Defaults and Foreclosures

A small percentage of mortgages are constantly in default because of death, divorce, or other financial difficulty of mortgagors. Some of the defaults go into foreclosure. If conditions are not too severe, the borrower can usually find someone to buy him out and take over his property, thus avoiding foreclosure. If current market conditions are extremely severe, lenders may have to take over many properties. This would be a very strong signal that the market is down, and new construction should not be started until economic conditions improve.

MARKET STUDY CONCLUSIONS

A real estate market analysis begins with the delineation of the market area and ends with the estimates of demand and of competition for the use under study. The study may be extended to include a feasibility analysis. Population and income projections from the base study are usually the key elements of long-run demand for most types of uses. Existing inventory and current rates of construction, conversion, and demolition are the key elements of supply. Current or short-run market indicators—vacancies, prices, costs, and mortgage defaults—give clues for immediate decisions by an investor or developer. The long- and short-run analyses of supply and demand should support and be consistent with the study conclusions.

The study report should be written in a clear manner. The data and logic in the report should lead the reader to the same conclusions reached by the analyst. Extraneous or nonpertinent data should not be included.

The study conclusions should blend the short-run and long-run market outlooks for the purpose of an investment, a development, or a lending decision. As we shall see in the chapter on real estate investment, the market-study conclusions provide the basis for projecting cash flows and the resale value of a property under study. If the market outlook is for decline or no growth in real estate needs, the productivity and income of the subject property is likely to hold fast or even decline. This, of course, means that the property is not likely to appreciate and may even decline in value. On the other hand, an optimistic projection probably means increasing cash flows and values. Even if the market is overbuilt, strong growth and demand will absorb the excess space over two or three years. Thus, the market study conclusions are critical to the advisability and value levels of real estate investments.

FEASIBILITY ANALYSIS

A **feasibility analysis** is a study to determine the practicality of a particular situation. It is the extension of the generality of the economic base and market analysis to a specific real estate development or investment problem. A feasibility analysis is a study of the profit potential in a proposed real estate project, with market, physical, locational, legal, social, governmental, and financial factors taken into account. The project

435

is considered feasible only if the value to be created exceeds the total costs to be incurred.

Everyone involved in an investment situation expects to benefit. The owner of the site or property wants to realize as much profit or value increase as possible. The user wants to get a property in a location that best serves his or her needs. The owner may become the user. The developer, brokers, architects, engineers, builders, lenders, and attorneys involved expect to receive reasonable fees or commissions. A feasibility analysis is made so that the initiator of action minimizes risk while getting the greatest benefits possible.

Feasibility analysis applies to three types of situations:

1. A site or property looking for a use
2. A use looking for a site or a property with certain types of improvements
3. An investor looking for the best profit opportunity available

Site Looking for a Use

Costs must be incurred in developing a site or modifying an improved property to suit the needs of a proposed use. The problem is to find a use able to realize enough value or benefits from the completed project to justify the costs. For example an office building might be constructed on a site at a total cost of $800,000. The present value of future rents or benefits must equal or exceed $800,000 for the project to be feasible. Or again, a developer has an option to buy an old, abandoned cannery for $1 million. It is located near the waterfront, which is a major tourist attraction. He is considering converting the cannery into a tourist shopping center at an additional cost of $2 million. The value in the new use must equal or exceed $3 million to justify the project. Thus, cost must be bumped against expected value.

The process of feasibility analysis in the case of a site looking for a use begins with selection of the three or four, or more, most likely uses for the property. The total costs involved in preparing the site or property for each use is then determined. By category, these costs would include the following:

1. Cost of site, or market value if already owned
2. Site preparation costs—soil tests, grading, landscaping
3. Fees of architects, engineers, attorneys
4. Brokerage commissions
5. Construction costs of improvements
6. Financing charges
7. Developer's profit
8. All other costs incidental to the development of the project

The project is feasible if a reliable tenant can be found to pay a rent high enough to justify the costs. It is feasible also if the owner expects to use the property personally and considers the costs reasonable and within his or her financial capability. If the project is to be rented to many tenants, the market analysis must show that sufficient demand exists for the space. And if the project is a conversion or rehabilitation, the higher rents or benefits must be sufficient to justify the costs of modification.

A feasibility analysis of a site looking for a use ends with the selection of the use giving the greatest value to the site. That use is its highest and best use. The selection of that use is the principle of comparative economic advantage in action. For example, alternative uses might indicate site values as follows: office building—$200,000; department store—$180,000; and hotel—$140,000. The owner, acting in self-interest, would almost certainly choose to construct the office building.

A Use Looking for a Site

A user expects to realize benefits from a site, its improvements, and its location. A user values a property on the basis of the future returns it will yield. The costs of renting or owning must be less than the value of the benefits to be realized for a property to be feasible. For example, after analysis of his situation, a merchant decides that the highest rent he can pay for a certain store is $24,000 per year. The owner wants $30,000. The property is not a feasible alternative for the merchant. Or, a developer estimates that apartment rentals prices justify a value of $27,000 per dwelling unit on a certain site. The site would cost $5,000 per dwelling unit, and improvement costs are estimated at $20,000 per dwelling unit. The $27,000 value exceeds the total costs of $25,000. The project is feasible.

The user begins with the results of the market analysis and estimates the amount of unsatisfied demand existing in a community. The demand might be for office space, retail trade area, or three-bedroom apartments. Several alternative sites are selected for analysis, based on their suitability for the use under study. Street patterns and traffic flows, lot size, location, zoning, actual or potential building size and shape, and neighborhood quality would be important considerations in selecting each of the sites. Based on the specific characteristics of each site, the amount of business to be conducted or the gross rental to be realized is estimated. From this, the amount of annual rental that can be paid for the property, or the value of the property, is calculated. The site or property best serving the user's needs is selected.

Unless the user is also the owner, not much attention is given to ensure that the property will be used in its highest and best use. In fact, a user will take a better property and location for his or her purposes than true rent-paying ability would justify. A feasibility analysis of a use looking for a site ends with the selection of a site that best meets the needs of the user.

Investor Looking for a Profit Opportunity

An investor may use market and feasibility analysis to locate, and to choose between, profit opportunities. In the simplest situation, the investor may be trying to select the best of two or three investment properties available. The use and sites have already been joined into a going operation. The techniques for analysis and comparison in this situation are discussed in the chapter on investment analysis.

In a more complex situation the investor may strive to join uses and sites for profits. Thus, the investors may determine from market analysis that demand for a supermarket exists in a neighborhood. Search produces the two or three best sites, which are tied up on options. The investor then approaches supermarket chains to induce one of them to locate a store on one of the sites under option. The effort ends when the store is built and put into operation, yielding a large commission on a long-term sale and leaseback arrangement to the investor.

SUMMARY

A real estate market analysis is a study to predict changes in the amount and types of real estate improvements needed in a community or area. Much judgment must be exercised in making and using a market study because the concepts, techniques, and applications are not yet well developed. Market studies are useful in determining when land at the urban fringe should be improved, as well as when the use of an improved site should be changed or increased in intensity. The study framework for an investment or development decision involves six steps:

1. Market area delineation
2. Analysis of the area's economy
3. Supply-and-demand analysis
4. Analysis of current market conditions
5. Projections and conclusions
6. Feasibility analysis

The range of competition is the prime consideration in delineating the market area. Economic base analysis involves determining and projecting those activities that drive the local economy. Economic base analysis provides the umbrella for market and feasibility analysis. Factors of real estate supply and demand must be studied to relate the economic base study to the use or site under study, on the basis of both a current and a long-run market outlook. The study conclusions should take account of all the foregoing considerations as they relate to the use under study. Feasibility analysis is the study of the profitability of a specific real estate proposal taking account of market, physical, locational, legal, governmental, and financial factors.

KEY TERMS

Base activity

Comparative economic advantage

Economic base

Economic-base analysis

Feasibility analysis

Locational quotient (LQ)

Market analysis

Service activity

QUESTIONS FOR REVIEW AND DISCUSSION

1. Explain briefly the nature of a real estate market study and the uses of a study to a developer, an investor or owner, and a prospective tenant. In other words, why analyze the real estate market?

2. Explain why urban areas grow and change? Then distinguish between changes in intensity of use, quality of use, and type of use relative to land-use succession.

3. List the six phases of a market study in sequence, and explain each phase briefly.

4. What considerations enter into delineating a market area?

5. In economic base analysis, what is a locational quotient? Explain the use of an LQ in identifying the economic base of a community.

6. Identify and explain briefly at least three supply and three demand factors of supply-and-demand analysis.

7. Identify and explain briefly the three types of situations for which feasibility analysis is suited.

8. Does a market study remove all the risk from a project for a developer or an investor? Discuss.

9. Is there a relationship between a market study, a feasibility study, and the highest and best use of a property? Explain.

10. What special factors would warrant consideration in making a market analysis for an office building? A shopping center? A supermarket? A warehouse?

REFERENCES

Area Economic Projections 1990. Washington, D.C.: Bureau of Economic Analysis, U.S. Department of Commerce, 1975. Projections of personal income, employment, and population to 1980 and 1990 for 425 geographic areas across the nation. Historical data for selected years back to 1950 are also included. An update is planned following the 1980 census. Provides a most convenient point of beginning for anyone doing a market study of an area.

Dasso, Jerome. "Economic Base Analysis for the Appraiser." *The Appraisal Journal,* July 1969, pp. 374–85. Case example of processing and projecting census data in an economic base analysis to estimate outlook for investment in a community.

Graaskamp, James A. *A Guide to Feasibility Analysis.* Chicago: Society of Real Estate Appraisers, 1970. Provides a threefold framework for feasibility analysis, related to client/investor objectives. The three components of the framework are legal-political-ethical constraints, physical-technical constraints, and financial constraints.

Messner, Stephen D.; Byrl N. Boyce; Harold G. Trimble; and Robert L. Ward. *Analyzing Real Estate Opportunities: Market and Feasibility Studies.* Chicago: RMNI, National Association of Realtors, 1977. A basic guide for making or interpreting market and feasibility studies, divided into five sections: (1) Use and Relevance of Studies, (2) Methods of Marketing and Feasibility Studies, (3) Financing and Leasing, (4) Case Studies, and (5) Annotated Bibliography. Case studies of shopping centers, office buildings, and a convenience food store are included. Also a fifty-six-page market analysis report is included as an exhibit. Easy to read and understand. A must for anyone involved with market and feasibility studies.

Rabianski, Joseph. "An Alternative Approach to Economic Base Analysis." *The Real Estate Appraiser,* September–October, 1977, pp. 49–54. Presents a conceptual framework for studying a community's economic base based on linkages to regional and national economies.

FIVE

REAL ESTATE INVESTMENT

Property Productivity Analysis

20

The value of a property depends primarily on its productivity. **Productivity** means the ability of the property to provide a flow of services and benefits. Productivity is the net result of a property's site, improvement, and locational characteristics. Ascertaining productivity is the first step toward determining a property's value.

PROPERTY PRODUCTIVITY

Real estate provides services or is productive in many ways. It provides services in the form of shelter for a homeowner and renter. These services may be in the form of fertile land that enables a farmer to grow corn, wheat, and cattle. Or they may be in the form of a well-located place of business, as for a jewelry store, a service station, or a warehouse. In all these cases the real estate serves a need and therefore has utility and value.

Utility—The Basis of Value

The ability of a property to render services that are in demand means that the property has utility. **Utility** is the usefulness of a thing based on its ability to satisfy a need. Utility can also be considered the benefit that comes with owning or using the thing. Utility, whether it is obtained from diamonds, wine, gasoline, medical service, or shelter, commands dollars in the marketplace. Thus, to say real estate has utility is to say that it has value.

To know how much value a property has requires a judgment of the quality, quantity, and duration of services that it can render. More detailed knowledge of the contributions of site, improvements, and location to productivity is required to make such a judgment. Even further, it is necessary to measure productivity in dollar terms to arrive at an estimate of the dollar value of a property. The dollar estimate of value is necessary for many real estate decisions and transactions. The value judgment is made after analyzing the property itself and its locational characteristics.

An owner, in self-interest, wants a property to realize its greatest value. And a property only realizes its greatest value when devoted to its highest and best use. **Highest and best use** is that legal, possible, and probable employment of realty which gives the greatest present value to the realty while preserving its utility.

How Productivity Is Realized

There are three ways in which the productivity of real estate is realized.

1. *Ownership for self-use.* Property is acquired for self-use as a house is bought by a family to provide them shelter. A store is built and occupied by a jeweler as a place of business. An insurance company acquires an office building to serve as a branch office. Ownership is desired to obtain greater security, to give greater flexibility, to avoid paying rent to someone else, or to obtain and control an advantageous location.

2. *Ownership for cash flow.* People frequently invest savings with an eye for a regular return on their money. Thus they acquire apartment houses, warehouses, office buildings, or shopping centers in order to rent out space. The return is generally stable and predictable and can be used to supplement occupational income and to reinvest for building an estate.

3. *Ownership for appreciation.* Raw land, vacant lots, and timberlands are often purchased because appreciation in value is anticipated. It is hoped that during the waiting period the property will earn enough to cover carrying costs, although that will not necessarily happen. Thus, in some cases, additional monies might have to be advanced also. The plan might call for the raw land to be developed into a subdivision at some future time.

Owners may hope to realize the benefits of property productivity in all three ways, and often do.

Sources of Productivity

Productivity results from a property's physical capability and its location. Physical capability refers to the type of services that the property can render and for how long the services can be rendered. Location refers to where the services are rendered relative to where they are in demand, as well as the quality of the services rendered.

The physical capability of a property depends entirely on its on-site characteristics. This means the site and the improvements on the site. Generally the improvements determine how a property will be used, and therefore they greatly influence its productivity. For example, an office building is constructed on a site. For all practical purposes, this precludes the property's use as a motel, a warehouse, or an apartment building. A new use is feasible only if it is so profitable that it can absorb the cost of conversion of the existing improvements for its needs.

How long improvements can render services—their durability—affects the quantity of services to be derived from a property. The size or extent of the improvements also directly affects the quantity of services to be rendered. That is, a 2,000-square-foot building does not compare with a 200,000-square-foot building in satisfying the needs of an insurance company as a home office.

How well a property renders services is termed its functional efficiency. **Functional efficiency** is the quality of services in a given use rendered by a property relative to the quality of services that could be provided by a new property designed for that use. Thus, an old gasoline service station converted into a drive-in restaurant is not likely to be as efficient as a new facility designed and built as a drive-in restaurant.

Location concerns the relation of the property to its surroundings. Location has two dimensions. One is the relation in terms of movement of people or goods to and from other properties (e.g., students going to and from a school, customers going to and from a supermarket). The second dimension involves the environment around the property, in an aesthetic sense. A school located in a park near a pleasant lake is preferred by most people over a school located in a slum area. This dimension of location is realized without moving from the site.

Location determines whether demand exists for the services that a property is capable of rendering. This is the principal reason that market and feasibility analysis studies are made before developing a property. Location also affects the costs of rendering the services. A hotel in the desert may be physically capable of rendering services, but if no demand exists, productivity cannot exist. And if the demand is present, the costs of getting workers, foods, water, and the like may be much higher than if the hotel were located near an urban community.

SITE ANALYSIS

Property analysis means the study of on-site characteristics of real estate as they relate to productivity. Road improvements and public utilities are necessary for the parcel to be productive and to have value and are therefore included as a part of property analysis. Property analysis begins with the site.

A complete listing of all factors or characteristics affecting site productivity is probably impossible. Some factors are physical, some are legal, some are economic. The following categories of factors account for those considered most important. Physical factors in site analysis tend to be less important to property productivity if the property has been developed and is in use. This is because the physical factors no longer determine the size and type of improvements to be added to the site. However, if the site is unimproved, physical factors are a primary determinant of the highest and best use to which a property might be developed.

Size and Shape

The size and shape of a site is of prime importance to its productivity, particularly in urban areas. Lots that are small or of odd or irregular shape are difficult to develop and can accommodate only a limited number of uses. As a consequence, their worth per unit of area is generally lower than for parcels of standard size and shape. For example, a lot that is triangular in shape does not lend itself to the siting of a rectangular building. As a result, either land is wasted or a triangular building is erected with higher construction costs and inefficient interior space arrangements. Long narrow lots are not desirable either; a lot 10 feet by 600 feet would not be practical as a site for a single-family residence even though it contained 6,000 square feet, a typical size lot in many communities.

Generally land value per unit of area declines as the size of parcels increases, and the method of measuring area changes. In rural areas land values are lower and size is stated in terms of acres (43,560 square feet) or sections (square miles of 640 acres each).

In certain cases a value increment, called plottage, or **plottage value,** can be realized by bringing two or more smaller parcels of land under one ownership. Plottage value means that the value of the several parcels, when combined, is greater than the sums of the values of the parcels taken individually under separate owners. Plottage comes about because the larger unit of land can be used more intensively or with lower costs than would be possible with the smaller parcels treated independently. Thus, combining two triangular business lots could provide a site able to accommodate a rectangular building. The benefit, as against two triangular-shaped buildings, would be lower construction costs and more efficient space arrangements. Another example of plottage would be the combining of two single-family lots to make a larger site on which a four-unit apartment building might be built, when allowed by the zoning ordinance.

Topography and Geology

A site must be able to physically accommodate, at a reasonable cost, the use to which it is put. The topography and geology of the earth's crust therefore determine the suitability of a site for support of buildings, or for cultivation, and may limit the uses to which a site can be put.

Topography, the contours and slopes of the surface, must generally not be unduly rough for business, industrial, or agricultural uses. Rough terrain can usually be adapted to residential developments even though the costs may be much greater than with level or gently rolling terrain. Rough terrain increases costs of putting in roads and streets, installing utilities, and landscaping, in addition to increasing building costs. Improved amenities—view and relative privacy—frequently result in builders of upper-income housing seeking hilly terrain even though the costs are greater. Topography also has an important bearing on the drainage and the susceptability to erosion of a parcel of land. This applies to adjoining land as well as to the subject site. The possibility of flooding is always an important item. Stagnant or polluted waters can be a ready source of mosquitos or disease and therefore a hazard to health.

Soil and subsoil conditions bear directly on the income-producing ability of farms. Fertile soils produce more and better crops and are therefore more valuable. In urban areas, marshy conditions or subsurface rock usually mean much greater difficulty, and expense, in development. Soil fertility tends to be of less importance. In urban fringe areas, not served by city sewer lines, the soils must be permeable to readily absorb septic tank effluent if healthy, relatively dense development, is to occur.

Topography and geology must work together to produce desirable sites. The contours of the land affect water flow and drainage. Subsoil conditions also affect drainage. Fertile soil eases landscaping problems. In developing a site, test borings help foretell excavation and foundation needs. Rocks, gullies, quicksand, cliffs, or bog underlayment present special problems in this sense.

Street Improvements and Public Utilities

Access to the street and road system is essential for each privately owned parcel of land in a community. The system facilitates movement between and among all sites and thus serves them all. Without ready access to and from a site, transportation costs would become excessively high to the point that most uses could not absorb them. Thus a farm on a good road or an industrial plant on a railroad and an interstate highway tends to be a prime property. The value of a farm or plant that is inaccessible except by foot is almost certain to be extremely low in comparison. And a completely inaccessible site, as in the snowbound Antarctic or the jungles of Brazil, has no value for all practical purposes.

In a similar sense, other public utilities are important to most sites. Telephone, gas, and electrical services are needed for rapid communication and for power. Sewer and water mains are necessary if septic tanks and wells cannot be accommodated. In many areas storm-water sewers must be installed to prevent periodic flooding.

The value of a site, on a comparative basis, is likely to be reduced by the market, where these various services are not immediately available. Other things equal, a site without water is worth less than a site with water. That means that the value or price of a site is generally on an "as is" condition. The penalty, or the amount of the reduction in value, depends on the specific market participants. The penalty should reflect the loss in benefits suffered because of the absence of the service. If improvements and services are in but not paid for, the value of the site is reduced by the amount of the unpaid costs or assessments.

Zoning and Other Legal Limitations on Use

The highest and best use of a site can be limited by zoning, deed restrictions, easements, leases, or liens. In the absence of limits or constraints on use, the highest value of a site and its highest and best use are determined by demand and by the supply of alternative sites. If the zoning is consistent with the use in demand, the site is likely to be developed to its highest and best use. If zoning is for a less intense use than the use in demand, the zoning controls. Of course, if the zoning is for a more intense use than the use in demand, the demand should control. To develop to the intensity allowed by the zoning ordinance would be to exceed the highest and best use. Likewise, deed restrictions or lease arrangements that are at odds with the use in demand may serve as limitations on the potential use and value of a site.

If several legal constraints apply to a site, the most limiting control takes precedence over all the others. Thus a site may be suitable by demand for a high-rise apartment building, zoned for a two-story apartment building, and limited by a deed restriction to development as a single-family residential site. The single-family use governs. If the deed restriction were removed, the zoning would control.

An easement or an awkward lease can reduce the productivity and therefore the value of a site just as surely as poor drainage, lack of access, or inconvenient size or shape. The cause is less tangible but the effect is just as real. And, as with most physical difficulties, the expenditure of additional monies can often solve the problem.

Title Encumbrances

Lack of clear title or other title problems can also limit the use and productivity of a site. For example, several brothers may inherit a property as tenants-in-common. Unless all the brothers with an interest in the property agree in writing to terms necessary for its development, efforts by an investor to develop it may be fruitless. Another example of an encumbrance limiting use and productivity would be a power-line easement across a site. Assume an easement limits construction on a site to 32 feet in height. Even though demand justifies a seven-story building, which would be allowed by the zoning, the use of the site would be limited to a three-story building. The productivity or flow of benefits from a three-story building is naturally much less than from a seven-story building. Thus, again, legal considerations can affect the productivity of a property just as much as physical considerations.

IMPROVEMENTS ANALYSIS

Improvements involve the main structure plus miscellaneous items such as garages, utility buildings, and landscaping. Improvements should be compatible with the highest and best use of the site and with one another.

447

Structural Analysis

Structures are the main on-site improvements for most real estate. They generally make up more than half of the cost or value of the total property. A primary purpose of structures is to provide shelter from the elements—wind, rain, sun, cold. Many modern buildings even provide year-round climate control for their inhabitants. Buildings also provide privacy. And they provide space for storage and for carrying on economic activities under controlled conditions. In fact, structures are increasingly designed to accommodate specific activities. Thus, a plant for the production of baby foods will differ greatly from a foundry. And an insurance office building will differ from a warehouse. An additional purpose of some structures is to project an image of prestige, as with a bank or a luxury hotel.

The concern of structural analysis is to weigh the value-generating characteristics of a building as they relate to its use and ability to provide services and benefits. In a more specific sense, the concern is with the amount of services provided, with how well the services will be rendered, and with how long the services will continue. This means that the size of the structure must be considered along with its functional utility, its appearance, and its durability. Building equipment must also be given attention.

Physical Capability and Durability

The size, efficiency, and physical soundness of a structure determines the quantity and duration of the services it renders. Other things equal, a large structure will give more services than a small one.

The physical soundness of a building depends on the quality of materials and workmanship used in its construction. A properly constructed building can render services for decades without the need of excessive maintenance costs. Loss in ability to render services—diminished productivity—results from **physical deterioration.** A building suffers physical deterioration in three ways:

1. Wear and tear through use—a ball going through a window, trim getting nicked from being bumped, or a stair railing torn loose.
2. Faults due to poor initial construction or damage as a result of acts of war, fire, explosion, or neglect.
3. Deterioration due to aging and actions of the elements. Examples are the need for replacement of a roof or for repainting. Damage due to storms or extreme temperatures is also included here.

Physical deterioration is one cause or source of property depreciation or loss in value. Thus, although the cause is physical, the effect is economic.

In general, physical deterioration is not a major cause in bringing the useful life of a building to an end. Buildings are more frequently demolished to clear the site for a higher and better use, hence the saying, "More buildings are torn down than fall down."

Functional Utility

The ability of a structure to provide useful services or benefits depends partially on its **functional utility.** To function means to work or operate. To have utility means to have the ability to satisfy a need. Thus, to evaluate a structure's ability to provide a useful service is to analyze the amount of functional utility that it contains. This judgment must be made in relationship to the nature of intended employment of the structure by a user. A dwelling unit is therefore tested against the needs and demands of family living and possibly for prestigious location. A warehouse is measured by the amount of storage it provides and the ease with which items can be put into or taken out of storage. A supermarket is tested against needs for storage, displays, checkout stations, and customer parking. The standard is a new property specifically designed for the intended use.

Functional efficiency is a measure of how well a building is suited to its actual or intended use. A property that performs well relative to a new property designed for the use is said to have a high functional efficiency. Any deficiency relative to the new property is functional obsolescence. **Functional obsolescence** is therefore the decreased ability of a property to provide the benefit or service relative to the new property designed for the use. Functional obsolescence results in diminished productivity because of higher costs of operation and maintenance, reduced ability to generate revenues, or lowered amenities. A five-bedroom house with only one bath has diminished productivity. Functional obsolescence might also be regarded as the relative inability of improvements to perform the functions for which they are intended or used. Current market standards of acceptability provide the basis of this judgment. Functional obsolescence is a major source or cause of property depreciation or loss in value.

The impact of new technology on business and social institutions results in the continuing functional obsolescence of buildings. Elevators caused walk-up apartment and office buildings to be outdated. The automobile, with its high demand for convenient parking space, gave rise to the shopping center and caused the decline of many downtown business districts. Motels replaced hotels for the same reason. New and better household appliances sharply reduced the need for household servants. Self-service supermarkets made the old corner groceries obsolete. Modern, clear-span office buildings and factories continually replace older structures with their many load-bearing walls and inefficient layouts.

The relation of the structure to the site should be taken into account in evaluating the functional utility of a property. Many older shopping centers provide too little parking space relative to sales space and are therefore relatively obsolete when compared to newer centers. An industrial plant with too little parking space for employees is also somewhat obsolete. A four-bedroom house on a small lot cannot have a yard large enough for the outdoor living demands of today. The house is too large for its site and is overimproved. Too small a structure is underimproved. In either event, some loss in value from the optimum occurs.

449

Functional utility is optimal when the site, structure, and equipment are combined in proper proportion with no distracting features. The building design should be suited to meet the requirements of typical users or purchasers in the price range and location. Equipment also should be in keeping with the use of the property.

Even building appearance is a consideration in functional utility. An old apartment house of forbidding appearance that deters tenants is functionally obsolete. Tastes change and architectural styles come and go. A property should meet reasonable standards of simplicity, harmony, and balance to minimize functional obsolescence due to appearance. Extreme architectural styles or bizarre colors detract from a property's general acceptability.

Miscellaneous Improvements

Other site improvements, besides those involving the main structure, frequently contribute to the productivity of a property. These include: (1) walks and driveways; (2) accessory buildings such as garages; (3) landscaping, including lawn, trees, shrubbery and gardens; (4) fences and terraces; and (5) retaining walls. These improvements must be considered in relation to the proposed uses of the property when studying its productivity.

LOCATIONAL ANALYSIS

A property's productivity and value depend on proper location as well as on physical capability. Location has two distinct meanings. One concerns convenience, accessibility, or the relative costs involved in getting to and from the site. The second, called exposure, concerns the environment surrounding the site. Location concerns relationships external to a property only. If these external factors are negative, or diminish the utility of a property, the property is said to have **locational obsolescence.** *Convenience,* or **convenience of location,** therefore means that the costs of getting to and from a property tend to be minimal. In like manner, **accessibility** means that a property is easy to get to or that the costs in time and money of getting to it are minimal.

Convenience

A social or economic activity takes place on a site as only one of many possible uses to which the land or property could be put. For example, a given site might be used for a residence, a professional office building, a gasoline service station, a dry-cleaning pickup station, or a tavern. What determines which use will win out in the competition among them?

Market demand provides the economic basis of the competing uses. The strength of market demand for each use determines the amount each can pay to buy or rent a site or a property. The use giving the site its highest value can be expected to win, other things equal. This is, of course, the highest and best use of the site. Many limiting considerations like zoning or the types of previous improvements, can substantially affect the winning use in the competition. If hotel improvements exist, for example, highest and best use as a bank is not likely to be possible.

If all possibilities are open, convenience or location is usually the dominant consideration in the competition between the alternative uses for which a site might be used.

LINKAGES. Social and economic activities are interdependent. Families in residences tend to be tied to schools, stores, churches, work centers, and friends in other dwelling units. Lawyers are typically in frequent contact with court proceedings and records, clients, abstracting and title companies, and financial institutions. A drive-in restaurant attracts customers, takes deliveries of food and drink, and is the daily workplace of its employees. Each of these relationships is termed a linkage. A **linkage,** for our purposes, is a relationship between two land-use activities that generates movement of people or goods between them.

A child going to school is a linkage. So is a man going to the office to work or a mother going to the store for ice cream. A car getting gas at a service station constitutes a linkage, as is wheat going from the farm to the flour mill. The movement of cars from a factory in Detroit to a distributor in Denver is a linkage. All involve movement of people or goods.

COSTS OF FRICTION. Moving people or goods between linked activities involves four types of costs. These costs, taken as a group, are termed **costs of friction.** Costs of friction are measured in time and energy as well as in dollars. Many costs of friction cannot be easily estimated in dollar terms.

1. *Transportation costs.* The out-of-pocket costs of movement are measured as fares on public transit or operating expenses for privately owned vehicles.

2. *Time costs of travel.* Time is required for a person or good to move from one site to another, from one economic activity to another. The speed of alternative transportation modes, traffic controls, congestion, and the efficiency of the street and road system all affect time costs of travel. The dollar cost of a trip can be calculated based on the time required for the trip and the value of the traveler's time. For goods, estimating the dollar cost of the trip is much more difficult. It is a function of lost business because of the good's not being on hand, of spoilage due to delays in transit, or of lost personnel or work time because of interrupted schedules.

3. *Terminal costs.* Many types of linkage involve expenses at one or both ends. **Terminal costs** include dollars spent for loading docks as well as for moving goods onto and from a truck or train. Storing an automobile during a downtown interview usually involves paying a parking fee, which is a terminal cost.

4. *Aggravation costs.* Traveler irritation and annoyances caused by delay, congestion, bumping and shoving, and heat or cold are costs of travel that, on a personal level, enter into the costs of friction. **Aggravation costs** are very difficult to measure in dollar terms.

The costs of fiction connected with locating an activity on a given site are measured in disutilities (dollars, time, aggravations). For each linkage the costs of friction equal the product of the costs of each trip times the frequency of the trips. Subjective judgment is often required for this calculation. The site providing relatively lowest total costs of friction provides, by definition, the greatest convenience or accessibility for a use.

EXAMPLES OF CONVENIENCE. The importance of convenience can best be shown with an example. Retail trade activity sharply shifted from central business districts to shopping centers following World War II. The prices charged in shopping centers were not any lower, and were possibly a little higher. The centers provided free parking and could be reached easily by auto. Congestion and delays were minimal compared to reaching the central business district. The out-of-pocket cost to reach the centers was in some cases greater than that required to reach the downtown area. It is not unusual for shoppers to go around the central business district to reach a center on the other side of town, for example. But over all, the centers were much more convenient for the population. And, as a result, the centers captured most of the dollar growth in retail sales while central business districts held steady.

A more recent example of the interrelationship between location and productivity is the revival of Atlantic City. In 1976, Atlantic City's economy was faltering and its famed hotels were in severe disrepair. In the fall of that year casino gambling was legalized for Atlantic City. Subsequently, the local economy surged and building remodeling and construction boomed. The nearness of Atlantic City to the population centers of the East enables it to tap a demand for gambling that formerly had to be satisfied through illegal local bookies or in the casinos of Nevada.[1]

Exposure

The environment surrounding a property may enhance or reduce its productivity. Thus a good view, pleasant breezes, or nearness to centers of prestige and fashion are said to give favorable exposure to a property and thereby make its ownership and use more desirable. On the other hand, the productivity of a property subject to loud or untimely noises, to foul-smelling odors and smoke, to unduly high property taxes, or to an unattractive view is reduced. It is said to have unfavorable exposure. Exposure affects the senses of people and is realized or experienced without moving from the site. Some considerations, such as the social mix of a neighborhood, may be considered favorable or unfavorable, depending on the user's perspective. In other words, **exposure** is the environment of a property as experienced or observed by an owner or user of the property.

FAVORABLE EXPOSURE. The primary benefits of exposure are aesthetic satisfactions and prestige. A good view, tree-lined streets, or a southeastern orientation are generally considered desirable attributes for residential areas. So, also,

---

[1] See "Gaming Fever: Atlantic City Bets Casinos Will Revive Its Faltering Economy," *Wall Street Journal,* June 22, 1977.

is stable, flood-free terrain. High ground tends to possess these attributes to a greater extent than do low areas. These factors coupled with an ability to out-bid low-income families, are the reasons that upper-income areas tend to dominate the hills in most urban areas.

Social and business prestige are important determinants of location also. In Washington, D.C., Georgetown or Chevy Chase addresses carry high social acceptance. The same is true of the Gold Coast north of the Chicago Loop. Every large metropolitan area has at least one or two premium areas. As might be expected, these are usually associated with desirable aesthetic qualities.

Locational prestige is also important for business activities. In New York, a Wall Street address suggests financial strength and stability. And a Madison Avenue address is important for acceptance in the world of advertising.

UNFAVORABLE EXPOSURE. A social or economic activity prefers not to locate in conditions that are distasteful, inharmonious, or objectionable. More than one slaughterhouse has been banned from a business district because it produced noxious odors. Slum areas are not inviting for high-income housing developments. Factories emitting excessive smoke cause residential areas downwind to become blighted. Polluted lakes and streams, trash dumps, open sewers, and sewerage-disposal plants are all undesirable neighbors for most land-use activities. The result of unfavorable exposure is usually lower land and property values.

Locational Dynamics

The elements of location are constantly changing. The following four types of change should be taken into account in any analyses to select a site for locating or relocating a specific social or economic activity. Failure to take account of them is likely to result in locational obsolescence. Only factors external to a property enter into locational obsolescence.

CHANGES IN LINKED ACTIVITIES. Tendencies and trends of linked activities to relocate must be noted and taken into account. For example, Sears Roebuck developed a policy of relocating at the edge of downtown areas or in the new shopping centers, following World War II. Montgomery Ward chose to be conservative and stay downtown. For over three decades, Sears far outstripped Montgomery Ward in growth, although the two firms started out approximately even.

CHANGES IN CHANNELS OF MOVEMENT. An activity that is tied to a movement channel should determine periodically if any changes are imminent. New modes of movement or new channels of movement mean new travel patterns. Thousands of motels, truck stops, and gasoline service stations were "done in" by the construction of the interstate highway system. The energy shortage could cause a shift toward modes of mass travel; this would probably increase the advantage of central or downtown locations for restaurants and motels. Drive-in restaurants would also probably be seriously hurt by the shift.

CHANGES IN NONLINKED ESTABLISHMENTS. The development, removal, or relocation of unrelated activities may have widespread effects on many nonlinked land uses. The development of a civic center may break up a retail shopping pattern. A large new office building may touch off a whole series of moves by attorneys, engineers, realtors, and business services, leaving numerous vacancies in the process. Lower rents in the older buildings tend to allow a shift in the makeup of local office users to such types of business as bill collectors, insurance adjustors, printing agencies, and cheap photography studios. An "innocent" newsstand owner may find that the clientele has largely left, forcing either a move or a change in operational methods.

CHANGES IN NATURE OF AN ACTIVITY. Structural and locational obsolescence should be taken into account whenever an activity is located or considering relocation. The influence of changes in technology and in ways of conducting business on the functional utility of a property was discussed earlier. The replacement of the corner grocery store by a supermarket because of a change in distribution methods was cited as an example of functional obsolescence because supermarkets can serve larger areas and must be located on or near major traffic arteries.

Protection from Adverse Land Uses

A social or economic activity can gain some protection from encroachment of undesirable land uses in several ways:

1. A site may be selected that provides physical barriers, such as freeways, a line of hills, or a river, to serve as a buffer against impending blight.

2. Legal action may be initiated to curtail or close down nuisance activities that create smog, dust, or unpleasant odors.

3. Requests may be made for enforcement of public and private land-use controls. And sometimes a site may be selected because of the protective planning, zoning, or deed restrictions that go with it.

MEASURING PROPERTY PRODUCTIVITY

The gross annual income for which a property can be rented serves as a crude index or measure of its productivity as judged by the market. Alternatively, the utility of a nonincome-producing property, like a one-family house or a vacant lot, is measured by the price for which it sells. The theory is simple: the greater the rental or sale price, the greater the utility or productivity of the property. Of course, each investor or home buyer must make individual subjective judgments of the utility possessed by each of several properties in comparing properties to get the best buy.

Income-Property Productivity

Property managers, investors, and others who work with income properties use an annual operating statement to measure property productivity. The statement shows the gross and the net operating income of the property. **Net**

operating income (NOI) is the amount left over after costs necessary to keep the property-earning income have been met.

An annual operating statement should be based on realistic estimates of income and expense. That is, the statement should reflect actual market behavior. For this reason the most useful and important accounting information for purposes of investment analyses is obtained from the operating statement. The annual operating statement of the Douglas Manor Apartments is representative (shown in figure 20–1). It provides the starting point for a series of income and expenses projections termed *cash flow analyses*. Cash flow analysis is taken up in detail in chapter 23.

FIGURE 20–1
Annual Operating Statement, Douglas Manor Apartments

GROSS SCHEDULED INCOME			$108,000
Less vacancy and credit losses (4%)			4,320
EFFECTIVE GROSS INCOME (EGI)			$103,680
Less operating expenses			
Fixed			
Property taxes	$20,908		
Insurance	1,446		
License and permits	256		
		$22,610	
Variable			
Gas, water, and electricity	$ 2,035		
Supplies	1,344		
Advertising	384		
Payroll, including payroll taxes	2,112		
Management (5% of EGI)	5,184		
Miscellaneous services	1,158		
Interior maintenance	1,845		
		$14,062	
Reserves for Replacements			
Roof	$ 640		
Elevator	1,664		
Repaint exterior	704		
		$ 3,008	
TOTAL EXPENSES		39,680	− $ 39,680
NET OPERATING INCOME (NOI)			$ 64,000

GROSS INCOME. The total rents that a property should earn in a year constitute its gross income. The use of "should" here is important. If the owner or manager leases the premises for less than their market rental, the gross income is not an accurate reflection of the property's productivity. This situation can occur because of a long-term lease or because of ignorance or incompetence on the part of the owner or manager. Market rent, also termed economic rent rather than contract rent, should therefore be used in estimating gross income for determining market value. **Market rent** is the number of dollars for which a property could be rented if made available to the market at the present time. Market rent is therefore determined by supply and demand conditions. **Contract rent** is the number of dollars to be paid in rent for a property based on a lease or rental agreement. Contract rent is likely to equal market rent at the time a lease is negotiated. Later, contract rent may exceed or fall below market rent owing to changing economic conditions that are not accommodated in the lease. Contract rent should be used in estimating gross income for a determination of investment value.

Properties frequently rent subunits of space on a month-to-month basis. The most obvious example of such use is an apartment house. However, office buildings, shopping centers, and even warehouses also operate on this basis. For example, the sample property, Douglas Manor Apartments, contains sixteen apartments—eight one-bedroom units and eight two-bedroom units. The rents are $525 and $600 per month, respectively. Gross scheduled income would therefore be calculated as follows:

	One-Bedroom Units	Two-Bedroom Units
Monthly rental per unit	525	600
Times number of months	x 12	x 12
Annual rental per unit	6,300	7,200
Times number of units	x 8	x 8
Gross scheduled income from units	$50,400	$57,600

The total gross scheduled income equals $108,000 ($50,400 plus $57,600).

If a subunit of space, such as an apartment, is not rented for a month, no income is earned. Also, if the space is rented but the tenant fails to pay, no income is realized. For this reason, the gross scheduled income of a property is reduced by the amount of income not realized. The term for this deduction is *vacancy and collection losses.* In the sample operating statement, Douglas Manor Apartments is expected not to collect 4 percent of gross scheduled income because of vacancy and collection losses, which traditionally run 4 percent in the area. A deduction of $4,320 is therefore made. The resulting figure is effective gross income. **Effective gross income (EGI)** is the amount of money the manager or owner actually collects.

OPERATING EXPENSES. Operating expenses are out-of-pocket costs necessary to provide services to tenants and to maintain the income stream. The costs fall into three general categories: fixed expenses, variable expenses, and reserve for replacements.

Property taxes and building insurance are the main two items of fixed costs. Fixed costs are outlays that remain at the same level, regardless of the intensity of use of the property. Property taxes, for example, are levied on an annual basis. They do not increase if occupancy climbs to 100 percent, nor do they decrease if occupancy drops to 65 percent.

Variable expenses, on the other hand, tend to fluctuate with the level of occupancy. More gas, water, electricity, and supplies are used with full occupancy than with 75 percent occupancy. Management is usually calculated as a percentage of the effective gross income rather than of the gross income. Calculation in this way gives the manager more reason to keep the property as fully rented as possible. It also causes the management fee to fluctuate with the level of occupancy. Finally, repairs and miscellaneous services tend to rise and fall with the number of tenants.

Many items of equipment and building parts have lives longer than one year but substantially shorter than the expected life of the building. Stoves, refrigerators, elevators, roofs, boilers, washers, dryers, carpeting, and air conditioning are examples. These items must be replaced periodically to maintain the property so that it can continue to earn income. The cost of replacement of these items is a periodic out-of-pocket expense. Judgment must be exercised in estimating the probable useful life of these items. Accountants used to believe that the annual deduction for replacement of equipment and building parts should be placed in a special account called **reserves for replacements.** Thus, when an item needed replacement, the money was available. The deductions are still made on the operating statement under that heading; however, the monies are not necessarily placed in a special account. The amount of a deduction is calculated by dividing the estimated cost of replacement of an item by its expected useful life. Thus, if a roof has an expected life of 15 years and costs $9,600 to replace, the annual cost is $9,600/15 years or $640 per year.

NET OPERATING INCOME. The amount left over after expenses to provide tenant services and to maintain the property have been met is called net operating income. This is the net amount a property can earn in a year in competition with other properties that offer similar services. In valuation theory, net operating income (NOI) assumes average or typical management. Net operating income directly reflects property productivity. As such, NOI is a basic input in income capitalization to find property value. In other words, it serves as an index of a property's productivity that can be translated into property value.

Net operating income is preferred to gross income as a measure of productivity because it is a standard concept. Differences in costs of operation or leasing terms are taken into account in reaching NOI. Thus, NOI allows comparison of the subject property's productivity with that of other properties. A prestige office building that generates high gross rents but also has extremely high operating costs can be compared to a more modest office building on a long-term, net lease.

NOI indicates what the property can do on its own. Hence, some items that are often considered by an owner-investor in analyzing an income property must not be included in the operating statement. Financing costs, owner's income taxes, depreciation, and corporation taxes are therefore excluded. These items, though important to the investor, do not affect the amount of NOI a property is able to generate.

Mortgaging a property does not increase its income-producing capability. Hence, financing costs must also be excluded from the annual operating statement. Likewise, the owner's income taxes on money earned from the property reflect the owner's tax situation and not the productivity of the property. The same is true if the property is held under corporate ownership; so corporate taxes should not be deducted as an operating expense. Other items to be excluded are outlays for capital improvements, business expenses of the owner in owner-occupied, income-producing properties, and personal property taxes of the owner.

Neither is building depreciation deducted as an operating expense, because it is not a current cash outlay. It does not affect productivity and is not necessary to produce gross income. Thus, its function as an expense differs from that of other operating expenses. Operating expenses are required to maintain the property's flow of services. Depreciation, nevertheless, is a loss in value, which is taken as an income tax deduction. This loss in value is further accounted for in the process of capitalization by adding to the rate of interest (return *on* capital) a rate for capital recovery (return *of* capital).

PRODUCTIVITY RATIOS. More operating data concerning revenues and costs of income properties are published with each passing year. It is therefore becoming increasingly easier to calculate ratios for analysis of income properties and their management.

Standardized accounting terms and formats are used in classifying and reporting the operating information. Considerable data are needed to judge the size and stability of the ratios. And considerable experience and caution is needed in interpreting the ratios. But a start has been made. And the potential usefulness of ratios is so great that it appears almost certain that this area of real estate analysis will be expanded.

Thus far the best operating data have been reported for apartment buildings, shopping centers, and hotels and motels. The Institute of Real Estate Management annually publishes *Apartment House Income-Expense Experience.* The Urban Land Institute publishes *Dollars and Cents of Shopping Centers* every third year and The Building Owner's and Manager's Association, and specialized accounting firms, periodically publish operating information on hotels and motels, office buildings, and other specialized property types.

Two of the more useful ratios for evaluating property productivity are the income ratio and the operating ratio. The **income ratio** is the proportion of gross scheduled income represented by net operating income.

$$\text{Income ratio} = \frac{\text{net operating income}}{\text{gross scheduled income}}$$

For the Douglas Manor Apartments the income ratio equals 59.3 percent.

$$\text{Income ratio} = \frac{\$64,000}{\$108,000} = .593 = 59.3\%$$

The higher the income ratio, the greater the productivity of the property. This might be the result of good management—keeping the property fully rented while keeping control of operating expenses. It might also be the result of high-quality construction that minimizes costs of repairs and maintenance. An alternative ratio emphasizing controls of expenses therefore becomes necessary for cost-control purposes.

The **operating ratio** reflects operating expenses as a percentage of gross scheduled income.

$$\text{Operating ratio} = \frac{\text{operating expenses}}{\text{gross scheduled income}}$$

$$= \frac{\$39,680}{\$108,000} = .367 = 36.7\%$$

The use of the operating ratio might be as follows. New apartment buildings typically have an operating ratio between 35 and 40 percent. As the building ages, costs of repairs and maintenance go up. And the ratio gradually increases toward 50 and eventually 60 percent. The ratio tells the experienced investor or lender if an operating statement is realistic. A ratio of 32 percent for a new apartment building would indicate that not all expenses were reported on the operating statement. Or the expenses might have been underestimated. Operating ratios vary from property type to property type, that is, from apartment house to office building to hotel, and so on.

Nonincome-Producing Property

The productivity of owner-occupied properties like single-family homes and churches cannot be measured in dollars of annual income. Productivity is realized through self-use. Hence, these property types are just not usually rented out. Vacant lots, timberlands, and owner-occupied stores and factories are other property types for which productivity measurement is difficult.

The productivity of some property types can be estimated by comparison, even though they are owner occupied. That is, the rent-producing capability of owner-occupied stores, warehouses, offices, and factories can be estimated by comparison with similar type properties that are rented out for income. For example, if a similar office building rents out for $16 per square foot per year, it's likely that the subject office building would rent out for about $16 per square foot per year. Based on this information and typical productivity ratios for the property type, the net operating income potential of the subject property can be estimated.

The productivity estimate of property types that are not usually rented out but that sell frequently can be based on comparative sale prices. Single-family residences are the classic example in this situation. A sale price is the capitalized expression of property productivity. That is, the price indicates the value for family living purposes placed on the services to be rendered by a one-family house by the buyer. In turn, the productivity of a six-year-old, four-bedroom, three-bath house can be estimated by comparison with prices recently paid in the market for similar houses. The value estimated represents the utility of the property to the typical person in the market for that type of property. This is also true for vacant lots.

Estimating the productivity of utility of churches and of other special-purpose properties is highly subjective. Almost no outside sales occur to provide a standard for judgment.

For the most part the productivity of timberlands and vacant lands come through value appreciation. Productivity can be measured by comparison with similar properties that have recently sold. Or the present value of the sale price can be calculated, with account taken of maintenance and disposition costs and taxes expected at the end of some projected holding period.

SUMMARY

Productivity is the ability of a property to render a flow of services and benefits. Productivity analysis is the first step toward ascertaining a property's value.

The benefits of productivity are realized through ownership for self-use, for cash flow, or for value appreciation. Productivity results from a property's physical capability to render services and from a property's location.

Property analysis means study of the on-site characteristics of real estate, with primary attention given the site and the structure. Major categories of study in site analyses are (1) size and shape, (2) topography and geology, (3) street improvements and public services, (4) zoning and other legal limitations on use, and (5) title encumbrances. Major categories of study in structural analysis are (1) physical capability and durability and (2) functional utility. The functional efficiency of a property is the quality of services rendered in a given use relative to the quality of services that could be rendered by a new property designed for that use.

Locational analysis concerns the convenience and exposure of a property or off-site characteristics. Convenience is measured in terms of the costs of movement involved in carrying on a social or economic activity on a site; the lower the costs, the greater the convenience. Costs of movement are (1) transportation costs, (2) time costs of travel, (3) terminal costs, and (4) aggravation costs. Exposure is the relation of the property to its environment. Favorable exposure means that the environment is pleasing or pretigious.

The amount of net operating income earned or the amount for which the property could be sold provides an index of a property's productivity. Net operating income equals gross scheduled income less vacancy and credit losses and less operating expenses. The income ratio (net operating income divided by gross scheduled income) and the operating ratio (operating expenses divided by gross scheduled income) are highly useful in analyzing and comparing the relative productivities of income properties. The three components of property depreciation are (1) physical deterioration, (2) functional obsolescence, and (3) locational obsolescence. These detract from a property's utility and prevent the property from realizing its highest and best use.

KEY TERMS

Accessibility	Linkage
Aggravation costs (of friction)	Locational obsolescence
Contract rent	Market rent
Convenience of location	Net operating income (NOI)
Costs of friction	Operating ratio
Effective gross income (EGI)	Physical deterioration
Exposure	Plottage value
Functional efficiency	Productivity
Functional obsolescence	Reserves for replacements
Functional utility	Terminal costs (of friction)
Highest and best use	Utility
Income ratio	

QUESTIONS FOR REVIEW AND DISCUSSION

1. What is property productivity? What is it based on? How is it realized? Explain.

2. Explain briefly how each of the following site characteristics relates to property productivity:
   (a) Size and shape
   (b) Topography and geology
   (c) Street improvements and public utilities
   (d) Zoning
   (e) Title encumbrances

3. Define the following concepts briefly, and then explain how each relates to the productivity of structures. Give examples where possible.
   (a) Physical capability, physical deterioration
   (b) Functional efficiency, functional obsolescence
   (c) Locational convenience, locational obsolescence

4. Four "costs of friction" are incurred in moving people or goods between linked activities. Identify and briefly explain the nature of each.

5. What does "exposure" mean to a property in a locational sense? Give at least one example of positive and negative exposure.

6. How is productivity measured for an income property? For a detached one-family residence?

461

7. Write up an outline showing the major sections of an annual operating statement for an income property. State briefly the nature of the inputs or items in each section.

8. Is all property productive? Does all property have value? Discuss.

9. Is a property's productivity related to economic and social activity on a regional basis? On a local basis? Discuss.

10. Is there a relationship between the energy crunch and the location of real estate? Explain or discuss.

REFERENCES

American Institute of Real Estate Appraisers. *The Appraisal of Real Estate.* 7th ed. Chicago: AIREA, 1978. The handbook of professional appraisers. Discusses the nature and meaning of most factors influencing the value of real estate. Chapters 17–19 pertain directly to the measurement and analysis of income and expenses. The style is straightforward for the most part, but considerable background in real estate is assumed at times.

Barlowe, Raleigh. *Land Resource Economics.* 3rd ed. Englewood Cliffs, N.J.: Prentice-Hall, 1978. Real property discussed in an economic framework. Chapters 5–10 particularly pertain to the productivity of real estate. For the advanced or serious reader.

Kinnard, William N., Jr. *Income Property Valuation.* Lexington, Mass.: Heath, 1971. The basic book on the principles and techniques of appraising income-producing real estate. Chapters 2, 6, 15, and 17 pertain directly to measuring the productivity of income properties. Moderately easy to read and understand.

Ratcliff, Richard U. *Real Estate Analysis.* New York: McGraw-Hill, 1961. This landmark book shifted the emphasis of real estate education to analysis for real estate decision making. Chapters 3, 4, and 6 directly concern the analysis and measurement of real estate productivity. Easy to read and understand.

Federal Taxes Affecting Real Estate

The art of taxation consists in so plucking the
goose as to obtain the largest amount of feathers
with the least amount of hissing.
Jean Baptiste Colbert

21

"Taxes are what we pay for civilized society," according to a 1904 U.S. Supreme Court ruling.[1] But in 1947 Judge Learned Hand said:

> Over and over again courts have said that there is nothing sinister in so arranging one's affairs as to keep taxes as low as possible. Everybody does so, rich or poor; and all do right, for nobody owes any public duty to pay more than the law demands: taxes are enforced exactions, not voluntary contributions. To demand more in the name of morals is mere cant.[2]

Thus, no person is obligated to place himself or herself in the highest possible tax-paying position. Rather, the prudent person is expected to practice **tax avoidance,** which means to plan and conduct affairs and transactions to minimize the amount of taxes paid. Such planning requires that the citizen be well-informed on tax law. Tax evasion, on the other hand, is illegal, and punishable by fine, imprisonment, or both. Padding expense accounts, making false and fraudulent claims, and failing to submit a return are forms of **tax evasion.**

---

[1] *Compania de Tobocas* v. *Collector,* 275 US87, 100, 1904.

[2] *Commissioner* v. *Newman,* 159 F. 2nd 848 (2d Cir., 1947).

This chapter sets forth, in generalized form, the federal tax regulations that most directly affect real estate. The basic concepts pertinent to a personal income tax return are presented first, to provide a framework. Then examples and explanations of how the concepts apply to real estate are given.

Tax law is very complex and sticky. Because of this it is sometimes called a bramblebush; everyone working in the field gets stuck at one time or another. Many books and manuals have been written to explain the subject. Millions of dollars are spent in tax litigation each year. No last word is possible because the law coming out of the tax courts is subject to change on a daily basis. Therefore, decisions should not be based solely on the material presented here. Further checks should be made with competent attorneys and accountants and other reliable sources. The tax law discussed here is as of late 1979.

The federal income tax laws are administered and enforced by the Internal Revenue Service, alternately referred to as the IRS or the "infernal revenue service." The IRS is a division of the U.S. Treasury Department. Everyone earning annual income above a certain minimum, currently $750, must file the Individual Income Tax Return, Form 1040.

Federal tax laws concerning corporate income and corporate-held real estate are generally beyond the scope of this book and therefore seldom discussed. Also, state taxes affecting real estate are not taken up here because valid generalization about them is not possible.

BASIC TAX CONCEPTS

Federal tax laws affect most real estate decisions regardless of the type of property involved. The effect becomes very apparent in the income reported and the tax paid. A summary discussion of income is a most logical place to begin discussion of how federal taxes affect real estate since it provides a point of reference to interrelate depreciation methods, tax shelters, capital gains, and methods of real estate disposition.

Types of Taxation of Income

Taxable income is divided into two classes: ordinary income and capital gains income from the sale of a noninventory asset. Each class has its own tax rates.

ORDINARY INCOME. Wages, salaries, commissions, professional fees, and business income are termed ordinary income. Income received as dividends, interest, rents, and royalties also fit into this category. Expenses incurred to generate rents and other types of business income and allowances for exemptions may be deducted in arriving at the amount of ordinary income that is taxable. Ordinary income is taxed at from 14 to 70 percent, depending on the amount of taxable income reported for the year. Corporations pay taxes at the rate of 17 percent on the first $25,000 of earnings, 20 percent on the second $25,000, 30 percent on the third $25,000, 40 percent on the fourth $25,000, and 46 percent on earnings in excess of $100,000.

CAPITAL GAINS INCOME. A capital gain or profit results from selling or exchanging a capital asset, such as real estate, for more than its book value. That is, any value in excess of book value in gifts and inheritances is not subject to capital gains treatment. *Book value,* for capital gains purposes, is value based on accounting calculations and events. For example, an investor pays $300,000 for an apartment property, on which $75,000 in tax depreciation is taken during a six-year ownership period. The investor then sells the property for $345,000. The realized capital gain or profit is $120,000, calculated as follows:

Sale price, EOY6		$345,000
Purchase price	$300,000	
Less tax depreciation	75,000	
Book value of property	$225,000	− 225,000
(technically called the tax basis or adjusted cost basis)		
Capital gain or profit		$120,000

The tax or bookkeeping depreciation accounts for $75,000 of the gain; market-value appreciation accounts for the other $45,000.

The rationale for distinct tax treatment of capital gains and losses is that the gain or loss takes place over more than one year. With our progressive income tax, the impact would be magnified if all the gain or loss were attributed to the year of sale or exchange. And it is not practical to revalue every capital asset each year to determine possible gain or loss. So the government simply applies special rules to gains and losses realized on the sale of capital assets held for longer than twelve months, termed long-term capital gains or losses. Capital gains or losses on assets held twelve months or less, termed short-term, are treated the same as ordinary income.

A gain must be realized to be taxable. A **realized gain** means that cash or boot is obtained in the sale or exchange of the capital asset. **Boot** is cash or the value of personal property given or received in an exchange to balance equities in the transaction. A known increase in value of a capital asset that is not realized as boot or cash is termed **recognized gain.** Recognized gain is not taxable until it is realized. That is, a recognized gain may be transferred from one property to another without being subjected to taxation in a tax-deferred exchange.

Since November 1, 1978, only one method of taxing long-term capital gains has applied. Very simply, 60 percent of any gain is not subject to taxation. Or, 40 percent of any long-term capital gain is added to other, ordinary, income, all of which is taxed according to ordinary-income tax rates. Therefore, for the capital gain of $120,000 cited above, $48,000 ($120,000 x 40% = $48,000) is taxable at ordinary-income tax rates. Assuming an investor in the 50 percent tax bracket, the tax on the $120,000 gain would be $24,000 ($48,000 x 50% = $24,000).

Tax Shelters

A **tax shelter** is a means of reducing taxes on income, either by deferring realization of the income or by changing the class of the income from ordinary to capital gains. Income realization may be deferred by using a bookkeeping loss or expense not involving an expenditure of cash to avoid paying taxes on income as it is received. Such expenses are sometimes termed "artificial losses." Tax depreciation on buildings is an example. The IRS recognizes buildings as wasting assets. It therefore permits owners to take an annual depreciation allowance to recover their investment in the wasting asset even though the building does not decline in value as judged by the market. The allowance is deducted as an expense from the income generated by the property. Land is not considered a wasting asset and therefore no depreciation expense may be taken against it. The market value of the property must not, in fact, decline. If it does, the depreciation allowance is really a recovery of the investment and no advantage has been gained. And, in turn, no capital gain or profit will be realized upon sale of the property.

Deferring or changing the class of income is particularly important when disposing of real property if capital gains are present. The amount of money is often very large. Thus, use of installment sales and tax-deferred exchanges come into play. A **tax-deferred exchange** is the trading of property held for productive use in a trade or business or for investment for a like kind of property held for productive use in a trade or business or for investment. No gain is recognized for tax purposes in a well-structured exchange and hence no tax must be paid. Taxes are only deferred in an installment sale. Methods of disposition are discussed later in this chapter.

CLASSES OF REAL ESTATE

For tax purposes, four classes of real estate are recognized: (1) property held for sale; (2) property held for use in trade or business; (3) property held for investment; and (4) property held for personal use. The class determines the tax treatment that applies to the property.

Property Held for Sale

Property held for sale is considered inventory for tax purposes and not a capital asset. Lots being held by a subdivider or condominiums being held by a builder are examples. The purpose of the owner is sales for profits as opposed to generation of income from rents or investment appreciation for capital gains. The owner is termed a **dealer.**

The tax treatment given dealer property is essentially the same as that given inventory of a merchant. Thus, houses held by a developer would be the equivalent of cars held by an automobile dealer. No depreciation allowance may be taken. All gains are treated as ordinary income and all losses as ordinary losses. That is, capital gains and losses are not recognized. A tax-deferred exchange is not recognized either.

Property Held for Use in Trade or Business

A service station owned by an oil company, an industrial plant owned by a manufacturer, or a store owned by a merchant are examples of property held for use in a trade or business. The real estate is considered a factor of production in much the same sense as equipment in a factory, rather than as merchandise held for sale. This is reflected in the tax treatment given the class, under section 1231 of the Internal Revenue Code.

1. Depreciation may be taken on the wasting asset portion of the property, along with other expenses of operating and maintaining the property.

2. Gains and losses may be taken as long-term gains and losses or as ordinary income and expenses, depending on which gives greater advantage to the taxpayer. In all likelihood, losses would be taken as ordinary losses because they could be used to offset income on a dollar-for-dollar basis. Also, as ordinary losses, they can be used to offset income in previous years to get a tax refund.

3. The property may be traded for like kind of real estate in a tax-free exchange. Thus, the possibility of avoiding capital gains taxes in relocating is available.

Real property that is rented or leased may be treated as 1231 property, with the owner considered to be in the "rental business," that is, in the business of owning and renting apartments or offices. Owners of apartment houses, stores, warehouses, shopping centers, and the like are therefore better off to take the 1231 classification. Long-term capital gain treatment may then be obtained, while capital losses may be used as a direct offset to other, ordinary income.

Property Held for Investment

Investment property is held primarily for capital appreciation rather than the production of income. Large tracts of land bought and held by investors fall into this class. Nominal income such as that from rental for grazing or signboards is insufficient to remove property from this classification to that of income property.

Owners of investment property face the following tax implications:

1. A depreciation allowance usually cannot be taken because the property does not produce income.

2. Interest payments may be taken as an expense only up to the amount of investment income earned by the owner or owners from this and other property. Interest payments beyond investment income must be capitalized, that is, added to the tax basis. All interest expense may be capitalized if the investor wishes.

3. The property may be traded on a tax-deferred exchange for other real estate.

4. Capital gains and losses may be realized.

Property Held for Personal Use

Holding property for personal use, as with a residence, has two serious tax limitations for an owner. The first is that no depreciation allowance may be taken as an income tax deduction. Second, if the property is sold for less than its adjusted tax basis, the loss may not be taken as a deduction or as an offset against other gains. Therefore, where a loss is expected, an owner may find it good strategy to convert the property to an investment or business property by renting it out before selling. A later section discusses tax treatment of a personal residence in more detail.

TAX BASIS

Basis is an expression of property value or cost for tax purposes that is determined at the time of acquisition. In an accounting sense, basis is book value. Basis is necessary to determine the amount of depreciation expense (tax shelter) that may be charged off for income tax purposes. Second, it is needed to determine the amount of gain or loss at the time of disposition. With time and change (the taking of depreciation, the making of improvements, and exchanging), tax basis must be adjusted to ascertain the gain or loss upon disposition of the property. After basis has been changed or modified, it is usually called **adjusted cost basis** (ACB).

Acquisition of Tax Basis

The initial purchase price or cost of real estate becomes its basis. The use of credit to help finance the purchase has no influence on the amount of basis available to the new owner. Thus, a property purchased for $200,000 has a basis of $200,000, even if a $150,000 mortgage loan is needed and used to help finance the purchase. Special rules, not taken up here, determine the basis to a new owner when property is acquired by gift, inheritance, exchange, or other means.

Allocation of Tax Basis

Only the wasting-asset portion of a real estate investment may be depreciated for income tax purposes. Thus a new owner must allocate the purchase price or basis to the land and the improvements. The ratio of this allocation must be the fair market values of the land and the improvements at time of acquisition, according to the IRS. Two methods of making this allocation are used most often:

1. The ratio of land value and improvement value to total property value as determined by the local tax assessor
2. A property value estimate with allocation to land and improvements provided by a qualified fee appraiser

The allocation process is quite simple. For example, assume a property is purchased for $200,000. It is assessed for $100,000, or 50 percent of market value. The assessor's records show an allocation of $15,000, or 15 percent, to the land and $85,000, or 85 percent, to the improvements. In turn, $170,000, or 85 percent, of the purchase price, can be depreciated by the new owner. This ratio or proportion process must also be used in allocating the tax basis of a property acquired in other ways.

Changes in Tax Basis

The tax basis of a property changes through time. Common ways of increasing basis are by making capital improvements, such as building an addition or installing an elevator. The purchase of adjacent property will increase the basis. And carrying expenses, property taxes, and loan interest can be capitalized to further increase basis for investment property. Taking depreciation, selling off a portion of a property, or an uninsured casualty loss (fire) decreases the basis.

An example may be helpful here. An investor buys two vacant lots for $40,000. He makes $120,000 worth of improvements to one lot. He sells the other for $60,000 and he takes $16,000 of depreciation. At this point, what is the adjusted cost basis of the property?

Action	Cost/Price	Change in Basis	Adjusted Cost Basis
Purchase lots	$ 40,000	+ 40,000	$ 40,000
Add improvements	120,000	+ 120,000	160,000
Sell lot 2	60,000	− 20,000	140,000
Take depreciation	16,000	− 16,000	124,000

The adjusted cost basis is $124,000. Note that in selling lot 2, only the basis attributed to lot 2 is deducted in making the adjustment to basis. The $40,000 profit on lot 2 (sale price less cost or $60,000 less $20,000) is reported as a long-term capital gain, provided lot 2 was held longer than twelve months.

TAX DEPRECIATION

The IRS recognizes three fundamental methods of calculating **tax depreciation:** straight line, declining balance, and sum-of-years digits (SOYD). The last two are considered accelerated or "fast write-off" methods and may be used only under limited conditions. The rules on when the methods may be used are given below, following the explanation of the methods themselves. We use a "standard property" in explaining the methods. This standard property's initial tax or cost basis (purchase price) is $640,000, of which $540,000 is allocated to depreciable improvements. The remaining economic or useful life of the improvements is taken as twenty-seven years. **Useful life** is the number of years over which the depreciable asset, the building, is expected to render services of economic value. Useful life is synonymous with economic life or remaining economic life. Most new realty improvements have a useful life of between forty and fifty years. The Internal Revenue Code gives specific details of acceptable useful life. No salvage value is considered to remain for the improvements at the end of the twenty-seven years. A schedule detailing each of the methods is given in figure 21–1.

Depreciation starts when an asset is placed in service for normal use. In the first and last year of service, only a proportional part of a year's depreciation may be taken. Thus, an actual depreciation schedule is not quite as neat as that shown in figure 21–1.

Depreciation Methods

STRAIGHT LINE. **Straight-line depreciation** is the write-off of an investment (tax basis) in a wasting asset by an equal amount each year over the remaining useful life of the asset. Land cost and expected salvage value of the improvements must be deducted before calculating the amount to be taken as a depreciation expense:

$$\frac{\text{Total investment} - (\text{land cost and salvage value})}{\text{Remaining useful life in years}} = \begin{array}{l}\text{annual}\\\text{depreciation}\\\text{expense}\end{array}$$

For the standard property, the annual write-off amounts to $20,000, calculated as follows:

$$\frac{\$640,000 - \$100,000}{27 \text{ years}} = \frac{\$540,000}{27 \text{ years}} = \$20,000/\text{year}$$

This amounts to a 3.7 percent depreciation rate in the first year; ($20,000/540,000 x 100 = 3.7037%).

DECLINING BALANCE. Various percentage rates of **declining-balance depreciation** are provided for in the federal tax code. These are 200, 150, and 125 percent. Only the 200 percent rate is demonstrated here, but the method of calculation is the same in all cases except for the differences in percentages. The higher the percentage, the faster the rate of depreciation and the greater the tax shelter advantage.

With 200 percent declining balance, the initial straight-line percentage is doubled or multiplied by 200 percent to get the annual factor. With the standard property this gives a 7.407 percent factor (3.7037% x 200% = 7.407%). The first year's allowable depreciation equals 7.407 percent of the basis of the wasting asset, or of $540,000; this amounts to $40,000. See figure 21–1. This first year's depreciation is deducted from the initial basis to get the declining balance at the beginning of the second year. In our example, the declining balance at the end of year 1, and the beginning of year 2, is $500,000. Taking our 7.407 percent times the $500,000 gives the allowable depreciation in the second year of $37,037, when calculated without a rounded figure. The declining balance at the beginning of year 3 is $462,963; the allowable depreciation in the third year is $34,294, or 7.407 percent of $462,963, again unrounded. This calculation procedure may be continued as long as the basis does not drop below the salvage value.

Application of Depreciation Methods: Straight Line, 200 Percent Declining Balance, and Sum-of-the-Years Digits to the Douglas Manor Apartment Building

Cost or tax basis (purchase price) $640,000
Less basis allocated to land 100,000 (15.6%)
Equals basis initially allocated to improvements for tax depreciation $540,000 (84.4%)

Remaining useful or economic life of improvements = 27 years
Assume no salvage value to improvements

DEPRECIATION METHOD

	STRAIGHT LINE			200% DECLINING BALANCE			SUM-OF-THE-YEARS DIGITS		
Year	Allowed Dep'n.	Accum. Dep'n.	ECY Basis	Allowed Dep'n.	Accum. Dep'n.	EOY Basis	Allowed Dep'n.	Accum. Dep'n.	EOY Basis
1	$20,000	$ 20,000	$520,000	$40,000	$ 40,000	$500,000	$38,571	$ 38,571	$501,429
2	20,000	40,000	500,000	37,037	77,037	462,963	37,143	75,714	464,286
3	20,000	60,000	480,000	34,294	111,331	428,669	35,714	111,428	428,572
4	20,000	80,000	460,000	31,753	143,084	396,916	34,286	145,714	394,286
5	20,000	100,000	440,000	29,401	172,485	367,515	32,857	178,571	361,429
6	20,000	120,000	420,000	27,223	199,708	340,292	31,429	210,000	330,000
7	20,000	140,000	400,000	25,207	224,915	315,085	30,000	240,000	300,000
8	20,000	160,000	380,000	23,340	248,255	291,745	28,571	268,571	271,429
9	20,000	180,000	360,000	21,611	269,866	270,134	27,143	295,714	244,286
10	20,000	200,000	340,000	20,010	289,876	250,124	25,714	321,428	218,572
11	20,000	220,000	320,000	18,528	308,404	231,596	24,286	345,714	194,286
12	20,000	240,000	300,000	17,155	325,559	214,441	22,857	368,571	171,429
13	20,000	260,000	280,000	15,885	341,444	198,556	21,429	390,000	150,000
14	20,300	280,000	260,000	14,708	356,152	183,848 *	20,000	410,000	130,000
15	20,000	300,000	240,000	14,142	370,294	169,706	18,571	428,571	111,429
16	20,000	320,000	220,000	14,142	384,436	155,564	17,143	445,714	94,286
17	20,000	340,000	200,000	14,142	398,578	141,422	15,715	461,429	78,571
18	20,000	360,000	180,000	14,142	412,720	127,280	14,286	475,715	64,285
19	20,000	380,000	160,000	14,142	426,862	113,138	12,857	488,572	51,428
20	20,000	400,000	140,000	14,142	441,004	98,996	11,428	500,000	40,000
21	20,000	420,000	120,000	14,142	455,146	84,854	10,000	510,000	30,000
22	20,000	440,000	100,000	14,142	469,288	70,712	8,571	518,571	21,429
23	20,000	460,000	80,000	14,142	483,430	56,570	7,143	525,714	14,286
24	20,000	480,000	60,000	14,142	497,572	42,428	5,714	531,428	8,572
25	20,000	500,000	40,000	14,142	511,714	28,286	4,286	535,714	4,286
26	20,000	520,000	20,000	14,143	525,857	14,143	2,857	538,571	1,429
27	20,000	540,000	0	14,143	540,000	0	1,429	540,000	0

* Conversion to straight-line depreciation method

With 150 percent declining-balance depreciation, the initial straight-line depreciation rate would be multiplied by 1.5; with 125 percent, by 1.25.

The taxpayer may shift back to straight-line depreciation based on the remaining economic life at any time. This is usually done when straight-line depreciation gives the taxpayer a faster write-off than would be obtained with the declining-balance method. This changeover occurs at the beginning of the fifteenth year in figure 21–1, as indicated by the heavy horizontal line. Based on the straight-line method, with twelve years of remaining economic life, the depreciation allowed calculates to $14,618. Thus, a changeover at this point usually works to the taxpayer's advantage. A taxpayer changing over to straight-line depreciation cannot revert back to the declining-balance method.

SUM-OF-THE-YEARS DIGITS. **Sum-of-the-years digits (SOYD)** *depreciation* is the accelerated write-off of a wasting asset according to a stipulated schedule of fractions. As with straight-line depreciation, salvage value is applied. The result is a steadily decreasing amount of depreciation allowance.

The denominator in the fractions equals the total or sum-of-the-years digits in the initial remaining useful life of the wasting asset. For example, with a remaining useful life of four years, the denominator is 10 or $4 + 3 + 2 + 1$. For long useful lives, a short-cut method of calculating the denominator is given by the formula:

$$\frac{(N)\,(N + 1)}{2} \text{ or } \frac{(4)\,(5)}{2} = \frac{20}{2} = 10$$

This denominator remains constant throughout all the computations.

The numerator equals the number of remaining years of useful or economic life. In the first year the fraction would therefore be 4/10, in the second year it would be 3/10, etc. The formula to calculate the depreciation then becomes:

$$\frac{\text{Remaining economic life of wasting asset}}{\text{Initial sum-of-the-years digits.}} \times \text{tax basis} = \begin{array}{l}\text{allowable}\\ \text{depreciation}\\ \text{expense}\end{array}$$

Applying the SOYD depreciation to the standard property with a remaining economic life of twenty-seven years, the denominator equals 378,

$$\frac{(N)\,(N + 1)}{2} = \frac{(27)\,(28)}{2} = \frac{756}{2} = 378$$

and the first year's tax depreciation allowance equals $38,571.

$$\$540,000 \times \frac{27}{378} = \$38,571.43, \text{ rounded to } \$38,571.$$

The depreciation allowance for year 2 would be $37,143.

$$\$540,000 \text{ x } \frac{26}{378} = \$37,142.86, \text{ rounded to } \$37,143.$$

Applicability of Depreciation Methods

   Tax depreciation allows a tax payer to recover the cost of an asset over its useful life. Tax depreciation may be taken only for property held for use in a trade or business or held for the production of income. Note that depreciation is not allowable on nonbusiness assets such as a personal residence. And as already noted, depreciation is not allowable in property held for sale, as by a dealer. Finally, depreciation may not be taken on land, and costs generally associated with land development or site preparation, such as grading, clearing, and general landscaping.

   Some distinctions must be noted to determine the specific rate at which depreciation may be taken on a property. New or first-user property is allowed faster write-off than used or second-user property. And residential, rental property is treated differently than non residential property, primarily commercial, and industrial property are.

   Figure 21–2 summarizes the rules for application of the methods. The indicated methods of rates are maximums. Any slower write-off method may be used. For example, new residential rental property qualifies for any method up to 200 percent declining balance. If a taxpayer considers it advantageous, 150 percent, 133 percent, or 190 percent of declining balance may be used. The most often used declining balance schedules are 200, 150, and 125 percent.

FIGURE 21–2
Eligibility of Depreciation Methods Applicable to Real Estate (methods indicated are maximums)

Property Type	"NEW" First Owner-User	"USED" Subsequent Owner-Users
	PROPERTY OWNERSHIP STATUS	
Residential Rental	Sum-of-Years-Digits or 200% Declining Balance	125% Declining Balance when remaining economic life 20 years or more. Straight Line when remaining economic life less than 20 years.
Nonresidential (primarily commercial and industrial)	150% Declining Balance	Straight Line

RESIDENTIAL RENTAL PROPERTY. First-owner-user or **"NEW" residential rental property** may be depreciated according to any recognized depreciation method or schedule. Sum-of-years digits (SOYD) and double declining balance offer the faster write-offs and are therefore usually preferred.

"**USED**" or second- and subsequent-owner property may be depreciated at a maximum rate of 125 percent declining balance, if the remaining economic life is twenty years or more. If the remaining economic life is less than twenty years, straight-line depreciation must be used.

To be classified as residential rental, a property must earn more than 80 percent of its rental income from dwelling units for nontransients. Hotels, motels, and resort condominiums, where more than half the units are used on a transient basis, therefore, do not qualify, and are termed **nonresidential property.**

NONRESIDENTIAL PROPERTY. The fastest depreciation schedule for nonresidential real estate is based on the 150 percent declining-balance method. It applies only to new or first-owner-user property. All subsequent owners are limited to the straight-line depreciation method.

FIRST OWNER-USER. The person holding title to an income property when it is initially rented or put to use is the **first owner-user.** Thus, if a builder-developer rents out space while trying to find a buyer for a property, he is the first owner-user. A buyer becomes a subsequent owner-user. However, if the builder sells the property before any rentals are made, the buyer gets the benefits of being the first owner-user. A buyer will normally be willing to pay more for first-owner-user status. The builder therefore should be reluctant to initiate renting if the prospects for a quick sale appear bright.

Depreciation Recapture

The current tax laws were written to encourage longer holding periods for real estate. With longer holding periods, it is believed that properties would be maintained in better condition by their owners. And in turn, blighted conditions and slums would be less likely to come about.

A concept of **depreciation recapture** was developed to encourage the longer holding period. *Recaptured depreciation* is depreciation that has been taken and then disallowed for purposes of calculating capital gains. This only happens upon the sale of the property. The full amount of gains or profits that are reported as recaptured depreciation are taxed at ordinary income tax rates rather than at the much lower capital gains rates. This higher tax rate is the penalty to the owner for not owning a property for a long time. After a specified holding period, no recapture is required.

Depreciation recapture occurs under two conditions. If a property has been owned for less than twelve months, all depreciation is disallowed and recaptured, and the gain from the sale is treated as ordinary income. In effect, the property is assumed to have been bought or developed for resale and is thus treated as inventory rather than an investment. Therefore, any and all depreciation expenses that have been taken on the property are recaptured and taxed at ordinary rates.

The second condition under which depreciation recapture occurs is when accelerated depreciation has been taken but the property has been owned only for several years. Tax depreciation that has been taken in excess of straight line is termed **excess depreciation.** Consider the property and schedule presented in figure 21-1. Assume a holding period of twelve years. According to the 200 percent declining-balance schedule, depreciation in the amount of $325,559 has been taken (accumulated). Under a straight-line schedule, only $240,000 would have been taken. The difference, $85,559, represents excess depreciation subject to recapture upon sale of the property.

For nonresidential property acquired after 1969, all excess depreciation is subject to recapture and taxation at ordinary income tax rates, with no time limit. For residential property, all excess depreciation is recaptured if the holding period has been between 12 and 100 months. For a holding period of from 100 to 200 months, the proportion of the recapture decreases by 1 percent per month. There is no excess depreciation recapture for a residential property held over 200 months (16⅔ years).

To return to our example, the investor sells the standard property of figure 21-1 at the end of twelve years. Excess depreciation equals $85,559. Because the investor owned the property 144 months at the time of the sale, only 56 percent of the $85,559, or $47,913, is subject to recapture as excess depreciation. The 56 percent is calculated as 200 months less 144 months.

FIGURE 21-3
Real Estate Depreciation Recapture Rules (Effective January 1, 1970)

Property Type	OWNERSHIP HOLDING PERIOD			
	Less than 12 Months	12–100 Months	100–200 Months	More than 200 Months
Residential Rental	No depreciation allowed. Any and all depreciation taken is "recaptured" and taxed at ordinary income tax rates.	Excess depreciation (depreciation taken that is greater than that which would have been taken on a straight-line schedule) is recaptured and taxed at ordinary income tax rates.	Excess depreciation subject to recapture reduced by 1% per month for each month held beyond 100 months. Remainder of excess depreciation is taxed as ordinary income.	No recapture.
Commercial-Industrial (nonresidential)	No depreciation allowed.	All excess depreciation, up to total gain on sale, is subject to recapture and taxation at ordinary income tax rates.		

Composite versus Component Depreciation

Thus far, we have focused our attention on composite depreciation. *Composite* means a combination of distinct parts or components to make up one whole thing, as a building. Thus, **composite depreciation** means to apply one depreciation rate to a building or other asset. The rate is intended to approximate the weighted average of the useful lives of the building shell and superstructure, plus the lesser components. Using a composite rate obviously simplifies depreciation computations, reporting, and record keeping.

However, a taxpayer may choose to depreciate a building and its components independently, using component depreciation. *Component* means one of the parts or elements of a whole. And **component depreciation** therefore means depreciation of the various parts of an asset, according to the useful life of each part. Component depreciation is being used by many investors to realize faster depreciation write-off because of the shorter useful lives of the many components, even though straight-line depreciation is used. And if straight-line depreciation is used, depreciation recapture need not be considered at time of property disposition. Of course, more computations are involved, and record keeping is more complex.

Briefly, straight-line component depreciation might look as follows:

Component	Cost or basis	Useful life in years	Annual allowable depreciation
Roof	$ 36,000	12	$ 3,000
Plumbing	60,000	15	4,000
Wiring	45,000	15	3,000
Heating & A/C	60,000	12	5,000
Roads & walks	60,000	12	5,000
Elevator	36,000	12	3,000
Building superstructure	243,000	27	9,000
Totals	$540,000	—	$31,000

This example is illustrative only. But the $31,000 on straight-line component depreciation compares favorably with the amounts obtainable on accelerated depreciation, according to figure 21–1; and the amount is continuous year after year while depreciation recapture is avoided on disposition.

TAX CREDITS

The Internal Revenue Code provides for an investment tax credit to encourage rehabilitation of older buildings. A *tax credit* is a dollar-for-dollar offset against taxes due and payable. Industrial, commercial, and other income-producing buildings (factories, office buildings, retail stores, hotels and motels) rehabilitated after October 31, 1978 qualify; however, residential rental structures do not qualify. To be eligible, twenty years must have elapsed since original construction or previous rehabilitation. The building must not have been abandoned. And 75 percent of the existing exterior walls must be retained. Cost of acquisition or enlargement of the property is not a recognized expense nor are expenses for exterior repairs. All interior rehabilitation expenses, such as plumbing, wiring, air conditioning, and heating, are recognized, however.

Ten percent of eligible expenditures qualify as a dollar-for-dollar offset against taxes payable, up to $25,000. That is, $250,000 in expenditures produce a tax credit of $25,000. Tax credits may be realized for expenditures beyond $250,000 as well, but at a slightly lower effective rate, which was set at 6 percent in 1979 and will increase to 9 percent beginning in 1982. The credit does not reduce the tax basis of the property.

An example is appropriate at this point. A limited partnership of ten people spends $3 million for the renovation of a small shopping center. Each partner gets a tax credit of 10 percent of $250,000, or $25,000. In addition, in 1982 and thereafter, 9 percent of the expenditures in excess of $250,000 qualify as a tax credit at 9 percent. In our example, 9 percent of the excess $50,000 equals $4,500. Thus, each partner gets a total tax credit of $29,500. In addition, the tax basis of each partner is increased by $300,000 by the renovation project. Taxes obviously are a very important consideration to a real estate investor.

DISPOSITION OF INCOME REAL ESTATE

After several years of ownership, it is usually advantageous for an investor to dispose of or "get out of" a specific property. The depreciation tax shelter has probably been used up. This change in position can be accomplished by cash sale, installment sale, or a tax-deferred exchange. Tax implications vary with each of these techniques.

Cash Sale

Cash sale, for our purposes, means that the seller gets money out of the property in the year of sale. Cash sale is usually desirable when the taxpayer wishes to change the makeup of his or her investment portfolio, with an increased emphasis on stocks, bonds, or oil leases. Also, it may be desirable if the taxpayer needs to release equity for personal reasons, such as to establish a trust fund or a retirement annuity.

All capital gains and excess depreciation recapture must be reported in the year of a cash sale and taxes paid accordingly. Because the tax bite is greatest in a cash sale, investors usually prefer to dispose of their properties by alternative methods.

Installment Sale

An **installment sale** takes place when the buyer makes payments over a number of years. This occurs when the sale is made on an installment land contract, or when the seller accepts a first or second purchase money mortgage for part of the price. Certain technical rules must be complied with for a seller to elect the installment method of reporting gain or profit on the sale and to thereby realize tax benefits.

THIRTY PERCENT RULE. The seller must not receive more than 30 percent of the purchase price in the year of sale to elect the installment method of reporting gain. If more than 30 percent is received in any form, all gain must be reported in the year of sale and taxes paid thereon as in a cash sale. This is true if even 31 percent of the contract price is received in the year of sale. Both direct and indirect payments are counted in the 30 percent. Thus, relief to the seller from liabilities such as taxes, accrued interest, or liens, including mortgage liens, are treated as payments to him or her. Many installment sales are therefore set up with a 29 percent down payment so that a margin of safety is built in.

A down payment of $29,000 on a $100,000 sale with the seller's taking back a purchase money mortgage would ordinarily qualify a transaction as an installment sale. Assume, however, that the transaction has been carelessly set up, and the buyer is required to pay $2,200 in property taxes for the seller. The seller would constructively receive $31,200. The transaction no longer qualifies, and the seller will be required to pay taxes on all gains from the sale with this year's income tax return.

REPORTING RULES. The gains on an installment sale are calculated in the same way that they are for a cash sale. And long-term capital gains continue to receive capital gains tax treatment in the year they are reported. Thus, gains are not only reported later, but they may be subject to a lower tax rate. However, if depreciation recapture is reported on the sale, the first amounts of gain reportable are all attributable to the depreciation recapture. This means a higher effective tax rate in the earlier years of the transaction.

Tax-deferred Exchange

The exchange of property for *like kind* of property without taxation of economic gains is allowed under federal tax law. The gain, though realized in an economic sense, is not recognized for tax purposes. A transaction of this type is frequently referred as a tax-free exchange. This is erroneous. The tax on the gain is just deferred until a later time.

Under current tax law the advantages of a well-structured exchange are very great. As a result, an ever-increasing proportion of income and investment property transactions are exchanges rather than sales. Because tax basis, market value, mortgages, and equities must all be taken account of, exchanges tend to be very complex. In fact, other than to stipulate elements of an exchange, the subject will not be pursued further here.

Three elements must be present in an exchange to qualify for nonrecognition of gain or loss:

1. The transaction must be an exchange as distinguished from a sale and separate purchase.

2. The exchange must be of business or investment assets.

3. The exchange must involve *like kinds* of property. City real estate may be exchanged for county property. A warehouse may be traded for a supermarket. But a tax-deferred exchange of real property for personal property is not recognized. Nor may "dealer" real estate be exchanged on a tax-deferred basis for investment real estate. **Like kind** therefore refers to business or investment property that is exchanged for business or investment property. A personal residence does not qualify as like kind of real estate with business or investment real estate.

Considerable planning is required to structure a tax-deferred exchange properly. Usually some unlike kinds of property, termed *boot,* must be added to balance the equities in the transaction. To the extent that boot is used and gain is recognized, taxes must be paid as a result of the transaction.

PERSONAL RESIDENCE

The owner-occupant of a personal residence does not get all the advantages that an owner-investor of other types of property realizes. An annual depreciation allowance may not be taken on a personal residence, for example. Also, a personal residence is *not* "like kind" of real estate in a tax-deferred exchange for business or investment property. However, interest payments on a mortgage loan and property taxes for a personal residence property can both be used as direct offsets against ordinary income. These deductions may be taken each year to reduce the home owner's income on which tax must be paid. Deductions must be itemized in the tax return to get the benefit. A home owner in the 30 percent tax bracket, with property tax payments of $1,500 and interest payments of $3,000 in a given year, pays $1,350 less income tax as a result. Interest and tax deductions therefore constitute a substantial incentive to home ownership.

In addition, the owner of a personal residence gets some tax relief in the area of capital gains not allowed owners of other kinds of real estate.

Relief of Sale and Repurchase

Homeowners must occasionally relocate as a result of job transfers or of economic necessity. The moves are therefore not necessarily made at a time of maximum advantage or by the choice of the taxpayer. The requirement to pay capital gains tax on each transfer could place a severe hardship on many families. Congress has therefore enacted special relief provisions to lessen the impact of sale of a personal residence.

Gain or profit on the sale of a personal residence is exempt from immediate taxation if a new residence of equal or greater value is purchased within the 36-month period beginning 18 months before and ending 18 months after the disposition of the old residence. This does not mean that all the cash proceeds from the sale must be reinvested in the new residence. The gain is also tax exempt if a new residence is built and occupied within 24 months, provided construction is started within 18 months of the sale. An overall replacement period of 42 months is therefore provided the taxpayer in changing residences.

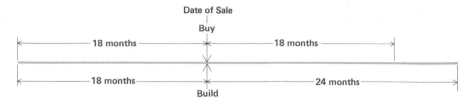

By way of example, John Able bought a Denver residence for $42,000 four years ago. In December of last year his company transferred him to Chicago. He promptly sold his old residence for $69,000 in January, realizing a gain of $27,000 ($69,000 less $42,000). In October of the same year, he purchased a new residence for $73,000. No tax need be paid on the $27,000 gain. However, should Mr. Able sell his Chicago house, any amount realized in excess of $46,000 ($73,000 less $27,000) would be taxable gain unless reinvested in a personal residence in the forty-two-month period discussed above. Alternatively, his investment in the Chicago residence could be considered to be the $42,000 initially paid for the Denver residence plus the $4,000 added over the Denver sale price.

The new residence must be occupied within the period stipulated. The replacement residence will not be considered a new residence if it is sold before disposition of the old or initial residence. And a condominium or a cooperative unit can qualify as a replacement residence. Note that only the purchase price of the new residence must exceed the *adjusted sale price* of the old; many of the dollars may be invested or spent in other directions, and made up by a larger mortgage loan on the new residence.

Relief on Sale by Elderly

Elderly citizens often need and want less living space because of smaller family size and reduced income. They may want to move to a smaller dwelling unit, to a retirement home, or to the home of a son or daughter. In all likelihood, the change would involve sale of the personal residence at a capital gain or profit, which would be taxable. However, on a once-in-a-lifetime election, a taxpayer, aged fifty-five or older, is exempt from taxation of profits from sale of a residence, within limits.

The Revenue Act of 1978 provides a one-time exemption from capital gain taxation on as much as $100,000 in gain realized from the sale of a personal residence. The residence must have been owned and used as the taxpayer's principal residence for at least five of the previous eight years to qualify. A married couple is treated as one taxpayer under this exclusion. Both spouses are treated as satisfying the requirements, if either meets the age, holding, and use provisions. The "one-time exemption" means that the exemption is used to avoid taxes on a gain of $30,000. The taxpayer may not later claim a second exemption of up to $70,000.

Adjusted Sale Price Defined

The adjusted or net sale price is used to determine the amount of gain recognized on the sale of a personal residence. It also determines the minimum amount that must be paid for a new residence to escape taxation of the gain. The **adjusted sale price** equals the full sale or contract price less selling expenses and less "fixing-up" expenses. Selling expenses are primarily brokerage fees, prepayment penalties, and legal fees.

Fixing-up expenses are noncapital outlays made to assist in the sale of the residence, such as painting, minor repairs, landscaping, and so on. The following conditions must be met for outlays to qualify as fixing-up expenses:

1. They must be for work performed on the residence in the 90-day period immediately before the sale date of the property.
2. They must be paid for within 30 days after the sale date.
3. They must not be capital in nature—that is, for substantial improvement, such as adding a room.

Thus, suppose the $69,000 were the contracted sale price received by Mr. Able. If selling expenses were $2,000 and fixing-up expenses were $1,000, the adjusted sale price of the old Denver residence would be $66,000. The gain would be reduced to $24,000, and if the new Chicago residence cost $66,000 or more, no capital gains tax would be payable.

Conversion to Income Property

The owner of a personal residence, upon moving, may wish to convert it to an income property rather than selling it. Rental income, tax shelter, and capital appreciation might all become available as a result. But the property cannot be represented as an income property, and depreciation taken, while it stands vacant and up for sale. The intent must be to convert to an income property as evidenced by the owner's affirmative actions. The property need not actually be rented; however, reaching the status of income property, rental, is prima-facie proof of the conversion.

Once a personal residence has been converted into an income property, the personal residence relief provisions discussed earlier are no longer available to the taxpayer. That is, should the property be sold shortly afterwards, taxes on any capital gain must be paid in the tax return for that year.

Energy Tax Incentives

Installing insulation or other energy-saving items entitles the owner of a personal residence to an income tax credit. A **tax credit** is a dollar-for-dollar offset against taxes payable. The energy-saving items must be installed in, or on the personal residence of, the taxpayer. The resident must be the first person to use the item, and the item must have an expected life of at least three years. Energy-saving items, in addition to insulation, include storm or thermal windows, caulking and weather stripping, and energy usage display, meter, and more energy-efficient furnace burners. The credit amounts to 15 percent of the first $2,000 of qualifying expenditures (maximum credit is $300) and is available to both owners and renters.

In addition, an income tax credit is available for qualifying solar and wind energy-equipment expenditures for installation on a new or used personal residence. The credit amounts to 30 percent of the first $2,000 and 20 percent of the next $8,000 of qualifying expenditures, with a maximum credit of $2,200. Original use of the property must begin with the taxpayer and be expected to remain in operation for five years.

SUMMARY

An investor may legally practice tax avoidance in arranging personal affairs so as to minimize the amount of income taxes payable. A prudent real estate investor therefore attempts to make optimum use of tax shelters in owning and disposing of properties. A tax shelter is a means of reducing taxes on income, either by deferring realization of the income or by changing the nature of the income from ordinary to capital gains. Ordinary income tax rates range from 14 to 70 percent, depending on an investor's tax bracket. And only 40 percent of long-term capital gains is subject to ordinary income tax rates. That is, 60 percent of long-term capital gains is sheltered.

A long-term capital gain results when the sale price less disposition costs exceeds the adjusted tax basis of a property that has been held longer than twelve months. Tax basis is the book value of the property. Taking tax depreciation is a major way that tax basis is reduced. Tax depreciation is a bookkeeping expense allowed by the IRS even though the property may not decline in value. Thus, tax depreciation often shelters income during ownership. Three methods of calculating tax depreciation are recognized: straight line, declining balance, and sum-of-the-years digits. Tax depreciation may not be taken on property held for sale or for personal use. A 10 percent tax credit may be taken for expenses incurred in rehabilitating commercial buildings.

The owner-occupant of a personal residence has a period of forty-two months within which to sell and acquire a new residence without payment of capital gains taxes. And interest payments on a mortgage loan and property taxes on the residence may be deducted from ordinary income to determine taxable income. On the other hand, an owner may not take tax depreciation on a residence while using it as a personal dwelling. And a personal residence is not "like kind" of real estate for a tax-deferred exchange for business or investment property.

KEY TERMS

Adjusted cost basis

Adjusted sale price

Boot

Capital gains income

Component depreciation

Composite depreciation

Dealer

Depreciation methods

  Straight line

  Declining balance

  Sum-of-the-years digits

Depreciation recapture

Excess depreciation

First owner-user

Installment sale

Like kind of property

NEW property

Nonresidential property

Ordinary income

Realized gain

Recognized gain

Residential rental property

Tax avoidance

Tax basis

Tax credit

Tax-deferred exchange

Tax depreciation

Tax evasion

Tax shelter

USED property

Useful life

QUESTIONS FOR REVIEW AND DISCUSSION

1. Distinguish between ordinary and capital gains incomes, and describe the methods of calculating tax payable on each.

2. What is a tax shelter? Give at least three examples or illustrations.

3. List the four classes of real estate for tax purposes, and briefly explain the tax treatment applicable to each.

4. What is basis? How is it initially established? How is it changed?

5. Explain briefly the calculation of depreciation by the straight-line, declining-balance, and SOYD methods. Then briefly explain when each method may be used.

6. Explain the difference between composite and component depreciation.

7. For a personal residence, explain the sale and repurchase or rollover provision to avoid capital gains taxes.

8. Are investment and market values of real estate influenced by tax factors? Discuss.

9. Is there a difference between depreciation for tax purposes and for appraisal purposes? If so, is there always a difference? Discuss.

REFERENCES

Dunham, Eugene F., Jr., "What Is a Tax Shelter?" *Real Estate Today,* October 1979, p. 43. A short and to-the-point discussion of three distinct types of tax shelters and of how an investor may take advantage of them.

Halperin, Jerome Y.; Francis J. Grey; Carl M. Moser; and Herbert A. Huen. *Tax Planning for Real Estate Transactions.* Chicago: FLI, National Association of Realtors, 1978. A comprehensive, and generally easy to read, guide to real estate. The Revenue Act of 1978 is included as an addendum.

Heath, John Jr. "A Tax Saving Opportunity for Real Estate Owners." *Real Estate Review,* spring 1979. Examples of opportunities that may be used to gain tax savings by owners of major facilities, including cases involving tax credits and component depreciation.

Ragas, Wade R., and Ivan J. Miestchovich, Jr. "Incentives for Historic Preservation in the 1976 Tax Reform Act." *Real Estate Review,* winter 1978. An in-depth look at tax credits and depreciation as incentives for the preservation of historical properties, including case examples.

Valachi, Donald V. "Real Estate Tax Topics." *Real Estate Review,* fall 1979. A lead-in article to exchanging and how it may be used to advantage by investors. Clearly written. Several other pertinent articles cited.

Appraising for Market Value

> Nothing can have value without being an objective of utility. If it is useless, the labor contained in it is useless, cannot be reckoned as labor, and cannot therefore create value.
> Karl Marx, *Capital*

22

Market value is the focal point of rational real estate decision making. Whether a person is buying, selling, investing, developing, lending, exchanging, renting, assessing, or acquiring property for public use, market value must be known for the decision and action to be sound. Therefore, anyone engaging in these activities needs a working knowledge of appraising principles and procedures. Real estate can be put to its highest, best, and hence most profitable use only if the principles and procedures are correctly applied in an appraisal.

An **appraisal** is an estimate or opinion of the value of a property, or some interest therein, rendered by an impartial person skilled in the analysis and valuation of real estate. The **appraisal process,** an orderly, well-conceived set of procedures, is used to make the estimate of value. An appraisal is usually followed by an appraisal report setting forth the value estimate along with any reservations or limiting conditions attached to it. Of course, a specific description of the property being evaluated and the date of the value estimate must also be included. Supporting data and analysis are also usually included as documentation of the value estimate.

A person who makes appraisals is known as an *appraiser* or a *valuer.* Many appraisers are employed on a full-time basis by a business or government. But the majority, termed *fee appraisers,* are self-employed professionals who contract with members of the general public to appraise properties for a fee.

The following are the main professional organizations of appraisers:

American Institute of Real Estate Appraisers

Appraisal Institute of Canada

Society of Real Estate Appraisers

American Society of Appraisers

The essential requirements for membership in any of these organizations include (1) a college education or its equivalent, (2) five years of appraisal experience, and (3) mastery of appraisal theory and practice as evidenced by passing stipulated examinations and submission of acceptable appraisal demonstration reports.

Obviously, all the theoretical and practical knowledge necessary to become a professional appraiser cannot be condensed into one chapter in an introductory real estate book. The objective of this chapter, therefore, is limited to defining terms and to providing a basic understanding of what constitutes a good appraisal.

THE NEED FOR APPRAISALS

The need for appraisals is universal. Everyone uses real estate and must pay for its use in one way or another, usually by purchase or rental. This means transactions or situations in which a decision must be made, an action taken, or a policy established. These situations or transactions usually turn on a value estimate. Almost all fit into one of the following classifications:

1. Transferring property ownership or possession
2. Financing a property interest
3. Taxation of property
4. Compensating for loss of a property interest
5. Determining a property utilization program

The buy-sell (transfer) and the financing are most important for purposes of brokerage and the sale of property rights. Further, almost all of these transactions or situations depend in some way on knowing the market value of the property of concern, termed the **subject property.** Thus, the value most usually sought in an appraisal is market value. Simply stated, **market value** is the most probable selling price of a real estate interest.

Transferring Ownership or Possession

Knowledge of market value is extremely important to both the owner and the prospective buyer in negotiating the sale of real estate. For example, assume that the market value or most likely selling price of an apartment building is $600,000. A prudent buyer would be very likely to open negotiations at a lower level, say $550,000, and would not want to pay very much in excess of $600,000 as negotiations progressed. The owner, as a prospective seller, certainly would not want to begin by offering to sell or list the property for less than $600,000. Most likely the initial asking price would tend toward $650,000 or $700,000. Further, the owner would not be likely to accept less than $600,000 unless the pressure to sell were very great.

Market value is also important in determining the rent paid for a property in a leasing arrangement; rent is usually a percentage of market value. In fact, some leases call for property reappraisal every five or ten years as the basis for a periodic adjustment in the rent. These leases are called *reappraisal leases.* Market-value estimates are also needed to establish a fair basis for tax-deferred exchanges of real property or a minimum bid in an auction sale. Further, market-value estimates are helpful in settling an estate in which a number of parcels are involved and in which several people are designated as heirs on a pro rata basis. In this situation, it is often preferable to assign properties to individual heirs rather than to sell the properties and distribute the proceeds to the heirs. If there were no objective value estimates, some of the heirs might believe that they received less than their fair share of the estate. Considerable bitterness and litigation could result, particularly if the value of the estate and the properties were very large.

Finally, an objective value estimate is needed as a basis for the reorganization or the merging of interests in which multiple properties or owners are involved. This need even extends to transactions such as corporate mergers, the issuance of new or additional stock by a corporation or trust, or corporate bankruptcy.

Financing a Property Interest

Large amounts of money are involved in making almost all real estate loans. The lender's first line of defense, or security, is the property. Therefore, the lender wants assurance that the most probable selling price of the property pledged as security is greater than the amount of the loan. For example, suppose a 90 percent loan was requested to finance the purchase of the apartment building mentioned earlier, which sold at the owner's initial asking price of $700,000. A $630,000 loan is implied, which is $30,000 more than the $600,000 market value and $90,000 more than $540,000, or 90 percent of market value. If the $630,000 loan were made, the lender would have little or no cushion if foreclosure became necessary within a few years. The risk to the lender would be much greater than implied by the 90 percent loan to sale price ratio.

Extending this line of reasoning, the prospective purchaser of mortgage bonds also wants assurance that adequate security or protection is provided by the property. Of course, insurers of mortgage loans, for example, the Federal Housing Administration, also want assurance that the security exceeds the initial principal by an established percentage.

Taxation of Property

In many taxing jurisdictions market value provides a basis for assigning assessed value to property, which in turn directly affects the property taxes payable by owners. If assessed value is supposed to equal 60 percent of market value, by policy, the apartment building with a $600,000 market value should have a $360,000 assessed value. If there is a 3 percent tax levy, the annual taxes on the duplex would equal $10,080. Each thousand dollars of overassessment would mean an additional $30 per year in taxes. Errors in estimating market value thus directly affect the amount of property taxes levied against a property.

The amount of annual depreciation allowance that may be taken in an income tax return depends on an appraisal to allocate the costs of assets, or basis, between land and depreciable improvements. The allocation is frequently made in direct relation to the distribution of *assessed* value between land and depreciable improvements. An investor may disagree with the assessor's distribution, in which case, an appraiser may be hired to make the determination. The appraiser may also be asked to provide the term or useful life of the depreciable assets and even the most appropriate depreciation schedule. The market value of gifts and inheritance must also be determined, if sufficiently large, to ascertain the amount of taxes payable to federal and state governments.

Compensation for Property Loss or Damage

Owners take out insurance to protect against risks of property loss or damage due to such natural disasters as fire, wind, flood, lightning, and earthquake. In some cases this insurance is for the cost of replacement or reproduction of the property rather than for market value. But if the loss is realized, the insurance adjustment or settlement depends on an appraisal.

Eminent domain takings constitute a continuing and major need for appraisals. If an entire property is condemned, the owner is entitled to just compensation equal to at least the market value of the property. If only part of the property is taken, the owner is usually entitled to compensation equal to the value of the part taken plus the amount of any damages to the remainder. Frequently the taking authority and the owner will each have two or three appraisals made as a basis for determining just compensation. If a settlement cannot be negotiated, the appraisers may have to testify at a court hearing.

Property Utilization Program

Real estate must be used to its highest and best use in order to give maximum owner benefits. Determining highest and best use involves investigating all alternative ways of using land or realty to find the one or several ways that give the greatest present value to the property. For all practical purposes, each investigation constitutes a market-value appraisal. This analysis is closely akin to market and feasibility analysis and should precede any decision or action concerning development or redevelopment of realty.

VALUE

Real property, or an interest in real property, must have five characteristics to have **value** in the real estate market. The first is utility, or the ability to satisfy human needs and desires, for example, by providing shelter, privacy, or income. The second is effective demand for the services or amenities that the property produces. Effective demand is people's need or desire for the service or amenity of the property, backed up by purchasing power or financial capability. The third is relative scarcity; the supply must be limited relative to demand. The fourth is transferability, meaning that the rights of ownership can be conveyed from one person to another with relative ease. Finally, the realty must be located in an environment of law and order so that when people invest in real property they will not sense a risk of loss because of legal or political uncertainty.

Market Value

The two most widely accepted meanings of value in real estate are (1) the amount in dollars, goods, or services for which a property may be exchanged, and (2) the present worth of future rights to the income or amenities generated by a property. The value under these definitions varies, depending on the person involved. In this sense, value is subjective or dependent on the nature or mental attitude of the person making the exchange or judgment.

If the viewpoint of the typical person exchanging or evaluating a property is taken, the resulting value estimate is the most probable selling price of the property. This definition of market value was given earlier. Market value can usually be estimated in an **objective** manner by methods shown later in this chapter. In applying the methods the following assumptions must be made about the market and the property:

1. Real estate buyers and sellers act with reasonable, but not perfect, knowledge. This is realistic because almost all market participants gather information about conditions before they act.

2. Buyers and sellers act competitively and rationally in their own best interests to maximize their income or satisfactions.

3. Buyers and sellers act independently of each other, that is, without collusion, fraud, or misrepresentation. If this were not the case, in some transactions the price would be severely distorted.

4. Buyers and sellers act without undue pressure; that is, they are typically motivated. This means that properties placed on the market turn over or sell within a reasonable period. Thus a forced sale or a sale occurring after the property has been exposed to the market for an extremely long time would not be considered typical.

5. Payment is made in cash in a manner consistent with the standards of the market; that is, the buyer utilizes financing on terms generally available in the locale.

Market Value versus Market Price

Market value does not necessarily equal market price. In fact, market value for a property may be greater than, equal to, or less than its sale price in an actual market transaction. **Market price** is an amount negotiated between a buyer and a seller, who were not necessarily well informed, free from pressure, or acting independently. Market price is an accomplished fact. *Market value,* on the other hand, is an estimated sale price made by an objective, experienced, knowledgeable appraiser. The estimate is made after looking at and studying a number of actual transactions and other market data. Market value is more akin to the most likely sale price for the property as of a given date.

Market Value versus Cost of Production

Market value may also be greater than, equal to, or less than the cost of a property. As used here, *cost* means the capital outlay (including overhead and financing expenses) for land, labor, materials, supervision, and profit necessary to bring a useful property into existence. In appraisal analysis, cost means the cost of production. It does not mean the cost of acquisition, that is, price.

A rational owner, subdivider, or builder should create lots or construct new buildings only if the expected market value equals or exceeds the cost of production. To subdivide or develop property or to remodel property otherwise would mean proceeding even though a loss were expected. Developing a major property without adequate market analysis also ignores the simple truth that cost does not necessarily mean value.

Value in Use versus Value in Exchange

Each property has a subjective value to anyone considering ownership and use of the property. **Value in use** is the worth of a property to a specific user, based on the utility of the property to the user. The utility may be based on expected amenities, income, or value enhancement. Value in use depends on the specific judgments, standards, or demands of the user. Thus, value in use is synonymous with **subjective value.** Value in use does not depend on identifiable market information.

Value in exchange, on the other hand, is based on the explicit actions of buyers and sellers. **Value in exchange** is the amount of money or purchasing power (in goods and services) for which the property most probably might be traded. Value in exchange is therefore synonymous with market value. Being based on observed or explicit actions, value in exchange is also the equivalent of **objective value.**

A rational investor-owner retains a property as long as value in use exceeds value in exchange. But with time, tax basis is used up for depreciation purposes, community change makes a location obsolete, or an owner decides to retire to the Sun Belt. Thus, for a variety of reasons, value in exchange or market value comes to equal or exceed value in use. At this point, disposition becomes advantageous and market activity results. Note that, in a special sense, value in exchange becomes value in use at the point where disposition becomes desirable.

PRINCIPLES OF APPRAISING

Over the years professional real estate appraisers have developed several principles of real estate valuation. Although only implied, the principles treat real property interests as a commodity and are therefore applied economic theory. The principles are as follows:

1. *Supply and demand.* The market value of real estate is determined by the interaction of supply and demand as of the date of the appraisal.

2. *Change.* The forces of supply and demand are dynamic and are constantly creating a new real estate environment, thereby leading to price and value fluctuations.

3. *Competition.* Prices are kept in line, and market values are established through the continuous rivalry and interaction of buyers, sellers, developers, and other market participants.

4. *Substitution.* A rational buyer will pay no more for a property than the cost of acquiring an equally desirable alternative property.

5. *Variable proportions.* Real estate reaches its point of maximum productivity, or highest and best use, when the factors of production (usually considered to be land, labor, capital, and management) are in balance with one another. (This is also termed the *principle of balance* or the *principle of increasing and decreasing returns.*)

6. *Contribution or marginal productivity.* The value of any factor of production, or component of a property, depends on how much its presence adds to the overall value of the property.

7. *Highest and best use.* For market-valuation purposes real estate should be appraised at its highest and best use.

8. *Conformity.* A property reaches its maximum value when it is located in an environment of physical, economic, and social homogeneity or of compatible and harmonious land uses.

9. *Anticipation.* Market value equals the present worth of future income or amenities generated by a property, as viewed by typical buyers and sellers.

The first four of these principles involve the real estate market. The next three principles apply primarily to the subject property itself. The eighth principle concerns the neighborhood or area around the property. The ninth principle looks at the property's productivity from the viewpoint of a typical buyer or seller.

The principles of substitution, change, contribution, and highest and best use are generally considered most important and therefore merit further explanation.

Substitution

The **principle of substitution** is: A rational buyer will pay no more for a property than the cost of acquiring an equally desirable alternative property. An equally desirable alternative means one of equal utility or productivity, with time costs or delays taken into account. In appraising, a buyer is presumed to have the following three alternatives:

1. Buying an existing property with utility equal to the subject property. This is the basis of the market or direct sales-comparison approach to estimating market value.

reproduction

replacement

2. Buying a site and adding improvements to produce a property with utility equal to the subject property. This is the basis of the cost approach to estimating market value.

3. Buying a property that produces an income stream of the same size and with the same risk as that produced by the subject property. This is the basis of the income approach to estimating market value.

Change

The **principle of change** is: The forces of supply and demand are dynamic and are constantly creating a new real estate environment, thereby leading to price and value fluctuation. That is, physical, social, political, and economic conditions are in a continuing state of transition: buildings suffer wear and tear, people move, laws change, and industries expand and contract. The appraiser's task is to recognize cause and effect in these forces by studying their trends and their effect on real property values. It is the principle of change that necessitates a specific date with each value estimate.

Contribution or Marginal Productivity

The **principle of contribution** is: The value of any factor of production, or component of a property, depends on how much its presence adds to the overall value of the property. Alternatively, the value of the factor or component can be measured by how much its absence detracts from the overall value. For example, the absence of a garage or a second bath reduces the value of a residence by some incremental amount. This principle provides the basis for making adjustments between properties in the direct sales-comparison or market approach in value. It also provides the basis for estimating depreciation due to property deficiencies or excesses in the cost approach.

Highest and Best Use

The **principle of highest and best use** is: Real estate should be appraised at its highest and best use for market-valuation purposes. Highest and best use is the legal, possible, and probable use of realty that will give it the greatest present value while preserving its utility.

The logic behind this principle is that a prudent owner will put a property to that use which yields the greatest value or return, that is, its highest and best use in the long run. To make a decision or take an action on any other basis would not be rational or in the self-interest of an owner or potential owner.

In applying this principle it must be recognized that the value of an improved property in its highest and best use may not be as great as that of the site, if valued as vacant and available for an alternative highest and best use. This would be the case if an improvement were not suited to the highest and best use of the site. The value of the site exceeding the value of the property would mean that the improvements made no contribution to value and should be removed. As long as the property value is greater, it pays the owner to continue the use dictated by the improvements.

THE APPRAISAL PROCESS

The possession of substantial business and real estate knowledge is a must in professional appraising for market value. In addition, a working knowledge of the principles of real estate appraising is needed. On a specific assignment the elements or steps listed below must be developed. The elements are presented here in simplified form only to point up the essential nature of real estate appraising. These elements make up what professional appraisers sometimes call the *appraisal process or framework*. These elements or steps, when taken in the order presented, provide for the systematic analysis of the facts that bear upon, or determine the market value of, real estate.

1. Definition of appraisal problem and planning alternative ways to solve it
2. Data collection and analysis — *comparables*
3. The sales-comparison approach to market value *cost*
4. The cost approach to market value *income*
5. The income approach to market value
6. The reconciliation of estimates reached under the above approaches into a market-value estimate

Defining the Problem

Generally, the appraisal problem should be defined jointly by the appraiser and by the owner or the owner's agent. In defining the problem, agreement must be reached on the following:

1. Identify, in a very specific manner, the subject property, preferably by address and by legal description.
2. Identify the specific legal rights to be valued: fee simple, leased fee, leasehold, or other.
3. Specify the purpose of the appraisal: sale, financing, insurance, condemnation, or other.
4. Specify the date for which the value estimate is desired.
5. Specify or define the value to be estimated: market value, assessed value, condemnation damages, or other. Market value is the objective in a large majority of fee appraisal assignments.

Making a Survey and Plan

The next step is to determine the scope, character, and amount of work involved. This determination is simple and routine in the valuation of a one-family residence, but a check with data sources, such as brokers, lenders, title companies, and other appraisers, is probably necessary when a major property or complex legal rights are involved. The highest and best use alternatives of the property must also be considered. Using the information obtained, the appraiser next determines which alternative approaches to value can be utilized, the amount of effort likely to be involved, and the fee. This determination constitutes the appraisal plan. The fee is usually cleared with the employer at this time.

Collecting and Organizing Data

The appraiser next collects and classifies data from many sources. This is a tedious but necessary task. The point of beginning is to inspect the subject property and then to write a description of it. If the subject property is an income property, a pro forma annual operating statement must be made up. With these data on the subject property in hand, the appraiser is in a much better position to collect data on comparable sales, cost, and capitalization rates. Once they are collected, the data are sorted according to the sales-comparison, cost, and income approaches. This sorting enables the appraiser to concentrate analysis on one approach at a time.

Analysis of the data must also be made for national, regional, community, and neighborhood data. This general analysis provides the setting for the more specific approaches. The focus and nature of much of this general analysis is discussed in earlier chapters. By way of summary review, the following considerations would be important in the analysis of a residential neighborhood.

A. Topography and physical improvements
    (1) rolling or flat terrains, (2) features of natural beauty, (3) draining facilities and quality of soil, (4) condition and contour of roads, (5) transportation and availability of all essential public utilities, (6) quality and housing design, (7) proximity to schools, stores, and recreational facilities

B. Nature and characteristics of population
    (1) living habits, (2) care of homes, (3) attitude toward government, (4) homogeneity of cultural interests, (5) percentage of homeowners

C. Economic data
    (1) homogeneity of professional or business interests, (2) index of earnings and income stability, (3) frequency of property turnover and market price trends, (4) tax and assessment levels, (5) building mortality, (6) vacancies, (7) percentage of area development.

With national, regional, city, and neighborhood data forming a *general* value background and serving as a guide to the economic health of the area under study, the *specific* measures of value under the cost, market, and income approaches may now be applied to the site and its improvements. These approaches are so basic to a market-value estimate that an entire section of this chapter is devoted to each. Following application of the approaches, the value estimates generated from each must be reconciled and a report written to complete the appraisal process.

MARKET APPROACH OR DIRECT-SALES-COMPARISON APPROACH

The market approach or **direct-sales-comparison approach** provides for the estimation of market value of a subject property by referring to recent sales, listings, and offerings of comparable properties. The underlying assumption is that an investor or potential owner will pay no more for the subject property than would probably have to be paid for another property of equal utility or desirability. The term direct-sales-comparisons approach used here is preferred to the term market approach because the cost and income approaches also rely on market data, although to a lesser degree.

The direct-sales-comparison approach to value involves the following four basic steps:

1. Selection of comparable sales
2. Selection of units of comparison and making necessary computations and comparisons.
3. Analysis to determine differences between each comparable property and the subject property, and adjusting as appropriate
4. Estimation of indicated market value of subject property (See figure 22–1.)

Adjustments

The main valuation principle in the market approach is substitution. The process is to discover recent sales of properties similar to, and competitive with, the subject property and then to adjust the prices to the subject property based on differences between the properties. Generally speaking, the greater the likeness between a comparable and a subject property, the fewer the necessary adjustments and the more reliable the resulting value estimate. If sufficient sales of comparable properties cannot be found, listing and offering prices of comparables may be used as a basis for the appraiser's value estimate.

Square footage is almost always used as a unit of comparison in making adjustments. In addition, number of rooms and number of units are usually used in comparing motels, hotels, and apartment buildings. Cubic footage is an important unit of comparison for warehouses and storage facilities. The number of frontage feet is often important in valuing vacant sites and commercial facilities.

Differences that require adjustment between comparables and a subject property fall into four general categories: (1) location, (2) property characteristics, (3) date of sale or value estimate, and (4) terms and conditions of sale. Locational adjustments mainly involve differences in neighborhoods or areas. Items of locational adjustment for one-family houses, for example, include age, kind, size, and condition of houses, zoning and prevalence of deed restrictions, and the general price ranges of houses in similar neighborhoods. Items of adjustment for property characteristics include size, age, condition, number of rooms, number of baths, the presence or absence and size of a garage or carport,

FIGURE 22–1
Elements or Steps in Market-value Estimating (Also Termed *the Appraisal Process* or *the Appraisal Framework*).

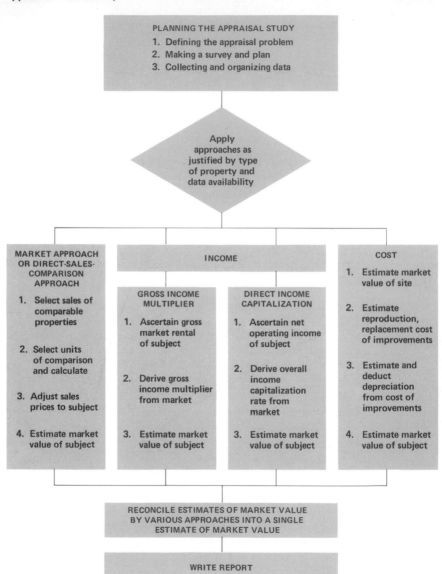

PLANNING THE APPRAISAL STUDY
1. Defining the appraisal problem
2. Making a survey and plan
3. Collecting and organizing data

Apply approaches as justified by type of property and data availability

MARKET APPROACH OR DIRECT-SALES-COMPARISON APPROACH
1. Select sales of comparable properties
2. Select units of comparison and calculate
3. Adjust sales prices to subject
4. Estimate market value of subject

INCOME

GROSS INCOME MULTIPLIER
1. Ascertain gross market rental of subject
2. Derive gross income multiplier from market
3. Estimate market value of subject

DIRECT INCOME CAPITALIZATION
1. Ascertain net operating income of subject
2. Derive overall income capitalization rate from market
3. Estimate market value of subject

COST
1. Estimate market value of site
2. Estimate reproduction, replacement cost of improvements
3. Estimate and deduct depreciation from cost of improvements
4. Estimate market value of subject

RECONCILE ESTIMATES OF MARKET VALUE BY VARIOUS APPROACHES INTO A SINGLE ESTIMATE OF MARKET VALUE

WRITE REPORT

and special features like fireplaces, air conditioning, or a swimming pool. An adjustment must be made for time of sale if market activity, money availability, or sale prices in general change between the date of sale of the comparable property and the date of the value estimate for the subject property. Finally, if a buyer or seller were under pressure, if an unusually high down payment were required, or if one party knew more about market conditions than the other, a terms-and-conditions adjustment would be necessary. Only sales of comparables that occurred before the date of the value estimate should be used in making adjustments; to use sales of a later date would give the appraiser greater market knowledge than that possessed by buyers and sellers as of the date of valuation.

An Example

Figure 22–2 gives an example of adjustments that might be made in the direct-sales-comparison approach to value as applied to an apartment house.

Figure 22–2
Direct-Sales-Comparison Adjustment Analysis of Apartment Properties

		COMPARABLE SALE		
Item of Comparison	Subject Property	730 Oakway	3320 Hilyard	1720 Park
Sale price	—	$610,000	$745,760	$680,000
Number of units	16	14	16	16
Sale price/unit	—	$43,571	$46,610	$42,500
Number of rooms/unit	4½	4½	4½	4½
ADJUSTMENTS				
1. Location	fair	fair	excellent	fair
2. Physical characteristics			−10%	
a. Condition	rundown	excellent	fair	excellent
		−10%	−5%	−10%
b. Garage	1½	1	2	1½
spaces/unit		+2%	−2%	—
3. Date of sale		current	2 months	4 months
			+2%	+4%
Net adjustment		−8%	−15%	−6
Adj. S.P./unit of subject		$40,085	$39,618	$39,995

Note that all adjustments are made from comparables to the subject property. The adjusted sale prices per unit represent the probable sale price of the subject property by comparison with each respective comparable property. The range is from $39,618 to $40,085. Using this information, an appraiser could justify an indicated market value for the subject property of $40,000/unit by the direct-sales-comparison approach. On an overall basis, the subject property, with 16 units, has indicated market value of $640,000.

$$16 \text{ units} \times \$40,000/\text{unit} = \$640,000.$$

Note also that comparisons are made on a per unit basis to take account of different size properties. That is, adjustments on a per unit make it possible to compare a fourteen-unit property with a sixteen-unit property or a twenty-unit property if other things are generally the same. Finally, recognize that comparisons and adjustments are actually much more complex than indicated here. Considerable judgment and experience are required. But our purpose here is primarily to illustrate the process.

Uses and Limitations

The direct-sales-comparison method is well suited to making an objective estimate of a property's market value. It depends directly on market information. The inclusion of several comparable sales almost ensures that the thinking and behavior of typical buyers and sellers are included in the resulting value estimate. Also, the approach takes account of varying financing terms, inflation, and other market elements that influence the typical purchaser. Courts place greater emphasis and reliance on this method than on any other method.

The method is most applicable when the market is active and when actual sales data are readily available. This means the direct-sales-comparison method is most appropriate for a property type that is widely bought and sold, such as vacant lots, one-family houses, and condominium units. In fact, lack of adequate market data is a major limitation of the method. By default, then, the method is not applicable to the kind of property that is only infrequently bought and sold or is of a unique character. Two other limitations are that sales of truly comparable properties must be selected and that the value indication is based on historical data. The assumption is that market forces and behavior of the past continue on into the present or to date of the value estimate.

INCOME APPROACH

The **income approach** uses a ratio, derived from the market, to convert income generated by a property into market value. The underlying assumption or principle is that a rational potential owner will pay no more for an income property than the cost of acquiring an alternative property capable of producing an income stream of the same size and with the same risk. One version of the income approach, termed the **gross income multiplier (GIM),** relates the total income generated by a property to its market value. A second version, termed **direct income-capitalization,** relates net operating income to market value. These are the two most basic versions of the income approach. Additional, more complex versions would be encountered in a book or course devoted exclusively to appraisal.

Gross Income Multiplier

The following basic steps are involved in using the GIM technique to find market value:

1. Ascertaining the current gross market rental of the subject property by comparing it with rented properties of similar utility
2. Deriving the market gross income multiplier by analyzing comparable properties that were sold while rented
3. Multiplying the current market rental of the subject property by the GIM to get an indication of the market value of the subject property

ASCERTAINING CURRENT MARKET RENTAL. Current market rental of the subject property is obtained by comparing the subject property with similar properties that are rented. **Market rent** means the amount that a property would command if exposed to the market for a reasonable time and rented by a reasonably knowledgeable tenant. Market rental is analogous to market value except that rental instead of a sale price is involved. Annual rental is commonly used for income properties. And adjustments are made in rental price from the comparable property to the subject property in much the same way that a sales price is adjusted from the comparable to the subject in the market approach to value. Thus, if rental prices for three comparable one-bedroom apartments, after adjustment to the subject, equal $510, $520, and $525, the subject may be considered to have a gross monthly market rental value of $525. This $525 would be multiplied by 12 to get the annual rental of $6,300 for the unit. And, if eight one bedroom units were in the building, the gross annual income for the units would amount to $50,400. In a similar manner, eight two bedroom units with a market rental of $600 per month would give an annual rental of $57,600 ($600 x 8 x 12). Gross annual rental for the property would equal $108,000 ($50,400 + $57,600).

DERIVING THE GIM. Dividing sales price by the monthly gross income gives the gross income multiplier. The calculations are made as follows to derive the GIM for sales of income houses.

$$\frac{\text{Sale price}}{\text{Gross income}} = \text{gross income multiplier (GIM)}$$

$$\text{Comparable A: } \frac{\$610,000}{\$101,400} = 6.02$$

$$\text{Comparable B: } \frac{\$745,760}{\$124,500} = 5.99$$

$$\text{Comparable C: } \frac{\$680,000}{\$113,200} = 6.01$$

A market GIM of 6.00 therefore seems reasonable for apartment houses in this particular neighborhood at this time. The GIM changes through time. A GIM once derived is not a "once and for all" rule of thumb that applies to all similar properties.

APPLYING THE GIM. The indicated market value of the subject property is $648,000, as determined by multiplying its gross income by the market GIM, for example:

$$\text{Gross income x market gross income multiplier} = \begin{array}{l}\text{indicated}\\\text{market value}\end{array}$$
$$\$108,000 \times 6.00 = \$648,000$$

Monthly rental income is usually used in making these calculations for one-family residences. The ratio is then called a *gross rent multiplier* (GRM).

USES AND LIMITATIONS. The multiplier technique is a quick, simple, and direct technique for estimating value whenever properties are rented at the same time they are sold, for instance, one-family residences and apartment buildings. Many appraisers use the technique early in their appraisal analysis to develop a quick idea of the market value of a property to aid their judgment in applying other techniques.

One limitation of the technique is that sales of rental properties are not always available for deriving the multiplier. Another limitation is that gross rents are used instead of net operating incomes. In addition, the ratio is subject to some distortion because adverse zoning, lack of maintenance, or heavy property taxes will negatively influence sale prices with little effect on rental levels. Rent controls or heavy operating costs, however, may hold down rented levels without influencing sale prices. Thus, unless the comparables are similar in all respects to the subject, a distorted GIM may be derived from the market. Finally, in deriving a GIM, the presence or absence of extras, for example, range, refrigerator, furniture, must be the same for the comparables as for the subject.

Direct Income-Capitalization

The direct income-capitalization approach is based on the premise that market value equals the present worth of future rights to income as judged by the typical investor. This means that the market value of a subject property depends directly on its annual net operating income (NOI). **Net operating income** is the dollar income of a property after deduction of maintenance and operating expenses but before deduction of interest and depreciation expenses. The conversion of expected future income payments into a lump-sum present value is termed **capitalization.** Direct income-capitalization is most meaningfully applied to investment properties (apartment buildings, office buildings, warehouses, stores).

Following are the five basic steps involved in the direct income-capitalization process:

1. Ascertaining the current gross market rental of the subject property by comparison with rental properties of similar utility

2. Estimating and deducting possible rent losses due to vacancies, bad debts, termed vacancy, and credit losses

3. Estimating and deducting fixed and variable expenses necessary to operate and maintain the property income stream to get net operating income

4. Deriving a **capitalization rate** from the market by analysis of sales of comparable income properties

5. Dividing the market capitalization rate into the net operating income of the subject property to obtain an indication of its market value

DERIVING THE CAPITALIZATION RATE. The first of the five steps ascertaining current market rental, is discussed as a part of the gross rent multiplier technique. Steps 2 and 3 are not immediately important to capitalization calculations, and therefore deductions for vacancy and credit losses and for costs of operation are not discussed any further. The discussion here centers on deriving a capitalization rate from the market, and subsequently applying it. Assuming comparable properties, the only information required about each property is its net operating income and its sale price. Dividing the sale price into the net operating income gives a ratio or capitalizaton rate. This ratio is termed an **overall capitalizaton rate** and is designated as "R," by convention. The equation is

$$\frac{\text{Net operating income}}{\text{sale price}} = \text{capitalization rate} = R$$

Using three comparable properties, the calculations are as follows:

$$\text{Comparable D: } \frac{\$59,400}{\$600,000} = 0.0990 \text{ or } 9.9\%$$

$$\text{Comparable D: } \frac{\$74,800}{\$740,000} = 0.1011 \text{ or } 10.11\%$$

$$\text{Comparable E: } \frac{\$46,500}{\$468,000} = 0.09935 \text{ or } 9.94\%$$

Using this information, we see that an overall capitalization rate of 10 percent seems reasonable.

APPLYING THE CAPITALIZATION RATE. Finding an indicated market value of the subject property merely involves dividing its NOI by the overall capitalization rate. The formula is

$$\frac{\text{Net operating income}}{\text{Overall capitalization rate}} = \frac{\text{NOI}}{R} = \text{market value}$$

For example, using the $64,000 net operating income from the operating statement for a hypothetical subject property, we obtain a value of $640,000.

$$\frac{\$64,000}{0.10} = \$640,000$$

USES AND LIMITATIONS. The income approach obviously is applicable only to income properties, such as apartment buildings, office buildings, and rented warehouses and store buildings. In fact, it is best suited to larger-income properties that have stable net operating incomes and that are sold fairly frequently. Because of the manner in which the capitalization rate is derived, the approach yields value indications very similar to those generated by the market approach.

One major limitation of the direct capitalization technique is that sales of some income properties occur only infrequently; thus the derivation of a capitalization rate must be based on limited information. In addition, obtaining or verifying the NOI of an income property that has been sold is often very difficult.

Moreover, chance for error is introduced in calculating net operating income for the subject property because estimates of expense items are often based on judgment; and any error in estimating NOI is magnified severalfold in the capitalization process. Finally, the technique is not useful for properties that are unique or that generate income in the form of amenities.

COST APPROACH

The **cost approach to value** provides for the estimation of market value of a subject property based on the cost of acquiring a vacant site and of constructing a building and other improvements in order to develop a property of equal utility. The underlying assumption is that a rational potential owner will pay no more for a subject property than the cost of producing a substitute property with equal utility and without any undue delay. Note that the cost involved is to the typical rational, informed purchaser and not to a contractor or builder. The cost approach is also sometimes called the *summation approach.*

The Basic Steps

The cost approach to value involves the following four basic steps:

1. Estimation of the market value of the site in its highest and best use
2. Estimation of the reproduction and/or replacement costs of improvements
3. Estimation of accrued depreciation

4. Estimation of indicated market value of the subject property by deducting depreciation from cost of new improvements and adding the value of the site

Land value is almost always established by the direct sales comparison with similar sites. The site should be valued in its highest and best use to avoid overlooking the fact that the value of the site may exceed the value of the property in an inappropriate use. Thus a highway site may have a market value of $28,000 in a commercial use, but the property's value (site plus structure) in its present use (residential), dictated by an old residence located thereon, may be $24,000. Obviously, the $28,000 value should be recognized and should control; that is, the residential structure should be torn down and the site converted to commercial use. If the present use is other than the highest and best use, as determined by the structure, then the site must be valued in its present use for the cost approach; the above comparison of values would then be made.

The most usual method of determining the cost of buildings is to multiply their area or cubic content by the current cost of construction per square foot or cubic foot. Two techniques of estimating cost new are used. The first, *cost of replacement new,* involves determining the cost of producing a building or other improvement with utility equal to that of the subject property's improvement. Modern materials, design, and layout may be used, but the utility must be the same. *Cost of reproduction new,* the second technique, involves determining the cost of producing an exact replica of the subject property's improvements, including materials, design, layout—everything. The current theory is that the cost of reproduction new should be used in appraising because functional obsolescence must be built into a structure before it can be deducted.

Depreciation is loss in value of a property due to diminished utility from replacement cost new or reproduction cost new. Three classes of depreciation are recognized in appraising. The first is *physical deterioration,* which is loss in value brought about by the wear and tear of use, acts of God, or actions of the elements. The second is *functional obsolesence,* which is loss in value of a property because of relative inability to provide a service, as compared to a new property properly designed for the same use. The cause may be poor layout and design or inefficient building equipment. In short, the improvements are old and out-of-date. The third class of depreciation is termed *economic, locational,* or *environmental obsolescence,* which is loss in value of a site or property because of external or environmental factors that unfavorably affect the flow of income or benefits from the property, including blight and declining demand. Note that we are talking of market depreciation here and not tax depreciation.

An Example

An example of the cost-of-reproduction-less-depreciation approach to market value is appropriate here. Assume the cost of producing the subject property in its present condition is estimated at $639,400. Thus the indicated market value by the cost approach is $639,400. But cost is not value. And only if market value exceeds cost would a buyer or investor choose this alternative.

Land value (by direct sales comparison)	$ 88,000	
plus landscaping, walks, drive, etc.	12,000	
Total site value	$100,000	$100,000
Reproduction cost of new improvements:		
Main structure: 24,800 sq. ft. @ $30/sq. ft.	$744,000	
Garage area: 6,000 sq. ft. @ $8.00/sq. ft.	48,000	
Misc. (blinds, storage areas, etc.)	41,600	
Total cost new	$833,600	
Less depreciation:		
Physical deterioration	$106,600	
Functional obsolescence	86,000	
Locational obsolescence	101,600	
Total depreciation	$294,200	−$294,200
Depreciated value of improvements	$539,400	$539,400
Indicated market value by cost approach		$639,400

Uses and Limitations

The cost approach to value has greatest application in estimating the value of unique or special-purpose properties that have little or no market, for example, churches, tank farms, or chemical plants. It is also well suited to new or nearly new properties where estimating depreciation is not too involved or difficult. The cost approach has long been used in assessing for property tax purposes, which involves mass appraising and, in the past, has demanded standardized methodology. Property insurance adjustors rely on the cost approach because improvements often are only partially damaged or destroyed and must be restored to their original design and layout, or else completely torn down. Finally, the approach is very suitable in analysis to determine the highest and best use of a vacant site.

One major limitation of the cost approach is that depreciation is very difficult, if not impossible, to measure for older properties. Another major limitation is the great difficulty in allowing for differences in quality of improvements that result from design and style, kind and quality of materials, and quality of workmanship. This limitation applies to both estimating cost new and estimating depreciation. Further even getting an accurate estimate of costs new is difficult because costs often vary substantially from one contractor to another. For the foregoing reasons, the cost approach is not as applicable as other approaches for older properties or properties that are frequently sold. Also, it is nearly impossible to find vacant-lot sales to serve as comparables in determining site value in older, established neighborhoods.

RECONCILIATION

Each approach yields a distinct indication of market value. For the apartment property discussed in this chapter, the approaches produced indications as follows:

Direct-sales-comparison approach	$640,000
Income approach	
Gross income multiplier technique	648,000
Direct income-capitalization technique	640,000
Cost less depreciation approach	639,400

These estimates must be reconciled into a single estimate of market value. **Reconciliation** is the process of resolving differences in indications of value and of reaching a final or single value estimate. Reconciliation was formerly termed *correlation* by appraisers. Reconciliation involves weighting and comparing the indications according to the quality of the available data and the appropriateness of the approach for the kind of property and the value being sought. That is, reconciliation is a thought and judgment process. It is not the averaging of the value indications.

The direct-sales-comparison approach is generally regarded as giving the most reliable indication of market value when data are available. The GIM, on the other hand, is often regarded as a rule-of-thumb technique. The direct income-capitalization technique and the cost less depreciation approach strongly support the direct-sales-comparison indication in our example. Therefore, a market-value judgment of $640,000 for the subject property would seem reasonable and defensible.

SUMMARY

Appraisals are needed for decisions in a number of circumstances or situations: (1) transferring of property ownership or possession, (2) financing a property interest, (3) taxation of property, (4) determining compensation for property loss or damage, and (5) developing a property utilization program.

The most common objective of an appraisal is to estimate the market value of a property. Market value is a property's most probable sale price. Market value may be greater than, equal to, or less than either the sale price or the cost of production of a property. The most important principles of market-value appraising are (1) substitution, (2) change, (3) contribution, and (4) highest and best use.

The three approaches to value are (1) market or direct-sales-comparison, (2) cost, and (3) income. The income approach is divided into the gross income multiplier and the direct income-capitalization techniques. All three approaches are based on the principle of substitution. Reconciliation is the resolution of the three indications of market value generated by the techniques into one estimate of market value.

KEY TERMS

Appraisal

Appraisal process

Capitalization

Capitalization rate

Cost approach to value

Cost of replacement

Cost of reproduction

Depreciation

Direct income-capitalization

Direct-sales-comparison approach to value

Gross income multiplier (GIM)

Income approach to value

Market price

Market rent

Market value

Net operating income (NOI)

Objective value

Overall capitalization rate ("R")

Principles of:

   Change

   Contribution

   Highest and best use

   Substitution

Reconciliation

Subject property

Subjective value

Value

Value in exchange

Value in use

QUESTIONS FOR REVIEW AND DISCUSSION

1. List and explain briefly three major reasons or needs for appraisals.

2. Define and/or distinguish among the following:
   market value   value in use
   market price   value in exchange
   cost of production   subjective value

3. List and explain at least three principles of market-value appraising, including the principle of substitution.

4. Give or briefly explain the following about the direct-sales-comparison approach to value:
   (a) The four basic steps
   (b) Two appropriate applications
   (c) Two major limitations

5. List and explain briefly the following about the income approach to value:
   (a) Three basic steps of GIM technique
   (b) The basic steps of the direct income-capitalization technique
   (c) Two appropriate applications of each
   (d) Two limitations of each

6. Explain the purpose and process of reconciliation.

7. Depreciation need not be considered in market-value appraising because it is more than offset by inflation. Discuss.

8. In what directions would the adjustments be for a comparable sale involving an extremely low down payment and a first and second mortgage? Explain your reasoning.

9. Is depreciation taken account of in the direct-sales-comparison and income-capitalization approaches to value? If so, how? Explain.

10. How do market values adjust or change in response to changes in demand? What is the relationship to estimates of value by appraisers? Discuss.

REFERENCES

Appraisal of Real Estate. 7th ed. Chicago: American Institute of Real Estate Appraisers, 1978. A basic guide to traditional methods of real estate appraising.

Kahn, Sanders A., and Frederick E. Case. *Real Estate Appraisal and Investment.* 2nd ed. New York: Ronald Press, 1977. As the title indicates, an integration of appraisal and investment theory. Contains four basic sections: (1) Introduction: basic appraisal factors, (2) Valuation techniques, (3) Specific appraisal assignment, and (4) Investment analysis. Generally to the point, pragmatic, and easy to read and understand.

Kinnard, William N., Jr. *Income Property Valuation.* Lexington, Mass.: Heath, 1971. The first book focusing strictly on the principles and techniques of appraising income-producing property. It is probably the best also. Well written. For the serious or advanced student.

Ratcliff, Richard U. *Valuation for Real Estate Decisions.* Santa Cruz, Calif.: Democrat Press, 1972. A theory book relating appraisal directly to real estate decision making. For the serious or advanced student.

Ring, Alfred A. *Valuation of Real Estate.* Englewood Cliffs, N.J.: Prentice-Hall, 1970. A basic source integrating the theory and practice of appraising. Easy to read and understand. Many excellent and clear examples.

Wendt, Paul F. *Real Estate Appraisal: Review and Outlook.* Athens: University of Georgia Press, 1974. The development of appraisal theory and practice discussed from an economic and a historical perspective. Well organized, generally easy to read and understand. A must have book for anyone seriously interested in appraisal on a continuing basis.

Real Estate Investment Analysis

Never follow the crowd.
Bernard Baruch, American financier and governmental adviser

23

This chapter covers the apex or high point in the investment cycle. In earlier sections we looked at various components of the real estate investment cycle: (1) defining ownership rights, (2) conveying ownership rights, (3) financing, and (4) real estate markets and the investment climate. In this section, we have thus far looked at topics closer to the investment decision: property productivity, investment tax considerations, and market-value determination. The making and implementing of the investment decision, taken up in this chapter, is the point in the cycle where our investor moves from passive theorizing to active commitment. Up to this point, costs are relatively low, and control is almost entirely with the investor. But now other people get involved, a large monetary commitment may be required, and the game gets serious. It also gets exciting. And the time span is quite short relative to the probable holding period of any property acquired.

In this chapter, we look at the advantages and disadvantages of real estate as an investment, at the characteristics of specific types of real estate as investments, and at investor types and goals. We also apply the methodology of determining investment value discussed earlier and of developing strategies of investing and negotiating. Section topics are as follows:

1. Nature of real estate as an investment
2. Property types and characteristics
3. Developing investment strategy
4. Determining investment value
5. Negotiation and rate of return

A few preliminary remarks are pertinent before we take up these topics.

First, the viewpoint is that of a real estate investor as against that of a speculator or developer. Judgment must be exercised to distinguish among these three roles because the line of demarcation is not always obvious or clear-cut. For our purposes, an **investor** puts money into real estate based on careful analysis, with the expectation of realizing income or profit over an extended period. In effect, an investor looks for both annual income and long-term capital gains. A **speculator** buys and sells realty with the expectation of realizing quick profits due to sharp price changes. A speculator is roughly synonymous with a dealer, operating with a short time horizon. A **developer** prepares and improves land for use, usually by the construction of buildings. A developer's time horizon is usually several years.

All three take risks, although speculator risks are generally considered the greatest. In fact, a speculator may be regarded as a risk seeker, hoping to beat the market and thereby realize higher profits. Speculators are sometimes considered to operate on the "bigger-fool" theory. The **bigger-fool theory** is that buyers pay current prices based on trends in market prices rather than on analysis of forces underlying value, with the expectation of reselling to a "bigger fool." The owner holding title when the bubble bursts is the biggest fool. The developer's viewpoint is discussed further in a later chapter on property development. The speculator's viewpoint is not discussed further, largely because valid generalization about it is difficult if not impossible. One person may wear all three hats, and act depending on the situation.

Second, investment in only one property is considered. This is considered reasonable for several reasons. Real estate is a "lumpy" investment, meaning that a large amount of equity investment is necessary to buy even one property. At the same time, usually only a small portion of all investment properties are offered in a market at any one time. Further, considerable analysis is required to evaluate even one property. In fact, a calculator is almost a must for the type of analysis presented here. Finally, only one property is needed to make a decision when an investor operates on a net present-value basis with a required rate of return. That is, if the investment value of the subject property exceeds market value at the required rate of return, an offer to purchase becomes a logical next step.

This chapter concludes with a discussion of negotiating strategy for a good reason. Even though the investment value exceeds market value, an investor wishes to pay no more for a property than necessary. In fact, purchase for less than investment value increases the rate of return to the investor, other things the same.

NATURE OF REAL ESTATE
AS AN INVESTMENT

Real estate has certain attributes, as an investment, which are discussed here as advantages or disadvantages, from the viewpoint of a proficient investor. A brief discussion of the financial management of real estate as an investment concludes this section.

Advantages

An *investment* is the act of putting money into property or a business to obtain income or profits. Real estate is like many other investments in its ability to provide periodic income and/or value appreciation. During the 1970s, however, real estate provided a much higher rate of return than stocks, bonds, and many other investment media. Of course, periodic losses and value depreciation are possible for real estate as well as for these other investments. Many of the advantages of real estate as an investment are in the traditions and institutions surrounding them. Let us look at some of the more important or obvious advantages.

LEVERAGE. As explained in an earlier chapter, positive *leverage* is the use of borrowed monies to increase the rate of return earned from an equity investment. This presumes that the investment earns at a higher rate than is paid on the borrowed monies. It doesn't matter whether the rate of return is from periodic income or from value enhancement. Traditionally, real estate investors borrow from 60 to 90 percent of the value of any properties owned or acquired, which is a much higher ratio of leverage than is available on most other investments.

The higher the leverage ratio, the higher is the rate of return to equity. For income property, this often means a higher dollar cash flow per dollar of equity investment. Also, a high leverage ratio increases the likelihood that tax depreciation will shelter most of the cash flow. Of course, a high loan-to-value ratio carries lots of risk to the investor-borrower if the property becomes distressed. For this reason, many investors negotiate for and get exculpation clauses in loans when borrowing money. An **exculpation clause** is a provision in a mortgage or trust deed holding the borrower blameless in default, and therefore limiting the borrower's personal liability. Without limited liability, the borrower might lose all personal assets if the investment fails. And of course, from the borrower's point of view, that isn't good.[1]

Leverage also enables an investor to control more property with a given amount of money. And by maintaining high leverage through slow repayment or frequent refinancing, an investor may pyramid investments more quickly. **Pyramiding** is controlling ever more property through reinvestment, refinancing, and exchanging, while keeping leverage at a maximum. The objective is to

---

[1] See Emanuel B. Halper, "People and Property: Mortgage Exculpation Clauses," *Real Estate Review,* summer 1978.

control the maximum value in property with given resources. Needless to say, pyramiding carries high risk of a total wipe-out during a recession.

TAX SHELTER. Real estate enjoys many tax-sheltering opportunities, as discussed in an earlier chapter. Tax depreciation, long-term capital gains, tax credits, installment sales, and tax-deferred exchanges all enable an investor to minimize or defer income taxes. These shelters concern federal taxation but often apply to taxation at other levels as well.

PURCHASING-POWER PROTECTION. Few investment media have equaled the inflationary protection offered by holdings of real estate. This protection has been specially evident during the steep inflationary period that began in 1964.

Whereas most capital assets have lost in terms of purchasing power of their dollar value, adequately improved realty, especially apartments, shopping centers, and selected commercial properties, have increased in terms of constant dollars. The rise is a result of rapidly increasing costs of construction and the rising cost of money as reflected in interest rates that have reached statutory usury levels in all fifty states. In the absence of rent and price controls, real property, like a ship upon the ocean waters, floats above its purchasing power-constant dollar line irrespective of depth or rise in the level of prices. It is this ability to hold its purchasing-power integrity that has in recent years popularized the demand for shares of real estate trusts and syndicates. For this holding power to be true of a specific parcel of income real estate, the property must be well located, have rentals that can be raised periodically, and not be subject to sudden sharp increases in operating costs.

PRIDE OF OWNERSHIP. The satisfaction of being an owner of real estate is important to many investors. They gain identity by being "in the game" or "shrewd operators." Some investors also realize great satisfaction from owning something tangible that can be touched, felt, and shown to friends and relatives.

CONTROL. An individual owner has immediate and direct control or power over realty. This control enables the owner or an agent to make continuing decisions about the property as a financial asset and as a productive property. Financial management is the concern of this entire book. Property management is discussed in chapter 25. This control also enables the investor to manage the property to meet personal goals, whether they are to maintain the property as a showpiece for pride of ownership or to operate the property for maximum rate of return.

ENTREPRENEURIAL PROFIT. A last important advantage is that profit may be realized by building or rehabilitating a property, and the profit is immediately invested in the property without being taxed. Thus, many investors also develop property. Other investors combine real estate investing with brokerage or property management.

Disadvantages

Lack of liquidity and ownership risks are the main disadvantages of real estate as an investment. *Risk* is the chance of damage, injury, or loss. Most risks associated with real estate investment may be classified as either business or financial. **Business risk** is the probability that projected or predicted levels of income will not be realized. **Financial risk** is the extra uncertainty created by the use of debt financing.

LACK OF LIQUIDITY. Investment **liquidity** is judged by the ease with which an asset can be converted to cash and the ratio of the conversion. Any asset, of course, can be converted into cash if the price is low enough. An asset is considered to have *high liquidity* when it can be sold for cash at or near its market value. High-value real estate is generally considered to have low liquidity.

Despite the ready availability of real estate syndicate and real estate investment trust shares on national stock exchanges, nonliquidity of real estate continues to be the economic Achilles' heel of real estate investment. Inability to adjust readily to economic market demands has caused real properties and especially urban lands to reach phenomenal "boom" levels of inflated value and conversely deep and lasting economic depressions. Real estate as a consequence has gained a "bearish" reputation. Where, however, a well-informed investor balances his or her investment portfolio so as to weather impending and generally short-range economic fluctuations, the relative nonliquidity of real estate is not a serious handicap to garnering the long-term benefits of net return and capital safety. Also, in an urgent situation, such as an opportunity for an alternative investment, an investor has the option to raise cash by refinancing or giving a second mortgage.

BUSINESS RISK. The productivity of a parcel of real estate is a function of the physical property, its location, its market, and economic conditions in general. Each of these factors is subject to fluctuation and change and to misinterpretation. Therefore, predicting productivity and income based on these factors involves some uncertainty or risk. For example, a new freeway or bridge can destroy the locational advantage of a service station; a new shopping center can undercut a downtown department store. Or, an unexpected decline in the economic base of a community can result in higher than expected vacancy rates for apartment houses. To the extent that events like these occur to adversely influence the productivity of a property, business risk is involved in owning property.

Fluctuation in projected income must not be confused with business risk, however, If fluctuations in productivity are certain and predictable, the investor must only take account of the lack of stability in the income prediction. For example, in many university communities, occupancy levels in student housing drop below 50 percent in the summer months. The investor can make calculations based on this fluctuation and thus have no uncertainty. In the analysis of business risk, the emphasis should be on the relative certainty of the prediction, not on the level or pattern of the prediction.

FINANCIAL RISK. An investor who does not borrow to help finance the purchase of ownership of a property has almost no financial risk. That is, if the investor buys the property entirely with his or her own funds, then the financial risk is reduced to meeting operating expenses. At the same time, no leverage is used, and the rate of return may be quite low. To increase the equity rate of return, the investor may choose to use leverage—that is, to mortgage the property and thereby reduce the equity investment in it. In doing this, both the investor and the lender relate the loan contract to the productivity characteristics of the property. Thus, a farm loan may call for one debt-service payment each fall, at which time the harvest is assumed to be sold. On the other hand, a loan on an apartment house that collects monthly rent from tenants is likely to call for monthly debt service.

The additional risk created by borrowing against the property is financial risk. The risk might be rather slight for a wealthy owner with strong financial carrying capacity. And of course, the higher the loan-to-value ratio, the higher the risk. This risk would also show up when annual debt-service requirements are related to net operating income. The higher debt service is as a proportion of net operating income (NOI), the greater the risk. Note that a change in the pattern of financing for a property does not influence the NOI, or productivity, of the property. Productivity and income are determined by the market; the financing pattern is the result of a decision by a specific owner.

MISCELLANEOUS RISKS. Several additional risks are involved in owning real estate, as follows. **Market risk** is the chance of a drop in market value. We have already pointed out that real estate tends to ride with inflation; therefore, market risk and **purchasing-power risk** are rather small for real estate. Market risk is much more applicable to securities. Legislative or political risks must be recognized as property or area specific. That is, all properties in an entire community are not likely to be affected. **Political risks** are uncertainties that arise from governmental actions. Examples are changes in zoning and initiation of rent controls.

RISK AND RATE OF RETURN. The amount of risk involved in owning a property is important in determining the value of the property. The equity rate of return expected by a specific investor should be, in part, a function of the risk involved in owning the property. A safe and sure return to the investor justifies a relatively low equity rate of return. As risk and uncertainty increase, the expected rate of return should also increase. Thus, an investor who borrows money to gain leverage assumes greater risk in return for the potential of a higher equity rate of return.

Comparing Investment Media

Real estate requires good financial management if the investor is to realize as many benefits and to avoid as many costs or disadvantages as possible. In fact, a prudent investor would compare the costs and benefits of all alternative investment media to determine that one or that combination that best serves his or her personal needs. Many subjective judgments would be involved in such a comparison. Therefore we'll limit our attention to real estate.

The real estate investment cycle has three phases: (1) acquisition and/or development, (2) property management and use, and (3) disposition. We devote considerable attention to the acquisition/development phase because most of the major decisions determining the success of an investment are made in this phase. It is much easier to finish right if you start right. The legal, financial, market, and tax factors in the cycle are many, complex, and often subtle. All must be taken into account. Therefore, the entire cycle must be taken into account for the investment decision.

Many costs are involved in real estate investing, and not all of them are dollar costs. Most dollar costs of acquisition and disposition are explained in chapter 8. Costs of operation are discussed in chapters 20 and 25. And chapter 24, on property development, contains cost information pertaining to improving real estate. Even so, some dollar costs have been overlooked and deserve brief attention here.

Costs incurred in finding and administering real estate are often overlooked by investors because the costs are not picked up as part of the transaction. Examples include investor payments for transportation, meals, lodging, telephone calls, and counselors while looking for, buying, and selling properties. These costs may be substantial and obviously deserve recognition when comparing investment media. Some of these expenses are tax deductible as well. Records of these out-of-pocket expenses therefore should be kept by an investor.

And more than money is involved in real estate investing. Considerable time for data collection and analysis, for negotiation, and for management is invested also. Aggravation costs are also sometimes incurred, as when an owner is harassed by tenants and others. An owner is wise to log these costs also and fix a dollar value to them. Only then can a truly valid comparison of investment media be made.

CHARACTERISTICS OF PROPERTY TYPES AS INVESTMENTS

We looked at general advantages and disadvantages of real estate as an investment in the previous section. By isolating several different property types, it is possible to make additional, more specific comments about real estate as an investment. These comments will help later when we discuss investor goals and strategy. The property types we look at briefly are vacant or raw land, residential rentals, office buildings, warehouses, small shopping centers, and hotels and motels. Figure 23–1 summarizes these comments.

Vacant or Raw Land

The supply of land is limited. Demand is growing. Therefore, investing in land is a sure thing. This analysis is generally valid, but it is also limited. Land is only one of several real estate alternatives open to an investor.

Rate of return from land must be realized through value appreciation, which involves supply and demand. The supply of land is limited. But the supply of urban land may be increased simply by extending roads, water and sewer lines, and electrical services. Demand for land depends on expansion of demand in the specific community or area. Location relative to local road and travel patterns goes far to determine the demand for a specific parcel of realty. Finally, planning, zoning, and probable highest and best use greatly determine chances for value enhancement.

Land is passive and illiquid as an investment medium. Low loan-to-value ratios make it difficult to leverage land very highly. Owning land gives no tax depreciation; carrying costs must be capitalized. And rate of return on the investment must be realized through value appreciation subject to capital gains tax treatment.

In that land earns little or no income, an investor must pay carrying costs from other income. Such an investment is sometimes called an "alligator" because it has to be fed. If the owner suffers reduced income, a distress sale may be necessary. The rate and amount of value appreciation likely to occur over a period adds additional risk to investment in land.

The most likely investors in land are speculators for short-term gains, and developers for long-term operating needs. Estates and others seeking a store of value and an easily managed hedge against inflation, are also likely investor types for vacant or raw land.

Apartments

Population and income levels are the primary determinants of value for residential real estate. Some apartment buildings also realize value based on status or prestige considerations. Location, in terms of convenience and of environment, also greatly influences value.

Apartments require moderately active attention as an investment. And apartments are more liquid than most realty investments because investors are more knowledgeable in residential properties than in other types of investment properties. The market is broader. Also, up to 90 percent, and sometimes higher, loan-to-value ratios may be obtained, giving high leverage. Tax depreciation is available to the investor, and if the property is new, accelerated depreciation may be taken. Rate of return is by both periodic income and value enhancement, which, in turn, are subject to ordinary and capital gains taxation.

The major risks in apartment investment are during the start-up period of new properties and in obtaining or providing quality management on a continuing basis. For large complexes, professional management is almost a must. It takes considerable know-how to manage these complexes and to avoid harassment from tenants and others.

High-income people are in a position to benefit most from accelerated depreciation. However, apartments are desirable as an investment for almost everyone. Smaller properties, roughly twelve units or less, may be managed and maintained by an owner with adequate time. Personal management gives the owner closer control and the value of the services rendered.

FIGURE 23–1
Generalized Characteristics of Real Property Investment Types

Property Type	Main Value Determinants	Investment Characteristics	Principal Risks	Most Likely Investor Type
VACANT OR RAW LAND	Expansion of demand Convenient location Travel patterns Planning/zoning/highest and best use	Passive Illiquid Limited leverage Rate of return by value appreciation No tax depreciation Capital gains taxation Expenses capitalized	Carrying costs: Must be fed, "Alligator" Distress sale possible Value appreciation uncertain ("Tax payer" may be used to help carry)	Speculator Developer Estate as store of value
RESIDENTIAL RENTALS (APARTMENTS)	Expanding population Rising incomes Location —convenience —favorable exposure Prestige, sometimes	Moderately active Moderately liquid High leverage, LVR R. of R. by periodic income and value appreciation Tax dep'n., accelerated possible Ordinary and capital gains taxation	Start-up when new Management (Probably necessary to hire professional for larger projects) Tenant harassment	High income benefiting from tax shelter Suitable for anyone but must be able to put up initial equity investment
OFFICE BUILDINGS	Expanding local economy Location linkages Prestige/status sometimes important Tenant-mix compatibility	Active, unless leased to one firm Moderately liquid R. of R. by periodic income and value appreciation Tax depreciation Ordinary and capital gains taxation	Start-up when new Management—high level of service required Competitive facilities Obsolescence Shift in location of business activity	High income needing tax shelter Suitable for anyone if professional management hired and if able to put up initial equity investment

Property Type	Main Value Determinants	Investment Characteristics	Principal Risks	Most Likely Investor Type
WAREHOUSES	Commercial/industrial activity Location for ease of movement Structural design to endure change	Mostly passive—often on long-term lease Moderate liquidity Moderate leverage R. of R. mainly by periodic income Tax depreciation Ordinary and capital gain taxation	Obsolescence due to changes in materials-handling, equipment techniques, and equipment	Retired—desiring high cash flow and limited management Anyone desiring tax shelter with adequate initial equity capital
NEIGHBORHOOD SHOPPING CENTERS	Community growth Effective demand —population —income Convenient location relative to competition Adequate parking Tenant mix relative to spending patterns and effective lease negotiation	Moderately active Liquidity limited Moderate leverage R. and R. by periodic income and value appreciation Tax depreciation Ordinary and capital gains taxation	Start-up—getting proper tenant mix Management—provide adequate level of service Vacancies Competitive facilities Obsolescence	High value, large equity investment likely, therefore reasonably wealthy Anyone able to use tax shelter plus other benefits
HOTELS/MOTELS	Location—linkages and convenience Demand—conference, tourist, resort, business Mix of facilities and services	Active Liquidity Moderate to poor leverage R. of R. by periodic income and value appreciation Tax depreciation Ordinary and capital gains taxation	Management—high tenant turnover (professional management almost a necessity) Competing facilities Larger than certain minimum size—economies of scale apply	Anyone able to use tax shelter and with adequate initial equity capital Smaller properties suitable for investors also willing to manage and maintain

Office Buildings

The value of office buildings depends heavily on the business health of the community or area. Location for convenient linkages, a compatible tenant mix, and a prestigious image also add to value.

Office buildings generally require active participation of an investor unless leased to a single firm. Tenant demands must be dealt with. Liquidity and leverage are generally moderate. Tax depreciation may be taken on improvements. Rate of return is by periodic income and value appreciation.

The main risks in owning an office building are during start-up, maintaining high-quality management, and obsolescence. These risks tend to be within the control of the owner. Shifts in location of business activity and development of competitive facilities are risks outside the direct influence of the owner.

Likely owners of large office buildings are wealthy or high-income investors. Moderate leverage means a high initial equity investment is required. Also, high-income owners gain more benefit from the tax depreciation. Syndicates may be organized, opening the investment opportunity to investors of more moderate means.

Warehouses

Warehouses obviously depend heavily on the level of commercial and industrial activity for value. Warehouses, to maintain value, must be designed and built to accommodate changes in methods of handling materials. Ceilings too low and aisles too narrow to accommodate fork trucks caused many warehouses to become obsolete in the 1950s and 1960s, for example. Warehouse value also depends on a location that allows easy movement throughout an area or community of the items or materials being stored and distributed.

Many warehouses are on long-term leases to one firm, and as a consequence, are a passive type of investment. Leverage and liquidity are moderate. Cash flow tends to be somewhat higher as a proportion of value than with some other improved properties because less value appreciation is expected. In turn, people desiring higher cash flow and limited management requirements find warehouses an excellent investment In most other respects, warehouses are similar to apartment and office buildings as investments.

Small Shopping Centers

The value of shopping centers depends heavily on adequate purchasing power in their tributary area, meaning people and incomes. The location must be convenient for the population and parking must be plentiful. Finally, the tenant mix must be suited to the demands of the population in the tributary area. Supermarkets, small variety and discount stores, restaurants, and gasoline stations are typical tenants.

Active management is required to establish and maintain a center as an investment. Effective lease negotiation is important. Liquidity is limited because few investors have the broad knowledge needed to manage a center; also, leverage is moderate. The tax treatment of shopping center investment is similar to that of office buildings. Vacancies and lease negotiation, obsolescence, and development of competitive facilities are the main risks of center ownership. Also, as with office buildings, a reasonably large equity investment is required. In other respects, any investor for periodic income and capital gain would find shopping center investment inviting.

Hotels / Motels

Hotels and motels depend primarily on tourist and business people for their demand. Tourists look to hotels and motels for rest, relaxation, and recreation. Traveling sales people and executives make up a large portion of the continuing clientele. And in recent years, business conferences have been in vogue. Having a location and the facilities to satisfy this demand with ease is a large determinant of the value of a hotel or motel.

Hotels and motels are active investments with limited liquidity and offer moderate-to-poor leverage. They receive treatment as business property for tax purposes.

Major risks in hotel/motel investment are maintaining adequate size and competent management. Economies of scale apply. And high tenant turnover means management must be effective. Obsolescence and the development of more adequate competing facilities are also major risks.

Large hotels and motels require considerable equity investment and are therefore limited to syndicates or wealthy investors. Smaller properties are suitable for less affluent investors who are also willing to personally manage and maintain the property.

DEVELOPING INVESTMENT STRATEGY

In chapter 1 we looked briefly at the decision-making process relative to the financial management of real estate. We now have the background and information to apply the process. We apply our knowledge by looking briefly at a young couple and an elderly couple as they identify investment goals and constraints and from there develop investment strategy. But first, we'll look at key variables in real estate investing.

Key Variables

Austin Jaffe and David Walters independently conducted sensitivity analysis of real estate investment to determine the most significant variables involved.[2] **Sensitivity analysis** is the study of the impact of various factors of an

---

[2] Austin Jaffe, *Property Management in Real Estate Investment Decision-Making.* (Lexington, Mass.: Heath, 1979), chaps. 5–7. David W. Walters, "Just How Important Is Property Management?" *Journal of Property Management,* July–August, 1973.

investment decision on the rate of return earned from a property or on the investment value of a property. The factors are varied under controlled conditions to determine which exerts the most influence, which the second most influence, and so forth. The results help an investor to know which are the most critical variables in an investment decision. The research results of Jaffe and Walters are very similar.

In Jaffe's and Walter's studies, the six most important variables were found to be (1) operating expenses, (2) loan-to-value ratio or leverage, (3) effective gross income, (4) property-value growth rate, (5) mortgage loan interest rate, and (6) purchase price. The significance of these variables to an investor are as follows. Property management is quite important to successful investment because operating costs (number 1) must be kept under control, while effective gross income (number 3) must be kept high. To keep EGI up, a manager must keep rents at market while keeping vacancy and collection losses low. Financing also showed up as important in that high leverage (number 2) gives substantial advantage and also keeps the interest rate low (number 5). The last two variables, property-value growth rate (number 4) and cost or purchase price (number 6), effectively mean buy low and sell high. Buying low is the result of good analysis and shrewd negotiation. Selling high is the result of managing a property well during ownership and shrewd negotiation on disposition.

The importance of variables drops off sharply after these first six. Other variables considered include loan term, tax depreciation method, life of improvements for tax depreciation, tax rate of investor, expected holding period of investment, and rate of return required by investor. While alternative tax depreciation rates do not show up as significant, it does not follow that tax depreciation is not significant to a successful investment.

Cast of Characters and Situations

Gerald and Nancy Investor are in their early thirties with two children, Kelly in first grade and Ulysses in second grade. Gerald is a financial executive with the Diamond Distributing Company, the operations of which are limited to his state. Nancy works half-time with the county as a biologist. Together they earn after-tax income of $36,000 per year. After purchasing a home several years ago, they began investing small amounts in other real estate, most of which has done well. They spend considerable time managing the several properties involved and would like some relief from this chore. They have gained considerable knowledge and experience and now wish to adopt a more logical or rational modus operandi.

Wendy Welloff, a wealthy widow, owns several quality pieces of real estate. She plans to marry Count Michael Scrapinski in the near future. A premarital property agreement is being arranged so that the estate of each will go to his or her respective heirs. That is, they do not plan to merge their property interests. While negotiating the property agreement, each recognized the need to develop an investment strategy. Count Scrapinski has had three previous wives.

Motivations and Goals

The basic human motivation is self-interest. Self-interest is equated with wealth maximization in economic and financial theory. In fact, self-interest takes such other forms as safety, comfort and convenience, concern for the welfare of others, and public altruism. Several of the more common human motivations and the implied goals for investment purposes are as follows:

Motivation	Goal or Objective
Gain/economy	Rate of return, wealth maximization
Protection/safety	Purchasing-power protection, hedge against inflation
Comfort/convenience	Rate of return mainly through cash flow, with avoidance of undue risk, personal effort, or personal stress
Personal identity/satisfaction	Entrepreneurial profit, as from developing property, power to control property and others, showpiece properties
Concern for welfare of others	Assist or help others, including relatives

Gerald and Nancy Investor have adequate income for their personal needs. Their goals are, as for most people, greater wealth, protection against inflation, and adequate time and money to travel. They want to avoid undue risk. They do not feel the need of greater personal identity through development and management of property.

Wendy Welloff has adequate funds for her own welfare and comfort, which she wants to preserve and to pass on to her children and their families. She also takes great pride in owning good properties.

Count Scrapinski enjoys comfort and convenience as well as taking risks. He is not too concerned with passing his wealth on to his heirs. He would like greater wealth but is not willing to give up the fun of playing the game of life.

Constraints

Common constraints of investors are as follows:

Financial/economic factors	Wealth
	Income level
	Risk of alternative investments
Personal factors	Age (time horizon)
	Energy level and work preferences
	Time availability
	Investment-analysis ability
	Executive ability
	Risk preference
	Location/mobility preferences

Wealth largely determines the level of a person's investing, unless the person has a great deal of ability to operate on other people's money. To operate on other people's money requires considerable persuasiveness and willingness to take risks. A high level of income makes it easier to accumulate savings for investment, if the investor holds down expenditures. For the wealthy investor, a real estate investment strategy makes sense only if it is related to the investor's overall strategy. For other investors, real estate may offer the quickest road to wealth.

Age, analytical ability, executive ability, energy level, work preferences, and time availability all act as constraints on an investor. A young person can afford a longer time horizon than an elderly person. A person with limited time or energy is probably best advised to invest in media requiring little effort. Likewise, a person with limited ability to analyze and administer investments is better off avoiding active investments, meaning most real estate investments. Risk and locational preferences are self-explanatory as personal constraints.

How do these constraints apply to our cast of characters?

Gerald and Nancy Investor have adequate income for their present needs, by their own standards. They do not have great wealth and therefore are not able to get into very large properties. They have experience in real estate investing and are willing to undertake reasonable risks of additional investing. They have adequate capital to get into a moderate-sized property, because of successful investments in the past. Both are satisfied with their work and the community; therefore their preference is to invest only locally. Gerry has adequate ability to analyze and administer active investments from a financial management viewpoint. They do not have adequate time or energy to personally manage a property on an everyday basis.

Wendy Welloff has considerable wealth, from which she obtains reasonable income. She does not have or want a steady job. She's knowledgeable and capable in real estate investing and willing to incur reasonable risks. Wendy, in her late fifties, is beginning to shorten her time horizon; more and more she's thinking of ways to pass as much of her wealth as possible to her children and grandchildren. Of course, she wants to continue to enjoy comforts and pleasures during her life. Wendy has adequate analytical and administrative ability to manage her investments quite successfully.

Count Scrapinski likes to be noticed and has a zest for life. He also likes to be involved with people. His interest in investments and ability to analyze and administer them is limited. But he is a promoter. Count Scrapinski earns a very adequate income as vice-president of public relations for a regional supermarket chain. However, he has accumulated only moderate wealth and, being nearly sixty, wants to retire soon. He must travel three or four months a year and therefore has little time for property management or investment. Also, the count feels strong ties to Urbandale and would like to be more limited in a locational sense.

Strategy

Briefly, we have concluded that Nancy and Gerald Investor have the knowledge and the capability to conduct a very successful investment program.

They have a reasonable amount of money. Their main constraints are wanting to invest locally and not wanting to manage property personally any longer. By selling off their smaller properties and refinancing one other property, they generate enough cash equity for a larger property, Douglas Manor, at $640,000. They thereby meet both constraints. Several of the smaller properties required considerable attention from them; larger properties may be managed by professionals at an acceptable percentage fee. The Investors now realize both cash flow and potential for equity appreciation. They also realize high leverage by investing in residential rental property. They sacrifice extra capital gains taxes to make the transition but consider the cost acceptable. Their purchase of Douglas Manor, documented earlier, culminates their transition. The Investors now have more time for family life, and Gerald is better able to attend to financial management of their investments rather than to everyday property management.

Owning an income property also gives tax shelter, which the Investors expect to need increasingly as their ordinary income goes up. The size, sixteen units, and high value, $640,000 or more, stretches the Investors slightly insofar as coming up with the initial cash equity is concerned. Fortunately, the age and condition of the property appear such that no unduly large expenditures or capital improvements are likely to be needed for several years.

Wendy Welloff sold off Douglas Manor because much of her depreciation shelter had been used up. Also, she wanted to release money to reinvest in vacant land for appreciation. She now earns considerable periodic income from investments. She wants to increase the portion coming from capital gains, and land investment provides the means. Also, she wants several smaller parcels of property that can more easily be passed on to heirs in an estate. Finally, she and the count believe they would make an excellent property development team when he retires. She can do the analysis and provide financing. He can take over individual parcels in a joint venture, limited partnership arrangement. He'll put up the risk capital and promote the development. Thus, the count will continue to be actively involved with people. They expect to travel in the off season.

DETERMINING INVESTMENT VALUE

Investment value represents the worth of a property to a specific individual or group. Personal or group assumptions or judgments about the property are considered to be included in this estimate of value. By way of contrast, the assumptions and judgments of the *typical investor* for the particular type property under consideration may be used in estimating market value. The theory and techniques of determining market value are taken up in a prior chapter. The elements and techniques needed to determine investment value on an after-tax basis are presented in this chapter in the form of a case property, Douglas Manor Apartments. The viewpoint of Gerald I. and Nancy O. Investor is used in the analysis of the case property.

The analysis is conducted in dollar terms only. An investor may have preferences over and above the economic analysis, but these should be exercised *after* the investment value of the property is known. In this way the investor is able to ascertain the cost of the preferences in making a decision. The analysis includes an eight-year after-tax cash flow projection, discounted at a 15 percent required rate of return to determine the net present value of the equity position. Subsequently, the internal rate of return and the payback period are calculated. Thus, all three of the more common and accepted methods of evaluating investments are discussed.

Data on Douglas Manor Apartments

Much of the data needed to determine investment value is discussed earlier in this book. A summary of these data, plus additional assumptions or inputs, for Douglas Manor Apartments follows.

1. Net operating income is $64,000, as presented in an operating statement in the chapter on property productivity analysis. Market analysis is assumed to justify the eight-year cash flow projection for Douglas Manor Apartments shown in figure 23–2. The cash flow projection gives own-

FIGURE 23–2
Projected Cash Flows and Value Levels, Douglas Manor Apartments

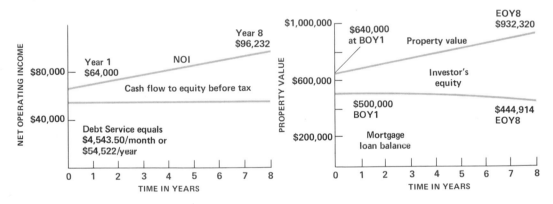

ership a time dimension in which NOI is assumed to increase by 6 percent per year.

2. Market value for Douglas Manor Apartments is taken at $640,000. This is assumed to be reached by dividing the $64,000 NOI by a capitalization rate of 10 percent, or .10. The market value is also the assumed purchase price for purposes of the depreciation schedule.

3. Improvements are assumed to make up 84.4 percent of the purchase price, or $540,000, and to have a remaining useful life for income tax purposes of twenty-seven years. Annual straight-line depreciation is $20,000. See

the schedule developed in the chapter on federal tax factors affecting real estate. Use of a straight-line depreciation schedule simplifies the calculations and avoids problems of depreciation recapture upon disposition.

4. The property is to be financed with a twenty-seven-year, 10 percent mortgage requiring monthly payments and made at a 78 percent loan-to-value ratio. The loan is therefore for $500,000 with debt service of $4,543.50 monthly or $54,522 yearly. We developed an amortization schedule for a loan of this amount and at these terms in the chapter on time value of money in real estate.

5. The Investors are assumed to be in the 50 percent tax bracket insofar as income from this property is concerned. In addition, the Investors have a minimum of 15 percent per year after-tax required rate of return on any equity investment.

6. The property is assumed to be held for eight years, during which time its market value increases by about 50 percent or over $320,000. Disposition costs upon resale are taken at 7 percent of sale price.

7. Time value of money factors from the appendix are used to calculate the present worth of future payments. By convention, monthly payments are assumed on mortgages unless otherwise stated.

In summary, the cash flows and value levels for Douglas Manor are shown in figure 23–2.

Figure 23–3 provides a visual summary or overview of the process by which investment value is determined. Investment value equals available credit financing plus the present value of **after-tax cash flows to equity.** After-tax cash flows are realized from annual income and **equity reversion.**

FIGURE 23–3
Investment Value Equals Available Credit Financing Plus the Present Value of Annual After-tax Cash Flows and of the After-tax Equity Reversion

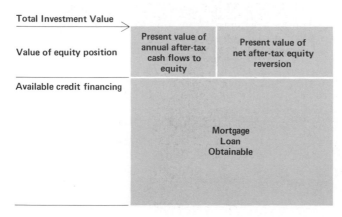

The Investment Value of After-Tax Cash Flow

The taxable income from real estate equals net operating income less the depreciation allowance and less interest paid on money borrowed to finance the property. See figure 23–4. Multiplying the taxable income times the tax rate gives the tax payable on income from the property.

For year 1 in figure 23–4, taxable income is actually a minus $5,786 because depreciation and interest exceed net operating income.

Net operating income	$64,000
Less depreciation	− 20,000
Less interest paid	− 49,786
Taxable income	[$ 5,786]
Income tax rate	.50
Income tax payable	[$ 2,893]

In turn, the income tax payable is a minus $2,893, or 50 percent of minus $5,786. The minus income or tax loss of $2,893 offsets $2,893 of taxes payable on income from other sources and therefore has a value to the investor equal to the tax savings, or $2,893. The effects of depreciation to shelter income and interest paid to leverage the property lead to this result. By year 8, NOI has increased and interest payments have declined so that a tax of $15,608 is payable on income from Douglas Manor Apartments.

The next step in valuing the annual cash flow from a property is to determine the actual after-tax income realized. Before-tax cash flow equals NOI less annual debt service. Subtracting the tax payable on the income from the property yields the after-tax cash flow that can be pocketed. Finally, because the cash is realized in the future, it must be discounted back to the present at the investor's desired rate of return.

For year 1 on figure 23–5, the before-tax cash plan to equity equals the NOI of $64,000 less annual mortgage debt service of $54,522, or $9,478. The minus income tax is deducted from this to give an after-tax cash income of $12,371.

Net operating income	$64,000
Less annual debt service	− 54,522
Before-tax cash flow to equity	$ 9,478
Less income tax payable	−[2,893]
After-tax cash flow to equity	$12,371
Times present value of one factor (15%, one year) (column 1)	x .8696
Investment value of after-tax cash flow	$10,759

FIGURE 23–4
Douglas Manor Cash Flow Projection and Calculation of Annual Tax on Income to Equity Owner in 50 Percent Tax Bracket

YEAR	1	2	3	4	5	6	7	8
Net operating income	$64,000	$67,840	$71,901	$76,225	$80,799	$85,646	$90,785	$96,232
— Tax depreciation	20,000	20,000	20,000	20,000	20,000	20,000	20,000	20,000
— Interest on loan	49,786	49,291	48,744	48,138	47,470	46,731	45,915	45,015
= Taxable income	$[5,786]	$[1,451]	$ 3,166	$ 8,087	$13,329	$18,915	$24,870	$31,217
x Investor's tax rate	.50	.50	.50	.50	.50	.50	.50	.50
= Income tax payable	$[2,893]	$ [726]	$ 1,583	$ 4,044	$ 6,664	$ 9,458	$12,435	$15,608

FIGURE 23–5
Calculation of the Investment Value of the Annual After-Tax Cash Flow to Equity from the Douglas Manor Apartments

YEAR	1	2	3	4	5	6	7	8
Net operating income	$64,000	$67,840	$71,910	$76,225	$80,799	$85,646	$90,785	$96,232
— Annual debt service	54,522	54,522	54,522	54,522	54,522	54,522	54,522	54,522
= Before-tax cash flow	$ 9,478	$13,318	$17,388	$21,703	$26,277	$31,124	$36,263	$41,710
— Income tax payable	[2,893]	[726]	1,583	4,044	6,664	9,458	12,435	15,608
= After-tax cash flow	$12,371	$14,044	$15,805	$17,659	$19,613	$21,666	$23,828	$26,102
x PVI Factor (15%)	.8696	.7561	.6575	.5718	.4972	.4323	.3759	.3269
= Present value of after-tax cash flow	$10,759	$10,619	$10,392	$10,097	$ 9,752	$ 9,366	$ 8,957	$ 8,533

By convention, the income is assumed to be received at the end of the year and is discounted with annual time value of money factors. The 15 percent, present value of one factor for one year is .8696; therefore the present value of the after-tax cash flow for year 1 is $10,759. For year 8, the present value of the after-tax cash flow is $8,533; the projected annual increase in NOI is more than offset by increasing income taxes and a decreasing present value of one factor.

The investment value of the projected cash flow for all eight years is $78,475. The investment value of the net equity reversion upon disposition is yet to be determined. The two together constitute the investment value of the equity position in Douglas Manor Apartments to Gerald and Nancy Investor. The value of the equity position plus available financing give the total investment value of the property for negotiating purposes.

Year	Present Value of Income
1	$10,759
2	10,619
3	10,392
4	10,097
5	9,752
6	9,366
7	8,957
8	8,533
Total	$78,475

The Investment Value of the After-Tax Equity Reversion

To determine the investment value of an income property, it is necessary to determine the present value of the after-tax equity reversion expected upon disposition, in addition to the present value of the expected annual after-tax cash flow. Some of this reversion will, of course, be a return of the initial cash investment. But to the extent that tax depreciation is taken in excess of market depreciation, capital gains are recognizable upon disposition. Also, to the extent that appreciation in the value of the property occurred during the ownership period, capital gains are generated. Capital gains are subject to taxation according to the rules set forth in the chapter on federal taxes affecting real estate. Costs must also be incurred in disposing of the property. Thus, the net equity reversion equals sale price less disposition costs, less the unamortized mortgage balance, and less capital gains taxes.

Let us look again at Douglas Manor Apartments. They are presumed to have increased in value by over 50 percent, so that a disposition sale price of $962,232 is realized. At the end of eight years, the mortgage balance equals $444,914. Disposition costs at 7 percent are estimated at $67,356.

The long-term capital gain equals $414,876, 40 percent of which is taxable.

Disposition price, EOY 8		$962,232
Less disposition costs @ 7%		67,356
Net disposition prices		$894,876
Less adjusted tax basis		
Purchase price	$640,000	
Depreciation (8 x $20,000)	−160,000	480,000
Long-term capital gain		$414,876
Proportion taxable		40%
Long-term capital gain taxable		$165,950
Investor's estimated marginal tax rate		67%
Tax payable on long-term capital gain		$111,187

The estimated overall tax rate applying to the capital gain is 67 percent. Thus, total taxes on this long-term capital gain are taken at $111,187. Because tax depreciation was taken on a straight-line schedule, no excess depreciation needs to be recaptured.

The following summary of the calculations shows that the net after-tax equity reversion amounts to $338,775.

Disposition price		$962,232
Less		
Disposition cost @ 7%	$ 67,356	
Loan balance, EOY 8	444,914	
Capital gains taxes	111,187	
	$623,457	623,457
Net after-tax equity reversion, EOY 8		$338,775

This equity reversion must now be brought back to time zero at the investor's required rate of return, 15 percent. The 15 percent, eight-year present value of one factor is .3269. The present value of the net after-tax equity reversion equals $110,746.

Net after-tax equity reversion	$338,775
PVI factor (15%, 8 years)	.3269
BOY 1 value of net after-tax equity reversion	$110,746

Total Investment Value

The value of the equity position under the stated condition equals the present value of the annual after-tax cash flows and of the net after-tax equity reversion. Total investment value equals equity value plus the obtainable mortgage. The total value of Douglas Manor Apartments to Gerald and Nancy Investor, based on a 15 percent rate of return to equity, equals $689,000, calculated as follows:

	Calculated	Rounded
Investment value of annual after-tax cash flow to equity	$ 78,475	$ 78,000
Investment value of net after-tax equity reversion	$110,746	$111,000
Investment value of equity position	$189,221	
Rounded		$189,000
Available mortgage loan		$500,000
Total investment value		$689,000

This means that the maximum the investors can pay for the property and still realize the objective of earning a 15 percent rate of return on cash invested is $689,000. Naturally, the investors would prefer to purchase the property for less. Figure 23–6 shows how these values combine to equal investment value.

FIGURE 23–6
Components of Investment Value

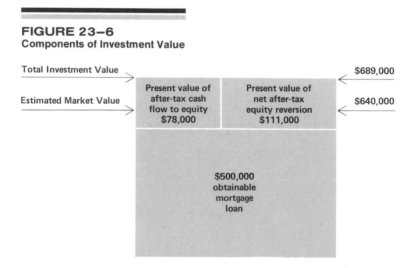

NEGOTIATION AND RATE OF RETURN

The most probable selling price of a property is its market value. An owner wants to sell for as much as possible and is not likely to accept less than market value. An interested investor wants to buy for as little as possible and is not likely to agree to pay more than market value. Undue pressure on a buyer or seller, differences in negotiating ability, lack of adequate information, and changing market conditions are considerations that might result in an agreed price being above or below market value.

The market value of Douglas Manor Apartments was estimated as $640,000. The investment value is $689,000. An investor needs both of these figures going into negotiations. If the property can be purchased for $640,000 or less, the investor accomplishes several things. The cash equity invested is reduced to $140,000, which means that the equity rate of return will be greater than 15 percent, if all other assumptions hold. In turn, the investor has nearly $50,000 left over, which might be invested in another property, possibly at 15 percent or more. Investing in more than one property also spreads the investor's risk.

Realized Equity Rate of Return

Assuming purchase of the property for $640,000 the equity rate of return can easily be calculated, assuming that no other factors vary. To begin with, an equity rate of return high enough to give a total investment value less than $640,000 must be used to discount the cash flows to equity, including the net after-tax equity reversion. A 20 percent rate is used here. After-tax cash flows calculated earlier and presented in figure 23–5 are used in that they are not influenced by an increase in the discount rate to 20 percent.

End of Year	Amount of After-Tax Cash Flow	Present Value of One Factor (20%)	Present Value of Payment
1	$ 10,759	.8333	$ 8,965
2	10,619	.6944	7,374
3	10,392	.5787	6,014
4	10,097	.4823	4,870
5	9,762	.4019	3,919
6	9,366	.3349	3,137
7	8,957	.2791	2,500
8	8,533	.2326	1,985
(reversion) 8	$338,775	.2326	78,799
Total equity investment value			$117,563
Available mortgage loan			500,000
Total property investment value round to $618,000			$617,563

Now the equity rate of return may be calculated. The total investment value of Douglas Manor Apartments at alternative equity rates of return are as follows:

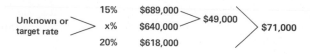

With purchase at $640,000, the expected equity rate of return is between 15 and 20 percent. In fact, it is approximately $49,000/$71,000 of the way from 15 percent to 20 percent. By interpolation:

$$15\% + 5\% \frac{\$49,000}{(\$71,000)} = x\%$$
$$15\% + 5\% (.690) = x\%$$
$$15\% + 3.45\% = x\%$$
$$18.45\% = x\%$$

In financial terms, 18.45 percent is the internal rate of return. The *internal rate of return*, IRR, is that rate of discount that makes future cash receipts equal to the initial cash investment.

The payback period for this investment is eight years. The after-tax cash flows do not equal initial cash equity investment until the property is sold. Thus, a five-year payback requirement would have rejected Douglas Manor as an investment. High property-value appreciation is the source of this result. And of course, that sort of faulty signal for acceptable investments is the reason payback period is not acceptable as an investment criteria.

Negotiating Strategy

According to the Jaffe and Walter studies mentioned earlier, purchase price and value appreciation are two of the most important items in a successful investment. Negotiation directly affects both of these figures, one when buying and the other when selling. What can an investor do to improve negotiating performance? Entire books have been written on negotiation, but for our purposes, four items stand out.

First, an investor must understand his or her personal goals and negotiating style. What are the relative priorities of the goals? What negotiating style best suits achieving the goals?

Second, the property must be understood. What is its highest value to me as a buyer-investor (investment value)? What is the lowest price at which I will sell, as an owner (market value, unless in distress)? What influence will terms have on these prices?

Third, know the opponent and his or her goals. In buying, look in the public records to find out how much the seller paid for the property and how long it has been owned. Is the owner's tax depreciation about used up? Also, estimate owner's mortgage balance and terms, if not included in the listing. Are there other liens against the property? How much pressure to sell is the owner under?

Last, in negotiating, remain objective. Losing one's temper or getting highly emotionally involved leads to mistakes and to failure to achieve goals. Have high expectations in the negotiations, be determined while pursuing them, but also be courteous. Recognize that no transaction occurs unless both parties expect to benefit. In buying, the property must have as high, or higher, a value in use to you than it does to the seller. The owner is selling because value in exchange exceeds value in use. And once a bargain is struck, look for ways to improve it by modifying terms. Cooperative negotiations are better for both parties in the long run.

SUMMARY

Real estate, like many investments, promises periodic income and value appreciation. The main advantages of real estate as an investment are (1) leverage, (2) tax shelter, (3) purchasing-power protection, (4) pride of ownership, and (5) control. For builders and developers, real estate investing also offers an opportunity for entrepreneurial profit. Disadvantages are lack of liquidity and risks—business, financial, market, and political. Business risk is the chance that predicted incomes will not be realized. Financial risk is the added uncertainty caused by use of debt financing. The most common property types of real estate for investment are vacant land, residential, office buildings, warehouses, hotels and motels, and small shopping centers. Each type has its own characteristics.

Sensitivity analysis shows that the key variables in income-property investing are (1) operating expenses, (2) leverage or loan-to-value ratio, (3) effective gross income, (4) property-value growth rate, (5) interest rate on loans, and (6) purchase price or cost. Wealth maximization is the primary investor goal according to financial theory. Other possible investor goals include purchasing-power protection, avoidance of risk and personal stress, power to control property and others, and pride of ownership. Common investor constraints are wealth or income level, risk avoidance, time availability, investor analytical and administrative ability, and locational preferences.

Investment value equals equity value plus obtainable debt financing. Equity value equals the present worth of periodic after-tax income to equity and of the net after-tax equity reversion. The investor's required rate of return is used in finding the present worth of the cash flow to equity. Many of the elements in the illustrative example are developed in earlier chapters.

KEY TERMS

After-tax cash flow to equity	Exculpation clause
After-tax equity reversion	Financial risk
Bigger-fool theory	Investment
Business risk	Investment value
Developer	Investor

Liquidity

Market risk

Political risks

Purchasing power risk

Pyramiding

Sensitivity analysis

Speculator

QUESTIONS FOR REVIEW AND DISCUSSION

1. Distinguish between an investor, a speculator, and a developer.

2. In what ways is real estate like other investments? List and explain briefly at least four advantages of real estate in comparison to most other investment media. What are the major risks or disadvantages of investing in real estate?

3. Compare vacant or raw land with an office building as an investment. On what basis or criteria should the comparison be made?

4. What are the six key variables in income-property investing, according to results of sensitivity analysis?

5. List and explain briefly at least five items that are commonly considered as constraints to a real estate investor.

6. Explain in general terms the process of determining the investment value of an income property.

7. Outline the accounting steps to calculate each of the following:
   (a) Tax payable on annual income from a property
   (b) Net after-tax equity reversion
   (c) Long-term capital gain or loss from sale of property

8. How might an investor best estimate the amount of a loan obtainable on a property of interest for purpose of analysis? Discuss.

9. Is there a difference between investment analysis and market-value analysis? Discuss.

10. It has been said that a skilled negotiator can buy for 20 percent less than a typical citizen. Does this apply to real estate as well? Discuss.

REFERENCES

Jaffe, Austin J., and C. F. Sirmans, Jr. *Real Estate Investment Decision Making.* Englewood Cliffs, N.J.: Prentice-Hall, 1981. Methodology of real estate investment analysis, including sensitivity analysis, explained in detail. For the advanced student.

Kinnard, William N., Jr. *Income Property Valuation.* Lexington, Mass.: Heath, 1971. A basic source on data collection and techniques of income property analysis. Useful whether market value or investment value is to be determined.

Messner, Stephen P.; Irving Schreiber; and Victor L. Lyon. *Marketing Investment Real Estate: Finance, Taxation, Techniques.* Chicago: Realtors' National Marketing Association, 1975. Written for the commercial investment real estate broker, this book concerns itself with fitting real estate into an investor's portfolio to achieve desired goals. Authors are a professor, an accountant, and a realtor, respectively. Includes discussion of sensitivity analysis, case problems, and exchanging. Reasonably easy to read and understand, given the technical nature of the content.

Real Estate Investing Letter: A Guide to Prudent Investing Boston: United Media International, Inc. A monthly letter explaining current trends and issues in real estate investing. Excellent reference for student and professional alike. Easy to read and understand.

Wiley, Robert J. *Real Estate Investment: Analysis and Strategy.* New York: Ronald Press, 1977. A logical discussion of the principles and methods for making real estate investment decisions. Many analytical techniques are explained. Knowledge of elementary algebra and accounting are assumed. Also, discusses in detail land, residential rentals, shopping centers, and motels as investments.

Property Development and Redevelopment

24

City building is just a privilege of citizenship.
Robert Thornton, Sr., former mayor of Dallas

Realty, or land, must produce a surplus, or margin of profit, to warrant its development or redevelopment. That is, a specific parcel of land is combined with other factors of production (labor, capital, and management) only if each of the factors stands to obtain a return sufficient to attract it to the project. Combining these factors in optimum proportions gives the highest value to the property, thereby constituting the highest and best use for the site.

Land that does not produce a margin of profit is termed **submarginal.** Deserts, jungles, arctic areas, and marshes are examples of submarginal lands. Realty may be submarginal in one use and yet produce a surplus in another. Thus, a parcel may have value as a residential lot and at the same time not have value as a site for a gasoline station.

Urban property development and redevelopment requires the combined skills of community planners, architects, civil engineers, attorneys, lenders, market analysts, investors, and developers. Projects need to gain the acceptance of appropriate governmental agencies and bodies to obtain the necessary approvals as they go through the developmental process. The developer acts as the manager or coordinator in the process. The developer is also typically the main risk taker in any project.

Competition to control and develop desirable properties is often very keen. Sometimes a site is acquired well ahead of the time it is to be developed. Advance acquisition preserves the site until it is "ripe" for development. A **ripe**

property is one that yields a profit to a developer after all other factors of production have been satisfied. With advance acquisition, **carrying costs,** (expenses and outlays of holding) must be met until the property is ripe. In downtown areas, sites are often devoted to interim uses, known as **taxpayers,** that cover most carrying costs, until the sites are ripe. Parking lots and one-story fast-food outlets are common taxpayers.

Real estate development projects, such as apartment houses, shopping centers, office buildings, and hotels are often designed and built as "one of a kind." When this happens, it is interesting to note that the total cost also becomes the average cost and the marginal cost. This is an economic anomaly that applies more to real estate development than to any other industry. It means that a developer must be extremely alert in each project as it builds from scratch. The developer is working in a batch process rather than a continuous-flow process.

Major topics of this chapter are as follows:

1. History and nature of property development
2. The property development process
3. Site selection and analysis
4. Residential land development
5. Income property development

HISTORY AND NATURE OF PROPERTY DEVELOPMENT

Property development adds to the supply of space in a community. Increasingly, development is subject to control by the community. Property development involves both breaking land into smaller parcels and adding improvements to the parcels. Growing or changing demand for space is the reason for land development. In this section we take a brief look at these considerations.

Development Practices

Before 1930, and particularly during the "boom" periods following World War I, land speculators took advantage of the naïveté of home buyers and the unconcern of community and governmental leaders, as evidenced during those years by lack of city planning, zoning, and subdivision controls. Subdivisions sprang up everywhere, principally in remote suburban places and often miles away from connecting utility-service lines and community water, sewage, and transportation systems. Generally, imposing pillars were erected at the entrance to the proposed subdivision. Promotional schemes were then set in motion and supported by extravagant advertising campaigns. Municipal authorities often fell for the bait and agreed to extend municipal services, to pave and curb the streets, to install street lights, and to provide schools and police and fire departments in order to meet the imminent "bandwagon" growth of the community.

Many cities and hundreds of smaller incorporated communities burdened their citizens with long-term bonded debt to finance the ill-fated improvements, hoping by quick action to attract a greater share of the migrating city dwellers whom the automobile was expected to set free. Except in isolated cases, the mad rush to the suburban hinterland never developed and thousands of once-imposing entrance pillars stand to this day as monuments to the fallacies of past subdivision practices.

The Great Depression of the 1930–40 decade brought home to citizens everywhere the costly consequences of the hasty faith that municipal leaders had placed in the overtures of fast-working real estate speculators. As an outcome of the debacle of the real estate boom, communities, with the aid of state *enabling acts* and indirect aid from federal agencies, have adopted safeguards to prevnt a recurrence of the runaway subdivisions and their attendant civic burdens. Today most cities provide for strict subdivision controls. Whenever areas are to be subdivided, assurance must be given that all costs, including the grading and paving of streets and the installation of conduits for municipal services, can and will be borne by the owners or developers. Generally, necessary land for schools and other civic facilities must be dedicated to public use. Proof of subdivision demand, too, must be established in many jurisdictions before authority to proceed with site improvements is granted. In many states statutes have been enacted regulating the methods and practices governing subdivision land sales and placing the owners and developers under detailed supervision. Statutes in some instances provide that collections made on installment contracts for the purchase of lots—in developments that are subject to statutory control—be held as trust funds to cover the cost of releasing such lots from the liens of existing encumbrances. Under these statutes, violators are subject to criminal prosecution or may be restrained from further lot sales in the affected subdivision.

However, even today abuses continue to occur, primarily in interstate land sales. Typical examples, cited by the Comptroller General in *Need for Improved Consumer Protection in Interstate Land Sales,* make the point.[1]

> A purchaser of a lakefront lot in Texas reported that there had never been any water in the manmade lake areas.
>
> A purchaser of a lot in Arizona attempted to resell his property but was told by the developer that he could not sell the lot until the subdivision was completely developed. He was not informed of this restriction when he purchased the lot.
>
> A purchaser of a lot in Florida reported that he was advised that monthly interest charges would be on the unpaid balance of the contract. He later learned that monthly interest was computed on the original balance due, without considering payments made.
>
> A purchaser of a lot in California reported that a drainage easement on his property had rendered the land useless.

---

[1] *Report to the Congress by the Comptroller General of the United States* (Washington, D.C., U.S. General Accounting Office, 1973), pp. 31–33.

Notwithstanding the above excesses, developers are generally much more responsible now than in the past. The public expects greater livability in its communities and buys from the developers offering the best values. Also, more land-use controls (community plans, zoning ordinances, subdivision regulations, building inspections) are in effect now than in the past. Consequently, the quality of development has steadily improved since World War II.

Subdividing versus Developing

Subdividing and *developing* are commonly used interchangeably. These terms have distinct meanings in practice, however. **Subdividing** means the breaking up of a large parcel of land into smaller sites for sale. The sites may be for one-family houses, office buildings, or warehouses. The subdividing must generally be done in accordance with subdivision regulations of the city, village, or county in which the land is located. A plat of the subdivision must be recorded to provide identification and a legal description for the smaller parcels. A **plat** is a plan or map of land showing actual or proposed property lines, setback lines, easements, and other pertinent information that is entered into the public record. A plat must be prepared by a surveyor or engineer or other licensed person.

Developing, on the other hand, is a broader concept. Developing is subdividing plus adding improvements, primarily buildings, to the land. **Land development** therefore means combining land and improvements to produce a completed operational property. Adding improvements to a site provided by a subdivider is also commonly termed developing.

Subdividing is a less intricate process than developing. Acquiring land at wholesale, obtaining necessary approvals, adding streets and utilities, and selling at retail make up the bulk of a subdivider's activities. Subdividing often requires little physical change to the land. Developing requires knowledge, planning, and commitment well beyond subdividing. A developer must arrange financing, obtain designs in accordance with community space requirements, supervise construction, and then dispose of the improved property. A developer must be more concerned with creating amenities or livability for the ultimate user of the realty. Many developers improve land for their own investment portfolio.

Land-Use Succession—The Reason for Development

Land, or real estate, tends to go to that use paying the owner the highest return (rent) or giving the owner the greatest value. There are examples around us all the time. Forest lands are cleared or marshes are drained to make way for farms. Farmland is developed into residential neighborhoods, shopping centers, and industrial parks. Older houses are remodeled and converted to office use. Old factories, mills, and canneries are often rehabilitated for shopping centers and other uses. Houses and stores are removed to make way for bridges and freeways.

Each successful change increases the productivity and value of the land involved and adds to the general welfare at the time it is made. In effect, realty is continually adjusting to changing social and economic needs, or demand. Or stated in other terms, each parcel is continually seeking its highest and best use. This principle is true for both urban and rural realty. The highest and best use will be realized unless prevented by institutional limitations (such as community plans and zoning ordinances) or by lack of owner insight and initiative. Thus, each parcel is subject to development and redevelopment, a process termed **land-use succession.**

The reason for land-use succession may better be visualized with the aid of a graph. Effectively, each new or succeeding use must be so productive or profitable that it can absorb the old use. Figure 24–1 illustrates the process. In the figure, use B might be a high-rise office building replacing an old, obsolete apartment building. The value of the site in office use is therefore great enough to absorb the value of the site in residential use plus the value of the depreciated building. Where remodeling is involved, the new use must absorb the value of the property in its old use plus the construction costs involved.

FIGURE 24–1
Land-use Succession Results When a New Use Is so Profitable that It Can Absorb the Value of the Property in Its Old Use

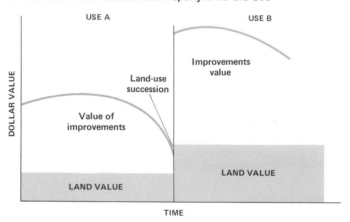

Our cities historically developed outward, or at the extensive margin, until recent years. The energy crunch of the early 1970s, and other factors, apparently brought about a turning point toward more growth upward, or at the intensive margin. Energy conservation means more-compact urban areas, or less travel, of course. Construction costs have inflated so rapidly that it is now often more economical to rehabilitate older buildings than to build them new. Rehabilitation is also advantageous because our cities are optimally located for the most part and involve a substantial infrastructure of streets, utilities, and civic buildings. And a centrally located older building is generally preferable to a new building at the urban fringe. Further, with zero population growth becoming a reality, it seems likely that high-quality space is going to be in greater demand than more space. Finally, tax incentives favor rehabilitation of existing buildings as against construction of new buildings for business uses. Thus, our present communities, with their houses, apartments, schools, recreational and cultural facilities, shopping centers, industrial districts, and churches all tied together by the transportation system, seem likely to endure for many years. And it seems likely that rehabilitation of existing structures will become increasingly more important relative to construction of new buildings.

THE PROPERTY DEVELOPMENT PROCESS

Successful property development requires a series of positive decisions by the many interests concerned with a particular project. First, the developer must judge that the project is feasible and coordinate the development process, much like a maestro. The land owner, if not the developer, must be satisfied as to price and terms for the land. Consumers or other users must be satisfied that the space provided suits their needs at an acceptable price. Planners and other public officials must accept the project as meeting applicable zoning and subdivision regulations and as being in the public interest generally. Realtors, financiers, engineers, architects, and attorneys must also solve problem situations to make the project go. The development process only moves forward with positive decisions and actions by the above players. One negative or "no-go" decision may shut down an entire project. Hence, the developer's skill in coordinating the many participants in a project is critical to its success. All elements in a project are interrelated, and a weakness or inadequacy in any one element may endanger the entire project.

These many decisions may be classified into a physical, institutional, and economic framework, as shown in figure 24–2. Study of figure 24–2 makes apparent the need for careful coordination in the development process. Institutional considerations break down into legal and governmental limitations and constraints. Zoning ordinances, subdivision regulations, and approvals by the planning commission are examples of governmental constraints. Legal constraints include options to purchase, obtaining clear title, and preparing private deed restrictions. Economic considerations include financing and marketing plans and actions. The process involves three stages: preliminary plans, final plans, and disposition or start-up. The process, as presented here, is schematic only. In fact, it varies from one project to another.

Preliminary Planning Stage

In the preliminary planning stage, a developer must search for a property suitable for improvement if one is not already owned. Once a property is located, its development possibilities must be checked out with the planning commission and other governmental agencies. A market analysis is necessary to ascertain the probable demand if the property were to be approved by local government agencies and the value, and probable cost, if the land were to be

FIGURE 24–2
The Property Development Process

Stage of Development	TYPE OF CONSIDERATION				
	PHYSICAL	INSTITUTIONAL		ECONOMIC	
	Physical design and development	Governmental	Legal	Financial	Marketing and promotion
PRELIMINARY PLANS	Locate property if not already owned	Discuss possibilities with planning agency and others	Arrange for option to purchase land if not owned	Make estimate of cost and value of land	Market analysis
	Complete preliminary design			Locate financial backing	Highest- and best-use analysis
		Tentative approvals		Feasibility analysis	
FINAL PLANS	Details of final plat	Work with planning and other agencies to get final approvals of proposed development	Develop land-use controls	Make up initial capital and operating budgets and solvency statement	Marketability study
					Develop marketing and promotional program based on market analysis
				Verify backing	
		Approvals obtained	Purchase land, if not owned	Make up final budgets	
DISPOSITION OR START-UP	Install utilities and streets	Record plat and controls		Recheck profit picture	Initiate marketing program
	Build houses, etc., if part of operation		Transfer parcels as sold	Pay bills, watch money come in	Rent space if ownership to be retained

purchased. If the situation looks right, an option to purchase is arranged with the owner. Assuming these constraints or limitations are satisfied, the highest and best use of the property must be determined and financial backing located. A preliminary plan is drawn up and submitted to the planning commission and other agencies for tentative approval. Upon receipt of tentative approval, the final planning stage is entered. No definite time limit applies in the preliminary planning stage, but several months to a couple of years is typical.

Final Planning Stage

In the final planning stage, details of the plat map to be recorded are worked out. This means removing or satisfying any reservations or conditions attached to the approval of the preliminary plan by governmental agencies. Private land-use controls must be written. Capital and operating budgets must be worked out to determine if the project is feasible and likely to leave the developer solvent. Based on these accounting statements, financial backing must be arranged if not already in hand. Also, concurrently, a marketing and promotional program must be drawn up. Toward the end of the final planning stage, governmental approvals must be in hand and final budgets firmed up. If everything continues to appear feasible, the land is purchased if not already owned. One year is usually the maximum time from preliminary plan approval to final plat approval. The maximum time will be stipulated in local regulations. If this time is exceeded, the developer is likely to have to begin all over again, which frequently involves having additional conditions attached to the project.

Disposition or Start-up Stage

Upon getting all approvals and recording the plat, the developer suddenly becomes largely independent of outside influences except for the market. Utilities and streets must be installed or a performance bond put up. Deed restrictions must also be recorded if appropriate and the marketing program must be initiated.

At this point lots can be sold if the project is an urban subdivision. Model dwellings must be built if the sale of homes is the nature of the developer's operations. And on sale, clear title must be conveyed. If the project is an income property being developed for use as an investment, space must be leased and a management plan initiated. The disposition stage continues until all parcels are sold or all space is rented out.

SITE SELECTION AND ANALYSIS

Judging a site suitable for development is probably the most basic decision of an investor-developer. Most other decisions in the development process flow from the site-selection decision. In many cases, the site-selection decision is made twice. Acquisition of the site or even committing resources to study a site and its potential for development is the first decision. Committing resources to subdivide and/or develop a site is the second one. The second decision is of greater importance than the first. An acquired site may be sold or held vacant as well as developed. Actually, developing a site involves a substantial commitment of resources.

In addition to site analysis, developmental studies include market analysis, highest-and-best-use analysis, feasibility analysis, marketability analysis, and investment analysis. Our main concern here is with site analysis. Major elements of consideration in site selection and analysis are

1. Location or sites
2. Accessibility
3. Size and shape
4. Physical characteristics
5. Utilities and services
6. Applicable public regulations
7. Cost or value

We consider these elements briefly as they apply to the major alternative uses of any site, namely residential, commercial, and industrial.

Residential

Location is the relation of a site to its environment, namely to other land uses. Showing a site on a vicinity map enables a developer to visualize its location relative to existing or future schools, churches, shopping centers, major roadways, and other urban facilities. Desirable residential location includes living amenities. Thus, adverse or conflicting land uses, such as air-polluting industrial plants, are best avoided. Location and accessibility are closely related. *Accessibility,* you will remember, is the relative ease of getting to and from a parcel. Most trips from homes are to schools, shopping facilities, places of work, and homes of friends or relatives. Thus, close proximity to schools and shopping is important. Most wage earners are willing to commute up to an hour if the neighborhood and living environment are otherwise acceptable. Beyond close proximity, immediate access to freeways and mass transit is important to having good accessibility.

Each site is unique in its size, shape, and physical characteristics. The size and shape of a parcel must accommodate reasonable layout for residential use. Similarly, the topography, soils, hydrology, trees and bushes, and other physical characteristics of a site must be suitable to residential development. The most desirable topography is gently rolling hills that allow adequate drainage and facilitate the creation of an interesting living environment. Fertile soils that support vegetation are also advantageous.

The relative availability of utilities, such as water, sanitary sewers, and storm sewers, is critical to most residential developments. These utilities may be provided through private or public systems, with public being much preferred to assure continuity of service at a reasonable cost. The installation of these utilities and of streets is a major cost in residential development. On the other hand, electrical and telephone services are extended to most urban sites at time of development, without costs to the project. In many areas, gas is available on a no-cost basis also.

Public regulation of development increased dramatically in the 1960s and 1970s, to become one of the major costs of development. The situation became so serious that in 1976, the Urban Land Institute published *The Permit Explosion* to state the seriousness of the situation and to encourage greater coordination in permitting procedures by public agencies. Permits add to development costs, both directly and indirectly. The direct cost is the charge made to obtain them, and the indirect cost is the long delay involved in getting the many required approvals and inspections. Also, increasing permit requirements tend to bar entry into development, making it easier for existing owners and developers to ask for and get higher prices.

Cost or value is a final major consideration in selecting a site for development. If the cost or asking price is so high that little developer profit is likely, all things considered, the site is unacceptable. On the other hand, if the value of an owned site on the market is higher than a developer considers justified, the site may be sold rather than developed.

Commercial

A distinct trade area is the prime consideration in locating a convenient commercial development. The size of the population and income levels must be examined in the market analysis and must justify the development. Then the most accessible site to the residences, one that cannot be readily cut off by competition, becomes important. Easy accessibility from several directions, without undue congestion and with easy entry onto the parcel itself, makes up a substantial part of this locational and accessibility need. High visibility to passing traffic is a location plus.

The size and shape must be suited to the type of development proposed. For example, a 5- to 10-acre site is needed for a neighborhood shopping center, while 80 to 100 acres or more are needed for a regional center. A large discount store might need 5 to 10 acres. Fast-food outlets and service stations increasingly need from 1 to 3 acres. Commercial sites must accommodate not only a necessary structure but also easy and adequate parking for customers.

A level site, at or slightly above street level, is desirable for commercial development. That is, uneven terrain, or sites substantially above or below street level, discourage entry by potential customers and are therefore avoided by developers. All urban utilities and services are necessary for most commercial development. Proper zoning and other public approvals must be obtained in developing a commercial center or district, as for other types of development. In addition, an environmental-impact statement is required. And finally, the cost or value of the site must be consistent with the proposed use to allow the developer an acceptable profit.

Industrial

Primary concerns in location and accessibility for industrial purposes are raw materials, labor, supplies and component parts, and the market for the finished product. Larger firms, such as metal and mineral processors, are tied to raw materials. Weight-gaining industries must locate near their markets. Most other manufacturers need only be sure of readily obtaining component parts, supplies, and services from suppliers. That makes proximity and access to a freeway or interstate highway highly important to them. Large plants may need railroad or water access in addition. Immediate airport access is becoming increasingly important. An adequate labor pool with appropriate skills is necessary for any plant. But except for the most specialized processes, labor may be readily obtained almost anywhere in the United States because of the high technical capability of our population.

An industrial park may occupy several hundred acres in a large metropolitan area. Of course, many parks and districts are much smaller. The size and shape of the parcel must accommodate a reasonable layout. That is, the parcel must not necessitate sites of odd and inefficient shape. The topography must be level for the most part, and the soil must have high load-bearing capability. That is, sites with soft ground, such as marshes, are best avoided as they may not be able to support large buildings and heavy machines.

All utilities are required in an industrial area. In many cases, the utilities may have to be oversize to handle the many wastes resulting from the processes. Likewise, gas and electrical services may have to be oversize.

Highly restrictive local air- and water-pollution regulations discourage industrial location in many areas. Some communities, in addition, have a "no-growth" attitude, which results in reluctance to accommodate the needs of prospective industries. An environmental-impact statement is required in creating any industrial park or district.

As with residential and commercial parcels, the cost or value of a site intended for industrial purposes must be in line with its profit potential.

RESIDENTIAL LAND DEVELOPMENT

Preparing land for use is an involved and time-consuming effort. In this section, we present several case examples or illustrations that point up some of the more important challenges or decisions of the residential developer.

1. Land use and layout
2. Private land-use controls
3. Local governmental controls
4. Financing
5. Land development costs
6. Budget requirements
7. Marketing

Land Use and Layout

For purposes of illustrating some of the problems and considerations that arise in connection with the subdividing and developing of a small tract of land located at the outer edge of a community of 40,000 people, a case study made for the purchaser of a 13-acre tract is briefly summarized. The problems were (1) to determine the highest and best use of the land, (2) to prepare and submit alternate subdivision and development plans, (3) to ascertain by market analysis the prices that the developed sites would command if exposed for sale, and (4) to establish the price or value per acre of the tract.

The problem of land use was solved without great difficulty, for the area was zoned residence "A" and thus legally restricted to residential uses. Zoning laws further provided that building sites must contain a minimum area of 10,000 square feet or be approximately 100 feet wide by 100 feet in depth. Streets had to be graded and paved and essential utilities had to be provided to make the sites eligible for federally insured and guaranteed mortgage loans.

A physical inspection of the area disclosed that the contour of the land was uneven and that moving of earth for filling would be necessary to level low spots. The area as a whole drained toward a small clear creek near the north border of the tract. To ascertain the elevation and exact physical contour of the land, a civil engineer was engaged to survey the area and to prepare a contour map showing specific elevations. The map thus secured was then submitted to a consulting architect for preparation of alternative subdivision plats that would best conform to the contours of the land. The architect was also instructed to determine the average amount of earth fill necessary to level the subdivision throughout to minimum required grades. The architect then superimposed his plat plans on the engineering contour map and presented his findings and suggestions for further analysis.

The two alternative plans submitted by the architect are reproduced for the reader's study. Plan A (fig. 24–3) shows the tract fronting approximately 740 feet on Archer Road and extending due north for 1135.2 feet on its western and 775.5 feet on its eastern boundary. The northern tract boundary as shown is 709.5 feet in length. Plan B, (fig. 24–4) called for a simple subdivision of the tract into nineteen lots. All land below an elevation of 80 feet (above sea level) was poorly drained, due to the existence of a high water table, and was deemed unfit for residential use. It was suggested that the creek area be landscaped and that the low areas be developed into a community park. To make plan B feasible, 4,000 cubic yards of earth had to be moved and filled. To keep developing costs at a minimum, only one semicircular road 25 feet in width was proposed under plan B.

Alternative plan A shows the same area with land contours and elevations altered after moving and filling 20,000 cubic yards of earth. Under this plan a more attractive subdivision was designed and lots available for homesite use were increased to twenty-two as shown. An additional center road, and the installation of a traffic isle, were suggested to increase pedestrian safety and to provide far greater privacy to residents.

Both plans were then costed out as follows:

547

FIGURE 24–3
Lot Layout A

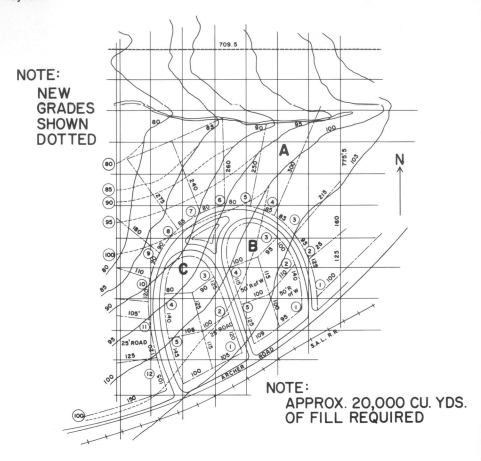

NOTE:
NEW
GRADES
SHOWN
DOTTED

NOTE:
APPROX. 20,000 CU. YDS.
OF FILL REQUIRED

		TOTAL COSTS UNDER:
Type of Improvement	Plan A	Plan B
Water mains	$ 19,200	$15,000
Sanitary sewers	27,000	21,000
Street grading and paving	36,000	22,500
Curbs and gutters	22,500	15,000
Earth moving and filling at $2.40 per cubic yard	48,000	9,600
Miscellaneous costs—legal, sales, and overheads	15,000	12,900
Total development costs, exclusive of cost of land and profits	$167,700	$96,000

FIGURE 24–4
Lot Layout B

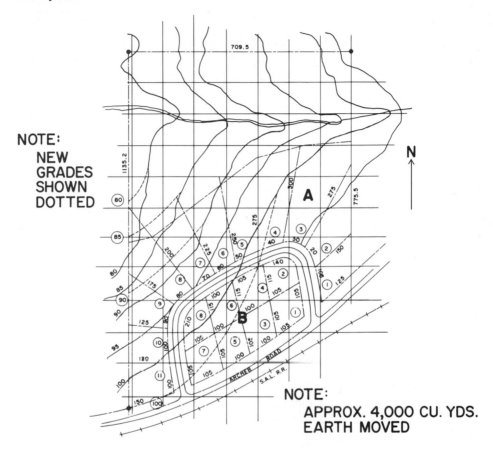

NOTE:
NEW
GRADES
SHOWN
DOTTED

NOTE:
APPROX. 4,000 CU. YDS.
EARTH MOVED

With this information at hand, a market survey was then undertaken to determine the value of the developed sites if exposed for sale at the time of study. In the determination of the value data, reliance was placed on comparable land sales and prices paid by buyers in equally desirable neighborhoods offering comparable homesite amenities. The technique employed was that illustrated in the chapter on appraising for market value.

The information secured via the market-comparison approach to value indicated that lots sold under plan B would average $8,250 per lot and yield a total of $156,750 for the nineteen lots. Under the more attractive layout of plan A, lots would yield an average price of $10,200 or a total of $224,400 for the twenty-two lots. Assuming that the purchaser or developer is entitled to a 10 percent profit based on actual development costs, the maximum price that could economically be offered to the owner for the tract of land was derived as follows:

	Plan A	Plan B
Total developing costs	$167,700	$ 96,000
Add developers' profit (10%)	16,770	9,600
Total costs and profits	184,470	105,600
Total market price of subdivision (based on lot sale values shown above)	224,400	156,750
Available for purchase of unimproved land	$ 39,930	$ 51,150

Although from a community and an aesthetic point of view, plan A proves more attractive, plan B indicates the highest and best use of the land. Because the tract in question contained approximately thirteen acres and plan B supports a land value of $51,150, a purchase price at the rate of $3,900 per acre was recommended. This case study is presented to provide a practical guide to the problems incident to subdividing and development and to demonstrate a method under which the profitableness of an undertaking can be checked with a fair degree of accuracy—prior, of course, to the acquisition of the land and expenditures for subdivision improvements.

Private Land-Use Controls

Increasingly, subdivisions and developments include private restrictions that govern land use and subject to which the land is sold to prospective users. Such restrictions are generally agreed upon by the owner or developer at the time the subdivision is platted and placed in the public records. All land subsequently deeded is then made subject to these restrictions, and reference to the page and book of record will appear in each deed.

Deed restrictions are especially important where the subdivision is not improved in its entirety or where building sites are to be developed by future land owners. Private subdivision controls or deed restriction is intended to protect and safeguard the interests of present owners against willful or inadvertent misuse of the land. Deed restrictions attach to the land and are successively deeded with the land and run as a rule for a period of about twenty to thirty years, after which the restrictions generally may be continued by a majority or two-thirds vote of the landowners of record. Deed restrictions must be just, reasonable, and legal, that is, not contrary to public policy or in violation of constitutional or statutory rights. Typical deed restrictions in a one-family subdivision may include the following:

1. Building sites may be improved only with one-family residences, not to exceed two and one-half stories in height.

2. Buildings must be set back not less than 20 feet from property building line, and not less than 8 feet from property side lines.

3. Only buildings containing 1,000 square feet of living area or more may be erected on a building site.

4. Occupancy of each structure is limited to one family.

5. Re-subdivision of lots is prohibited, and no more than one dwelling may be erected on each lot.

6. Buildings must conform in design to the neighborhood, and approval of building plans must be secured from the subdivision building committee, duly approved by a majority of property owners. Building sites may not be used for erection of temporary residences, trailers, or structures moved from other locations.

7. The keeping of animals, other than those classed as domesticated, is prohibited.

8. Observance of these covenants, subject to which the land is deeded, may be enforced by any one or more owners of subdivision land through appropriate notice and court action.

9. These covenants shall remain in force from February 1, 1979, to February 1, 1999, and shall be subject to renewal for two additional twenty-year periods, unless changed by a vote of two-thirds of the property owners at the time of expiration.

Deed restrictions, well intended as they may be, do not automatically enforce themselves. A neighborhood or subdivision "vigilance committee" must be organized to guard against violations and to secure court enforcement, if necessary, to protect the interests of affected owners. Where size of the subdivision warrants it, a neighborhood or civic organization may be founded not only to safeguard proper land use in the area, as provided in the restrictions, but also to promote owners' interests, as citizens, in matters of communitywide importance, or in matters concerning specific administrative or civic functions.

Local Governmental Controls

In addition to municipal subdivisions and development controls imposed through zoning ordinances under which street width, type, occupancy, and setback of structures are regulated, additional controls are exercised by health, fire, and building-safety departments, which inspect improvements to insure compliance with health and safety standards. Since 1935 one of the most effective though indirect methods of assuring sound subdivision and development practices has been used by the Federal Housing Administration, which is under legislative mandate to promote and encourage the development of basically sound residential areas. FHA's indirect controls are achieved by threat of withholding mortgage loan insurance from any residential area that does not comply with minimum development standards. These regulations are applied with particular stringency in subdivisions that have been planned since World War

II. The regulations are by no means arbitrary. In fact, they are quite flexible and subject to review and modification by regional offices to meet local needs, customs, and climatic conditions. Generally, the regulations are in the interest of all concerned and are designed to prolong the life of the area for residential use and to guard against practices that may hasten site deterioration or promote slum conditions. The following are some of the more important FHA minimum subdivision standards to which newly developed areas must conform to be eligible for mortgage loan insurance.

1. Streets must be of approved width and properly paved. Curved street patterns to avoid through traffic and to promote greater privacy are recommended.

2. The area must be free from hazards caused by excessive dust, noise, heavy through traffic, or other detrimental forces. Where the residential area is adjacent to nonconforming commercial or industrial uses, effective artificial barriers (parks or playgrounds) must be provided to shield and protect the area.

3. Subdivision must have ready access to adequate shopping and recreational facilities, schools, churches, and transportation service.

4. Essential utilities, such as water, electricity, sewage disposal, and area drainage, must be present and approved by city or county health authorities.

5. Lots must be of minimum size, generally at least 5,000 sq. ft. (50' x 100') in size, although the larger 100' x 120' plots are recommended.

6. Structures must be of approved design, must meet minimum construction standards, and must vary in elevation sufficiently to improve neighborhood appearance. Row houses, for instance, except in areas classified as "temporary" or "emergency" would not be authorized for loan insurance.

7. Buildings must be uniform in setback from street or building property line. Lawns must be "sprigged," and a minimum of landscaping in front and on sides of the homes must be provided.

As a service to subdividers, developers, and builders, regional FHA offices furnish aid and offer helpful suggestions free of charge. Thus a developer may send the proposed subdivision and plot plans to the regional office for check or modification and approval. Trained specialists generally study the plan in relation to land contour, elevation, drainage, and the community environment and then offer changes intended to improve the subdivision layout and to increase the benefits to future homeowners. Even the placement of buildings, changes in the variety of design, and building color variation are suggested to make the appearance of structures pleasing to the eye and thus increase the amenities of living and pride of ownership among the occupants. Before approval is granted, proof must be supplied that the existing and potential demand for homesites warrants the proposed subdivision. The intention is to discourage purely speculative undertakings.

Financing

Only in exceptional instances is an urban or suburban area subdivided or developed without the aid of borrowed funds. Generally, the subdivider or real estate operator acquires the "raw" land with equity (owner) funds and then seeks aid through mortgage financing to carry out the development of the project area. The raw land, as was noted above, requires only a fraction of the total cost that the land and improvement in their final stage of development represent. Compared with total value of land and building improvements, suburban land in its raw stage represents generally not more than 3 to 5 percent of the completed development costs. To secure the remaining 95 to 97 percent of project funds poses the financial problem. There are many plans under which investment funds may be borrowed in the market. In some instances, the improvement funds are sought by individuals who assume personal liability for borrowed funds or by partnerships or syndicates that are organized for the purpose of carrying out the subdivision and development plans. In most instances, however, the corporate form of ownership is preferred, especially where the project involves large tracts of land. A typical and orderly procedure for financing land improvements may be carried out as follows:

1. The raw land is acquired with owner's or equity funds at a price substantiated by income and cost calculations, as demonstrated above. The developer then proceeds with surveying, plotting, and filing of the proposed subdivision plan.

2. Once the plat is accepted and approved by municipal authorities and also by FHA regional representatives as a subdivision eligible for mortgage loan insurance (subject to completion of specified site improvements), the developer or developing company may borrow improvement funds over short-term periods of one to three years, offering the entire project land holdings as security under a "blanket" mortgage. Under this blanket mortgage, funds will be made available for land improvement purposes to the maximum agreed upon. This mortgage customarily provides for the release of individual sites from the lien of the mortgage, upon payment of agreed principal sums. This arrangement permits sale of building or improved homesites to individual buyers free and clear of mortgage encumbrances. This blanket mortgage, as a rule, also contains provisions under which it will assume a junior security position in case mortgage funds are obtained and invested for building construction on a given site or plot, either by the developer or by future homeowners.

3. Once the subdivision is improved with streets, utilities, and so forth, the developers may proceed with building-financing plans as follows:
   (a) They may offer the individual building sites for sale directly or through brokers, releasing each lot from the blanket mortgage as stated above.
   (b) They may offer the sites to builders for a nominal down payment under a long-term land purchase contract, which provides for payment

of the balance of the purchase price upon erection and sale of the proposed structure. In most instances, builders require title to the land when they, too, seek mortgage funds for building-construction purposes. Where this is the case, the developers take back a junior mortgage or merely retain an equitable lien against the property. The building site under such arrangements must be freed from the blanket mortgage, or the latter, as provided, must assume a secondary lien position.

(c) The developers may hire their own contractors and subcontractors and proceed with the erection of a few model homes. The necessary funds are generally secured through construction mortgage loans or building loan mortgages where the improvements are built to order for approved mortgagors. The builder may also secure an FHA building mortgage loan commitment and borrow funds against the insurance thus offered to the lender. Where the market is active and a ready demand exists for homes in the proposed subdivision, the third method of financing the building improvements may prove most advantageous.

Land Development Costs

References are often made to the seemingly large spread existing between the developers' land costs on a per acre basis and their asking price per front foot of a lot; often these references are inaccurate and unfair. Few purchasers of homesites realize the great amount of work and the expenditures that are required to "produce" land even in a modest urban or suburban development. Analysis of development costs reveals that the sale price of a site in an average development may yield three to four times the cost of the raw land if the undertaking is to prove financially successful. Although it is difficult to set forth with accuracy specific development costs that would apply to all the various economic areas of the nation, an attempt will be made to set forth concrete measures of the kind and amount of expenditures that may be anticipated when subdividing and developing a project area. Caution, however, need be exercised in accepting dollar expenditures as typical or representative. Costs obviously vary with lot and street width, population density, kind and number of utility services, and mode and quality of development improvements. The cost figures presented below, nevertheless, should prove enlightening to those who are unaware of the expenses involved in such projects.

Assume that a 40-acre tract of land is planned as a residential development and that under the highest and best land use it appears best to subdivide the area into 120 lots, each measuring 100 feet by 120 feet, or about 3 lots per acre. Assuming further that the balance of the land is devoted to streets, traffic isles, and other public uses, then typical development cost per improved lot in a medium-sized community might be as follows:

Based on the above illustration, each lot in this hypothetical subdivision would have to sell for at least $10,000 to return the direct and out-of-pocket costs, assuming (as some people do) that land is "free"—a gift of God—and that the developers are not entitled to any reward for their efforts or for risking their

Type of Improvement	Development Cost per Lot
Water mains	2,600
Sanitary sewers	3,200
Street grading and asphalt (30') paving	1,900
Curbs and gutters	800
Other costs including survey, legal, filing, sales, brokerage, and overhead	1,500
Total cost exclusive of land cost and developer's profits	$10,000
Add cost of raw land ($6,000 per acre)	2,000
Developers' profit—approximately 10%	1,200
Fair sales price—per lot	$13,200

capital in providing improvements. Assuming, for purposes of this illustration, a reasonable land cost of $6,000 per acre and a 10 percent return to the developers, the lots would have to bring $13,200 each to make the enterprise financially worthwhile. The above cost allocations indicate that the proportion of raw land costs to total lot improvements costs equal, in this case, 15 percent. Developers generally consider a 20 percent ratio a maximum for residential properties.

In the derivation of the above lot improvement costs, it is assumed that the water mains and sanitary sewer facilities serve lots on both sides of the street and that only one-half of the street paving and curbing costs are assignable to each lot. It is further assumed that no costs will be incurred by the developers for the installation of sidewalks or for the extension of gas, electric, or telephone utilities and that no expenditures are required for other public or recreational facilities. Should further costs be incurred, they must, of course, be added proportionally to the sales price of each lot.

As indicated above, density of population affects in an important way site development costs. Although utility-service mains must be larger and streets wider and paving stronger as density increases, the utility-service and street-grading and paving costs decline on a per capita basis as the population per lot or acre increases. However, a point of diminishing returns is reached when "crowding" occurs, and oversize installations are required to care for abnormal loads.

Subdivider-Builder Costs

In recent years most of the land subdivided near large urban centers has been developed by operative builders who sell homes ready for occupancy. The builder usually erects a number of model homes, each with a different layout. From these basic plans, variation in structural appearance of additional buildings is achieved by slight changes in façades, dormers, orientation, and exterior finish. Such building practice avoids the monotony of structural design so often seen in older sections of most cities.

A modern large-scale development requires a careful analysis of all costs to be incurred from date of purchase of the raw land to date of sale of the finished residences. As an illustration of this type of development, the following actual case may be considered. The builder in this instance acquired fairly level suburban land at a cost of $13,000 per acre, each of which provided 4½ building plots 60′ x 100′ in size after meeting street and sidewalk requirements. The building plans called for a frame structure containing seven rooms, including three bedrooms and a basement playroom. The house was furnished with one bath, a 40-gallon automatic water heater, an oil burner, and an attached garage. The structure was faced with a brick-and-wood front and asbestos shingle siding; it contained 22,500 cubic feet in volume. A budget to establish the selling price per property follows.

A. Developing costs per acre
   1. *Engineering and survey fees*
      Outline survey
      Topographical map
      Subdivision map
      Test holes, etc. $ 550
   2. *Draining dump area*
      Cost of land used for this purpose, excavation, earth moving, concrete curbs, and chain link fence   2,400
   3. *Subgrading of roads*   700
   4. *Drainage*
      Catch basins, manholes, underground pipes, concrete head walk required by Department of Public Works   2,200
   5. *Park area*   600
   6. *Road paving*
      Class A road in conformity with county specifications   9,400
   7. *Sidewalks*   4,150
   8. *Curbs*   3,200
   9. *Water mains*   6,600
  10. *Miscellaneous*
      Street signs
      Monuments
      County inspection fees, etc.   500

Total cost per acre	$29,750	
Cost of raw land per acre	13,000	
Total cost of land and improvements, per acre	$42,750	
Total cost per 60′ x 100′ plot (4½ to the acre)	9,500	$ 9,500

B. Total cost per structure
   The dwelling was built to the specifications outlined above, excluding profit, at a cost of $2.40 per cubic foot, or $54,000 for the 22,500 cubic feet of the building.

Building (net cost)	$54,000	
Profit—10%	5,400	
	$59,400	$59,400
Indicated selling price		$68,900

    The profit margin noted may be altered by a number of factors, such as fortunate purchase of land at a lower price, extras added to suit some purchasers, competition in the area, and other conditions.

It must be remembered that the illustration above is of a typical dwelling on an average lot. Purchasers select the house from a model, contract for an identical house decorated to suit, often with extras such as fireplace, double garage, additional bath, and plumbing lines to attic for future expansion. A lot selected from the development plan, too, may cost much more or less than the average depending on orientation, shade trees, or elevation. These variable factors may contribute to the construction of a large number of properties each originating from one of the basic plans, but each differing in selling price from the others.

Marketing

Marketing begins as soon as the development is made presentable—that is, when the ground is cleared, streets and service utilities installed, signs and markers put in place, and other work completed to make the land attractive. It is always advisable to erect a few model homes—perhaps one house for every twenty lots—to invite inspection by prospects and curiosity seekers and to provide a show of activity. Model homes have proved almost indispensable as selling aids in the marketing of homes and building sites of a development project.

Although most developers have their own regular sales force, cooperating real estate brokers often participate in the direct advertising and selling campaign. Compensation for them may be a fixed amount per unit or on a commission basis, derived as a percentage of the gross amount of sales. The good will and cooperation of real estate brokers in a community often are essential to the successful marketing of large subdivisions or when building improvements must be liquidated readily to secure necessary funds for payments of mortgage obligations or for further employment in the project development.

INCOME PROPERTY DEVELOPMENT

The discussion thus far has centered largely on subdivision and development of land, primarily for one-family residential use. Some suburban areas necessitate development of "self-contained" projects, however. Therefore, it is important to discuss development for income property uses—industrial, commercial, and multifamily residential—that may be retained as investments.

Multifamily Residential Development

Many real estate projects are developed for operation and retention as an investment by an owner. The analysis for this decision is generally the same as for purchasing an investment property in that investment value must exceed cost to make the proposal feasible. Some differences are involved, however. For a first user on a residential property, tax depreciation may be taken on a 200 percent declining basis, which, used as tax shelter, should increase the project's feasibility. Actual development costs are used instead of the purchase price in the comparison for feasibility. Further, instead of negotiating the price with a seller, the developer negotiates construction costs with contractors. The developer is therefore in a position to make tradeoffs between costs of construction and costs of operation to get the situation giving greatest personal advantage.

For illustration purposes, a summary of project costs for a proposed Glen Springs Apartment Project is given in figure 24–5. The total estimated costs amount to $4,300,000. Until the project is built, exact costs will be unknown.

Figure 24–6 shows the income and operating statement for the Glen Springs Apartment project. The statement gives an operating ratio (operating expense divided by effective gross income) of 35.5 percent, which may be a little lean, even for a new property. However, the vacancy and credit loss allowance, at 5 percent, may give a little extra leeway.

Applying an overall capitalization rate, R, of 10 percent to the NOI of $435,000 gives an indicated market value of $4,350,000:

$$\frac{\text{NOI}}{R} = \frac{\$435,000}{.10} = \$4,350,000$$

FIGURE 24–5
Project Costs Glen Springs Apartment Project

Land		$ 200,000
Land development—utilities, etc.		200,000
Improvements:		
Building costs:		
Apartment space	264,140 sq. ft. @ $9.50	2,509,000
Balconies and corridors	49,560 sq. ft. @ $4.00	198,000
Stairs—open	5,880 sq. ft. @ $5.00	29,000
Elevator shafts	29,054 sq. ft. @ $0.50	15,000
Elevators	10 sq. ft. @ $13,000	130,000
Appliances, stove, etc.	170 units @ $1,000	170,000
Carpet and draperies		134,000
Recreational facilities		84,000
Contractor's fee		150,000
Architectural services		65,000
Total improvement costs		$3,484,000
Financing and legal costs:		
Mortgage fees		90,000
Construction loan interest		135,000
Taxes during construction		4,000
Risk insurance		4,000
Title and recording		10,000
Miscellaneous—legal		15,000
Total finance costs		$ 258,000
Developer's fee		$ 150,000
Contingencies—1%		$ 40,000
Total project costs		$4,332,000
Rounded to		$4,300,000

This exceeds the $4,300,000 development cost, indicating that the project is feasible on a preliminary basis. Refined calculations along the lines illustrated in the chapter on investment analysis could be used to determine more specifically whether the project is a desirable investment alternative. This refined analysis would involve discounting after-tax cash flows.

FIGURE 24–6
Income and Operating Expense Statement Glen Springs Apartment Project

Gross Scheduled Income			
60—1-bedroom, 1½-bath apts. @ $290		$ 17,400	
77—2-bedroom, 2½-bath apts. @ 360		27,720	
33—3-bedroom, 2½-bath apts. @ 425		14,025	
170 apartment units		$ 59,145	
$59,145 per month times 12			$709,740
Less 5% vacancy and collection loss			35,487
Equals Effective Gross Income (EGI)			$674,253
Less operating expenses:			
Fixed			
Real estate taxes		106,000	
Hazard insurance		4,500	
		$110,500	$110,500
Variable:			
Utilities		16,200	
Management @ 5%		33,700	
Selling and advertising		3,000	
Resident manager		10,560	
Janitor and yardman		15,600	
Workmen's comp. and soc. sec.		2,350	
Decorating and repairs		16,800	
Other—pool, etc.		1,943	
Elevator service		3,600	
		$103,753	103,753
Reserves for Replacements:			25,000
Total operating expenses		$239,253	239,253
Net Operating Income (NOI)			$435,000

Commercial Property Development

Whenever land is to be allocated to competing uses, care must be taken not to violate the economic law of highest and best land use. Because the highest and best use is always determined by the present worth of *future* rights to income or amenities, consideration must be given to the actual demand for the uses and purposes to which certain sites are dedicated in the overall subdivision plan. Because business properties are known to bring a much higher price per unit of land, it is a common error to overprovide the amount of space required for commercial use. Simply designing an area as business property does not make it one. There must be a demand for business property, and that demand generally is in direct proportion to the number of people, or, better, families residing in the area. The reasonable relationship of number of families to number and kind of retail and service establishments can best be judged by a study of the spending pattern of the people in the area under analysis. An illustration seems in order. Personal consumption expenditures for the U.S., by product or service, are given in figure 17–10 on a percentage basis. On the average, individuals allocate their disposable incomes to goods and services as shown in that figure. This information provides a basis for determining if the commercial needs of a community or a trade area are being adequately met.

Studies of expenditure patterns for specific areas need to be made, of course, with more detailed breakdowns of expenditures. Differences from one area to another should be expected.

The spending pattern of families is important because such data can serve as a guide in determining the number of retail establishments best suited to an area. In comparing average family spending for the state of New York with the state of Florida, for example, outlays for food and general merchandise may be almost identical, but outlays for apparel stores, automotive, building material, and drugs may be significantly different. This can be accounted for by differences in climate, geographic distances between cities, modes of construction (also influenced by climate), and average age of citizens, the latter influencing drugstore outlays.

Assuming the subdivision and developing of a self-contained neighborhood in a suburban area in which a maximum of 1,000 families will reside, sound subdivision policy might call for a maximum of twenty-three retail stores, distributed as follows:

Number of Stores	Kind of Retail or Service Establishment
3	Food stores
1	Bakery
2	Apparel stores
1	Drugstore
2	Eating places
1	Furniture and household
2	Automotive supplies
2	Gasoline service station
1	Lumber, building materials, and hardware
1	Package liquor store
2	Barbershops
2	Beauty parlors
1	Shoe repair
1	Variety
1	Dry cleaning and pressing

The kind and number of retail establishments depend, in a specific situation, on community custom, climate, and general characteristics of the inhabitants.

Intelligent subdivision planning further requires an analysis of demand for the number and kind of rental and apartment units and for the number and kind of park, school, church, recreational, and civic facilities essential to make the development self-contained. Here, too, reference should be made to studies of other and similarly located suburban subdivisions, whose proven plans may serve as a guide in the proposed allocation of the subject land to alternative and often competing uses. In general, it is considered good policy to provide a buffer zone between the single-family residential and commercial areas. It is in this buffer zone that apartment, rental, and transient occupants may best be housed. Parks and recreational areas, too, provide effective protection against the "spilling" of inharmonious uses into the section reserved for single-family residential occupancy. The residents, it must be remembered, comprise the core or heart of the subdivision, and when their welfare is impaired, the development as a whole will suffer.

Industrial Property Development

Industrial parks and districts are often developed by railroads, utility companies, or public service corporations. Private developers need considerable experience and financial capability before entering this field of competition because of the nature of the competition and of the specialized and highly technical analysis required.

The market for industrial property is regional and national. This means that national contacts are also necessary for this line of activity.

SUMMARY

All factors of production (land, labor, capital, and management) must receive a reasonable return in a proposed development to make it feasible. The developer provides the management in the project. A subdivider breaks a large parcel of land into smaller units, while a developer adds improvements in addition to subdividing. The reason for property development and redevelopment is land-use succession, or upgrading parcels to different and more intense uses.

Three stages are involved in the property development process: (1) preliminary planning, (2) final planning, and (3) disposition or start-up. Physical, governmental, legal, financial, and marketing considerations must be taken into account in each stage. Gently rolling terrain, well located and well served by utilities and services is preferable for residential development. A commercial site must be easily accessible, well located, relatively level, and slightly above street level. High visibility to passing traffic is also desirable. Industrial sites depend on truck and rail transport, an adequate labor supply, and adequate utilities and services.

Important decisions in the development of residential land involves type of use and physical layout of the tract, nature and type of private controls, financing, development costs, budget requirements, and the marketing program. Careful attention to the amount of space devoted to each use is required in commercial land development, if the overall highest and best use of the site is to be realized. Where income properties are to be developed and retained as investments, cash flow analysis, as demonstrated in chapter 23, should be used in evaluating projects.

KEY TERMS

Carrying costs	Ripe property
Land development	Subdividing
Land-use succession	Submarginal
Plat	Taxpayers

QUESTIONS FOR REVIEW AND DISCUSSION

1. Define and explain the relationships between *carrying costs, taxpayer,* and *a ripe property.*
2. Distinguish between subdividing and developing property.
3. Explain land-use succession and its relationship to property development.
4. Locate and briefly discuss activities in each of the three stages of the property development process.
5. List five or six elements of consideration in site analysis and selection. Explain each as it applies to selecting a site for residential development. For commercial development. For industrial development.
6. Discuss the property development process as it applies to a one-family residential project.
7. What is the five-year outlook for your community's economic and social development? What sections or areas of your community are being developed now? What type of development is it? What are the trends?
8. Do zoning and other land-use controls affect a developer's profits? If so, how? Discuss.
9. Do we need planning, zoning, subdivision regulations, and other land-use controls? Discuss.
10. Is advance acquisition of land productive? Discuss. Is it socially desirable?

REFERENCES

McMahon, John. *Property Development.* New York: McGraw-Hill, 1976. An easy-to-read overview of property development with an emphasis on the types of decisions involved.

Messner, Stephen D.; Byrl Boyce; Harold Trimble; and Robert Ward. *Analyzing Real Estate Opportunities: Market and Feasibility Studies.* Chicago: RMNI, NAR, 1977. A book of theory and case studies to show the relevance of market and feasibility studies to actual developments. Use of case studies gives depth and application to techniques. Some areas are technical in nature.

National Association of Home Builders. *Land Development Manual.* Washington, D.C.: NAHB, 1974. A how-to manual in property development, primarily for one-family residences. Very pragmatic. Easy to read.

Urban Land Institute. Community Builders Handbook Series. *Residential Development Handbook,* 1978. *Shopping Center Development Handbook,* 1977. *Industrial Development Handbook,* 1975. Washington, D.C.: Urban Land Institute. Three handbooks written for and based on experiences of the major developers in this country. Clearly written, easy to read. Much useful information for anyone interested in these areas of development.

SIX

REAL ESTATE OWNERSHIP AND ADMINISTRATION

Property Management

Considerable effort and attention are needed to make real property productive on a continuing basis. An owner must personally provide or buy (contract for) the effort and attention. The objective of this chapter is to provide an overview of routine activities and long-term decisions involved in property ownership and management.

In an earlier chapter we noted that three of the six most important variables in income property investing are directly related to property management. These three variables are (1) maximizing the property's gross income, (2) controlling operating expenses, and (3) maintaining leverage. Maximizing gross income may be accomplished by merchandising the property properly and by periodically adapting the property to change. For an investor, these variables translate into balancing periodic income and obtaining capital gain at optimum levels.

The basic function of property management, therefore, is to balance periodic cash flow against preservation of property value, to maximize rate of return on the investment. The concern here is primarily with income property; therefore, attention is not given to vacant land or owner-occupied properties. Further, the concern here is to provide an overview of property management; it is not to give a detailed explanation of principles and techniques of everyday routine. Major topics in this overview are as follows:

1. Managing property as an investment
2. Managing property as a business
3. Property assessments and taxes
4. Property insurance
5. Management requirements by property type

MANAGING PROPERTY AS AN INVESTMENT

The three major issues in managing a property as a long-term investment to maximize rate of return are

1. Arranging for routine administration of the property
2. Maintaining leverage
3. Adapting the property to market and environmental change

On an overall basis, to maintain an acceptable rate of return, attention must be given to four investment-administration functions.

1. Select a competent manager to maintain the property's cash flow and value. Thus, the results of a manager's efforts show up in the property. The results also show up in the adequacy of periodic reports to the owner. The objective is to have routine details attended to by the manager while having items requiring financial decisions brought to the attention of the owner at the appropriate time.

2. Periodically analyze the property's productivity to the investor on an after-tax rate-of-return basis. The objective is to ascertain if a sale or an exchange is in order. At such time as a higher rate of return may be earned by investing in and owning another property, a shift in investment is usually justified. The analysis must include transaction costs involved in changing investments. The methodology for analysis of this type is the same as explained in the chapter on real estate investment.

3. If a sale or exchange is not justified, adjusting the financing on the property to increase leverage and rate of return should be considered. The chance for a higher rate of return must be weighed against the higher financial risks to be incurred. Again, the objective is to optimize the investor's rate of return.

4. Periodically analyze the property's productivity relative to changing market and environmental conditions. The possibility of investing additional capital to change the use, to modernize the building, or to make an addition to the property is included here. The objective is to optimize the rate of return earned on the investment in the property or to enhance the value for disposition and possible capital gain.

A property manager or a real estate consultant may be called upon to do much of the analysis needed for these decisions. But because the decisions are major, with long-term implications and effects, they should be made by the owner or owners.

Good management, from the investment-administration point of view, begins before expenditures are made in the development of a site, or before a property is acquired for investment purposes. The objective is to determine in advance of any financial commitments the greatest possible net return the property will yield under the highest and best land use and over the economic life of the structures and improvements. This net return must then be related to the investment in order to ascertain whether the *rate* of return is commensurate with the risk assumed in the financial venture. When the return *on* the investment is deemed adequate—that is, competitive with alternative forms of investment—and the return of the investment is sufficient to equal anticipated periodic accrued property depreciation, the development or purchase of the property is in order.

The tax position of the individual owner or corporation and the extent to which a property continues to provide adequate tax shelter to equity owners have become increasingly important in the managerial decision-making process. In all instances that involve taking advantage of accelerated depreciation tax allowances, an investment property, within ten years of ownership, may cease to provide meaningful tax shelter and, in fact, may yield insufficient cash flow to meet tax liabilities. When this investment position is reached and deemed critical, good investment-administration policy calls for an exchange or sale and purchase of like properties to reestablish a profitable tax basis for maintaining the cash flow at desired levels.

MANAGING PROPERTY AS A BUSINESS

Property management, in a routine sense, seeks optimization of after-tax cash flow on a continuing basis while maintaining the property's value. Cash flow is optimized by keeping effective gross income high and operating expenses low. The objective is not to minimize operating expense, per se, but rather to operate at a point of optimum efficiency and economy.

The property manager, if working for an owner, is an agent. On the other hand, a property manager contracting with several owners to manage their properties is an independent contractor. In either case, the property manager's role is to satisfy both the owner and the tenants.

For the most part, the property manager assumes all executive functions involved in the operation and physical care of the property, thereby relieving the owner of all labor and details associated with day-to-day operation of the property. The principal functions of the manager include:

1. Merchandise space to secure suitable tenants at the best rents obtainable
2. Collect rents

3. Tenant relations
4. Purchase operating supplies and equipment
5. Employee relations
6. Maintain property
7. Keep proper accounts and render periodic reports
8. Look after property assessment and taxation levels
9. Maintain adequate insurance protection

The first seven of these functions are discussed in this section. Property taxation and insurance are so significant as operating costs that a separate section is devoted to each. These functions are all economically interrelated and all bear on the overall success of the property management effort. Also, they are all subject to critical review and control by a manager or an owner.

Merchandise Space

The marketing of space is in essence a merchandising problem. The space-seeking tenant, as a rule, is familiar with the city, with the neighborhood in which the property is located, with prevailing rentals on a per room or per square foot basis, with availability of competitive space, and with the locational advantages and disadvantages of the subject property. To secure the prospect as a tenant, the manager or his or her representative must be able to "sell" the space by matching the service opportunities that the property has to offer with the specific needs and requirements that the prospect seeks to satisfy.

Merchandising of space, contrary to common belief, is more difficult than outright selling. In the latter case, when a property sale is consummated the broker is through with the deal and may turn to other properties with renewed vigor and initiative. In merchandising space, the "sale" normally is for a limited time and periodically renewals must be renegotiated. The property manager is thus aware that any representations must be truthful and the services offered adequate in order that the tenant may remain sold as long as possible.

RENT SCHEDULE. The first and perhaps most important step in the marketing of space is the establishment of a **rental schedule.** In theory the price of space should be based on operating costs, fixed charges, and a fair rate of return *on* the investment and *of* the investment (amortization) over the economic life of the property. In practice, rental prices are established by space supply and demand. Although in the long run rentals must be compensatory and fully meet operating costs and investment charges (if new space is to be forthcoming), in the short run space values fluctuate widely, depending on forces affecting tenant space demand (purchasing power) in relation to the relatively inflexible space supply of apartment and commercial properties.

Rental schedules for the various units of space offered are most realistically established on a market-comparison basis. This is done by rating the subject property in relation to like properties in similar neighborhoods for which accurate rental data are available. The comparison approach, though simple in application, relies on sound judgment for effective application. Comparison is generally made with a number of typical space units, and price adjustments for the subject property are based on quantitative and qualitative differences. For example, in the pricing of an apartment unit, consideration should be given to the following: area of floor space, number of bathrooms, quality of construction, decorative features, floor location, type and quality of elevator service, nature and quality of janitorial services, reputation of building and characteristics of tenants, location of building in relation to public conveniences, and quality rating of neighborhood and neighborhood trends. Assuming that a standard unit in an ideal neighborhood rents for $500 per month and the comparative rating for the subject property, after due consideration of the factors enumerated above, is 90 percent, then the estimated fair rental is judged to be $450 per month. If a detailed comparison is made for each space unit with six or more selected and comparable units, a fairly accurate and competitive rental schedule can be established and submitted for the owner's approval.[1]

ADVERTISING AND TENANT SELECTION. The next step in the marketing of space is the determination of the kind of tenants to be secured and the policy to be followed in advertising the types of units and services offered. Every effort should be made to attract qualified tenants who appear homogeneous in living characteristics. Tenants react on each other and, as a whole, add or detract from the amenities of living and the congenial atmosphere that is conducive to pride of occupancy and a feeling of belonging. Some buildings may be deemed best suited for young couples with children; others may be best for older and retired people who cherish an atmosphere of quiet restfulness. The fact that an attempt is made to suit the facilities of the building to the housing needs and requirements of the tenant makes a favorable impression upon the prospect and generally contributes importantly to the development of tenant good will and to the furtherance of good public relations. If the rental schedule is properly prepared and the building space effectively advertised, one out of every five eligible prospects calling at the property should as a rule become a building tenant.[2] If the ratio of tenants to prospects is greater or smaller, the space units may be underpriced or overpriced.

Collection of Rents

The collection of rents need not pose a problem if the credit rating of each tenant, before his or her acceptance, is carefully checked and if the collection policy is clearly explained and firmly adhered to. In most communities with a population of 10,000 and over, credit bureaus have been established, and it is

---

[1] Students of management and those seeking to perfect their judgment in rental schedule preparation should study the rental formula developed by Leo J. Sheridan and William Karkow, two well-known Chicago building managers. Copies of the Sheridan-Karkow formula are available through the National Association of Building Owners and Managers, Chicago.

[2] See James C. Downs, Jr., *Principles of Real Estate Management,* 11th ed., chap. 8, "Merchandising Residential Space" (Chicago: Institute of Real Estate Management, 1975).

possible to secure from them, at nominal cost, a credit record of the prospective tenant. Credit reports, as a rule, serve as an excellent safeguard against acceptance of tenants who have demonstrated financial instability. It is also wise policy to request references and to check with property owners from whom the applicant has rented in the immediate past. If the applicant, for instance, has not given proper "vacate" notice at a previous place of residence, or failed to pay the rent, the application should, of course, be rejected or an advance deposit of an extra month's rent be required.

A firm collection policy is basic to successful management. At the outset, tenants should be impressed with the importance of making payments on time at the start of the rental period as specified in the lease agreement. Tenants may also be informed that periodic statements are not sent and that it is their obligation to submit payment on the due date to the manager's office. In many cases, however, notices are sent. It is deemed good policy, for record purposes, to issue rental receipts even though payments are received by check. Such receipts permit uniform rental auditing and provide a ready reference for bookkeeping purposes.

A procedure for follow-up of past-due rentals should be rigidly and uniformly adhered to. A statement for past-due rents should be sent to delinquent tenants within five to ten days after the rental due date. This due notice may be followed with a final notice a week or ten days later. If this notice is ignored or not satisfactorily acted upon, legal proceedings are then in order to obtain possession or to collect the unpaid rent.

Tenant Relations

Clear communications and an open manner go far to establish and maintain cordial tenant relations. And cordial tenant relations go far in making rent collections easier, avoiding the organization of tenant unions, and obtaining tenant cooperation in general. Prompt and courteous attention to tenant requests is important in this respect, though all requests may not be met. Downs says that 90 percent of all tenant requests are reasonable.[3] If a request cannot be met, the tenant should be immediately so informed.

Purchases, Wages, and Expenditures for Repairs

The manager's responsibility is to supervise and authorize the prudent expenditure of money essential to the operation and maintenance of the building. Many expenditures are routine, such as the wages of employees and the bills for light, heat, power, and other recurring items. Even in meeting these expenditures, operational practices can be reviewed and economy practiced.

In meeting expenditures for repairs, the manager may refer all work to a general contractor who assumes all responsibility for carrying out the needed work, or the manager may purchase and stock required materials and hire skilled workers to attend to the repairs under his or her general supervision. The

---

[3] Ibid., p. 355.

former practice is recommended when buildings under one management are small in size and number. With large buildings and extensive scope of managerial functions, the latter practice may prove more economical. Service, too, can be restored and repairs attended to more promptly where workers and technicians are subject to direct control. Where the practice of attending directly to repairs is followed, a repair voucher order should be issued for each job and an accurate record kept of labor and materials used. The owner is then billed for actual expenditures plus a nominal overhead service charge (5 to 10 percent) for job superintendence. The direct control of purchases, wages, and expenditures for repairs, provided the size and number of buildings managed warrant it, should prove more economical and more efficient in the maintenance and restoration of building service.

Employee Relations

The success of property management depends to a great extent upon other people—that is, people upon whom the property manager must rely as employees or associates. It is therefore of utmost importance that the selection and training of personnel be given special care and consideration. Employees, although not vested with agency responsibility, indirectly represent the owner, and their conduct and serviceability affect public relations and tenant good will.

In selecting personnel, consideration should be given to the following:

1. Is the applicant technically qualified?
2. Is the person sufficiently interested in this work to make it a career?
3. Is the compensation offered at least as high as that earned for similar work in the applicant's prior position?
4. Is the applicant congenial, emotionally adjusted, and worthy of becoming a member of the firm's "family"?
5. Does the applicant display an interest in growing with the firm?

These questions, of course, cannot be satisfactorily answered solely by the facts disclosed during the initial interview. A follow-up of the applicant's experience and personnel records and direct interviews with prior employers may supply the needed information. The initial care and trouble assumed in the hiring of employees is more than repaid in the economy that flows from the effective teamwork of competent and well-adjusted personnel. Proper personnel selection, too, reduces employee turnover and minimizes organizational inefficiency. The important fact should be kept in mind that it takes weeks and even months to effectively train an employee and that, as a consequence, changes in personnel will prove expensive. Initial care in hiring employees should receive the due attention that it merits.

The careful selection of an employee should be followed with a well-thought-out and effective training program. The employee should be given an opportunity to meet coworkers, to sense pride in his or her work, and to acquire a feeling of belonging to an organization that "cares." Where the executive, because of stress of work, is unable to instruct the new employee, a manual should be prepared in which the overall objectives of the organization are clearly stated. The manual should also set forth the conditions of employment, hours of work, holidays, sick leave, and vacation as well as complete instructions covering duties and responsibilities of the specific job to which the employee is assigned. All employees, of course, should be informed that they are expected to give unstintingly of the time for which they are paid and that their work must prove worth their hire.

Maintain Property

Good property management demands a thorough knowledge of building service and maintenance requirements. Service is a big word. In the effective accomplishment of it, the interests of the owner and those of the tenants must be properly balanced. It is in the physical care of the property that the service interests of the owner and those of the tenants merge. The owner is interested in having the manager give the structure constant care and attention in order that property investment may yield the highest possible net return over the life of the building. The tenants, on the other hand, are entitled to reasonable building service performance. The manager's pride and concern about good service generally invites tenant cooperation and stimulates proper building use rather than abuse. Tenants, by and large, are reasonable in their demands, and complaints where voiced should be attended to promptly. No matter how small the request may be, good managerial policy calls for attending to it at once. Never should a request for service be ignored. Prompt action is essential in building good will not only with the tenants but also with the property owner, whose interests are at stake.

The building should be kept clean and attractive at all times. Inspection of the property should be made at regular intervals. It should be seen to that the janitor is on the job and carrying out janitorial duties. Halls should be kept lighted and elevators running. Heating systems and building service utilities must be kept in proper order. Constant watch should be kept for possible defects around the property. Flaws and hazards should be checked for in sidewalks, stairs, flooring, roofing, wiring, plumbing, or anywhere inattention may cause an accident. The maintenance problems and repairs referred to above apply only to buildings that are rented to a number of tenants and where the landlord controls portions of the building. In some cases, the tenant agrees to attend to all repairs, and consequently the owner is not liable for damages. The question of liability for damages is more fully discussed in the chapter on leases.

Keep Proper Accounts and Render Periodic Reports

One of the prime requirements of good management is the maintenance of an adequate system of accounts by means of which an orderly presentation of monthly activities, detailed as to income and expenditures, can be submitted to the owners. Accounting, although principally intended to provide statements of assets and liabilities and interim schedules of income and expenses, is also an important aid in providing a historical record of continuing property control and occupancy as well as data useful in the determination of management policy. In selecting the appropriate accounting system, careful thought should be given to the type of forms and accounts best suited to the orderly and efficient operation of the property and to the types of records to be maintained for the reporting of required facts and figures.

Owner's statements, depending on size and number of properties managed, may be presented in summary or detailed (also known as *transcript*) form. Modern practice sanctions the detail reporting method. Under this method the owner is furnished a monthly statement which may contain property income and expense data as follows:

MONTHLY PROPERTY MANAGEMENT REPORT

Name of building ....

Location ....

Statement for the month of .... 19 ....

And accounts receivable as of .... 19 ....

Number of units rented ....

Number of units vacant ....

RENTAL INFORMATION AND RECEIPTS

Property	Name of Tenant	Rent per Month	Arrears	Amount Paid	Arrears at Close	Remarks

DISBURSEMENTS AND DISTRIBUTION

Work Done or Article Bought Contractor or Vendor	Capital or Cost	Pay-roll	Fuel	Water Gas Elec-tricity	Gen-eral Sup-plies	Insur-ance & Taxes	Main-tenance & Repairs	Com-mis-sions	Total

Amount Collected $_____

Less Amount Disbursed $_____

Net Amount Deposited $_____

Where the manager is charged with the duty of maintaining social security and withholding tax records and the filing of governmental reports, auxiliary accounting records should be kept and periodically submitted for the owner's check and approval. All funds received and those held for the owner's account should be deposited in a separate trust account and under no circumstances should such monies be deposited with the manager's personal or business funds.

PROPERTY ASSESSMENT AND TAXATION

Property taxation to support local government is an unavoidable fixed cost against real estate, equal to from 1 to 8 percent of market value. New Jersey, Massachusetts, Wisconsin, and Maryland traditionally tax at high rates while Florida, Louisiana, Mississippi, and Nevada tax at comparatively low rates, according to a study by Professor Stephen E. Lile of Western Kentucky University. The best most owners can do is get overassessments lowered to avoid overpaying taxes. The intent here is to explain property taxes as they affect ownership of realty. We do this by looking at assessment and taxation procedures, and we conclude with a discussion of challenging an assessed value.

The Property-Taxation Process

The property-taxation process has three major phases, from an owner's viewpoint. These are

1. Property valuation and assessment
2. Budget and tax levy
3. Tax billing and collection

In the assessment phase, all real estate in a township, a city, or county is appraised for market value. Each parcel is then assigned an assessed value, which is typically a legally required or generally agreed-upon proportion of the market value. **Assessed value** is the worth of a property for taxation purposes. Nationally the ratio runs about one-third of market value. The ratio may run higher or lower than this. In Oregon and Florida, by state law, assessed value is 100 percent of market value. The assessed values of all properties in a tax district, when added together, constitute the **tax base** for the district.

Each fiscal year a budget summarizing the financial needs of each tax district is put together. The tax district may be a school district, a park district, a city, a village, or an entire county. The portion of the budget to be financed by property taxes is estimated and divided by the assessed value of the properties in the district to calculate the tax levy rate. The levy rate is the amount of taxes per $100 of assessed value. The **levy** is the number of dollars to be paid in taxes by a property, based on its assessed value and the tax districts in which it is located. Levying taxes on each property completes the budget and levy phase.

In the third phase, a tax roll is made up listing taxes levied against properties by section or subdivision, block, and lot. All outstanding liens for taxes (and also for special assessments for local improvements and water charges) can be readily ascertained by this method. This is preferred to listing properties by owner's name, which would necessitate a search against the names of owners for some time in the past to ascertain the existence of tax arrears. Individual property owners are also billed for taxes and assessments in the third phase. Payment of the taxes due completes the tax cycle from the viewpoint of an individual property owner. Failure to pay results in a lien against the property, which may eventually be enforced by sale of the property or some interest in it.

VALUATION AND ASSESSMENT. The tax is apportioned to various properties in proportion to the value of each. Thus, it is necessary for the taxing body, acting through its representatives, to examine and appraise all taxable property equitably. Various methods of appraisal are used, some of which take the property at a fraction of real market value, such as one-half, two-thirds, or three-fourths. Others take the value to be the amount for which the property would sell at a forced sale, and again others use as a basis the full market value of the property. Many large cities use the last method, which is generally coming to be recognized as the only one that is fair and equitable. Full market value has been defined as "the price that one who wishes to buy, but is not compelled to buy, would pay to a seller willing but not compelled to sell." Prices paid at auction sales, particularly forced sales, do not usually measure true market value, and neither do prices paid for property by those who have a need for that particular property only.

The assessor, in valuing property, frequently separates the values of land and buildings. The land is valued on the basis of the value of a standard or typical lot, that is, a lot of the size usually marketed in the vicinity. If the assessor fairly determines the value of such a lot, the value is allocated to all similar lots. It will of course be seen that in the valuation of lots in cities and villages, each street, and in fact each block, must be considered separately. Main thoroughfares and business streets create values in excess of those on side streets and in residential districts. Corners, corner influences, plottage, and similar circumstances are taken into account in order that the assessor may make an equitable appraisement, one that is fair and just both to the taxpayer and to the community. In certain cities maps are published by the tax departments giving the front foot value of land in each block of the entire city.

Although all lots in a block may have the same value, the buildings may be different in both size and character. In the valuation of buildings, the tax assessor must consider whether they are new or old and whether they are or are not the proper improvement for the land. New buildings are usually worth their cost of production, and the assessment is computed on that basis. As the age of a building increases, allowance is made for depreciation. When the land value remains stationary and the building depreciates through age, the total valuation of land and building will tend to decrease from year to year. In many localities, land increases in value as time goes on, owing to its availability for a better building—that is to say, one producing a greater rental. The assessed valuation of the lot improved with an old building will increase, but the total of land and building will remain the same. In such cases the building is assessed, not at its cost less depreciation but at *the amount it adds to the value of the land*. This condition may progress so that a once-valuable building adds merely a nominal amount to the value of the land.

Assessors are expected to consider the rent a building is capable of producing. It has been stated as a principle that an improved parcel of real estate is never worth more than its capitalized rental value unless the value of the land alone exceeds this capitalized sum.

After each property has been appraised by these various methods, the assessor compares and analyzes the conclusions to assign it an assessed value. Increasingly, assessed value is some proportion of market value. Therefore, the assessor's thought process in assigning an assessed value very closely parallels that discussed in the section on correlation analysis in the chapter on appraising for market value.

The assessed value assigned a property directly affects the amount of taxes to be paid on it. For example, assume a community in which the tax or levy rate runs 3 percent of the assessed value. A property assessed at $60,000 would have a tax bill of $1,800. But if the owner gets the assessed value reduced to $45,000, the tax bill drops to $1,350, a saving of $450.

BUDGET AND TAX LEVY. A *budget* is a statement of probable revenue and expenditure and of financial proposals for the ensuing year as presented to, or passed upon, by a legislative body. It is customary, in the preparation of a budget, for each branch or department of the government to prepare in detail an estimate of the amount it requires for the period under consideration. This estimate and those of other departments are analyzed and amended, usually decreased, by the legislative body. After consideration of all estimates, the final figures are assembled, and the total represents the amount of money the political body appropriates for its use for the period. Usually there are revenues derived from sources other than taxation, and these, estimated as closely as possible, are deducted from the total of the budget. The remaining amount represents the sum that must be raised by taxation on property within the jurisdiction. In some states there is a tax on personal property. In others, since the enactment of income tax laws, so much personal property is exempt that the direct tax falls almost entirely upon real property.

In large cities there is usually one annual tax levy, which provides funds for all purposes for which the city raises money. In other localities there are various tax levies, which may be all or some of the following:

1. *State tax.* The expenses of the state government are met to a large extent by special taxes such as income taxes, inheritance taxes, corporation taxes, stock transfer taxes, and automobile taxes. If these taxes do not provide the state with sufficient funds, a direct tax is levied in some states by counties, based upon the value of the taxable property in each county.

2. *County tax.* Each county of the state raises money by taxation for the expenses of the county government and its courts, penal institutions, hospitals, care of the poor, roads, and bridges.

3. *Town tax.* Local town government provides for its needs by taxation. Frequently state, county, township, and town taxes are levied and collected at the same time.

4. *School tax.* The school tax is often a separate levy by school districts for the purpose of maintaining the public schools. The appropriation for which the tax is levied is usually voted by the taxpaying residents of the district.

5. *Highway tax.* The highway tax is usually made by highway commissioners for the upkeep and repair of the roads within the district.

6. *City or village tax.* Incorporated cites and villages within a county provide for their recurring expenses by a separate and independent tax levy.

To ascertain the amount of tax levied against a particular piece of property, a tax rate must be determined. To arrive at the tax rate, two factors are used: the budget or amount of money to be raised and the total valuation of taxable property within the district. The total amount to be raised by taxation divided by the total assessed valuation gives the rate, or millage. A *mill* is a monetary unit equal to one-thousandth part of the dollar. The rate, or millage, applied to the value of a particular parcel of real estate gives the amount of taxes chargeable to it. For example, assume the budget to be $9,600,000, the value of the property $80,000,000, and the amount derived from revenues other than taxes for real estate $7,200,000. The tax rate would be determined by deducting $7,200,000 from $9,600,000, which would leave $2,400,000 to be derived from property taxes. Dividing $2,400,000 by $80,000,000 gives a tax rate of 3 percent, or 30 mills per dollar, or $30 per $1,000 of assessed valuation. Calculations for a typical property tax bill are shown below.

Property of taxpayer		
Value of land		$10,000
Value of building	$35,000	
Less depreciation	5,000	
Depreciated building value		$30,000
Total property value		$40,000
Less homestead exemption	$ 5,000	
veteran's exemption	1,000	
Total exemption		6,000
Taxable property—assessed value		$34,000
County rate = 4.4 mills		
City rate = 8.6 mills		
School rate = 17.0 mills		
Total rate = 30.0 mills		
Tax for 19___ $34,000 x .03 = $1,020		

BILLING AND COLLECTION. The procedure for tax billing and collection differs among the various states. Some states bill annually on a calendar-year basis; others authorize separate billing by school, municipal, county, and sanitary tax authorities. When separate tax billing is the practice, the tax burden is spread by statutory provision over budget years, which may end in spring, summer, and fall. Thus school taxes may be billed in September, sanitation taxes in April, and county taxes in July.

In some states, taxes are due when billed and become a lien against the property that takes priority over all other private liens, including mortgages, that are on public records or pending under court action. Most states provide a grace period of thirty to ninety days, during which time taxes may be paid without penalty. Some states offer a 1 to 4 percent declining discount if taxes are paid during the first few months of billing. After the discount period, taxes are deemed due and payable, and penalties for late payment accrue in accordance with statutory law.

There are several methods of enforcing the payment of taxes. The property on which taxes are unpaid may be sold at public auction. At such auction sale the property is struck down to the highest bidder. The sale, however, is subject to the right of the former owner to redeem the property from the sale by paying the amount of taxes, penalties, and interest within a certain time. Sometimes the sale takes the form of a lien against the property for a period of years. In most communities, the law permits the city to sell a lien on the property after taxes, assessments, or water rates have remained unpaid for a certain time. A list of all properties upon which there are arrears of taxes, assessments, or water rates is made up, and the date of sale is advertised. At such a sale the purchaser acquires not the property itself but a lien upon it. The bidding at the sale is by rates of interest; the person bidding the lowest rate of interest (which must not exceed a maximum rate set by law) becomes the owner of the lien. That person then has what is virtually the same as a first mortgage on the property, which has, as a rule, two or three years to run and bears interest at the rate he or she bid at the sale. The interest is payable semiannually. If there is a default in the payment of interest or in the payment of subsequent taxes or assessments on the property, or if the principal is not paid off at maturity, the lien may be foreclosed by an action similar to an action for the foreclosure of a mortgage. By this method of enforcing the payment of taxes, assessments, and water rates, the city has been successful in obtaining the payment of the arrears. The only disadvantage that may be noticed about this method of enforcing payment of taxes is the fact that it has allowed certain people to purchase the tax liens, not for the purpose of making an investment at a fair rate of interest but rather for the purpose of making a profit through charges for legal services in connection with the foreclosure of the liens. In an action to foreclose the lien, the owner and all persons interested are made parties to the action and must be served. This procedure gives the owners notice and an opportunity to pay the liens, penalties, legal charges, and interest and thus avoid actual sale of the property.

In some instances of titles that are defective, the tax lien foreclosure may be the most satisfactory method of clearing the title. Where such is the case, delinquencies will be deliberately allowed to accumulate; the tax lien will be bought and foreclosed by an interested party who will become the owner on the foreclosure sale and thus secure the property with a clear, marketable title.[4]

---

[4] Foreclosures of tax liens *in rem* (that is, against the property rather than the owner and lien-ors) are now protected by law in many jurisdictions. This procedure greatly simplifies the process and saves time and expense.

Challenging the Assessment Value

Each county and community generally follows a statutory tax calendar in accordance with which dates are set for the completion of the property assessment rolls, and for periods of three to six weeks, during which time the assessment rolls are open for public inspection. As a rule, notices of protest may be filed during the inspection period. Upon closing of the books, a board of review hears and considers protests made by property owners. Where relief is denied and the owner feels aggrieved, he or she may then petition the court for a judicial review.

BOARD OF REVIEW. The value assigned to real property by a tax official is merely the opinion of that official as to its value. The owner of the property may not agree with such opinion and feel that the property has been assessed too high. The owner may challenge the assessment and is entitled to a hearing on the objections. In making a protest of this kind, the owner is advised to analyze the assessment as to land and building and see which is erroneous. Land may be assessed too high for one of two reasons: Either a mistake has been made (in which case a correction is easily obtained), or the wrong unit of value has been applied. A change in the latter requires more care, for a reduction in the unit of value will affect the assessment on neighboring property also. A reduction in the assessed valuation of one lot usually results in a reduction of the value of adjoining lots also, often of all the lots in an entire block. Evidence of value may be offered by a taxpayer by way of information as to sales, mortgages, and so forth, and his contention may be supported by such evidence.

If the taxpayer's protest is based upon a claim of overassessment of the building, he or she has a fair chance of obtaining a reduction. Every building is considered separately, with the result that a reduction of assessed value of one does not necessarily mean that others must be reduced also. In making a claim of this kind, the owner may offer as evidence proof of the cost of the building, its rental, physical condition, sales price, mortgages, and so forth.

COURT REVIEW. The action of the tax officials is subject to review by the court. If an owner believes that the assessed value of his or her property is too high and is unable to secure a reduction upon protest to the officials, an appeal may then be made to the courts. This is a proceeding a certiorari; that is to say, it is a proceeding whereby the tax officials are required to produce their records and to certify to them to the court in order that the court may determine whether the officials have proceeded according to the principles of law by which they are bound. The court does not usually fix the assessed value, but it may criticize the administrative officers and give directions as to how they must proceed. It is, of course, also possible that the court will sustain the tax officials and find that they have proceeded according to law in fixing the assessed value, or it may direct the reduction of its assessed value.

PROPERTY INSURANCE

The primary function of insurance is to substitute certainty for uncertainty by shifting the risk of a disastrous event to an insurance company. A payment, termed an *insurance premium,* is made to the company as compensation for its acceptance of the risk. A policy contract between the individual and the company stipulates the amount of term or period of time of the insurance protection. The insurance company, of course, insures many individuals against the same risk. The overall effect is to spread the cost of the disastrous event, which normally would fall on one individual, over many individuals exposed to the same hazard.

Manager's Insurance Responsibility

The property manager's responsibility includes protecting the owner against all major insurable risks. An owner expects the management firm to relieve him or her of most details incident to the ownership of the property. As the owner's representative, the manager should be capable of determining and evaluating the risks involved and should make every effort to secure the best and most economical protection available in the insurance market.

Standard insurance-coverage contracts that the manager should consider in the protection of the client's property include the following:

1. *Standard fire insurance.* This policy protects the insured against all direct losses or damages to real property by fire excepting those losses caused by perils or forces specifically excluded in the policy.

2. *Extended coverage.* The inclusion of **extended coverage** is a recommended practice. It provides for broader protection and includes risk compensation for losses due to perils of explosion, windstorm, hail, riot, civil disturbances, aircraft, vehicles, and other causes.

3. *General liability.* This policy insures the owner against liability imposed by law for damages due to injuries caused to the persons or properties of others.

4. *Workmen's compensation.* This type of employee protection against injury is mandatory in most states and varies in accordance with state law.

5. *Inland marine insurance.* This is available to cover personal property losses and, more generally, damages to property that is mobile in nature.

6. *Casualty insurance.* This protects the insured against losses due to theft, burglary, plate-glass breakage, and elevator, steam-boiler, machinery, and similar accidents. Under this form of insurance, policies are also issued to cover a variety of accident and health injuries.

7. *Rent insurance and consequential losses.* This type of insurance is also referred to as **business interruptions insurance.** It compensates the owner for consequential losses incident to damage or destruction of the property.

The manager's responsibility, as agent for the owner, is to keep accurate records of all insurance policies and to arrange for renewals well in advance of date of policy expiration. Care must be taken that insurance coverage is in proper relation to current property replacement costs and that dollar price changes due to increased construction costs or monetary inflation have been considered on or before the date of policy renewal. Good management, too, can assist in keeping fire insurance down to a minimum by eliminating fire hazards as much as possible. Sometimes the character of a tenant's business increases the insurance rate on the building. This fact should be recognized in setting the appropriate rent. Generally tenants agree to pay the additional premium caused by their mode of occupancy.

A study of insurance price schedules offered by competing companies may suggest ways of securing rate reductions. As a rule, liability insurance is carried so that any claim for damages is defended by the insurance company, and loss, if any, is borne by them. Rent insurance is entirely optional with the owner. Many owners do not wish to carry it, being willing to assume the risk of a loss of rents in case of fire.

Buying Insurance

The most important consideration in obtaining insurance for the typical property owner is the selection of the agent or broker. Price, or the amount of the policy premium, and the reputation and financial capability of the insurance company are obviously important also. But the agent aids in the choice of the company and the type and adequacy of insurance coverage to be obtained. The agent helps to balance the costs against the risks to obtain the best insurance program possible within the owner's capability. The agent also services the policy on a continuing basis and is the owner's liaison with the company in the event of a claim of loss. Obviously the relationship involves considerable trust. If the trust in the relationship is lost, the owner should seriously consider changing to another agent.

THE BUSINESS OF PROPERTY INSURANCE. The constant search for means to eliminate uncertainty and to shift the risks of ownership to agencies or companies best qualified to cope with them has caused the business of property insurance to develop into a highly important but complex and involved specialty. Because of its almost indispensable nature, insurance as a business is designated a **public calling** and the formation, operation, and solicitation of the insurance business are subject to stringent regulation under the laws of most states.

Because of the necessity for reliability and continuity in meeting hazard obligations, insurance as a business is carried on by corporations organized under special state laws. Generally, articles of incorporation and information regarding the scope of business, number and par value of shares, and other required data must be filed with the proper state official. As a rule, periodic reports and audits of operations are made additional requirements in order to protect the public interest.

The insurance business, almost in its entirety, is accounted for by two principal types of carriers: (1) cooperative or mutual insurance organizations, and (2) proprietary or stock companies.

The cooperative or mutual organization is a nonprofit organization and operates for the benefit of its members. Insurance premiums are intended to cover losses of calculated risks and costs of general operation and business overhead. Surplus, if any, resulting from superior management or extra hazard control of the insured is returned as pro rata dividend at the end of the contract period. This form of cooperative insurance has proved economically successful in areas where the hazards were homogeneous and where unanimity of member interest permitted risk control and mutual cooperation. In the field of life insurance, the cooperative or mutual organizations have taken a leading role.

The proprietary insurance companies, or stock ownership enterprises, are known as **professional risk bearers.** This form of company is organized to apply business principles and practices to the field of insurance and to yield in return a profit to its owners or proprietors. This form of organization not only has proved to be competitive to the "mutual" companies in the field of life insurance but also seems better adapted to deal with heterogeneous hazards that commonly prevail in the field of property insurance.

SELECTING THE AGENT OR BROKER. The very nature of the insurance business compels insurance companies to diversify their risks and to seek policyholders in far-flung areas as a safeguard against large-scale peril in a single region or community. The common-sense policy not to put all the risks in one basket necessitates insurance operations at great distances from office headquarters. Although many companies have established branch offices in the larger communities, the greater share of the insurance business is dependent on services of company agents or insurance brokers. Then, too, the characteristics of the business are such that insurance must be *sold*—it is rarely bought by individual business people or property owners. Generally, individuals give their insurance business to agents or brokers on the basis of professional confidence, personal acquaintance or friendship.

Insurance agents and brokers must demonstrate competency by qualifying for an insurance agent's or broker's license in most states, usually by passing an examination. The important distinction is whether the agent must represent the company or whether the agent, as a broker, independent of any one insurance company, is in a position to represent the property owner. Obviously the latter is to be preferred.

Legally, the agent is the representative of the insurance company and owes it his or her loyalty. An agent, too, is generally charged with the responsibility for protecting the company's interests and should confine his or her operations to the insurance offerings of the company or companies represented. For her or his services the agent is compensated by payment of a commission on new insurance and on renewals of existing policies. In fact, the agent may be called a salesperson for one or more insurance companies. The powers of such a person, as a rule, are limited to securing applications, delivering insurance policies, and collecting premiums. Acceptance of risks and settlement of losses are legally the sole responsibilities of the insurance companies and not those of their agents.

The insurance broker, on the other hand, is an independent operator and expert adviser who serves the interests of clients always. The broker generally studies the insurance needs by inspecting clients' premises and then bargains with selected insurance carriers for the best terms and lowest rate obtainable. Often the broker will suggest improvements in the physical conditions of the property, such as the installation of a sprinkler system or the elimination of a hazard that may bring about a lower class rate and thus profitable savings in insurance premiums. The broker generally, because of his or her independence, is free to place insurance business anywhere and prefers companies that he or she considers financially strong, prompt in settlement of losses, and otherwise competitive in rates and broker commission payments.

RATES. Insurance is based on the law of averages. It would be difficult indeed to try to foretell, where many risks of the same nature are involved, how many would suffer loss in the period of one year and how extensive the loss would be. With 10,000 or 20,000 similar buildings, however, all with the same type risk and with proper statistics on hand, it would be easy to forecast with a great degree of accuracy the number of buildings that would suffer loss and the total extent of the damage to be expected. Knowing the total amount of the losses and the total value of the buildings, an insurance company could fairly easily calulate the rate per hundred dollars of value that should be used and, using that rate, could find the premium that should be charged each building, based on its value, in order to collect just sufficient funds to meet the expected loss. In actual practice, however, this rate would have to be increased to take care of the expense necessary to run an insurance company and to allow the company a fair profit from prudent underwriting.

There are a number of different types of rates, but the better-known ones are minimum, or class, rates and specific rates. **Minimum rated risks** take in whole groups of buildings of similar construction and hazard and give them the same rate. For instance, brick dwellings in a certain territory would all have the same rate, frame dwellings another. Many apartments of similar construction have the same rate as well as many store and dwelling properties. These rates are the lowest that can be had unless the rate for the entire class is lowered.

Other buildings, such as mercantile and manufacturing buildings, are **specifically rated.** That means a rate is promulgated by the use of a schedule to reflect the condition and occupancy of the building at the time it is inspected by the rating organization. Owners of properties that are specifically rated should always secure a schedule or "makeup" of their fire insurance rate. When this is received, it should be gone over thoroughly by an expert to make certain all the charges that go to make up the rate are in order. It may be that a hazardous tenant has left the building or that certain faults of management have been corrected since the rate was promulgated. If that is so, and it appears the rate is too high, a new rate should be applied for. The expert would also make a study of existing physical conditions to determine whether fire protection devices (such as sprinklers) or building alterations (such as fireproofing) would make a sufficient rate saving to justify the high cost of installation.

COINSURANCE. When rates are figured for various risks, consideration must be given to the premium those rates will produce. The premiums produced are dependent on the amount of insurance purchased. Ordinarily, the greater the amount of insurance purchased, the lower the rate that is necessary to produce sufficient reserve to meet anticipated loss. Now it is a well-known fact that in territory that enjoys fire protection, most losses are partial, and yet there is always the danger in individual cases of total loss. Knowing that most losses are partial, a person might feel that it was unnecessary to carry more than a nominal amount of insurance. On a building worth $10,000, such a person, therefore, might carry $2,000 insurance at a rate of $1 per hundred and a premium of $20. Another person, not knowing that most losses are partial, and desiring better protection, would insure for the full value, or $10,000, also at $1 per hundred, with a premium of $100. In the event of a $2,000 loss, if no **coinsurance** clause was in the policy, each would receive this amount, although the latter paid considerably more for the policy. It can be argued, of course, that the latter received a greater limit of protection; but inasmuch as most of the losses are partial, the danger of a total loss was not as great as the danger of a loss on the first few thousand at risk. Therefore, if the rate charged was the correct one for the first $2,000, it was excessive for the coverage over that amount. To equalize this distribution of the cost of insurance among policyholders and to penalize those going underinsured, the coinsurance or average clause was introduced and made a part of the policy. The clauses generally used are the 80, 90, or 100 percent average clauses. Of these, the 80 percent average clause is the one generally attached to the policy.

Many people think that an 80 percent coinsurance clause means that the insurance company will pay only 80 percent of any loss. Others feel that in the event of total loss, they would be able to collect 80 percent of the face amount of the policy. Both of these ideas, of course, are wrong. The usual 80 percent coinsurance, or typical, clause reads in part, "This company shall not be liable for a greater proportion of any loss or damage to the property described herein than the sum hereby insured bears to eighty percent (80%) of the actual cash value of said property at the time such loss shall happen, nor for more than the proportion that this policy bears to the total insurance thereon."

Various factors can enter into the determination of actual cash value, but under ordinary conditions it will be sufficient to consider actual cash value as replacement value, less depreciation. To illustrate the operation of the 80 percent average clause, consider the following example. A and B both own buildings, the actual cash value of each being $10,000. A carries $8,000 insurance, B carries $4,000 insurance. Both suffer a $2,000 loss, as shown in the calculations below:

	A's Company	B's Company
Actual cash value of building	$10,000	$10,000
Insurance required to be carried to meet requirements of the 80%		
Average clause (80% of $10,000)	8,000	8,000
Insurance actually carried	8,000	4,000
Actual loss	2,000	2,000

    A should and did carry $8,000 insurance. His company, therefore, pays 8,000/8,000 of the $2,000 loss, or $2,000.

    B should carry $8,000 insurance but only carried $4,000. His company, therefore, pays 4,000/8,000 of the $2,000 loss, or $1,000.

A carried the correct amount of insurance and therefore received the full amount of his loss without any penalty of coinsurance. B carried only one-half of the amount of insurance required by the average clause and therefore became a coinsurer with the insurance company for 50 percent of the loss.

It should be remembered that if sufficient insurance is carried to meet the requirement of the average clause, for all intents and purposes, in the event of a loss the policy can be considered as written without any coinsurance feature and will pay dollar for dollar any loss up to its face amount. The clause penalizes only when insufficient insurance is carried. It should also be noted that the average clause does not limit the amount of insurance the owner is permitted to take out. The owner can insure for full value regardless of what clause is used.

In unprotected territory—that is, territory without benefits of fire protection—the average clause is usually not required in the policy. The probable reason is that without fire protection almost any fire would in all likelihood result in a total loss, and therefore it would obviously not benefit the insurance companies to insist that large amounts of insurance be carried. In states or jurisdictions where regulations provide for "full" value insurance, the coinsurance concept is not applicable. Value for insurance purposes is ascertained by the agent. The owner may request higher coverage, but losses are limited to value as measured by cost of replacement less accrued depreciation based on age and conditions at time of loss.

RISK MANAGEMENT AND SELF-INSURANCE. Ultimately, an owner is responsible for the proper management of risk. By default, an owner in effect is self-insured for risks not covered by insurance. We have discussed only a few of the many forms of insurance protection available to owners. Property owners or their managers should carefully analyze the risks they believe they are subject to and consult a broker or agent, arranging for that person to make a thorough survey of insurance needs. Then they should follow the broker's recommendations for proper coverage. If this is intelligently done, and adequate insurance is carried to meet the hazards to which an owner is subject, he or she will have purchased, at comparatively small cost, security and protection against the possibility of sudden and severe financial loss.

Loss Adjustments

When a loss occurs, the insured should immediately notify the insurance company of such loss and protect the property from further damage. He or she should then secure the estimate of several competent builders to ascertain the cost to repair the damage. One of the estimates should then be sent to the insurance company to be compared with the insurance company's estimate. If there are differences, the insured or a representative and the company adjuster discuss those differences with a view to reaching a compromise settlement. In the vast majority of cases, this settlement is reached in a friendly fashion. If by any chance the differences are so great that the insured and the insurance company cannot reconcile them, then it is necessary for each to select an appraiser. The appraisers select an umpire, but in the event they cannot agree on an umpire, then, on the request of the insured or the insurance company, one may be selected by a judge of a court of record in the state in which the property covered is located. An award arrived at by the appraisers or by the appraisers and the umpire will then determine the amount of actual cash value and loss. An insured is permitted to make temporary repairs to prevent further damage but should not proceed with the complete restoration of the damaged premises until the loss has been adjusted or at least until the insurance company grants permission to commence the permanent repairs.

MANAGEMENT REQUIREMENTS BY PROPERTY TYPE

Each property type has some management requirements that are unique to it. Apartment buildings are the most commonly managed property types in our society, and so they serve as "the standard" in our discussion. Our look at management of alternative property types is brief, intended only to highlight differences. Much deeper study of, and experience with, alternative property types and their management requirements is needed to qualify as a professional manager. The Institute of Real Estate Management, (IREM), the Building Owners and Managers Association (BOMA), the Urban Land Institute (ULI), and the International Council of Shopping Centers (ICSC) are excellent sources of more information on property management.

Residential

Much of the discussion in this chapter thus far has focused on the management of an apartment building. Lease arrangements are typically month to month or, if written, for one to three years. Physical maintenance, with periodic adjustment to changing environment or market, is needed to retain the property's tenants and therefore its value.

Many apartment buildings are being converted to condominiums or cooperatives. The physical building remains the same; yet, some aspects of management take on special importance. What are these unique aspects?

Condominiums and cooperatives have almost the same operating and maintenance requirements as apartment buildings. The main difference is form of ownership and tenancy. Thus, the manager serves the tenant-owners rather than an absentee-owner. This owner-occupancy means that the interior of each unit is maintained by its owner. The manager's duties involve administration or maintenance of common areas. The security of the premises is an important area of responsibility. The managers need not be concerned with maintaining occupancy.

The administrative duties of the manager include keeping account of costs and assessing the costs to individual units. The manager also advises the owners' association, which at times means balancing opposing interests. Time-share condominiums require more intensive management than other condominium developments. Also, closer attention to payment of debt service, and taxes by individual tenants is needed of a manager of a cooperative project; nonpayment by one proprietary tenant may cause a lien to be placed against the interests of all the tenants.

Commercial

Commercial space is rented in units of varying size, running from a small cubicle for a newsstand or an office to a multistory building. Except for the smallest units of space, the leases usually are complex, requiring considerable negotiation, and are for an extended number of years. Office building leases usually contain an escalation clause. An **escalation clause** increases rents to cover increasing costs of taxes, insurance, and operation. The appearance, cleanliness, and efficiency of office buildings must be carefully monitored to maintain the prestige and the rent levels. Stores and shopping centers are likely to be rented on percentage leases. Administrative reports to the owner are often involved with commercial properties because of the variety in tenants and spaces rented.

Industrial

Industrial properties, except for warehouses, tend to be special-purpose properties requiring a large capital investment. For this reason, many must be built to specification for the owner-user. That is, others are frequently not willing to incur the risk of building and leasing a special-purpose property. In turn, after the property is a going operation, the owner may enter into a sale and lease-back arrangement with an investor. Even so, the value of a special-purpose property is closely tied to the success and financial capability of the firm renting the space. Little property management is involved where a property is entirely accepted by one tenant, as the tenant is likely to be responsible for property taxes, insurance, and maintenance.

Warehouses tend to be rented on a lease for several years. And, for the most part, warehouse leases are more similar to commercial leases than to leases for other industrial property.

SUMMARY

In the financial management of a real estate investment to maximize rate of return, it is necessary to (1) maintain leverage, (2) adapt the property to market and environmental change, and (3) arrange for administration of the property as a business. The function of property management, in a routine sense, is to balance cash flow (keep net operating income high) against preservation of the value of the property, in order to operate at optimum rate of return. The principal functions of a manager include: (1) merchandise space, (2) collect rents, (3) tenant relations, (4) purchase operating supplies and equipment, (5) employee relations, (6) keep proper accounts and render periodic reports, (7) maintain the physical property, (8) look after the property's assessment and taxation levels, and (9) maintain adequate insurance protection. A manager frequently needs to consult with an owner and to obtain outside assistance concerning the last two functions; each involves complex issues and is extremely important to the overall operation of the property. The three phases of the property taxation process are (1) valuation and assessment, (2) budget and tax levy, and (3) billing and collecting.

Form of ownership and tenancy is the main distinction between management of apartments as against condominiums and cooperatives. Management concerns with commercial properties derive from the greater variety in the units of space rented and form the extreme complexity of the leases negotiated. Among other things, office building leases often have escalation clauses to cover increasing costs of taxes, insurance, and operation. Retail space, on the other hand, is often rented on a percentage-of-sales lease. Being special purpose, industrial properties, as a rule, are rented on a sale and lease-back arrangement, when rented. Warehouses are more general purpose and tend to be an exception to this rule.

KEY TERMS

Assessed value	Minimum rated risk
Business interruption insurance	Professional risk bearers
Coinsurance	Public calling
Escalation clause	Rental schedule
Extended coverage	Specifically rated risks
Levy	Tax base

QUESTIONS FOR REVIEW AND DISCUSSION

1. List and discuss briefly the three key issues in managing a property as a long-term investment.

2. List and explain briefly five important but routine functions of a manager in operating a property as a business.

3. What are the three major phases in the property taxation process? What is the manager's (and owner's) concern about this process? What and when is action necessary relative to this process?

4. Name at least four different types of risks involved in owning and operating a property. Is insurance available to protect an owner from each of these risks?

5. What issues are involved in buying insurance?

6. What is coinsurance? Explain.

7. Name at least one unique aspect of managing each of the following: condominiums, office buildings, retail space, and industrial buildings.

8. What criteria would be most important in hiring a property manager? Would the nature of the property make any difference? Discuss.

9. How far should a property manager go in analyzing financial alternatives and recommending alternative decisions to an owner? Discuss.

10. How might an owner account for time spent in seeking out and managing investment properties? Discuss.

REFERENCES

Downs, James C., Jr. *Principles of Real Estate Management.* 11th ed. Chicago: Institute of Real Estate Management, 1975. Traditional treatment of real estate management, including the marketing and administrative processes involved. Generally easy to read and understand. A must-have for anyone seriously interested in property management.

Garrigan, Richard T. "The Case for Rising Residential Rents." *Real Estate Review,* fall 1978. Inflation calls the time, and apartment house developers and managers must dance to it. Explains process to test feasibility of developing or acquiring an investment, taking rent increases into account. Also, discusses importance of location to a successful investment. Generally easy to read; calculations shown. Related directly to maintaining the value of a property for capital gain.

Jaffe, Austin J. *Property Management in Real Estate Investment Decision-Making.* Lexington, Mass.: Heath, 1979. Professor Jaffe's doctoral dissertation. This study goes far in explaining the theoretical relationships among variables used in real estate investment analysis. The study involved examining the literature of computerized real estate modeling, developing a sensitivity analysis model, obtaining empirical data, and testing for significant variables. Important for the serious student of real estate investment and management.

Property Management. Institute of Real Estate Management, National Association of Realtors, Chicago. Monthly periodical of professional property managers. Excellent for keeping current in the field. Generally easy to read.

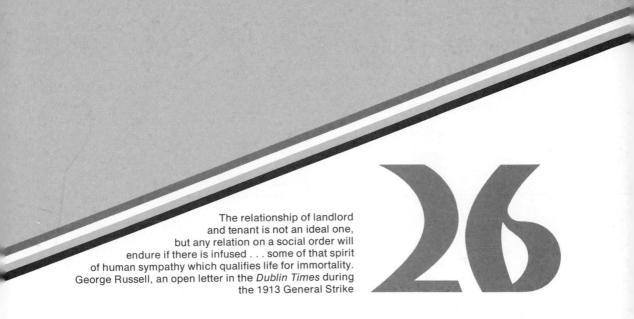

Leases and Leasing

The relationship of landlord and tenant is not an ideal one, but any relation on a social order will endure if there is infused . . . some of that spirit of human sympathy which qualifies life for immortality.
George Russell, an open letter in the *Dublin Times* during the 1913 General Strike

26

This chapter covers the basic terminology of, the kinds of, the typical **covenants** or clauses of, and the ways to terminate leases. Some brief attention is also given to the relative negotiating positions of the parties and to some of the broader issues involved in negotiation, mainly tenant unions and rent controls. Parties acting in self-interest continue to be taken as given.

One important consideration, from the viewpoint of a tenant, is omitted from this discussion—locational analysis. Location, or the relation of a land use to its environment, including other land-use activities, is generally considered the key to value in real estate. This is true for any property, whether operated by an owner or a tenant. Locational analysis is discussed in the chapter on property productivity.

The locational analysis involved in selecting a site for a land use is essentially the same whether control of the premises is to be gained by purchase or by rental. That is, the locational analysis involved in selecting a site for a supermarket, a gasoline service station, or a warehouse would be the same whether purchase or rental was being considered. Leasing, of course, requires no equity investment in real estate. Thus, the tenant may retain or free money for business purposes or other uses. Lower transaction cost and greater flexibility of location can usually be realized by renting, although a long-term lease would negate the latter point.

Major topics taken up in this chapter are as follows:

1. Basic terms and concepts
2. Kinds of leases
3. Typical lease covenants/clauses
4. Termination of leases
5. Lease negotiations

BASIC TERMS AND CONCEPTS

As noted in the chapter on ownership, four distinct tenancies may be held in a leasehold estate.

1. Tenancy for years
2. Tenancy from period to period, or periodic tenancy
3. Tenancy at will
4. Tenancy at sufferance

The rights of the lessee become weaker when the lessee goes from a tenancy for years to a tenancy at sufferance. The emphasis here is on tenancy for years and periodic tenancy. *Tenancy,* again, means the manner or conditions under which a property is held. And, in everyday language, the party who hires or rents a property is the **tenant** or **lessee.**

The agreement under which a tenant hires a property from a landlord is a **lease.** That is, a *lease* is a contract under which a tenant goes into possession of a property or a unit of space for a certain period of time in return for payments to the landlord. The time that the tenant may hold possession is called the **term.** The amount to be paid to the landlord is known as **rent.** Rent is usually stated in dollars per month or per year. A lease may be an oral agreement under which the property is rented for a short term or it may be a lengthy document containing many special provisions and covenants. Most fraud statutes require a lease for more than one year to be in writing. It follows that a lease for one year or less may be oral. Written or oral, a leasehold interest is legally personal property.

The party selling the right of occupancy and use in a lease is the **lessor** or **landlord.** The landlord or lessor is usually, but not necessarily, the owner of the property. The lessor may be a tenant of the owner who enters into an agreement to sublet the premises to subtenants. This type of agreement establishes an estate, often known as a **sandwich leasehold** which is illustrated in figure 26–1. The original tenant has become sandwiched in between the user of the premises or "top" lessee and the owner of the property or leased fee—the landlord.

Tenancies for years and a periodic tenancy are easily the most common types of rental arrangements. Some additional discussion of each therefore seems appropriate.

FIGURE 26–1
Sandwich Leasehold

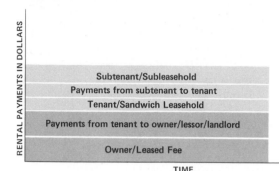

RENTAL PAYMENTS IN DOLLARS

Subtenant/Subleasehold
Payments from subtenant to tenant
Tenant/Sandwich Leasehold
Payments from tenant to owner/lessor/landlord
Owner/Leased Fee

TIME

Tenancy for Years

A leasing agreement for a specific or definite period of time is a *tenancy for years*. A tenancy for years is usually for more than one year and therefore usually written. The term may actually be for one month, six months, one year, or more than ten years. A written lease for nine months creates a tenancy for years as well as a lease for ninety-nine years. In both cases, the time of occupancy and use is definite. The tenant is required to vacate the property and return possession to the landlord at the end of the lease. The landlord is not required to give notice to the tenant. A tenant continuing in possession beyond the end of the lease is a holdover. The landlord may dispossess or elect to hold the tenant for a further period of one year. The landlord may also enter into a specific agreement with the tenant that if possession continues, it is a month-to-month tenancy. In the absence of an agreement of this kind, the acceptance of rent by the landlord from a holdover is usually construed as a renewal of the lease by the landlord for one year, regardless of the number of years in the term of the original lease.

Periodic Tenancy

A tenancy of uncertain duration, for example, month to month or year to year is termed a periodic tenancy or tenancy from year to year or period to period. The tenancy is usually from month to month in urban areas. The tenancy continues until either the landlord or tenant gives notice of termination. Usually, the rental period determines the length of notice required. That is, a week's notice is required to end a week-to-week tenancy. A month's notice is required to end a month-to-month tenancy. A notice of from one to six months is likely to be required to terminate a year-to-year tenancy.

If rental payments are accepted from a holdover tenant for years and if there is no new lease agreement, a tenancy from year to year is created. Courts generally hold that a holdover tenancy can never be longer than a year, probably because no new written contract is made. However, a tenant holding over from a tenancy for years, where rental payments are accepted monthly, is likely to create a month-to-month tenancy.

KINDS OF LEASES

Leases are classified according to several systems that are sometimes inconsistent with each other. At times this inconsistency causes confusion. The main alternative classification systems are presented here, despite the possibility of confusion.

Broadly speaking, leases are classified as either short-term or long-term leases. This division, based on length of time and terms of use, is rather arbitrary and has no particular legal significance. Generally, however, commercial or industrial leases extending over ten or more years may appropriately be referred to as long-term leases. These leases, as a rule, are lengthy documents containing many special provisions and landlord-tenant convenants. At the same time, a three-year lease for an apartment would be considered a long-term lease. And a ground lease, defined later in this section, would be considered long term only if it exceeded twenty-one years.

The most usual lease classification system is by rental-payment method. **Ground leases** and sale-and-leaseback arrangements are also classifications of leases. Again, these classifications may overlap and therefore are not mutually exclusive. For example, a sale-and-leaseback arrangement might actually be a ground lease calling for a net rental.

Rental-Payment Classifications

The most frequently used rental-payment plans are as follows.

1. Flat, straight, or fixed
2. Graduated
3. Percentage
4. Index (or escalated)
5. Net
6. Reappraisal

FLAT LEASE. An agreement calling for a fixed rental to be paid periodically throughout its entire life or term is a **flat lease,** also called *straight* or *fixed rental.* This arrangement, which at one time enjoyed wide use and popularity, has come into gradual disuse for long-term leasing purposes. The reason, no doubt, is inflation. In selling a property the owner can reinvest the equity in another property. But in a lease, payments are received over future years. Thus, when rentals are fixed in amount, a declining dollar value deprives the landlord (owner) of a fair return in proportion to the value of the property as measured in constant dollars. Consequently, the use of the flat, or straight, lease is increasingly restricted to short-term, month-to-month leases or, at maximum, yearly leases. A flat lease calling for the lessor to pay all property charges as taxes, insurance, and maintenance is termed a **gross lease.**

GRADUATED LEASE. A lease calling for periodic increases in the rental is termed a **graduated lease.** This lease is intended to give the tenant an opportunity to lighten operating expenses during the early, formative years of a business enterprise and to give the landlord an opportunity to participate in future business growth through successively higher rental payments. These lease agreements should be evaluated carefully because excessive rents without growth may cause business failure and bankruptcy. This arrangement is also termed a *step-up lease.* Conceivably, a similar arrangement might also be used to "step down" rentals for an older property.

PERCENTAGE LEASE. An agreement whereby rent is a specified proportion of sales or income, generated through tenant use of a property, is a **percentage lease.** A "floor" or minimum rent may be included in a percentage lease, to assure an owner of some basic income from the property.

The percentage lease based on gross sales lease has gained steadily in popularity; it is used most frequently for commercial leasing. The tenant agrees to pay a stipulated percentage of gross sales from goods and services sold on the premises. Generally, leases of this kind provide for a minimum rental ranging from 40 to 80 percent of amounts considered fair in relation to property value. Percentage rentals may range from as low as 2 percent of gross sales for department stores or supermarkets to as high as 75 percent for parking lot operations.

Negotiating a percentage lease requires experienced people to make the resulting agreement equitable to the parties. The landlord-owner's rental income is directly related to the business success of the tenant's operations. Lease clauses or covenants are therefore generally included to ensure, so far as possible, continuous and effective store operation. Agreement on methods of accounting for gross sales or receipts and on a periodic audit is also generally included. The landlord, in turn, is expected to promise to maintain the property in prime operating condition and to exclude competitors from other nearby owned properties.

Percentage leases are best used where changing sales figures, usually due to growth or inflation, are expected. Sometimes the percentage figure that was designated for rent increases; usually this occurs when the growth of sales is expected to exceed the rate of inflation because of the high rate of growth in the area. In effect, the agreement is saying that the property has a prime location resulting in greater sales, and the rent should therefore be higher.

INDEX LEASE. Index leases, or escalation leases, have also come into vogue in recent years as a result of high and continuous inflation. An **index lease** either provides for rental adjustment in direct proportion to increases in taxes, insurance, and operating costs or provides for rental increments in proportion to changes in cost-of-living or wholesale price indexes as periodically published by the United States Department of Commerce. Index leases are more likely to be used where property value is going up but no easy measure of its increase is available because few sales are made. Examples are warehouses, factories, or office buildings.

NET LEASE. A rental agreement requiring the tenant to pay all maintenance costs, insurance premiums, and property taxes is a **net lease.** Net leases generally run for ten years or more. A net lease assures an owner of a certain rate of return from an investment while shifting the burden of meeting increasing operating costs and taxes to the tenant. Net leases are deemed suitable for large office, commercial, and industrial properties. Net leases are preferred by investment trusts and insurance companies that acquire real estate under purchase-and-leaseback agreements.

REAPPRAISAL LEASE. The **reappraisal lease** establishes rentals as a percentage of property value at fixed intervals, usually three to five years. The reappraisal lease is rarely used today because it has proven expensive to maintain and has been the cause of lengthy litigation in which value agreements were difficult to arbitrate because of divergent appraisal estimates and opinions.

Ground Lease

A **ground lease** is an agreement giving use and occupancy of a vacant site or unimproved land in return for rental payments. The agreement usually contains a provision that a building is to be erected on the land by the tenant. Frequently it contains a further provision for the disposition of the building at the end of the term. The building, although erected at the expense of the tenant, legally becomes real estate and therefore, unless otherwise provided, becomes the property of the landlord. The tenant, of course, has the right of possession. The lease may provide that the landlord, at the expiration of the term, will pay the tenant all or part of the cost or appraised value of the building. In the absence of such a provision, the term of the lease, including renewal privileges, must give the tenant time to amortize the entire cost of the building during the period of occupancy. Ground rent is often a certain percentage of the value of the land. The tenant pays all taxes and other charges, the landlord's rent being net. No set rules govern ground leases. Each bargain is specifically negotiated by the parties concerned. The provisions mentioned above merely suggest what may be agreed upon.

Sale and Leaseback

The transfer of title to a property for consideration (sale) with the simultaneous renting back to the seller (leaseback) on specified terms is a *sale-and-leaseback* arrangement. From the buyer's viewpoint, the arrangement is a *purchase and leaseback.* In recent years more and more businesses and corporate entities have found it profitable to sell their real estate holdings and thus free additional capital for expansion of their business operations, while leasing back the properties thus sold under custom-designed long-term agreements. Institutional investors, principally nationally known insurance companies, have found that real estate occupied on a long-term basis by reliable tenants with high credit ratings is an excellent and secure investment. Consequently, sale-and-leaseback transactions have increased significantly. At the time of a sale-and-leaseback closing, the parties to the transaction in effect exchange instruments. The seller, generally a business corporation, deeds the realty to the buyer, an insurance company, or like investor, and the buyer in turn leases the property to the seller under mutually agreed-upon terms.

As a rule, such long-term leases extend from twenty to thirty years with options to renew for like or lesser succeeding periods. The lease terms usually require the tenant to pay all operating expenses, including taxes, maintenance, and insurance, thus yielding a net return or cash flow to the buyer-lessor. This often yields a return in excess of that obtainable from a like sum invested in high-grade corporate bonds or government securities to the buyer-landlord.

Sale-and-leaseback transactions have proven mutually advantageous. The lessee-seller, in effect, obtains 100 percent financing, realizing cash far in excess of that obtainable under conventional mortgage refinancing. Further, the seller-lessee now enjoys significant income tax advantages since the entire rent becomes tax deductible as a cost of business operations. Such deductions are considerably larger than the sum total of owners' deductions allowable for interest on mortgage debt, real estate taxes, and permissible deductions for depreciation on older buildings and improvements.

TYPICAL LEASE COVENANTS / CLAUSES

A lease must contain the essential elements of a valid contract to be enforceable. The contract spells out the rights and obligations of both the landlord and the tenant. Many of these rights and obligations are standard; others must be negotiated according to the situation.

The amount of rent to be paid is the immediate consideration in lease negotiations. The amount is negotiated against the rights and obligations of the landlord and the tenant under the lease as well as against the size and quality of the space provided and the amount of services provided by the owner-landlord.

Essential Elements of a Lease

No particular wording or form of agreement is required by statute to create a valid lease. It is sufficient in law, if the intention is expressed, to transfer from one to another possession of certain real property for a determinate length of time. Substance, not form, is what counts. A contract is not a lease merely because it is designated as such. The following items are necessary to create an enforceable landlord-tenant agreement:

1. A lessor and lessee with contractual capacity
2. An agreement to let and take
3. Sufficient description of premises

4. Term

5. Consideration

6. An execution such as required by statute

7. A delivery and an acceptance

Most of these provisions carry over from our earlier discussion of contracts and deeds. A few differences need to be noted, however. The contract may continue to be valid even though the amount of rent and term may be omitted. Without a term, a periodic tenancy may be created rather than an intended tenancy for years. The amount of rent payable may be evidenced by actual performance of the parties even though not stated. Legally, the tenant-lessee need not sign; taking possession of the premises is evidence of acceptance and agreement. Statute requirements for execution may require witnesses, seal, acknowledgment, and recording.

Leases for three years or more are recordable in most states. In that possession gives actual notice of a tenant's claim in most states, recording is not always important. And some leases are not recorded because the parties wish to avoid revealing rents, terms, and other contents. For this situation, "a memorandum of lease" may be recorded instead of the actual lease, in several states. See figure 26–2 for a typical apartment lease.

Landlord Rights and Obligations

The covenant in the lease specifically made by a landlord is that of quiet enjoyment. There are implied covenants of possession and sometimes fitness for use. Historically, there is no warranty in the lease of a whole or detached house of habitability or suitability. If a landlord leases an apartment in an apartment building or an office in an office building, there is an implied covenant that the portions of the building used by all of the tenants are fit for the use for which they are intended. In recent years many states have passed landlord-tenant laws requiring that the premises be kept in good repair. In some cases, failure to maintain the property gives the tenant the right to withhold rental payments and to apply the payments toward maintenance of the premises.

The implied covenant of possession is that the tenant can hold possession against everyone, including the landlord. Under the terms of the lease, the landlord is usually allowed the right to show the property to another tenant or to a purchaser for a short period before the expiration of the lease, and also the lease usually gives the landlord the right to enter and make necessary repairs or comply with the requirements of governmental authorities. The important point for the tenant is that it is incumbent upon the landlord to accord possession to the tenant for the term of the lease, subject only to its conditions.

Tenant Rights and Obligations

The tenant also gets certain rights and incurs certain obligations in making a lease. When a lease is being made for many years, the covenants are particularly important. They define the flexibility of the parties, particularly the

FIGURE 26–2

FORM No. 818
STEVENS-NESS LAW PUBLISHING CO., PORTLAND, OR. 97204
TO-8B

RENTAL AGREEMENT
(Dwelling Unit—Residence Oregon)

26-12

THIS AGREEMENT, entered into in duplicate this 10th day of September, 19 81, by and between Everready Real Estate Management Co., lessor, and Otto and Mary Mobile, lessee;

WITNESSETH: That for and in consideration of the payment of the rents and the performance of the terms of lessee's covenants herein contained, lessor does hereby demise and let unto the lessee and lessee hires from lessor for use as a residence those certain premises described as Unit 11, Douglas Manor
located at 2001 Century Drive, Urbandale, Anystate
☒ on a month to month tenancy beginning 16 September, 19 81 } (Indicate
☐ for a term of commencing , 19 , and ending , 19 } which)
at a rental of $ 520.00 per month, payable monthly in advance on the 1st day of each and every month. Rents are payable at the following address: Everready Management Co, 41 East Third, Urbandale, Anystate 00000
It is hereby agreed that if rent is unpaid after four (4) days following due date, the lessee shall pay a late charge of $1.00 per day computed to include the first day due and continuing until both rent and late charges are fully paid. Any dishonored check shall be treated as unpaid rent and shall be subject to the same late charge plus $5.00 as a special handling fee and must be made good by cash, money order or certified check within 24 hours of notification.
It is further mutually agreed between the parties as follows:

1. Said aforementioned premises shall be occupied by no more than two adults and two children;
2. Lessee shall not violate any city ordinance or state law in or about said premises;
3. Lessee shall not sub-let the demised premises, or any part thereof, or assign this lease without the lessor's written consent;
4. If lessee fails to pay rent or other charges promptly when due, or to comply with any other term or condition hereof, lessor at lessor's option, and after proper written notice, may terminate this tenancy;
5. Lessee shall maintain the premises in a clean and sanitary condition at all times, and upon the termination of the tenancy shall surrender same to lessor in as good condition as when received, ordinary wear and tear and damage by the elements excepted; a fee is herewith paid, no part of which is refundable, for cleaning up and restoring the premises in the amount of $ 200.00
6. There shall be working locks on all outside doors; lessor shall provide lessee with keys for same;
7. Lessee ☒, Lessor☐ shall properly cultivate, care for and adequately water the lawn, shrubbery and grounds;
8. Lessor shall supply electric wiring, plumbing facilities capable of producing hot and cold running water and adequate heating facilities;
9. Lessee shall pay for all natural gas, electricity, and telephone service. All other services will be paid for by Lessor and Lessee as follows:

	Lessee	Lessor		Lessee	Lessor
Water	☒	☐	Garbage Service	☐	☒
Sewer	☐	☒	Cable tv	☒	☐

10. Lessee agrees to assume all liability for, and to hold lessor harmless from, all damages and all costs and fees in the defense thereof, caused by the negligence or willful act of lessee or lessee's invitees or guests, in or upon any part of the demised premises, and to be responsible for any damage or breakage to lessee's equipment, fixtures or appliances therein or thereon, not caused by lessor's misconduct or willful neglect.
11. Nothing herein shall be construed as waiving any of the rights provided by law of either party hereto;
12. In the event any suit or action is brought to collect any of said rents or to enforce any provision of this agreement or to repossess said premises, reasonable attorney's fees may be awarded by the trial court to the prevailing party in such suit or action together with costs and necessary disbursements; and on appeal, if any, similar reasonable attorney's fees, costs and disbursements may be awarded by the appellate court to the party prevailing on such appeal;
13. If the lessee, or someone in the lessee's control, irreparably endangers the health or safety of the lessor or other tenants or irreparably damages or threatens immediate irreparable damage to the dwelling unit, the lessor, after 24 hours' written notice specifying the causes, may immediately terminate the rental agreement and take possession in the manner provided in ORS 105.105 to 105.160;
14. Lessee shall not allow any undriveable vehicle to remain on the premises for more than 24 hours. No car repairs are to be made on the premises, including minor maintenance such as an oil change;
15. Property of the tenant left on the premises after surrender or abandonment of the premises, or termination of this rental agreement by any means except court order, shall be deemed abandoned. Upon 15 days notice to tenant, in writing, landlord shall have the right to store, sell or otherwise dispose of any such property as provided by law, unless within said 15-day period tenant removes the property. Failure to remove the

property within 15 days will be conclusive evidence of abandonment.
16. The owner (or agent for service) is Everready Real Estate Mgt. Co.
Address 41 East Third
Urbandale, Anystate 00000 Phone 345-4330
The manager is H. "Handy" Overseer
Address 41 East Third
Urbandale, Anystate Phone 345-4331
17. Any holding over by the lessee after the expiration of the term of this rental agreement or any extension thereof, shall be as a tenancy from month to month and not otherwise;
18. If this is a month-to-month tenancy only, then, except as otherwise provided by statute, this agreement may be terminated by either party giving the other at anytime not less than 30 days' notice in writing prior to the date designated in the tenancy termination notice, whereupon the tenancy shall terminate on the date designated;
19. Lessor acknowledges receipt of the sum of $ 400.00 as a security deposit, of which the lessor may claim all or part thereof reasonably necessary to remedy lessee's defaults in the performance of this rental agreement (including nonpayment of past-due rent) and to repair damage to the premises caused by lessee, not including ordinary wear and tear. To claim all or part of said deposit, lessor shall give lessee, within thirty (30) days after termination of the tenancy, a written accounting which states specifically the basis or bases of the claim, and the portion not so claimed shall be returned to lessee within said thirty days. Lessor may recover damages in excess of said deposit to which lessor may be entitled. Lessor also acknowledges receipt of the sum of $ N.A. to insure the return of keys to said dwelling unit; said sum to be refunded upon the return of all such keys;
20. Pets are allowed ☒, not allowed ☐ (indicate which). If allowed to consist of one cat
Lessee will be held responsible for all damage caused by pets and pay an additional non-refundable fee of $ 100.00 prior to bringing a pet onto the leased premises.
21. Lessee further agrees that failure by the lessor at any time to require performance by the lessee of any provision hereof shall in no way affect lessor's right hereunder to enforce the same, nor shall any waiver by said lessor of any breach of any provision hereof be held to be a waiver of any succeeding breach of any provision, or as a waiver of the provision itself.
22. The following personal property is included and to be left upon the premises when tenancy is terminated range, refrigerator electric globes, carpeting, drapes, fire alarm.

23. Additional provisions:
Door to kitchen cabinet to be repaired

Lessee Further Agrees {
1. That he has personally inspected the premises and finds them satisfactory at the time of execution of this agreement;
2. That he has read this agreement and all the stipulations contained in the lease agreement.
3. That no promises have been made to him except as contained in this agreement and lease, except the following: None

IN WITNESS WHEREOF, the parties hereto have executed this agreement in duplicate the day and year first above written and lessee, by affixing his signature hereto, acknowledges receipt of one copy of the executed documents.

/s/Handy Overseer

/s/Otto Mobile

Lessor   Lessee

for Everready Real Estate Management Co.
The words lessee and lessor shall include the plural as well as the singular.

/s/Mary Mobile
*See S-N Form Nos. 829, 971, 972, 973.

tenant. The landlord has only one major obligation—to provide quiet and peaceful possession and use of the premises. The tenant has certain automatic rights, as follows, unless otherwise agreed to in the lease.

1. Use the premises in any legal manner
2. Make no security deposit
3. Right to sublet
4. Right to assign
5. Right to mortgage
6. Right of redemption

USE OF PREMISES. Unless the lease contains a restriction, the tenant may use the premises in any legal manner. The tenant may not, however, interfere with occupants of other parts of the building. Illegal use would permit an action for dispossession by the landlord, and a lease specifically made for an illegal purpose would not be enforceable by either party. The purpose for which the premises are to be used is often stated in the lease, for example, "private dwelling," "boardinghouse," "retail drugstore," and so on. If it is desired to limit the use of the property to a specified purpose, it is well to have the lease state that the premises shall be used for the purpose mentioned, and *for no other*. It has been held in court cases, where the lease simply stated that the tenant was to use the premises for a certain trade, that he could use it for other trades. The lease may contain a covenant that the premises may not be used for any purpose that is extra hazardous, objectionable, detrimental to the neighborhood, or similarly undesirable. Note that the tenant may also legally vacate or give up use of the property, termed **abandonment,** before the lease expires; however the tenant continues to be liable for rental payments.

SECURITY DEPOSITS. A landlord, to assure the making of an important lease, may properly require the tenant to furnish security performance of the terms of the lease. This security may be in the form of cash or negotiable securities, or it may be in the form of a bond executed by personal sureties or a surety company. There is no rule on the amount of the security, but it is usually in proportion to the amount of rent required by the lease. The security may be a sum equal to the rent for one month or several months, or even a year or more. Increasingly, the law says that the tenant is entitled to receive interest at a certain rate on any cash **security deposits.** Unless a security deposit clearly appears to have been intended by the parties as liquidated damages, the lessor may retain only so much of the deposit as equals the amount of damages suffered.

A transfer of the property to another owner by the lessor does not, of itself, include the security deposit. The lessor's convenant to return the deposit to the lessee is personal. Of course, this liability may be otherwise stipulated in the lease.

RIGHT TO SUBLET. A rerenting of space held under a lease is **subletting** or **subleasing.** The rerental may be of part or of all the premises, for part or all of the term. The right to sublet is implied unless specifically stated otherwise. A landlord may include a clause against subletting, to maintain control of property occupancy.

ASSIGNMENT OF LEASE. A tenant may also assign rights held under a lease unless a specific covenant to the contrary is included in the lease. *Assignment* means to transfer rights in a contract to another. A landlord may rent based on the financial stability of the tenant and include a clause against assignment. Even so, given a stable alternate tenant, a landlord may waive the clause and agree to a proposed assignment. A lease, once assigned, is thereafter generally considered freely assignable. Thus, an investor-owner allowing assignment might be wise to include a statement against further assignments in the agreement allowing the assignment. In any event, the usual rule is that the original tenant-lessee can be held liable for rents under a lease even though it has been assigned.

MORTGAGING THE LEASEHOLD. The tenant's rights in a lease is a leasehold, which may be mortgaged unless the lease says otherwise. In almost all states a mortgage on a lease is a conveyance that comes under the provisions of the recording act and is, therefore, recorded in the same manner as a mortgage on real property and not as a chattel mortgage. In some jurisdictions it is considered a chattel mortgage. In the absence of a statute or legal decision in any particular state, a lender is likely to record the lien as both a real and chattel mortgage. Unless otherwise agreed, the mortgage lien would not have any greater claim on the property than that held by the tenant under the lease.

RIGHT OF REDEMPTION. In some states the law provides that if a tenant is dispossessed when more than five years of his lease are unexpired, the tenant has a right to come in at any time after the dispossess and pay up all arrears and again obtain possession of the property. That is to say, the lessee has a **right of redemption.** In a personally negotiated lease the tenant usually waives this right of redemption. The advantage of getting a waiver is that it enables the landlord to be rid of a tenant who does not meet obligations promptly. This enables the landlord to obtain another tenant without fear of the first tenant's coming in and reclaiming the property under the right of redemption.

Jointly Negotiated Covenants

A landlord and tenant negotiate many points in making a lease. The importance of any one item depends on the property, the proposed use, and other circumstances. The following points come up quite often but are not automatically included in a lease.

LEASE-PURCHASE OPTION. A provision giving the tenant the right to purchase the premises at a certain price during the term of the lease is called a **lease option** or *lease-purchase option.* Frequently the rental for the first year applies to the purchase price if the option to purchase is exercised within the first year. A lease option is used when an owner wants to sell to a tenant, but the tenant does not have an adequate down payment. A lease option gives a tenant in possession a right to purchase that has priority over any other prospective purchaser's right to purchase.

RIGHT OF RENEWAL. A right of one or more renewals may be included in a lease. The length of each renewal and a means to determine the rent to be paid on renewal are best negotiated as part of the initial lease. In that way, uncertainty is avoided by both the tenant and the landlord. This avoidance allows the tenant a more stable basis for planning operations; and it gives the owner more certainty of income, which translates into a more stable property value.

SUBORDINATION. A lease of property is subject to mortgages and other liens upon the property of record when the lease is made; that is, such liens are superior to the rights of the tenant. When the lease is made, the tenant usually takes possession of the property and may also record the lease. Either would give notice, to persons thereafter concerned with the property, of the rights of the tenant. A mortgage made after the lease would therefore be subordinate to the lease. *Subordinate* means to be inferior or lower in priority of claim. Thus, a mortgage lien may be subordinate to a lease and a lease may be subordinate to a mortgage lien. The first recorded usually has priority of claim. Leases often provide that they shall be subordinate to mortgages up to a certain amount, and this provision may permit the landlord to increase existing mortgages up to the agreed amount. The provision in the lease should be that the tenant will execute necessary agreements to effect such subordination. On the other hand, a vacant site may be leased on which the tenant proposes to build substantial improvements. The lessee may negotiate a clause for the investor-landlord to subordinate the fee ownership position to the proposed mortgage, up to an agreed amount.

In any event, the owner, the tenant, and a tentative lender should be aware of the significance of a subordinated position. There is a case on record in which a bank loaned $82,000 on a piece of property and ignored the rights of the people in possession. The mortgage was afterwards foreclosed. It was then found that the property was occupied by tenants under a ten-year lease, with an option of a further renewal of thirteen years, at an annual rental of $6,000. A rent of $6,000 is entirely inadequate for a property worth more than $82,000. This lease was especially disadvantageous in that it had a long time to run at the low rental.

LIABILITY AFTER REENTRY. An owner may include a provision that if a tenant is dispossessed by summary proceedings or if the tenant abandons the property, the landlord may sublease the premises as an agent of the tenant. Then, if the landlord reenters and takes possession, the landlord has the option of holding the tenant liable for the rent until the end of the term of the lease. The landlord may relet the premises as the agent of the tenant; in such a case the landlord credits the tenant with the amount collected from the sublessee. A clause of this kind prevents absolute termination of the lease by a summary proceeding or the landlord's reentry.

IMPROVEMENTS AND REPAIRS. All improvements become the property of the landlord when they are made, unless otherwise agreed. It is proper in some cases to provide that some or all improvements may be removed at, or prior to, the expiration of the lease. Fixtures and machinery installed by the tenant are usually considered personal property and are removable when the tenant vacates. The lease usually provides that no alterations to the buildings may be made without prior consent of the landlord.

The general rule is that neither party to a lease is required to make repairs, but the tenant is required to surrender the premises at the expiration of the term in as good a condition as they were in at the beginning of the lease, reasonable wear and tear and damage by the elements excepted. Occasionally the lease provides that the landlord shall make certain repairs only. There is no legal requirement that the landlord make the ordinary repairs for the upkeep of the property, except that the building must be kept tenable. If a building becomes untenable, the tenant may move out on the ground of having been constructively evicted.

LIENS. The tenant may make repairs, alterations, or improvements to the premises with the consent of the landlord. The landlord should guard against the tenant's neglecting to pay for the work performed and the consequent filing of mechanic's liens by those who did the work. The law in some states permits mechanics and materialmen under such circumstances to enforce their liens against the landlord's property, although they may not be able to hold the landlord personally liable. Whenever work of this kind is contemplated, the lease should provide that if such a lien is filed, the landlord may pay it and add it to the next installment of rent falling due under the lease. This may result in a dispossess of the tenant for nonpayment of rent unless the tenant reimburses the landlord for the amount paid to free the property from the lien.

The landlord may demand further protection from liens by requiring that the tenant deposit cash or file a bond as a guarantee that the cost of the repair or construction work will be paid. This requirement is very important in leases that provide that the tenant is to make any extensive repairs, alterations, or improvements.

DAMAGE CLAIMS. Agreement is desirable in a lease as to which party (landlord or tenant) is liable for claims developing from ownership, occupation, or use of the property. These claims may be by persons injured on the property, or they may be by persons damaged away from the property, as when a fire spreads from the property. With liability clarified, the party bearing the risk may obtain protection through insurance. The responsibility for injuries received upon the premises may fall on either the landlord or the tenant. The general rule is that the party with custody and control of the premises where the accident occurs is liable for damages, if any. Consequently, a tenant with control and possession of an entire building is responsible for any injury caused by a negligent condition of the building. In apartment houses or other buildings in which there are several tenants each tenant usually has custody and control of an apartment or other space in the building, but the landlord retains the custody and control of those parts of the building that are used in common by the tenants, namely, the roof, halls, stairways, and entrance. In such a building the tenants are responsible only for injuries arising from negligence in their apartments, while the landlord is liable for injuries sustained on roof, halls, stairways, or entry.

In the absence of an agreement on damages, the general rule is that whenever a landlord would be liable to a tenant, the landlord is liable to anyone able to "stand in the tenant's shoes." Thus, assume a landlord fails to maintain a stairway properly. Claims for damages suffered by relatives, friends, employees, or business visitors of the tenant as well as by the tenant may then be filed and enforced against the landlord. It must be borne in mind, of course, that neither the landlord nor the tenant is liable for an injury caused by a negligent condition existing in the building unless either actually knew or should have known of the condition. Finally, neither the landlord nor the tenant is responsible for an accident unless it was caused by negligence on the part of either of them.

DAMAGE/DESTRUCTION OF PREMISES. Unless otherwise agreed in a lease of land or a site, a tenant must continue to pay rent even if a building or other improvements are destroyed by fire, flood, wind, or other acts of God. This rule does not apply to a lease of an apartment, office, or some other portion of a building. Such an arrangement is not a lease of land. In the event that partial destruction makes a property untenantable or unuseable, the landlord must repair in a "reasonable" time. And if the premises are damaged and made unsuitable for occupancy before the tenant takes possession, the tenant may end the lease without liability to the landlord. A damage clause in a lease would, of course, enable the parties to clearly define their relationship and to protect themselves accordingly. In the absence of such a clause, settlement through negotiation and litigation becomes necessary, and that is often costly.

COMPLIANCE WITH GOVERNMENTAL REGULATIONS. Police power allows governmental regulation of the use, occupancy, and condition of real estate. Depending on the nature and duration of a proposed lease, a landlord and tenant may include a clause concerning responsibility for compliance with such regulations. With greater control by the tenant, as with a long-term ground lease, greater responsibility for compliance is likely to shift to the tenant.

TERMINATION OF LEASES

It is possible to terminate leases by using any one of the following devices:

1. End of term
2. Mutual agreement, either expressed or implied
3. Breach of conditions/eviction
4. Exercise of eminent domain
5. Destruction of property
6. Bankruptcy of lessee
7. Foreclosure of mortgage

Term Expiration

Written leases end on the last day of their term, without notice. Tenancies from period to period and at will continue, or are self-renewing, until notice of termination is given. The usual amount of notice required is one rental period; thus a month's notice is required to end a month-to-month tenancy.

Mutual Agreement

A tenant may offer to surrender possession of the premises to the landlord before the end of the lease. If such offer is accepted, the lease is terminated. Termination by surrender and acceptance may be by express or implied agreement as well as by oral or written agreement. With a recorded lease, the parties are advised to write out, sign, and record any agreement to surrender.

Breach of Conditions / Eviction

A breach of conditions, followed by **dispossess proceedings,** may terminate a lease. The conditions of a lease may be divided into two classes, those for which the landlord dispossesses the tenant by summary proceedings and those for which summary proceedings may not be brought. Summary (brief) dispossess proceedings may be used to terminate a lease for the following reasons:

1. Nonpayment of rent.
2. Holding over at the end of the term.
3. Unlawful use of the premises.
4. Nonpayment of taxes, assessments, or other charges when, under the terms of the lease, the tenant undertook to pay them.
5. The tenant in certain cases takes the benefit of an insolvent act or is adjudged a bankrupt

The right to recover possession from a tenant through the summary proceeding, known as dispossess, is one given by statute and is not a common-law right. Upon a decision by the court that a serious breach of conditions exists, a warrant for dispossess is issued. A tenant not immediately withdrawing from the property may be forcibly removed by a local law official, such as a sheriff.

For breach of other conditions of a lease, possession may be obtained only by means of a lengthy and expensive ejectment action. A lease, however, may be so drawn as to contain provisions that bring every condition and covenant into the class for which summary dispossess may be obtained.

EVICTION. An eviction may be either actual or constructive. An **actual eviction** occurs if the tenant is ousted from the premises, in whole or in part, by act of the landlord or by paramount title. **Constructive eviction** occurs when the physical condition of the leased premises has changed, owing to some act or failure to act of the landlord, so that the tenant is unable to occupy the premises for the purpose intended. No claim of constructive eviction will be allowed unless the tenant actually removes from the premises while the conditions exists.

If the tenant removes and can prove a valid case, the lease is terminated. The tenant may also be able to recover damages for the landlord's breach of the covenant of quiet enjoyment.

There may be constructive eviction from a portion of the premises only. And the tenant may take advantage of the fact that a lease is a complete contract by removing from the entire premises. The tenant may also retain possession of the remainder and refuse to pay rent until restored to possession of the entire premises.

The tenant's contention of constructive eviction must rest upon some act or omission of the landlord by which the tenant is deprived of the use of the property for the purpose or in the manner contemplated by the lease. The erection by the landlord of a building on adjoining property as a result of which the tenant's light was diminished would not be constructive eviction. But storage of materials on the sidewalk in front of the tenant's premises that interferes with the tenant's use of the premises may be construed as constructive eviction. Failure of the landlord to furnish steam heat or other services contemplated by the lease usually amounts to constructive eviction.

Eminent Domain or Property Destruction

When leased property is taken for public purposes under the right of eminent domain, leases on it terminate. The tenant is given an opportunity to prove the value of the unexpired term of the lease in the proceeding under which the property is taken and may receive an award for it.

Under the common law, the destruction of a building by fire or otherwise would not terminate a lease or relieve the tenant of the liability to pay rent. However, nearly all of the states have passed laws providing that the destruction of the entire property terminates the lease, if the tenant removes from the property immediately.

Bankruptcy or Mortgage Foreclosure

Frequently the lease provides for termination upon bankruptcy of the tenant or lessee. If, however, the lease does not end upon bankruptcy of the lessee, termination depends on the action of the trustee in bankruptcy. Rejection of the lease as an asset constitutes a breach of the lease and brings it to an end. The lessor may then assert a claim for future rents, which are probable and dischargeable in the bankruptcy proceeding. Where the trustee accepts the lease as an asset of the bankrupt, the lease, of course, is not terminated.

The foreclosure of a mortgage or other lien terminates a **leasehold estate,** provided the lease is subsequent or subordinate to the lien being foreclosed. The lessee must be made a party in the foreclosure suit for this to occur.

LEASE NEGOTIATIONS

Tenants and landlords need each other. Landlords have space to sell. Tenants need places to live or to do business. Both benefit when the right tenant gets the right space. The tenant gets greater satisfaction or does more business. The landlord gets higher rent, and in turn higher property value.

At the same time, the interests of tenants and landlords are in direct conflict. The negotiation between them goes on continuously, in one form or another. Two important developments of this negotiation/competition—tenant unions and rent controls—are outside the traditional landlord-tenant relationship as reflected in earlier portions of this chapter. A brief look at the nature and implications of these developments seems warranted.

Tenant Unions

Tenant unions came into being because of abusive practices by some landlords. In apartment house operation, particularly, the landlord is generally both more knowledgeable and stronger financially than any individual tenant. The situation is similar to that of a large employer with many individual employees. Organizing into unions increases the bargaining power of the tenants.

Tenant unions usually seek to negotiate (1) better leases and conditions for tenants and (2) a grievance procedure for dissatisfied tenants. Tenant unions have successfully called rent strikes, meaning rent withholding. The occasion of a rent strike might involve lack of security against criminal acts on the premises, wrongful eviction of tenants, or building code violations as when a serious fire hazard exists. Courts have held that if rents are paid in escrow in such strikes, retaliatory evictions are illegal. A **retaliatory eviction** is removing a tenant from a property as punishment for the tenant's asserting his or her rights. Thus landlords may not get even with tenants for joining tenant unions, reporting violatoins of building codes or other local regulations, or for legally withholding rents. The movement toward tenant unions seems healthy for responsible landlords and for society as a whole as well as for tenants.

Rent Control

Rent control is governmental limitation on the amount that owners may charge for apartments or other dwelling units. Rent control is sought, often by tenant unions, on the argument that housing is a unique good that is required by everyone. Housing is unique in that everyone needs basic shelter, for which there is no real substitute. The same is not true of other goods. Many substitutes exist for foodstuffs like pork, apples, and bread, or clothing like pants, shirts, and shoes. Consumers can always shift to less expensive food or shop elsewhere for clothing items. Further, housing tends to be unique in that the supply cannot be expanded quickly in response to increased demand. Thus, tenants have little choice but to pay increased rents when demand outruns supply.

Rent control is legally carried out under the police power authority of governments. The effect of controls is to transfer value or wealth from landlords to tenants. Except in wartime, when the factors of production for building new housing are not available, the arguments against appear to greatly outweight the arguments for rent control. In wartime, the emergency affects everyone. The supply of housing can be increased only at the expense of the war effort. Allowing landlords to gouge tenants under these circumstances would be grossly unfair. In peacetime, the factors of production are available, and only time is needed for the supply of housing to increase in response to greater demand.

Rent control benefits those with a low income and the elderly at the expense of property owners. But providing relief or welfare for these people should fall on the whole of society rather than on property owners. In fact, the costs of controls to society as a whole greatly outweigh the benefits. On this, both liberal and conservative economists agree. Gunnar Myrdal, a labor-oriented economist, who won a Nobel Prize in 1974, has this view. "Rent control has in certain western countries constituted, maybe, the worst example of poor planning by governments lacking courage and vision."[1] Frederick Hayek, a very conservative economist, and also a Nobel Prize Winner, has a similar view. "If this account seems to boil down to a catalogue of inequities to be laid at the door of rent control, that is no mere coincidence, but inevitable. . . . I doubt very much whether theoretical research into the same problem carried out by someone of a different political-economic persuasion than myself could lead to a different conclusion."[2]

What are the implications of rent control? Assuming inflation, the immediate effect is to squeeze the profits of a landlord. This leads to neglect of property maintenance and repairs. Property values drop due to limited rents also. Property taxes to local government drop, resulting in a tighter budget and reduced services. Owners seek relief through efforts to convert to condominiums or to demolish and rebuild in a use that is not subject to control. If their efforts are unsuccessful and all profits are squeezed out of ownership, properties are abandoned. Thus, severe blight and slums result. The effect is one more step toward decline in the neighborhood life cycle. In the meantime, investors develop new housing projects only in locations or communities without controls. And lenders avoid making loans on properties in rent control areas. Again, blight and urban deterioration result.

The loss of local tax revenue is documented by a study of the Boston area by George Sternlieb and others. Thus, artificially lower rents for a few tenants can only mean higher taxes for everyone else. The abandonment of properties by owners in some large cities is also well known. Is it any wonder that Assar Lindbeck, author of *The Political Economy of the New Left,* concluded, "In many cases rent control appears to be the most efficient technique presently known to destroy a city—except for bombing"?[3]

[1] Sven Oydenfelt, "The Rise and Fall of Swedish Rent Control," in *Rent Control, A Popular Paradox, Evidence on the Economic Effects of Rent Control* (Vancouver, B.C.: The Fraser Institute, 1975) p. 169.

[2] A. F. Hayek, "The Repercussion of Rent Restrictions," in *Rent Control,* p. 80.

[3] George Sternlieb et al., *The Realities of Rent Control in the Greater Boston Area* (New Brunswick, N.J.: Center for Urban Policy Research, Rutgers University, 1974), p. 78.

SUMMARY

A contract in which a landlord exchanges space for rent from a tenant is a lease. The main kinds of leases, based on rent payment plans, are flat, graduated, percentage, index, net, and reappraisal. The percentage lease is increasing in popularity because it provides to an owner a means of sharing in inflated property value. Ground lease and sale and leaseback arrangements are also important ways of renting property.

Typical covenants in a lease concern (1) use of the premises, (2) security deposits, (3) subletting, (4) assignment, (5) mortgaging, and (6) redemption. Covenants requiring joint negotiation by a landlord and tenant include (1) lease-option, (2) rights of renewal, (3) subordination, (4) requirements for improvements and repairs, (5) damage claims by others, (6) eminent domain, and (7) property destruction.

Tenant unions negotiate leases and grievance procedures for renters more effectively than can individual tenants. Rent strikes are legal in most states if the withheld rents are placed in escrow. Retaliatory eviction by landlords against tenants seeking their rights is illegal. The impact of tenant unions appears positive for real estate, except for their support of rent control. A ceiling on rents results in a squeeze on owner profits, less maintenance, lower values, reduced local tax revenues and services, and eventually blight and slums. Also, rent control discourages new construction where applicable. In short, control of rents can only lead to urban disaster.

KEY TERMS

Abandonment

Actual eviction

Constructive eviction

Dispossess proceedings

Extension

Flat lease

Graduated lease

Gross lease

Ground lease

Index lease

Lease

Lease option

Leasehold estate

Lessee/tenant

Lessor/landlord

Net lease

Percentage lease

Reappraisal lease

Rent

Retaliatory eviction

Right of redemption

Sandwich leasehold

Security deposit

Sublease/sublet

Term

609

QUESTIONS FOR REVIEW AND DISCUSSION

1. Explain the basic nature and terminology of leasing, including a clear distinction between tenancy for years and tenancy from year to year.

2. List and explain these rental-payment-plan leases.
   (a) Percentage
   (b) Flat
   (c) Net
   (d) Graduated
   (e) Index
   (f) Reappraisal

3. Explain the following concepts or clauses as they relate to leasing.
   (a) Use of premises
   (b) Right to sublet
   (c) Right to assign
   (d) Right to mortgage
   (e) Lease option
   (f) Subordination

4. List and explain at least four ways a lease may be terminated.

5. Define and/or distinguish between market rent and contract rent. Are these two kinds of rent ever equal? If so, when?

6. A property is under lease on a long-term, step-up lease. The neighborhood deteriorates, and the property value declines. Who benefits, if anyone? Explain.

7. Compare the advantages of leasing with buying a business property. Is there a time when either is clearly more appropriate?

8. Who benefits from rent controls? Who loses? In general, are rent controls desirable from a societal point of view? Are rent controls ever desirable?

REFERENCES

Kratovil, Robert, and Raymond J. Werner. *Real Estate Law,* 7th ed. Englewood Cliffs, N.J.: Prentice-Hall, 1979. Comprehensive coverage of real estate law in interesting style that includes many cases. Chapter 37, "Landlord and Tenant," gives considerable depth to the law of leases.

National Association of Realtors. *Rent Control: A Non-solution.* Chicago: NAR, 1977. The legal justification, the theory, and the effects of rent controls are discussed, with case studies from Washington, D.C., New York City, and Boston.

"Leasing: Space for Success." *Real Estate Today.* August 1978. A series of seven articles on commercial leasing by David R. Stambaugh, R. Alan Bullock, R. L. Greer, H. Peter Larson, III, and Elliot I. Young. Insight and comment by people in the business of leasing.

Realtors National Marketing Institute. *Guide to Commercial Property Leasing.* Chicago: RMNI, NAR, 1977. Comprehensive coverage of leasing practices and clauses; very useful reference; in easy-to-use format.

U.S. Department of Housing and Urban Development. *Wise Rental Practices.* Washington, D.C.: HUD, 1977. A short (22-page) objective, easily read brochure on important considerations in renting an apartment. Excellent for inexperienced landlords or tenants. Free.

Home Ownership: Condominiums, Cooperatives, Mobile Homes, and One-Family Residences

27

> The fellow who owns his own home is always just coming out of the hardware store.
> Kim Hubbard, *Bartlett's Unfamiliar Quotations*

Traditionally, home ownership has meant holding title to a detached one-family residence. Since World War II, however, condominiums, cooperatives, and mobile homes have become much more widely accepted for owner occupancy. Currently, about 65 percent of all residential units are owner occupied, as shown in figure 27–1. This figure is up from about 47 percent in 1900 and 55 percent in 1950. Over this same time, the number of people per occupied unit declined from 4.8 to 2.8. Clearly our population is better housed than ever before in our history.

The objective of this chapter is to present an overview and comparison of the main forms of home ownership in our society. This overview should enable the reader to make the best choice in housing when the occasion comes up. Major topics in this chapter are

1. To own or not to own
2. One-family home ownership
3. Ownership in a multifamily development
4. Mobile home ownership

FIGURE 27–1
Occupied Housing Units—Tenure and Population per Occupied Unit: 1900 to 1970
(In thousands, except percent. Prior to 1960, excludes Alaska and Hawaii)

| | | | OWNER OCCUPIED | | RENTER OCCUPIED | | |
Year	Total Population	Total	Number	Percent	Number	Percent	Population per Occupied Unit
1900	76,212,168	15,964	7,455	46.7	8,509	53.3	4.8
1910	92,228,496	20,256	9,301	45.9	10,954	54.1	4.5
1920	106,021,537	24,352	11,114	45.6	13,238	54.4	4.3
1930	123,202,624	29,905	14,280	47.8	15,624	52.2	4.1
1940	132,164,569	34,855	15,196	43.6	19,659	56.4	3.8
1950	151,325,798	42,855	23,560	55.0	19,266	45.0	3.4
1960	179,323,175	53,024	32,797	61.9	20,227	38.1	3.3
1970	203,211,926	63,450	39,885	62.9	23,565	37.1	3.1
1980*	222,000,000	80,135	52,088	65.0	28,047	35.0	2.8

* 1980 estimates by authors based on latest available data.
Source: U.S. Bureau of the Census, *U.S. Census of Population of Housing: 1960 and 1970.*

TO OWN OR NOT TO OWN

People—families or individuals—must live somewhere. But home ownership does not necessarily follow.

Renting a dwelling unit is certainly appropriate for individuals or families who want or need high mobility. Renting may be desirable if freedom from management concerns is desired. And renting may be an advantage if the tenant has an alternative need or use for the money that would otherwise be needed as a down payment on a home. Someone starting a business or going to college, for example, is probably entirely justified in renting a place to live.

To own or not to own eventually becomes the basic question for most people, however. The place to begin finding the answer is in a study of the reasons for home ownership.

Why Own a Home?

A strong case can be made for home ownership based on social and political considerations alone. And people often "feel" so strong a basic instinct and desire to own their own home that they are motivated to search for and acquire their own residence. There are many additional compelling reasons for home ownership, the most important of which follow.

SECURITY. The renter is always insecure. The rent may be raised, or the landlord may want possession. The homeowner is "set." Conditions may change, the economic cycle may go up or down, but there is a roof over one's head, and if payments are met regularly, no one can disturb the home owner; there will never be an eviction notice.

CREDIT. Home ownership improves one's credit standing. It makes for stability and better employment relations. As a home owner reduces the mortgage, he or she comes to be known as a "property owner" whose patronage is solicited; further, his or her credit rating may be counted as a financial asset.

THRIFT AND SAVING. Home ownership encourages saving, for the mortgage amortization provisions are specifically designed to increase the owner's equity at a rate faster than depreciation, i.e., loss in the value of the home. The home owner, too, must set aside sums to meet various payments, and the thrift habit becomes ingrained.

INDEPENDENCE. It is a wonderful feeling indeed for a home owner to stand on a piece of Mother Earth and know it is his or her own, no matter how modest the realm. To a large extent home owners can do as they wish—there is no landlord.

PEACE OF MIND. As soon as the initial payment on the home is made, the owner begins building up an equity, and this provides peace of mind. To be sure, there are payments to make, but the renter also has obligations each month. The great difference is that the renters are building up nothing.

COMMUNITY MAINTENANCE. A community in which homes are largely owner occupied generally reflects better care of properties, better landscaping, cleaner thoroughfares, and stability of home and property investments. As a rule, a home owner wants a nice home.

ADVENTURE. Home ownership, as well as the selection of a home, is one of the most interesting adventures in family life. It involves, in most instances, the largest single financial transaction that a family undertakes. It is indeed adventurous not only to invest one's life savings but also to roam around the community or countryside to find the best location, to choose a plot, and to select the design and layout of a home, if one is to be built, or to look at the innumerable buildings already constructed in anticipation of the home purchaser's demands.

COMMUNITY INTEREST. With home ownership, an entirely new world is opened to the buyer, who learns about values and prices, contracts, and building materials. As he or she considers the tax bill and governmental action that directly or indirectly touch upon the home, it becomes natural to inquire into civic affairs—how government is run and its local problems—and soon the home owner develops a feeling of belonging, which often leads to an active part in community affairs.

FUN. It is a delight to own one's home; to have a place in which to entertain and do the things a tenant may be prohibited from doing. The children can play about as they please without any complaint from landlords.

CREATIVE INSTINCT. The ownership of a home gives the owner an opportunity to play with ideas. People do not design or build their rented quarters—they take them as they find them—and very often simply because they are the best they can get for the price or are most conveniently located. Home owners are people who satisfy their instinctive desire to develop their own background. If building, the architectural design and layout may be what the home owner wishes. Even purchasing an old dwelling may bring into play ideas of alteration and remodeling.

When to Buy a Home

There is no specific time, period, or age at which home ownership can be recommended to any individual or group. The price of a home reflects market conditions as influenced by the supply and demand for housing. But the value of the home to the owner necessitates an analysis of personal factors and a consideration of subjective elements that enter into the evaluation process and the price to be paid for the home. There are, however, a few general considerations that are presented here to guide the home purchaser.

1. Before purchasing a home at any time, consideration should be given to the permanency of employment and stability of income. Purchasing late in life is a hazard if a decrease in earning power comes with age.

2. Prospective home purchasers who have heretofore lived in apartments should, where possible, rent a home first before undertaking a hasty purchase. Home ownership imposes many obligations in regard to home care and maintenance, which the purchaser may not be physically or emotionally prepared to undertake. Unless an abode means more than a mere place in which to sleep and eat, home ownership may prove both irritating and burdensome.

3. Purchase or building a home is best avoided during periods of active housing or building demand or at any time when a housing shortage encourages the payment of premiums to gain immediate possession. It should be remembered that homes purchased at inflated prices generally impose equally inflated monthly financial obligations, which must be borne over long debt periods (twenty or more years) irrespective of hardships that may occur during depression years. The specter of wholesale foreclosures of homes ill-purchased and ill-financed is bound to haunt the buyer if this rule is disregarded.

4. Further consideration should be given to the purchaser's willingness to live in the selected spot for many years to come, because the resale of the property may prove expensive. Unfortunately and too often the purchase of a home is considered an investment. In reality a home is a consumer's item which may diminish in value (not necessarily in price) with age and use as do other consumer commodities.

Where to Buy a Home

A prominent real estate broker was once asked to name three principles that should guide a purchaser in the selection of a home. His answer was as follows: (1) location, (2) location, and (3) location. At first impression it may appear that this answer was lightly and perhaps facetiously formulated, but when consideration is given to some of the peculiar characteristics of real estate the answer becomes meaningful. Location can contribute to making or breaking the conditions that are conducive to maximum enjoyment of the pleasures and amenities of living that arise out of home ownership.

There is no one scale of values that can be recommended as a guide to all present or prospective home owners concerning where to buy a home. Likes and dislikes, tastes, and conditions vary depending upon size of family, type of employment, costs of transportation, price of land, utility requirements, social habits, and personal characteristics of the purchaser. Proximity to place of work, no doubt, is of prime importance to all breadwinners, but other factors, both economic and social, may make living in the country and commuting to the city preferable to the confinement and lack of privacy that are the lot of the urban dweller.

In order to create an awareness of the more significant conditions to which careful consideration should be given by the purchaser, a listing of important items is presented as a guide to effective and successful evaluation of the home location. By comparing the relative value weights of two or more suggested and available locations in relation to family needs and living comforts, the home owner can wisely make an effective choice. The relative weights assigned to location factors as seen through the eyes of a typical home owner are itemized as follows:

Item	Relative Weight
Proximity to place of work	15
Quality of available schools	10
Distance to school	5
Nearness to church of own choice	5
Neighborhood—reptuation and characteristics	10
Degree of owner occupancy and owner's pride in area	5
Quality and proximity of shopping area	5
Tansportation (public) facilities and cost	5
City tax structure	10
Zoning stability	5
Availablity of necessary utilities	5
Recreation opportunities	5
Extent of neighborhood development	5
Nature of terrain—drainage and topography	5
Absence of noise, traffic, smoke, and dust	10
Effective fire and police protection	10

Each family, of course, has problems of its own, and the weights suggested above are purely relative and should be varied according to the specific needs with which each purchaser is confronted. In any event, a scale of values carefully selected and considered should act as a deterrent to hasty purchase and forestall the sweat and tears that otherwise may blot the joys that should be inherent in a home of one's own.

The Costs of Home Ownership

Many home owners fail to consider the "real" costs of operating a home. Among the financial sacrifices to be counted as a cost of home ownership should be the following:

1. Income foregone on equity investment in the home
2. Interest on borrowed capital
3. Depreciation of home investment
4. Maintenance and repairs of home
5. Real estate taxes and assessments
6. Fire and other hazard insurance
7. Utilities—such as water, garbage, and sewage disposal, where not included as part of the tax-paid city services

Assuming the purchase of a $100,000 home, where the buyer paid $10,000 down and $2,000 in title closing charges and obtained a $90,000 mortgage that is to be amortized monthly over a twenty-five-year period with interest at 12 percent per annum, typical monthly costs of home ownership would be nearly $1,500, calculated as follows:

1. Income foregone on equity and purchase (closing costs) investment of $12,000 @ 12% per year or 1% per month	$120.00
2. Interest on borrowed capital (mortgage loan) at 12% per year on $90,000, or 1% per month	900.00
3. Depreciation of building improvements @ 1½ percent per year on $80,000 (building-to-land ratio assumed as 4 to 1)	100.00
4. Maintenance and repair—estimated average monthly expenditures over life of home (painting, roof replacement, etc.)	100.00
5. Real estate taxes (these vary widely; for this illustration 3% of purchase price per year is estimated)	250.00
6. Fire and hazard insurance	16.00
7. Water, garbage, and sanitary sewage	9.00
Total monthly cost of owning a $100,000 home	$1,495.00

In that a cost of $1,500 per month would apply to a $100,000 home, a $50,000 home would probably cost about $750 per month. That is, the cost can be apportioned quickly to homes of other values. Note that the cost can vary widely because so many variables are involved, though cost of capital makes up about two-thirds of the total.

It is important to differentiate between **costs and expenses of home ownership.** *Costs* are the sum total of all the sacrifices in terms of dollars whether paid for or not by the home owner during a given period. *Expenses,* on the other hand, include only those charges that the home owner actually expends. The above-priced house, for instance, would be advertised as $10,000 down and $947.88 per month (covering monthly interest and mortgage amortization charges). No mention is made, as a rule, of closing costs nor of maintenance, repairs, taxes, or insurance expenditures. Even when the out-of-pocket payments covering taxes and insurance are included, the expenses of home owneship fall 20 to 25 percent short of real ownership costs as shown above.

Also, mortgage amortization payments should not be considered as home ownership costs. As the mortgage principal declines, the equity interest of the home owner increases, at least to the extent that payments on the mortgage exceed accrued depreciation on the home. Overall costs, however, remain relatively constant; savings in mortgage interest—as the mortgage principal diminishes—are offset by corresponding losses in income foregone on the increasing equity investment. But even when considering the real costs of home ownership, the amenities to those who purchase wisely make home ownership a sound investment. This is especially true during periods of inflation when "big" dollars borrowed under a fixed-interest mortgage are paid off with "small" dollars out of future, and generally higher (inflated), dollar incomes.

ONE-FAMILY HOME OWNERSHIP

One-family home ownership is generally considered most desirable. Privacy and plenty of room or space are more readily available on a per family basis. However, a 1974 study made for the Department of Housing and Urban Development concludes that the one-family residence is 40 percent more expensive than multifamily housing, on a per unit basis. However, the study, made by the Real Estate Research Corporation of Chicago, is based on six fictional neighborhoods. So the findings are not specifically applicable to any community or project. Further, most of the savings attributed to multifamily, high-density development came by comparing small apartments with large houses. In other words, the standard of comparison strongly favored multifamily housing.

According to the 1970 U.S. Census of about 40 million owner-occupied dwelling units, 35.66 million, or nearly 90 percent, were one-family units. Thus, the one-family house is easily the dominant type of owner-occupied dwelling in the United States. And the one-family house is the only type of dwelling unit to which the buy or build decision seriously applies.

To Buy or Build

Once the price range of a home and the neighborhood in which it is to be located are decided upon, the typical home seeker is confronted with the query whether to build or whether to purchase a ready-made new or old home. There is no one answer to this problem. Due consideration must be given first to the financial situation of the purchaser and second to the advantages and disadvantages that underlie each purchase plan.

In building a new home, the purchaser must be prepared to meet the hazards of unexpected outlays which often prove the killjoy of the thrills that normally accompany the construction of a home. It is difficult to conceive of other investment ventures in which so large a share of a family's savings or income is involved and in which cost understatements prevail so commonly as in the building trades. The difficulty generally rests in the misunderstanding arising from a builder's conception of a house and an owner's conception of a home. To the average purchaser, a house is not a home unless it contains the basic requisites, including blinds, cabinets, appliances, landscaping, and other features that are deemed essential to agreeable living. The aspirations, hopes, fears, and anxiety that are the lot of the typical home builder are well set forth, though in caricature, in Eric Hodgins's *Mr. Blandings Builds His Dream House,* to which the reader is referred.

Those more budget minded and who must know beforehand the costs that home ownership necessitates are best served through the purchase of an existing house. Though the joy of planning and the thrill of watching the new home take form are foregone, the savings and economies resulting from the purchase of an already-built house and the comforting ability to inspect the investment before dollar commitments are made often prove quite rewarding.

The reasons why a ready-built new home may prove more satisfactory to the average purchaser are as follows:

1. Builders can erect a number of houses cheaper than they can an isolated one. Part of this saving, which may amount to 5 percent or more of the total purchase price, is generally passed on to the buyer.
2. Builders, as a rule, secure better lot locations and at more favorable prices.
3. A planned "dream house" may turn out to be a financial nightmare. The cost of a ready-built house is readily known.
4. The home buyer has no headaches during home construction. Ready-made homes are available for inspection, and if the purchaser does not like it, he need not buy it.
5. Flaws in ready-built homes have matured and can be detected without difficulty by an expert architect or builder, either of whom should be called upon in an advisory capacity by the buyer.

If the building is old there are further economies that often accrue to the purchaser:

1. Prices of old homes reflect a discount for lack of newness (and conversely there is an absence of premium for new conditions).
2. General sales resistance resulting from changes in modes of construction and home design causes old homes to sell at lowered prices.
3. Old homes show settlement and other flaws that have developed as the house matures, and allowance is made in the price to reflect such shortcomings.

4. Older homes are likely to be located nearer the center of an urban area, giving economies in movement about the city.

There are, of course, disadvantages in purchasing a ready-built home, which the wise buyer should also consider. For instance:

1. Homes built in anticipation of demand are built for profit, hence speculation.
2. The design of ready-built homes is standard and intended to please the average buyer—that is, every Tom, Dick, and Harry. There is little individuality or homelike quality in mass-produced homes.
3. In ready-built homes, the needs of families must be subordinated to available space and design.
4. The quality of construction of mass-produced homes may be inferior to that obtained where construction is supervised by an architect representing the buyer.

Types of Homes

When one approaches the problem of acquiring a home, no better advice can be given than to look at all the available papers, pamphlets, and literature on the subject of houses. Many magazines feature home construction, design, and layout. It is always the desire of home buyers to have a home that is popular and in the current mode. They will find, very soon after they begin to study the pictures, that they are developing a style and popularity consciousness. It is also desirable to note the cost, so that they may keep to the type and size of building that will fit the purse.

Not only must the type that the home buyer selects fit purse and family requirements, but a type of building shouldn't be fixed until the lot on which the house will be built is selected. The topography of the lot will often have important bearing. For example, a lot that has considerable contour, with a difference in ground level of as much as one story between the front and back of the house, will make entirely different the handling of the basement. On a flat lot, the basement will be simply for service, whereas on a lot that is one story different in level, the basement will be so arranged that the service rooms will be segregated and several rooms for real family use will be placed in the basement. Then, too, the home buyer must carefully bear in mind a number of the elements of value, such as the necessity of having a fair ratio of land cost to building cost, and the further necessity of selecting a type of building that is harmonious with the neighborhood as to both type and cost of other homes.

Prefabricated Homes

This is a subject that is engaging the very serious attention of everyone in the building construction business and should be of concern to real estate people and home buyers. Simply stated, the prefabricated house is a building cut and constructed for the most part in a factory, then shipped to the plot upon which it is to be erected, and there put together on the foundation. There are many variations of the method and scheme of prefabrication, and a brief explanation may be helpful. Let it be assumed that the owner of a lot intends to erect a frame building. Ordinarily there would be plans and specifications prepared and submitted to a building contractor, who would give an estimate of the cost of supplying the material and erecting the building. If the estimate is satisfactory, a contract is entered into for the building construction. The contractor then orders the material, and to a large extent the material is delivered at the location of the house in standard sizes and lengths. The carpenters then cut the lumber and put the house together. This process, of course, means that each building operation is a separate unit. It is about the most expensive way to construct a building.

Considerable expense is saved by developers who erect a number of buildings at a time, all following about the same general plan. Even the builder erecting one building will have certain parts of the work handled "at the mill." These would be such items as window frames and sash, doors and door frames.

The theory of prefabrication is that a great deal of the work ordinarily done on the job can be done in a factory in wholesale quantities and sold to the homeowner at a great saving. The home owner selects the type of house desired. Most of the prefabrication organizations have a number of designs. The owner, having selected a certain design, receives all the lumber needed for the erection of that house "ready-cut," so that to a very large extent all the carpenters have to do is fit the various pieces together and erect the house very rapidly. Some of the companies undertake as a part of their service the actual erection of the house. In the case of a garage, a truck with workmen and materials will appear in the morning and before the end of the day the garage is completed and has its first coat of paint. Some of the organizations will supply not only the ready-cut lumber but the proper amount of every single item, such as nails, plaster, and paint. Many organizations go to the extent of supplying the walls, both interior and exterior, in completed panels ready to be fastened together.

The market for, and manufacture of, prefabricated housing is steadily expanding. The one thing, more than any other, delaying progress is the opposition of organized labor as to how and where it may be used and as to what extent prefabrication of interior fixtures may be carried. Then, too, there is the unreadiness of the general public to accept the "ready-to-wear" idea of a home. Homes, as a matter of fact, are about the only things that have not yet been standardized. People still seem to desire individuality. As soon as the public realizes the great savings that may be had, there will be many more houses of the prefabricated type.

The obstacles to prefabricated houses are slowly being disposed of, but some of them may well be pointed out. Lightweight materials must be devised, or transportation difficulties and expenses will eat up too much of the saving. Lots are of various shapes and sizes, and the contour of the ground is often not level. This condition creates engineering problems that cannot be overcome by prefabricated house plans that are too rigid. The house designs must be many and varied so as to take into consideration the fundamentally different types desirable in various parts of the country. The companies that sell these houses will have to give careful thought to the problem of financing and distribution. In many localities, building and other ordinances are so drawn (sometimes intentionally) as to make it almost impossible to erect prefabricated homes.

Importance of Professional Aid

The home purchaser is well advised to have all steps toward home ownership guided by competent professional aid, which real estate brokers, appraisers, architects, and lawyers are prepared to offer. The real estate brokers are generally first contacted, because most lots and houses are offered for sale through their intervening services. The question is often raised: Why deal through a broker? Can't the commission be saved by negotiating directly with the seller? Those who take this narrow view fail to realize that the broker renders necessary and important economic services for which the commission paid represents well-earned compensation. Some of the more important brokerage services that benefit the buyer and seller may be stated as follows:

Broker's Services Benefiting Buyer

1. Aid in speeding the selection of a home by offering valuable advice regarding city growth, neighborhood pattern, population and housing characteristics, value range, and kind of homes offered in the market

2. Limiting inspection of homes to those that fit the pocketbook of the purchaser

3. Safeguarding overpayment—for few brokers will waste time and money marketing overpriced properties

4. Satisfaction of purchaser is in mind, for each satisfied buyer is a potential seller and client for related services that brokers are prepared to offer in fields of management, insurance, financing, leasing, and selling

5. Help in arranging financing of purchase

Broker's Services Benefiting Seller

1. Advising as to reasonable asking price for the property offered for sale

2. Reaching wider market through contacts with established brokers' and cobrokers' channels in other communities

3. Separating the "suspects" from the "prospects" and thus saving annoyance resulting from sightseers and curiosity seekers who enjoy "house window-shopping"

4. Limiting visits to inspect homes to prearranged hours, thus saving inconvenience and possible embarrassment to occupying family

5. Attending to actual negotiations, contract preparations, and details concerned with closing of title and transfer of property rights

Although the intervening services of an established broker mitigate the chances of paying more than the property is worth, it should be remembered that the broker, in his or her capacity as agent, is duty-bound to secure for the principal—the seller—the highest price that market conditions warrant. How then should purchasers proceed to safeguard their interests? The answer, of course, lies in the employment of professional aid that will directly serve the buyer. After all, homes currently average well above $50,000 in price, and no such sum should be committed without independent check as to the marketability of the investment at the offered price.

Perhaps one of the best safeguards that the buyer may adopt is to make the purchase contract contingent upon procurement of a maximum FHA, VA, or conventional mortgage loan. For where such loans are offered and bear a fair relation to purchase price, the buyer can rest assured that the sales price is fair and represents a conservative long-term value estimate. Where such contract provisions are denied, the purchaser should take recourse to employment of an independent appraiser who should be requested to submit a narrative report setting forth fully the reasoning underlying the value estimate and the conditions and assumptions of his or her value judgment. Because such professional services can be secured at fees that rarely exceed one-half of 1 percent of the purchase price of a home, it appears foolhardy to make a large and significant investment without the professional aid of a competent appraiser The valuation of the home should, of course, take place in advance of contract commitments, for once the purchaser signs on the dotted line, a change of mind may prove costly and legally burdensome.

The Work of the Architect

Whenever a home is to be erected in the conventional way, or a larger building for commercial or industrial use is contemplated, the work of the architect is important. This person is consulted by those who wish to erect a building on land they own and by those who contemplate the purchase of land for a building operation. The owner determines the type of building to be erected—that is, whether it is to be a private dwelling, an apartment house, or a commercial building, and then furnishes the architect with a diagram or description of the plot. From this information, the architect advises concerning the size and shape of the proposed building, the arrangement of the rooms, and its probable cost. This information often assists in determining whether or not the building will be a success commercially or meet the needs of the home owner.

The architect is employed to draw finished plans and specifications for proposed buildings and for alterations and additions to existing buildings. He or she prepares and approves contracts for the work to be performed; aproves payments to contractors and watches the progress of the building during construction; and guards the interests of the employer against fraud, overcharges, inferior work, delays, and violations of law. The architect's work is sometimes in the interests of the mortgagee, reporting to the mortgagee on the quality of the material and the workmanship of the building. The architect often furnishes figures to be used as a basis for fixing the amount to be loaned. If the mortgage is advanced as a building loan, the advances are often made on certificates of the architect.

When the architect is employed to superintend the construction, he or she may reject any part of the work not conforming to the specifications. In considering the rejection of any work, or in deciding any controversy between owner and contractor, the architect must be impartial; judgment should be fair to both sides, even though he or she is retained and paid by the owner.

In many places, the authorities require certain certificates to be issued before a new building may be used for the purpose for which it was constructed. These may include a building-department certificate, showing that the building code has not been violated; a tenement-house department certificate, permitting occupancy of the building by three or more families; certificates of boards of fire underwriters and departments of gas and electricity as to electric wiring, motors, and fixtures; and, in the case of factories and loft buildings, certificates showing the weight that the various floors will sustain.

OWNERSHIP IN A MULTIFAMILY DEVELOPMENT

Half of the United States population lived in urban areas in 1920. By 1950, almost two-thirds lived in urban areas. Currently about three-fourths of the population live in places of 2,500 inhabitants or more. Further, the U.S. had 172 urbanized areas containing more than 100,000 persons in 1970; these accounted for 55 percent of the total population. The density of population in large population centers tends to be much greater than in smaller urban areas. And prices for land and housing tend to be much higher in large metropolitan areas, in turn. The extensive amount of land needed per one-family house thus becomes financially too costly for most home owners. For example, assume raw land costs $5,000 per acre in a small urban area and $20,000 per acre in a metropolitan area. If four one-family houses were built per acre on the small urban area, the per-dwelling unit cost of land would be $1,250. In the metropolitan area, the cost of land per unit would be $5,000. However, if multifamily units were built at a density of fifteen dwelling units per acre in the metropolitan area, the per-unit land cost would drop to $1,333. This example is oversimplified. But it does point up that greater intensity of use is needed when land costs are high, if the cost of land per dwelling unit is to be kept at a comparable level. The acceptance of this fact by people who wish to realize home ownership has led to increasingly greater reliance on condominiums and cooperatives for home ownership.

A given multifamily property can be owned as an income property (apartment building), a condominium, or a cooperative. The property may be the same, but the legal form of ownership varies greatly under these three alternatives. Considerable attention has been given to analyzing an income property in previous sections. Thus, attention here focuses on the condominium and cooperative forms of ownership only.

Ownership in a multifamily development provides freedom from concern for exterior management of a property in most cases. Also, people sometimes feel more secure because they live in close proximity to others. This feeling of security extends to the individual unit during the absence of the owner. That is, the units are close together, and the neighbors presumably know each other's comings and goings. Thus, suspicious activity in a unit when the owner is normally absent is more easily detected.

Condominium Ownership

Ownership of an equity interest in a condominium unit is directly equivalent to ownership of an equity interest in a one-family house, except for sharing in the cost of operation and governance of common areas. The owner of a condominium unit may obtain a mortgage loan against the unit on an individual basis. Each condominium unit is assessed for property tax purposes on an individual basis. And changes in the value of the unit, plus or minus, work to the gain or loss of the owner. A condominium unit is even owned on a fee or fee simple basis, with unrestricted right of sale or disposition.

The common areas of a condominium development are owned jointly with the other fee owners. Common areas ordinarily include the land and areas or portions of the structures not described as units. The interest of an individual owner in the common areas is defined as an individual percentage of the total based on the unit value ratio. The unit value ratio is obtained by dividing the appraised value of a unit by the total appraised value of all units. The unit value ratio is also used to apportion operating costs of the commons and voting power to individual condominium units.

CREATION. In a legal sense, condominium ownership is created by a special condominium law that permits individual dwelling-unit estates to be established within a total and larger property estate. The individual estates are technically established by use of vertical and horizontal planes (surfaces), which are usually identified, vertically, as the walls (not room partitions) of the unit, and horizontally, as the floors and ceilings of the unit. The exact location of the building or buildings on the site and the exact location of the unit within the building are described in the plat (location map) and in the architectural plans. Each is also described in legal language in a master deed. After all the individual unit estates have been described in the total property estate, all of what remains, such as the land and the structural parts of the buildings, become a common estate to be owned jointly by the owners of the individual unit estates. Thus, each condominium owner owns his or her individual unit estate and an undivided interest in the common estate.

Recording of the master deed extends the condominium laws of the state in which the condominium is located to the property. The master deed also establishes an association to look after the use and maintenance of the common estate. The association is governed by a board of directors or managers, elected from among the owners of the individual unit estates. The internal government of the total property is controlled by the bylaws, which are recorded with the master deed. The bylaws can usually be changed by a vote of the majority of individual owners. However, changes in the master deed normally require the consent of all owners.

CAUTIONS. Home ownership through the condominium arrangement can turn sour for a number of reasons. Problems such as the following are increasingly showing up in residential condominium developments.

Excessive operating costs and management fees frequently occur. Monthly payments for maintenance, repairs, and operation turn out to be two and sometimes three times the amount indicated by a salesperson at the time of purchase. Excessive management fees may be arranged by a developer on a long-term contract before selling units. And the management performance may be inferior. For example, the Point East Condominium Development in North Miami Beach ended up paying the developer $60,000 a year *not* to manage the project. The condominium owners found out it was less costly to do their own managing.

Recreational leases are sometimes built into the development to catch the unsuspecting buyer. The result is that condominium owners pay rent for years for recreational facilities they thought they had purchased. In one case, a 502-unit high-rise development in Miami Beach was committed to pay a developer over $300,000 per year land rent on a 99-year lease for a swimming pool. The assessed value of the land in question was $82,000.

Recreational facilities such as swimming pools, tennis courts, sauna facilities, and other amenities are sometimes not built or provided as promised. In some cases condominium buyers are asked to pay for facilities they thought they were getting in the base price. At one expensive development in Washington, D.C., residents were asked to put up an extra $3,000 for each parking space desired or needed.

In buying a condominium unit, prospective purchasers are advised to give attention to the following points:

1. To avoid unreasonable operating costs and management fees
   (a) Check with the assessor about actual or expected property taxes.
   (b) Make sure that an experienced management firm of good reputation will operate the property. Avoid any tie-in with the developer.
   (c) Make sure charges for operation and maintenance of common areas are realistic. If too low, poor service and shoddy maintenance is sure to result.

2. To avoid extra rental charges for recreational facilities, parking facilities, and other amenities or facilities
   (a) Ask about and check out all lease situations; determine if any fee ownership of land is involved. If so, what arrangement? Lease arrangements do not necessarily mean problems, but knowledge of their existence is important.

3. To avoid paying later for needed facilities that were assumed to be part of the purchase price
   (a) Check out the reputation of the builder or developer with the local realty board, Better Business Bureau, or tenants on the property.
   (b) Beware of promises of swimming pools, tennis courts, parking facilities, and other facilities. A good developer installs these facilities to

begin with; a bad developer may still be looking for ways to finance these "extras" while trying to sell the units.

(c) Make sure you know what is being bought. Normally a buyer gets a unit plus a share of the common elements.

Cooperative Ownership

Ownership in a cooperative housing development is really ownership of a membership certificate or stock in a corporation or trust that holds title to the property of concern. Owning the certificate or stock carries with it the exclusive right to occupy a dwelling unit in the property and to participate in the operation of the cooperative directly as an elected board member or indirectly as a voter. The owner of shares in a cooperative development thus occupies the dwelling unit under a **proprietary lease,** meaning a lease with the attributes of ownership. Rights under the certificate are usually governed by personal property laws.

The cooperative corporation or trust holds fee title to the dwelling units and directly assumes mortgage, tax, and other obligations necessary to finance and operate the development. Members do not have any *direct liability* for these items. Only elected board members can act officially for the corporation. The board is usually small in number (five to seven members) so the membership can elect its most reasonable and talented people to make decisions. The small number also makes for quicker decisions. The corporation or trust has the same rights and responsibilities as an individual before the law. The articles of incorporation or trust agreement and the bylaws of a cooperative are specially designed so the cooperative can be owned and operated by its member-stockholders. Each member usually has one vote in governing the cooperative.

In financing the property, the cooperative borrows the money and becomes the mortgager. Property taxes are levied against the corporation or trust as the owner. And responsibility for operating the property—collecting rents, maintaining the common areas, paying insurance and taxes, etc.—rests with the corporation.

OCCUPANCY AGREEMENT. The cooperative enters into the proprietary lease or occupancy agreement with individual members. The occupancy agreement spells out the rights and obligations of the cooperative to the member and of the member to the cooperative. It basically gives the member an exclusive right to occupy a unit, participate in the government of the property, and receive tax benefits and equity increases in return for financial and personal support of the cooperative. The occupancy agreement together with the membership certificate is therefore the basis of cooperative home ownership.

Operating costs, tax benefits, and changes in equity value are allocated on a proportionate share basis. A **proportionate share** is determined by dividing the valuation placed on a specific dwelling unit by the total valuation of the development at the time the cooperative takes title to the property. If all the assets of the cooperative are sold, members in occupancy at the time are entitled to their proportionate share of the amount remaining after all obligations have been paid. The membership certificate or stock of a shareholder deciding to leave the cooperative is sold in accordance with a transfer value and rules set forth in the bylaws of the corporation or trust. The sale is frequently subject to the approval of the board of directors. And sale of the membership share is a sale of personal property.

CAUTIONS. Two concerns stand out in considering home ownership through a cooperative arrangement. If some tenant-owners fail to pay their share of mortgage debt service and property taxes, the cooperative is the responsible party. This means the other tenant-owners must make up the difference or run the risk of foreclosure and possibly losing some of their equity. The second concern is that sometimes a tenant-owner, upon deciding to leave the cooperative, can recover only the initial equity investment plus equity build-up due to mortgage amortization during the period of ownership. That is, any equity build-up due to property appreciation accrues to the cooperative and the continuing tenant-owners.

Condominium versus Cooperative

Both the condominium and cooperative form of ownership provide the benefits of home ownership with freedom of responsibility from exterior property maintenance and care. A pro rata share of operating expenses, property taxes, and insurance must be paid under each form. In both forms, taxes and interest payments on financing may be taken and used as deductions in income tax returns.

The major difference between condominium and cooperative ownership is the relative independence of the group. In condominium ownership, units are owned in fee simple. In turn, each owner is assessed and taxed on his or her specific unit without regard to the actions of other owners. In cooperative ownership, the corporation or trust owns the property. A mortgage or tax lien against the property is therefore the obligation of the corporation or trust. The implication of this is that the failure of one owner to pay taxes or meet debt service becomes a burden to the other shareholders in the cooperative. They must make up the deficiency to protect their own interests. This group liability also extends to mechanic's liens or operating expenses. In addition, the condominium owner has greater freedom of disposition of his or her unit. And, in a cooperative, the property may be refinanced on a two-thirds vote, which may not be consistent with the desires of an individual owner. This greater freedom of action and freedom from dependence on the group has led to much greater popularity of condominium ownership in recent years.

MOBILE HOME OWNERSHIP

A distinction must be made between the two types of mobile dwelling units: the less-expensive travel trailers, and the modern mobile homes, which contain up to four bedrooms and two baths and which measure up to 14 feet in width (expandable to 28 feet, called double-wide) and up to 70 feet in length. Although travel trailers and mobile homes are often built by the same manufacturers, the former are strictly personal fixtures with some of the features of an automobile. The latter, once positioned in place, have been declared by statute in a number of states to possess the characteristics of realty.

Among the people who prefer mobile homes are military personnel, construction workers, student couples, retired citizens, economy-minded couples, and vacationers who like a home away from home. In the latter category, especially, a significant increase in demand for mobile homes is anticipated. Just as the ownership of two cars per family has become the rule rather than the exception, so the ownership of two homes is rapidly becoming an accepted status symbol among members of the affluent society. According to findings published by the National Association of Real Estate Brokers in September 1970, more than 25,000 mobile home parks with more than 2 million spaces were established in designated subdivisions of towns and cities of the United States. These parks expanded by some 1,100 parks each year. Some of these parks housed as many as 2,000 mobile homes and formed separate and incorporated communities complete with mayor, councilpersons, police and fire departments, and related community utilities and services. In 1975, an estimated 9 million Americans were living in nearly 4 million mobile homes.

The prices of mobile homes in 1980 ranged from $12,000 to $20,000 for 800 to 1,000 square feet of living space. This works out to about $15 to $20 per square foot of living space. For luxury models of the double-wide variety, where two 14-foot-wide models are placed side by side and combined to form one mobile home with over 1,400 square feet of floor space, the price of the home, delivered and assembled, reached a high of $60,000. Because of trucking, these so-called mobile homes are no longer truly mobile. In fact, judging by the quality of construction and the sumptuousness of interior furnishings, the motto of the mobile home industry appears to be: "Less Mobility and More Home for Your Money." Therefore, mobile homes should legally be classified as realty rather than personalty as is increasingly the case.

Mobile homes, as previously stated, are no longer solely a means of temporary shelter. They have come to be recognized as a form of permanent shelter much like conventional homes in competing residential environments except for density of housing. Of the estimated 25,000 mobile parks, the greatest number are concentrated in Florida, California, and the southwestern states. The maximum density, unless otherwise controlled by zoning laws, is ten trailer spaces per acre. The Mobile Home Manufacturers Association estimates park development cost at $3,000–$5,000 per space, depending on number and quality of utility facilities including paving, landscaping, and community recreation facilities. As a rule, these mobile parks are situated at the fringe of the urban community where raw land costs do not exceed $2,000 to $4,000 per acre. Although in some instances spaces for mobile homes can be purchased outright, the general practice is to rent the space at costs averaging $100 to $250 per month, varying with the number of service facilities provided, exclusive of utility costs for water, gas, telephone, and electricity, which are paid by the renter. In a few luxury locations, such as seashore or golf club areas, monthly rentals are as high as $400 or even more. Park owners often derive additional income from the sale of bottled gas, coin-operated laundries, and food-vending machines.

Mobile Home Advantages

The mobile home industry offers economies of mass production to people desiring to own their own home. These economies are largely unavailable in the conventional house market. Manufacturers of "shell" homes (complete except for interior finishing) and prefabricated homes, it is true, have attempted to introduce production-line methods into housing construction. However, over-restrictive local building codes, backed by craft unions that fear loss of their jobs to outside workers, have negated the savings that could result from home preconstruction. The mobile home, because it is classified as *personalty* rather than as *realty* in most jurisdictions, has so far escaped and promises to continue to escape the restrictions to which other prefabricated housing is subjected.

Other main advantages offered by the mobile home relative to traditional housing are as follows:

1. Low price with a low down payment. Cost is about half that of conventional housing. And the down payment and other moving-in costs are about one-fourth that of conventional housing.

2. Land does not have to be bought; rather, a lot is rented at from $100 to $250 per month.

3. Financing is much more readily available, although the interest rate is usually higher.

4. The mobile home is often classified and taxed as personal property. The annual tax per dwelling unit thus may run from $150 to $250, whereas the annual tax on a one-family house typically runs from $500 to $1,000 per year.

However, an unpublished study by Professor Philip Weitzman of the City University of New York concludes that to own a two-bedroom mobile home actually costs only 11 percent less than to own a three-bedroom house, over a fifteen-year period. The cost of owning a mobile home is higher than seems true at first glance because mobile homes depreciate in value more rapidly and because interest rates on financing are usually much higher.

The mobile home also differs from conventional housing in that it is finished inside and out to the last detail before leaving the factory. All furniture and furnishings, including rugs, draperies, and blinds, are in place and contained in the quoted and delivered price. Savings obtained through belt-line assembly are further increased by wholesale pricing of kitchen, heating, and cooling equipment. Mobile homes, as stated previously, are designed luxuriously to offer more and more home quality and less and less mobility. This trend is borne out by statistics gathered by the MHMA to show that the typical "mobile" home stays in place, on the average, for over five years. Surveys indicate that 80 percent of those living in mobile homes have not moved in the preceding five years, and of those who moved, 44 percent did so because of job changes.[1] Mobile home living appeals to the younger married couples and to the above-middle-aged group in the semi-retired or retired class. Statistics indicate that 55 percent of mobile home residents are skilled workers or persons of professional background. Questionnaires confirm that the compactness of mobile home construction offers more utility and convenience in the use of space than does the construction of conventional homes. Because of the welded-unit-body construction, upkeep is more economical. Built-in bureaus, beds, and appliances make housekeeping easier for senior citizens and for busy working couples.

The appeal of mobile home living is widespread. To large numbers of retired persons, mobile parks are a kind of new Eden, offering community spirit and friendly atmosphere generated by like-minded neighbors, a feeling unmatched in any area containing conventional homes of smaller size and number. Young couples, too, find mobile living an ideal way to begin their home-making adventure. A single purchase includes not only the roof over their heads but all the furniture and bulky appliances such as stove, refrigerator, washing machine, and many optional extras. Surveys of mobile parks indicate fewer children than in conventional homes and higher income per family and more formal education than the national average.

Buying a Mobile Home

There are some important considerations in shopping for a mobile home: (1) shop for a site, (2) shop for value, and (3) shop for safety.

SHOP FOR A SITE. Over half of all occupied mobile homes in the United States are located on individual lots. The balance are located in mobile home parks. Some areas or states discourage or do not allow locating mobile homes on individual sites. And these same areas may strongly discourage mobile home parks. So, before buying a mobile home, a site suitable to the aspiring owner-occupant must be located.

Several critical questions that need acceptable answers in shopping for a site are as follows:

1. What facilities or services are offered? Many parks provide a clubhouse, swimming pool, golf course, and other extras. The tenant will pay for these whether or not they are used. Other items to check for are street lights, fire-alarm boxes and hydrants, an emergency building for windstorms, underground wiring, and underground oil or gas tanks.

2. What is the quality of the site? Lots should be level and well drained, with adequate parking facilities. The concrete slab should be four inches thick, with sturdy wind anchors. Assuming good layout, density should not ex-

---

[1] See Art S. Leitch, "The Mobile Home Boom," *Successful Sales Slant,* no. 17, September 1970, National Institute of Real Estate Brokers, Chicago, Ill.

ceed six or seven sites per acre. What water, sewerage, and electrical services are provided?

3. How much is the rent, including cost of utilities and services? Rental charges here include entrance fees, setup charges, refuse collection, and TV cable, plus possible charges for recreational facilities, laundry facilities, and gas, oil, or electricity.

4. Is the park subject to flooding? Check with longtime residents. Also check the location relative to the nearest body of water and drainage facilities.

5. What miscellaneous services are provided, such as babysitting, day care, or bulk-storage facilities?

6. What type of residents occupy the park? Are the residents elderly, students, construction workers? Are they suitable to your needs?

SHOP FOR VALUE. After locating a site, a potential owner is ready to shop for a mobile home. Obviously, family size and income level will be prime determinants of the unit to be purchased. Beyond these considerations, attention to the following points is important to obtain the best value for the money:

1. Check dealer reputation with local banks, business associations, or occupants of several units of the brand or type being considered. A dealer with a poor reputation is not likely to have a good product.

2. In shopping, ascertain exactly what is included in the purchase price and what is not. Make up and use a written checklist in shopping.

3. Compare for quality. For example, the heavier a unit, the higher its quality is likely to be. Check the thickness and quality of the insulation, the capacity of the furnace and water heater, and the size and spacing of beams used in the walls, floor, and roof.

4. Before signing any contract, demand a manufacturer's *written* warranty on the unit, usually for one year. Also, note any *fine-print* exclusions.

5. Check into the terms and cost of financing. Typically, a loan runs to a maximum of twelve years.

SHOP FOR SAFETY. Mobile homes are especially susceptible to fire and wind hazards. Mobile homes are constructed of plywood, which can be dangerously flammable. As a result, mobile home fires do two to three times more dollar damage per fire than fires in one-family homes. Mobile homes are light relative to their side surface area. As a result, wind damage to mobile homes runs twenty to thirty times that of conventional homes, depending on the area of the country.

Fire protection can be gained by use of gypsum board interiors, smoke detectors, and easy-exist windows. Wind protection can be gained by strong, well-located straps or wires tied to sturdy anchors in the concrete base at the site. The 1974 Mobile Home Construction and Safety Standards Act calls for the Department of Housing and Urban Development to draw up safety standards similar to those now applicable to autos. These standards, when drawn up and implemented, should raise the quality of mobile homes. Note, however, that mobile homes built before the standards go into effect may be of low quality.

Financing of Mobile Homes

Loans for mobile homes are as readily obtainable as loans for the purchase of automobiles. As a rule, large sales agencies as well as commercial banks finance mobile homes freely. Dealers of mobile homes generally are able to obtain loans of 90 percent of cost including transportation of the mobile home, or they may elect to pay cash where the manufacturer's price concessions warrant it. Some manufacturers have their own financing subsidiaries to facilitate sale and promotion of their products. Approximately 80 percent of mobile homes are purchased on credit by the user, as are 80 percent of conventional homes. Loan maturities are relatively short, however, and range up to twelve years at rates comparable to automobile loan rates. Like automobile dealers, mobile home dealers arrange for trade-ins, and an increasing number of dealer transactions involve used mobile homes. Trade-ins for new models, however, represent only a small fraction of mobile home sales.

Some basic guides to financing a mobile home are as follows:

1. Choose a mobile home unit that can be afforded, which usually means that value or purchase price should equal no more than four times personal, stabilized income.

2. If loan payments turn out to be excessive, try to arrange alternative terms immediately. Mobile homes are personal property for the purposes of the purchase contract. Repossession takes much less time than with a one-family home financed with a mortgage loan.

The Future of Mobile Homes

The outlook for continued expansion of the mobile home industry and for increased use of this mode of housing in all states throughout North America is excellent. Planning agencies increasingly encourage mobile park developments as a means of slowing community obsolescence and decay. Some planners go so far as to refer to mobile housing as "renewable housing" that tends to self-modernize a park community. The theory is that residents will be likely to trade old models for new, thus upgrading the environment as it ages. Only the future can show whether this theory is valid.

SUMMARY

About 65 percent of all dwelling units in the United States are owner-occupied. Ninety percent of all owner-occupied units are one-family residences, with the remainder split about evenly between ownership of multifamily units and mobile homes.

Reasons for owning a home include security of a place to live, thrift or savings, and peace of mind. There is no clear rule as to when home ownership is justified. Much depends on the felt need for ownership and on the stability of income. Important considerations in choosing where to buy a home include proximity to place of work, quality of schools available, neighborhood reputaton, absence of pollution, traffic, and other nuisances, and effectiveness of fire and police protection. The cost of home ownership is the sum total of all sacrifices in terms of dollars during a given period, whether they are out-of-pocket expenses or not. The expenses of home ownership include only out-of-pocket payments.

Owner occupancy of a one-family residence is generally considered most desirable because greater privacy and more living area is realized. However, the cost per dwelling unit may be up to 40 percent greater. Ownership in a multifamily development gives freedom from exterior maintenance and care while retaining the benefits of home ownership. A condominium unit is owned in fee simple on an individual basis. A cooperative property is owned by the corporation, with units occupied by shareholders under proprietary leases. All owners are therefore dependent on group cooperation and action. Because of the greater freedom of action and less dependence on the group, condominium ownership is usually preferred to cooperative ownership.

Military personnel, construction workers, student couples, retired citizens, and vacationers dominate as owners of mobile homes. The main advantages of mobile home ownership are low price and low down payment, ready financing, and generally lower property taxes. Important steps in buying a mobile home are shopping for a site, shopping for value, and shopping for safety. One study concluded that mobile home ownership is only 11 percent less than ownership of a one-family residence. The lower cost has led to mobile homes as the only route to ownership for most low-income families.

KEY TERMS

Costs of home ownership

Expenses of home ownership

Proportionate share

Proprietary lease

QUESTIONS FOR REVIEW AND DISCUSSION

1. State and explain briefly at least six reasons for home ownership.

2. List at least six important elements of location for a home, as viewed by typical home owners, and indicate their relative weights. Do you agree with the relative weighting given in the chapter? Why or why not?

3. Costs of home ownership increased dramatically in the last decade. Does this increase have any implications as to the type of housing owned in our socety? As to the proportion of our citizens who become home owners? Discuss.

4. Is it better to buy or build? Discuss.

5. Is it better to own or rent? Discuss.

6. What advantages does owning a home in a multifamily development (con-

dominium, cooperative) have over owning a detached one-family residence, if any?

7. Compare ownership of a condominium and a cooperative unit.

8. List and explain briefly the major advantages of mobile home living. Then explain the need to shop for value and for safety in buying a mobile home.

9. Where are the major areas of detached one-family housing, multiple-family housing, and mobile home housing in your community? Are there any trends in their areas of dominance?

REFERENCES

Fallain, James R., Jr., and Raymond J. Struyk. "Is the American Dream Really Threatened?" *Real Estate Review,* winter 1979. A portion of a study prepared for HUD's Office of Policy Development and Research. Contains data on home ownership trends broken down by income, race, location, and household types. Also examines the affordability of housing by a typical citizen; concludes no problem exists. Easy to read and understand.

Harrison, Henry S. *Houses: The Illustrated Guide to Construction, Design, and System.* Chicago: RMNI, National Association of Realtors, 1973. An easy-to-read manual on housing types and their construction.

U.S. Department of Labor. *Rent or Buy.* Washington, D.C., 1974. Bulletin 1823. A pamphlet describing methods of comparing costs and benefits of owning with costs and benefits of renting. Easy to read. Many terms defined.

U.S. League of Savings Associations. *Saving and Loan Fact Book.* Chicago: U.S. League of Savings Associations. An annual publication of the U.S. Savings League. Contains considerable background on the financing and construction of housing, and other real estate improvements. An excellent reference. Easy to read. Many charts and tables.

Real Estate Trends and Outlook

28

> I never think of the future; it comes soon enough.
> Albert Einstein

Real estate is in a constant state of change. As knowledge advances, as technology develops, or as our social and economic needs and priorities shift, the institution of real estate changes. The previous chapters have provided information about real estate as it is today. This chapter discusses bits and pieces of information that indicate the changes in real estate likely to occur in the next five to ten years. Perhaps, as a result of this chapter, analysts and decision makers will be able to do a better job than they have in the past of anticipating trends and taking them into account.

The trends predicted here are based on insights of the authors from information available to them at time of publication. The trends and outlook are discussed as they affect real estate as (1) a body of knowledge or field of study, (2) a business activity or occupation, and (3) a commodity or physical asset. Those are the three definitions of real estate given in chapter 1.

Two major forces or principles seem to underly these trends. The first principle is, use land resources in our society in the most efficient manner so as to maximize total satisfaction or welfare. The second—which is really an extension of the first—is, balance development and use of our land resources between the private and public sectors of the economy so that marginal utilities or marginal satisfactions are equalized. While the ideal promised by these two principles may never be realized, adjustments that are in keeping with them will increase total utility realized from land resources in our society and culture.

OUTLOOK FOR REAL ESTATE
AS A FIELD OF STUDY

There are two interrelated trends that are likely to have an increasingly significant impact on real estate as a field of study. The first is the ever-widening use of calculations and computers in real estate analysis and business. The second is the development of an integrated body of knowledge that will make for faster and better real estate decisions. The two trends are interrelated in that the application of good theory requires fast and accurate calculations and, at times, quick access to large amounts of data. In turn, these two trends have many implications for real estate as a business and as a commodity.

Computers and calculators make possible very rapid storage, manipulation, and retrieval of data. They also make it possible to perform complex calculations quickly and accurately.[1] That, in turn, means that the theory and the practice of real estate can be brought much closer together. In turn, the standards of practice in real estate are likely to be even more demanding, whether the activity be office management, sales management, or investment analysis.

With the availability of quick recall of data and rapid calculations, analysts and decision makers are able to take account of more information. But a consistent means of relating the information becomes necessary to make it meaningful. Hence, an integrated body of knowledge, or theory, of real estate becomes a logical next step. The organization and content of this book provide the basis of an integrated body of theory for decision making, although this book alone can't supply all the answers.

Real estate centers are likely to be created in most states, and they will facilitate the move toward improved real estate analysis and decision making. Such centers collect, organize, and disseminate data on local areas. They often provide extension courses and services to assist practitioners in obtaining and understanding information and theory as it relates to their individual needs. Centers associated with universities also provide a professional image for their graduates.[2]

OUTLOOK FOR REAL ESTATE
AS A BUSINESS

Three items stand out as indicators of trends in real estate as a business. The first is more federal legislation along the lines of the Real Estate Settlement Procedures Act, and truth in lending laws are to be expected. The second is better ways of doing business by better selection of personnel, new technology and integrated theory. The third is more investment in U.S. real estate by foreigners.

---

[1] See James Verner and Jerome Dasso, "Computer Applications in Real Estate Brokerage," *Real Estate Today,* May 1980.

[2] See Arthur Wright and Jerome Dasso, "Promoting Professionalism Through Real Estate Centers," *Real Estate Today,* November 1979.

Consumer Protection

A federal agency for consumer advocacy appears to be the main objective of the consumer protection movement. The exact nature and function of any agency for consumer advocacy to be established is not clear, but it would almost certainly be freewheeling and wide ranging. Real estate would be just one of many business activities affected.

The demand for consumer protection appears strong. Two specific items of federal consumer protection legislation likely to be passed in the next couple years are the Uniform Land Transactions Act, ULTA, and the National Condominium Standards Act. Also, disclosure of neighborhood mortgage lending policies by financial institutions is likely to be required.

UNIFORM LAND TRANSACTIONS ACT. Three articles toward a Uniform Land Transactions Act were adopted by the Uniform State Laws Commission in 1975. The three articles concern contracts and conveyances, secured transactions, and definitions and purpose of the proposed act. Articles not accepted concerned public land records, liens, condominiums, and conveyancing, recording, and priorities. The American Bar Association and the National Association of Realtors are both vitally interested in the legislation. The exact form and time of acceptance of an entire act is uncertain, but the need for uniform land transaction legislation seems definitely recognized.

NATIONAL CONDOMINIUM STANDARDS. Condominium ownership of residential units is popular and growing rapidly, according to a HUD report. From 1970 to 1974, condominium ownership in the U.S. increased fifteenfold to 1.25 million units housing approximately 3 million people. Condominium ownership is subject to many problems, however, the greatest of which is operation and maintenance by the owners. Other problems include shoddy construction, overly complicated legal documents, and adverse long-term recreational leases. In addition, tenants are frequently left without a housing unit as a result of conversion of apartment houses into condominium developments.

To correct widespread abuses in the sale and operation of condominium developments, William Proxmire, chairman of the Senate Banking, Housing, and Urban Affairs Committee, has introduced legislation with provisions along the lines given below. The National Association of Realtors supports condominium legislation, but prefers enforcement by state agencies.

1. *Conversions.* Adequate written notice to be given a tenant to vacate the premises when conversion of an apartment building into condominiums is scheduled. An option for the tenant to buy the unit might also be required.

2. *Disclosures and warranties.* Buyers to be advised of "full material circumstances and features" about the project and receive a two-year plan and budget for maintaining the common elements (grounds, hallways, recreation facilities). In addition, a two-year warranty on the entire project and a one-year warranty on each unit would be required. A reserve fund for

repair *and* replacement of common elements to be established as backing to the warranty.

3. *Control.* Control of common elements must be given unit owners within one year of initial occupancy. And any manager desired by the unit owners may be hired within six months after control of common elements is taken over.

MORTGAGE DISCLOSURE. Required disclosure by mortgage lenders of mortgage loans by zip code areas appears imminent at the time of this writing, based on a bill passed by the U.S. Senate. The purpose of the disclosure is to discourage neighborhood *redlining,* which is the lender's practice of refusing to make mortgage loans in certain neighborhoods because of high risk or lack of profit potential. In other words, the neighborhood is redlined, or crossed out, for lending purposes by the financial institution.

Public disclosure of loan and no-loan areas presumably would permit consumers and local governments to threaten fund withdrawal from lenders practicing redlining. That is, residents of redlined neighborhoods could withdraw funds from financial institutions not making loans in their areas.

The initial bill involves disclosure, and not regulation, of lending practices. However, opponents insist that regulation would eventually follow. California, Illinois, and Massachusetts have state laws against redlining that are more stringent than the proposed federal laws.

Brokerage Operations

Two developments stand out as indicators of the future of brokerage operations. The first involves better selection of personnel. The second concerns franchised brokerage.

PERSONNEL SELECTION. Real estate sales personnel have traditionally been hired on a random basis by brokers. Of course, some brokers were more selective and did a better job of hiring than others. Professor B. E. Tsagris of California State University at Fullerton recently completed research concerning attributes possessed by successful sales personnel as rated by buyers. Attributes that successful sales representatives invariably possess, according to the study, are professional attitude, knowledge of real estate, use of understandable terms, genuine desire to serve, willingness to keep trying, and selection of properly priced homes. All sales representatives rated about evenly on manners, appearance, and property knowledge. Buyers apparently object strongly to excess aggressiveness in salespeople.

The study, *The Public Image of a Real Estate Agent: An Expanded Update,* may be obtained from the Real Estate Research Institute, California State University, Fullerton, California.

Progressive brokers increasingly have prospective sales personnel examined by professional testing services before hiring them and putting them through a training program. The information provided by Professor Tsagris should greatly improve screening procedures for selecting people most likely to be successful in real estate sales work. The practice of test screening new personnel seems likely to continue and increase.

NATIONAL BROKERAGE. Red Carpet, Previews, and Century 21 are leaders in franchising real estate brokerage operations on a national basis. National brokerage organizations have the advantage of client referral from one community to another. The client benefits because of greater confidence and trust in the brokerage operation based on past experience. In the past, no easy referral system was available. Eventually, national brokerage operations could dominate the market.

USE OF IMPROVED TECHNOLOGY AND THEORY. Use of computers and calculators is likely to be a competitive necessity for survival by investors and practitioners alike. Fast and accurate computations using the investment analysis model presented in earlier chapters is now feasible and operational. As discounted cash flow technologies become more widely accepted and used, better decisions should result. Financial management of real estate to maximize self-interest becomes ever more operational. Others, not using the new technology and integrated theory, and therefore flying blind, seem likely to get by-passed in the competition. The new technology seems sure to affect sales management, property management, appraisal, and finance for similar reasons.

Investment and Administration

Foreign capital invested in United States real estate comes mainly from Great Britain, West Germany, Japan, France, and the Mideast, according to recent reports. Investment by oil-producing nations in U.S. real estate accounts for about 8 percent of U.S. long-term private investment. Kuwait is mentioned specifically as being a heavy investor. Investments from non-Arab nations are reported to be declining, while investment from Arab nations appears to be increasing.

The July 16, 1975, issue of *Appraisal Briefs* indicated that investment in real estate, both domestic and foreign, is increasingly being made by institutions (banks, pension funds, and insurance companies). Greater institutionalization of investment and more foreign investment in U.S. real estate mean that real estate is increasingly becoming a commodity of national and international markets. Decisions on investment and administration of properties will be needed on a continuing basis. Some states are passing laws to limit foreign ownership of their lands, for example, a 1979 Iowa law prohibiting foreigners from buying land to farm in that state beginning January 1980.

This trend to broader markets and ownership almost certainly means that better real estate investment information and analysis will be needed in the future. Investor decision makers removed from the local market must rely heavily on reports for their information and analysis. The investments are generally very high in dollar value, and the decisions are major. Pressure for high-quality information and analysis seems sure to follow. Consequently, improved analysis for real estate decisions promises to be a dominant trend in the future.

OUTLOOK FOR REAL ESTATE
AS A COMMODITY

The amount of land in the United States and the world is fixed, for all practical purposes. The population of the United States is expected to climb to nearly 280 million people over the next fifty years in spite of a zero-population-growth birth rate. This means that the density of population in the 48 contiguous states will be about 90 people per square mile, compared to 60.1 in 1960 and 25.6 in 1900. In addition, the U.S. has changed from having a population with a strong rural orientation to having a population that is over 75 percent urban and obviously concerned with urban problems. All of this means that more and more people are crowding into a very small portion (about 3 percent) of our land area.

The crowding is reflected in the types of dwelling units occupied and the forms of ownership of dwelling units. The crowding is also reflected in an increasing concern with maintaining the quality of life and improving resource usage, both in the United States and throughout the world.

Shift in Housing Mix and Ownership

Zero population growth means smaller-sized family units. The strong movement of millions of people to the cities means a much higher density of population in the urban centers. The higher density takes the form of more multifamily housing, whether apartments, cooperatives, or condominiums. A comparison of 1970 and 1977 data from the annual housing survey conducted by the Department of Housing and Urban Development and the Bureau of the Census points up the trend. The trend is away from one-family and small multifamily structures. Mobile homes and larger multifamily buildings are picking up the slack. However, a larger portion of the population is entering the home-buying age (30–44) and one-family housing construction again is increasing as a percentage of the total.

FIGURE 28–1
Types of Housing Units Occupied Year-round in the United States (percent)

	One-Family Home	Mobile Home	MULTIFAMILY DWELLING UNITS 2–4	5 or more	Total
1970	69.1	3.1	13.3	14.5	100
1977	67.3	4.6	12.9	15.2	100

Source: U.S. Department of Housing and Urban Development and U.S. Department of Commerce, Bureau of the Census, *Annual Housing Survey,* 1977 (Series H–150–77), Washington, D.C.: Government Printing Office, 1979.

Maintaining Quality of Life

Population growth is causing even greater pressure for ways to preserve and enhance the quality of life in the United States. Methods used to maintain quality of life include growth policies, legislation for land-use planning and environmental controls, and urban renewal programs.

GROWTH POLICIES. Movement of people from one state or community to another sometimes causes severe growth problems for the receiving community or state. California and Florida were two outstanding examples of rapid-growth states in the 1950s and 1960s. Mass regional migration (from state to state) has slowed since 1970. But within states, population shifts are still occurring. For example, in 1975, the census figures show that populations of thirty-seven of the nation's fifty-eight largest cities had fallen since 1970. Heavy losers were Minneapolis, off 12 percent; St. Louis, off 10.3 percent; and Cleveland, off 9.6 percent.

The movement is to the suburbs for relief from crime, poor services, and high taxes. The movement to small cities in the suburbs causes traffic congestion, need for new schools and sanitation facilities, and and a general lowering of quality of life for the residents of the suburbs.

Petaluma, California, a suburb of San Francisco with a 1971 population of 30,500 people, was one city threatened with population overflow. Petaluma enacted a five-year plan to permit no more than 500 new dwelling units per year, or to limit growth to about 2,000 new residents per year. Builders sued the city for violation of people's constitutional "right to travel" and won in district court. The case attracted national attention. A court of appeals reversed the ruling, holding that Petaluma has a right to preserve its small-town character, its open spaces, and its low density of population and to grow at an orderly and deliberate pace. The Petaluma plan serves as an indication of the strong desire of people to insulate themselves from the world and to maintain a desired quality of life. As long as the Petaluma plan is upheld in the courts, other suburban communities are almost certain to emulate it.

ENVIRONMENTAL QUALITY. The desire to maintain quality of life is also evidenced in the considerable legislation introduced at the federal level to deal with land-use planning, clean air and water, and energy conservation in recent years. The National Environmental Policy Act requires environmental-impact statements for all major development projects. If the impact will be too detrimental to the environment, a project may be turned down. Additional legislation proposed includes a National Land Use Planning and Resource Conservation Bill to provide financial and technical assistance to states and localities to establish standard land-use planning procedures.

Also, Congress recently passed two amendments to strengthen the Clean Air Act and a separate bill to control indirect sources of air pollution by requiring preconstruction reviews of proposed facilities that attract automobiles (large multifamily projects, shopping centers, airports, and highways). Three federal programs involving pure water and waste disposal are (1) Water Quality Management Basin Plans, (2) Area Waste Treatment Management Planning, and

(3) the National Pollutant Discharge Elimination System. The first is concerned with maintaining pure water, the second involves treatment of waste according to the Water Pollution Control Act Amendment, and the third is concerned with the discharge of liquid wastes into navigable waters. These three programs are likely to be expanded and coordinated in the next few years. Almost certainly, air, water, and land-use controls are going to get more stringent as our population mounts and presses more strongly on our environment.

ENERGY CONSERVATION. Bills are introduced into every session of Congress concerning both energy disclosure and energy conservation. An energy disclosure law would require informing prospective renters and buyers of the annual operating costs of energy systems in housing. One of the provisions of a recently passed energy conservation law is a subsidy for installation of insulation and weather stripping in housing. This type of legislation appears to be only in its beginning stages. Tax incentives seem likely to be enacted on a general basis to encourage greater use of insulation and better building design to conserve energy.

URBAN RENEWAL. The Housing and Community Development Act of 1974 provided for phasing out the federal urban renewal program. The program was initiated in 1949 to clear slums, to remove blight, and to improve the quality of the urban environment generally. According to a recent HUD study, the urban renewal program was not too successful. The program did help communities strengthen their economies, improve their competitive positions, and expand their tax bases. Some physical blight was removed from urban areas, and a favorable climate for public and private investment was created. However, major social problems and a slow turnover of renewal lands stamped the program as generally not successful. Only projects in or near central business districts seem likely to have success in the future, according to the study.

The need for urban renewal is still with us. The means of accomplishing renewal is being shifted from direct governmental programs to governmentally assisted housing. With government assistance, all citizens should be able to afford housing of a certain minimum standard or quality. Housing codes can also be strictly enforced when governmental housing assistance is provided. The expected net result is improvement of substandard units to standard or removal of the substandard units from the housing supply. Presumably, urban renewal will therefore be accomplished by market forces and strict code enforcement.

Metric Conversion

The U.S. appears to be firmly established on a course to metric conversion. The country is out of step with the rest of the world in its system of weights and measures and needs to convert to continue to participate in world markets. Conversion will probably take at least a decade. In 1976, wines and liquor were converted to metric measure. Many machine parts for export are already designed according to metric measures. Gasoline and other domestic products seem sure to follow. And somewhere down the line, land measurements and building blueprints will be in the metric system. Tables for conversion to and from the metric system are included in the Appendix of this book.

Time-Share Ownership of Condominiums

Recreational condominiums are generally expensive to purchase and maintain. Some developers provided management services to owners to rent the units out when they are not in use. This device was intended to generate income for the owners to cover carrying expenses as well as to give them some tax depreciation on such a unit in that it was being operated as an income property. But lack of demand for recreational units during recessions caused many owners severe cash flow problems. Some owners lost their equity in their units because of inability to meet debt-service and maintenance costs.

Developers in Hawaii and the Carolinas use a technique that gets around these problems. They sell the same condominium unit to many different owners on a time-share basis. For example, they build a very attractive unit for $75,000 and sell it to twenty-five different owners for $4,000 each or a total of $100,000. Each owner gets an exclusive right of use of a $100,000 condominium for fifteen days each year. That is, one owner might buy the right of use from June 16 to June 30. Under this arrangement little financing is necessary because the people buying the units pay cash from savings or personal borrowing. Time owners must pay maintenance costs for their fifteen-day period only. Decorating and remodeling is done when an owner fails to use the unit during his or her time for some reason. Other considerations are involved in this technique, but these are the essential points.

REFERENCES

Kahn, Herman, and others. *The Next 200 Years.* New York: Morrow, 1976. A brief overview of events since 1776, when the United States achieved independence and Adam Smith wrote *Wealth of Nations,* and a look into the future concerning the outlook for mankind. Generally easy to read.

McMahan, John. *Real Estate Review.* "Tomorrow's Changing Demand for Real Estate," "The Future of the Real Estate Industry; Changing Supply Patterns," "The Future of the Real Estate Industry: New Directions and New Roles." Three easy-to-read articles on what will be built and where, on the availability and cost of resources, and on the future regulation and rules of participants in the real estate industry.

Warner, Arthur E. *Continuing Education in Real Estate: A Survey of Current Status and Evaluation of Future Needs.* Columbia, S.C.: Center for Real Estate and Urban Economic Studies, University of South Carolina. An overview of continuing educational requirements for licensing, with a chapter pertaining to requirements in accounting and law.

SEVEN

APPENDICES

General Real Estate Information

A–1
REAL ESTATE SALES
TRANSACTION CHECKLIST

Facts to Ascertain before Drawing a Contract of Sale

1. Date of contract.
2. Name and address of seller.
3. Is seller a citizen, of full age, and competent?
4. Name of seller's spouse and whether that person is of full age.
5. Name and residence of purchaser.
6. Description of the property.
7. The purchase price.
   (a) Amount to be paid on signing contract.
   (b) Amount to be paid on delivery of deed.
   (c) Existing mortgage or mortgages and details thereof.
   (d) Purchase money mortgage, if any, and details thereof.
8. What kind of deed is to be delivered: full covenant, quitclaim, or bargain and sale?

9. What agreement has been made with reference to any specific personal property—i.e., gas ranges, heaters, machinery, partitions, fixtures, coal, wood, window shades, screens, carpets, rugs, and hangings?

10. Is purchaser to assume the mortgage or take the property subject to it?

11. Are any exceptions or reservations to be inserted?

12. Are any special clauses to be inserted?

13. Stipulations and agreements with reference to tenancies and rights of persons in possession, including compliance with any governmental regulations in force.

14. Stipulations and agreements, if any, to be inserted with reference to the state of facts a survey would show—i.e., party walls, encroachments, easements, and so forth.

15. What items are to be adjusted on the closing of title?

16. Name of the broker who brought about the sale, his or her address, the amount of commission and who is to pay it, and whether or not a clause covering the foregoing facts is to be inserted in the contract.

17. Are any alterations or changes being made, or have they been made, in street lines, name, or grade?

18. Are condemnations or assessment proceedings contemplated or pending, or has an award been made?

19. Who is to draw the purchase-money mortgage and who is to pay the expense thereof?

20. Are there any covenants, restrictions, and consents affecting the title?

21. What stipulation or agreement is to be made with reference to violations of sanitation laws, building code, or the like?

22. The place and date on which the title is to be closed.

23. Is time to be of the essence in the contract?

24. Are any alterations to be made in the premises between the date of the contract and the date of closing?

25. Amount of fire and hazard insurance, payment of premium, and rights and obligations of parties in case of fire or damage to premises from other causes during the contract period.

Upon the Closing of Title, the Seller Should be Prepared with the Following

1. Seller's copy of the contract.

2. The latest receipted bills for taxes, water, and assessments.

3. Latest possible meter readings of water, gas, and electric utilities.

4. Receipts for last payment of interest on mortgages.

5. Originals and certificates of all fire, liability, and other insurance policies.

6. Estoppel certificates from the holder of any mortgage that has been reduced, showing the amount due and the date to which interest is paid.

7. Any subordination agreements that may be called for in the contract.

8. Satisfaction pieces of mechanic's liens, chattel mortgages, judgments, or mortgages that are to be paid at or before the closing.

9. List of names of tenants, amounts of rents paid and unpaid, dates when rents are due, and assignment of unpaid rents.

10. Assignment of leases.

11. Letters to tenants to pay all subsequent rent to the purchaser.

12. Affidavit of title.

13. Authority to execute deed if the seller is acting through an agent.

14. Bill of sale of personal property covered by the contract.

15. Seller's last deed.

16. Any unrecorded instruments that affect the title, including extension agreements.

17. Deed and other instruments that the seller is to deliver or prepare.

Upon the Closing of Title, the Purchaser Should Do the Following

1. Have purchaser's copy of contract.

2. Obtain abstract of title.

3. Obtain report of title.

4. Examine deed to see if it conforms to the contract.

5. Compare description.

6. See that deed is properly executed.

7. Have sufficient cash or certified checks to make payments required by contract.

8. See that all liens that must be removed are properly disposed of.

9. Obtain names and details with reference to tenants and rents.

10. Obtain assignment of unpaid rents and assignment of leases.

11. Obtain and examine estoppel certificates with reference to mortgages that have been reduced.

12. Obtain letter to tenants.

    Obtain affidavit of title.

14. Obtain and examine authority if the seller acts through an agent.

15. Obtain bill of sale of personal property covered by the contract.

16. Examine survey.

17. See if report of title shows any covenants, restrictions, or consents affecting the title or use of the property.

18. Have bills for any unpaid tax, utilities, or assessments, and have interest computed up to the date of closing.

19. Make adjustments as called for in the contract.

20. Examine purchase-money mortgage and duly execute same.

21. Have damage award, if any, for public improvements assigned to the purchaser.

22. Obtain any unrecorded instruments affecting the title including extension agreements.

A–2
CODE OF ETHICS
NATIONAL ASSOCIATION
OF REALTORS®*

Revised and approved by the delegate body of the Association at its 67th annual convention, November 14, 1974.

PREAMBLE . . . Under all is the land. Upon its wise utilization and widely allocated ownership depend the survival and growth of free institutions and of our civilization. The REALTOR® should recognize that the interests of the nation and its citizens require the highest and best use of the land and the widest distribution of land ownership. They require the creation of adequate housing, the building of functioning cities, the development of productive industries and farms, and the preservation of a healthful environment.

Such interests impose obligations beyond those of ordinary commerce. They impose grave social responsibility and a patriotic duty to which the REALTOR® should dedicate himself, and for which he should be diligent in preparing himself. The REALTOR®, therefore, is zealous to maintain and improve the standards of his calling and shares with his fellow-REALTORS® a common responsibility for its integrity and honor. The term REALTOR® has come to connote competency, fairness, and high integrity resulting from adherence to a lofty ideal of moral conduct in business relations. No inducement of profit and no instruction from clients ever can justify departure from this ideal.

In the interpretation of his obligation, a REALTOR® can take no safer guide than that which has been handed down through the centuries, embodied in the Golden Rule, "Whatsoever ye would that men should do to you, do ye even so to them."

Accepting this standard as his own, every REALTOR® pledges himself to observe its spirit in all of his activities and to conduct his business in accordance with the tenets set forth below.

ARTICLE 1. The REALTOR® should keep himself informed on matters affecting real estate in his community, the state, and nation so that he may be able to contribute responsibly to public thinking on such matters.

ARTICLE 2. In justice to those who place their interests in his care, the REALTOR® should endeavor always to be informed regarding laws, proposed legislation, governmental regulations, public policies, and current market conditions in order to be in a position to advise his clients properly.

ARTICLE 3. It is the duty of the REALTOR® to protect the public against fraud, misrepresentation, and unethical practices in real estate transactions. He should endeavor to eliminate in his community any practices which could be damaging to the public or bring discredit to the real estate profession. The REALTOR® should assist the governmental agency charged with regulating the practices of brokers and salesmen in his state.

ARTICLE 4. The REALTOR® should seek no unfair advantage over other REALTORS® and should conduct his business so as to avoid controversies with other REALTORS®.

ARTICLE 5. In the best interests of society, of his associates, and his own business, the REALTOR® should willingly share with other REALTORS® the lessons of his experience and study for the benefit of the public, and should be loyal to the Board of REALTORS® of his community and active in its work.

ARTICLE 6. To prevent dissension and misunderstanding and to assure better service to the owner, the REALTOR® should urge the exclusive listing of property unless contrary to the best interest of the owner.

ARTICLE 7. In accepting employment as an agent, the REALTOR® pledges himself to protect and promote the interests of the client. This obligation of absolute fidelity to the client's interests is primary, but it does not relieve the REALTOR® of the obligation to treat fairly all parties to the transaction.

ARTICLE 8. The REALTOR® shall not accept compensation from more than one party, even if permitted by law, without the full knowledge of all parties to the transaction.

ARTICLE 9. The REALTOR® shall avoid exaggeration, misrepresentation, or concealment of pertinent facts. He has an affirmative obligation to discover adverse factors that a reasonably competent and diligent investigation would disclose.

ARTICLE 10. The REALTOR® shall not deny equal services to any person for reasons of race, creed, sex, or country of national origin. The REALTOR® shall not be a party to any plan or agreement to discriminate against a person or persons on the basis of race, creed, sex, or country of national origin.

ARTICLE 11. A REALTOR® is expected to provide a level of competent service in keeping with the Standards of Practice in those fields in which the REALTOR® customarily engages.

The REALTOR® shall not undertake to provide specialized professional services concerning a type of property or service that is outside his field of competence unless he engages the assistance of one who is competent on such types of property or service, or unless the facts are fully disclosed to the client. Any person engaged to provide such assistance shall be so identified to the client and his contribution to the assignment should be set forth.

The REALTOR® shall refer to the Standards of Practice of the National Association as to the degree of competence that a client has a right to expect the REALTOR® to possess, taking into consideration the complexity of the problem, the availability of expert assistance, and the opportunities for experience available to the REALTOR®.

ARTICLE 12. The REALTOR® shall not undertake to provide professional services concerning a property or its value where he has a present or contemplated interest unless such interest is specifically disclosed to all affected parties.

ARTICLE 13. The REALTOR® shall not acquire an interest in or buy for himself, any member of his immediate family, his firm or any member thereof, or any entity in which he has a substantial ownership interest, property listed with him, without making the true position known to the listing owner. In selling property owned by himself, or in which he has any interest, the REALTOR® shall reveal the facts of his ownership or interest to the purchaser.

ARTICLE 14. In the event of a controversy between REALTORS® associated with different firms, arising out of their relationship as REALTORS®, the REALTORS® shall submit the dispute to arbitration in accordance with the regulations of their board or boards rather than litigate the matter.

ARTICLE 15. If a REALTOR® is charged with unethical practice or is asked to present evidence in any disciplinary proceeding or investigation, he shall place all pertinent facts before the proper tribunal of the member board or affiliated institute, society, or council of which he is a member.

ARTICLE 16. When acting as agent, the REALTOR® shall not accept any commission, rebate, or profit on expenditures made for his principal-owner, without the principal's knowledge and consent.

ARTICLE 17. The REALTOR® shall not engage in activities that constitute the unauthorized practice of law and shall recommend that legal counsel be obtained when the interest of any party to the transaction requires it.

ARTICLE 18. The REALTOR® shall keep in a special account in an appropriate financial institution, separated from his own funds, monies coming into his possession in trust for other persons, such as escrows, trust funds, clients' monies, and other like items.

ARTICLE 19. The REALTOR® shall be careful at all times to present a true picture in his advertising and representations to the public. He shall neither advertise without disclosing his name nor permit any person associated with him to use individual names or telephone numbers, unless such person's connection with the REALTOR® is obvious in the advertisement.

ARTICLE 20. The REALTOR®, for the protection of all parties, shall see that financial obligations and commitments regarding real estate transactions are in writing, expressing the exact agreement of the parties. A copy of each agreement shall be furnished to each party upon his signing such agreement.

ARTICLE 21. The REALTOR® shall not engage in any practice or take any action inconsistent with the agency of another REALTOR®.

ARTICLE 22. In the sale of property which is exclusively listed with a REALTOR®, the REALTOR® shall utilize the services of other brokers upon mutually agreed upon terms when it is in the best interests of the client.

Negotiations concerning property which is listed exclusively shall be carried on with the listing broker, not with the owner, except with the consent of the listing broker.

ARTICLE 23. The REALTOR® shall not publicly disparage the business practice of a competitor nor volunteer an opinion of a competitor's transaction. If his opinion is sought and if the REALTOR® deems it appropriate to respond, such opinion shall be rendered with strict professional integrity and courtesy.

ARTICLE 24. The REALTOR® shall not directly or indirectly solicit the services or affiliation of an employee or independent contractor in the organization of another REALTOR® without prior notice to said REALTOR®.

Where the word REALTOR® is used in this Code and Preamble, it shall be deemed to include REALTOR®-ASSOCIATE. Pronouns shall be considered to include REALTORS® and REALTOR®-ASSOCIATES of both genders.

The Code of Ethics was adopted in 1913. Amended at the Annual Convention in 1924, 1928, 1950, 1951, 1952, 1955, 1956, 1961, 1962, and 1974.

A–3
LAND MEASURES
AND CONVERSION TABLES

Rules for Measuring Land

The following rules will be found of service in many cases that may arise in land parceling, particularly in the computation of areas:

To find the area of a four-sided tract, whose sides are perpendicular to each other (called a rectangle): Multiply the length by the width. The product will be the area.

To find the area of a four-sided tract, whose opposite sides are parallel, but whose angles are not necessarily right angles (called a parallelogram): Multiply the base by the perpendicular height. The product will be the area.

To find the area of a three-sided tract (called a triangle): Multiply the base by half of the perpendicular height. The product will be the area.

To find the area of a four-sided tract, having two of its sides parallel (called a trapezoid): Multiply half the sum of the two parallel sides by the perpendicular distance between these sides. The product will be the area.

To ascertain the contents of a tract bounded by four straight lines, and in which no two lines are parallel to each other, the length of each line is known, and the two opposite angles are supplements of each other (called a trapezium): Add all the four sides together, and halve their sum; subtract separately each side from that sum; multiply the four remainders thus obtained continually together, and extract the square root of the last product. The result will be the contents or area of the tract. Or divide the tract by lines into triangles and trapezoids, and ascertain and add together their several areas, the sum of which will be the area of the tract proposed.

Land bounded by an irregular line, such as a stream of water or a winding road, is measured as follows. Draw a base line as near as practicable to the actual line of the road or stream; at different places in the base line, equidistant from each other, take the distance to the line of the stream or road. Add the sum of all the intermediate lines (or breadths) to half the sum of the first breadth and the last breadth, and multiply the sum thus obtained by the common distance between the breadths. The result will be the area of the land in question.

Should the breadths be measured at unequal distances on the base line, add all the breadths together, and divide their amount by the number of breadths for the mean breadth, and multiply the quotient so obtained by the length of the base line.

MEASUREMENT TABLES

Table of Linear Measure

12 inches (in.)	= 1 foot	ft.
3 feet	= 1 yard	yd.
5½ yards or 16½ feet	= 1 rod	rd.
40 rods	= 1 furlong	fur.
8 furlongs, 320 rods, or 5,280 feet	= 1 statute mile	mi.

Table of Area Measure

144 square inches (sq. in.)	= 1 square foot	sq. ft.
9 square feet	= 1 square yard	sq. yd.
30¼ square yards	= 1 square rod	sq. rd.
40 square rods	= 1 rood	R.
4 rods or 43,560 square feet	= 1 acre	A.
640 acres	= 1 square mile	sq. mi.

Table of Surveyor's Linear Measure

7.92 inches (in.)	= 1 link	l.
25 links	= 1 rod	rd.
4 rods or 66 feet	= 1 chain	ch.
80 chains	= 1 mile	mi.

Table of Surveyor's Area Measures

625 square links (sq. l.)	= 1 pole	P.
16 poles	= 1 square chain	sq. ch.
10 square chains	= 1 acre	A.
640 acres	= 1 square mile	sq. mi.
36 square miles (6 mi. square)	= 1 township	Tp.

Note: 1 acre in square form equals 208.71 feet on each side.

CONVERSION TO METRIC MEASURES

U.S. Unit	Symbol	Multiply by	Symbol	Metric Unit
LENGTH				
inch	in.	2.540	cm.	centimeter
feet	ft.	0.3048	m.	meter
yard	yd.	0.9144	m.	meter
rod	rd.	5.0292	m.	meter
mile	mi.	1.609	km.	kilometer
AREA				
square inch	in.^{2}	6.5416	cm.^{2}	square centimeter
square foot	ft.^{2}	0.0929	m.^{2}	square meter
square yard	yd.^{2}	0.836	m.^{2}	square meter
acre	A.	0.4047	ha.	hectares (10,000 m.^{2})
square mile	mi.^{2}	2.590	km.^{2}	square kilometer
VOLUME				
cubic inch	in.^{3}	16.387	cm.^{3}	cubic centimeters
cubic foot	ft.^{3}	0.028	m.^{3}	cubic meters
cubic yard	yd.^{3}	0.765	m.^{3}	cubic meters
WEIGHT				
ounce	oz.	28.350	g.	gram
pound	lb.	0.4536	kg.	kllogram
ton, short (2,000 lbs.)	ton	0.9072	t.	tonnes (1,000 kg.)

CONVERSION FROM METRIC MEASURES

Metric Unit	Symbol	Multiply by	Symbol	U.S. Unit
LENGTH				
millimeter	mm.	0.0394	in.	inch
centimeter	cm.	0.3937	in.	inch
meter	m.	3.2808	ft.	foot
meter	m.	1.0936	yd.	yard
kilometer	km.	0.6213	mi.	mile

Metric Unit	Symbol	Multiply by	Symbol	U.S. Unit
AREA				
square centimeter	cm.^{2}	0.155	in.^{2}	square inch
square meter	m.^{2}	1.196	yd.^{2}	square yard
hectares (10,000 m.^{2})	ha.	2.471	A.	acre
square kilometer	km.^{2}	0.386	mi.^{2}	square mile
VOLUME				
cubic centimeters	cm.^{3}	0.061	in.^{3}	cubic inch
cubic meters	m.^{3}	35.714	ft.^{3}	cubic foot
cubic meters	m.^{3}	1.307	yd.^{3}	cubic yard
WEIGHT				
gram	g.	0.035	oz.	ounce
kilogram	kg.	2.2046	lb.	pound
tonnes (1,000 kg.)	t.	1.1023	ton	short ton

APPENDIX A–4
SAMPLE MORTGAGE LOAN
AMORTIZATION SCHEDULE

$10,000 MORTGAGE LOAN AMORTIZATION SCHEDULE

INTEREST RATE = 9 PERCENT
TERM = 25 YEARS = 300 MONTHS
LEVEL MONTHLY PAYMENT = $83.92

Payment Number	Amount of Interest	Amount of Principal Repaid	Principal Balance End of Period
1	$75.000	$ 8.92	$9991.08
2	74.9331	8.9869	9982.09
3	74.8657	9.0543	9973.04
4	74.7978	9.12221	9963.92
5	74.7294	9.19063	9954.73
6	74.6604	9.25956	9945.47
7	74.591	9.329	9936.14
8	74.521	9.39897	9926.74
9	74.4505	9.46946	9917.27
10	74.3795	9.54048	9907.73
11	74.308	9.61204	9898.12
12	74.2359	9.68413	9888.43
13	74.1632	9.75676	9878.68
14	74.0901	9.82993	9868.85
15	74.0163	9.90366	9858.94
16	73.9421	9.97794	9848.96
17	73.8672	10.0528	9838.91
18	73.7918	10.1282	9828.78

Payment Number	Amount of Interest	Amount of Principal Repaid	Principal Balance End of Period
19	73.7159	10.2041	9818.58
20	73.6393	10.2807	9808.30
21	73.5622	10.3578	9797.94
22	73.4846	10.4354	9787.51
23	73.4063	10.5137	9776.99
24	73.3274	10.5926	9766.40
25	73.248	10.672	9755.73
26	73.168	10.752	9744.97
27	73.0873	10.8327	9734.14
28	73.0061	10.9139	9723.23
29	72.9242	10.9958	9712.23
30	72.8417	11.0783	9701.15
31	72.7587	11.1613	9689.99
32	72.6749	11.2451	9678.75
33	72.5906	11.3294	9667.42
34	72.5056	11.4144	9656.00
35	72.42	11.50	9644.50
36	72.3338	11.5862	9632.92
37	72.2469	11.6731	9621.25
38	72.1593	11.7607	9609.48
39	72.0711	11.8489	9597.64
40	71.9823	11.9377	9585.70
41	71.8927	12.0273	9573.67
42	71.8025	12.1175	9561.55
43	71.7116	12.2084	9549.34
44	71.6201	12.2999	9537.04
45	71.5278	12.3922	9524.65
46	71.4349	12.4851	9512.17
47	71.3413	12.5787	9499.59
48	71.2469	12.6731	9486.92
49	71.1519	12.7681	9474.15
50	71.0561	12.8639	9461.28
51	70.9596	12.9604	9448.32
52	70.8624	13.0576	9435.27
53	70.7645	13.1555	9422.11
54	70.6658	13.2542	9408.86
55	70.5664	13.3536	9395.50
56	70.4663	13.4537	9382.05
57	70.3654	13.5546	9368.49
58	70.2637	13.6563	9354.84
59	70.1613	13.7587	9341.08
60	70.0581	13.8619	9327.22
61	69.9541	13.9659	9313.25
62	69.8494	14.0706	9299.18
63	69.7439	14.1761	9285.00
64	69.6375	14.2825	9270.72
65	69.5304	14.3896	9256.33
66	69.4225	14.4975	9241.84
67	69.3138	14.6062	9227.23
68	69.2042	14.7158	9212.51

Payment Number	Amount of Interest	Amount of Principal Repaid	Principal Balance End of Period
69	69.0938	14.8262	9197.69
70	68.9827	14.9373	9182.75
71	68.8706	15.0494	9167.70
72	68.7578	15.1623	9152.54
73	68.644	15.276	9137.26
74	68.5295	15.3905	9121.87
75	68.414	15.506	9106.37
76	68.2977	15.6223	9090.74
77	68.1806	15.7394	9075.00
78	68.0625	15.8575	9059.15
79	67.9436	15.9764	9043.17
80	67.8238	16.0962	9027.07
81	67.7031	16.2169	9010.86
82	67.5814	16.3386	8994.52
83	67.4589	16.4611	8978.06
84	67.3354	16.5846	8961.47
85	67.211	16.709	8944.76
86	67.0857	16.8343	8927.93
87	66.9595	16.9605	8910.97
88	66.8323	17.0877	8893.88
89	66.7041	17.2159	8876.66
90	66.575	17.345	8859.32
91	66.4449	17.4751	8841.84
92	66.3138	17.6062	8824.24
93	66.1818	17.7382	8806.50
94	66.0488	17.8712	8788.63
95	65.9147	18.0053	8770.62
96	65.7797	18.1403	8752.48
97	65.6436	18.2764	8734.21
98	65.5066	18.4134	8715.79
99	65.3685	18.5515	8697.24
100	65.2293	18.6907	8678.55
101	65.0891	18.8309	8659.72
102	64.9479	18.9721	8640.75
103	64.8056	19.1144	8621.63
104	64.6623	19.2577	8602.38
105	64.5178	19.4022	8582.97
106	64.3723	19.5477	8563.43
107	64.2257	19.6943	8543.73
108	64.078	19.842	8523.89
109	63.9292	19.9908	8503.90
110	63.7792	20.1408	8483.76
111	63.6282	20.2918	8463.47
112	63.476	20.444	8443.02
113	63.3227	20.5973	8422.43
114	63.1682	20.7518	8401.67
115	63.0126	20.9074	8380.77
116	62.8557	21.0643	8359.70
117	62.6978	21.2222	8338.48
118	62.5386	21.3814	8317.10

Payment Number	Amount of Interest	Amount of Principal Repaid	Principal Balance End of Period
119	62.3782	21.5418	8295.56
120	62.2167	21.7033	8273.85
121	62.0539	21.8661	8251.99
122	61.8899	22.0301	8229.96
123	61.7247	22.1953	8207.76
124	61.5582	22.3618	8185.40
125	61.3905	22.5295	8162.87
126	61.2215	22.6985	8140.17
127	61.0513	22.8687	8117.30
128	60.8798	23.0402	8094.26
129	60.707	23.213	8071.05
130	60.5329	23.3871	8047.66
131	60.3575	23.5625	8024.10
132	60.1808	23.7392	8000.36
133	60.0027	23.9173	7976.44
134	59.8233	24.0967	7952.35
135	59.6426	24.2774	7928.07
136	59.4605	24.4595	7903.61
137	59.2771	24.6429	7878.97
138	59.0923	24.8277	7854.14
139	58.906	25.014	7829.13
140	58.7184	25.2016	7803.92
141	58.5294	25.3906	7778.53
142	58.339	25.581	7752.95
143	58.1471	25.7729	7727.18
144	57.9538	25.9662	7701.21
145	57.7591	26.1609	7675.05
146	57.5629	26.3571	7648.70
147	57.3652	26.5548	7622.14
148	57.1661	26.7539	7595.39
149	56.9654	26.9546	7568.43
150	56.7632	27.1568	7541.28
151	56.5596	27.3604	7513.92
152	56.3544	27.5656	7486.35
153	56.1476	27.7724	7458.58
154	55.9393	27.9807	7430.60
155	55.7295	28.1905	7402.41
156	55.518	28.402	7374.00
157	55.305	28.615	7345.39
158	55.0904	28.8296	7316.56
159	54.8742	29.0458	7287.51
160	54.6564	29.2636	7258.25
161	54.4369	29.4831	7228.77
162	54.2157	29.7043	7199.06
163	53.993	29.927	7169.14
164	53.7685	30.1515	7138.98
165	53.5424	30.3776	7108.61
166	53.3145	30.6055	7078.00
167	53.085	30.835	7047.17
168	52.8537	31.0663	7016.10

Payment Number	Amount of Interest	Amount of Principal Repaid	Principal Balance End of Period
169	52.6207	31.2993	6984.80
170	52.386	31.534	6953.27
171	52.1495	31.7705	6921.50
172	51.9112	32.0088	6889.49
173	51.6712	32.2488	6857.24
174	51.4293	32.4907	6824.75
175	51.1856	32.7344	6792.01
176	50.9401	32.9799	6759.03
177	50.6927	33.2273	6725.81
178	50.4435	33.4765	6692.33
179	50.1925	33.7275	6658.60
180	49.9395	33.9805	6624.62
181	49.6847	34.2353	6590.39
182	49.4279	34.4921	6555.89
183	49.1692	34.7508	6521.14
184	48.9086	35.0114	6486.13
185	48.646	35.274	6450.86
186	48.3814	35.5386	6415.32
187	48.1149	35.8051	6379.51
188	47.8464	36.0736	6343.44
189	47.5758	36.3442	6307.10
190	47.3032	36.6168	6270.48
191	47.0286	36.8914	6233.59
192	46.7519	37.1681	6196.42
193	46.4731	37.4469	6158.97
194	46.1923	37.7277	6121.25
195	45.9093	38.0107	6083.23
190	45.6243	38.2957	6044.94
197	45.337	38.583	6006.36
198	45.0477	38.8723	5967.48
199	44.7561	39.1639	5928.32
200	44.4624	39.4576	5888.86
201	44.1665	39.7535	5849.11
202	43.8683	40.0517	5809.06
203	43.5679	40.3521	5768.70
204	43.2653	40.6547	5728.05
205	42.9604	40.9596	5687.09
206	42.6532	41.2668	5645.82
207	42.3437	41.5763	5604.25
208	42.0319	41.8881	5562.36
209	41.7177	42.2023	5520.16
210	41.4012	42.5188	5477.64
211	41.0823	42.8377	5434.80
212	40.761	43.159	5391.64
213	40.4373	43.4827	5348.16
214	40.1112	43.8088	5304.35
215	39.7826	44.1374	5260.21
216	39.4516	44.4684	5215.74
217	39.1181	44.8019	5170.94
218	38.7821	45.1379	5125.80

Payment Number	Amount of Interest	Amount of Principal Repaid	Principal Balance End of Period
219	38.4435	45.4765	5080.33
220	38.1025	45.8175	5034.51
221	37.7588	46.1612	4988.35
222	37.4126	46.5074	4941.84
223	37.0638	46.8562	4894.99
224	36.7124	47.2076	4847.78
225	36.3583	47.5617	4800.22
226	36.0016	47.9184	4752.30
227	35.6422	48.2778	4704.02
228	35.2802	48.6398	4655.38
229	34.9154	49.0046	4606.38
230	34.5478	49.3722	4557.00
231	34.1775	49.7425	4507.26
232	33.8045	50.1155	4457.15
233	33.4286	50.4914	4406.65
234	33.0499	50.8701	4355.78
235	32.6684	51.2516	4304.53
236	32.284	51.636	4252.90
237	31.8967	52.0233	4200.87
238	31.5065	52.4135	4148.46
239	31.1134	52.8066	4095.65
240	30.7174	53.2026	4042.45
241	30.3184	53.6016	3988.85
242	29.9164	54.0036	3934.85
243	29.5113	54.4087	3880.44
244	29.1033	54.8167	3825.62
245	28.6921	55.2279	3770.39
246	28.2779	55.6421	3714.75
247	27.8606	56.0594	3658.69
248	27.4402	56.4798	3602.21
249	27.0166	56.9034	3545.31
250	26.5898	57.3302	3487.98
251	26.1598	57.7602	3430.22
252	25.7266	58.1934	3372.02
253	25.2902	58.6298	3313.39
254	24.8505	59.0695	3254.32
255	24.4074	59.5126	3194.81
256	23.9611	59.9589	3134.85
257	23.5114	60.4086	3074.44
258	23.0583	60.8617	3013.58
259	22.6019	61.3181	2952.26
260	22.142	61.778	2890.49
261	21.6786	62.2414	2828.24
262	21.2118	62.7082	2765.54
263	20.7415	63.1785	2702.36
264	20.2677	63.6523	2638.71
265	19.7903	64.1297	2574.58
266	19.3093	64.6107	2509.97
267	18.8247	65.0953	2444.87
268	18.3365	65.5835	2379.29

$10,000 MORTGAGE LOAN AMORTIZATION SCHEDULE (continued)

Payment Number	Amount of Interest	Amount of Principal Repaid	Principal Balance End of Period
269	17.8447	66.0753	2313.21
270	17.3491	66.5709	2246.64
271	16.8498	67.0702	2179.57
272	16.3468	67.5732	2112.00
273	15.84	68.08	2043.92
274	15.3294	68.5906	1975.33
275	14.8149	69.1051	1906.22
276	14.2967	69.6233	1836.60
277	13.7745	70.1455	1766.45
278	13.2484	70.6716	1695.78
279	12.7184	71.2016	1624.58
280	12.1843	71.7357	1552.84
281	11.6463	72.2737	1480.57
282	11.1043	72.8157	1407.75
283	10.5582	73.3618	1334.39
284	10.0079	73.9121	1260.48
285	9.4536	74.4664	1186.01
286	8.89511	75.0249	1110.99
287	8.33242	75.5876	1035.40
288	7.76551	76.1545	959.247
289	7.19435	76.7256	882.522
290	6.61891	77.3011	805.22
291	6.03915	77.8808	727.34
292	5.45505	78.465	648.875
293	4.86656	79.0534	569.821
294	4.27366	79.6463	490.175
295	3.67631	80.2437	409.931
296	3.07448	80.8455	329.086
297	2.46814	81.4519	247.634
298	1.85725	82.0627	165.571
299	1.24178	82.6782	82.8928
300	0.621696	82.8928	0
LAST PAYMENT IS	83.5145		

A–5
FORMS AND DOCUMENTS

These forms are typical of those used in real estate transactions. In most cases, blanks have been completed to give a clearer idea of the use of the forms. However, the completed forms are intended only as examples and not as having applicability in any particular state. We extend particular appreciation to the Stevens-Ness Law Publishing Company for their permission to use many of the forms reproduced below as well as several used in the text.

The following forms are included in this appendix:

1. Contract between real estate broker and salesperson
2. Option to purchase

661

3. Binder
4. Contract for deed (land contract)
5. Acknowledgment of act or deed
6. Affidavit or voluntary written declaration sworn to before a notary public.
7. Assignment of a contract by direct endorsement on the contract
8. Satisfaction of mortgage

FIGURE A–1

Contract between Real Estate Broker and Salesperson

THIS AGREEMENT, Made and entered into this 10th day of October , 19 78 , between Ivan Everready, Realtor , doing business as Everready Realty Company , hereinafter called the "broker," and Harvey Hustle , hereinafter called the "salesman";

WITNESSETH:

The broker is duly registered, licensed and actively engaged in business as a real estate broker under the laws of the state of Anystate with his principal office in said state at No. 41 East Third , City of Urbandale ; said office is equipped with telephone, furnishings and facilities suitable for the said business.

The salesman is a duly registered real estate salesperson
(State whether real estate salesman, associate broker, holder of a temporary permit or other appropriate description.)
under the laws of said state and is duly authorized to deal with the public as a real estate salesman.

NOW, THEREFORE, in view of the premises and in consideration of the mutual promises of the parties hereinafter set forth, the parties hereto agree:

1. From the date hereof and until the termination of this agreement, the parties hereto hereby do associate themselves as broker and salesman. With respect to the clients and customers of the broker and all other persons, the salesman shall be a sub-agent only with powers limited by this agreement. It is expressly understood and agreed that the salesman is and shall be an independent contractor and not an employee, partner or joint adventurer with the broker.

2. The broker agrees to make all his listings, both current and future, available to the salesman, except those which the broker temporarily in his sole discretion may wish some other salesman to handle, and agrees to cooperate with the salesman and to assist him in his work by advice and instruction. The broker further agrees that the salesman may share with other salesmen and employees the facilities of the broker's office.

3. The salesman agrees to work diligently and use his best efforts in the name of the broker to sell, exchange, lease and rent listed properties, to purchase and take options on real estate for the broker's clients, to serve the real estate needs of the broker's clients and customers, to obtain additional listings and customers for the broker and

otherwise to promote the broker's business to the end that each of the parties hereto may derive the greatest profit possible from their association. The salesman agrees to conduct his business and regulate his habits so as to maintain his own reputation in the community and to increase the good will and reputation of the broker.

4. Both parties hereto agree to conform to and abide by all laws, rules, regulations and codes of ethics that are binding upon or applicable to real estate brokers and salesmen in their dealings with each other and with the public and other brokers and salesmen.

5. The commissions to be charged for services performed shall be at the rates generally prevalent in the community, except in those cases where in particular transactions the broker may enter into special contracts relative to items which he undertakes to handle. It is expressly understood that the broker in his discretion may arrange with other brokers to share commissions on the sale of specific properties. The parties hereto recognize that some transactions may present peculiar difficulties which require the services of surveyors, experts, specialists, accountants, attorneys, the use of the long distance telephone and telegraphic service or other expense, for the cost of which the broker is not reimbursed by the client or customer; such expenses on any transaction in which a commission is earned shall be deemed a part of the cost of that transaction and paid out of the commission thereon before any division thereof. In each transaction where services rendered by the salesman shall result in the earning by the broker of a commission, or part thereof, there shall first be deducted from the commission collected by the broker on that particular transaction the listing fee, if any is due, mentioned in the 6th paragraph of this agreement, as well as the unreimbursed expenses of that transaction hereinabove described, and the following percentage of the balance of the commission collected by the broker shall be paid to the salesman:

Except as provided in the 8th paragraph hereof, the expense of surveyors, experts, specialists, accountants, attorneys, telegrams and telephone tolls on transactions in which a commission is *not* earned shall be paid by the broker. The expense of attorney's fees and costs which are incurred in the collection of or attempts to collect a commission in which the salesman is entitled to a share shall be paid by the parties hereto in the same proportion as above provided for the division of commissions on that particular transaction. Where two or more salesmen participate in any transaction in which a commission is earned, or claim to have done so, the salesman's said percentage or share of the commission shall accrue to the participating salesman and be divided according to agreement between them; if there is no such agreement, the share of each participating salesman shall be determined by arbitration as hereinafter provided. In those cases where the property of the broker is sold through the efforts of the salesman, the compensation of the salesman shall be agreed upon by the broker and the salesman. In those cases where property of the salesman is sold through the broker's organization, the salesman shall pay to the broker a sum equal to one-half of the regular commission on the selling price of the property so sold. In no case shall the broker be liable to the salesman for any commission, or part thereof (except in those transactions involving the broker's own property), unless the same shall have been collected by the broker. Settlements between the broker and salesman as to commissions earned and collected shall be made at the close of each transaction except as to deferred commissions or collections, on which a written accounting shall be rendered and settlement made on or before the 10th day of each month for all receipts of the previous month.

6. Where the salesman takes additional listings and if the property so listed is sold (by whomsoever sold) while this contract is in force and effect and the commission is collected by the broker, the salesman shall be entitled to a listing fee equal to the following percentages of the commission so collected:

```
intra office - 33-1/3%

inter office - 25%
```

the salesman recognizes that other salesmen in the broker's organization may become entitled to a listing fee on the sale of properties listed by them.

7. The parties further agree that on any deal when the seller or client is unable to pay the commission, or any part thereof, in cash, the broker in his sole discretion may accept notes, mortgages or securities in lieu of cash; in any such event the broker shall not be liable to the salesman for that part of the commission represented by such notes, mortgages or securities unless and until the broker shall have realized cash thereon. Upon any such collection being made, the broker's actual out-of-pocket expense in effecting such collection shall first be deducted and retained by the broker and the salesman shall be paid his said percentage of the balance of the sums (principal and interest) collected.

8. The salesman shall have no authority to bind the broker by any promise or representation, unless specifically authorized in a particular transaction. The salesman shall have no authority to hire surveyors, experts, specialists, accountants or attorneys in any transaction or to incur the expense of telegrams or long distance telephone tolls at any time without the broker's prior written approval; such expenses incurred by the salesman without such approval shall be paid by the salesman. Except as herein provided, the salesman shall not be liable to the broker for any part of the office expense or for signs, advertising, telephones or utilities and the broker shall not be liable to the salesman for any expense incurred by the salesman.

9. All advertising shall be under the direct supervision and in the name of the broker. The salesman shall not publish any advertising under his own name in any manner, either directly or indirectly. All offers to purchase, exchange, option, rent, lease or forfeit obtained by the salesman shall be submitted immediately to the broker. Closing of all transactions shall be handled by or under the direct supervision of the broker. No option shall be taken except in the name of the broker or his nominee. Suits for commissions shall be maintained only in the name of the broker. Without the broker's written consent, the salesman shall not buy for himself, either directly or indirectly, or take options to purchase any property listed with the broker or any person associated with the broker.

10. The salesman shall have no power to forfeit or declare forfeited earnest money deposited by any purchaser, that power being expressly reserved to the broker. Should the broker declare any such deposit forfeited and if the salesman ultimately may be entitled to a share of the commission on the transaction, then in the absence of a settlement with and release from the depositor, the broker shall deposit the moneys so forfeited in his Clients Trust Account (if he has not already done so) and shall not be obligated to pay any share of the commission on that transaction to the salesman unless and until he has secured a written release from the depositor or has received assurances and security satisfactory to the broker that the salesman will return the salesman's share of the commission in the event it should ultimately be determined that the broker was not entitled to declare such forfeiture.

11. The broker shall have the right in his sole discretion at any time to cancel any deal signed up by the salesman, to release the parties thereto, to return deposits of earnest money and documents and generally to settle, adjust and compromise suits, actions, disputes and controversies in which the salesman is interested or to which he is a party, without the consent of the salesman and the salesman shall have no claim against the broker by reason of any such settlement, adjustment or compromise. In the event charges are made or a lawsuit is filed against the broker growing out of the conduct of the salesman in any transaction, the salesman agrees to pay the expense of defending against any such claims or law suits, to pay any judgments entered in such law suits and generally to save the broker harmless therefrom.

12. The salesman agrees to furnish his own transportation in his performance of this agreement; also, that at all times while this contract is in force and effect he will carry, maintain and keep in effect, at his own expense, public liability insurance insuring both the salesman and the broker against all liability for damage to person or property in connection with the use and operation of the salesman's car or cars in said business; the amount of said liability insurance shall be not less than $ 250,000 for injury to one person, $ 500,000 for injuries arising out of any one accident and $ 200,000 for property damage; satisfactory evidence that said insurance is in effect shall be furnished to the broker.

13. In case of a controversy between the salesman herein and another salesman in the broker's organization, which the parties to said controversy are unable to settle between themselves, the matters in dispute shall be submitted to arbitration in which the broker shall be the sole arbitrator; the decision of the broker in any such arbitration shall be final, binding and conclusive upon the salesmen involved in said controversy; the broker shall serve as arbitrator without compensation. In case a controversy should arise between the parties hereto relative to any matter arising out of this contract, which they are unable to settle between themselves, the matters in dispute shall be submitted to arbitration before a board of three arbitrators; each of the parties hereto shall select one arbitrator and the two thus chosen shall select the third arbitrator; the decision of the majority of said board of arbitration shall be final, binding and conclusive upon all parties hereto. The expense of said arbitration, including the fees of the arbitrators, shall be paid by the party or parties to such controversy as the majority of said board of arbitration may designate. In any arbitration under this paragraph each party to the controversy shall have the right to appear in person or by attorney and to summon and examine witnesses.

14. This contract and the association created hereby may be terminated by either party hereto for any reason at any time upon notice given to the other, but the right of the salesman to any commission which accrued prior to said notice shall not be divested by the termination thereof. The fact that arbitration proceedings are pending pursuant to the preceding paragraph at the time said notice is given shall not preclude either party hereto from canceling the agreement effective forthwith. Upon such termination, (1) the salesman shall return to the broker all writings, documents and property belonging to the broker and (2) all listings of property procured by the salesman shall become the absolute property of the broker without further liability for listing commissions. After the termination of this contract, the salesman shall not use to his own advantage or to the advantage of any other person or corporation, without the broker's written consent, any information gained from the files or business of the broker.

15. If the salesman is a licensed associate broker, he agrees that while this contract is in effect he will not engage in any act in the capacity of broker.

16.

17. In construing this agreement, it is understood that the broker herein may be more than one person or a corporation and that, therefore, if the context so requires, the singular pronoun shall be taken to mean and include the plural, the masculine, the feminine and the neuter and that generally all grammatical changes shall be made, assumed and implied to make the provisions hereof apply equally to corporations and to more than one individual.

IN WITNESS WHEREOF, the parties hereto have executed these presents in duplicate on this, the day and year first above written.

/s/Ivan Everready

_____
Broker

/s/Harvey Hustle

_____
Salesman

AGREEMENT

Between Real Estate Broker and Salesman

(FORM No. 650)

Dated ...., 19......

STEVENS-NESS LAW PUB. CO., PORTLAND, ORE.

781

FORM No. 74—OPTION—No Commission to Agent.   STEVENS-NESS LAW PUBLISHING CO., PORTLAND, OR. 97

TT

OPTION

KNOW ALL MEN BY THESE PRESENTS, That Wendy Welloff, Unit 77, Condominum Towers, Urbandale, Anystate 00000 hereinafter called owner, in consideration of Dollars ($ 20,000.00) to owner paid by P. O. Tential , hereinafter called the purchaser, has given and granted and does hereby give and grant unto the said purchaser, his executors, administrators and assigns, the sole, exclusive and irrevocable option to and including midnight on 30th day of November , 19 81 , to purchase the following described property in the city of Urbandale , County of Rustic , State of Anystate Zip 00000 , to-wit:

Douglas Manor, 2001 Century Drive
(Lots 16 and 17, Block 3, Edgewood South Subdivision)

at and for a purchase price of Seven Hundred Thousand Dollars ($ 700,000) payable at the following times, to-wit: $ 50,000 additional at the time the purchaser elects to purchase said property, said sum to be paid not later than the date above fixed for the expiration of this option; $ 30,000 of said purchase price to be paid by November 30th , 19 81 , and the balance to be paid as follows, to-wit: $600,000 at closing which is to be held on or before December 31st, 1981.

Within five (5) days after the purchaser elects to exercise this option and makes the first payment above provided, owner agrees to furnish said purchaser title insurance prepared by a reputable title insurance company insuring in the amount of said purchase price good marketable title in the owner free and clear of all incumbrances whatsoever excepting only as hereinafter stated. The purchaser shall have days after the delivery of said title insurance in which to examine same, and owner is to have thirty (30) days after written notice of defects is delivered to owner to remedy same.

Upon the payment of said purchase price, owner agrees to convey the above described property to the said purchaser by a good and sufficient deed containing covenants of general warranty, said property to be conveyed free of all incumbrances of every nature and description except easements of record filed as part of the subdivision

Owner further covenants and agrees to and with the said purchaser and to and with his heirs and assigns, that the undersigned are the owners of said property and have a valid right to sell and convey the same and to contract so to do.

Time is of the essence of this contract, and should the said purchaser fail for any reason whatsoever to elect to purchase said property on or before the expiration of the time above stated, then this contract shall be absolutely null and void and of no further force or effect.

DATED July 4th , 19 81

/s/Wendy Welloff

_____ OWNER   _____ OWNER

_____ OWNER   _____ OWNER

STATE OF _____ , County of _____) ss. _____ , 19 ____

Personally appeared the within named _____

and acknowledged the foregoing instrument to be _____ voluntary act and deed.

Before me: _____

[SEAL]   Notary Public for _____ My Commission Expires _____

THIS AGREEMENT made and entered into between Wendy Welloff
_____, as Seller, and the undersigned as Buyer. Buyer agrees
to purchase Douglas Manor, 2001 Century Drive, Urbandale, Anystate
at the price of $ 640,000.$\underline{00}$, with a deposit of $ 16,000.$\underline{00}$
_____, receipt of which is hereby acknowledged, and $ 16,000.$\underline{00}$
_____ when a more formal contract is agreed to by Seller and
Buyer, which is to be on or about April 1st, 1982. The Buyer
agrees to pay $32,000.$\underline{00}$ in cash at closing, and $500,000
by assuming and agreeing to pay existing mortgage for that amount
now on subject property. The balance of $76,000 is to be
paid by Buyer as follows: a five year straight term loan from seller to
buyer with interest to be paid at one percent per month, secured by a second
trust deed . In the event
the Seller is not willing to accept the above price and terms,
the deposit is to be forthwith returned. In the event the Seller
accepts and the Buyer does not comply, the deposit shall be
forfeited.
Closing to be in escrow, with escrow charges to be shared equally between
buyer and seller. Lack of marketable title shall give buyer valid reason to
void this contract.
This agreement is approved and accepted by the Seller, who
agrees to pay Ivan M. Everready, Kealtor , licensed
real estate broker, $28,600 ~~% of the purchase price~~
as commission.

Date: February 31st, 1982

/s/Harvey Hustle

Harvey Hustle, Sales Representative

/s/Nancy Investor
Buyer

/s/Gerald Investor
Buyer

/s/Wendy Welloff
Seller

FORM No. 854—CONTRACT—REAL ESTATE—Partial Payments—Deed in Escrow.

STEVENS-NESS LAW PUBLISHING CO., PORTLAND, OR. 97204

TT

38

CONTRACT—REAL ESTATE

THIS CONTRACT, Made this 31st *day of* February , *19* 82 , *between*
Wendy Welloff, Unit 77, Condomium Towers, Urbandale, Anystate
, *hereinafter called the seller,*

and Gerald & Nancy Investor, 3278 Exotic Drive, Urbandale, Anystate
00000 , *hereinafter called the buyer,*

WITNESSETH: That in consideration of the mutual covenants and agreements herein contained, the seller agrees to sell unto the buyer and the buyer agrees to purchase from the seller all of the following described lands and premises situated in Rustic *County, State of* Anystate , *to-wit:*

Douglas Manor, 2001 Century Drive, Urbandale
(Lots 16 & 17, Block 3, Edgewood South Subdivision)

for the sum of Six Hundred Forty Thousand and no/100 *Dollars ($* 640,000 *)* *(hereinafter called the purchase price) on account of which* thirty two thousand and no/100 *Dollars ($* 32,000 *) is paid on the execution hereof (the receipt of which hereby is acknowledged by the seller), and the remainder to be paid at the times and in amounts as follows, to-wit:*

Equal installments of $7,402.$\frac{40}{}$ on the first day of each month for sixty (60) months, at the end of which the buyer is to arrange financing for the remaining balance of five hundred thousand dollars ($500,000) from another source, for which title will be conveyed.

All of said purchase price may be paid at any time; all deferred balances shall bear interest at the rate of one (1) *per cent per* month *from* March 1st, 1982 *until paid, interest to be paid* monthly *and* * *in addition to being included in the minimum regular payments above required. Taxes on said premises for the current tax year shall be prorated between the parties hereto as of this date.*

The buyer warrants to and covenants with the seller that the real property described in this contract is (B)
(A) primarily for buyer's personal, family, household or agricultural purposes,
(B) for an organization or (even if buyer is a natural person) is for business or commercial purposes other than agricultural purposes.

The buyer shall be entitled to possession of said lands on 1 March , *19* 02 , *and may retain such possession so long as he is not in default under the terms of this contract. The buyer agrees that at all times he will keep the buildings on said premises, now or hereafter erected, in good condition and repair and will not suffer or permit any waste or strip thereof; that he will keep said premises free from mechanic's and all other liens and save the seller harmless therefrom and reimburse seller for all costs and attorney's fees incurred by him in defending against any such liens; that he will pay all taxes hereafter levied against said property, as well as all water rents, public charges and municipal liens which hereafter lawfully may be imposed upon said premises, all promptly before the same or any part thereof become past due; that at buyer's expense, he will insure and keep insured all buildings now or hereafter erected on said premises against loss or damage by fire (with extended coverage) in an amount not less than $* *in a company or companies satisfactory to the seller, with loss payable first to the seller and then to the buyer as their respective interests may appear and all policies of insurance to be delivered as soon as insured to the escrow agent hereinafter named. Now if the buyer shall fail to pay any such liens, costs, water rents, taxes, or charges or to procure and pay for such insurance, the seller may do so and any payment so made shall be added to and become a part of the debt secured by this contract and shall bear interest at the rate aforesaid, without waiver, however, of any right arising to the seller for buyer's breach of contract.*
The seller has exhibited unto the buyer a title insurance policy insuring marketable title in and to said premises in the seller; seller's title has been examined by the buyer and is accepted and approved by him.
Contemporaneously herewith, the seller has executed a good and sufficient deed (the form of which hereby is approved by the buyer) conveying the above described real estate in fee simple unto the buyer, his heirs and assigns, free and clear of incumbrances as of the date hereof, excepting the easements, building and other restrictions now of record, if any, and none other

and has placed said deed, together with an executed copy of this contract and the title insurance policy mentioned above, in escrow with Hifidelity Escrow Services, Urbandale *escrow agent, with instructions to deliver said deed, together with the fire and title insurance policies, to the order of the buyer, his heirs and assigns, upon the payment of the purchase price and full compliance by the buyer with the terms of this agreement. The buyer agrees to pay the balance of said purchase price and the respective installments thereof, promptly at the times provided therefor, to the said escrow agent for the use and benefit of the seller. The escrow fee of the escrow agent shall be paid by the seller and buyer in equal shares; the collection charges of said agent shall be paid by the* buyer

(Continued on reverse)

IMPORTANT NOTICE: Delete, by lining out, whichever phrase and whichever warranty (A) or (B) is not applicable. If warranty (A) is applicable and if the seller is a creditor, as such word is defined in the Truth-in-Lending Act and Regulation Z, the seller MUST comply with the Act and Regulation by making required disclosures; for this purpose, use Stevens-Ness Form No. 1308 or similar unless the contract will become a first lien to finance the purchase of a dwelling in which event use Stevens-Ness Form No. 1307 or similar.

FIGURE A–5
Acknowledgment of Act or Deed

STATE OF ____Any state____ On this, the ___15th___ day of __December__, __1980__
COUNTY OF _____Rustic_____, _____
_____Wendy Welloff_____ personally appeared before me and
acknowledged the foregoing instrument as his/her voluntary act and deed.

/s/Alfred B. Culbertson

Notary Public

FIGURE A–6
Affidavit or Voluntary Written Declaration Sworn to Before Notary Public

STATE OF ____Any state____ DATE: __10th__ day of _____May_____
COUNTY OF _____Rustic_____ 19 _81_
_____Alexander Loquacious_____ personally appeared before me this
day and, after being duly sworn, says that: (Here the fact or facts affirmed or
agreed to by the person making the affidavit are stated)

/s/Alexander Loquacious

signature of person making affidavit

Subscribed and sworn before me this day:

/s/Albert B. Culbertson

signature of notary public

FIGURE A–7
Assignment of a Contract by Direct Endorsement on the Contract

For Value Received, I, ____Wendy Welloff____, hereby assign all my rights, title,
and interests in and to this contract to _____Edward L. Magnet_____
as of this __20th__ day of _____January_____, 19 _82_.

/s/Wendy Welloff

670

KNOW ALL MEN BY THESE PRESENTS,

that

(Insert residence, if individual, or principal office,

if corporation, giving street and street number)

___We___ HEREBY CERTIFY that the following Mortgage IS PAID, and do

_____ hereby consent that the same be discharged of record.

Mortgage dated the ___15th___ day of ___January___, 19__81__, made by

___Gerald and Nancy Investor, H&W___ to ___Urbandale Savings and Loan Asso.___

in the principal sum of $___500,000___ and recorded on the ___15th___

day of ___January___, 19__81__, in Liber ___one___ of Section

__1981__ of Mortgages, page ___531___, in the office of the ___Recorder___

of the ___County of Rustic, Florida___ which mortgage has not been assigned

of record. Dated the ___1st___ day of ___March___, ___2006___.

In Presence Of:

_____/s/John L. Lewis_____

_____

Time Value of Money Tables

B

These time value of money tables show annual and monthly factors for the present value of one, present value of one per period, and principal recovery at the following interest rates:

5%	11%
6%	12%
7%	15%
8%	20%
9%	25%
10%	30%

MONTHLY
Effective rate = 0.417%   Base = 1.00417

ANNUAL
Effective rate = 5.000%   Base = 1.05000

	PV1 PRESENT VALUE OF ONE	PV1/P PRESENT VALUE OF ONE PER PERIOD	PR PRINCIPAL RECOVERY			PV1 PRESENT VALUE OF ONE	PV1/P PRESENT VALUE OF ONE PER PERIOD	PR PRINCIPAL RECOVERY	
MONTH				MONTH	YEAR				YEAR
1	C.995851	0.995851	1.004167	1	1	0.952381	0.952381	1.050000	1
2	C.991718	1.987569	0.503127	2	2	0.907029	1.859410	0.537805	2
3	C.987603	2.975173	0.336115	3	3	0.863838	2.723248	0.367209	3
4	C.983500	3.958678	0.252610	4	4	0.822702	3.545950	0.282012	4
5	0.979425	4.938103	0.202507	5	5	0.783526	4.329477	0.230975	5
6	C.975351	5.913463	0.169106	6					
					6	0.746215	5.075692	0.197017	6
7	C.971313	6.884777	0.145248	7	7	0.710681	5.786373	0.172820	7
8	0.967283	7.852060	0.127355	8	8	0.676839	6.463213	0.154722	8
9	0.963269	8.815329	0.113439	9	9	0.644609	7.107821	0.140690	9
10	0.959272	9.774602	0.102306	10	10	0.613913	7.721735	0.129505	10
11	0.955292	10.729894	0.093158	11					
YEAR				MONTH	11	0.584679	8.306414	0.120389	11
1	0.951328	11.681222	0.085607	12	12	0.556837	8.863251	0.112825	12
2	C.905025	22.793898	0.043871	24	13	0.530321	9.393573	0.106456	13
3	0.860976	33.365701	0.029971	36	14	0.505068	9.898640	0.101024	14
4	C.819071	43.422955	0.023029	48	15	0.481017	10.379657	0.096342	15
5	C.779205	52.990705	0.018871	60					
					16	0.458111	10.837769	0.092270	16
6	C.741280	62.092776	0.016105	72	17	0.436297	11.274066	0.088699	17
7	0.705201	70.751833	0.014134	84	18	0.415521	11.689586	0.085546	18
8	C.670677	78.989438	0.012660	96	19	0.395734	12.085320	0.082745	19
9	C.638225	86.826105	0.011517	108	20	0.376889	12.462209	0.080243	20
10	0.607161	94.281347	0.010607	120					
					21	0.358942	12.821152	0.077996	21
11	0.577609	101.373729	0.009864	132	22	0.341850	13.163002	0.075971	22
12	0.549496	108.120913	0.009249	144	23	0.325571	13.488573	0.074137	23
13	0.522751	114.539699	0.008731	156	24	0.310068	13.798641	0.072471	24
14	0.497308	120.646071	0.008289	168	25	0.295303	14.093943	0.070952	25
15	0.473103	126.455236	0.007908	180					
					26	0.281241	14.375184	0.069564	26
16	C.450076	141.981658	0.007577	192	27	0.267848	14.643032	0.068292	27
17	0.423170	137.239100	0.007287	204	28	0.255094	14.898126	0.067123	28
18	0.407331	142.240652	0.007030	216	29	0.242946	15.141072	0.066046	29
19	0.387505	146.998771	0.006803	228	30	0.231377	15.372450	0.065051	30
20	C.368644	151.525303	0.006600	240					
					31	0.220359	15.592809	0.064132	31
21	0.350702	155.831521	0.006417	252	32	0.209866	15.802675	0.063280	32
22	0.333635	159.928147	0.006253	264	33	0.199872	16.002548	0.062490	33
23	0.317394	163.825304	0.006104	276	34	0.190355	16.192902	0.061755	34
24	0.301946	167.532935	0.005969	288	35	0.181290	16.374193	0.061072	35
25	0.287250	171.060033	0.005846	300					
					36	0.172657	16.546850	0.060434	36
26	0.273209	174.415461	0.005733	312	37	0.164436	16.711286	0.059840	37
27	0.259968	177.607575	0.005630	324	38	0.156605	16.867891	0.059284	38
28	0.247315	180.644322	0.005536	336	39	0.149148	17.017039	0.058765	39
29	0.235278	183.533266	0.005449	348	40	0.142046	17.159084	0.058278	40
30	0.223827	186.281600	0.005368	360					
					41	0.135282	17.294366	0.057822	41
31	0.212933	188.896167	0.005294	372	42	0.128840	17.423206	0.057395	42
32	0.202569	191.383479	0.005225	384	43	0.122704	17.545910	0.056993	43
33	0.192709	193.749729	0.005161	396	44	0.116861	17.662771	0.056616	44
34	0.183330	196.000810	0.005102	408	45	0.111296	17.774068	0.056262	45
35	0.174407	198.142326	0.005047	420					
					46	0.105997	17.880064	0.055928	46
36	0.165918	200.179611	0.004996	432	47	0.100949	17.981014	0.055614	47
37	0.157843	202.117738	0.004948	444	48	0.096142	18.077156	0.055318	48
38	0.150160	203.961532	0.004903	456	49	0.091564	18.168719	0.055040	49
39	0.142852	205.715586	0.004861	468	50	0.087204	18.255923	0.054777	50
40	C.135899	207.384267	0.004822	480					

MONTHLY   Effective rate = 0.500%   Base = 1.00500

ANNUAL   Effective rate = 6.000%   Base = 1.06000

	PV1 PRESENT VALUE OF ONE	PV1/P PRESENT VALUE OF ONE PER PERIOD	PR PRINCIPAL RECOVERY	
MONTH				MONTH
1	0.995025	0.995025	1.005000	1
2	0.990075	1.985099	0.503753	2
3	0.985149	2.970248	0.336672	3
4	0.980248	3.950496	0.253133	4
5	0.975371	4.925866	0.203010	5
6	0.970518	5.896384	0.169595	6
7	0.965690	6.862074	0.145729	7
8	0.960885	7.822959	0.127829	8
9	0.956105	8.779064	0.113907	9
10	0.951348	9.730412	0.102771	10
11	0.946615	10.677027	0.093659	11
YEAR				MONTH
1	0.941905	11.618932	0.086066	12
2	0.887186	22.562866	0.044321	24
3	0.835645	32.871016	0.030422	36
4	0.787098	42.580317	0.023485	48
5	0.741372	51.725560	0.019333	60
6	0.698302	60.339512	0.016573	72
7	0.657735	68.453040	0.014609	84
8	0.619524	76.095215	0.013141	96
9	0.583533	83.293421	0.012006	108
10	0.549633	90.073449	0.011102	120
11	0.517702	96.459594	0.010367	132
12	0.487626	102.474738	0.009759	144
13	0.459298	108.140434	0.009247	156
14	0.432615	113.476980	0.008812	168
15	0.407482	118.503507	0.008439	180
16	0.383810	123.238017	0.008114	192
17	0.361513	127.697477	0.007831	204
18	0.340511	131.897867	0.007582	216
19	0.320729	135.854236	0.007361	228
20	0.302096	139.580761	0.007164	240
21	0.284546	143.090794	0.006989	252
22	0.268015	146.356914	0.006831	264
23	0.252445	149.510966	0.006688	276
24	0.237779	152.444108	0.006560	288
25	0.223960	155.200850	0.006443	300
26	0.210954	157.809091	0.006337	312
27	0.198699	160.260156	0.006240	324
28	0.187156	162.568827	0.006151	336
29	0.176283	164.743377	0.006070	348
30	0.166042	166.791597	0.005996	360
31	0.156396	168.720826	0.005927	372
32	0.147310	170.537977	0.005864	384
33	0.138752	172.249562	0.005806	396
34	0.130691	173.861713	0.005752	408
35	0.123099	175.380206	0.005702	420
36	0.115947	176.810483	0.005656	432
37	0.109212	178.157668	0.005613	444
38	0.102867	179.426589	0.005573	456
39	0.096891	180.621793	0.005536	468
40	0.091262	181.747562	0.005502	480

	PV1 PRESENT VALUE OF ONE	PV1/P PRESENT VALUE OF ONE PER PERIOD	PR PRINCIPAL RECOVERY	
YEAR				YEAR
1	0.943396	0.943396	1.060000	1
2	0.889996	1.833393	0.545437	2
3	0.839619	2.673012	0.374110	3
4	0.792094	3.465106	0.288591	4
5	0.747258	4.212364	0.237396	5
6	0.704961	4.917324	0.203363	6
7	0.665057	5.582381	0.179135	7
8	0.627412	6.209794	0.161036	8
9	0.591898	6.801692	0.147022	9
10	0.558395	7.360087	0.135868	10
11	0.526787	7.886874	0.126793	11
12	0.496969	8.383843	0.119277	12
13	0.468839	8.852682	0.112960	13
14	0.442301	9.294983	0.107585	14
15	0.417265	9.712248	0.102963	15
16	0.393646	10.105895	0.098952	16
17	0.371364	10.477259	0.095445	17
18	0.350344	10.827603	0.092357	18
19	0.330513	11.158116	0.089621	19
20	0.311805	11.469920	0.087185	20
21	0.294155	11.764076	0.085005	21
22	0.277505	12.041581	0.083046	22
23	0.261797	12.303378	0.081278	23
24	0.246978	12.550356	0.079679	24
25	0.232999	12.783355	0.078227	25
26	0.219810	13.003165	0.076904	26
27	0.207368	13.210533	0.075697	27
28	0.195630	13.406163	0.074593	28
29	0.184557	13.590720	0.073580	29
30	0.174110	13.764830	0.072649	30
31	0.164255	13.929084	0.071792	31
32	0.154957	14.084042	0.071002	32
33	0.146186	14.230228	0.070273	33
34	0.137911	14.368140	0.069598	34
35	0.130105	14.498245	0.068974	35
36	0.122741	14.620985	0.068395	36
37	0.115793	14.736779	0.067857	37
38	0.109239	14.846017	0.067358	38
39	0.103055	14.949073	0.066894	39
40	0.097222	15.046295	0.066462	40
41	0.091719	15.138014	0.066059	41
42	0.086527	15.224541	0.065683	42
43	0.081630	15.306171	0.065333	43
44	0.077009	15.383180	0.065006	44
45	0.072650	15.455830	0.064701	45
46	0.068538	15.524368	0.064415	46
47	0.064658	15.589026	0.064148	47
48	0.060998	15.650024	0.063898	48
49	0.057546	15.707570	0.063664	49
50	0.054288	15.761858	0.063444	50

7%   7%

MONTHLY
Effective rate = 0.583%   Base = 1.00583

ANNUAL
Effective rate = 7.000%   Base = 1.07000

	PV1 PRESENT VALUE OF ONE	PV1/P PRESENT VALUE OF ONE PER PERIOD	PR PRINCIPAL RECOVERY			PV1 PRESENT VALUE OF ONE	PV1/P PRESENT VALUE OF ONE PER PERIOD	PR PRINCIPAL RECOVERY	
MONTH				MONTH	YEAR				YEAR
1	0.994200	0.994200	1.005833	1	1	0.934579	0.934579	1.070000	1
2	0.988435	1.982635	0.504379	2	2	0.873439	1.808018	0.553092	2
3	0.982702	2.965337	0.337230	3	3	0.816298	2.624316	0.381052	3
4	0.977003	3.942340	0.253656	4	4	0.762895	3.387211	0.295228	4
5	0.971337	4.913677	0.203514	5	5	0.712986	4.100197	0.243891	5
6	0.965704	5.879381	0.170086	6					
					6	0.666342	4.766539	0.209796	6
7	0.960103	6.839484	0.146210	7	7	0.622750	5.389289	0.185553	7
8	0.954535	7.794019	0.128304	8	8	0.582009	5.971298	0.167468	8
9	0.948999	8.743018	0.114377	9	9	0.543934	6.515232	0.153486	9
10	0.943495	9.686513	0.103236	10	10	0.508349	7.023581	0.142378	10
11	0.938024	10.624537	0.094122	11					
YEAR				MONTH	11	0.475093	7.498674	0.133357	11
1	0.932583	11.557120	0.086527	12	12	0.444012	7.942686	0.125902	12
2	0.869712	22.335099	0.044773	24	13	0.414964	8.357650	0.119651	13
3	0.811079	32.386404	0.030877	36	14	0.387817	8.745467	0.114345	14
4	0.756399	41.760200	0.023946	48	15	0.362446	9.107913	0.109795	15
5	0.705405	50.501992	0.019801	60					
					16	0.338735	9.446648	0.105858	16
6	0.657849	58.654442	0.017049	72	17	0.316574	9.763222	0.102425	17
7	0.613499	66.257283	0.015093	84	18	0.295864	10.059086	0.099413	18
8	0.572139	73.347566	0.013634	96	19	0.276508	10.335594	0.096753	19
9	0.533567	79.955846	0.012506	108	20	0.258419	10.594013	0.094393	20
10	0.497590	86.126350	0.011611	120					
					21	0.241513	10.835526	0.092289	21
11	0.464050	91.877129	0.010884	132	22	0.225713	11.061239	0.090406	22
12	0.432765	97.240210	0.010284	144	23	0.210947	11.272186	0.088714	23
13	0.403590	102.241731	0.009781	156	24	0.197147	11.469333	0.087189	24
14	0.376381	106.906067	0.009354	168	25	0.184249	11.653582	0.085811	25
15	0.351007	111.255950	0.008988	180					
					26	0.172195	11.825777	0.084561	26
16	0.327343	115.312578	0.008672	192	27	0.160930	11.986708	0.083426	27
17	0.305275	119.095723	0.008397	204	28	0.150402	12.137110	0.082392	28
18	0.284654	122.623820	0.008156	216	29	0.140563	12.277673	0.081449	29
19	0.265501	125.914066	0.007942	228	30	0.131367	12.409040	0.080586	30
20	0.247602	128.982495	0.007753	240					
					31	0.122773	12.531813	0.079797	31
21	0.230910	131.844061	0.007585	252	32	0.114741	12.646554	0.079073	32
22	0.215342	134.512751	0.007434	264	33	0.107235	12.753788	0.078400	33
23	0.200825	137.001448	0.007299	276	34	0.100219	12.854008	0.077797	34
24	0.187286	139.322404	0.007178	288	35	0.093663	12.947671	0.077234	35
25	0.174660	141.486889	0.007068	300					
					36	0.087535	13.035206	0.076715	36
26	0.162885	143.505452	0.006968	312	37	0.081809	13.117015	0.076237	37
27	0.151904	145.387930	0.006878	324	38	0.076457	13.193472	0.075795	38
28	0.141663	147.143498	0.006796	336	39	0.071455	13.264927	0.075387	39
29	0.132112	148.780712	0.006721	348	40	0.066780	13.331707	0.075009	40
30	0.123206	150.307551	0.006653	360					
					41	0.062412	13.394119	0.074660	41
31	0.114900	151.731455	0.006591	372	42	0.058329	13.452447	0.074336	42
32	0.107154	153.059365	0.006533	384	43	0.054513	13.506960	0.074036	43
33	0.099930	154.297751	0.006481	396	44	0.050946	13.557906	0.073758	44
34	0.093193	155.452650	0.006433	408	45	0.047613	13.605520	0.073500	45
35	0.086910	156.529689	0.006389	420					
					46	0.044499	13.650018	0.073260	46
36	0.081051	157.534119	0.006348	432	47	0.041587	13.691606	0.073037	47
37	0.075587	158.470833	0.006310	444	48	0.038867	13.730472	0.072831	48
38	0.070491	159.344397	0.006276	456	49	0.036324	13.766797	0.072639	49
39	0.065739	160.159088	0.006244	468	50	0.033948	13.800744	0.072460	50
40	0.061307	160.918817	0.006214	480					

MONTHLY
Effective rate = 0.667%   Base = 1.00667

ANNUAL
Effective rate = 8.000%   Base = 1.08000

	PV1 PRESENT VALUE OF ONE	PV1/P PRESENT VALUE OF ONE PER PERIOD	PR PRINCIPAL RECOVERY			PV1 PRESENT VALUE OF ONE	PV1/P PRESENT VALUE OF ONE PER PERIOD	PR PRINCIPAL RECOVERY	
MONTH				MONTH	YEAR				YEAR
1	0.993377	0.993377	1.006667	1	1	0.925926	0.925926	1.080000	1
2	0.986799	1.980176	0.505006	2	2	0.857339	1.783265	0.560769	2
3	0.980264	2.960440	0.337788	3	3	0.793832	2.577097	0.388034	3
4	0.973772	3.934212	0.254181	4	4	0.735030	3.312127	0.301921	4
5	0.967323	4.901535	0.204018	5	5	0.680583	3.992710	0.250456	5
6	0.960917	5.862452	0.170577	6					
					6	0.630170	4.622879	0.216315	6
7	0.954553	6.817005	0.146692	7	7	0.583490	5.206370	0.192072	7
8	0.948232	7.765237	0.128779	8	8	0.540269	5.746639	0.174015	8
9	0.941952	8.707189	0.114848	9	9	0.500249	6.246888	0.160080	9
10	0.935714	9.642903	0.103703	10	10	0.463193	6.710081	0.149029	10
11	0.929517	10.572420	0.094586	11					
YEAR				MONTH	11	0.428883	7.138964	0.140076	11
1	0.923361	11.495782	0.086988	12	12	0.397114	7.536078	0.132695	12
2	0.852596	22.110543	0.045227	24	13	0.367698	7.903775	0.126522	13
3	0.787255	31.911805	0.031336	36	14	0.340461	8.244236	0.121297	14
4	0.726921	40.961912	0.024413	48	15	0.315242	8.559478	0.116830	15
5	0.671210	49.318432	0.020276	60					
					16	0.291890	8.851368	0.112977	16
6	0.619770	57.034520	0.017533	72	17	0.270269	9.121637	0.109629	17
7	0.572272	64.159258	0.015586	84	18	0.250249	9.371886	0.106702	18
8	0.528413	70.737967	0.014137	96	19	0.231712	9.603598	0.104128	19
9	0.487917	76.812493	0.013019	108	20	0.214548	9.818146	0.101852	20
10	0.450523	82.421476	0.012133	120					
					21	0.198656	10.016802	0.099832	21
11	0.415996	87.600595	0.011415	132	22	0.183940	10.200743	0.098032	22
12	0.384115	92.382793	0.010825	144	23	0.170315	10.371058	0.096422	23
13	0.354677	96.798491	0.010331	156	24	0.157699	10.528757	0.094978	24
14	0.327455	100.875776	0.009913	168	25	0.146018	10.674775	0.093679	25
15	0.302396	104.640584	0.009557	180					
					26	0.135202	10.809977	0.092507	26
16	0.279221	108.116862	0.009249	192	27	0.125187	10.935163	0.091448	27
17	0.257822	111.326724	0.008983	204	28	0.115914	11.051077	0.090489	28
18	0.238065	114.290586	0.008750	216	29	0.107327	11.158405	0.089619	29
19	0.215818	117.023302	0.008545	228	30	0.099377	11.257782	0.088827	30
20	0.202971	119.554280	0.008364	240					
					31	0.092016	11.349798	0.088107	31
21	0.187416	121.837594	0.008204	252	32	0.085200	11.434998	0.087451	32
22	0.173053	124.042087	0.008062	264	33	0.078889	11.513887	0.086852	33
23	0.159790	126.031462	0.007935	276	34	0.073045	11.586932	0.086304	34
24	0.147544	127.868374	0.007821	288	35	0.067635	11.654567	0.085803	35
25	0.136236	129.564508	0.007718	300					
					36	0.062625	11.717191	0.085345	36
26	0.125796	131.130653	0.007626	312	37	0.057986	11.775177	0.084924	37
27	0.116155	132.576770	0.007543	324	38	0.053690	11.828867	0.084539	38
28	0.107253	133.912060	0.007468	336	39	0.049713	11.878581	0.084185	39
29	0.099033	135.145014	0.007399	348	40	0.046031	11.924612	0.083860	40
30	0.091443	136.283477	0.007338	360					
					41	0.042621	11.967233	0.083562	41
31	0.084435	137.334690	0.007281	372	42	0.039464	12.006697	0.083287	42
32	0.077964	138.305339	0.007230	384	43	0.036541	12.043238	0.083034	43
33	0.071989	139.201599	0.007184	396	44	0.033834	12.077072	0.082802	44
34	0.066472	140.029171	0.007141	408	45	0.031328	12.108400	0.082587	45
35	0.061376	140.793319	0.007103	420					
					46	0.029007	12.137407	0.082390	46
36	0.056674	141.498904	0.007067	432	47	0.026859	12.164266	0.082208	47
37	0.052330	142.150414	0.007035	444	48	0.024869	12.189135	0.082040	48
38	0.048320	142.751993	0.007005	456	49	0.023027	12.212162	0.081886	49
39	0.044617	143.307468	0.006978	468	50	0.021321	12.233483	0.081743	50
40	0.041197	143.820372	0.006953	480					

MONTHLY
Effective rate = 0.750%   Base = 1.00750

ANNUAL
Effective rate = 9.000%   Base = 1.09000

	PV1 PRESENT VALUE OF ONE	PV1/P PRESENT VALUE OF ONE PER PERIOD	PR PRINCIPAL RECOVERY			PV1 PRESENT VALUE OF ONE	PV1/P PRESENT VALUE OF ONE PER PERIOD	PR PRINCIPAL RECOVERY	
MONTH				MONTH	YEAR				YEAR
1	0.992556	0.992556	1.007500	1	1	0.917431	0.917431	1.090000	1
2	0.985167	1.977723	0.505632	2	2	0.841680	1.759111	0.568469	2
3	0.977833	2.955556	0.338346	3	3	0.772183	2.531295	0.395055	3
4	0.970554	3.926110	0.254705	4	4	0.708425	3.239720	0.308669	4
5	0.963329	4.889440	0.204522	5	5	0.649931	3.889651	0.257092	5
6	0.956158	5.845598	0.171069	6					
					6	0.596267	4.485918	0.222920	6
7	0.949040	6.794638	0.147175	7	7	0.547034	5.032953	0.198691	7
8	0.941975	7.736613	0.129256	8	8	0.501866	5.534819	0.180674	8
9	0.934963	8.671576	0.115319	9	9	0.460428	5.995247	0.166799	9
10	0.928003	9.599580	0.104171	10	10	0.422411	6.417657	0.155820	10
11	0.921095	10.520674	0.095051	11					
YEAR				MONTH	11	0.387533	6.805190	0.146947	11
1	0.914238	11.434913	0.087451	12	12	0.355535	7.160725	0.139651	12
2	0.835831	21.889146	0.045685	24	13	0.326179	7.486903	0.133567	13
3	0.764149	31.446805	0.031800	36	14	0.299246	7.786150	0.128433	14
4	0.698614	40.184781	0.024885	48	15	0.274538	8.066688	0.124059	15
5	0.638700	48.173372	0.020758	60					
					16	0.251870	8.312557	0.120300	16
6	0.583924	55.476847	0.018026	72	17	0.231073	8.543631	0.117046	17
7	0.533845	62.153902	0.016089	84	18	0.211994	8.755624	0.114212	18
8	0.488002	68.258435	0.014650	96	19	0.194490	8.950114	0.111730	19
9	0.446205	73.835377	0.013543	108	20	0.178431	9.128545	0.109546	20
10	0.407937	78.941688	0.012668	120					
					21	0.163698	9.292243	0.107617	21
11	0.372952	83.606414	0.011961	132	22	0.150182	9.442424	0.105905	22
12	0.340967	87.871086	0.011380	144	23	0.137781	9.580206	0.104382	23
13	0.311725	91.770011	0.010897	156	24	0.126405	9.706611	0.103023	24
14	0.284991	95.334556	0.010489	168	25	0.115968	9.822578	0.101806	25
15	0.260549	98.593400	0.010143	180					
					26	0.106392	9.928971	0.100715	26
16	0.238204	101.572760	0.009845	192	27	0.097608	10.026579	0.099735	27
17	0.217775	104.296604	0.009588	204	28	0.089548	10.116127	0.098852	28
18	0.199099	106.786846	0.009364	216	29	0.082155	10.198282	0.098056	29
19	0.182023	109.063520	0.009169	228	30	0.075371	10.273653	0.097336	30
20	0.166413	111.144942	0.008997	240					
					31	0.069148	10.342801	0.096686	31
21	0.152141	113.047858	0.008846	252	32	0.063438	10.406239	0.096096	32
22	0.139093	114.787576	0.008712	264	33	0.058200	10.464439	0.095562	33
23	0.127164	116.378093	0.008593	276	34	0.053395	10.517834	0.095077	34
24	0.116258	117.832204	0.008487	288	35	0.048986	10.566820	0.094636	35
25	0.106288	119.161608	0.008392	300					
					36	0.044941	10.611761	0.094235	36
26	0.097172	120.376999	0.008307	312	37	0.041231	10.652992	0.093870	37
27	0.088839	121.488157	0.008231	324	38	0.037826	10.690818	0.093538	38
28	0.081220	122.504019	0.008163	336	39	0.034703	10.725521	0.093236	39
29	0.074254	123.432760	0.008102	348	40	0.031838	10.757359	0.092960	40
30	0.067886	124.281849	0.008046	360					
					41	0.029209	10.786567	0.092708	41
31	0.062064	125.058120	0.007996	372	42	0.026797	10.813364	0.092478	42
32	0.056741	125.767815	0.007951	384	43	0.024584	10.837949	0.092268	43
33	0.051875	126.416646	0.007910	396	44	0.022555	10.860503	0.092077	44
34	0.047426	127.009832	0.007873	408	45	0.020692	10.881196	0.091902	45
35	0.043359	127.552146	0.007840	420					
					46	0.018984	10.900179	0.091742	46
36	0.039640	128.047949	0.007810	432	47	0.017416	10.917596	0.091595	47
37	0.036241	128.501232	0.007782	444	48	0.015978	10.933574	0.091461	48
38	0.033133	128.915640	0.007757	456	49	0.014659	10.948233	0.091339	49
39	0.030291	129.294508	0.007734	468	50	0.013449	10.961681	0.091227	50
40	0.027693	129.640883	0.007714	480					

MONTHLY
Effective rate = 0.833% Base = 1.00833

ANNUAL
Effective rate = 10.000% Base = 1.10000

	PV1 PRESENT VALUE OF ONE	PV1/P PRESENT VALUE OF ONE PER PERIOD	PR PRINCIPAL RECOVERY			PV1 PRESENT VALUE OF ONE	PV1/P PRESENT VALUE OF ONE PER PERIOD	PR PRINCIPAL RECOVERY	
MONTH				**MONTH**	**YEAR**				**YEAR**
1	0.991736	0.991736	1.008333	1	1	0.909091	0.909091	1.100000	1
2	0.983539	1.975279	0.506259	2	2	0.826446	1.735537	0.576190	2
3	0.975411	2.950686	0.338904	3	3	0.751315	2.486852	0.402115	3
4	0.967350	3.918036	0.255230	4	4	0.683013	3.169865	0.315471	4
5	0.959355	4.877391	0.205028	5	5	0.620921	3.790787	0.263797	5
6	0.951427	5.828817	0.171561	6					
					6	0.564474	4.355260	0.229607	6
7	0.943563	6.772381	0.147659	7	7	0.513158	4.868419	0.205406	7
8	0.935765	7.708146	0.129733	8	8	0.466507	5.334926	0.187444	8
9	0.928032	8.636178	0.115792	9	9	0.424098	5.759023	0.173641	9
10	0.920362	9.556540	0.104640	10	10	0.385543	6.144567	0.162745	10
11	0.912756	10.469296	0.095517	11					
YEAR				**MONTH**	11	0.350494	6.495061	0.153963	11
1	0.905212	11.374508	0.087916	12	12	0.318631	6.813691	0.146763	12
2	0.819410	21.670854	0.046145	24	13	0.289664	7.103356	0.140779	13
3	0.741740	30.991235	0.032267	36	14	0.263331	7.366687	0.135746	14
4	0.671432	39.428159	0.025363	48	15	0.239392	7.606079	0.131474	15
5	0.607789	47.065367	0.021247	60					
					16	0.217629	7.823708	0.127817	16
6	0.550178	53.978663	0.018526	72	17	0.197845	8.021552	0.124664	17
7	0.498028	60.236604	0.016601	84	18	0.179859	8.201411	0.121930	18
8	0.450821	65.901485	0.015174	96	19	0.163508	8.364919	0.119547	19
9	0.408089	71.029350	0.014079	108	20	0.148644	8.513563	0.117460	20
10	0.369407	75.671158	0.013215	120					
					21	0.135131	8.648693	0.115624	21
11	0.334392	79.872980	0.012520	132	22	0.122846	8.771539	0.114005	22
12	0.302656	83.676522	0.011951	144	23	0.111678	8.883217	0.112572	23
13	0.274004	87.119535	0.011478	156	24	0.101526	8.984743	0.111300	24
14	0.248032	90.236193	0.011082	168	25	0.092296	9.077039	0.110168	25
15	0.224521	93.057430	0.010746	180					
					26	0.083905	9.160944	0.109159	26
16	0.203239	95.611249	0.010459	192	27	0.076278	9.237222	0.108258	27
17	0.183975	97.922998	0.010212	204	28	0.069343	9.306565	0.107451	28
18	0.166536	100.015622	0.009998	216	29	0.063039	9.369605	0.106728	29
19	0.150751	101.905891	0.009813	228	30	0.057309	9.426913	0.106079	30
20	0.136461	103.624607	0.009650	240					
					31	0.052099	9.479012	0.105496	31
21	0.123527	105.176789	0.009508	252	32	0.047362	9.526374	0.104972	32
22	0.111818	106.581844	0.009382	264	33	0.043057	9.569431	0.104499	33
23	0.101219	107.853716	0.009272	276	34	0.039142	9.608573	0.104074	34
24	0.091625	109.005031	0.009174	288	35	0.035584	9.644158	0.103690	35
25	0.082940	110.047210	0.009087	300					
					36	0.032349	9.676507	0.103343	36
26	0.075078	110.990615	0.009010	312	37	0.029408	9.705915	0.103030	37
27	0.067962	111.844591	0.008941	324	38	0.026735	9.732650	0.102747	38
28	0.061520	112.617620	0.008880	336	39	0.024304	9.756954	0.102491	39
29	0.055688	113.317376	0.008825	348	40	0.022095	9.779049	0.102259	40
30	0.050410	113.950804	0.008776	360					
					41	0.020086	9.799136	0.102050	41
31	0.045632	114.524191	0.008732	372	42	0.018260	9.817396	0.101860	42
32	0.041306	115.043228	0.008692	384	43	0.016600	9.833996	0.101688	43
33	0.037391	115.513066	0.008657	396	44	0.015091	9.849087	0.101532	44
34	0.033847	115.938370	0.008625	408	45	0.013719	9.862806	0.101391	45
35	0.030639	116.323360	0.008597	420					
					46	0.012472	9.875278	0.101263	46
36	0.027734	116.671858	0.008571	432	47	0.011338	9.886617	0.101147	47
37	0.025105	116.987323	0.008548	444	48	0.010307	9.896924	0.101041	48
38	0.022726	117.272886	0.008527	456	49	0.009370	9.906294	0.100946	49
39	0.020572	117.531380	0.008508	468	50	0.008519	9.914813	0.100859	50
40	0.018622	117.765373	0.008491	480					

MONTHLY
Effective rate = 0.917%   Base = 1.00917

ANNUAL
Effective rate = 11.000%   Base = 1.11000

	PV1 PRESENT VALUE OF ONE	PV1/P PRESENT VALUE OF ONE PER PERIOD	PR PRINCIPAL RECOVERY			PV1 PRESENT VALUE OF ONE	PV1/P PRESENT VALUE OF ONE PER PERIOD	PR PRINCIPAL RECOVERY	
MONTH				MONTH	YEAR				YEAR
1	C.990917	0.990917	1.C09167	1	1	0.900901	0.900901	1.110000	1
2	C.981916	1.972832	0.5C6885	2	2	0.811622	1.712523	0.583934	2
3	C.972997	2.945829	0.339463	3	3	0.731191	2.443715	0.409213	3
4	0.964138	3.909987	0.255755	4	4	0.658731	3.102446	0.322326	4
5	0.955401	4.865388	0.205533	5	5	0.593451	3.695897	0.270570	5
6	C.946722	5.812110	0.172055	6					
					6	0.534641	4.230538	0.236377	6
7	0.938123	6.750233	0.148143	7	7	0.481658	4.712196	0.212215	7
8	0.929602	7.679835	0.130211	8	8	0.433926	5.146122	0.194321	8
9	0.921158	8.600992	0.116266	9	9	0.390925	5.537047	0.180602	9
10	C.912790	9.513782	0.105111	10	10	0.352184	5.889232	0.169801	10
11	0.904499	10.418282	0.C95985	11					
YEAR				MONTH	11	0.317283	6.206515	0.161121	11
1	0.896283	11.314565	0.088382	12	12	0.285841	6.492356	0.154027	12
2	0.8C3323	21.453618	0.C46608	24	13	0.257514	6.749870	0.148151	13
3	0.720005	30.544874	0.032739	36	14	0.231995	6.981865	0.143228	14
4	0.645329	38.691420	0.C25846	48	15	0.209004	7.190869	0.139065	15
5	C.578397	45.993032	0.C21742	60					
					16	0.188292	7.379161	0.135517	16
6	C.518408	52.537344	0.C19034	72	17	0.169633	7.548794	0.132471	17
7	0.464640	58.402900	0.017122	84	18	0.152822	7.701616	0.129843	18
8	0.416449	63.680099	0.C15708	96	19	0.137678	7.839294	0.127563	19
9	0.373250	68.372038	0.C14626	108	20	0.124034	7.963327	0.125570	20
10	0.334543	72.595270	0.013775	120					
					21	0.111742	8.075069	0.123838	21
11	0.299845	76.380481	0.013092	132	22	0.100669	8.175738	0.122313	22
12	0.268746	79.773102	0.012536	144	23	0.090692	8.266431	0.120971	23
13	0.240873	82.813851	0.012075	156	24	0.C81705	8.348135	0.119787	24
14	0.215890	85.539223	0.C11691	168	25	0.073608	8.421744	0.118740	25
15	0.193499	87.981928	0.C11366	180					
					26	0.066314	8.488057	0.117813	26
16	0.173430	90.171284	0.011090	192	27	0.059742	8.547799	0.116989	27
17	0.155442	92.133566	0.010854	204	28	0.053822	8.601621	0.116257	28
18	0.139320	93.892326	0.010650	216	29	0.048488	8.650109	0.115605	29
19	0.124870	95.466674	0.010475	228	30	0.043683	8.693791	0.115025	30
20	0.111919	96.881527	0.C10322	240					
					31	0.039354	8.733145	0.114506	31
21	0.100311	98.147844	0.010189	252	32	0.035454	8.768599	0.114043	32
22	0.089907	99.282823	0.010072	264	33	0.031940	8.800540	0.113629	33
23	0.080582	100.300085	0.009970	276	34	0.028775	8.829315	0.113259	34
24	0.072225	101.211840	0.CC9880	288	35	0.025924	8.855238	0.112928	35
25	0.064734	102.029030	0.C09801	300					
					36	0.023355	8.878593	0.112630	36
26	0.058020	102.761464	0.C09731	312	37	0.021040	8.899633	0.112364	37
27	0.052002	103.417933	0.C09670	324	38	0.018955	8.918588	0.112125	38
28	0.046609	104.006314	0.009615	336	39	0.017077	8.935665	0.111911	39
29	0.041775	104.533670	0.C09566	348	40	0.015384	8.951049	0.111719	40
30	0.037442	105.006331	0.C09523	360					
					41	0.013860	8.964909	0.111546	41
31	0.033558	105.429969	0.CC9485	372	42	0.012486	8.977396	0.111391	42
32	0.030078	105.805668	0.009451	384	43	0.011249	8.988645	0.111251	43
33	0.026958	106.149966	0.009421	396	44	0.010134	8.998779	0.111126	44
34	0.024162	106.455008	0.009394	408	45	0.009130	9.007909	0.111014	45
35	0.021656	106.728393	0.C09370	420					
					46	0.008225	9.016134	0.110912	46
36	0.019410	106.973424	0.C09348	432	47	0.007410	9.023544	0.110821	47
37	0.017397	107.193041	0.CC9329	444	48	0.006676	9.030219	0.110739	48
38	0.015593	107.389680	0.009312	456	49	0.006014	9.036234	0.110666	49
39	0.013975	107.566304	0.C09297	468	50	0.005418	9.041652	0.110599	50
40	0.012526	107.724429	0.C09283	480					

MONTHLY
Effective rate = 1.000%   Base = 1.01000

ANNUAL
Effective rate = 12.000%   Base = 1.12000

	PV1 PRESENT VALUE OF ONE	PV1/P PRESENT VALUE OF ONE PER PERIOD	PR PRINCIPAL RECOVERY			PV1 PRESENT VALUE OF ONE	PV1/P PRESENT VALUE OF ONE PER PERIOD	PR PRINCIPAL RECOVERY	
MONTH				MONTH	YEAR				YEAR
1	0.990099	0.990099	1.010000	1	1	0.892857	0.892857	1.120000	1
2	0.980296	1.970395	0.507512	2	2	0.797194	1.690051	0.591698	2
3	0.970590	2.940985	0.340022	3	3	0.711780	2.401831	0.416349	3
4	0.960980	3.901966	0.256281	4	4	0.635518	3.037349	0.329234	4
5	0.951466	4.853431	0.206040	5	5	0.567427	3.604776	0.277410	5
6	0.942045	5.795476	0.172548	6					
					6	0.506631	4.111407	0.243226	6
7	0.932718	6.728194	0.148628	7	7	0.452349	4.563756	0.219118	7
8	0.923483	7.651678	0.130690	8	8	0.403883	4.967639	0.201303	8
9	0.914340	8.566018	0.116740	9	9	0.360610	5.328249	0.187679	9
10	0.905287	9.471304	0.105582	10	10	0.321973	5.650223	0.176984	10
11	0.896324	10.367628	0.096454	11					
YEAR				MONTH	11	0.287476	5.937699	0.168415	11
1	0.887449	11.255077	0.088849	12	12	0.256675	6.194374	0.161437	12
2	0.787566	21.243387	0.047073	24	13	0.229174	6.423548	0.155677	13
3	0.698925	30.107504	0.033214	36	14	0.204620	6.628168	0.150871	14
4	0.620260	37.973958	0.026334	48	15	0.182696	6.810864	0.146824	15
5	0.550450	44.955036	0.022244	60					
					16	0.163122	6.973985	0.143390	16
6	0.488450	51.150339	0.019550	72	17	0.145644	7.119630	0.140457	17
7	0.433515	56.648449	0.017653	84	18	0.130040	7.249669	0.137937	18
8	0.384723	61.527699	0.016253	96	19	0.116107	7.365776	0.135763	19
9	0.341422	65.857765	0.015184	108	20	0.103667	7.469443	0.133879	20
10	0.302995	69.700517	0.014347	120					
					21	0.092560	7.562002	0.132240	21
11	0.268892	73.110740	0.013678	132	22	0.082642	7.644645	0.130811	22
12	0.238628	76.137151	0.013134	144	23	0.073788	7.718433	0.129560	23
13	0.211771	78.822931	0.012687	156	24	0.065882	7.784315	0.128463	24
14	0.187936	81.206425	0.012314	168	25	0.058823	7.843138	0.127500	25
15	0.166783	83.321655	0.012002	180					
					26	0.052521	7.895659	0.126652	26
16	0.148012	85.198814	0.011737	192	27	0.046894	7.942552	0.125904	27
17	0.131353	86.864698	0.011512	204	28	0.041869	7.984422	0.125244	28
18	0.116569	88.343084	0.011320	216	29	0.037383	8.021805	0.124660	29
19	0.103449	89.655078	0.011154	228	30	0.033378	8.055183	0.124144	30
20	0.091806	90.819405	0.011011	240					
					31	0.029802	8.084984	0.123686	31
21	0.081473	91.852686	0.010887	252	32	0.026609	8.111593	0.123280	32
22	0.072303	92.769671	0.010779	264	33	0.023758	8.135351	0.122920	33
23	0.064165	93.583449	0.010686	276	34	0.021212	8.156563	0.122601	34
24	0.056943	94.305653	0.010604	288	35	0.018940	8.175503	0.122317	35
25	0.050534	94.946538	0.010532	300					
					36	0.016910	8.192413	0.122064	36
26	0.044847	95.515307	0.010470	312	37	0.015098	8.207511	0.121840	37
27	0.039799	96.020061	0.010414	324	38	0.013481	8.220992	0.121640	38
28	0.035320	96.468005	0.010366	336	39	0.012036	8.233029	0.121462	39
29	0.031345	96.865552	0.010324	348	40	0.010747	8.243775	0.121304	40
30	0.027817	97.218317	0.010286	360					
					41	0.009595	8.253371	0.121163	41
31	0.024686	97.531396	0.010253	372	42	0.008567	8.261938	0.121037	42
32	0.021907	97.809257	0.010224	384	43	0.007649	8.269587	0.120925	43
33	0.019442	98.055807	0.010198	396	44	0.006830	8.276417	0.120825	44
34	0.017254	98.274626	0.010176	408	45	0.006098	8.282515	0.120736	45
35	0.015312	98.468816	0.010155	420					
					46	0.005445	8.287960	0.120657	46
36	0.013588	98.641150	0.010138	432	47	0.004861	8.292821	0.120586	47
37	0.012059	98.794068	0.010122	444	48	0.004340	8.297162	0.120523	48
38	0.010702	98.929813	0.010108	456	49	0.003875	8.301037	0.120467	49
39	0.009497	99.050261	0.010096	468	50	0.003460	8.304497	0.120417	50
40	0.008426	99.157153	0.010085	480					

15%   # 15%

MONTHLY
Effective rate = 1.250%   Base = 1.01250

ANNUAL
Effective rate = 15.000%   Base = 1.15000

	PV1 PRESENT VALUE OF ONE	PV1/P PRESENT VALUE OF ONE PER PERIOD	PR PRINCIPAL RECOVERY			PV1 PRESENT VALUE OF ONE	PV1/P PRESENT VALUE OF ONE PER PERIOD	PR PRINCIPAL RECOVERY	
MONTH					YEAR				
1	0.987654	0.987654	1.012500	1	1	0.869565	0.869565	1.150000	1
2	0.975461	1.963115	0.509394	2	2	0.756144	1.625709	0.615116	2
3	0.963418	2.920534	0.341701	3	3	0.657516	2.283225	0.437977	3
4	0.951524	3.878058	0.257861	4	4	0.571753	2.854978	0.350265	4
5	0.939777	4.817835	0.207562	5	5	0.497177	3.352155	0.298316	5
6	0.928175	5.746010	0.174034	6					
					6	0.432328	3.784482	0.264237	6
7	0.916716	6.662726	0.150089	7	7	0.375937	4.160419	0.240360	7
8	0.905398	7.568124	0.132133	8	8	0.326902	4.487321	0.222850	8
9	0.894221	8.462345	0.118171	9	9	0.284262	4.771584	0.209574	9
10	0.883181	9.345526	0.107003	10	10	0.247185	5.018768	0.199252	10
11	0.872277	10.217803	0.097868	11					
YEAR				MONTH	11	0.214943	5.233711	0.191069	11
1	0.861509	11.079312	0.090258	12	12	0.186907	5.420618	0.184481	12
2	0.742157	20.624234	0.048487	24	13	0.162528	5.583146	0.179110	13
3	0.639409	28.347266	0.034665	36	14	0.141329	5.724475	0.174689	14
4	0.550856	35.931479	0.027831	48	15	0.122894	5.847369	0.171017	15
5	0.474568	42.034590	0.023790	60					
					16	0.106865	5.954234	0.167948	16
6	0.408844	47.292471	0.021145	72	17	0.092926	6.047160	0.165367	17
7	0.352223	51.822182	0.019297	84	18	0.080805	6.127965	0.163186	18
8	0.303443	55.724566	0.017945	96	19	0.070265	6.198230	0.161336	19
9	0.261419	59.086503	0.016924	108	20	0.061100	6.259331	0.159761	20
10	0.225214	61.982641	0.016133	120					
					21	0.053131	6.312461	0.158417	21
11	0.194024	64.478062	0.015509	132	22	0.046201	6.358662	0.157266	22
12	0.167153	66.627715	0.015009	144	23	0.040174	6.398836	0.156278	23
13	0.144004	68.479660	0.014603	156	24	0.034934	6.433771	0.155430	24
14	0.124061	70.075126	0.014270	168	25	0.030378	6.464148	0.154699	25
15	0.106879	71.449634	0.013996	180					
					26	0.026415	6.490563	0.154070	26
16	0.092078	72.633785	0.013768	192	27	0.022970	6.513533	0.153527	27
17	0.079326	73.653941	0.013577	204	28	0.019974	6.533507	0.153057	28
18	0.068340	74.532014	0.013417	216	29	0.017369	6.550876	0.152651	29
19	0.058875	75.289970	0.013282	228	30	0.015103	6.565979	0.152300	30
20	0.050722	75.942261	0.013168	240					
					31	0.013133	6.579112	0.151996	31
21	0.043697	76.504226	0.013071	252	32	0.011420	6.590532	0.151733	32
22	0.037645	76.988559	0.012909	264	33	0.009930	6.600462	0.151505	33
23	0.032432	77.405444	0.012919	276	34	0.008635	6.609097	0.151307	34
24	0.027940	77.764766	0.012859	288	35	0.007509	6.616606	0.151135	35
25	0.024071	78.074325	0.012808	300					
					36	0.006529	6.623136	0.150986	36
26	0.020737	78.341012	0.012765	312	37	0.005678	6.628814	0.150857	37
27	0.017865	78.570166	0.012727	324	38	0.004937	6.633751	0.150744	38
28	0.015391	78.768701	0.012695	336	39	0.004293	6.638044	0.150647	39
29	0.013260	78.939224	0.012668	348	40	0.003733	6.641777	0.150562	40
30	0.011423	79.086130	0.012644	360					
					41	0.003246	6.645024	0.150489	41
31	0.009841	79.212691	0.012624	372	42	0.002823	6.647846	0.150425	42
32	0.008476	79.321725	0.012607	384	43	0.002455	6.650301	0.150369	43
33	0.007304	79.415659	0.012592	396	44	0.002134	6.652436	0.150321	44
34	0.006293	79.496563	0.012579	408	45	0.001856	6.654292	0.150279	45
35	0.005421	79.566300	0.012568	420					
					46	0.001614	6.655906	0.150243	46
36	0.004670	79.626302	0.012559	432	47	0.001403	6.657309	0.150211	47
37	0.004024	79.678106	0.012550	444	48	0.001220	6.658530	0.150183	48
38	0.003466	79.722684	0.012543	456	49	0.001061	6.659591	0.150159	49
39	0.002986	79.761083	0.012537	468	50	0.000923	6.660514	0.150139	50
40	0.002573	79.794173	0.012532	480					

MONTHLY
Effective rate = 1.667% Base = 1.01667

ANNUAL
Effective rate = 20.000% Base = 1.20000

	PV1 PRESENT VALUE OF ONE	PV1/P PRESENT VALUE OF ONE PER PERIOD	PR PRINCIPAL RECOVERY	
MONTH				
1	0.983607	0.983607	1.016667	1
2	0.967482	1.951088	0.512534	2
3	0.951621	2.902710	0.344506	3
4	0.936021	3.838731	0.260503	4
5	0.920677	4.759408	0.210110	5
6	0.905583	5.664991	0.176523	6
7	0.890738	6.555729	0.152538	7
8	0.876136	7.431864	0.134556	8
9	0.861773	8.293637	0.120574	9
10	0.847645	9.141282	0.109394	10
11	0.833749	9.975032	0.100250	11
YEAR				MONTH
1	0.820081	10.795113	0.092635	12
2	0.672534	19.647985	0.050896	24
3	0.551532	26.908061	0.037164	36
4	0.452301	32.861914	0.030430	48
5	0.370924	37.744558	0.026494	60
6	0.304168	41.748724	0.023953	72
7	0.249459	45.032466	0.022206	84
8	0.204577	47.725402	0.020953	96
9	0.167769	49.933828	0.020027	108
10	0.137585	51.744918	0.019326	120
11	0.112831	53.230159	0.018786	132
12	0.092530	54.448177	0.018366	144
13	0.075882	55.447052	0.018035	156
14	0.062230	56.266210	0.017773	168
15	0.051033	56.937986	0.017563	180
16	0.041852	57.488898	0.017395	192
17	0.034322	57.946690	0.017259	204
18	0.028147	58.311196	0.017149	216
19	0.023082	58.615042	0.017060	228
20	0.018930	58.864220	0.016988	240
21	0.015524	59.068566	0.016929	252
22	0.012731	59.236146	0.016882	264
23	0.010440	59.373570	0.016843	276
24	0.008562	59.486280	0.016811	288
25	0.007021	59.578706	0.016785	300
26	0.005758	59.654503	0.016763	312
27	0.004722	59.716662	0.016746	324
28	0.003873	59.767638	0.016731	336
29	0.003176	59.809443	0.016720	348
30	0.002604	59.843720	0.016710	360
31	0.002136	59.871841	0.016702	372
32	0.001752	59.894897	0.016696	384
33	0.001436	59.913805	0.016691	396
34	0.001178	59.929312	0.016686	408
35	0.000966	59.942028	0.016683	420
36	0.000792	59.952456	0.016680	432
37	0.000650	59.961009	0.016678	444
38	0.000533	59.968022	0.016676	456
39	0.000437	59.973774	0.016674	468
40	0.000358	59.978491	0.016673	480

	PV1 PRESENT VALUE OF ONE	PV1/P PRESENT VALUE OF ONE PER PERIOD	PR PRINCIPAL RECOVERY	
YEAR				YEAR
1	0.833333	0.833333	1.200000	1
2	0.694444	1.527778	0.654545	2
3	0.578704	2.106481	0.474725	3
4	0.482253	2.588734	0.388289	4
5	0.401878	2.990612	0.334380	5
6	0.334898	3.325510	0.300706	6
7	0.279082	3.604591	0.277424	7
8	0.232568	3.837159	0.260609	8
9	0.193807	4.030966	0.248079	9
10	0.161506	4.192472	0.238523	10
11	0.134588	4.327060	0.231104	11
12	0.112157	4.439216	0.225265	12
13	0.093464	4.532680	0.220620	13
14	0.077887	4.610567	0.216893	14
15	0.064905	4.675472	0.213882	15
16	0.054088	4.729560	0.211436	16
17	0.045073	4.774633	0.209440	17
18	0.037561	4.812194	0.207805	18
19	0.031301	4.843495	0.206462	19
20	0.026084	4.869579	0.205357	20
21	0.021737	4.891316	0.204444	21
22	0.018114	4.909430	0.203690	22
23	0.015095	4.924525	0.203065	23
24	0.012579	4.937104	0.202548	24
25	0.010483	4.947586	0.202119	25
26	0.008735	4.956322	0.201763	26
27	0.007280	4.963601	0.201467	27
28	0.006066	4.969668	0.201221	28
29	0.005055	4.974723	0.201016	29
30	0.004213	4.978936	0.200846	30
31	0.003511	4.982446	0.200705	31
32	0.002925	4.985372	0.200587	32
33	0.002438	4.987810	0.200489	33
34	0.002032	4.989841	0.200407	34
35	0.001693	4.991534	0.200339	35
36	0.001411	4.992945	0.200283	36
37	0.001176	4.994121	0.200235	37
38	0.000980	4.995100	0.200196	38
39	0.000816	4.995917	0.200163	39
40	0.000680	4.996597	0.200136	40
41	0.000567	4.997164	0.200113	41
42	0.000472	4.997637	0.200095	42
43	0.000394	4.998030	0.200079	43
44	0.000328	4.998359	0.200066	44
45	0.000273	4.998632	0.200055	45
46	0.000228	4.998860	0.200046	46
47	0.000190	4.999050	0.200038	47
48	0.000158	4.999208	0.200032	48
49	0.000132	4.999340	0.200026	49
50	0.000110	4.999450	0.200022	50

PV1 PRESENT VALUE OF ONE	PV1/P PRESENT VALUE OF ONE PER PERIOD	PR PRINCIPAL RECOVERY	MONTH		PV1 PRESENT VALUE OF ONE	PV1/P PRESENT VALUE OF ONE PER PERIOD	PR PRINCIPAL RECOVERY	YEAR
MONTH				**YEAR**				
0.979592	0.979592	1.020833	1	1	0.800000	0.800000	1.250000	1
0.959600	1.939192	0.515679	2	2	0.640000	1.440000	0.694444	2
0.940016	2.879208	0.347318	3	3	0.512000	1.952000	0.512295	3
0.920832	3.800041	0.263155	4	4	0.409600	2.361600	0.423442	4
0.902040	4.702081	0.212672	5	5	0.327680	2.689280	0.371847	5
0.883631	5.585712	0.179028	6					
				6	0.262144	2.951424	0.338820	6
0.865598	6.451310	0.155007	7	7	0.209715	3.161139	0.316342	7
0.847932	7.299242	0.137001	8	8	0.167772	3.328911	0.300399	8
0.830628	8.129870	0.123003	9	9	0.134218	3.463129	0.288756	9
0.813676	8.943546	0.111812	10	10	0.107374	3.570503	0.280073	10
0.797070	9.740616	0.102663	11					
YEAR				11	0.085899	3.656402	0.273493	11
0.780804	10.521420	0.095044	12 **MONTH**	12	0.068719	3.725122	0.268448	12
0.609654	18.736584	0.053372	24	13	0.054976	3.780097	0.264543	13
0.476020	25.151014	0.039760	36	14	0.043980	3.824077	0.261501	14
0.371679	30.155425	0.033157	48	15	0.035184	3.859262	0.259117	15
0.290208	34.070011	0.029351	60					
				16	0.028147	3.887409	0.257241	16
0.226595	37.123411	0.026937	72	17	0.022518	3.909927	0.255759	17
0.176927	39.507517	0.025312	84	18	0.018014	3.927942	0.254588	18
0.138145	41.369036	0.024173	96	19	0.014412	3.942353	0.253650	19
0.107864	42.822517	0.023352	108	20	0.011529	3.953883	0.252915	20
0.084221	43.957400	0.022749	120					
				21	0.009223	3.963106	0.252327	21
0.065760	44.843522	0.022300	132	22	0.007379	3.970485	0.251858	22
0.051346	45.535408	0.021961	144	23	0.005903	3.976388	0.251485	23
0.040091	46.075836	0.021703	156	24	0.004722	3.981110	0.251186	24
0.031303	46.497448	0.021507	168	25	0.003778	3.984888	0.250948	25
0.024442	46.826800	0.021355	180					
				26	0.003022	3.987910	0.250758	26
0.019084	47.063959	0.021239	192	27	0.002418	3.990328	0.250606	27
0.014901	47.284750	0.021148	204	28	0.001934	3.992262	0.250485	28
0.011635	47.441529	0.021079	216	29	0.001547	3.993810	0.250387	29
0.009084	47.563942	0.021024	228	30	0.001238	3.995048	0.250310	30
0.007093	47.659522	0.020982	240					
				31	0.000990	3.996038	0.250248	31
0.005538	47.734152	0.020949	252	32	0.000792	3.996830	0.250198	32
0.004324	47.792423	0.020924	264	33	0.000634	3.997464	0.250159	33
0.003376	47.837922	0.020904	276	34	0.000507	3.997971	0.250127	34
0.002636	47.873447	0.020888	288	35	0.000406	3.998377	0.250101	35
0.002058	47.901185	0.020876	300					
				36	0.000325	3.998701	0.250081	36
0.001607	47.922843	0.020867	312	37	0.000260	3.998961	0.250065	37
0.001255	47.939754	0.020860	324	38	0.000208	3.999169	0.250052	38
0.000980	47.952958	0.020854	336	39	0.000166	3.999335	0.250042	39
0.000765	47.963208	0.020849	348	40	0.000133	3.999468	0.250033	40
0.000597	47.971318	0.020846	360					
				41	0.000106	3.999574	0.250027	41
0.000466	47.977603	0.020843	372	42	0.000085	3.999659	0.250021	42
0.000364	47.982511	0.020841	384	43	0.000068	3.999727	0.250017	43
0.000284	47.986342	0.020839	396	44	0.000054	3.999782	0.250014	44
0.000222	47.989334	0.020838	408	45	0.000044	3.999825	0.250011	45
0.000173	47.991671	0.020837	420					
				46	0.000035	3.999860	0.250009	46
0.000135	47.993495	0.020836	432	47	0.000028	3.999888	0.250007	47
0.000106	47.994919	0.020836	444	48	0.000022	3.999910	0.250006	48
0.000083	47.996031	0.020835	456	49	0.000018	3.999928	0.250005	49
0.000064	47.996899	0.020835	468	50	0.000014	3.999942	0.250004	50
0.000050	47.997577	0.020834	480					

MONTHLY
Effective rate = 2.500% Base = 1.02500

ANNUAL
Effective rate = 30.000% Base = 1.30000

PV1 PRESENT VALUE OF ONE	PV1/P PRESENT VALUE OF ONE PER PERIOD	PR PRINCIPAL RECOVERY	MONTH		PV1 PRESENT VALUE OF ONE	PV1/P PRESENT VALUE OF ONE PER PERIOD	PR PRINCIPAL RECOVERY	YEAR
MONTH					YEAR			
0.975610	0.975610	1.025000	1	1	0.769231	0.769231	1.300000	1
0.951814	1.927424	0.518827	2	2	0.591716	1.360947	0.734783	2
0.928599	2.856024	0.350137	3	3	0.455166	1.816113	0.550627	3
0.905951	3.761974	0.265818	4	4	0.350128	2.166240	0.461629	4
0.883854	4.645828	0.215247	5	5	0.269329	2.435570	0.410582	5
0.862297	5.508125	0.181550	6					
				6	0.207176	2.642746	0.378394	6
0.841265	6.349390	0.157495	7	7	0.159366	2.802112	0.356874	7
0.820747	7.170137	0.139467	8	8	0.122589	2.924701	0.341915	8
0.800728	7.970865	0.125457	9	9	0.094300	3.019001	0.331235	9
0.781198	8.752064	0.114259	10	10	0.072538	3.091539	0.323463	10
0.762145	9.514208	0.105106	11					
YEAR			MONTH	11	0.055799	3.147338	0.317729	11
0.743556	10.257764	0.097487	12	12	0.042922	3.190260	0.313454	12
0.552875	17.884985	0.055913	24	13	0.033017	3.223276	0.310243	13
0.411094	23.556250	0.042452	36	14	0.025398	3.248674	0.307818	14
0.305671	27.773152	0.036006	48	15	0.019537	3.268211	0.305978	15
0.227284	30.908654	0.032353	60					
				16	0.015028	3.283239	0.304577	16
0.168998	33.240075	0.030084	72	17	0.011560	3.294799	0.303509	17
0.125659	34.973616	0.028553	84	18	0.008892	3.303691	0.302692	18
0.093435	36.262601	0.027577	96	19	0.006840	3.310532	0.302066	19
0.069474	37.221034	0.026867	108	20	0.005262	3.315794	0.301587	20
0.051658	37.933682	0.026362	120					
				21	0.004048	3.319841	0.301219	21
0.038410	38.463575	0.025999	132	22	0.003113	3.322955	0.300937	22
0.028560	38.857581	0.025735	144	23	0.002395	3.325350	0.300720	23
0.021236	39.150546	0.025542	156	24	0.001842	3.327192	0.300546	24
0.015790	39.368382	0.025401	168	25	0.001417	3.328609	0.300426	25
0.011741	39.530355	0.025297	180					
				26	0.001090	3.329699	0.300327	26
0.008730	39.650791	0.025220	192	27	0.000839	3.330538	0.300252	27
0.006491	39.740342	0.025163	204	28	0.000645	3.331183	0.300194	28
0.004827	39.806928	0.025121	216	29	0.000496	3.331679	0.300149	29
0.003589	39.856438	0.025090	228	30	0.000382	3.332061	0.300115	30
0.002669	39.893252	0.025067	240					
				31	0.000294	3.332354	0.300088	31
0.001984	39.920625	0.025050	252	32	0.000226	3.332580	0.300068	32
0.001475	39.940979	0.025037	264	33	0.000174	3.332754	0.300052	33
0.001097	39.956113	0.025027	276	34	0.000134	3.332887	0.300040	34
0.000816	39.967360	0.025020	288	35	0.000103	3.332990	0.300031	35
0.000607	39.975733	0.025015	300					
				36	0.000079	3.333069	0.300024	36
0.000451	39.981954	0.025011	312	37	0.000061	3.333130	0.300018	37
0.000335	39.986580	0.025008	324	38	0.000047	3.333177	0.300014	38
0.000249	39.990020	0.025006	336	39	0.000036	3.333213	0.300011	39
0.000185	39.992578	0.025005	348	40	0.000028	3.333240	0.300008	40
0.000138	39.994479	0.025003	360					
				41	0.000021	3.333262	0.300006	41
0.000102	39.995893	0.025003	372	42	0.000016	3.333278	0.300005	42
0.000076	39.996945	0.025002	384	43	0.000013	3.333291	0.300004	43
0.000057	39.997727	0.025001	396	44	0.000010	3.333300	0.300003	44
0.000042	39.998308	0.025001	408	45	0.000007	3.333308	0.300002	45
0.000031	39.998740	0.025001	420					
				46	0.000006	3.333314	0.300002	46
0.000023	39.999062	0.025001	432	47	0.000004	3.333318	0.300001	47
0.000017	39.999301	0.025000	444	48	0.000003	3.333321	0.300001	48
0.000013	39.999478	0.025000	456	49	0.000003	3.333324	0.300001	49
0.000010	39.999610	0.025000	468	50	0.000002	3.333326	0.300001	50
0.000007	39.999709	0.025000	480					

Glossary

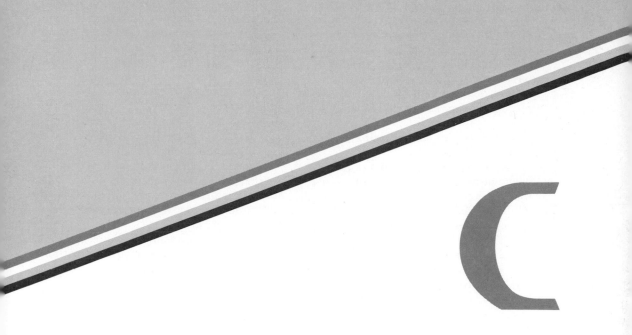

Many real estate terms use the following key words. When one of these key words appears in a term in the glossary, look up the key word first. If two or more of these key words appear in a term, the term is defined under one of them.

cost, costs   mortgage
capital   property
deed   rent
depreciation   tax
equity   tenancy
lease   title
lien   utility
listing   value
market   zoning

Abandonment. Vacating or giving up use of, or rights in, real property. Also the vacating by a tenant of premises before a lease expires without consent of the landlord.

Absolute Fee Simple. *See* Fee.

Abstract of Title. A digest of conveyances, transfers, wills, and other legal proceedings pertinent to title of a property, such as liens, charges, or encumbrances.

Acceleration Clause. A provision in a trust

685

deed, mortgage loan contract, or land contract giving the lender the right to declare the entire remaining balance due and payable immediately because of a violation of one of the covenants in the contract. The most common reasons for a lender to invoke the clause are failure to make scheduled payments (default), sale of the property, or demolition of buildings on the property. Also known as Alienation Clause.

Acceptance. Receiving and agreeing to the terms of a deed.

Access. The approach or way to a property or the means of entrance into or out of the property.

Accessibility. Relative cost (in time and money) of getting to and from a property. A property that is easy to get to is regarded as having good accessibility, i.e., convenience of location.

Accountability. Responsibility for money or property, including the maintaining of records concerning such money or property.

Accretion. Accumulation in an owner's land area due to water action, e.g., a stream.

Accrued Expense. A charge owed and not yet paid, such as interest or property taxes.

Acknowledgment. A formal declaration by a person executing an instrument that such act is intended as a free and voluntary act made before a duly authorized officer.

Acre. A measure of land area containing 43,560 square feet.

Actual Eviction. *See* Eviction.

Actual Knowledge or Notice. A claim of interest in, or ownership of, realty imputed as known to all the world because the claimant was or is in possession of the property.

Ad Valorem. According to value; the basis of real estate taxation.

Adjusted Cost Basis. Book value in an accounting sense. Value or cost of an asset for income tax purposes. The tax basis of property after taking account of time and change involved in owning and managing of the property. Also referred to as Tax Basis.

Adjusted Sale Price. The full sale or contract price less selling expenses and less "fixing-up" expenses.

Administrative Process. A series of five steps to guide action: (1) make decision to accomplish an objective, (2) organize resources, (3) exert leadership, (4) manage operations, and (5) reevaluate periodically.

Administrator. A person appointed by a probate court to settle the estate of a deceased person.

Advance Commitment. An agreement to purchase or make a government-underwritten mortgage on a property before (in advance of) construction.

Adverse Land Use. A land-use activity that is incompatible with, or has a negative effect on, nearby properties. For example, a used-car lot in a neighborhood of one-family residences.

Adverse Possession. The right of an occupant of land to acquire title against the real owner, under color of title, where possession has been actual, continuous, hostile, visible, and distinct for the statutory period.

Advertising. *General or Name.* Paid promotional material and efforts intended to place the advertiser's name and business before the public.
Institutional. Paid promotional material and efforts to create good will and confidence in real estate as a profession.
Specific. Paid promotional materials and efforts to achieve a limited goal, such as selling a particular house, lot, store, or warehouse.

Affidavit. A written statement or declaration sworn to before a public-office holder with authority to administer an oath or affirmation.

Of Heirship. A written statement setting forth the heirs or distributers of a decedent who died intestate, signed and sworn to, under oath, by a person or persons claiming property through inheritance.

Of Title. A written statement of ownership, signed and sworn to under oath by the person or persons purporting to be the owners.

After-Tax Cash Flow to Equity. Net operating income less debt service and less tax liability on income from the investment, taken period by period.

After-Tax Equity Rate of Return. The annual yield rate earned or expected on an equity investment with taxes on income from the investment taken into account. *See* Internal Rate of Return. Also referred to as After-Tax Equity Yield Rate.

After-Tax Equity Reversion. The actual or estimated sale price of a property less transaction costs, less outstanding debt, and less disposition taxes (primarily capital gains taxes).

Agency. In real estate, a fiduciary relationship in which one party (the agent-broker) acts as the representative of the other (the principal-owner) in negotiating the sale, purchase, leasing, or exchanging of property. Also, the relationship between a broker-principal and a salesperson-agent.

Law of. The legal rights, duties, and liabilities of principal, agent, and third parties as a result of the relationships between them.

Agent. A person who represents another (a principal) by the latter's authority.

Aggravation Costs. Driver or passenger irritation and annoyance during a linkage trip caused by delay, congestion, bumping and shoving, heat, cold, etc.

Agreement of Sale. *See* Sales Contract.

AIDA. Acronym for the intended effect of advertising: (1) attention, (2) interest, (3) desire, and (4) action (to contact owner or broker).

Air Rights. The right to inclusive and undisturbed use and control of a designated air space within the perimeter of a stated land area and within stated elevations. Such rights may be acquired for the construction of a building above the land or building of another, or for the protection of the light and air of an existing or proposed structure on an adjoining lot. The right to exclusive use, control, and quiet enjoyment of air space within stated elevations over a specific parcel of land.

Alienation. The transfer of property title to another, as by sale or gift.

ALTA Title Insurance Policy. A broad-coverage form of title insurance, suggested by the American Land Title Association, designed to protect against any defect in title not specifically excluded and whether recorded or not. Specific risks such as matters of survey, unrecorded mechanic's liens, water and mineral rights, and rights of parties in possession are automatically covered.

Amenities. Pleasing, nonmonetary satisfactions and benefits generated by a property, e.g., a pleasant view.

Amortization. The systematic repayment of borrowed money.

Annual Percentage Rate (APR). The yearly cost of credit in percentage terms.

Annuity. A series of payments to be received or paid through time.

Apartment. A room or group of rooms set apart for occupancy as a dwelling.

Appraisal. An estimate or opinion of value of a property, or some interest therein, rendered by a person skilled in property analysis and valuation, usually accompanied by an appraisal report setting forth the estimate of value and any reservations or conditions attached to it. Also referred to as Valuation.

Appraisal Process. An orderly, well-conceived set of procedures for valuing real estate.

Appraiser. One who makes value estimates.

Appreciation. Increase in value or worth of a property, usually because of locational advantage or inflation; the opposite of depreciation.

Appurtenance. That which has been added to or becomes a part of property; usually passes with it when it is sold, leased, or devised, as an easement.

Architect. A person who designs and oversees construction of real estate improvements.

Assess. To place an official value on property for *ad valorem* tax purposes. Assessed value. *See* Value, Assessed.

Assessed Value. *See* Value, Assessed.

Assessed Value-Sales Price Ratio. Relation of assessed value of a sample of sold property to actual sales prices for the properties.

Assessment. The official value placed on a parcel of property for *ad valorem* tax purposes.

Assessment Cycle or Period. The frequency with which all property in a tax district is reassessed or is supposed to be reassessed.

Assessment Roll. *See* Tax Roll.

Assessor. A government official who places assessed values on property for *ad valorem* tax purposes.

Assignment. A transfer of one's rights under a contract, as a transfer of lender's rights in a mortgage or of a tenant's right of occupancy on a lease.

Attachment. Seizure of property by court order, usually to ensure its availability to satisfy a plaintiff or complainant in the event a judgment against the owner is obtained in a pending suit.

Attorney-in-Fact. A person authorized to act for another under a power of attorney.

Balloon Payment. The unamortized principal of a mortgage or other type of loan, which is paid off in a lump sum.

Base Activity. The economic activity producing goods or services for export outside an area or community in return for money or income.

Base Line. An imaginary east-west line through the initial point of a principal meridian, from which township lines are established in the government survey system.

Basis. *See* Tax Basis.

Basis, Allocation of. Assigning initial basis to land, improvements, and personal property.

Before-Tax Cash Flow to Equity. Cash available to an owner-investor, period by period, after deducting operating expenses and debt service. Also referred to as Cash Throwoff.

Before-Tax Equity Reversion. The actual or estimated sale price of a property less transaction costs and less outstanding debt, usually a mortgage loan.

Bench Mark. A fixed point-of-known elevation used as a reference by surveyors.

Bequest. A gift of personal property through a will, a legacy.

Bigger-Fool Theory. Refers to the practice by which buyers pay current prices for investments without analysis and with the expectation of reselling to a "bigger fool." The owner, when the bubble of speculation bursts, is the biggest fool.

Bill of Sale. An agreement or statement that articles of personal property have been sold or transferred to a certain person or party.

Binder. An acknowledgment of an earnest

money deposit by a buyer plus a written brief agreement to enter into a longer written contract for the sale of real estate. Also referred to as an Earnest Money Receipt or an Offer to Purchase.

Blight. The decay, withering away, or decline in the quality of a neighborhood.

Blockbusting. Inducing neighborhood residents to sell their property at depressed prices by introducing people of another race or class into the neighborhood, thereby taking advantage of fears and prejudices.

Bona Fide. In good faith, without fraud.

Boot. Cash or the market value of personal property offered or received in a tax-deferred exchange to balance equities, unlike property.

Borrower Risk. Chance of loss in mortgage lending due to perils associated with the borrower. The main items of analysis to determine the risks are (a) credit rating, (b) assets, (c) earning capacity or income, and (d) motivation.

BOY. Beginning of year, as BOY1; a designation of time for time-value-of-money purposes.

Breach of Contract. Failure to perform or live up to the terms of a contract.

Broker, Real Estate. A licensed person engaged to negotiate the sale, purchase, leasing, or exchange of realty, or to arrange the financing thereof, for a fee or commission.

Broker's Bond. A bond, put up by a licensed broker or salesperson, to insure return of money, obtained fraudulently, to a client.

Buffer Strip. A parcel of land, frequently unimproved except for landscaping, to ease the transition from one land use (residential) to another (industrial) that is considered incompatible or inharmonious.

Building Code. A local or state government ordinance regulating the construction, alteration, and maintenance of structures within the jurisdiction.

Bulk Transfer. Sale of a large amount of materials, supplies, merchandise, or other inventory outside the usual course or way of doing business.

Business Interruption Insurance. Insurance to compensate a business owner for loss of income due to a fire, flood, or other peril.

Business Risk. The chance that projected levels of income will not be realized.

Buyer's Market. The supply of goods and services strongly exceeds the demand, enabling buyers to bargain for and get lower prices.

Canadian Rollover Mortgage Loan. Periodic financing and refinancing of a property with short-term loans at the current interest rate.

Canvassing. Contacting property owners, in person or by telephone and without a prior appointment, to obtain a listing agreement.

Capital Budgeting. Making decisions about capital and scheduling its use for long-term investments.

Capital Gains Income. The amount by which the net proceeds on resale of realty or other capital assets exceeds the adjusted cost or tax basis (book value).

Capital Markets. Creation and exchanges for money of long-term (more than one year) debt instruments (bonds, mortgages, commercial paper) and of stocks.

Capital Rationing. Allocating or budgeting financial resources to the most acceptable or desirable projects or investments.

Capitalization. The conversion or discounting of expected future income payments into a lump-sum present value.

Capitalization Rate. A ratio of income to value; a combination of discount rate and a capital recovery rate. When divided into income, as from a property, a present or capitalized value for the property results.

Carrying Cost. Expenses and outlays to be met until a property is ripe for development or redevelopment.

Cash Flow. The net result of cash receipts and disbursements taken period by period for an investment; may be on a before-tax or after-tax basis.

Cash Flow to Equity. *See* After-Tax and Before-Tax Cash Flow to Equity.

Cash Throwoff. *See* Before-Tax Cash Flow to Equity.

Caveat Emptor. "Let the buyer beware," meaning that one examines and purchases property at one's own risk.

Central Business District. The downtown or core area of an urban community where retail, financial, governmental, and service activities are concentrated.

Certificate of Occupancy. An official statement, required in many municipalities for new or rehabilitated buildings, stating that required inspections of construction, plumbing, electrical wiring, etc., have been passed and the property is fit for use.

Certification of Title. *See* Title.

Chain of Title. *See* Title.

Change, Principle of. The forces of supply and demand are constantly creating a new real estate environment, thereby leading to price and value fluctuation.

Chattel. Personal property, such as household goods or fixtures.

Client. A principal, usually a property owner, who employs a broker.

Closing. Sales, financing, title. Bringing a transaction to a conclusion. Examples are the exchange of purchase price for a deed in a title closing or the exchange of mortgage funds for a mortgage lien and note. Also, getting an interested buyer to put up earnest money and to sign an offer to purchase a property.

Closing Statement. A summary of financial adjustments between a buyer and seller, including the amount of the net difference between them, which is usually paid by cash or check at the closing.

Cloud on the Title. *See* Title, Cloud on.

Coinsurance. A clause in fire insurance policies to encourage purchase of adequate coverage. If a certain percentage of value is not insured against loss, the property owner is presumed to share the risk of loss with the insurance company.

Comingling of Funds. Illegally combining or mixing, often in the same bank account, monies held in trust for clients and personal monies.

Commission. Payment due a real estate broker or salesperson for services rendered in such capacity.

Commitment. A pledge, promise, or letter of agreement to make a loan.

Common Law. Body of law that grew up from custom and decided cases (English law) rather than from codified law (Roman law); a system of law based on precedent.

Community Property. *See* Property, Community.

Community Shopping Center. A retail trade facility, from 10 to 30 acres, that provides a limited line of shopping goods (apparel and furniture) in addition to convenience goods; often anchored by a small department store.

Comparative Economic Advantage. The activity giving the greatest gain or benefit to an area or community.

Competent Party. A person legally considered qualified or fit to enter into a binding contract.

Component Depreciation. Depreciation that is calculated by applying a distinct rate against each part or component of an asset, according to its useful life.

Composite Depreciation. Depreciation that is calculated by applying one rate against an entire building or asset.

Compound Interest. *See* Time Value of Money.

Concentric-Circle Theory. An explanation of urban growth and structure in which a central city is surrounded by circles of varied economic activities.

Concession. Giving up or yielding a right or benefit in making a contract, e.g., not requiring a security deposit in making a lease.

Condemnation Taking private property for public use or purposes with compensation to the owner, under the right of eminent domain.

Conditional Commitment. An agreement, with certain limiting provisions, to make a loan.

Conditional Use Permit. *See* Zoning Exception.

Condominium. Fee ownership of a unit of space in developed realty plus an undivided interest in common areas owned jointly with other condominium owners in the development.

Conduit. The transfer of income from one legal entity to another when only the final recipient incurs tax liability; a form of ownership that funnels or directs profits from a property to an investor-owner without the need for payment of taxes in between. A real estate investment trust is considered a conduit, while a corporation is not.

Confiscation. The taking of property by a government without compensation.

Conforming Use. A use of land that is consistent with the zoning of the property.

Consideration. Anything of value given or received in a contractual agreement. Money, services, personal or real property, and even love and affection qualify.

Construction Cycle. A regular, rhythmic rise and fall in real estate building and development activity.

Construction Loan. A short-term loan to finance construction or development of realty; upon completion of construction a permanent loan is obtained.

Constructive Eviction. *See* Eviction.

Constructive Knowledge or Notice. Notice presumed of everyone, by law, as consequence of properly making documents and other information a part of the public record.

Consumer Choice. The selection of goods and services for personal use and not for resale or use in a productive process.

Consumer Price Index. A measure of the relative costs of living, which differs from time to time or place to place.

Contingency. An event of chance, usually considered to carry negative consequences.

Contract. A legally binding agreement between competent parties calling for them to do or not to do some specific thing, for consideration.

Contract Interest Rate. The agreed rate of interest in a specific note or loan.

Contract Rent. *See* Rent, Contract.

Contract Zoning. Limiting the use by deed restriction or side agreement to a more restrictive use than allowed by a new zoning classification simultaneously granted by a public agency.

Contractor. In construction, one who contracts to build structures and other realty improvements.

Contribution, Principle of. The value of any factor of production or component of a property depends on how much its presence adds to the overall worth of a property or its absence detracts from the overall worth.

Convenience. *See* Accessibility.

Conventional. Customary or ordinary. For example, a conventional mortgage loan is made without government insurance or guarantee and conforms to accepted standards of mutual consent between a lender and a borrower.

Conveyance. The transfer of an interest in real property by deed, mortgage, or lease, but not including a will.

Cooperative Ownership of a membership certificate or stock in a corporation or trust, which carries the right to occupy a specific dwelling unit or other unit of space under a proprietary lease.

Cooperative Ownership. Ownership of shares in a cooperative venture entitling the owner to occupy and use specific space unit, usually an apartment; under a proprietary lease.

Corporation. An entity or organization, created by operation of law, with rights of doing business essentially the same as those of an individual. The entity has continuous existence regardless of that of its owners and limits liability of owners to the amount invested in the organization. The entity ceases to exist only if dissolved according to proper legal process.

Corporeal Right. A visible, tangible right in realty, such as occupancy.

Cost. The amount of money, or price paid or obligated, for anything.
Approach. An appraisal procedure using depreciated replacement costs of improvements and fixtures plus land value as a basis for estimating market value of the subject property. The underlying assumption is that an investor will pay no more for a property than the cost of a site, plus the cost of improvements, necessary to provide a substitute property with utility comparable to that of the subject property. Also referred to as Summation Approach.

Of Capital. The price paid for the use of money; may be an actual or imputed rate of return. For a mortgage loan, the interest rate is the cost; for equity capital, the required rate of return is set by the best alternative use of the money.
Of Replacement. The outlay or amount of money required to construct a substitute, of comparable utility, for existing buildings or improvements.
Of Replacement Less Depreciation. Cost of replacement new less decreased utility due to physical, functional, or locational causes.
Of Reproduction. The outlay or amount of money required to construct an exact duplicate of existing buildings or improvements.

Costs, Selling or Transaction. Expenses incurred in disposition of a property, such as broker's commission, escrow charges, and legal fees.

Costs of Friction. Costs of moving goods or people between linked land-use activities. Included are transportation costs, time costs of travel, terminal costs, and aggravation costs.

Costs of Home Ownership. Total of all financial sacrifices to own a home, such as interest, depreciation, taxes, and maintenance.

Covenant. A promise. For example, in a warranty deed, the grantor promises that no encumbrances exist against the property being conveyed except those stated.

Covenants. A promise or clause in a contract.

Credit. A bookkeeping entry in a person's favor, as in a closing statement.

Credit Financing. Making loans to others, as to help finance the purchase of a property.

Cul de sac. A dead-end street with a large turnaround at the closed end.

Curtesy. A husband's right or interest in his wife's real estate upon her death.

Customer. Buyer of listed property.

Damages. In eminent domain, the loss in value to the remainder after a partial taking of a property.

Dealer. One whose primary purpose and activity is to buy, develop, or hold real estate for sale to customers for profit.

Debit. On a closing statement, an entry in someone else's favor; what is owed to someone else.

Debt Financing. The borrowing of money to help pay the purchase price of a property or an investment.

Debt Service. The periodic payment on a loan for interest and principal repayment.

Decedent. A dead person.

Decision-Making Process. A series of steps for orderly decision making: (1) recognize problem situation, (2) collect pertinent information, (3) identify problem clearly, (4) pose alternatives, and (5) make decision.

Dedication A giving of land or property to some public use and the acceptance for such use by and on behalf of the public. Example: land for a park or school.

Deed. A legal instrument that, when properly executed and delivered, transfers or conveys title, or an interest in realty, from the grantor to the grantee.

Administrator's. A nonstatutory deed used to convey property of a person who died intestate.

Bargain and Sale. A legal instrument to convey title in which, by implication, the grantor asserts ownership of title or an interest in the realty, as described, but makes no other covenants or claims, unless stated.

Cession. A nonstatutory deed to convey street rights to a municipality by an abutting owner.

Committee's. A nonstatutory deed to transfer or convey property of infants and incompetents whose affairs are managed by a court-appointed committee.

Confirmation. A deed to correct information or a defect cited and recorded in a previous deed. Also referred to as a Correction Deed.

Executor's. A deed to convey title in settling the estate or affairs of a person.

Grant. A deed in which the grantor warrants, by implication, that ownership has not already been conveyed to another, that the title is free from encumbrances except those stated, and that any title later acquired by the grantor is conveyed to the grantee.

Guardian's. A nonstatutory deed used by a guardian to convey the interest of an infant or ward in realty, upon permission of the court.

Nonstatutory. A long form deed, written for special purposes or to cover unique situations, as when a guardian acts for a dependent or court ward.

Quitclaim. A legal instrument whereby the grantor transfers rights in a property, if any, to the grantee, without warranty of title or interest.

Referee's in Foreclosure. An instrument used following a foreclosure sale in which an officer of the court conveys the mortgagor's interest with no other supporting covenants.

Referee's in Partition. An instrument used following a partition judgment and sale in which an officer of the court conveys the interests of the former joint owners with no other supporting covenants.

Release. A deed used to remove or negate a mortgage lien, a dower interest, a remainder interest, or a reverter. Also referred to as a Mortgage Release.

Special Warranty. A deed which only covenants that title has not been impaired, except as noted, by any acts of the grantor.

Statutory. A short form of deed in which covenants and warranties are implied as though written in full because the deed is approved or provided for in the state statutes.

Surrender. A nonstatutory deed to convey an estate for years or a life estate to a remainderman or a holder of a reversionary interest.

Trust. A legal instrument conveying title, or an interest in realty to a third party (trustee) to be held as security for a debt owed a lender-beneficiary. Also referred to as a Deed of Trust or a Trust-Deed-in-the-Nature-of-a-Mortgage.

Warranty. A deed conveying title, or an interest in realty, that covenants that the grantor has good title, free of encumbrances except as stated, which the grantee should be able to quietly enjoy and which the grantor will protect against other claimants, if necessary. Also known as General Warranty Deed.

Deed in Lieu of Foreclosure. An owner-borrower conveyance of equity interest to a lender when in default, to avoid foreclosure costs and procedures when equity is less than the expected costs of foreclosure.

Deed of Reconveyance. A deed from the trustee returning title to the owner-borrower-trustor to clear a trust deed; the equivalent of mortgage release or satisfaction piece. Also known as a Deed of Release.

Deed Restriction. A covenant or condition entered in the public record to limit the nature or intensity of land or realty.

Default. Failure to fulfill or live up to the terms of an agreement or contract, as a mortgage loan contract; most often the failure to make the scheduled periodic payments to service the loan.

In Prior Mortgage Clause. A provision in a second mortgage giving the mortgagee the right to pay debt service, etc., on default of the first mortgage by the mortgagor.

Defeasance. An instrument that offsets the effect of some other deed or of an estate.

Defeasance Clause. A mortgage provision returning clear title to the borrower-mortgagor after all terms of the loan, including repayment, have been met.

Defendant. The party against whom a lawsuit is filed; the party required to respond or give an answer in a legal action.

Deficiency Judgment. A judicial decree in favor of the lender for that portion of a mortgage debt that remains unsatisfied after default, foreclosure, and sale of the property pledged as security.

Delivery. An act by a grantor showing intent to make a deed effective.

Demand. A desire to own or use something, such as realty. The quantity of goods or services wanted at a given price is effective demand.

Demographic. Relating to population characteristics and study.

Demography. Study of population characteristics, trends, and patterns.

Depletion. Using up or exhausting a resource, as the taking of oil from a well.

Depreciation. Loss or decline in value of an asset; loss in market value of property because of physical deterioration, functional obsolescence, or locational obsolescence; for bookkeeping and income tax purposes, a deduction from gross income to provide for the recapture of investment in a wasting asset, or for the gradual wasting away of an asset other than land.

Accelerated. A method of calculating

tax depreciation that gives a higher allowance in the early years than the straight-line method.

Curable. Describes physical deterioration or functionally obsolete items that add more to value if corrected than the cost of correction. Example: broken window.

Declining Balance. For income tax purposes a writing off of tax basis in a wasting asset by a fixed percent each year.

Double-Declining-Balance Method of. For income tax purposes, a writing off of tax basis in a wasting asset by double the percentage calculated in the first year for straight-line depreciation.

Economic, Locational, or Environmental. Decrease in value or worth in value of a property due to factors external to or outside the property. Also referred to as Economic or Locational Obsolescence.

Functional Obsolescence. The loss in value because a property cannot render a service in a given use as well as a new property designed for the use.

Functional Obsolescence—Curable. A functional deficiency that, if corrected, adds more to property value than the cost of correction.

Functional Obsolescence—Incurable. A functional deficiency that would cost more to correct than the correction would add to value.

Incurable. Physical deterioration or functional obsolescence items that would cost more to correct than the correction would add to value.

Locational Obsolescence. Diminished utility and value of a site or property because external factors and environment unfavorably affect its income or income potential. These external factors include blight, change in transportation routes, excessive taxes, or encroachment of inharmonious land uses. Also referred to as Economic or Environmental Obsolescence.

Physical Deterioration. The loss in value because of physical deterioration or impairment brought about by use in service, acts of God, or actions of the elements.

Physical Deterioration—Curable. An item of physical deterioration that can be corrected at a cost less than the increase in value resulting from the correction.

Physical Deterioration—Incurable. Items of physical deterioration for which the cost to correct exceeds the increase in value resulting from the correction.

Recapture. Depreciation that has been taken by an accelerated schedule and then disallowed for income tax purposes at time of sale; this means that the owner must report the recaptured depreciation as ordinary income and pay taxes accordingly in the year of sale.

Straight Line. The annual write-off of an investment (basis) in a wasting asset by an equal amount each year over its remaining useful life.

Sum-of-the-Years Digits (SOYD). For income tax purposes, an accelerated write-off of tax basis in a wasting asset, according to a stipulated schedule of fractions available to first user only. For long useful lives, the denominator can be calculated according to the following formula, when N = remaining useful life. This method is available to *first* user only.

$$\frac{(N)(N+1)}{2} = \frac{(4)(5)}{2} = \frac{20}{2} = 10$$

Depreciation, Component. *See* Component Depreciation.

Depreciation, Composite. *See* Composite Depreciation.

Descent. A transfer of property title according to inheritance laws because the owner died without a will.

Developer. One who prepares and improves land for use as by subdividing and adding buildings.

Development Charge. Fee imposed on a subdivider or developer to pay the costs of new roads, utility lines, etc., necessitated by a new subdivision or structure.

Devise. A gift of real property through a will.

Direct Income Capitalization. Determining market value by devising an overall capitalization rate from the market and applying it to the subject property in a direct or straightforward manner.

Direct Sales-Comparison Approach to Value. An appraisal procedure using sale prices of properties similar to a subject property as a basis for estimating the market value of the subject property. The underlying assumption is that an investor will pay no more for a property than would have to be paid for a similar property of comparable utility. Also known as Market Approach to Value.

Direction of Least Resistance. An explanation of urban growth and structure, in which a city grows in the direction of greatest attraction or least resistance, or their resultants.

Disclosed Principal. A principal known or identified to a third party by an agent.

Discount. To reduce the value of a future payment or series of future payments, e.g., to make an adjustment for the difference in time of receipt and the rate of discounting.

Discount Rate. The percentage used in time value of money calculations to find the present value of a future payment. The percentage charge member banks must pay the Federal Reserve when borrowing.

Discounted Cash Flow Analysis. Analysis using TVM factors to solve financing problems, e.g., calculating the present value of anticipated future cash flows generated by a property by discounting them at a desired rate of return.

Discounted Rate of Return. *See* Internal Rate of Return.

Disintermediation. The process when savers withdraw money from savings or time accounts for direct investment in stocks, bonds, and other securities.

Dispersing Force. An influence for scatteration of people and activites, as for example, some people desire space and isolation.

Dispossess Proceeding. A legal action to recover possession from a tenant for default or breach of contract.

Donee. A person receiving a gift.

Donor. A person giving a gift.

Double-Entry Bookkeeping. An accounting system in which a credit entry is made for every debit entry; in turn, total debits equal total credits.

Doubling up. The occupancy of one dwelling unit by two or more families.

Dower. A wife's right in her husband's real estate; the right is "inchoate" or inactive during his lifetime. At his death, the right becomes "consummate," or effective.

Dual/Divided Agency. An agency that represents two principals, which is illegal except with knowledge and consent of both.

Durability. The ability of land or realty to render services or to exist for a long time.

Durability of Investment. *See* Fixity of Investment.

Duration of Loan. The life or contract period of a loan; the time over which a loan is to be repaid.

Earnest Money. A down payment of money or other consideration made as evidence of good faith in offering to purchase real estate.

Easement. A nonpossessory right or privilege to use the land of another for certain purposes such as party driveways, ingress and egress, or drainage.

Easement Appurtenant. The right of an owner of a dominant estate to use adjacent land of another, termed a servient estate, for stipulated purposes.

Easement in Gross. The right to use the land of another without the need of owning an adjacent or dominant estate. An easement granted a utility company for power or sewer lines is an example.

Easy Money. A money supply large enough to meet the economy's needs with interest rates being stable or falling.

Economic Base. The economic activity of an area or community that exports goods and/or services in return for money or income. Often the activity for which a community is famous, as beer for Milwaukee, autos for Detroit, or government for Washington, D.C.

Economic Base Analysis. The study of basic and nonbasic economic activities of an area or community to predict population, income, and demand for real estate facilities.

Economic Capacity of Land. The relative ability of a site to absorb human and capital resources in keeping with the principal of proportionality.

Economic Force. An influence for change growing out of people's efforts to use and allocate limited resources to satisfy needs and wants.

Economic Life. The number of years over which realty improvements are expected to render services of economic value, e.g., earn rents that exceed costs of operation. Also referred to as Useful Life.

Economic Rent. *See* Rent, Economic.

Economics. Science and study of the allocation and reallocation of limited resources among competing human needs to maximize human satisfactions.

Economies of Scale. Producing larger output and thereby reducing the cost per unit of output.

Effective Demand. Potential demand armed with purchasing power or the ability to pay. Demand for space that enters into and influences the market.

Effective Gross Income. Revenues actually collected in operating an income property; gross scheduled income less allowances for vacancies and credit losses (failure to collect payments even though space was rented).

Efficient Market. A market in which changes in information are quickly reflected in each property's probable selling price or value.

Emblements. Vegetation requiring annual cultivation, as for example corn, tomatoes or cabbage. They are deemed to be personal property.

Eminent Domain. The right of a government, or quasi-governmental agency, to take private property for public uses or purposes upon payment of reasonable or just compensation and without the consent of the owner.

Enabling Acts. Express authority from a state legislative body for a local governmental body to carry on a certain activity such as land-use planning or zoning.

Encroachment. A building, part of a building, or other object that intrudes upon or invades a highway or sidewalk or trespasses upon property of another.

Encumbrance. Any cloud against clear, free title to property that makes it less than marketable or freely acceptable to a buyer and therefore less valuable. Outstanding mortgage loans, liens, easements, or unpaid taxes are all regarded as clouds or encumbrances on title.

Environment. The physical, legal, social, economic, and political makeup surrounding a parcel of realty that influence its value.

Environmental Impact Study (EIS). An investigation and analysis to determine the long-run effects of a proposed land use on its surroundings.

EOY. End of year, as EOY1; a designation of time for time-value-of-money purposes.

Equitable Right of Redemption. A borrower's right to recover a mortgaged property, prior to foreclosure, upon payment of debt, interest, and miscellaneous costs of the lender. Also known as the equity of redemption.

Equity. The disposition value of a property less any liens or encumbrances against the property and less transaction costs; the owner's interest in a property.

Equity Build-Up. The increase in the owner's interest because of mortgage loan amortization or appreciation in the total value of a property.

Equity Kicker. An equity interest in a property given a mortgage lender to obtain a mortgage on said property.

Equity Rate of Return. Average annual percentage rate of earning on an equity investment expected or realized over the holding period.

Equity of Redemption. The right of a borrower to recover mortgaged property by paying the debt, even after default but before foreclosure sale. Also, the right of a tenant to reclaim occupancy, if dispossessed and more than five years remain on the lease. Also known as Equitable Right of Redemption.

Equity Yield. The total return to equity investment.

Erosion. The wearing away of land through processes of nature, as by streams and winds.

Escalation Clause. A provision in a contract, to adjust, usually increase, payments based on some index or level of costs.

Escheat. Reversion of property to the state because no heirs are available and the owner made no will disposing of the property to others.

Escrow. The depositing of money, legal instruments (deeds), or other valuables and instructions with a third party to be held until acts or conditions of a contractual agreement are performed or satisfied.

Estate. A right or interest in property. Also known as Tenancy. Also, the property of a deceased person.

Estoppel Certificate. A written statement that, when signed and given to another person, legally prevents the person signing from subsequently saying that the facts are different from those set forth.

Eviction. The removal of a tenant from possession of realty. Actual eviction results from direct actions of the landlord; constructive eviction occurs when the physical condition makes occupancy hazardous and/or makes the premises unsuitable for the purpose intended.

Excess Condemnation. The taking of more property by a public body than is physically needed for a proposed improvement under the right of eminent domain.

Excess Depreciation. Tax depreciation taken over and above straight line.

Exchange, Tax-Deferred. The trading of a productive property used in a business or held as an investment for a like kind of a property for productive use in a business or held as an investment without the payment of any taxes on the economic gain or profit realized on the property transferred.

Exculpation Clause. A provision as in a mortgage loan agreement holding the borrower blameless in default and thereby limiting the borrower's personal liability. The property serves as the main security for the loan.

Executor. A person empowered by a court to carry out the terms and provisions of a will.

Expenses, Fixed Operating. Costs of operating a property that remain relatively stable during the period of concern and must be paid whether the property earns revenues or not. Property taxes and insurance are the most obvious examples.

Expenses of Home Ownership. Charges to own a home that require an actual monetary outlay.

Exposure. The environment as experienced or observed from a property and therefore a locational consideration. An aesthetic benefit, such as a good view, is termed favorable exposure. Location in a blighted neighborhood or where smoke or noxious odors prevail constitute unfavorable exposure.

Extended Coverage Insurance. Insurance against losses from other than fire; that is, from wind, rain, hail, explosion, rust, smoke, etc.

Extension. The continuation of a contract or arrangement, such as the right of renewal of a lease.

Extensive Margin. The point at which it is just barely financially feasible (profitable) to convert rural land to urban uses. The extensive margin is symbolized by land subdivision and development at the urban fringe. See Intensive Margin.

External Economies of Scale. Locating a production facility at a place where specialized materials and services are readily available to reduce the cost per unit.

Fair Cash Value. Comparable to market value.

Fair Housing Laws. Laws to ensure equality of treatment regardless of sex, race, color, religion, or national origin.

Fannie Mae. A government-sponsored, privately owned corporation that supplements private mortgage market operations by buying and selling FHA, VA, and conventional loans. Also known as FNMA or Federal National Mortgage Association.

Feasibility Analysis. The investigation to determine whether an investment or development should be undertaken. A study of the profit potential in a proposed real estate project.

Feasible. An economically reasonable, profitable, or worthwhile project, plan, or undertaking.

Fee, Fee Simple, Fee Simple Absolute. The most complete type of private ownership of an interest in real estate; includes all rights of possession, control, use, and disposition even by inheritance; limitations are police power, taxation, eminent domain, and escheat.

FHA. Federal Housing Administration. An agency of the federal government that functions as an insurer of mortgage loans.

FHLMC. *See* Freddie Mac.

Fiduciary Relationship. Occupying a position of trust and confidence to handle a financial transaction for another in good faith. Examples: guardian-ward or broker-owner.

Filtering. The change in ownership and/or occupancy of housing from one income group to another. Filtering down means that lower-income groups occupy the units.

Finance Charge. Total of all costs a consumer or borrower must pay, directly or indirectly, to obtain credit.

Financial Management of Real Estate. Using and administering realty to maximize self-interest, which is usually taken as maximizing wealth.

Financial Markets. Creation and exchange for money of financial claims, such as bonds, bills, and mortgages.

Financial Risk. Extra uncertainty or chance of loss to an owner created by the use of debt financing (borrowing) in purchasing an investment.

Financing Statement. A legal document signifying a debt encumbrance on personal property as fixtures, prepared in accordance with the Uniform Commercial Code, for filing in the public record.

Firm Commitment. A definite offer to make a loan at stated terms and conditions.

First Owner-User. The person holding title to income property when it is initially rented or put into use.

Fixed Costs. *See* Expenses, Fixed.

Fixed-Rate Mortgage Loan. A loan at one stated interest rate over its life.

Fixing-Up Expenses. Noncapital outlays made to assist in the sale of a residence, such as painting, minor repairs, or landscaping.

Fixity of Investment. An economic characteristic of realty; the long time required to recover the investment in a property.

Fixity of Location. Physical immobility of a parcel of real estate; the implication is that demand must come to the parcel for real estate to render a production service.

Fixture. An item of personal property that is annexed, attached, affixed to, or installed in real property. Examples are furnaces, plumbing fixtures, hot-water heaters, draperies, and wall-to-wall carpeting. If certain tests regarding nature of annexation, nature of use, and intent of parties are met, the item is regarded as realty. This determination is important at time of sale, of mortgaging, of lease termination, and of assessment for property tax purposes.

Flat Lease. *See* Lease, Flat.

Floor-Area Ratio (FAR) Zoning. Zoning for density by limiting the relation of building coverage to parcel area to a fixed number.

FNMA. *See* Fannie Mae.

Force. An influence for change, which involves strength or magnitude and direction.

Foreclosure. A legal process initiated by a mortgagee or other lien creditor, upon default by an owner-debtor, to force sale of the property and immediate payment of the debt.

Foundation. The supporting portion of a structure below the first-floor construction, or below grade, including the footings.

Fraud. Deceiving or misrepresenting. Using an untruth to gain an advantage in negotiations for a business transaction.

Freddie Mac. A secondary mortgage market facility affiliated with the Federal Home Loan Bank System, authorized to buy and sell conventional, FHA, and VA loans. Also known as Federal Home Loan Mortgage Corporation or FHLMC.

Freehold. An estate held in fee simple or for life.

Functional Area. A place where some specialized activity, such as retail trade, occurs in business districts and shopping centers.

Functional Efficiency. The cost and quality of services rendered by a property in a particular use relative to the cost and quality of services rendered by a new property designed for that use. A measure of how well a property is suited to its actual or intended use. *See also* Utility, Functional.

Functional Obsolescence. *See* Depreciation.

Fungible. Substitutable: one specimen or part may be used in place of another in satisfying an obligation or contract, e.g., money or wheat. Real property rights are often not considered fungible.

General Partner. The operating or managing partner in a limited partnership.

Ginnie Mae. A federal government corporation designed to handle special assistance functions for certain FHA and VA loans and to guarantee certain securities backed by mortgage loans. Also known as GNMA or Government National Mortgage Association.

GNMA. *See* Ginnie Mae.

Good Will. The reputation a trade or business has built up by rendering willing, reliable service.

Graduated Lease. *See* Lease, Graduated.

Graduated-Payment Mortgage Loan. A loan with debt service starting low and gradually increasing over a stated period, usually five to ten years.

Grant. Conveying an interest in property to another.

Grantee. The person or party to whom real estate is conveyed; the buyer.

Grantor. The person or party conveying an interest in realty, as in a deed signed by a seller.

Gross Income. Estimated potential revenues that a property can earn before deductions for vacancies, credit losses, and expenses.

Gross Income Multiplier (GIM). The ratio between the sale price and the annual gross income of an income property.

$$\frac{\text{Sale price}}{\text{Annual gross income}} = \frac{\text{gross income}}{\text{multiplier (GIM)}}$$

The GIM derived in this way can be used as a means of estimating the market value of an unsold property. Gross income x GIM = indicated market value.

Gross Lease. *See* Lease, Gross.

Gross National Product (GNP). Total value of all goods and services produced in an economy at current prices.

Ground Lease. *See* Lease, Ground.

Guide Meridian. Imaginary north-south line parallel to principal meridian, with adjustments for earths curvature at each standard parallel.

Habendum Clause. A statement, beginning with "to have and to hold," in a deed of the interest conveyed (life estate or fee).

Hazard. The source or cause of a disastrous event, such as fire, flood, earthquake, wind, or workman's injury.

Heir. One who receives property of a deceased person, either by will or by law of descent when an owner dies intestate (without a will).

Heterogencity. The realty characteristic of unlikeness between one property and another in location, size and shape, topography, etc.

Highest and Best Use. The legal, possible, and probable employment of land that will give the greatest present value to land or realty while preserving its utility. Or, roughly, that use which will give the greatest net return from land if no difference in risk is present.

Highest and Best Use, Principle of. Real estate must be appraised in its highest and best use in determining its market value.

Homestead. Real estate occupied by an owner as a home.

Homestead Exemption Right. A reservation of a homestead that precludes attachment or forced sale for nonpayment of debt, except for mortgage and tax liens. In a few states, property taxes are reduced or not applied to homesteads.

Homogeneous. Made of the same or similar kind, as a neighborhood of similar types of housing.

Hundred Percent Location. The commercial site with the greatest amount of traffic going by, hence the site likely to generate the greatest amount of sales. Presumably this is the most desirable and the most valuable site for commercial purposes.

Immobility. The characteristic of a site that it has a fixed physical location.

Improved Land. Land readied for development as by the installation of sewers, water, roads, etc. Also, land on which buildings have been erected.

Improvements. Buildings, sewer, water and power lines, or roads to make a property marketable and/or productive.

Improvement Costs. The expenses incurred or dollar outlays to make a site productive. Outlays for buildings, driveways, and landscaping are obvious examples.

Income. *See* Gross, Net Operating, Net Spendable, Net Taxable, Ordinary.

Income Approach to Value. An appraisal procedure using capitalization of expected future income or utility (amenities) as a basis for estimating market value of the subject property. The underlying assumption is that the investor will pay no more for the subject property than would have to be paid for another property with an income stream of comparable amount, duration, and certainty.

Income Property. Realty that produces monetary income on a continuing basis.

Income Ratio. For an income property: net operating income divided by gross scheduled income.

Increasing and Diminishing Returns, Law of. An economic law relating input and output. Initially each additional unit of input is regarded as producing an increasingly larger amount of output; this is increasing returns. Eventually the amount of output per unit of input declines; this is diminishing returns. Generally, additional units of input will be added as long as the value of the marginal output exceeds the cost of the marginal input.

Independent Contractor. A person retaining control over work details while performing a service or accomplishing a result for an employer, e.g., a broker engaged to sell a property for an owner or a sales person engaged by a broker.

Indestructibility. The characteristic of land or space that it cannot be destroyed; it goes on forever.

Index Lease. A lease providing for changes in rent payments in direct proportion to changes in an independent index, such as the consumer price index.

Infrastructure. *See* Urban Infrastructure.

Injunction. A court order requiring one to pursue or to stop a certain course of action.

Installment Sale. The transfer of property to another for two or more payments, or installments. If 30 percent or less of the sale price is received in the first year of the sale, income taxes on profits can be prorated according to the period in which payments are received. The transaction may involve a land contract or a purchase money mortgage.

Institution. An established principal, law, organization, custom, or belief.

Institutional Force. An influence for change generated by the acceptance by people of certain principles, laws, or beliefs.

Insurance. Shifting the risk of financial loss

caused by a disastrous event (fire or death) to another party (insurance company) in return for a fee (premium).

Insurance Premium. A payment to an insurance company as compensation for its acceptance of risk.

Intensity of Use. The relative amount of human and capital resources added to a site.

Intensive Margin. The point at which it is just barely financially feasible (profitable) to use urban land more intensely, e.g., replacing old houses with a high-rise office building. *See* Extensive Margin.

Interdependence. An economic characteristic of realty; each site has a mutual interaction of uses, improvements, and value with surrounding parcels.

Interest. Rent or a charge paid for the use of money, e.g., a mortgage loan, a share or right in property.

Interest Due (in advance). Interest calculated and accruing at the beginning of each period.

Interest in Arrears. Interest accruing and calculated at the end of each period.

Interest Rate. The amount paid to borrow money, usually calculated as a percentage per month or year of the amount borrowed.

Intermediary. A go-between; one who acts between two parties, as a bank does between savers and borrowers.

Intermediation. The process that occurs when savers place monies in savings or time accounts at financial institutions, which in turn invest the funds in loans and other investments. *See also* Disintermediation.

Internal Economies of Scale. Producing a larger output, through use of specialized labor and machinery, to reduce cost per unit of output.

Internal Rate of Return (IRR). The rate of return that discounts and equates future cash flows to the initial cash investment. In more complex situations, it is the rate of discount that equates the present value of expected cash outflows (amount of investment) with expected cash inflows (return *of* and return *on* investment). It is the same return referred to as equity rate of return earned over the holding period of the investment.

Internal Revenue Code, U.S. Laws and regulations governing the filing of tax returns with the United States Treasury. Important sections for purposes of real estate are

453	Installment sales
1031	Tax-deferred exchanges
1231	Property used in trade or business qualifying for capital gains treatment
1245	Depreciation recapture on disposition of personal property
1250	Depreciation recapture on disposition of real property

Intestate. The legal status of a person dying without a will or last testament.

Investment. An outlay of money (or something of value) for income or profit, over a long term, as opposed to a short term for speculation.

Investment Value. The worth of a property to a specific investor based on available financing, desired rate of return, and other assumptions unique to the investor.

Investor. One who puts money into real estate based on careful analysis with the expectation of realizing income or profit over an extended period.

Investor's Rate of Return Method. Average annual *cash flow* from a property divided by the initial cash investment; a crude measure for ranking or accepting an investment. *See* Equity Rate of Return in contrast.

Joint Tenancy. *See* Tenancy, Joint.

Joint Venture. The development of or investment in property by two or more individuals or organizations on a partnership cooperative basis where both the risks and the benefits of ownership are shared.

Judgment. A court decree of indebtedness to another and fixing the amount.

Just Compensation. Payment to an owner for property taken in condemnation proceedings, usually the market value of the realty taken.

Labor Specialization. Labor that concentrates on a specific function or end, e.g., an electrician versus general laborer.

Land. The solid part, or crust, of the earth. Provides minerals, living and growing area, and support for buildings, etc. Often used interchangeably with realty.

Land Contract. A written agreement for the purchase and payment of real property over an extended period of time, with title remaining in the seller until the terms of the arrangement are satisfied. Also known as Contract for Deed or Installment Land Contract.

Land Development. Combining land and improvements to produce a completed, operational property.

Land Economics. Study of the allocation and use of land resources to meet people's needs and desires.

Land Use. The employment of land for such productive purposes as agriculture, housing, industry, or commerce. Stores, factories, houses, roads, or parks are all examples of a land use.

Control. Public and private efforts and directives to regulate, limit, and guide the use of land. Examples: zoning ordinances, subdivision regulations, and deed restrictions.

Planning. The development of long-term schemes for the use of land together with ways and means of implementation.

Land-Use Control. A means, public or private, to regulate and guide the use of realty.

Land-Use Succession. The process of land development and redevelopment, as owners strive to maximize value of their properties.

Landlord. *See* Lessor.

Law. A body of rules and regulations established and enforced by governments.

Lease. An agreement giving possession and use of land or realty in return for a specified rental payment.

Flat, Fixed or Straight. An agreement calling for level periodic rental payments throughout its term.

Graduated or Step-Up. An agreement calling for periodic rental increases during its term.

Gross. A lease calling for a single payment of rent to the landlord, who is then responsible for taxes, insurance, maintenance, etc.

Ground. A lease giving use and occupancy of a vacant site or unimproved land.

Index or Escalated. An agreement providing for rental adjustments based on changes in a neutral index, such as the consumer price index.

Net. A lease in which all payments to the owner are equivalent to net operating income; tenant pays all property taxes, insurance, and maintenance costs.

Percentage. An agreement wherein the rental payment is based on a percentage of sales or income generated by a property.

Proprietary. A lease, with the attributes of ownership, under which a tenant-shareholder in a cooperative occupies a specific apartment or unit of space. Also known as Occupancy Agreement.

Reappraisal. An agreement with rental payments equal to a fixed percentage of market value, as determined by periodic reevaluation, usually three to five years.

Sandwich. A leasing arrangement in which a lessee rerents the property to another party putting himself or herself in the middle, or "sandwich," position.

Lease Option. A provision in a lease giving the tenant the right to purchase the property at a specific price for a specified time.

Leased Fee. The interest or position of a landlord in a leased property, made up primarily of the rights to receive rental payments during the lease term and ultimately to repossess the property at the end of the lease term.

Leasehold/Leasehold Estate. The interest or rights of a lessee or tenant in a leased property, including rights of use and possession for a specified period of time in return for the payment of rent.

Leasehold, Sandwich. A lessee interest in real property between the user of the premises or "top" lessee and the owner of the premises or lessor.

Legacy. Personal property disposed of by a will.

Legal Description. A specific and unique identification of a parcel of real estate that is recognized and approved by law.

Lessee. A person to whom property is rented under a lease; a tenant.

Lessor. One who owns the right to use and occupy realty, which is transferred to another (a lessee) under a lease agreement; a landlord.

Leverage. Use of borrowed funds to magnify or put leverage on the rate of return on an equity investment. Economic analogy to the physical use of a lever to gain a mechanical advantage.

Levy. The amount of property tax payable on a property in a fiscal year, usually 2 to 5 percent of value, depending on the jurisdiction.

Liability. A disadvantage or drawback; a legal responsibility and obligation to another.

License. Privilege to use or enter onto premises granted by someone in legal possession of realty.

Lien. A claim, enforceable at law, to have a debt or charge satisfied out of property belonging to the debtor. Examples are mortgages, taxes, judgments, and attachments.

General. A claim that affects all property of a debtor.

Involuntary. A lien imposed against property without the owner's consent.

Judgment. A claim against property resulting from a court judgment.

Junior. A lien subsequent in priority to a lien or liens previously entered and recorded.

Mechanic's. A statutory lien in favor of those who performed work or furnished materials toward the improvement of realty.

Mortgage. A pledge of realty as security for a mortgage loan.

Specific. A claim that only applies or affects a certain property or group of properties.

Surety Bail Bond. A recorded notice that an owner's equity in a property has been put up as bail to secure the release of someone arrested on a criminal charge.

Tax. A claim against property due to nonpayment of income, inheritance, or property taxes.

Vendee's. A buyer's claim against property of a seller for any money paid under a contract of sale, with subsequent default by the seller.

Vendor's. A seller's claim against a property conveyed to a buyer who subsequently failed to pay the agreed purchase price in full.

Lien Release. A legal instrument to remove or discharge a judgment, mortgage, or other lien as a claim against property.

Lien Waiver. A legal document that, if signed by a contractor, subcontractor, worker, or material supplier, signifies that payment for goods or services rendered in the construction of a property has been received and that any right to place a lien against the property for nonpayment is given up.

Life Estate. An ownership interest of use and enjoyment in real estate limited to the lifetime of a certain person.

Like-Kind Property. Property that can be traded or exchanged without any recognition of capital gains in the transaction. All real estate is like-kind property, except that owned by a dealer and that used as a personal residence.

Limited Partner. *See* Partnership, Limited.

Linkage. A relationship between two land uses that generates movement of goods or people between them.

Lintel. A horizontal structural member that supports the load over an opening, such as a door or window.

Liquidated Damages. Penalty provided for in a contract in the event of nonperformance by one of the parties.

Liquidity. Ease of converting an asset into cash, with account taken of the ratio of cash realized relative to the value of the investment.

Lis pen dens. Notice of a suit pending.

Listing. An oral or written agreement between an owner and a broker employing the broker to sell or lease real estate. In most states the agreement must be in writing to be enforceable.
   Certified. Employment of a broker to sell realty at an appraised (certified) value obtained from a professional appraiser.
   Exclusive Agency. Employment of one broker to sell or rent realty for a commission, with the owner retaining the right to personally sell or rent the property and pay no commission.
   Exclusive Right to Sell. Employment of one broker to sell or rent realty, with a commission to be paid the broker regardless of who sells or rents the property, owner included.
   Multiple. The arrangement among a group of real estate brokers whereby each broker brings listings to the attention of the other members, so that if a sale results, the commission is divided between the broker bringing the listing and the broker making the sale, with a small percentage going to the multiple-listing organization.
   Net. Agreement whereby the owner agrees to sell or rent at a fixed or minimum price, with any excess to be considered as the broker's commission.
   Open. Making opportunity to sell or rent realty available to many brokers, with compensation only to that broker who actually sells or rents the property.

Loan Commitment. *See* Commitment.

Loan Constant, Annual Mortgage. *See* Mortgage Constant.

Loan Discount. An amount off of or a reduction from the principal balance due or face amount of a loan.

Loan Premium. An amount added to or over and above the principal balance due or face amount of a loan.

Loan-to-Value Ratio (LVR). The proportion of property value financed by a mortgage loan, usually expressed as a percentage.

Location. Economically, the relationship of a property to its environment or surroundings. Important considerations are accessibility, exposure, and personal preferences. *See also* Situs. A physical or legal description of property.

Locational Analysis. Identification and

study of environment, situs, linkages, accessibility, and other external factors as they relate to the use, utility, and value of a site or property.

Locational Obsolescence. *See* Depreciation.

Locational Quotient (LQ). A ratio; the percentage of local activity of an industry relative to or divided by national activity in the same industry. Any amount in the ratio in excess of one indicates base economic activity.

Lot. A distinct parcel of land.

Loyalty. Faithful performance as an agent.

Maggie Mae. A private secondary mortgage company. The legal name is Mortgage Guarantee Insurance Corporation (MGIC).

Management by Exception. Focusing attention, as an executive or manager, on substantial deviations from expected performance or results; by so doing, the manager gives attention to items or considerations of greatest concern and benefit to the operation.

Management by Objective (MBO). Making decisions and organizing resources to achieve priority-ranked objectives, such as profits or growth.

Manager. A person who operates properties for owners.

Market. The bringing together or communication between people interested in buying, selling, or exchanging a commodity or service. Real property rights constitute the commodity in the real estate market.

Market, Primary Mortgage. A market made up of lenders who supply mortgage funds directly to borrowers; examples are savings and loan associations and banks.

Market, Secondary Mortgage. A market in mortgages made up of mortgage bankers and brokers who originate loans, and lenders, such as insurance companies and mutual savings banks, who place or invest funds.

Market Analysis. A study of supply, demand, and prices to predict changes in the amount and types of real estate facilities needed in a community or area.

Market Approach to Value. *See* Direct Sales-Comparison Approach to Value.

Market Area. The geographic range of competition for a particular type of real estate, taking account of physical, social, legal, and economic elements.

Market Interest Rate. Rate charged by lenders in making loans in the current market.

Market Price. The amount actually paid or payable in a buy-sell transaction.

Market Rent. *See* Rent, Economic.

Market Risk. Chance of loss due to a drop in the market value of a property.

Market Value. *See* Value, Market.

Master Plan. A comprehensive plan setting forth ways and means by which a community can adjust its physical makeup to social and economic change.

Metes and Bounds. A legal description of realty in which the boundaries are defined by directions and distances.

Middleman. A broker acting for a buyer and seller, both having full knowledge of the double agency.

Minimum-Rated Risk. A risk rating of property based on building type and other characteristics, which is the lowest rate obtainable for the property type.

Mobile Home. A year-round, fully equipped dwelling unit on wheels that may be towed from city to city without violating state highway regulations.

Mobile Home Park. A facility equipped with sewer, water, and electrical connections for individual "pads" to accommodate mobile homes on a year-round basis.

Modification. *See* Interdependence.

Monetary Policy. Adjustments in the nation's money supply to achieve an acceptable balance in the national goals of full employment, economic growth, and price stability.

Money Markets. The creation and exchange for money of short-term (less than one year) money instruments, e.g., notes.

Monument. A fixed object, such as a large boulder, to mark real estate boundaries.

Moral Suasion. Efforts by political leaders to tighten or ease credit without direct regulation, for instance, by persuading bankers to hold to or change certain policies.

Mortgage. A pledge of real property as security for a debt or obligation.

Amortizing. A mortgage loan contract in which the periodic debt service is expected to pay interest on the loan and to repay the principal over the life of the agreement.

Blanket. One mortgage covering two or more pieces of property pledged as security for the debt.

Certificate of Reduction. A statement by the Mortgagee (lender) giving the interest rate and exact principal balances as of a given time.

Construction or Building Loan. A loan to aid an owner or a builder to finance erection of a structure.

Conventional. A mortgage loan made by a financial institution without FHA insurance or a VA guarantee.

FHA. A mortgage loan in which the lender is insured againt loss by the Federal Housing Administration for a fee or charge paid by the borrower.

First. A mortgage that has priority over all other mortgages as a lien on the property.

Junior. A mortgage subsequent in priority to other mortgages as a lien; this may be a third or fourth mortgage in priority.

Open-End. A mortgage contract providing for subsequent advances from a lender up to, but not exceeding, the original amount of the loan.

Package. A mortgage contract providing for accepting fixtures and building equipment as collateral.

Participation. A mortgage loan in which two or more persons or institutions are lenders.

Purchase Money Mortgage (PMM). A mortgage given by a buyer to a seller to cover all or a portion of the purchase price of a property.

Seasoned. A mortgage loan two to three years old on which the borrower has a good record of meeting debt service and of maintaining the property.

Second. A mortgage subsequent in priority to a first mortgage as a lien.

Subject to a. Describes a case in which a buyer takes title to a property on which a mortgage loan exists but does not take over legal responsibility for the mortgage or its debt service; in case of default, the lender has no recourse against the buyer-owner for satisfaction.

Term or Straight. A nonamortizing mortgage, generally for three to five years, with interest payable quarterly or semiannually.

Trust Deed. See Trust Deed.

VA or "GI." A mortgage contract made with eligible veterans and certain others in which the lender is guaranteed against loss on loans by the Veterans' Administration.

Variable Rate. A mortgage loan interest rate that increases or decreases directly with fluctuations in an index beyond the control of the lender, such as the prime rate or bond market rate.

Wraparound. A refinancing mortgage whereby a lender assumes responsibility for debt service on an existing mortgage while making a new, larger second or junior mortgage to the property owner-borrower at a higher interest rate. In effect, the new mortgage "wraps around" the existing mortgage on the property.

Mortgage Assignment. A written transfer of ownership of a mortgage loan contract from one lender to another.

Mortgage Assumption. Agreement by the grantee (usually a buyer) of real estate to accept responsibility and become liable for payment of an existing mortgage against the property.

Mortgage Banker. A person who makes mortgage loans with the expectation of reselling them to an institutional lender while retaining the right to service them for a fee.

Mortgage Broker. A person who, for a fee, obtains mortgage money for a potential borrower or who finds a willing borrower for a potential lender.

Mortgage Consolidation Agreement. A contract whereby two or more mortgages are consolidated into a single mortgage lien.

Mortgage Constant. Total annual debt service on an amortizing mortgage loan, expressed as a proportion or percentage of the initial amount of the loan.

Mortgage Default. *See* Default.

Mortgage Extension. An agreement between the lender and the borrower to extend the life of a term loan without reduction or prepayment in the interim.

Mortgage Release. The release of part of mortgaged realty from the mortgage lien; that is, part of the mortgaged premises is no longer pledged as security for the loan.

Mortgage Satisfaction. Receipt acknowledging payment, to be recorded and thereby terminating the mortgage lien against the property. Also known as Lien Release.

Mortgage Share (Participation) Agreement. A contract setting forth the portions of a participation mortgage owned by the parties involved.

Mortgage Spreading Agreement. A contract extending a mortgage lien to properties not previously included, thereby increasing the security given a lender.

Mortgage Warehousing. An arrangement often used by mortgage bankers whereby several mortgages are initiated with funds obtained on short-term credit for later resale to a large institutional lender or investor, such as an insurance company.

Mortgagee. The lender in a mortgage loan contract, in whose favor the property is pledged as security.

Mortgagor. The borrower in a mortgage loan contract, who pledges property as security.

Mortgagor/Mortgagee Index. Public-record summary showing parties giving and receiving mortgages.

Most Probable Selling Price. The amount at which a property would most likely be sold if exposed to the market for a reasonable time. Synonymous with market value.

Multiple-Nuclei Theory. An explanation of urban growth and structure, in which clusters of development (functional areas) such as business districts, manufacturing districts, and residential neighborhoods combine to make up a city.

Multiple-Use Zoning. A classification allowing several compatible but different uses in the same zoning district.

Neighborhood. An area made up of a group of similar-type business enterprises, houses, or people, often surrounded by well-defined natural or manmade boundaries.

Neighborhood Shopping Center. A retail trade facility, from 5 to 15 acres in area, that primarily provides convenience goods (food, drugs, hardware) to its immediate environment or neighborhood.

Net Lease. *See* Lease, Net.

Net Operating Income (NOI). Earnings of an income property after operating and maintenance expenses are deducted but before interest and depreciation deductions are taken. Also known as Net Income before Recapture (NIBR).

Net Present Value. The present value of future benefits from an investment less the cost of the investment.

Net Spendable Income. Money left over from a property after operating expenses and debt service have been provided for and after state and federal income taxes have been paid. Net operating income less loan payments and less federal and state income taxes.

Net Taxable Income. The income from a property actually subject to taxation; net operating income less interest on loans and less tax depreciation.

New Property. Income property in the same ownership as when initially rented or put into use; important for income tax depreciation purposes.

Nonassumption Clause. A conventional mortgage clause stating that the property of an owner-borrower cannot be sold to, and the mortgage assumed by, a third party without the consent of the lender.

Nonconforming Use. A land use not in agreement with the applicable zoning; may be legal or illegal.

Nonperformance. Failure to fulfill a contract or agreement; also termed breach of contract.

Nonresidential Property. Property earning *less* than 80 percent of its rental income from nontransients or "permanent" residents.

Objective Value. Value of a property dependent on standards, judgments, and demands of the typical owner-user, as judged by the amount paid for similar properties in the market; synonymous with market value or value in exchange.

Obsolescence. Impairment of desirability and usefulness brought about by economic or functional changes.

Obsolete. No longer useful or desirable though physically sound.

Open-Housing Law. A federal law declaring real estate a "public interest" commodity and therefore stipulating that all housing offered for sale or rent through real estate agents must be "open" to all without discrimination based on race, color, creed, or national origin.

Open Market Operations. The buying and selling of money instruments by the Fed to regulate the money supply and influence the interest rate.

Open Occupancy. Refers to residential rental property not restricted by race, creed, color, or national origin.

Operating Expenses. Out-of-pocket costs incurred to maintain a property and to keep it productive of services and income. Examples are water, electricity, supplies, redecoration outlays, taxes, insurance, and management.

Operating Income. *See* Net Operating Income.

Operating Ratio. For an income property: operating expenses divided by gross scheduled income.

Operating Statement. An accounting report of income and expenses for a property, usually based on a time period of one year. The broad format is as follows:

Gross income (GI)

Less vacancy and credit losses

(V&CL)
Equals effective gross income (EGI)
Less operating expenses
Equals net operating income (NOI)

Opinion of Title. *See* Title, Certification of.

Opportunity Cost. The best alternative earning or benefit that is foregone in selecting or deciding among several alternatives.

Option. An agreement whereby an owner agrees to sell property at a stipulated price to a potential buyer within a specified length of time. The potential buyer will usually have paid a fee or price to obtain the right of purchase.

Ordinance. A law or regulation enacted by a local governmental unit.

Ordinary Income. Income from wages, salaries, commissions, professional fees, interest, rents, royalties, and dividends (noncapital gains income) subject to federal taxation at regular rate.

Overall Capitalization Rate. Net operating income divided by sale price, a ratio customarily designated as "R."

Partial Interest. An interest in real property that is less than a tenancy in severalty.

Partial Taking. In eminent domain, the acquisition of less than an entire property.

Partially Amortizing Mortgage Loan. A loan calling for systematic repayment of a portion of the principal, with a balloon or balance to be repaid at some future time.

Partnership. An organizational arrangement whereby two or more people join together to conduct business without forming a corporation and with profits and losses shared according to contributions of capital and expertise.

Partnership, General. *See* Partnership.

Partnership. Limited. A partnership arrangement whereby some members, termed limited or silent partners, are exempt by law from liability in excess of their contribution. Silent partners cannot participate in management under penalty of losing their limited liability status. The managing partners are termed operating or general partners.

Party Wall. A wall built along the line between adjoining properties in which the respective owners share a common right of use.

Patent. A conveyance or grant of property from the U.S. government.

Payback Period. Number of years required to recover an initial capital investment.

Percentage Lease. *See* Lease, Percentage.

Perfect Market. A market in which all information concerning future benefits and risks for each property is available to all participants.

Performance Bond. Insurance or security, put up by a party to a contract, to guarantee specific and proper completion of the contract.

Performance Standards. Criteria used relative to land-use tests to ascertain whether a proposed land use will be acceptable in a specific zone. Tests pertain to items like noise, air pollution, and traffic generation.

Performance Zoning. Establishing zoning districts by standards relating to density, appearance, and traffic generation rather than to use.

Personal Income. Money earned by persons from all sources, with money for social security deducted.

Personalty. Any property that does not fit the definition of realty.

Physical Deterioration. *See* Depreciation.

PIIT. Acronym for payments to a lender that cover principal, interest, insurance, and taxes on a property. Sometimes PITI.

Plaintiff. The complainant and complaining party in a lawsuit.

Planned Unit Development. Development

of property with overall density the same as, or slightly greater than, conventional development but in which, because of flexibility in the zoning ordinance, the improvements may be clustered, with open, common areas between.

Planner. One who coordinates community or area development.

Planning, by City, County, Urban, State, or Regional Authorities. Devising ways and means of achieving goals and objectives considered desirable for the jurisdiction. Planning usually concerns land use, transportation, and community services and facilities.

Plat. A plan or map of a tract of land showing actual or proposed property lines, easements, setback lines, etc., entered into the public record, as for a subdivision.

Plottage. *See* Value, Plottage.

Points. Discount or premium made on the origination or the sale of mortgage loan. Each point equals 1 percent of the loan amount.

Police Power. The limitation of private rights in property by a government, without compensation to the owner, based on need to protect public health, welfare, safety, or morals.

Political Force. Influence for change generated by our efforts to organize and manage ourselves and others through government and laws.

Political Risk. Chance of loss in property ownership or value due to decisions or actions of a governmental body, e.g., a change in zoning.

Portfolio Risk. Chance of loss in owning and managing a large number of investments due to (a) administrative, (b) investment, and (c) mix or diversification perils.

Possessory Interest. A right to occupy and use realty.

Potential Demand. Latent or unrealized desire for a good, such as real estate. Tentative quality and quantity of demand for space.

Power of Attorney. Granting authority to an agent under a formal, sealed instrument. The agent receiving this authority is called an attorney-in-fact.

Power of Sale. The right of a trustee to sell property in default on a trust deed loan, without court proceedings.

Prepaid Expense. A charge paid in advance, e.g., rent or an insurance premium.

Prepayment Clause. A provision in a loan contract setting forth the conditions under which the loan can be prepaid. If the borrower can prepay any time, the contract is said to have a "prepayment privilege." If the borrower must pay for the right to prepay, such as 3 percent of the remaining or unamortized principal, the contract is said to have a "prepayment penalty."

Prescriptive Rights. *See* Adverse Possession.

Present Value. The current monetary value of future benefits or income; the discounted value of future payments.

Present-Value Analysis. *See* Discounted Cash Flow Analysis.

Present Value of One (PV1). A time-value-of-money multiplier used to convert a single payment to be received in the future into a current lump-sum value.

Present Value of One per Period (PV1/P). A time-value-of-money multiplier used to convert a series of equal or level payments, to be received in the future, into a current, lump-sum value.

Price. The amount of one item or commodity traded for another, usually the amount of money.

Primary Lender. Financial institutions originating loans, thereby supplying funds directly to borrowers.

Prime Rate. The interest (or discount) rate

a commercial bank charges higher-credit borrowers on loans to them.

Principal. A person who employs another (an agent) as a representative. *See* Agency. Also, the capital amount of a loan or investment, which amount must be recovered over the term of the loan or investment before any interest or profit can be earned.

Principal Meridian. An imaginary north-south line in the government survey system.

Principal Recovery (PR) Factor. A time-value-of-money multiplier to convert a current, lump-sum principal value, such as a mortgage loan, into a series of equal, periodic payments, sufficient for amortization over the loan period or term.

Principal Risk. The chance that a monetary investment will be worth less than expected in terms of purchasing power when recovered.

Probate. To prove or establish the validity of a will.

Procuring Cause of Sale. A requirement for a broker to claim and collect a commission for the sale of realty from an owner-principal. A sale brought about primarily, immediately, and efficiently by the actions and efforts of a broker is considered to qualify the broker for the commission.

Productivity. In real estate, the capacity of a property to provide a flow of services and benefits in the form of shelter, fertile soil, or advantageous location.

Professional Risk Bearer. Insurance company owned and operated as a profit-making enterprise rather than as a cooperative or mutual organization operated for its members.

Profitability Index. The present value of future cash flows divided by the initial cash investment; the index must exceed 1 for the investment to be acceptable.

Promissory Note. A statement acknowledging a debt and the terms under which it is to be repaid, signed by the debtor or borrower.

Property. The right or interest of an individual in lands and chattels to the exclusion of all others. Real property rights include possession, control, enjoyment, and disposition.
Common. Land or realty owned equally by all members of a group, a community, or the public.
Community. Property, real or personal, acquired by a husband and wife, individually or jointly during their marriage, that belongs to them equally.
Personal. Ownership of or holding title to chattels or non-real estate items such as automobiles, accounts receivable, goodwill, or clothes.
Real. Ownership of or holding title to real estate.

Property, Separate. Property that is specifically excluded from community property, e.g., property owned prior to marriage or received by gift or inheritance after marriage.

Property Brief. Written summary of pertinent information and facts about a property.

Property Description. *See* Legal Description.

Property Risks. Chance of loss in mortgage lending due to perils of properties involved. The risk has three main sources: (a) on-site characteristics, (b) location, and (c) market.

Proportionality, Principle of. Real estate reaches its maximum productivity, or highest and best use, when factors of production are in balance with one another. Also known as principle of balance, of variable proportions, and of increasing and decreasing returns.

Proportionate Share. Allocation of taxes,

maintenance, and other costs involved in a condominium or cooperative according to the relative share of value of each owner.

Proprietary Lease. A lease with the attributes of ownership.

Proration. A division or distribution of proportionate shares, e.g., the prorated adjustments of taxes, insurance, and interest in a title closing.

Public Calling. A business rendering a necessary service, such as insurance, and therefore subject to strict regulation as to formation, operation, and solicitation.

Puffing. The presentation and promotion of a property in the best light possible by a salesperson who is trying to sell the property; statements made by a salesperson about a property that tend to be exaggerated.

Purchasing-Power Risk. The chance that future dollars will be worth less than current dollars in terms of purchasing power for goods and services.

Pyramiding. A financial technique or program for controlling properties or corporations with a limited amount of equity. Also, an estate-building program whereby an investor strives to use leverage and prudent financial management to increase wealth as fast as possible.

Qualified Fee. A limitation on ownership of realty that may cause title to transfer to another person.

Quality of Use. The nature of the use and benefits to be realized from a property—an old house versus a new one.

Question of Fact. In court proceedings, the interpretation of evidence as fact or absolute reality (actual events, conditions, or actions), as by a jury in contrast to interpretation based on legal principle.

Question of Law. In court proceedings, the interpretation of evidence according to legal principles or established rules of law, as by a judge; concern with the letter of the law.

Quitclaim. *See* Deed, Quitclaim.

Range. A column of townships, six miles wide, east or west, of a principal meridian.

Rational Being. An individual acting in a logical and reasonable manner to maximize personal advantage or self-interest.

Ready, Willing, and Able Buyer. A purchaser acceptable to a seller or capable of meeting the seller's tems.

Real Estate. An asset, commodity, or type of property, more accurately classified as "realty," that begins with land and includes all "permanent" improvements to the land. A field of study concerning the description and analysis of the physical, economic, and legal aspects of realty, or real estate as defined above. An occupation or form of business activity that involves realty or real property.

Real Estate Cycle. A rhythmic rise and fall in sales of existing real estate.

Real Estate Investment Trust (REIT). A means of holding real estate with limited liability similar to a corporation and with the ability to pass profits to owners without payment of corporate taxes: thus, the trust is said to be a "conduit."

Real Estate Market. *See* Market.

Real Property. *See* Property, Real.

Realized Gain. A capital gain in the sale or exchange of an asset, the amount of which is received in cash or boot and is therefore subject to taxation. For contrast, *see* Recognized Gain.

Realtor®. A broker or salesperson, affiliated with the National Association of Realtors®. A word to designate an active member of a local real estate board affiliated with the National Association of Realtors®.

Realty. Land and all appurtenances and permanent improvements added thereto, such as easements and buildings.

Reappraised Lease. *See* Lease, Reappraisal.

Recast. Keeping the same loan but modifying debt service by changing the interest rate or the amortization period.

Receiver. A person appointed by the court to take possession and control of a property involved in a legal suit, as in foreclosure.

Recission. Act of rescinding or canceling, as to have title reconveyed to a grantor in a buy-sell transaction.

Recognized Gain. A capital gain in the sale or exchange of an asset realized in like property; that is, not in cash or boot. Therefore not subject to taxation. *See* Realized Gain.

Reconciliation. In appraising, the process of resolving differences in indications of market value to reach a final or single estimate of value.

Reconveyance, Deed of. A deed from a trustee to a borrower to offset a trust deed; similar in function to a mortgage satisfaction.

Recording. Entering a legal instrument or document, such as a mortgage or deed, into the public record to give constructive notice to all the interests involved.

Rectangular or Government Survey. A system of land description or identification utilizing surveying lines running north and south, called meridians, and running east and west, called base lines. The system applies in thirty states.

Redemption, Equity of. *See* Equity of Redemption.

Redemption, Right of. A right to recover property for a limited time after a mortgage foreclosure sale by payment of the price plus back interest plus foreclosure costs. *See also* Equity of Redemption. Also, right to recover a leased property.

Refinance. To obtain a new, and usually larger, loan at new terms.

Regional Shopping Center. A retail trade facility, from 40 acres up, that carries a wide variety of shopping goods, with at least one large department store; the equivalent of a central business district for shopping purposes.

Regulation Z. Truth-in-lending laws concerning consumer loans, published by the Federal Reserve Boards.

Rehabilitation. The restoration of property to good condition with a change in the floor plan or style of architecture.

REIT. *See* Real Estate Investment Trust.

Reliction. Usable land becoming available to an owner owing to a gradual recession of waters. Gradual increase in land of an owner owing to the receding of water. *See also* Accretion.

Remainder. A future possessory interest in realty; what is left at the termination of a life estate.

Remainderman. The owner of a remainder interest in realty.

Remaining Economic Life. The remaining number of years over which realty improvements are expected to render services of economic value. Also known as Remaining Useful Life.

Rent. Consideration given for the use of space or realty, usually stated in terms of dollars per month or year.

Rent, Contract. The amount of money paid for the use of land or realty based on agreement or contract.

Rent, Economic or Market; Rental Value. The amount of money that space would bring if it were being rented currently for is highest and best use.

Rent Triangle. A schedule or graphic illustration depicting the decreasing amount of rent a land use can pay as an increasing amount of space is devoted to the use.

Rental Schedule. A listing of rents to be received for space in a property.

Reserve for Replacements. An amount deducted as an expense in the annual operating statement to pay for the replacement of short-life items necessary to maintain a property's earning ability. Examples of replacement items are elevators, roofs, boilers, stoves, and washers.

Reserve Requirements. The level of monetary reserves required of financial institutions. Raising requirements tightens the money supply, and vice versa.

Residential Rental Property. For income tax purposes, property earning *more than* 80 percent of its rental income from dwelling units for nontransients.

RESPA. Real Estate Settlement Procedures Act, a federal law applying to institutionally made first-mortgage loans to finance the purchase or ownership of one-family residences.

Restrictive Condition with Reverter. A limitation on ownership that may result in the title's being returned to the grantor or to the heirs of the grantor.

Restrictive Covenant Condition. A private limitation on the use and occupancy of realty, often included in a recorded deed or subdivision plat; it is binding on subsequent owners of the property.

Retaliatory Eviction. Removal of a tenant from a property as punishment for the tenant's asserting his or her rights; generally considered illegal.

Reversion, Reversionary Right. The right to recover complete and exclusive use and/or ownership of real property, as at the end of a lease or easement.

Reverter Clause. A condition in a deed restriction calling for title to return to grantor if the restriction is violated.

Right of Eminent Domain. *See* Eminent Domain.

Right of Recission. A borrower's right to cancel or repeal a loan, as under regulation Z.

Right of Way. A privilege or right to cross the land of another, as with an easement for ingress-egress. Also a strip of land for a highway, railroad, or power line.

Riparian Rights. The right of an owner of land bordering a stream or lake to continue the use and enjoyment of the waters therein.

Ripe Property. One that yields a profit to a developer after improvements have been added and all other factors of production have been satisfied.

Risk. The chance of loss on an investment or from a hazard such as fire, flood, or vandalism.

Rolling Option. An option to purchase land that remains alive as long as a certain minimum amount is purchased each year or during some stipulated time period. Often used by subdividers and developers.

Rule of 72. Divide 72 by the interest rate to get the number of years to double a value by compounding, or to halve a future value by discounting.

Sale and Leaseback. The transfer of title of a property for consideration (sale) with the simultaneous renting back to the seller (leaseback) at a stipulated rent for a specified time.

Sale Contract. A written agreement concerning the transfer of ownership interests in realty, setting forth the price, the terms, and the rights and obligations of the parties, and signed by buyer and seller.

Sale Price. *See* Market Price.

Salesperson. An individual working as an agent for a broker to buy, sell, or exchange property for a fee.

Sandwich Leasehold. *See* Leasehold, Sandwich.

Satisfaction Piece. *See* Mortgage Satisfaction.

Scarcity. Inadequacy in supply of land for a given use or in a desired location.

Scenic Easement. An easement limiting use of realty in order to preserve the natural and historical attractiveness of the immediate environment or area.

Secondary Lender. A party or institution that buys existing mortgage loans or originates loans through someone else.

Secondary Mortgage Market. The buying and selling of existing mortgage loans.

Section. A square mile of land area containing 640 acres.

Secured Transaction. The pledging of personal property by a buyer to a seller or lender as collateral for a loan to buy the property.

Security Deposit. Cash, negotiable securities, or a bond placed with a landlord to assure care and maintenance by the tenant.

Seizin. Possession of realty by the owner or titleholder, who has the right to sell or convey same to another.

Self-Interest. A motivation causing each of us to strive to maximize our satisfactions.

Seller's Market. When the demand for goods and services strongly exceeds the supply, enabling sellers to bargain for and get higher prices, we have a seller's market.

Sensitivity Analysis. A study of the impact of various factors in an investment decision on the rate of return to be earned from, or the investment value of, a property.

Separate Property. *See* Property, Separate and Property, Community.

Service Activity. The economic activity producing goods or services for consumption or use within an area or community.

Severability. A contract provision that invalidation of one clause will not affect the validity of other clauses; each clause is a distinct and independent obligation of the parties involved.

Severance Damages. The loss in market value of the remainder area after a partial taking due to the taking (severance) or the construction of the proposed improvements.

Site. A parcel of land including road improvements and public utilities that make it ready and available for use; for an improved property, the land plus road and utility improvements only.

Site Analysis. The identification and study of characteristics, such as size and shape, topography, and road improvements, that affect the value and marketability of a site.

Situs. Locational relationships external to a property that affect value. Crucial locational considerations are accessibility, exposure, and personal preference.

SMSA. *See* Standard Metropolitan Statistical Area.

Social Force. An influence for change generated by the physical and psychological needs and desires of human beings.

Soil Capability. The relative suitability of a soil for crops or for road or building support.

Special Assessment. A charge against real estate to cover the proportionate cost of an improvement, such as a street or sewer, which benefits the property.

Special-Purpose Property. A unique type of property, such as a church, cemetery, or golf course.

Special Unit Permit. The right to introduce a use not otherwise allowed in a zoning district where a definite need exists and guidelines are agreed upon.

Specific Performance. A remedy, under court order, compelling the defendant to carry out, or live up to, the terms of an agreement or contract.

Specific Rated Risk. A risk rating of a

property based on the condition and occupancy at the time of inspection by a rating organization or team.

Speculator. One who buys and sells realty expecting to realize large, quick profits due to price changes.

Squatter. One who settles on land without any claim of title or right to do so.

Standard Metropolitan Statistical Area (SMSA). A central city with a minimum population of 50,000, or two contiguous cities with a combined population of 50,000 or more, and the county or counties in which they are located; may include surrounding areas if they are economically integrated with the urban centers.

Standard Parallels. Imaginary east-west lines running parallel to, and at 24-mile intervals north and south of, a base line.

Standby Commitment. An agreement to buy a loan from another lender without the other lender's being obligated to sell.

Statute of Frauds. Legislation requiring, among other things, that any contract creating or transferring an interest in land or realty be in writing. Applies to sales contracts, mortgages, creation of easements, and leases in excess of one year. The intent is to prevent perjured testimony and fraudulent proofs by not allowing oral testimony to alter or vary the terms of the written agreement.

Statute of Limitations. Legislation setting the maximum time allowed to file a legal suit after a cause of action arises. Thus, title to real property by adverse possession is gained under the statute of limitations.

Statutory Right of Redemption. *See* Redemption, Statutory Right of.

Steering. Guiding home seekers to specific properties or areas so as to create or avoid a blockbusting situation; an illegal act under fair housing laws.

Strict Foreclosure. Lender-mortgagee taking over a mortgaged property on default rather than seeking its disposition through a judicial sale.

Structural Analysis. The identification and study of characteristics, such as size, shape, layout, equipment, and physical durability, that affect a building's ability to provide services and benefits and, hence, its value.

Subdivider. One who splits land up into building sites.

Subdivision. The breaking up of a tract of land into smaller sites or plots in accordance with community regulations. Sites may be for homes, small office buildings, warehouses, etc.

Subdivision Regulation. Local laws governing the conversion of raw land into building sites.

Subject Property. The property under study, as in a feasibility analysis or an appraisal.

Subjective Value. Value dependent on the specific judgments, standards, and demands of a user. *See* Value in Use.

Sublease/Sublet. A rerenting of space held under a lease to a third party.

Submarginal Land. Land yielding no margin of profit to an owner-operator-user.

Subordination. Clause in a lease or mortgage that stipulates that a lien, subsequent in time, is to have priority. For example, a lessee grants a right of prior claim on a property to a lender-mortgagee.

Subpoena. A legal notice requiring a witness to appear and give testimony.

Substitution, Principle of. A rational buyer will pay no more for a property than the cost of acquiring an equally desirable alternative property.

Suit for Possession. A legal action to gain

or regain possession and use of a property.

Summation Approach. *See* Cost Approach.

Supply. The amount of a commodity available. The quantity of goods or services offered for sale at a given price.

Survey. The process by which a parcel of land is measured and its area ascertained. *See also* Rectangular Survey.

Syndicate. A combining of personal and financial abilities of two or more people to conduct business and to make investments; as a group they are able to accomplish ends that each alone could not undertake and complete.

Syndication. A grouping together of parties or legal entities for a business endeavor, as to develop realty.

Take-Out Letter/Commitment. The statement of terms for, and agreement to make, an advance commitment for a loan, signed by the lender.

Tax Avoidance. The administration of one's affairs and the planning of transactions with income tax regulations and tax court rulings in mind to minimize the amount of taxes to be paid.

Tax Base. The total assessed value of all property in a tax district.

Tax Basis. Cost or value of a property at the time it is acquired; book value.

Tax Capitalization. The discounted present value of all future taxes incurred or avoided because of over- or under-assessment.

Tax Credit. A dollar-for-dollar offset or allowance against taxes due and payable.

Tax-Deferred Exchange. The trading of a property for a *like kind* of property without taxation of economic gains.

Tax Depreciation. A deductible expense for tax purposes, to allow recovery of the cost of an asset over its useful life.

Tax Evasion. Using illegal means to escape payment of taxes, such as failure to submit a return, making false and fraudulent claims, or padding expense accounts.

Tax-Exempt Property. Property not subject to taxation because it is owned by a governmental unit or a nonprofit institution or because of statutes, such as homestead laws.

Tax Levy. A charge made against a property in the form of a tax for the operation of state or local government. Also, the total revenue to be obtained from the tax.

Tax Lien. *See* Lien, Tax.

Tax Roll. The official listing of all property in a jurisdiction, giving legal description, owner, assessed value, and the amount of taxes due and payable.

Tax Shelter. Using a bookkeeping expense of investment depreciation to protect, or avoid paying taxes on, income. It is implied or taken for granted that the investment actually maintains or increases in value during ownership.

"Taxpayer." A building of one or two stories constructed on a site to enable the property to generate enough income to pay real estate taxes until the erection of a skyscraper becomes feasible.

Tenancy. The nature of a right to hold, possess, or use property as by lease or ownership.

At Sufferance. Initially occupying or using realty by legal means and afterward remaining in possession without any justification but with implied consent of the owner.

At Will. Occupying or using realty subject to termination at the will of either the owner or tenant.

By the Entirety. Ownership of realty by husband and wife, who are regarded as one person. No disposition of any interest can take place without the consent of both. The property passes to the survivor in the event of the death of one of them.

Definite. A tenancy of certain duration.

For Years (or One Year). A tenancy for a specific period of time, usually agreed to in writing.

In Common. The ownership of realty by two or more persons, each of whom has an undivided interest, with right of inheritance upon death of the other.

In Severalty. Ownership of realty by one person.

Indefinite. A tenancy of uncertain duration.

Joint. Undivided ownership of realty by two or more persons with survivorship. That is, if one owner dies, his or her interest passes to the remaining owners and not to the heirs of the deceased.

Tenant. A person who occupies or uses real estate under a lease (lessee).

Tenant, Holdover. A tenant who remains in possession of leased property after the expiration of the lease term.

Tenement, Dominant. The benefiting property in an easement.

Tenement, Servient. The property losing rights in an easement, as by giving right of access to a dominant tenement.

Tenure. The right of use and possession of realty.

Term. The time a tenant may occupy a property under a lease. Also, the life of a mortgage loan.

Terminal Costs. Expenses and outlays required at the ends of linkage trips, such as for parking, loading docks, and loading and unloading.

Testate. Leaving a valid will at death.

Third Party. The person negotiating or contracting with the agent of a principal.

Tier. East-west rows of townships north or south of a baseline.

Tight Money. When money for mortgages is scarce, relatively unavailable, and lent at a high interest rate.

Time Costs of Travel. The value of the time period required to move a person or goods from one linked site to another.

Time Is of the Essence. A phrase that, if included in a contract, makes failure to perform by a specified date a material breach or violation of the agreement.

Time Value of Money (TVM). The relating of payments and value at different times by compounding or discounting at a certain interest or discount rate. The relationship depends on the rate, the frequency of compounding, and the total time period involved. Also known as Compound Interest.

Title. Ownership of property. For real estate, a lawful claim, supported by evidence of ownership.

Title, Certification of. An opinion that title is good rendered by an attorney or other qualified person who has examined the abstract of title and other records and information.

Title, Chain of. The succession of all previous holders of title (owners) back to some accepted starting point.

Title, Cloud on. An outstanding claim or encumbrance that, if valid, would affect or impair the owner's title; a mortgage or judgment.

Title, Marketable. Title to real property that is readily salable to an interested, reasonable, prudent, intelligent buyer at market value.

Title Assurance. Evidence or documentation to give confidence or certainty as to the quality of title.

Title by Accretion. Acquiring ownership to soil attaching to land as a result of natural causes, as by a river's action.

Title Closing. Final settlement in the exchange of purchase price for a deed. *See* Closing.

Title Company. A company organized to ensure title to real property.

Title Evidence. Documentary proof of ownership.

Title Examination or Search. An investigation of public records to ascertain the status of title or ownership of a specific parcel of real estate. Items of concern include liens, easements, and other encumbrances that might detract from the quality of title.

Title Insurance. Protection against financial loss due to defects in the title of real property that existed but were not known at the time of purchase of the insurance policy.

Title Report. The results of a title search. Includes the name of the owner and the legal description of a property plus the status of taxes and other liens and encumbrances affecting the property. Results of a property survey may also be included.

Torrens System. A method of land-title registration in which clear title is established with a governmental authority, which subsequently issues title certificates to owners as evidence of their claims.

Tort. A wrongful or damaging act against another, for which legal action may be initiated.

Town/Township. In the rectangular survey system, an area of land 6 miles square.

Trade Area. The area from which a retail or service property draws most of its customers.

Trade Fixtures. Personal property installed by a tenant that is removable at the end of a business lease.

Tradeoff. A giving up of one alternative or advantage to gain another considered more desirable.

Trading on the Equity. *See* Leverage.

Traffic Count. The number of people or vehicles passing a given point in an hour or a day.

Transferable Development Rights. The assignment of development rights from one parcel to another parcel.

Transportation Costs. Out-of-pocket expenses for travel between linked land-use activities.

Trespass. The illegal act of entering onto the land of another without permission.

Trust. A fiduciary arrangement whereby property is turned over to an individual or institution (a trustee) to be held and administered for the profit and/or advantage of another person, termed a beneficiary.

Trust Agreement. The written contract setting forth the terms of a trust arrangement.

Trust Deed. *See* Deed, Trust.

Trustee. The person or institution administering and controlling property under trust agreement.

Type of Use. Nature of land use on a site, e.g., residential—one-family, multifamily—or commercial—store, office building, or shopping center.

Undisclosed Principal. A principal, unknown to a third party, acting through an agent, who appears to be acting in self-interest.

Uniform Commercial Code. A set of laws governing the sale, financing, and security of personal property in commercial transactions.

Urban Infrastructure. The basic facilities of a community, including schools, sewer and water systems, power and communication systems (electricity and telephone services), and transportation systems (streets, freeways and subways).

Urban Land Economics. Study of the allocation and use of urban landed space to meet the needs and desires of citizens in the community.

Urban Renewal. The conservation, rehabilitation, and redevelopment of urban real estate facilities. Also, a continuing program to achieve these goals, sponsored by the federal and local governments.

Urbanizing Force. An influence toward the concentration of people, buildings, and machines, e.g., trade, education, or manufacturing.

Used Property. Property held by a second or subsequent owner.

Useful Life. *See* Economic Life; Remaining Economic Life.

Usury. Charging more than the legal rate of interest for the use of money.

Utilities. Community services rendered by public utility companies, such as providing gas, water, electricity, and telephone.

Utility. The ability of an economic good or service to satisfy human needs and desires. In real estate, the ability of a property to render services that are in demand. Also, the benefit or satisfaction that comes with owning or using realty. Utility is the basis of value.

Utility, Diminishing. Decreasing satisfaction realized with the acquisition or consumption of each succeeding unit of an economic good or service.

Utility, Functional. The ability of a property to render services in a given use based on current market tastes and standards. Depends on interior layout, sizes and types of rooms, attractiveness, and accessibility.

Utility, Marginal. The addition to total utility realized by the last unit of a good or service acquired or consumed. In general, as more units are acquired or consumed, the smaller the incremental addition to total utility.

VA. Veterans' Administration, a federal government agency that aids veterans in obtaining housing, primarily by guaranteeing loans with low down payments.

Vacancy and Credit Losses (V&CL). A deduction from potential revenues of an income property because of unrented units or because of nonpayment of rent by tenants for the time they used space.

Valuation. *See* Appraisal.

Value. The worth of a thing as measured in exchange for goods, services, or money. The estimated or assigned worth of a thing because of its scarcity and desirability or usefulness. The present worth of future benefits or ownership.

Appraised. The worth of a thing (property) as estimated by a qualified appraiser. *See also* Appraisal.

Assessed. The worth or amount of dollars assigned a property for property taxation purposes usually varies with the market value of the property and may be a pecentage of market value, fixed by statute.

Book. The capital amount at which a property is carried in accounting records. Usually it is original cost less deductions for depreciation and plus outlays for improvements. *See* Basis, Adjusted Cost.

Capitalized. A value estimate reached through a capitalization process; the present worth of expected future benefits or income.

Market. A term synonymous with fair market value. The price at which a property will sell, assuming a knowledgeable buyer and seller both operating with reasonable knowledge and without undue pressure. The most probable selling price of a property or thing.

Plottage. Bringing two or more parcels of real estate together so that their combined value is greater than the sum of the values of the parcels when taken individually under separate owners. The increment of value created by combining two or more parcels of real estate.

Value after the Taking. Market value of the remaining lands in condemnation proceedings, assuming a partial taking and assuming the proposed improvements or changes have been completed.

Value before the Taking. Market value of an entire property before the taking in eminent domain or condemnation proceedings.

Value in Exchange. The worth of a property in money or purchasing power (in goods and services) to the typical owner or user in the market. Synonymous with market value.

Value in Use. The worth of a property to a specific user, based on its utility to the user.

Vendee. The buyer or purchaser, as of real estate.

Vendor. The seller.

Void Contract. A contract legally invalid and unenforceable.

Voidable Contract. A contract that may be enforced or declared invalid by one of the parties, as by a minor.

Waste. Damage to property through neglect or otherwise.

Water Rights. A right to a stipulated amount of water from a stream, lake, or reservoir.

Will. A legal statement concerning the disposition of a person's property after death.

Yield. The rate of return or amount of return expected or earned on an investment.

Zoning. A division of a government unit into districts for regulation of: (1) nature of land use (residential, commercial, etc.); (2) intensity of land use; and (3) height, bulk, and appearance of structure.

Density. Limiting the number of families per unit of land area in a given zone rather than the number per structure.

Exclusionary. Zoning designed to keep low-income and moderately low-income groups out of a residential district by setting large minimum-lot size and floor-area requirements, and high construction-quality standards.

Spot. An area or parcel, usually small, zoned for a use that is inconsistent with the rationale of the entire zoning ordinance or plan.

Zoning Exception. Permitting a nonconforming use into a zone because of an urgent need, under conditions that protect the area and public interests. Example: a power substation in a residential neighborhood. Also known as Conditional Use Permit.

Zoning Map. A map showing the various zones of permitted land uses under a zoning ordinance.

Zoning Ordinance. Legal regulations to implement a zoning plan to control the use and character of real estate. Usually includes text and a zoning map.

Zoning Variance. A deviation from the zoning ordinance that is granted because strict enforcement would result in undue hardship on a property owner.

INDEX

H

I